The Bible Speaks Today

Series Editors: J. A. Motyer (OT)
John R. W. Stott (NT)

The Message of Acts

The Spirit, the Church & the World

Titles in this series

OLD TESTAMENT

The Message of **Genesis 1—11**
David Atkinson

The Message of **Genesis 12—50**
Joyce G. Baldwin

The Message of **Deuteronomy**
Raymond Brown

The Message of **Judges**
Michael Wilcock

The Message of **Ruth**
David Atkinson

The Message of **Chronicles**
Michael Wilcock

The Message of **Job**
David Atkinson

The Message of **Ecclesiastes**
Derek Kidner

The Message of **Jeremiah**
Derek Kidner

The Message of **Daniel**
Ronald S. Wallace

The Message of **Hosea**
Derek Kidner

The Message of **Amos**
J. A. Motyer

NEW TESTAMENT

The Message of the **Sermon on the Mount (Matthew 5—7)**
John R. W. Stott

The Message of **Mark**
Donald English

The Message of **Luke**
Michael Wilcock

The Message of **John**
Bruce Milne

The Message of **Acts**
John R. W. Stott

The Message of **1 Corinthians**
David Prior

The Message of **2 Corinthians**
Paul Barnett

The Message of **Galatians**
John R. W. Stott

The Message of **Ephesians**
John R. W. Stott

The Message of **Philippians**
J. A. Motyer

The Message of **Colossians & Philemon**
R. C. Lucas

The Message of **1 & 2 Thessalonians**
John R. W. Stott

The Message of **2 Timothy**
John R. W. Stott

The Message of **Hebrews**
Raymond Brown

The Message of **James**
J. A. Motyer

The Message of **1 Peter**
Edmund P. Clowney

The Message of **John's Letters**
David Jackman

The Message of **Revelation**
Michael Wilcock

The Message of Acts

The Spirit, the Church & the World

John R. W. Stott

With Study Guide

Inter-Varsity Press
Leicester, England
Downers Grove, Illinois, U.S.A.

InterVarsity Press
38 De Montfort Street, Leicester LE1 7GP, England
P.O. Box 1400, Downers Grove, Illinois 60515, U.S.A.

InterVarsity Press®, USA, is the book-publishing division of InterVarsity Christian Fellowship®, a student movement active on campus at hundreds of universities, colleges and schools of nursing in the United States of America, and a member movement of the International Fellowship of Evangelical Students. For information about local and regional activities, write Public Relations Dept., InterVarsity Christian Fellowship, 6400 Schroeder Rd., P.O. Box 7895, Madison, WI 53707-7895.

Inter-Varsity Press, England, is the publishing division of the Universities and Colleges Christian Fellowship (formerly the Inter-Varsity Fellowship), a student movement linking Christian Unions in universities and colleges throughout the United Kingdom and the Republic of Ireland, and a member movement of the International Fellowship of Evangelical Students. For information about local and national activities in Great Britain write to UCCF, 38 De Montfort Street, Leicester LE1 7GP.

USA ISBN 0-8308-1236-9
USA ISBN 0-87784-925-0 (set of The Bible Speaks Today)
UK ISBN 0-85110-926-4

Printed in the United States of America ∞

Library of Congress Cataloging-in-Publication Data

Stott, John R. W.
The message of Acts: the Spirit, the church, and the world/John Stott.
p. cm.—(The Bible speaks today)
Originally published: Leicester, England: Universities and Colleges Christian Fellowship.
Includes bibliographical references.
ISBN 0-8308-1236-9
1. Bible. N.T. Acts—Commentaries. 2. Holy Spirit—Biblical teaching. 3. Mission of the church—Biblical teaching. 4. Church and the world—Biblical teaching. I. Title. II. Title: Spirit, the church, and the world. III. Series.
BS2625.3.S86 1994
226.6'07—dc20 *94-426*
CIP

British Library Cataloguing in Publication Data

A catalogue record for this book is available from the British Library.

---

16 15 14 13 12 11 10 9 8 7 6 5 4 3 2 1
07 06 05 04 03 02 01 00 99 98 97 96 95 94

General preface

The Bible Speaks Today describes a series of both Old Testament and New Testament expositions, which are characterized by a threefold ideal: to expound the biblical text with accuracy, to relate it to contemporary life and to be readable.

These books are, therefore, not 'commentaries', for the commentary seeks rather to elucidate the text than to apply it, and tends to be a work rather of reference than of literature. Nor, on the other hand, do they contain the kind of 'sermons' which attempt to be contemporary and readable without taking Scripture seriously enough.

The contributors to this series are all united in their convictions that God still speaks through what he has spoken, and that nothing is more necessary for the life, health and growth of Christians than that they should hear what the Spirit is saying to them through his ancient – yet ever modern – Word.

J. A. Motyer
J. R. W. Stott
Series Editors

AUTHOR'S PREFACE

Thank God for *The Acts of the Apostles*! The New Testament would be greatly impoverished without it. We are given four accounts of Jesus, but only one of the early church. So the Acts occupies an indispensable place in the Bible.

The value of the Acts

It is important, first, for its historical record. Luke begins his story with the outpouring of the Spirit on the Day of Pentecost and the honeymoon period of the Spirit-filled community, which was abruptly terminated by the opposition of the Jewish authorities. He goes on to describe the transition stage in which the foundations were laid for the Gentile mission by Stephen's martyrdom and Philip's evangelism, the conversions of Saul and Cornelius, and the founding of the first Greek church in Antioch. From this international city and church the world-wide Christian mission was launched. Paul and Barnabas evangelized Cyprus and Galatia; the Council of Jerusalem acknowledged the legitimacy of Gentile conversion; Europe was reached during the second missionary journey (including Athens and Corinth) and Ephesus on the third. Then Paul was arrested in Jerusalem, and this was followed by a series of court trials, his appeal to Caesar, and the long sea voyage to Rome, the city of his dreams. There Luke leaves him, restricted to his own rented house, but unrestricted in his preaching of the gospel. Without the Acts we could not have reconstructed the course of Paul's intrepid missionary career or known how the gospel spread to the strategic cities of the Roman world.

The Acts is also important, however, for the contemporary inspiration which it brings us. Calvin called it 'a kind of vast treasure'.[1] Martyn Lloyd-Jones referred to it as 'that most lyrical of books', and added: 'Live in that book, I exhort you: it is a tonic, the greatest tonic I know of in the realm of the Spirit.'[2] It has, in fact, been a salutary exercise for the Christian church of every

[1] Calvin, I, p. 20.

[2] *The Christian Warfare* by Martyn Lloyd-Jones (Banner of Truth, 1976), p. 274.

century to compare itself with the church of the first, and to seek to recapture something of its confidence, enthusiasm, vision and power. At the same time, we must be realistic. There is a danger lest we romanticize the early church, speaking of it with bated breath as if it had no blemishes. For then we shall miss the rivalries, hypocrisies, immoralities and heresies which troubled the church then as now. Nevertheless, one thing is certain. Christ's church had been overwhelmed by the Holy Spirit, who thrust it out to witness.

The literature of the Acts

Because of its unique importance, the Acts has attracted an enormous literature, and it would be almost impossible for anybody to read it all. I have enjoyed some of the older commentators, who nowadays are often neglected. I am thinking of John Chrysostom's fifty-five homilies on the Acts preached in Constantinople in AD 400 and of John Calvin's two volumes written in sixteenth-century Geneva. I have appreciated the pithy comments of Johann Albrecht Bengel of the eighteenth century, the godly and clear-headed insights of J. A. Alexander, the brilliant Princeton linguist of the nineteenth century, and the archaeological expertise of Sir William Ramsay, who wrote ten books between 1893 and 1915 bearing on Luke and/or Paul, the best-known being *St Paul the Traveller and the Roman Citizen* (1895). I have also struggled with the critical postures of liberal works like the five volumes edited by F. J. Foakes-Jackson and Kirsopp Lake under the title *The Beginnings of Christianity* (1920–32) and the 700 pages of Ernst Haenchen's scholarly treatment (1956).

Among contemporary conservative authors I have specially profited from the commentaries by F. F. Bruce (Greek, 1951; English, 1954), Howard Marshall (1980) and Richard Longenecker (1981). I particularly regret that the late Dr Colin Hemer's *magnum opus* entitled *The Book of Acts in the Setting of Hellenistic History* (1989), ably edited by Conrad Gempf, was published too late for me to study thoroughly; I have been able, as this manuscript is being prepared for the press, to spend only a morning in the perusal of it. This has enabled me to refer the reader to a number of Dr Hemer's discussions. The wealth of recent archaeological discovery (especially from papyri, inscriptions and coins), which he has painstakingly collected and sifted, will make his work a standard reference book for many years to come. Encyclopaedic in knowledge, conscientious in research and cautious in judgment, Colin Hemer has put all students of Acts in his debt.

It is easy to echo the sentiment of Sir William Ramsay, who wrote: 'It is impossible to find anything to say about Acts that has not been said before by somebody.'[3] Then how on earth can one justify adding yet another volume to the extensive library on Acts? If anything distinctive can be claimed about this book it is that, whereas all commentaries seek to elucidate the original meaning of the text, the commentary on Acts I have written is committed also to its contemporary application. I have tried, therefore, to address myself with integrity to some of the main questions which the Acts raises for today's Christians, such as the baptism of the Spirit and charismatic gifts, signs and wonders, the economic sharing of the first Christian community in Jerusalem, church discipline, the diversity of ministries, Christian conversion, racial prejudice, missionary principles, the cost of Christian unity, motives and methods in evangelism, the call to suffer for Christ, church and state, and divine providence.

The interpretation of the Acts

But can we leap the gap of nineteen centuries between the apostles and us, and apply the Acts text to ourselves without manipulating it to suit our own preconceived opinions? Yes, it is right to affirm that the Word of God is always relevant. But this does not mean that we may simply 'read off' the text as if it was originally addressed to us in our context. We have to recognize the historical particularities of Scripture, especially of the 'salvation-history' which it records. In one sense, for example, the Day of Pentecost was unique and is unrepeatable, because the outpouring of the Spirit on that day was the final act of Jesus following those equally unique and unrepeatable events, his death, resurrection and ascension. Similarly unique in some respects was the ministry of the apostles, whom Jesus appointed to be the pioneer teachers and the foundation of the church.[4] We have no liberty to copy everything they did.

It is in this connection that I need to say something about the difference between didactic and narrative parts of Scripture, and about the importance of allowing the didactic to control our interpretation of the narrative. For what I wrote about this in *Baptism and Fullness* has been misunderstood by some, and I will

[3] Ramsay, *St Paul*, p. viii.
[4] See Eph. 2:20.

try to clarify it.[5] I am emphatically not saying that biblical narrative has nothing to teach us, for of course 'all Scripture is God-breathed and profitable'.[6] Moreover, what happened to others in former times has been recorded for our instruction.[7] The question, however, is *how* are we going to interpret these narrative passages? For some of them are not self-interpreting, and contain within themselves few if any clues as to what we are intended to learn from them. Are they necessarily normative? Is the behaviour or experience recorded in them meant to be copied? or perhaps avoided?

I am not referring only to charismatic questions like the gift of the Spirit to the Samaritans (Acts 8). The same query has to be raised in regard to other descriptive passages. For example, are we to make local church elections by drawing lots, because this was what they did when choosing an apostle to replace Judas (1:23–26)? Are we to hold our possessions in common, sell our goods and share the proceeds with the needy, as the members of the early church in Jerusalem did (2:44–45; 4:32ff.)? Again, are we to expect at our conversion to see a bright light and hear an audible voice, as Saul of Tarsus did (9:3ff.)? It should be clear from these examples that not everything that people are recorded in the Acts as having done or experienced is meant to be replicated in our lives. So how shall we decide? It is here that the didactic must guide us in evaluating and interpreting the descriptive. We have to look for teaching on the issue, first in the immediate context (within the narrative itself), then in what the author writes elsewhere, and finally in the broader context of Scripture as a whole. For instance, the apostle Peter's plain statement to Ananias that his property, both before and after its sale, was his own and at his disposal (5:4), will prevent us from regarding all Christian possessions as being necessarily held in common.

The biblical text used throughout this book is that of the New International Version. Sometimes it appears as a block before the exposition. But when the full text is incorporated within the ex-

[5] See *Baptism and Fullness* (IVP, second edition 1975), pp. 15–17. Roger Stronstad in his *The Charismatic Theology of St Luke* (Hendrickson, 1984) writes of those who allege 'an unbiblical dichotomy between the so-called descriptive and didactic passages of Scripture' (p. 6) and appears to include me among them. But I plead 'not guilty'! I am not denying that historical narratives have a didactic purpose, for of course Luke was both a historian and a theologian; I am rather affirming that a narrative's didactic purpose is not always apparent within itself and so often needs interpretative help from elsewhere in Scripture.

[6] 2 Tim. 3:16. [7] Rom. 15:4; 1 Cor 10:11

position, it has not been thought necessary to include it independently as well.

I am grateful to many people for helping to bring this book to birth. I thank those who over a number of years have patiently listened to my clumsy attempts to expound the Acts and have thus served as a valuable sounding board. I mention the Summer School students at Regent College, Vancouver, in July 1979, and in particular those members of the Evangelical Fellowship of the Church in Wales who stoically submitted to annual instalments which went on for thirteen years. Next, I appreciate the helpfulness of the three official IVP readers of the manuscript – John Marsh, Colin Duriez and especially Conrad Gempf, who is himself extremely knowledgeable in Acts and who combed my manuscript with meticulous thoroughness and made a number of shrewd suggestions, many of which I have adopted. Another reader to whom I am greatly indebted is Todd Shy, my current student assistant. He has worked diligently through the typescript more than once, made perceptive comments, checked the NIV text and the footnotes, and compiled the list of abbreviations and the bibliography. Last but not least, I express my continuing gratitude to my able and tireless secretary of 33 years' standing, Frances Whitehead, whose task of typing and correcting has been made less tedious and more enjoyable by the versatile magic of her Apple Macintosh Plus.

John Stott
Easter 1989

CHIEF ABBREVIATIONS

AV	The Authorized (King James') Version of the Bible (1611).
BAGD	Walter Bauer, *A Greek-English Lexicon of the New Testament and Other Early Christian Literature*, translated and adapted by William F. Arndt and F. Wilbur Gingrich, 2nd edition, revised and augmented by F. Wilbur Gingrich and Frederick W. Danker from Bauer's fifth edition, 1958 (University of Chicago Press, 1979).
BC	*The Beginnings of Christianity, Part I: The Acts of the Apostles*, 5 volumes, ed. F. J. Foakes-Jackson and Kirsopp Lake (Macmillan: vol. I, 1920; vol. II, 1922; vol. III, 1926; vols. IV and V, 1932; Baker reprint, 1979).
GT	*A Greek-English Lexicon of the New Testament* by C. L. W. Grimm and J. H. Thayer (T. & T. Clark, 1901).
HDB	*A Dictionary of the Bible*, ed. James Hastings, 5 volumes (T. & T. Clark, 1898–1904).
JB	The Jerusalem Bible (1966).
JBP	*The New Testament in Modern English* by J. B. Phillips (Collins, 1958).
LXX	The Old Testament in Greek according to the Septuagint, 3rd century BC.
NEB	The New English Bible (NT 1961, 2nd edition 1970; OT 1970).
NIV	The New International Version of the Bible (1973, 1978, 1984).
RSV	The Revised Standard Version of the Bible (NT 1946, 2nd edition 1971; OT 1952).
TDNT	*Theological Dictionary of the New Testament*, ed. G. Kittel and G. Friedrich, translated into English by G. W. Bromiley, 10 vols. (Eerdmans, 1964–76).

BIBLIOGRAPHY

Alexander, J. A., *A Commentary on the Acts of the Apostles* (1857; Banner of Truth, 1963, volumes I and II together).

Barclay, William, *The Acts of the Apostles*, in *The Daily Study Bible* (St Andrew Press, 1953; 2nd edition, 1955).

Barrett, C. K., *Luke the Historian in Recent Study* (Epworth, 1961).

Baur, F. C., *Paul, The Apostle of Jesus Christ, His Life and Works*, in 2 volumes (translated into English, 1836; London: Williams & Norgate, 1873–75).

Bengel, Johann Albrecht, *Gnomon of the New Testament*, vol. II, 1742; translated into English by Andrew R. Fausset (T. & T. Clark, 6th edition, 1866).

Blaiklock, E. M., *Cities of the New Testament* (Pickering & Inglis, 1965).

The Acts of the Apostles: An Historical Commentary (Tyndale Press, 1959).

Bruce, F. F., *The Acts of the Apostles: The Greek Text with Introduction and Commentary* (Tyndale Press, 1951).

Commentary on the Book of the Acts: The English Text with Introduction, Exposition and Notes, in *The New London Commentary on the New Testament* (Marshall, Morgan and Scott/Eerdmans, 1954).

The Speeches in the Acts of the Apostles (Tyndale Press, 1943). *Referred to in the text as *Speeches* (1).

'The Speeches in Acts – Thirty Years After', in *Reconciliation and Hope: New Testament Essays on Atonement and Eschatology*, essays in honour of L. L. Morris, ed. Robert Banks (Paternoster Press, 1974). *Referred to in the text as *Speeches* (2).

Cadbury, Henry, *The Making of Luke-Acts* (Macmillan, 1927; 2nd edition, SPCK, 1958).

Calvin, John, *The Acts of the Apostles*, an exposition in 2 volumes: vol. I, chapters 1–13 (originally 1552; translated into English, 1965); vol. II, chapters 14–28 (originally 1554; translated into English 1966); ed. D. W. and T. F. Torrance (Oliver and Boyd).

Chrysostom, John, *The Homilies on the Acts of the Apostles*,

preached in Constantinople in AD 400; from *A Select Library of the Nicene and Post-Nicene Fathers*, ed. Philip Schaff, vol. XI, 1851 (Eerdmans reprint, 1975).
Coggan, Donald, *Paul: Portrait of a Revolutionary* (Hodder & Stoughton, 1984).
Conybeare, W. J. and J. S. Howson, *The Life and Epistles of St Paul* (Longmans Green, new edition, 1880).
Conzelmann, Hans, *The Theology of St Luke* (Faber, 1960; being the English translation of *Die Mitte der Zeit*, 1954).
Dibelius, Martin, *Studies in the Acts of the Apostles* (originally written between 1923 and his death in 1947, published in 1951; translated into English, SCM, 1956).
Dunn, James D. G., *Baptism in the Holy Spirit* (SCM Press, 1970).
Jesus and the Spirit: A Study of the Religious and Charismatic Experience of Jesus and the First Christians as Reflected in the New Testament (SCM, 1975).
Dupont, Dom Jacques, *The Salvation of the Gentiles: Essays on the Acts of the Apostles* (1967; translated into English by Paulist Press, 1979).
Edersheim, Alfred, *The Life and Times of Jesus the Messiah*, 2 volumes (Longmans, 1883).
Sketches of Jewish Social Life in the Days of Christ (Religious Tract Society, undated).
Farrar, F. W., *The Life and Work of St Paul* (Cassell, popular edition, 1891).
Gärtner, Bertil, *The Areopagus Speech and Natural Revelation* (Uppsala, 1955).
Gasque, W. Ward, 'The Book of Acts and History', in *Unity and Diversity in New Testament Theology*, essays in honour of G. E. Ladd, ed. Robert A. Guelich (Eerdmans, 1978).
A History of the Criticism of the Acts of the Apostles (Mohr, Tübingen/Eerdmans, 1975).
Gasque, W. Ward and Ralph P. Martin, eds., *Apostolic History and the Gospel: Biblical and Historical Essays* (Paternoster, 1970).
Gomme, A. W., *A Historical Commentary on Thucydides*, in 5 volumes, vol. I (1945), vol. II & III (1956), vol. IV (1970) and vol. V (1981) by A. W. Gomme, A. Andrews and K. J. Dovey (Oxford: Clarendon Press).
Green, Michael, *Evangelism in the Early Church* (1970; Highland, 1984).
I Believe in the Holy Spirit (Hodder & Stoughton, revised edition, 1985).
The Meaning of Salvation (Hodder & Stoughton, 1965).

Haenchen, Ernst, *The Acts of the Apostles: A Commentary* (1956; 14th German edition, 1965; translated into English, Basil Blackwell, 1971).

Hanson, R. P. C., *The Acts* (1967; Oxford, Clarendon Press, 1982).

Harnack, Adolf, *The Acts of the Apostles* (translated into English, Williams & Norgate, London, 1909).

Luke the Physician (1906; translated into English, Williams & Norgate, London, 1907).

Hemer, Colin, *The Book of Acts in the Setting of Hellenistic History*, ed. Conrad H. Gempf (Tübingen: Mohr, 1989).

Hengel, Martin, *Acts and the History of Earliest Christianity* (SCM, 1979).

Hobart, W. K., *The Medical Language of St Luke* (Dublin University Press, 1882; reprinted by Baker, 1954).

Horton, Stanley M., *The Book of Acts: A Commentary* (Springfield, Missouri: Gospel Publishing House, 1981).

Irenaeus, *Against Heresies*, in *The Ante-Nicene Fathers*, vol. I, ed. Alexander Roberts and James Donaldson (1885; Eerdmans, 1981).

James, M. R., translation of *The Apocryphal New Testament* (Oxford, Clarendon Press, 1924; corrected edition, 1953).

Josephus, Flavius, *The Antiquities of the Jews*, *c.* AD 93–94, translated by William Whiston, 1737; from *Josephus: Complete Works* (Pickering & Inglis, 1981).

The Wars of the Jews, *c.* 78–79, translated by William Whiston, 1737; from *Josephus: Complete Works* (Pickering & Inglis, 1981).

Keck, Leander E. and J. Louis Martyn, eds., *Studies in Luke-Acts* (Abingdon, 1966; SPCK, 1968; Fortress, 1980).

Knowling, R. J., *The Acts of the Apostles*, in *The Expositor's Greek Testament* (Hodder & Stoughton, 1900; 2nd edition, 1901).

Lenski, R. C. H., *The Interpretation of the Acts of the Apostles* (1934; Augsburg, 1961).

Longenecker, Richard N., *The Acts of the Apostles: Introduction, Text and Exposition*, in *The Expositor's Bible Commentary*, ed. Frank Gaebelein, vol. 9 (Regency Reference Library, Zondervan, 1981).

Biblical Exegesis in the Apostolic Period (Eerdmans, 1975).

Marshall, I. Howard, *The Acts of the Apostles: An Introduction and Commentary*, in *Tyndale New Testament Commentaries* (new series, IVP, 1980).

Luke: Historian and Theologian (Paternoster, 1970).

Metzger, Bruce M., *A Textual Commentary on the Greek New Testament* (United Bible Societies, corrected edition, 1975).

Morgan, G. Campbell, *The Acts of the Apostles* (Fleming H. Revell, 1924; Pickering & Inglis, 1946).
Morton, H. V., *In the Steps of St Paul* (Richard Cowan, 1936).
Neil, William, *The Acts of the Apostles*, in the *New Century Bible* (Oliphants/Marshall, Morgan and Scott, 1973).
Pierson, A. T., *The Acts of the Holy Spirit* (Marshall, Morgan and Scott, 1895).
Rackham, R. B., *The Acts of the Apostles: An Exposition*, in the *Westminster Commentaries Series* (Methuen, 1901; 4th edition, 1909).
Ramsay, Sir William M., *The Church in the Roman Empire before AD 170* (Hodder & Stoughton, 1893).
The Cities of St Paul: Their Influence on his Life and Thought (Hodder & Stoughton, 1907).
St Paul the Traveller and the Roman Citizen (Hodder & Stoughton, 1895; 11th edition, undated).
Ridderbos, H. N., *The Speeches of Peter in the Acts of the Apostles* (Tyndale Press, 1962).
Sherwin-White, A. N., *Roman Society and Roman Law in the New Testament* (Oxford University Press, 1963; Baker, 1978).
Smith, James, *The Voyage and Shipwreck of St Paul*, revised and corrected by Walter E. Smith (4th edition, Longmans, 1880).
Stanton, Graham N., *Jesus of Nazareth in New Testament Preaching* (Cambridge University Press, 1974).
Stonehouse, N. B., *Paul before the Areopagus: and other New Testament Studies* (Tyndale Press, 1957).
Stronstad, Roger, *The Charismatic Theology of St Luke* (Hendrickson, 1984).
Torrey, C. C., *The Composition and Date of Acts* (Harvard University Press, 1916).
Vermes, Geza, *The Dead Sea Scrolls in English* (1962; 2nd edition, Penguin, 1975).
Walker, Thomas, *The Acts of the Apostles* (1910; Moody Press, 1965).
Williams, C. S. C., *A Commentary on the Acts of the Apostles*, in *Black's New Testament Commentaries* (A. & C. Black, 1957; 2nd edition, 1964).

A CHRONOLOGICAL TABLE*

Acts narrative		*Roman Empire*	
AD		**AD**	
30	The crucifixion, resurrection and ascension of Jesus (1:1–11)	**14–37**	Tiberius, emperor
	Pentecost (2:1–41)	**26–36**	Pontius Pilate, procurator of Judea
32, 33	Stephen is stoned (7:54–60); Saul is converted (9:1–19)		
35 or 36	Paul's first visit to Jerusalem (9:26–28; Gal. 1:18–20)		
		37–41	Caligula, emperor
43 or 44	James the apostle is executed (12:1–2)	**41–44**	Herod Agrippa I, king of Judea
46 or 47	Paul's second visit to Jerusalem (11:27–30; Gal. 2:1–10)	**41–54**	Claudius, emperor
		45–47	Famine in Judea
47, 48	The first missionary journey (13 – 14)		
49	The Council of Jerusalem (15:1–30)	**49**	Claudius expels Jews from Rome
	The second missionary journey begins (15:36ff.)	**50–*c.* 93**	Herod Agrippa II, tetrarch of Northern territory
50–52	Paul in Corinth (18:1–18a)	**51–52**	Gallio, proconsul of Achaia
52	Paul returns to Syrian Antioch via Ephesus and Caesarea (18:18b–22)		
	The third missionary journey begins (18:23ff.)		

52–55	Paul in Ephesus (19:1 – 20:1a)	**52–59**	Felix, procurator of Judea
55–56	Paul in Macedonia (20:1b–2a)	**54–68**	Nero, emperor
56–57	Paul winters in Corinth (20:2b–3a)		
57	The voyage to Jerusalem, via Macedonia, Troas and Miletus (20:3b – 21:17) Paul is arrested in Jerusalem (21:27–36) and tried before Felix (24:1–22)		
57–59	Paul's Caesarean imprisonment (23:23 – 24:27)		
59	Paul is tried before Festus and Agrippa (25:6 – 26:32)	**59–61**	Festus, procurator of Judea
59–60	The voyage to Rome (27:1 – 28:16)		
60–62	Paul's Roman imprisonment (28:16ff.)		
64	The probable martyrdoms of Peter and Paul in Rome	**64**	Nero begins persecution of Christians
		70	Fall of Jerusalem

(* Based on the work of Colin Hemer, pp. 159–175 and 251–270, and used by permission.)

INTRODUCTION

1. Introduction to Luke (Luke 1:1–4)

Before reading any book it is helpful to know the author's purpose in writing it. The biblical books are no exception to this rule. So why did Luke write?

He actually wrote two books. The first was his Gospel, which ancient and unassailed tradition attributes to his authorship and which is almost certainly the 'former book' referred to at the beginning of Acts. So the Acts was his second book. The two form an obvious pair. Both are dedicated to Theophilus and both are written in the same literary Greek style. Further, as Henry J. Cadbury pointed out sixty years ago, Luke regarded the Acts as 'neither an appendix nor an afterthought', but as forming with his gospel 'a single continuous work'. Cadbury went on to suggest that, 'in order to emphasize the historic unity of the two volumes . . . the expression "Luke-Acts" is perhaps justifiable'.[1]

Reverting to the question why Luke wrote his two-volume work on the origins of Christianity, at least three answers may be given. He wrote as a Christian historian, as a diplomat and as a theologian-evangelist.

a. Luke the historian

It is true that the more destructive critics of the past had little or no confidence in Luke's historical reliability. F. C. Baur, for example, leader of the 'Tübingen School' in the middle of the last century, wrote that certain statements in the Acts 'can only be looked at as intentional deviations from historical truth in the interest of the special tendency which they possess'.[2] And the very unorthodox Adolf Harnack (1851–1930), who could describe the Acts as 'this great historical work',[3] also wrote in the same book

[1] Cadbury, pp. 8–11. [2] Baur, I, p. 109. [3] Harnack, *Luke*, pp. 121, 146.

that Luke 'affords gross instances of carelessness, and often of complete confusion in the narrative'.[4]

There are a number of reasons, however, why we should be sceptical of this scepticism. To begin with, Luke claimed in his preface to the Gospel to be writing accurate history, and it is generally agreed that he intended this to cover both volumes. For 'it was the custom in antiquity', whenever a work was divided into more than one volume, 'to prefix to the first a preface for the whole'. In consequence, Luke 1:1–4 'is the real preface to Acts as well as to the Gospel'.[5] Here it is:

Many have undertaken to draw up an account of the things that have been fulfilled among us, [2]just as they were handed down to us by those who from the first were eye-witnesses and servants of the word. [3]Therefore, since I myself have carefully investigated everything from the beginning, it seemed good also to me to write an orderly account for you, most excellent Theophilus, [4]so that you may know the certainty of the things you have been taught.

In this important statement Luke delineates five successive stages:

First came the historical events. Luke calls them certain 'things that have been fulfilled among us' (1). And if 'fulfilled' is the right translation, it seems to indicate that these events were neither random nor unexpected, but took place in fulfilment of Old Testament prophecy.

Next Luke mentions the contemporary eyewitnesses, for the things 'fulfilled among us' were then 'handed down to us by those who from the first were eyewitnesses and servants of the word' (2). Here Luke excludes himself, for, although he was an eyewitness of much that he will record in the second part of the Acts, he did not belong to the group who were eyewitnesses 'from the first'. These were the apostles, who were witnesses of the historic Jesus and who then handed down (the meaning of 'tradition') to others what they had themselves seen and heard.

The third stage was Luke's own personal researches. Although he belonged to the second generation who had received the 'tradition' about Jesus from the apostolic eyewitnesses, he had not accepted it uncritically. On the contrary, he had 'carefully investigated everything from the beginning' (3).

Fourthly, after the events, the eyewitness tradition and the investigation came the writing. 'Many have undertaken to draw up an account' of these things (1), he says, and now 'it seemed good also to me to write an orderly account' (3). The 'many' authors doubtless included Mark.

[4] *Ibid.*, p. 112. [5] *BC*, II, pp. 491–492.

Fifthly, the writing would have readers, among them Theophilus whom Luke addresses, 'so that you may know the certainty of the things you have been taught' (4). Thus the events which had been accomplished, witnessed, transmitted, investigated and written down were (and still are) to be the ground of Christian faith and assurance.

Moreover, the Luke who claimed to be writing history was well qualified to do so, for he was an educated doctor,[6] a travelling companion of Paul, and had resided in Palestine for at least two years.

Even in those far-off days doctors underwent quite a rigorous training, and Luke's stylish Greek is that of a cultured person. There is also some evidence in Luke-Acts of the vocabulary and powers of observation which one would expect to find in a member of the medical profession. In 1882 the Irish scholar W. K. Hobart wrote his book *The Medical Language of St Luke*, whose aim was to show that Luke was 'well acquainted with the language of the Greek medical schools'[7] and that 'the prevailing tinge of medical diction' reveals a medical author throughout both Gospel and Acts.[8] Adolf Harnack endorsed this theory.[9] More recent critics have rejected it, however. H. J. Cadbury in several studies, after scrutinizing Hobart's list of supposedly medical words used by Luke, pointed out that they belonged not so much to a technical medical vocabulary as to the repertoire of any educated Greek. The truth probably lies at neither of these extremes. Although Luke's medical background cannot be proved by his vocabulary, yet some residue of medical interest and terminology does seem to be discernible in his writing. 'Instinctively Luke uses medical words', wrote William Barclay,[10] and proceeded to give examples in both the Gospel[11] and the Acts.[12]

Another reason for crediting Luke's claim to be writing history is that he was a travelling companion of Paul's. It is well known that several times in the Acts narrative Luke changes from the third person plural ('they') to the first person plural ('we'), and that by these 'we-sections' he unobtrusively draws attention to his presence, in each case in the company of Paul. The first took them from Troas to Philippi, where the gospel was planted in European soil (16:10–17); the second from Philippi to Jerusalem after the conclusion of the last missionary journey (20:5–15 and 21:1–18); and the third from Jerusalem to Rome by sea (27:1 – 28:16). During these periods Luke will have had ample opportunity to hear and

[6] Col. 4:14. [7] Hobart, p. xxix. [8] *Ibid.*, p. xxxvi.
[9] *E.g.* in *Luke the Physician*. See his conclusion on p. 198.
[10] Barclay, p. xiv. [11] *Ibid., e.g.* Lk. 4:35; 9.38; 18:25.
[12] *Ibid., e.g.* Acts 3:7; 8:7; 9:33; 13:11; 14:8 and 28:8–9.

absorb Paul's teaching, and to write a personal travelogue of his experiences from which he could later draw.

In addition to being a doctor and a friend of Paul's, Luke had a third qualification for writing history, namely his residence in Palestine. It happened like this. Luke arrived in Jerusalem with Paul (21:17) and left with him on their voyage to Rome (27:1). In between was a period of more than two years, during which Paul was held a prisoner in Caesarea (24:27), while Luke was a free man. How did he use this time? It would be reasonable to guess that he travelled the length and breadth of Palestine, gathering material for his Gospel and for the early Jerusalem-based chapters of the Acts. He will have familiarized himself as a Gentile with Jewish history, customs and festivals, and he will have visited the places made sacred by the ministry of Jesus and the birth of the Christian community. Harnack was impressed by his personal knowledge of Nazareth (its hill and synagogue), Capernaum (and the centurion who built its synagogue), Jerusalem (with its nearby Mount of Olives and villages, and its 'Synagogue of the Freedmen'), the temple (its courts, gates and porticoes), Emmaus (sixty stadia distant), Lydda, Joppa, Caesarea and other towns.[13]

Since, for Luke's understanding of the early history, people were even more important than places, he will surely also have interviewed many eyewitnesses. Some of them will have known Jesus, including perhaps the now elderly Virgin Mary herself, since Luke's birth and infancy narrative, including the intimacies of the Annunciation, is told from her viewpoint and must go back ultimately to her. Others will have been associated with the beginnings of the Jerusalem church like John Mark and his mother, Philip, the apostles Peter and John, and James the Lord's brother; they will have been able to give Luke firsthand information about the Ascension, the Day of Pentecost, the early preaching of the gospel, the opposition of the Sanhedrin, the martyrdom of Stephen, the conversion of Cornelius, the execution of the apostle James and the imprisonment and release of Peter. So it is not surprising that the first half of the Acts has a 'very noticeable Semitic colouring'.[14]

[13] Harnack, *Acts*, chapter 2, especially pp. 71–87. He concludes: 'The geographical and chronological references and notices in the book show the circumspection, the care, the consistency, and the trustworthiness of the writer' (p. 112). For Luke's specific local knowledge of places, people and circumstances relating to Paul's travels (Acts 13 – 28), see Hemer, pp. 108–158.

[14] Quoted from the Harvard scholar C. C. Torrey, who in his *The Composition and Date of Acts* (1916) developed the interesting theory (though it has failed to convince) that 'the earliest documents of this Jewish-Christian community would have been written in Aramaic, the vernacular', and that Luke would have made a 'special search for Semitic documents, as the primitive and authentic sources, in order to render them into Greek' (p. 5).

We have good reasons, then, to have confidence in Luke's claim to be writing history, and professional historians and archaeologists have been among the most doughty defenders of his reliability. Sir William Ramsay, for example, who had at first been an admiring student of the radical critic F. C. Baur, was later led by his own researches to change his mind. He tells us in his *St Paul the Traveller and the Roman Citizen* (1895) that he began his investigation 'without any prejudice in favour of the conclusion' which he later reached, but 'on the contrary . . . with a mind unfavourable to it'.[15] Yet he was able to give reasons 'for placing the author of Acts among the historians of the first rank'.[16]

Nearly seventy years later A. N. Sherwin-White, who was Reader in ancient history at Oxford University and described himself as 'a professional Graeco-Roman historian',[17] strongly affirmed the accuracy of Luke's background knowledge. He wrote about the Acts:

> The historical framework is exact. In terms of time and place the details are precise and correct. One walks the streets and market-places, the theatres and assemblies of first-century Ephesus or Thessalonica, Corinth or Philippi, with the author of Acts. The great men of the cities, the magistrates, the mob and the mob-leader are all there. . . . It is similar with the narrative of Paul's judicial experiences before the tribunals of Gallio, Felix and Festus. As documents these narratives belong to the same historical series as the record of provincial and imperial trials in epigraphical and literary sources of the first and early second centuries AD.[18]

Here is his conclusion: 'For Acts the confirmation of historicity is overwhelming. . . . Any attempt to reject its basic historicity even in matters of detail must now appear absurd. Roman historians have long taken it for granted.'[19]

b. *Luke the diplomat*

The writing of history cannot have been Luke's only purpose, for the history he gives us is selective and incomplete. He tells us about Peter, John, James the Lord's brother and Paul, but nothing about the other apostles, except that James the son of Zebedee was beheaded. He describes the spread of the gospel north and west of Jerusalem, but writes nothing about its progress east and south, except for the conversion of the Ethiopian. He portrays the

[15] Ramsay, *St Paul*, pp. 7, 8. [16] *Ibid.*, p. 4.
[17] Sherwin-White, p. 186. [18] *Ibid.*, pp. 120–121.
[19] *Ibid.*, p. 189. See also the wealth of information in Hemer's chapter 5, 'Evidence from Historical Details in Acts' (pp. 159–220).

Palestinian church in the early post-Pentecost period, but then follows instead the expansion of the Gentile mission under the leadership of Paul. So Luke is more than a historian. He is, in fact, a sensitive Christian 'diplomat' in relation to both church and state.

First, Luke develops a political apologetic, because he is deeply concerned about the attitude of the Roman authorities towards Christianity. He therefore goes out of his way to defend Christianity against criticism. The authorities, he argues, have nothing to fear from Christians, for they are neither seditious nor subversive, but on the contrary legally innocent and morally harmless. More positively, they exercise a wholesome influence on society.

Perhaps this is why both Luke's volumes are addressed to Theophilus. Although the adjective *theophilēs*, meaning either 'loved by God' or 'loving God' (BAGD), could symbolize every Christian reader, it is more likely to be the name of a specific person. And although the adjective *kratistos* (*most excellent*, Lk. 1:3) could be either just 'a polite form of address with no official connotation', or the 'honorary form of address used to persons who hold a higher official or social position than the speaker' (BAGD), the latter seems more likely because it occurs later in relation to the procurators Felix (23:26; 24:3) and Festus (26:25). A modern equivalent might be 'Your Excellency' (NEB). Some scholars have gone on to suggest that Theophilus was a specific Roman official who had heard anti-Christian slanders, while B. H. Streeter thought the word was 'a prudential pseudonym', in fact (he guessed) 'the secret name by which Flavius Clemens was known in the Roman Church'.[20]

In any case, Luke repeatedly makes three points of political apologetic. First, Roman officials were consistently friendly to Christianity, and some had even become Christians, like the centurion at the cross, the centurion Cornelius, and Sergius Paulus, proconsul of Cyprus. Secondly, the Roman authorities could find no fault in either Jesus or his apostles. Jesus had been accused of sedition, but neither Herod nor Pilate could discover any basis for the accusation. As for Paul, in Philippi the magistrates apologized to him, in Corinth the proconsul Gallio refused to adjudicate, and in Ephesus the town clerk declared Paul and his friends to be innocent. Then Felix, Festus and Agrippa all failed to convict him of any offence – three acquittals corresponding to the three times Luke says Pilate had declared Jesus innocent.[21]

In the third place, the Roman authorities conceded that Christianity was a *religio licita* (a lawful or licensed religion) because it

[20] *The Four Gospels: A Study of Origins* by B. H. Streeter (Macmillan, 1924), pp. 534–539.

[21] Lk. 23:4, 14, 22.

was not a new religion (which would need to be approved by the state) but rather the purest form of Judaism (which had enjoyed religious freedom under the Romans since the second century BC). The coming of Christ was the fulfilment of Old Testament prophecy, and the Christian community enjoyed direct continuity with the Old Testament people of God.

This, then, was Luke's political apologetic. He produced evidence to show that Christianity was harmless (because some Roman officials had embraced it themselves), innocent (because Roman judges could find no basis for prosecution) and lawful (because it was the true fulfilment of Judaism). Christians should always be able on similar grounds to claim the protection of the state. I am reminded of a statement made in 1972 by the Baptist believers of Piryatin to Mr N. V. Podgorny, Chairman of the Praesidium of the Supreme Soviet of the USSR, and Mr L. I. Brezhnev, General Secretary of the Communist Party. Quoting articles of the USSR constitution and the Universal Declaration of Human Rights, together with particular laws and juridical interpretations, the Evangelical Christian Baptists of Piryatin claimed the right to freedom of conscience and confession, and declared that they did not break the law 'because there is nothing harmful, nothing opposed to the government, nothing fanatical in our activity, but only that which is spiritually useful and healthy, just, honest, peaceful in accordance with the teaching of Jesus Christ'.[22]

The second example of Luke's 'diplomacy' is that he was a peacemaker in the church. He wanted to demonstrate by his narrative that the early church was a united church, that the peril of division between Jewish and Samaritan Christians, and between Jewish and Gentile Christians, was providentially avoided, and that the apostles Peter, James and Paul were in fundamental agreement about the gospel.

It was Matthias Schneckenburger in his *Über den Zweck der Apostelgeschichte* (1841) who made 'the first elaborate investigation into the purpose of Acts'.[23] He believed that Luke was defending Paul against Jewish-Christian criticism of his mission to the Gentiles by emphasizing his Jewish practices and his good relations with the Jerusalem church. He was also at pains to demonstrate their 'parallel miracles, visions, sufferings and speeches',[24] in order 'to make Paul equal to Peter'.[25]

F. C. Baur went much further. He saw Acts as having a precise,

[22] Quoted in *Religion in Communist Lands*, Jan.-Feb., 1973 (published by Keston College).

[23] See the article by A. J. Mattill entitled 'The Purpose of Acts: Schneckenburger reconsidered' in Gasque and Martin, pp. 108–122.

[24] *Ibid.*, p. 110. [25] *Ibid.*, p. 111.

'tendentious' purpose. On the rather flimsy foundation of the Corinthian factions ('I follow Paul . . . I follow Peter . . .', 1 Cor. 1:12) he constructed an elaborate theory that the early church was torn apart by conflict between original Jewish Christianity represented by Peter and later Gentile Christianity represented by Paul. He regarded Acts as a second-century attempt by a 'Paulinist' (a follower and champion of Paul) to minimize, and even deny, the supposed hostility between the two leading apostles and so to reconcile Jewish and Gentile Christians to one another. He portrayed Paul as a faithful Jew, who kept the law and believed the prophets, and Peter as the evangelist through whom the first Gentile was converted. The two apostles are thus seen in harmony, not at loggerheads, with each other. In fact, Luke attempted to reconcile the 'two opposing parties by making Paul appear as Petrine as possible, and, correspondingly, Peter appear as Pauline as possible . . .'.[26]

It is generally agreed that F. C. Baur and his successors in the Tübingen School carried their theory much too far. There is really no evidence that in the early church there were two Christianities (Jewish and Gentile) headed by two apostles (Peter and Paul) in irreconcilable opposition to each other. Baur was probably influenced by Hegel's dialectical understanding of history in terms of a recurring conflict between thesis and antithesis. There certainly was tension between Jewish and Gentile Christians, and because of the activity of the Judaizers a serious split did seem possible until the issue was settled by the Council of Jerusalem. Luke does not hide this. Certainly too, in Antioch, Paul publicly opposed Peter to his face,[27] because of his withdrawal from fellowship with Gentile believers. But this confrontation was exceptional and temporary; Paul wrote about it to the Galatians in the past tense. Peter recovered from his momentary lapse. The reconciliation between the two leading apostles was real, not fictitious, and the thrust of Acts, Galatians 1 and 2, and 1 Corinthians 15:11 is on the agreement of the apostles about the gospel.

Luke did not invent this apostolic harmony, as Baur argued: he rather observed it and recorded it. It is evident that he gives prominence in his story to Peter (chapters 1–12) and to Paul (chapters 13–28). It seems very probable as well that he deliberately presents them as exercising parallel rather than divergent ministries. The similarities are remarkable. Thus, both Peter and Paul were filled with the Holy Spirit (4:8 and 9:17; 13:9); both preached the word of God with boldness (4:13, 31 and 9:27, 29); both bore witness

[26] Dr Ward Gasque's translation of F. C. Baur in his very thorough *A History of the Criticism of the Acts of the Apostles*, p. 326.

[27] Gal. 2:11.

before Jewish audiences to Jesus crucified, risen and reigning, in fulfilment of Scripture, as the way of salvation (*e.g.* 2:22ff. and 13:16ff.); both preached to Gentiles as well as Jews (10:34ff. and 13:46ff.); both received visions which gave vital direction to the church's developing mission (10:9ff.; 16:9); both were imprisoned for their testimony to Jesus and then miraculously set free (12:7ff. and 16:25ff.); both healed a congenital cripple, Peter in Jerusalem and Paul in Lystra (3:2ff. and 14:8ff.); both healed other sick people (9:41 and 28:8); both exorcized evil spirits (5:16 and 16:18); both possessed such extraordinary powers that people were healed by Peter's shadow and by Paul's handkerchiefs and aprons (5:15 and 19:12); both raised the dead, Tabitha in Joppa by Peter and Eutychus in Troas by Paul (9:36ff. and 20:7ff.); both called down God's judgment on a sorcerer/false teacher, Peter on Simon Magus in Samaria and Paul on Elymas in Paphos (8:20ff. and 13:6ff.); and both refused the worship of their fellow human beings, Peter that of Cornelius and Paul that of the Lystrans (10:25–26 and 14:11ff.).

It is true that these parallels are scattered through Acts and are not put in direct juxtaposition to each other. Yet there they are. They can hardly be accidental. Luke surely includes them in his narrative in order to show by his portraiture of Peter and Paul that they were both apostles of Christ, with the same commission, gospel and authentication. It is in this way that he may be called a 'peacemaker', who demonstrated the unity of the apostolic church.

c. *Luke the theologian-evangelist*

The value of 'redaction-criticism' is that it portrays the authors of the Gospels and the Acts not as unimaginative 'scissors and paste' editors, but as theologians in their own right, who conscientiously selected, arranged and presented their material in order to serve their particular pastoral purpose. It was in the 1950s that redaction-criticism began to be applied to the Acts, first by Martin Dibelius (1951), next by Hans Conzelmann (1954)[28] and then by Ernst Haenchen (1956) in his commentary. Unfortunately, these German scholars believed that Luke pursued his theological concerns at the expense of his historical reliability. Professor Howard Marshall, however, who has built on their work (while at the same time subjecting it to a rigorous critique), especially in his fine study *Luke: Historian and Theologian* (1970), urges that we must not set Luke the historian and Luke the theologian in opposition to each other, for he was both, and in fact each emphasis requires the other:

> Luke is *both* historian *and* theologian, and . . . the best term to describe him is 'evangelist', a term which, we believe, includes

[28] *Die Mitte de Zeit* (1954), whose English title is *The Theology of St. Luke* (1960).

> both of the others. . . . As a theologian Luke was concerned that his message about Jesus and the early church should be based upon reliable history. . . . He used his history in the service of his theology.[29]

Again, Luke was 'both a reliable historian and a good theologian. . . . We believe that the validity of his theology stands or falls with the reliability of the history on which it is based. . . . Luke's concern is with the saving significance of the history rather than with the history itself as bare facts'.[30]

In particular, then, Luke was a theologian of salvation. Salvation, wrote Howard Marshall, 'is the central motif in Lucan theology',[31] both in the Gospel (in which we see it accomplished) and in the Acts (in which we see it proclaimed). Michael Green had drawn attention to this in his *The Meaning of Salvation*. 'It is hard to overestimate the importance of salvation in the writings of Luke . . .', he wrote. 'It is astonishing . . . that in view of the frequency with which Luke uses salvation terminology, more attention has not been paid to it.'[32]

Luke's theology of salvation is already adumbrated in the 'Song of Simeon' or *Nunc Dimittis* which he records in his Gospel.[33] Three fundamental truths stand out.

First, *salvation has been prepared by God.* In speaking to God, Simeon referred to 'your salvation, which you have prepared in the sight of all people' (Lk. 2:30–31). Far from being an afterthought, it had been planned and promised for centuries. The same emphasis recurs throughout the Acts. In the sermons of Peter and Paul, not to mention Stephen's defence, Jesus' death, resurrection, reign and Spirit-gift are all seen as the culmination of centuries of prophetic promise.

Secondly, *salvation is bestowed by Christ.* When Simeon spoke to God of 'your salvation', which he had seen with his own eyes, he was referring to the baby Jesus whom he held in his arms and who had been 'born a Saviour' (Lk. 2:11). Jesus himself later made the unequivocal statement that he had come 'to seek and to save what was lost' (Lk. 19:10), and he illustrated it by his three famous parables of human lostness (Lk. 15:1–32). Then after his death and resurrection his apostles declared that forgiveness of sins was available to all who would repent and believe in Jesus (Acts 2:38–39; 13:38–39). Indeed, salvation was to be found in no-one else (Acts 4:12). For God had exalted Jesus to his right hand 'as Prince and Saviour that he might give repentance and forgiveness of sins . . .' (Acts 5:31).

[29] Marshall, *Luke*, pp. 18–19. [30] *Ibid.*, p. 85. [31] *Ibid.*, p. 93.
[32] Green, *The Meaning of Salvation*, pp. 125–131. [33] Lk. 2:29–32.

Thirdly, *salvation is offered to all peoples*. As Simeon put it, it has been prepared 'in the presence of all the peoples' (literally), to be both a light to the nations and the glory of Israel (Lk. 2:31–32). Without doubt it is this truth on which Luke lays his major emphasis. In Luke 3:6, in reference to John the Baptist, he continues his quotation from Isaiah 40 beyond where Matthew and Mark stop, in order to include the statement 'all flesh will see God's salvation'. In Acts 2:17 he records Peter's quotation of God's promise through Joel: 'I will pour out my Spirit on all flesh.' These two words *pasa sarx*, 'all flesh' or 'all humankind', stand as a signpost near the beginning of each of Luke's two volumes, in both cases embedded in an Old Testament prophecy, to point to Luke's principal message. Jesus is the Saviour of the world; nobody is beyond the embrace of his love. In his Gospel, Luke shows Jesus' compassion for those sections of the community whom others despised, namely women and children, the poor, the sick, the sinful and the outcast, Samaritans and Gentiles, while in the Acts Luke explains how Paul came to turn to the Gentiles, and describes the gospel's triumphal progress from Jerusalem the capital of Jewry to Rome the capital of the world.

The prominence given to the universal offer of the gospel comes with particular appropriateness from the pen of Luke. For he is the only Gentile contributor to the New Testament.[34] Well-educated and widely travelled, he is the only Gospel-writer who calls the Sea of Galilee a 'lake', because he is able to compare it with the Great Sea, the Mediterranean. He has the broad horizons of the Graeco-Roman world, its history as well as its geography. So he sets his story of Jesus and of the early church against the background of contemporary secular events. And he uses the word *oikoumenē*, 'the inhabited earth', more often (eight times) than all the other New Testament writers together.

But Luke the theologian of salvation is essentially the evangelist. For he proclaims the gospel of salvation from God in Christ for all people. Hence his inclusion in the Acts of so many sermons and addresses, especially by Peter and Paul. He not only shows them preaching to their original hearers, but also enables them to preach to us who, centuries later, listen to them. For as Peter said on the Day of Pentecost, the promise of salvation is for us too, and for every generation, indeed 'for all whom the Lord our God will call' (Acts 2:39).

[34] Col. 4:10ff. For Luke's emphasis on the world-wide expansion of the church see especially Dupont's *The Salvation of the Gentiles*.

2. Introduction to the Acts (Acts 1:1–5)

After our general introduction to Luke, and to his purposes in writing, we come now more particularly to the Acts and to its preface. We need to note carefully the way in which Luke understood both the relation between his two volumes and the foundation role exercised by the apostles.

a. Luke's two volumes

In my former book, Theophilus, I wrote about all that Jesus began to do and to teach ²until the day he was taken up to heaven, after giving instructions through the Holy Spirit to the apostles he had chosen.

Here Luke tells us how he thinks of his two-volume work on the origins of Christianity, which constitutes approximately one quarter of the New Testament. He does not regard volume one as the story of *Jesus Christ* from his birth through his sufferings and death to his triumphant resurrection and ascension, and volume two as the story of *the church of Jesus Christ* from its birth in Jerusalem through its sufferings by persecution to its triumphant conquest of Rome some thirty years later. For the contrasting parallel he draws between his two volumes was not between Christ and his church, but between two stages of the ministry of the same Christ. In his *former book* he has written *about all that Jesus began to do and to teach until the day he was taken up to heaven*, since he was 'powerful in word and deed before God and all the people';[35] in this his second book (he implies) he will write about what Jesus continued to do and to teach after his ascension, especially through the apostles whose sermons and authenticating 'signs and wonders' Luke will faithfully record. Thus Jesus' ministry on earth, exercised personally and publicly, was followed by his ministry from heaven, exercised through his Holy Spirit by his apostles. Moreover, the watershed between the two was the ascension. Not only did it conclude Luke's first book[36] and introduce his second (Acts 1:9), but it terminated Jesus' earthly ministry and inaugurated his heavenly ministry.

What, then, is the correct title for Luke's second volume? Its popular name, especially in the United States, is 'the Book of Acts', and this is justified by the fourth-century Codex Sinaiticus in which it is headed simply *Praxeis*, 'Acts'. But this neither tells us whose acts Luke is portraying, nor helps to distinguish his book from the later apocryphal works like the second-century *Acts of John*, *Acts of Paul* and *Acts of Peter*, and the third-century *Acts of Andrew*

[35] Lk. 24:19. [36] Lk. 24:51.

and *Acts of Thomas*. These were pious romances intended to enhance the reputation of the apostle concerned, especially by legendary miracles, and usually to promote under his patronage some unorthodox tendency.[37]

The traditional title since the second century has been 'The Acts of (the) Apostles', with or without the definite article. And certainly it is apostles who occupy the centre of Luke's stage – first Peter and John (chapters 1–8), then Peter on his own (chapters 10–12), James as chairman of the Jerusalem Council (chapter 15), and especially Paul (chapters 9 and 13–28). Yet this title is too man-centred; it omits the divine power by which the apostles spoke and acted.

Others have proposed the title 'The Acts of the Holy Spirit', for example, Johann Albrecht Bengel in the eighteenth century. He wrote that Luke's second volume 'describes not so much the Acts of the Apostles as the Acts of the Holy Spirit, even as the former treatise contains the Acts of Jesus Christ'.[38] The concept was popularized by Arthur T. Pierson whose commentary (1895) was published with this title:

> This book we may, perhaps, venture to call the *Acts of the Holy Spirit*, for from first to last it is the record of his advent and activity. Here he is seen coming and working. . . . But (*sc.* only) one true Actor and Agent is here recognized, all other so-called actors or workers being merely his instruments, an agent being one who acts, an instrument being that through which he acts.[39]

Pierson ends his book with a stirring challenge:

> Church of Christ! The records of these acts of the Holy Ghost have never reached completeness. This is the one book which has no proper close, because it waits for new chapters to be added so fast and so far as the people of God shall reinstate the blessed Spirit in his holy seat of control.[40]

This, to be sure, is a healthy corrective. Throughout Luke's narrative there are references to the promise, gift, outpouring, baptism, fullness, power, witness and guidance of the Holy Spirit. It would be impossible to explain the progress of the gospel apart from the work of the Spirit. Nevertheless, if the title 'the Acts of the Apostles' over-emphasizes the human element, 'the Acts of the Holy Spirit' over-emphasizes the divine, since it overlooks the apostles as the chief characters through whom the Spirit worked. It is also inconsistent with Luke's first verse which implies that the

[37] James, pp. 228–438. [38] Bengel, p. 512. [39] Pierson, p. 18.
[40] *Ibid.*, pp. 141–142.

acts and words he reports are those of the ascended Christ working through the Holy Spirit who, as Luke knows, is 'the Spirit of Jesus' (Acts 16:7). The most accurate (though cumbersome) title, then, which does justice to Luke's own statement in verses 1 and 2, would be something like 'The Continuing Words and Deeds of Jesus by his Spirit through his Apostles'.

Luke's first two verses are, therefore, extremely significant. It is no exaggeration to say that they set Christianity apart from all other religions. These regard their founder as having completed his ministry during his lifetime; Luke says Jesus only began his. True, he finished the work of atonement, yet that end was also a beginning. For after his resurrection, ascension and gift of the Spirit he continued his work, first and foremost through the unique foundation ministry of his chosen apostles and subsequently through the post-apostolic church of every period and place. This, then, is the kind of Jesus Christ we believe in: he is both the historical Jesus who lived and the contemporary Jesus who lives. The Jesus of history began his ministry on earth; the Christ of glory has been active through his Spirit ever since, according to his promise to be with his people 'always, to the very end of the age'.[41]

b. The foundation ministry of the apostles

He was taken up to heaven, after giving instructions through the Holy Spirit to the apostles he had chosen. [3]*After his suffering, he showed himself to these men and gave many convincing proofs that he was alive. He appeared to them over a period of forty days and spoke about the kingdom of God.* [4]*On one occasion, while he was eating with them, he gave them this command: 'Do not leave Jerusalem, but wait for the gift my Father promised, which you have heard me speak about.* [5]*For John baptised with water, but in a few days you will be baptised with the Holy Spirit.'*

We have already noted that the ascension was the watershed between the two phases – earthly and heavenly – of the ministry of Jesus Christ. Now we need to note that he was not *taken up to heaven*, until *after* he had given *instructions through the Holy Spirit to the apostles he had chosen*. This is clearly emphasized in the Greek sentence, which reads literally: 'until the day when, having instructed his chosen apostles through the Holy Spirit, he was taken up.' Thus, before ending his personal ministry on earth, Jesus deliberately made provision for its continuance, still on earth (through the apostles) but from heaven (through the Holy Spirit). Because the apostles occupied a unique position, they also received a unique equipment. Luke outlines four stages.

[41] Mt. 28:20.

(i) Jesus chose them

They were *the apostles he had chosen* (2). Luke has used the same verb *eklegomai* in his account of Jesus' calling and choice of the Twelve, 'whom he also designated apostles',[42] and he is about to use it again when two men are proposed to fill the vacancy left by Judas and the believers pray 'Lord, . . . show us which of these two you have chosen' (24). Significantly, the same verb is also used later in connection with Paul. The risen Lord describes him to Ananias as 'my chosen instrument to carry my name before the Gentiles . . .' (9:15), and Ananias conveys this message to Paul: 'The God of our fathers has chosen you . . . You will be his witness . . .' (22:14–15). It is thus emphasized that all the apostles (the Twelve, Matthias and Paul) were neither self-appointed, nor appointed by any human being, committee, synod or church, but were directly and personally chosen and appointed by Jesus Christ himself.

(ii) Jesus showed himself to them

The other evangelists have indicated that Jesus appointed the Twelve 'that they might be with him' and so be uniquely qualified to bear witness to him.[43] The foundation witnesses had to be eyewitnesses.[44] Judas' successor, Peter said, had to be someone who had been with the Twelve 'the whole time the Lord Jesus went in and out among us, beginning from John's baptism to the time when Jesus was taken up from us' (1:21–22). And in particular he must be 'a witness with us of his resurrection' (1:22, *cf.* 10:41). So, *after his suffering*, the risen Lord *showed himself to these men* (3). Luke stresses this. Jesus *gave* them *many convincing proofs* (*tekmērion* is a 'convincing, decisive proof' – BAGD) *that he was alive*, which continued *over a period of forty days*. During this time *he appeared to them* (becoming visible), *spoke about the kingdom of God* (so that they heard as well as saw him) and *on one occasion* at least *was eating with them*, which indicates that he was no ghost, but could be touched (10:41).[45] He thus presented himself to their senses: their eyes, ears and hands. Such an objective experience of the risen Lord was an indispensable qualification of an apostle, which explains why Paul could be one[46] and James[47] and why there have been no comparable apostles since and can be none today.

(iii) Jesus commanded or commissioned them

In addition to speaking to them about the kingdom of God (3) and the Holy Spirit (4–5), which we shall consider further in the next chapter, he gave them certain *instructions through the Holy Spirit*

[42] Lk. 6:13; *cf.* Jn. 6:70. [43] Mk. 3:14; Jn. 15:27; *cf.* Acts 22:14–15.
[44] Lk. 1:2. [45] *Cf.* Lk. 24:41–43 and Jn. 21:10ff.
[46] 1 Cor. 9:1; 15:8ff. [47] 1 Cor. 15:7.

(who inspired all his teaching[48]). What were these instructions? It is interesting that the Bezan or Western text[49] answers this question by adding 'the apostles whom he had chosen and commanded to preach the gospel'. If this is correct, then the risen Lord's instruction was none other than his great commission, which Luke has already recorded at the end of his gospel in terms of preaching repentance and forgiveness in his name to all nations,[50] and which Jesus will soon repeat in terms of being his witnesses to the ends of the earth (1:8). This, then, adds a further feature to the portrait of an apostle. *Apostolos* was an envoy, delegate or ambassador, sent out with a message and carrying the authority of the sender. Thus Jesus chose his apostles, and showed himself to them after the resurrection, as preliminaries to sending them out to preach and teach in his name.

(iv) Jesus promised them the Holy Spirit

In the Upper Room, according to John, Jesus had already promised the apostles that the Spirit of truth would both remind them of what he had taught them[51] and supplement it with what he had not been able to teach them.[52] Now Jesus commands them to wait in Jerusalem until the promised gift has been received (4). It was his Father's promise (4a, presumably through such Old Testament prophecies as Joel 2:28ff., Is. 32:15 and Ezk. 36:27), his own (since Jesus had himself repeated it during his ministry, 4b), and John the Baptist's, who had called the 'gift' or 'promise' a 'baptism' (5). Jesus now echoes John's words and adds that the thrice-repeated promise ('the promised Holy Spirit', 2:33) is to be fulfilled *in a few days*. So they must wait. Not till God has fulfilled his promise and they have been 'clothed with power from on high', can they fulfil their commission.[53]

Here, then, was the fourfold equipment of the apostles of Christ.

[48] *Cf.* Lk. 4:18.

[49] Acts was known to the early church in two Greek texts, the 'Alexandrian', especially in the great fourth- and fifth-century codices (Sinaiticus, Vaticanus and Alexandrinus) and the 'Western', especially in the fifth- or sixth-century Codex Bezae (which is kept in the Cambridge University Library), although its existence has been traced back at least to the second century. The latter differs from the former as being in size longer (about 1,500 more words), in style smoother, and in content more colourful. Some scholars think Luke himself issued two editions of Acts, beginning either with a rough draft which he later abbreviated or with a concise draft which he later elaborated. Others think Luke produced only one original, which was deliberately amended by a later scribe (either by expansion or by contraction). 'In all probability', writes C. K. Barrett, 'each has something to contribute to our knowledge of Luke's text' (*Luke the Historian in Recent Study*, p. 8). For a thorough discussion see Metzger, pp. 259–272, Haenchen, pp. 50–60 and Hemer, pp. 193–201.

[50] Lk. 24:47. [51] Jn. 14:26. [52] Jn. 16:12ff. [53] Lk. 24:49.

Of course in a secondary sense all the disciples of Jesus can claim that he has chosen us, revealed himself to us, commissioned us as his witnesses, and both promised and given us his Spirit. Nevertheless, it is not to these general privileges that Luke is referring here, but to the special qualifications of an apostle – a personal appointment as an apostle by Jesus, an eyewitness experience of the historical Jesus, an authorizing and commissioning by Jesus to speak in his name, and the empowering Spirit of Jesus to inspire their teaching. It was primarily these uniquely qualified men through whom Jesus continued 'to do and to teach', and to whom Luke intends to introduce us in the Acts.

A. IN JERUSALEM
Acts 1:6—6:7

1. Waiting for Pentecost
1:6-26

The major event of the early chapters of the Acts took place on the Day of Pentecost, when the now-exalted Lord Jesus performed the last work of his saving career (until his coming again) and 'poured out' the Holy Spirit on his waiting people. His life, death, resurrection and ascension all culminated in this great gift, which the prophets had foretold and which would be recognized as the chief evidence that God's kingdom had been inaugurated. For this conclusion of Christ's work on earth was also a fresh beginning. Just as the Spirit came upon Jesus to equip him for his public ministry,[1] so now the Spirit was to come upon his people to equip them for theirs. The Holy Spirit would not only apply to them the salvation which Jesus had achieved by his death and resurrection but would impel them to proclaim throughout the world the good news of this salvation. Salvation is given to be shared.

Before the Day of Pentecost, however, there was to be a time of waiting, for forty days between the resurrection and the ascension of Jesus (1:3), and for ten more between Ascension and Pentecost. Jesus' instructions were quite clear, and Luke repeats them for emphasis, first at the end of his Gospel and then at the beginning of Acts. 'Stay in the city until you have been clothed with power from on high.'[2] 'Do not leave Jerusalem, but wait for the gift my Father promised, which you have heard me speak about' (1:4). During the fifty-day waiting period, however, they were not inactive. On the contrary, Luke singles out for comment four important events. First, they received their commission (1:6–8). Secondly, they saw Christ go into heaven (1:9–12). Thirdly, they persevered together in prayer, presumably for the Spirit to come (1:13–14). Fourthly, they replaced Judas with Matthias as the twelfth apostle (1:21–26). Not that we are to think of these as human activities only. For it is Christ who commissioned them, ascended into

[1] Lk. 3:21–22; 4:14, 18. [2] Lk. 24:49

heaven, promised them the Spirit they prayed for, and chose the new apostle. Dr Richard Longenecker goes further and sees these four factors as comprising what he calls 'the constitutive elements of the Christian mission', namely the mandate to witness, the ascended Lord who directs the mission from heaven, the centrality of the apostles in this task, and the coming of the Spirit to empower them.[3] Only when these four elements were in place could the mission begin.

1. They received their commission (1:6–8)

So when they met together, they asked him, 'Lord, are you at this time going to restore the kingdom to Israel?'

7He said to them: 'It is not for you to know the times or dates the Father has set by his own authority. 8But you will receive power when the Holy Spirit comes on you; and you will be my witnesses in Jerusalem, and in all Judea and Samaria, and to the ends of the earth.'

During the forty days in which the risen Lord 'showed himself' to the apostles, and 'gave many convincing proofs that he was alive' (3), Luke indicates what he taught them. First, he spoke to them 'about the kingdom of God' (3), which had been the burden of his message during his public ministry and indeed (judging from the present participle *legōn*, 'speaking') continued to be after his resurrection. Secondly, he told them to wait for the gift or baptism of the Spirit, which had been promised by him, the Father and the Baptist, and which they would now receive 'in a few days' (4–5).

It appears, then, that Jesus' two main topics of conversation between his resurrection and his ascension were the kingdom of God and the Spirit of God. It seems probable that he also related them to each other, for certainly the prophets had often associated them. When God establishes the kingdom of the Messiah, they said, he will pour out his Spirit; this generous effusion and universal enjoyment of the Spirit will be one of the major signs and blessings of his rule; and indeed the Spirit of God will make the rule of God a living and present reality to his people.[4]

So then the question which the apostles put to Jesus when they met together (*Lord, are you at this time going to restore the kingdom to Israel?*, 6) was not altogether the *non sequitur* it sounds. For if the Spirit was about to come, as he had said, did this not imply that the kingdom was about to come too? The mistake they

[3] Longenecker, *Acts*, pp. 253ff.

[4] *E.g.* Is. 32:15ff.; 35:6ff.; 43:19ff.; 44:3; Ezk. 11:19; 36:26–27; 37:11ff.; 39:29; Joel 2:28–29.

made was to misunderstand both the nature of the kingdom and the relation between the kingdom and the Spirit. Their question must have filled Jesus with dismay. Were they still so lacking in perception? As Calvin commented, 'there are as many errors in this question as words'.[5] The verb, the noun and the adverb of their sentence all betray doctrinal confusion about the kingdom. For the verb *restore* shows that they were expecting a political and territorial kingdom; the noun *Israel* that they were expecting a national kingdom; and the adverbial clause *at this time* that they were expecting its immediate establishment. In his reply (7–8) Jesus corrected their mistaken notions of the kingdom's nature, extent and arrival.[6]

a. *The kingdom of God is spiritual in its character*

In the English language, of course, a 'kingdom' is usually a territorial sphere which can be located on a map, like the Hashemite kingdom of Jordan, the Hindu kingdom of Nepal, the Buddhist kingdom of Thailand, or the United Kingdom. But the kingdom of God is not a territorial concept. It does not – and cannot – figure on any map. Yet this is what the apostles were still envisaging by confusing the kingdom of God with the kingdom of Israel. They were like the members of Israel's righteous remnant whom Luke mentions in his Gospel as 'waiting for the kingdom of God' or 'the consolation of Israel',[7] and like the Emmaus couple who 'had hoped that he [Jesus] was the one who was going to redeem Israel',[8] but had become disillusioned because of the cross. The apostles' hope, however, had evidently been rekindled by the resurrection. They were still dreaming of political dominion, of the

[5] Calvin, I, p. 29.

[6] In the exposition of these verses I am following what may justly be termed the 'reformed' perspective, namely that the New Testament authors understood the Old Testament prophecies concerning the seed of Abraham, the promised land and the kingdom as having been fulfilled in Christ. Although Paul does predict a widespread turning of Jews to Christ before the end (Rom. 11:25ff.), he does not link it with the land. Indeed, the New Testament contains no clear promise of a Jewish return to the land. I fully recognize that the 'dispensational' view is different. It holds that the Old Testament promises relating to the Jewish occupation of the land will be (in fact, are already being) fulfilled literally, and that in the New Testament this is indicated by Mark 13:28ff. (the blossoming of the fig tree, symbolizing Israel) and Luke 21:24 (the trampling of Jerusalem by the Gentiles 'until the times of the Gentiles are fulfilled', implying that after this period Jerusalem will be rebuilt). In the dispensational view, therefore, the apostles were correct to ask about the restoration of the kingdom to Israel, for it will one day be fully restored to them (probably during a literal millennial reign of Christ on earth). In this case, what Jesus rebuked them for was not their expectation of a national kingdom but only their desire to know 'times and dates', together perhaps with their consequent lack of concern for world mission.

[7] Lk. 23:51; *cf.* 2:25, 38. [8] Lk. 24:21.

re-establishment of the monarchy, of Israel's liberation from the colonial yoke of Rome.

In his reply Jesus reverted to the topic of the Holy Spirit. He spoke of the Spirit coming upon them and giving them power to be his witnesses (8). In Charles Williams' notable words, he departed 'scattering promises of power'.[9] It is important to remember that his promise that they would *receive power* was part of his reply to their question about the kingdom. For the exercise of power is inherent in the concept of a kingdom. But power in God's kingdom is different from power in human kingdoms. The reference to the Holy Spirit defines its nature. The kingdom of God is his rule set up in the lives of his people by the Holy Spirit. It is spread by witnesses, not by soldiers, through a gospel of peace, not a declaration of war, and by the work of the Spirit, not by force of arms, political intrigue or revolutionary violence. At the same time, in rejecting the politicizing of the kingdom, we must beware of the opposite extreme of super-spiritualizing it, as if God's rule operates only in heaven and not on earth. The fact is that, although it must not be identified with any political ideology or programme, it has radical political and social implications. Kingdom values come into collision with secular values. And the citizens of God's kingdom steadfastly deny to Caesar the supreme loyalty for which he hungers, but which they insist on giving to Jesus alone.

b. The kingdom of God is international in its membership

The apostles still cherished narrow, nationalistic aspirations. They asked Jesus if he was about to restore to Israel her national independence, which the Maccabees had regained in the second century BC for a brief intoxicating period, only to lose it again.

In his reply Jesus broadened their horizons. He promised that the Holy Spirit would empower them to be his witnesses. They would begin indeed in Jerusalem, the national capital in which he had been condemned and crucified, and which they were not to leave before the Spirit came. They would continue in the immediate environs of Judea. But then the Christian mission would radiate out from that centre, in accordance with the ancient prophecy that 'the law will go out from Zion, the word of the Lord from Jerusalem',[10] first to despised Samaria, and then far beyond Palestine to the Gentile nations, indeed *to the ends of the earth*. The thesis of Johannes Blauw in his book *The Missionary Nature of the Church* is that the Old Testament perspective was one of concern for the nations (God made them, and they will come and bow

[9] *He Came Down From Heaven* by Charles Williams (1938; Eerdmans, 1984), p. 82.

[10] Is. 2:3 = Mi. 4:2.

down to him), but not of mission to the nations (going out to win them). Even the Old Testament vision of the latter days is of a 'pilgrimage of the nations' to Mount Zion: 'all nations will stream to it.'[11] Only in the New Testament, Blauw adds, is a 'centripetal missionary consciousness' replaced by a 'centrifugal missionary activity', and 'the great turning-point is the Resurrection, after which Jesus receives universal authority and gives his people a universal commission to go and disciple the nations'.[12]

The risen Lord's mandate to mission begins to be fulfilled in the Acts. Indeed, as many commentators have pointed out, Acts 1:8 is a kind of 'Table of Contents' for the book. Chapters 1–7 describe events in Jerusalem, chapter 8 mentions the scattering of the disciples 'throughout Judea and Samaria' (8:1), and goes on to record the evangelization of a Samaritan city by Philip (8:5–24) and of 'many Samaritan villages' by the apostles Peter and John (8:25), while the conversion of Saul in chapter 9 leads on in the rest of the book to his missionary expeditions, and finally to his journey to Rome. For Christ's kingdom, while not incompatible with patriotism, tolerates no narrow nationalisms. He rules over an international community in which race, nation, rank and sex are no barriers to fellowship. And when his kingdom is consummated at the end, the countless redeemed company will be seen to be drawn 'from every nation, tribe, people and language'.[13]

c. *The kingdom of God is gradual in its expansion*

The apostles' question included a specific reference to time: 'Lord, are you *at this time* going to restore the kingdom to Israel?'(1:6). Or (NEB) 'is this the time when you are to establish once again the sovereignty of Israel?' This had been the expectation of many during Jesus' public ministry, as Luke makes clear in his Gospel. He records a parable which (he explains) Jesus told 'because he was near Jerusalem and the people thought that the kingdom of God was going to appear at once'.[14] So the apostles asked if Jesus would do now after his resurrection what they had hoped he would do in his lifetime; and would he do it immediately?

The Lord's reply was twofold. First, *it is not for you to know the times or dates the Father has set by his own authority* (7). 'Times' (*chronoi*) or 'dates' (*kairoi*) together make up God's plan, 'the *times* or critical moments of its history and the *seasons* or epochs of its orderly development'.[15] The apostles' question

[11] Is. 2:2–3.

[12] *The Missionary Nature of the Church* by Johannes Blauw (1962; Eerdmans 1974), especially pp. 34, 54, 66, 83–84.

[13] Rev. 7:9. [14] Lk. 19:11.

[15] Rackham, p. 7. *Cf.* also Conzelmann's *The Theology of St Luke.*

betrayed either curiosity or impatience or both. For the Father himself had fixed the times by his own authority, and the Son had confessed that he did not know the day and hour of his return (*parousia*).[16] So they must curb their inquisitiveness and be willing to be left in ignorance. It is not only in relation to the fulfilment of prophecy, but to many other undisclosed truths as well, that Jesus still says to us 'it is not for you to know'. The 'secret things' belong to God, and we should not pry into them; it is the 'revealed things' which belong to us, and with these we should rest content.[17]

Secondly, although they were not to know the times or dates, what they should know was that they would receive power so that, between the Spirit's coming and the Son's coming again, they were to be his witnesses in ever-widening circles. In fact, the whole interim period between Pentecost and the Parousia (however long or short) is to be filled with the world-wide mission of the church in the power of the Spirit. Christ's followers were both to announce what he had achieved at his first coming and to summon people to repent and believe in preparation for his second coming. They were to be his witnesses 'to the ends of the earth' (1:8) and 'to the very end of the age'.[18] This was a major theme of Bishop Lesslie Newbigin in his book *The Household of God:*

> The Church is the pilgrim people of God. It is on the move – hastening to the ends of the earth to beseech all men to be reconciled to God, and hastening to the end of time to meet its Lord who will gather all into one. . . . It cannot be understood rightly except in a perspective which is at once missionary and eschatological.[19]

We have no liberty to stop until both ends have been reached. Indeed the two ends, Jesus taught, would coincide, since only when the gospel of the kingdom has been preached in the whole world as a testimony to all nations, only then 'will the end come'.[20]

So this was the substance of the Lord's teaching (as we know also from the Gospels) during the forty days between the resurrection and the ascension: when the Spirit came in power, the long promised reign of God, which Jesus had himself inaugurated and proclaimed, would begin to spread. It would be spiritual in its character (transforming the lives and values of its citizens), international in its membership (including Gentiles as well as Jews) and gradual in its expansion (beginning at once in Jerusalem, and then growing until it reaches the end of both time and earthly space). This vision and commission must have given clear direction to the

[16] Mk. 13:32. [17] Dt. 29:29. [18] Mt. 28:20.
[19] *The Household of God* by Lesslie Newbigin (SCM, 1953), p. 25.
[20] Mt. 24:14; *cf.* Mk. 13:10.

disciples' prayers during their ten days of waiting for Pentecost. But before the Spirit could come, the Son must go. This is Luke's next topic.

2. They saw Jesus go into heaven (1:9–12)

After he said this, he was taken up before their very eyes, and a
cloud hid him from their sight.
[10]*They were looking intently up into the sky as he was going,*
when suddenly two men dressed in white stood beside them. [11] *'Men*
of Galilee,' they said, 'why do you stand here looking into the sky?
This same Jesus, who has been taken from you into heaven, will
come back in the same way you have seen him go into heaven.'
[12]*Then they returned to Jerusalem from the hill called the Mount*
of Olives, a Sabbath day's walk from the city.

At least three questions form in our minds as we read this story of the 'ascension' of Jesus – literary, historical and theological. First, do not Luke's two accounts of the ascension[21] contradict each other? Secondly, did the ascension of Jesus literally happen? Thirdly, if it did, has it any permanent significance?

a. Did Luke contradict himself?

It is certainly appropriate, as we have already seen, that Luke should conclude his first volume and introduce his second with the same event, the ascension of Jesus, since it was both the end of his earthly ministry and the prelude to his continuing ministry from heaven through the Spirit. It is antecedently improbable, however, that the same author, telling the same story, should contradict himself. Yet this is what some modern scholars assert. Ernst Haenchen writes, for example: 'Two Ascensions – one on Easter Day (Lk. 24:51), the other forty days after (Acts 1:9) – are one too many.'[22] But in fact there are no substantial discrepancies, and a harmonization of the two accounts is possible, without forcing the evidence.

It is true that in his Gospel, Luke makes no mention of the forty days. But it is gratuitous to suggest that he must therefore have forgotten them, or that he thought that the resurrection and the ascension occurred on the same day. No, in the Gospel he is simply giving a condensed account of the resurrection appearances, without feeling the need to note their different times and circumstances. He is indubitably recording one ascension, not two.

It is also true that each account includes details which the other omits, the Acts version being fuller than that in the Gospel. For

[21] Lk. 24:50ff.; Acts 1:9ff. [22] Haenchen, p. 145.

example, at the end of the Gospel the ascending Christ raised his hands to bless them, and they worshipped him.[23] Luke omits these actions at the beginning of his second volume, but adds there the cloud which hid him from their sight, and the appearance and message of 'the two men dressed in white', presumed to be angels. Yet these features of the story supplement, and do not contradict, each other.

It is true, thirdly, that the Acts account seems to imply that Jesus ascended from the Mount of Olives (1:12), which is correctly said to be 'a Sabbath day's walk from the city', namely (according to the Mishnah) 2,000 cubits or (NIV margin) about three-quarters of a mile (about 1,100 metres)', whereas the Gospel account says that Jesus 'led them out to the vicinity of Bethany',[24] the village on the east slope of the mount, which is two or three miles further away from Jerusalem. Conzelmann declares that the latter 'flatly contradicts the geographical reference in Acts 1:12',[25] and Haenchen assumes that Luke 'did not possess any exact notion of the topography of Jerusalem'.[26] But Luke's Gospel statement may well be intentionally vague. He does not say that Jesus ascended from Bethany, but only that he led the apostles in that direction, *heōs pros* being quite properly rendered by NIV 'to the vicinity of Bethany'.

Having looked at what are said to be the three main discrepancies (regarding date, details and place), we may now note five points which the two accounts affirm in common. (i) Both say that the ascension of Jesus followed his commission to the apostles to be his witnesses. (ii) Both say that it took place outside and east of Jerusalem, somewhere on the Mount of Olives. (iii) Both say that Jesus 'was taken up into heaven', the passive voice indicating that the ascension like the resurrection was an act of the Father, who first raised him from the dead and then exalted him to heaven. As Chrysostom put it, 'the royal chariot (was) sent for him'.[27] (iv) Both say that the apostles 'returned to Jerusalem' afterwards, the Gospel adding 'with great joy'. (v) And both say that they then waited for the Spirit to come, in accordance with the Lord's plain command and promise. Thus the evident agreements are greater than the apparent disagreements. The latter are sufficiently explained by supposing that Luke used his editorial freedom in selecting different details from the account or accounts he had heard, without wishing to repeat himself word for word.

b. Did the ascension really happen?

Many people nowadays, even within the church, deny the histor-

[23] Lk 24:50ff [24] Lk 24:50 [25] Conzelmann, p. 94
[26] Haenchen, p 150 [27] Chrysostom, Homily II, p. 14

icity of the ascension. Belief in a literal ascension would have been understandable in Luke's day, they say, when people imagined heaven to be 'up there', so that Jesus had to be 'taken up' in order to get there. But that was a pre-scientific age; we have an altogether different cosmology. Must we not therefore 'demythologize' the ascension? Then we can retain the truth that Jesus 'went to the Father', while at the same time stripping it of its 'primitive mythological clothing' which depicts it as a kind of 'lift-off', followed by an ascent into the sky. Besides, Luke is the only Gospel-writer who tells the story of the ascension. The others omit it. In fact the New Testament authors in general hardly distinguish between the resurrection and the ascension; they seem to regard them as the same event, or perhaps two aspects of the same event. So Harnack could write that 'the account of the Ascension is quite useless to the historian'.[28] Even William Neil, who is usually quite conservative in his conclusions, tells his readers (without argument) that Luke, knowing that 'theological truth can often be best conveyed by imaginative word-pictures', is not to be interpreted literally. 'It would be a grave misunderstanding of Luke's mind and purpose to regard his account of the Ascension of Christ as other than symbolic and poetic.'[29]

A number of sound reasons can be given, however, why we should reject this attempt to discredit the ascension as a literal, historical event.

First, miracles do not need precedents to validate them. The classical argument of the eighteenth-century deists was that we can believe strange happenings outside our experience only if we can produce something analogous to them within our experience. This 'principle of analogy', if correct, would be enough in itself to disprove many of the biblical miracles, for we have no experience (for example) of somebody walking on water, multiplying loaves and fishes, rising from the dead or ascending into heaven. An ascension, in particular, would defy the law of gravity, which in our experience operates always and everywhere. The principle of analogy, however, has no relevance to the resurrection and ascension of Jesus, since both were *sui generis*. We are not claiming that people frequently (or even occasionally) rise from the dead and ascend into heaven, but that both events have happened once. The fact that we can produce no analogies before or since confirms their truth, rather than undermining it.

Secondly, the ascension is everywhere assumed in the New Testament. Although Luke is the only evangelist who describes it (Mark 16:19 is not an authentic part of Mark's Gospel, but a later addition

[28] Harnack, *Acts*, p. 241. [29] Neil, p. 66.

to it), it is incorrect to say that it is otherwise unknown. John records the risen Jesus as telling Mary Magdalene to stop clinging to him because he has not yet ascended to the Father.[30] Peter in his Pentecost sermon speaks of Jesus having been 'exalted to the right hand of God' as something different from and subsequent to his resurrection (Acts 2:31ff.), and he confirms it in his first letter.[31] Paul frequently writes of the exaltation of Jesus to the supreme place of honour and power, and distinguishes it from his resurrection.[32] And in the Epistle to the Hebrews the rising and the reigning of Jesus are not confused.[33]

Thirdly, Luke tells the story of the ascension with simplicity and sobriety. All the extravagances associated with the Apocryphal Gospels are missing. There is no embroidery such as we find in legends. There is no evidence of poetry or symbolism. Even Haenchen admits this: 'the story is unsentimental, almost uncannily austere.'[34] It reads like history, and as if Luke intended us to accept it as history.

Fourthly, Luke emphasizes the presence of eyewitnesses, and repeatedly refers to what they saw with their own eyes: 'he was taken up *before their very eyes*, and a cloud hid him *from their sight*. They were *looking intently* up into the sky as he was going. . .'. The two angels then said to them, 'Why do you stand here *looking* into the sky? This same Jesus . . . will come back in the same way you have *seen him go* into heaven.' Five times in this extremely brief account it is stressed that the ascension took place visibly. Luke has not piled up these phrases for nothing. He has much to say in his two-volume work about the importance for the verification of the gospel of the apostolic eyewitnesses. And here he plainly includes the ascension of Jesus within the range of historical truths to which the eyewitnesses could (and did) testify. Indeed, when Judas is replaced, Peter will make John's baptism and Jesus' ascension the beginning and end of the public ministry to which the apostles must bear witness (1:22).

Fifthly, no alternative explanation is available of the cessation of the resurrection appearances and of the final disappearance of Jesus from the earth. What happened to him, then, and why did his appearances stop? What was the origin of the tradition that they

[30] Jn. 20:17. [31] 1 Pet. 3:21–22.

[32] *E.g.* 1 Cor. 15:1–28; Eph. 1:18–23; Phil. 2:9–11; 3:10, 20; Col. 3:1; *cf.* 1 Tim. 3:16.

[33] *E.g.* Heb. 1:3; 4:14ff.; 8:1; 9:11ff. 13:20.

[34] Haenchen, p. 151. As an example of an extravagant description consider the end of the *Epistle to the Apostles*, which has been dated about AD 160: 'there was thunder and lightning and an earthquake, and the heavens parted asunder, and there appeared a bright cloud which bore him up' (James, p. 503).

lasted for precisely forty days? In default of any other answer to these questions, we prefer the explanation for which there is evidence, namely that the forty-day period began with his resurrection and terminated with his ascension.

Sixthly, the visible, historical ascension had a readily intelligible purpose. Jesus had no need to take a journey in space, and it is silly of some critics to ridicule his ascension by representing him as the first cosmonaut. No, in the transition from his earthly to his heavenly state, Jesus could perfectly well have vanished, as on other occasions, and 'gone to the Father' secretly and invisibly. The reason for a public and visible ascension is surely that he wanted them to know that he had gone for good. During the forty days he had kept appearing, disappearing and reappearing. But now this interim period was over. This time his departure was final. So they were not to wait around for his next resurrection appearance. Instead, they were to wait for somebody else, the Holy Spirit (1:4). For he would come only after Jesus had gone, and then they could get on with their mission in the power he would give them.

At all events, the manner of his going (a visible ascension) had its desired effect. The apostles returned to Jerusalem and waited for the Spirit to come.

c. *What is the permanent value of the ascension story?*

We have seen what the visible ascension did for the apostles; what can it do for us? If we were to give a thorough answer to this question, we would need to bring different strands of teaching together from all the New Testament authors, including the completed sacrifice and continuing intercession of our Great High Priest described in Hebrews, the glorification of the Son of man taught by John, the cosmic lordship emphasized by Paul and the final triumph when his enemies will become his footstool, foretold by Psalm 110:1, and endorsed by those who quote it. But it is not with these truths that Luke is concerned. In order to understand his primary interest as he tells the ascension story, we shall need to pay attention to those *two men dressed in white* (10) who *stood beside them* (the apostles) and spoke to them. Luke calls them 'men' because that is how they appeared, but their shining dress and authoritative tone indicate that they were angels. In his Gospel, Luke has recorded the ministry of angels at several crucial moments in his story. They announced and attended the birth of Jesus.[35] According to some manuscripts an angel appeared in the garden of Gethsemane to strengthen him.[36] And 'two men in clothes that gleamed like lightning', later identified as angels, proclaimed his

[35] Lk. 1:26ff.; 2:9–10, 13–15. [36] Lk. 22:43.

resurrection to the women.[37] So it was entirely appropriate that angels should now appear to interpret his ascension. They asked the apostles a searching question: *Men of Galilee, why do you stand here looking into the sky?* (11a). The expression 'into the sky' or 'into heaven' (AV, RSV) occurs four times in verses 10 and 11; its repetition, especially in the angels' implied reproof, emphasizes that the apostles were not to be sky-scanners. Two reasons are given.

First, Jesus will come again. *This same Jesus, who has been taken from you into heaven, will come back in the same way you have seen him go into heaven* (11b). The implication seems to be that they will not bring him back by gazing up into the sky. He has gone, and they must let him go; he will return in his own good time, and in the same way. To this angelic assurance of the Parousia we must attach full weight. But we must also be cautious in our interpretation of *houtos* (this *same* Jesus) and *houtōs* (in the *same* way). We should not press these words into meaning that the Parousia will be like a film of the ascension played backwards, or that he will return to exactly the same spot on the Mount of Olives and will be wearing the same clothes. It is only by letting Scripture interpret Scripture that we shall discern the similarities and dissimilarities between the ascension and the Parousia. 'This same Jesus' certainly indicates that his coming will be personal, the Eternal Son still possessing his glorified human nature and body. And 'in the same way' indicates that his coming will also be visible and glorious. They had seen him go; they would see him come. Luke recorded Jesus as saying so himself: 'they will see the Son of Man coming in a cloud with power and great glory.'[38] The same cloud which had hidden him from their sight (1:9), which had previously enveloped him and the three intimate apostles on the Mount of Transfiguration,[39] and which throughout the Old Testament was the symbol of Yahweh's glorious presence, would be the chariot of his coming as it had been of his going.

Yet there will also be important differences between his going and his coming. Although his coming will be personal, it will not be private like his ascension. Only the eleven apostles saw him go, but when he comes 'every eye will see him'.[40] Instead of returning alone (as when he went), millions of holy ones – both human and angelic – will form his retinue.[41] And in place of a localized coming ('There he is!' or 'Here he is!'), it will be 'like the lightning, which flashes and lights up the sky from one end to the other.'[42]

Secondly, the angels implied, until Christ comes again, the apostles must get on with their witness, for that was their mandate.

[37] Lk. 24:4ff., 23. [38] Lk 21:27. [39] Lk. 9:34.
[40] Rev. 1:7. [41] Lk. 9:26; *cf.* 1 Thes. 4:14ff.; 2 Thes. 1:7.
[42] Lk. 17:23–24.

There was something fundamentally anomalous about their gazing up into the *sky* when they had been commissioned to go to the ends of the *earth*. It was the earth not the sky which was to be their preoccupation. Their calling was to be witnesses not stargazers. The vision they were to cultivate was not upwards in nostalgia to the heaven which had received Jesus, but outwards in compassion to a lost world which needed him. It is the same for us. Curiosity about heaven and its occupants, speculation about prophecy and its fulfilment, an obsession with 'times and seasons' – these are aberrations which distract us from our God-given mission. Christ will come personally, visibly, gloriously. Of that we have been assured. Other details can wait. Meanwhile, we have work to do in the power of the Spirit.

The remedy for unprofitable spiritual stargazing lies in a Christian theology of history, an understanding of the order of events in the divine programme. First, Jesus returned to heaven (Ascension). Secondly, the Holy Spirit came (Pentecost). Thirdly, the church goes out to witness (Mission). Fourthly, Jesus will come back (Parousia). Whenever we forget one of these events, or put them in the wrong sequence, confusion reigns. We need especially to remember that between the ascension and the Parousia, the disappearance and the reappearance of Jesus, there stretches a period of unknown length which is to be filled with the church's worldwide, Spirit-empowered witness to him. We need to hear the implied message of the angels: 'You have seen him go. You will see him come. But between that going and coming there must be another. The Spirit must come, and you must go – into the world for Christ.'

Looking back, I think we may say that the apostles committed two opposite errors, which both had to be corrected. First, they were hoping for political power (the restoration of the kingdom to Israel). Secondly, they were gazing up into the sky (preoccupied with the heavenly Jesus). Both were false fantasies. The first is the error of the politicist, who dreams of establishing Utopia on earth. The second is the error of the pietist, who dreams only of heavenly bliss. The first vision is too earthy, and the second too heavenly. Is it fanciful to see a parallel here between Luke's Gospel and the Acts? Just as at the beginning of the Gospel Jesus in the Judean desert turned away from false ends and means, so at the beginning of the Acts the apostles before Pentecost had to turn away from both a false activism and a false pietism. And in their place, as the remedy for them, there was (and is) witness to Jesus in the power of the Spirit, with all that this implies of earthly responsibility and heavenly enabling.

3. They prayed for the Spirit to come (1:12–14)

Then they returned to Jerusalem . . . [13]*When they arrived, they went upstairs to the room where they were staying. Those present were Peter, John, James and Andrew; Philip and Thomas, Bartholomew and Matthew; James son of Alphaeus and Simon the Zealot, and Judas son of James.* [14]*They all joined together constantly in prayer, along with the women and Mary the mother of Jesus, and with his brothers.*

Their walk back to Jerusalem, being only the kilometre permitted on the sabbath, will not have taken them more than a quarter of an hour. Luke then tells us how they occupied the next ten days before Pentecost. In his Gospel he says 'they stayed continually at the temple, praising God',[43] and in the Acts that in the room where they were lodging, 'they all joined together constantly in prayer' (14). It was a healthy combination: continuous praise in the temple, and continuous prayer in the home. Luke does not tell us whether the upstairs room was the 'large upper room, all furnished',[44] in which Jesus had spent his last evening with the Twelve, or whether it was the house of Mary the mother of John Mark, in which later many members of the Jerusalem church gathered to pray (Acts 12:12), or some other room. What he does tell us is that their prayers had two characteristics which, Calvin comments, are 'two essentials for true prayer, namely that they persevered, and were of one mind'.[45] I will take them in the opposite order.

a. Their prayer was united

Who were these people who met to pray? Luke says that they were 'a group numbering about a hundred and twenty' (15). Professor Howard Marshall suggests that the reason why the number is mentioned is that 'in Jewish law a minimum of 120 Jewish men was required to establish a community with its own council'; so already the disciples were numerous enough 'to form a new community'.[46] Others have detected symbolism in the number, since the twelve tribes and the twelve apostles make twelve an obvious symbol of the church, and 120 is 12 x 10, as the 144,000 of the Book of Revelation is 12 x 12 x 1000. Yet others suggest that the 120 must have been only a percentage of the total believing community, since on one occasion 'more than 500' had seen the risen Lord at the same time,[47] although, to be sure, this may have been in Galilee. At all events, the 120 included the eleven surviving

[43] Lk. 24:53. [44] Lk. 22:12. [45] Calvin, I, p. 38.
[46] Marshall, *Acts*, p. 64. [47] 1 Cor. 15:6.

apostles. Luke lists them (13), as he has done in his Gospel.[48] And the list is the same, with only minor variations. For example, the inner circle of four, who had been named in the Gospel as pairs of brothers, 'Simon and Andrew, James and John', are now *Peter, John, James and Andrew*, putting first those who were to become the leading apostles, and also separating the natural brothers as if to hint that a new brotherhood in Christ has replaced the old kinship (see verse 16, 'Brothers . . .'). The next two pairs are also rearranged, although no reason is apparent. Instead of 'Philip, Bartholomew, Matthew, Thomas',[49] Luke writes *Philip and Thomas, Bartholomew and Matthew*. The remaining apostles are the same, except that of course the traitor Judas is omitted.

In addition to the eleven apostles are mentioned *the women* (14), presumably meaning Mary Magdalene, Joanna (whose husband managed Herod's household) and Susanna – the trio Luke has named in the Gospel[50] as 'helping to support them [*sc.* Jesus and the Twelve] out of their own means', together perhaps with 'Mary the mother of James' and the others who found the tomb empty[51] and to whom the risen Lord later revealed himself.[52] Then, placed separately as occupying a position of particular honour, Luke adds *Mary the mother of Jesus*, whose unique role in the birth of Jesus he has described in the first two chapters of his Gospel, together with *his brothers* (14), who had not believed in him during his earlier ministry,[53] but who now – perhaps because of the private resurrection appearance to one of them, James[54] – are numbered among the believers.

All these (the apostles, the women, the mother and brothers of Jesus, and the rest who made the number up to 120) *joined together constantly in prayer*. 'Together' translates *homothymadon*, a favourite word of Luke's, which he uses ten times and which occurs only once elsewhere in the New Testament. It could mean simply that the disciples met in the same place, or were doing the same thing, namely praying. But it later describes both united prayer (4:24) and a united decision (15:25), so that the 'togetherness' implied seems to go beyond mere assembly and activity to agreement about what they were praying for. They prayed 'with one mind or purpose or impulse' (BAGD).

b. Their prayer was persevering

The verb translated *joined . . . constantly* (*proskartereō*) means to be 'busy' or 'persistent' in all activity. Luke uses it later both of the new converts who 'devoted themselves to' the apostles' teaching

[48] Lk. 6:14–16. [49] Lk. 6:14–15. [50] Lk. 8:2–3. [51] Lk. 24:10, 22.
[52] *Cf.* Mt. 28:8ff. [53] Cf. Mk. 3:21, 31–34; Jn. 7:5. [54] 1 Cor. 15:7.

(2:42) and of the apostles who determined to give priority to prayer and preaching (6:4). Here he uses it of perseverance in prayer, as Paul does several times.[55]

There can be little doubt that the grounds of this unity and perseverance in prayer were the command and promise of Jesus. He had promised to send them the Spirit soon (1:4, 5, 8). He had commanded them to wait for him to come and then to begin their witness. We learn, therefore, that God's promises do not render prayer superfluous. On the contrary, it is only his promises which give us the warrant to pray and the confidence that he will hear and answer.

4. They replaced Judas with Matthias as an apostle (1:15–26)

In those days Peter stood up among the believers (a group numbering about a hundred and twenty) [16]and said, 'Brothers, the Scripture had to be fulfilled which the Holy Spirit spoke long ago through the mouth of David concerning Judas, who served as guide for those who arrested Jesus – [17]he was one of our number and shared in this ministry.'

[18](With the reward he got for his wickedness, Judas bought a field; there he fell headlong, his body burst open and all his intestines spilled out. [19]Everyone in Jerusalem heard about this, so they called that field in their language Akeldama, that is, Field of Blood.)

[20]'For,' said Peter, 'it is written in the Book of Psalms,

> *' "May his place be deserted;*
> *let there be no-one to dwell in it,"*

and,

> *' "May another take his place of leadership."*

[21]Therefore it is necessary to choose one of the men who have been with us the whole time the Lord Jesus went in and out among us, [22]beginning from John's baptism to the time when Jesus was taken up from us. For one of these must become a witness with us of his resurrection.'

[23]So they proposed two men: Joseph called Barsabbas (also known as Justus) and Matthias. [24]Then they prayed, 'Lord, you know everyone's heart. Show us which of these two you have chosen [25]to take over this apostolic ministry, which Judas left to go where he belongs.' [26]Then they drew lots, and the lot fell to Matthias; so he was added to the eleven apostles.

Having recorded the Lord's commission to witness, his ascension,

[55] *E.g.* Rom. 12:12 and Col. 4:2.

and the disciples' persevering prayers, Luke draws our attention to only one further action before Pentecost (*in those days* is vague enough to date it at any point between Ascension and Pentecost), namely the appointment of another apostle in place of Judas. We have to consider the need for such an appointment (the defection and death of Judas), the warrant for it (the fulfilment of Scripture) and the choice which was made (Matthias).

a. The death of Judas (1:18–19)

Verses 18 and 19 do not appear to be part of Peter's speech, for they interrupt the sequence of his thought. Moreover, as an Aramaic speaker addressing Aramaic speakers, Peter would not have needed to translate the word *Akeldama* (19). But Luke, writing for Gentile readers, would need to explain its meaning. So these two verses are best understood as an editorial parenthesis, in which Luke acquaints his readers with the circumstances of Judas' death. This is how RSV, NEB and NIV take it.

Luke is outspoken in calling Judas' betrayal of Jesus an act of *wickedness* (*adikia*, 18), 'infamy' (JBP) or 'villainy' (NEB), or a 'crime' (JB). Yet some people express their sympathy for him because his role was predicted and therefore (it is thought) foreordained. But this is not so. Calvin himself, for all his emphasis on the sovereignty of God, wrote: 'Judas may not be excused on the ground that what befell him was prophesied, since he fell away not through the compulsion of the prophecy but through the wickedness of his own heart.'[56]

In the Gospels only Matthew records what happened to Judas,[57] and he and Luke appear to be drawing on independent traditions. But their accounts are not as divergent as some argue, and it is certainly not necessary to say with R. P. C. Hanson that 'they cannot both be true'.[58] Both say that Judas died a miserable death, that a field was bought with the money paid him (thirty silver coins), and that it was called 'The Field of Blood'. The apparent discrepancies concern how he died, who bought the field and why it was called 'Blood Field'.

First, the manner of Judas' death. Matthew writes that he committed suicide: 'he went away and hanged himself.'[59] Luke writes that *he fell headlong, his body burst open and all his intestines spilled out* (18b). Attempts to harmonize these statements go back at least to Augustine. It is perfectly possible to suppose that after he had hanged himself, his dead body either fell headlong (the usual meaning of *prēnēs*), assuming that the rope or tree branch broke, or 'swelled up' (following a different derivation of *prēnēs*, which

[56] Calvin, I, p. 40. [57] Mt. 27:3–5. [58] Hanson, p. 60. [59] Mt. 27:5.

BAGD declares 'linguistically possible', *cf.* RSV margin, JBP), and in either case ruptured.

Secondly, there is the question who bought the field. Matthew says that Judas, filled with remorse, tried to return the money to the priests and (when they refused to accept it) threw it into the temple and left. He adds that later the priests picked up the money and with it bought the potter's field. Luke, on the other hand, says that *with the reward he got for his wickedness, Judas bought a field* (18a). So did the priests purchase the field, or did Judas? It is reasonable to answer that both did, the priests entering into the transaction, but with money which belonged to Judas. For, as Edersheim wrote, 'by a fiction of law the money was still considered to be Judas', and to have been applied by him in the purchase of the well-known "potter's field" '.[60]

Thirdly, why did the field purchased come to be known as 'The Field of Blood'? Matthew's answer is that it had been bought with 'blood money';[61] Luke gives no explicit reason, but implies that it was because Judas' blood had been spilled there. Evidently different traditions developed (as so often happens) as to how the field got its name, so that different people called it 'Blood Field' for different reasons.

It is fair to conclude that these independent accounts of Judas' death are not incompatible, and to agree with J. A. Alexander: 'there is scarcely an American or English jury that would scruple to receive these two accounts as perfectly consistent.'[62]

b. The fulfilment of Scripture (1:15–17, 20)

The warrant for replacing Judas was Old Testament Scripture. This was Peter's conviction, which he expressed to the believers: *Brothers, the Scripture had to be fulfilled which the Holy Spirit spoke long ago through the mouth of David concerning Judas* (16). We need to recall that, according to Luke, the risen Lord had both opened the Scriptures to his disciples and opened their minds to understand the Scriptures.[63] In consequence, since the resurrection they had begun to have a new grasp of how the Old Testament foretold the sufferings and glory, rejection and reign of the Messiah. And, stimulated by Jesus' explanations, they will during the fifty days of waiting have searched the Scriptures for further light. We know that various lists of Old Testament 'testimonies' to the Messiah were later compiled and circulated. But the process will have begun immediately after the resurrection.

Peter goes on to quote from two Psalms (Pss. 69 and 109), the

[60] Edersheim, *Life and Times*, II, p. 575. [61] Mt. 27:6.
[62] Alexander, I, p. 28. [63] Lk. 24:25–27, 32, 45–49.

first explaining what had happened (Judas' defection and death) and the second what they should do about it (replace him). Psalm 69 is applied to Jesus five times in the New Testament. In it an innocent sufferer describes how his enemies hate and insult him without cause (Ps. 69:4), and how he is consumed with zeal for God's house (Ps. 69:9). These verses are both quoted in John's Gospel, verse 4 by Jesus himself[64] and verse 9 by his disciples,[65] while Paul twice refers this psalm to Jesus.[66] Towards its end (Ps. 69:24) the psalmist utters a prayer that God's judgment will fall on these wicked and impenitent people. Peter individualizes this text and applies it to Judas on whom indeed God's judgment had fallen: *May his place be deserted; let there be no-one to dwell in it* (20a). Psalm 109 is similar. It concerns 'wicked and deceitful men' who without justification hate, slander and attack the writer. Then one particular person is singled out, perhaps the ringleader, and God's judgment on him is requested (Ps. 109:8): *May another take his place of leadership* (20b). This verse too, on what Dr Longenecker calls 'the commonly accepted exegetical principle of analogous subject',[67] Peter applies to Judas.

These two scriptures seemed to Peter and the believers adequate general guidance on the need to replace Judas. Perhaps there was an additional factor, which Luke mentions in his Gospel,[68] namely that Jesus drew a parallel between the twelve apostles and the twelve tribes of Israel. If the early church was to be accepted as enjoying direct continuity with, indeed as being the fulfilment of, Old Testament Israel, the number of its founders must not be depleted. A few years later it was not deemed necessary to replace James, for he had not defected, but had been faithful unto death (12:1–2).

c. *The choice of Matthias (1:21–26)*

Peter's proposal that a twelfth apostle be chosen to replace Judas (21–22) throws light on his understanding of apostleship, to which reference was made in the previous chapter.

First, the apostolic ministry (25, *this apostolic ministry*, as NIV renders *diakonia* and *apostolē*) was to be 'a witness to his resurrection' (22b, RSV). His resurrection was early recognized as the divine vindication of both his person and his work, and Luke describes how with great power 'the apostles continued to testify to the resurrection of the Lord Jesus' (Acts 4:33; *cf.* 13:30–31).

Secondly, the apostolic qualification was therefore to have been a witness of the resurrection to which they were called to bear

[64] Jn. 15:25. [65] Jn. 2:17. [66] Rom. 11:9–10; 15:3.
[67] Longenecker, *Acts*, p. 264. [68] Lk. 22:28–30.

witness (*e.g.* 2:32; 3:15; 10:40–42). It was indispensable to have seen the risen Lord, which is why Paul was later added to the apostolic band.[69] But Judas' replacement as a member of the foundation Twelve, whose responsibility was to safeguard the true tradition about Jesus, needed a fuller qualification than this. He must, Peter explained, *have been with us the whole time the Lord Jesus went in and out among us, beginning from John's baptism to the time when Jesus was taken up from us* (21–22; *cf.* 10:39; 13:31). This is why I cannot agree with Campbell Morgan who (following others) wrote: 'The election of Matthias was wrong. . . . He was a good man, but the wrong man for this position. . . . I am not prepared to omit Paul from the twelve, believing that he was God's man for the filling of the gap.'[70] But Luke gives no hint at all that a mistake was made, in spite of the fact that Paul was obviously his hero. Besides, Paul did not have the fuller qualification which Peter laid down.

Thirdly, the apostolic appointment was by the Lord Jesus himself. It had been he who chose the original Twelve.[71] So he must choose Judas' replacement. True, the 120 believers were told to do the choosing (21). But what they did was to sift possible candidates and from them nominate two, namely Joseph (whose other name was Barsabbas in Hebrew and Justus in Latin) and Matthias, of neither of whom do we know anything, although Eusebius says that both were members of the Seventy. Then they prayed to Jesus as Lord, calling him (literally) everybody's 'heart-knower', *kardiagnōstēs*, a word Luke later uses of God,[72] and asked him to show them which of the two he had already chosen (24). *Then they drew lots* (26), a method of discerning God's will which was sanctioned in the Old Testament,[73] but which does not appear to have been used after the Spirit had come.[74] Matthias was chosen; *so he was added to the eleven apostles*.

It is instructive to note the cluster of factors which contributed to the discovery of God's will in this matter. First came the general leading of Scripture that a replacement should be made (16–21). Next, they used their common sense that if Judas' substitute was to have the same apostolic ministry he must also have the same qualifications, including an eyewitness experience of Jesus and a personal appointment by him. This sound deductive reasoning led to the nomination of Joseph and Matthias. Thirdly, they prayed. For though Jesus had gone, he was still accessible to them by prayer

[69] 1 Cor. 9:1; 15:8–9. [70] Morgan, pp. 19, 20. [71] Lk. 6:12–13; Acts 1:2.
[72] Acts 15:8; *cf.* 1 Sa. 16:7; Rev. 2:23.
[73] *E.g.* Lv. 16:8; Nu. 26:55; Pr. 16:33; Lk. 1:9.
[74] Chrysostom explained the use of lots by saying 'for the Spirit was not yet sent' (Homily III, p. 19).

and was acknowledged as having a knowledge of hearts which they lacked. Finally, they drew lots, by which they trusted Jesus to make his choice known. Leaving aside this fourth factor, because the Spirit has now been given us, the remaining three (Scripture, common sense and prayer) constitute a wholesome combination through which God may be trusted to guide us today.

The stage is now set for the Day of Pentecost. The apostles have received Christ's commission and seen his ascension. The apostolic team is complete again, ready to be his chosen witnesses. Only one thing is missing: the Spirit has not yet come. Though the place left vacant by Judas has been filled by Matthias, the place left vacant by Jesus has not yet been filled by the Spirit. So we leave Luke's first chapter of the Acts with the 120 waiting in Jerusalem, persevering in prayer with one heart and mind, poised ready to fulfil Christ's command just as soon as he has fulfilled his promise.

2. The Day of Pentecost 2:1-47

Without the Holy Spirit, Christian discipleship would be inconceivable, even impossible. There can be no life without the life-giver, no understanding without the Spirit of truth, no fellowship without the unity of the Spirit, no Christlikeness of character apart from his fruit, and no effective witness without his power. As a body without breath is a corpse, so the church without the Spirit is dead.

Luke is well aware of this. Of the four evangelists it is he who lays the heaviest emphasis on the Spirit. Near the beginning of each part of his two-volume work he demonstrates the indispensability of the Holy Spirit's enabling. Just as the Holy Spirit descended upon Jesus when John baptized him, so that he entered his public ministry 'full of the Holy Spirit', 'led by the Spirit', 'in the power of the Spirit' and 'anointed' by the Spirit (Lk. 3:21–22; 4:1, 14, 18), so now the same Spirit came upon the disciples of Jesus to equip them for their mission in the world (Acts 1:5, 8; 2:33). In the early chapters of the Acts Luke refers to the promise, the gift, the baptism, the power and the fullness of the Spirit in the experience of God's people. The terms are many and interchangeable; the reality is one, and there is no substitute for it.

Yet this reality is multi-faceted, and there are at least four ways in which we may think of the Day of Pentecost. First, it was the final act of the saving ministry of Jesus before the Parousia. He who was born into our humanity, lived our life, died for our sins, rose from the dead and ascended into heaven, now sent his Spirit to his people to constitute them his body and to work out in them what he had won for them. In this sense the Day of Pentecost is unrepeatable. Christmas Day, Good Friday, Easter Day, Ascension Day and Whit Sunday are annual celebrations, but the birth, death, resurrection, ascension and Spirit-gift they commemorate happened once and for all. Secondly, Pentecost brought to the apostles the equipment they needed for their special role. Christ had appointed them to be his primary and authoritative witnesses, and had promised them the reminding and teaching ministry of the Holy Spirit (John 14 – 16). Pentecost was the fulfilment of that promise. Thirdly, Pentecost was the inauguration of the new era of the Spirit. Although his coming was a unique and unrepeatable historical event, all the people of God can now always and everywhere benefit from his ministry. Although he equipped the apostles to be the primary witnesses, he also equips us to be secondary witnesses. Although the inspiration of the Spirit was given to the apostles alone, the fullness of the Spirit is for us all. Fourthly, Pentecost has been called – and rightly – the first 'revival', using this word to denote one of those altogether unusual visitations of God, in which a whole community becomes vividly aware of his immediate, overpowering presence. It may be, therefore, that not only the physical phenomena (2ff.), but the deep conviction of sin (37), the 3,000 conversions (41) and the widespread sense of awe (43) were signs of 'revival'. We must be careful, however, not to use this possibility as an excuse to lower our expectations, or to relegate to the category of the exceptional what God may intend to be the church's normal experience. The wind and the fire were abnormal, and probably the languages too; the new life and joy, fellowship and worship, freedom, boldness and power were not.[1]

Acts 2 has three sections. It begins with Luke's description of the Pentecost event itself (1–13), continues with the explanation of the event which Peter gives in his sermon (14–41), and ends with its effects in the life of the Jerusalem church (42–47).

1. Luke's narrative: the event of Pentecost (2:1–13)

Luke's narrative opens with a brief, matter-of-fact reference to the time and place of the Spirit's coming. *They were all together in one place*, he writes, and is evidently not concerned to enlarge on this. We do not know, therefore, if the 'house' of verse 2 is still the upper room (Acts 1:13; 2:46b) or one of the many rooms or halls of the temple (Lk. 24:53; Acts 2:46a). The time is precise, however; it was *when the day of Pentecost came* (1). This feast had two meanings, one agricultural and the other historical. Originally, it was the middle of the three annual Jewish harvest festivals,[2] and

[1] A failure to grasp, and distinguish between, these four meanings of the Pentecost event lies, I suspect, behind the continuing tensions between 'charismatic' and 'non-charismatic' Christians. For example, Roger Stronstad is surely right to emphasize the 'vocational' aspect of the gift of the Spirit, namely that he 'anoints' and 'equips' people for their ministry. This was particularly evident in the case of the apostles. Roger Stronstad seems to me to overstate his case, however, by arguing that according to Luke's theology, the Spirit was given neither for salvation, nor for sanctification, but exclusively for service (Stronstad, pp. 1, 12, 83).

[2] Dt. 16:16.

was called either the Feast of Harvest,[3] because it celebrated the completion of the grain harvest, or the Feast of Weeks or Pentecost, because it took place seven weeks or fifty days (*pentēkostos* means 'fiftieth') after the Passover, which was when the grain harvesting began.[4] Towards the end of the inter-testamental period, however, it began also to be observed as the anniversary of the giving of the law at Mount Sinai, because this was reckoned as having happened fifty days after the Exodus.

It is tempting, therefore, to find the double symbolism of harvesting and law-giving in the Day of Pentecost. Certainly there was a great harvest of 3,000 souls that day, the first-fruits of the Christian mission. As Chrysostom put it, 'the time was come to put in the sickle of the word; for here, as the sickle, keen-edged, came the Spirit down'.[5] Certainly too the prophets regarded as almost identical Yahweh's two New Covenant promises, 'I will put my Spirit in you'[6] and 'I will put my law in their minds and write it on their hearts',[7] since what the Spirit does when he enters our hearts is to write God's law there, as Paul clearly taught. Nevertheless, Luke does not draw out this double symbolism. So we cannot be sure whether it was important to him, even though Jewish tradition associated wind, fire and voices with Mount Sinai,[8] the three phenomena which he is about to describe.

a. The three phenomena

Suddenly, Luke says, the great event took place. The Spirit of God came upon them. And his coming was accompanied by three supernatural signs – a sound, a sight and strange speech. First, there came from heaven *a sound like the blowing of a violent wind*, and it (*i.e.* the noise) *filled the whole house where they were sitting* (2). Secondly, there appeared to them visibly *what seemed to be tongues of fire*, which *separated and came to rest on each of them* (3), becoming for each an individual possession. Thirdly, *all of them were filled with the Holy Spirit and began to speak in other tongues* (*i.e.* languages of some kind) *as the Spirit enabled them* (4).

These three experiences seemed like natural phenomena (wind, fire and speech); yet they were supernatural both in origin and in character. The noise was not wind, but sounded like it; the sight was not fire but resembled it; and the speech was in languages which were not ordinary but in some way 'other'. Again, three of their higher senses were affected, in that they heard the wind-like sound, saw the fire-like apparition and spoke the 'other' languages. Yet what they experienced was more than sensory; it was signific-

[3] Ex. 23:16. [4] Ex. 34:22; Lv. 23:15ff.; Nu. 28:26.
[5] Chrysostom, Homily IV, p. 25. [6] Ezk. 36:27. [7] Je. 31:33.
[8] *Cf.* Heb. 12:18–19.

ant. So they sought to understand it. 'What does this mean?' the people later asked (12). If we allow other parts of Scripture to guide our interpretation, it seems that these three signs at least represented the new era of the Spirit which had begun (John the Baptist had bracketed wind and fire[9]) and the new work which he had come to do. If so, the noise like wind may have symbolized *power* (such as Jesus had promised them for witness, Lk. 24:49; Acts 1:8), the sight like fire *purity* (like the live coal which cleansed Isaiah, 6:6–7) and the speech in other languages the *universality* of the Christian church. In what follows nothing more is said about the phenomena like wind and fire; Luke concentrates on the third, the languages.

5Now there were staying in Jerusalem God-fearing Jews from every nation under heaven. 6When they heard this sound, a crowd came together in bewilderment, because each one heard them speaking in his own language. 7Utterly amazed, they asked: 'Are not all these men who are speaking Galileans? 8Then how is it that each of us hears them in his own native language?'

Luke's emphasis is on the international nature of the crowd which collected. They were all *God-fearing Jews*, and they were all *staying* (that is, residing) *in Jerusalem* (5). Yet they had not been born there; they came from the dispersion, *from every nation under heaven* (5). That we must not press Luke's 'every nation' literally to include, for example, American Indians, Australian aboriginals and New Zealand Maoris, is plain from what follows. He was speaking, as the biblical writers normally did, from his own horizon not ours, and was referring to the Graeco-Roman world situated round the Mediterranean basin, indeed to every nation in which there were Jews.

Luke's list comprises five groupings, as he moves with his mind's eye approximately from East to West. First, he mentions *Parthians, Medes and Elamites* and *residents of Mesopotamia* (9a), that is, peoples from the Caspian Sea westwards, many of whom will have been descended from the Jewish exiles who had been transported there in the eighth and sixth centuries BC. Secondly, in verses 9b–10a, Luke refers to five areas of what we call Asia Minor or Turkey, namely *Cappadocia* (east), *Pontus* (north), *and Asia* (west), *Phrygia and Pamphylia* (south). Because *Judea* (9) comes oddly between Mesopotamia and Cappadocia, some commentators think Luke is using the word to refer to a wider area like the whole of Palestine and Syria, even including Armenia, while others follow an Old Latin version which reads *Joudaioi* ('Jews') instead of *Joudaian* ('Judea'), and so translate 'the Jews inhabiting Mesopotamia and

[9] Lk. 3:16.

The Near East in the first century AD

Cappadocia *etc.*'. The third group (10b) is North African, namely *Egypt and the parts of Libya near Cyrene* (its chief city), the fourth (10c–11a) is *visitors from Rome* across the Mediterranean (*both Jews and converts to Judaism*), and the fifth, which looks like an afterthought, is *Cretans and Arabs* (11b).[10]

This was the international, multi-lingual crowd which gathered round the 120 believers. *We hear them declaring the wonders of God*, they said, *in our own tongues* (11c), that is, *each . . . in his own native language* (8). Yet the speakers were known to be Galileans (7), who had a reputation for being uncultured.[11] They also 'had difficulty pronouncing gutturals and had the habit of swallowing syllables when speaking; so they were looked down upon by the people of Jerusalem as being provincial'.[12] It is not surprising, therefore, that the crowd's reaction was one of bewilderment (6). Indeed, *amazed and perplexed, they asked one another, 'What does this mean?'* (12). *Some, however*, a minority who for some reason understood none of the languages, *made fun of them and said, 'They have had too much wine'* (13).

b. Glossolalia

What exactly was this third phenomenon which Luke stresses, and as a result of which people heard God's wonders in their vernacular? How does Luke understand *glossolalia*? We begin our answer negatively.

First, it was not the result of intoxication, of drinking too much *gleukos*, 'sweet new wine' (13, BAGD). Peter is emphatic on this point: 'These men are not drunk, as you suppose. It's only nine in the morning!' (15). As early in the day as that, Haenchen comments, 'even drunkards and wassailers have not yet begun to imbibe'.[13] Besides, the Jews fasted during festivals until the morning services were over. Nor, we must add, did the believers' experience of the Spirit's fullness *seem* to them or *look* to others like intoxication, because they had lost control of their normal mental and physical functions. No, the fruit of the Spirit is 'self-control',[14] not the loss of it. Besides, only 'some' (13) made this remark, and though they said it, they do not seem to have meant it. For, Luke

[10] Because of the somewhat strange order in which Luke lists the nations, some scholars have suggested that he may have been following an ancient 'astrological geography' like that of the fourth-century Paul of Alexandria, who tabulated the nations according to the twelve signs of the zodiac. For a sober evaluation of this speculation see Bruce Metzger's essay in Gasque and Martin, pp. 123–133.

[11] *Cf.* Jn. 1:46; 7:52.

[12] Longenecker, *Acts*, p. 272. See also Mt. 26:73 and Lk. 22:59 for references to the peculiar Galilean accent.

[13] Haenchen, p. 178. [14] Gal. 5:23.

says, they 'made fun of them'. It was more a jest than a serious comment.

Secondly, it was not a mistake or a miracle of hearing, in contrast to speaking, so that the audience supposed that the believers spoke in other languages when they did not.[15] Some of Luke's statements seem to support this theory: 'each one *heard* them speaking in his own language' (6); 'how is it that each of us *hears* them in his own native language?' (8); and 'we *hear* them declaring the wonders of God in our own tongues!' (11). When, however, Luke writes his own descriptive narrative, he puts the matter beyond dispute: they 'began to *speak* in other tongues as the Spirit enabled them' (4). *Glossolalia* was indeed a phenomenon of hearing, but only because it was first a phenomenon of speech.

Thirdly, it was not a case of incoherent utterance. Liberal commentators, who begin with a prejudice against miracles, suggest that the 120 believers broke into unintelligible, ecstatic speech, and that Luke (who had visited Corinth with Paul) mistakenly supposed that it was literal languages. Thus Luke got in a muddle and confused two quite different things. What he thought was languages was in reality 'inarticulate ecstatic babbling'[16] or 'a flood of unintelligible sounds in no known language'.[17] Those of us who have confidence in Luke as a reliable historian, however, let alone as an inspired contributor to the New Testament, conclude that it is not he who is mistaken, but rather his rationalistic interpreters.

Fourthly, and positively, the *glossolalia* on the Day of Pentecost was a supernatural ability to speak in recognizable languages. Some think that these were Aramaic, Greek and Latin, which would all have been spoken in multi-lingual Galilee; that 'other languages' means 'languages other than Hebrew' (the sacred biblical language which would have seemed appropriate to the occasion); and that the crowd's astonishment was aroused by God's wonders not the languages, by the content not the medium of the communication. This is plausible, and could be said to do justice to Luke's account. On the other hand, his emphasis is more on the linguistic media (4, 6, 8, 11) than on the message (12); it is natural to translate 'other languages' as 'other than their mother tongue' rather than 'other than Hebrew'; the list of fifteen regions in verses 9–11 leads one to expect a wider range of languages than Aramaic, Greek and Latin; and the crowd's astonishment seems due to the fact that the languages, which to the speakers were 'other' (4), *i.e.* foreign, were yet to the hearers their 'own' (6, 11), indeed their 'own native language' (8), in which they were born (see AV). I conclude, there-

[15] *E.g.* 'many present thought they recognized words of praise to God in other languages' (Dunn, *Jesus*, pp. 151f.).

[16] Neil, p. 71. [17] Barclay, p. 15.

fore, that the miracle of Pentecost, although it may have included the substance of what the one hundred and twenty spoke (*the wonders of God*), was primarily the medium of their speech (foreign languages they had never learned).

So far I have concentrated on Luke's own understanding of *glossolalia* on the Day of Pentecost, which can be discovered only by the exegesis of Acts 2. Presumably, the *glossolalia* to which he refers in Acts 10:46 and 19:6 was the same speaking of foreign languages, since he uses the same vocabulary (though most manuscripts omit the adjective 'other'). What, then, about the references to tongue-speaking in 1 Corinthians 12 and 14? Are the phenomena mentioned in Acts and 1 Corinthians the same or different? We must try to reach our answer with reference to the biblical text rather than to contemporary claims.

Some think the phenomena were in several ways different. First, they were different in *direction*, *glossolalia* in Acts being in some sense the public 'declaring' (11) of God's wonders, sharing them with others, while in 1 Corinthians the tongue-speaker 'does not speak to men but to God'.[18] Secondly, they were different in *character*, *glossolalia* in Acts being languages which were understood by groups of listeners, while in 1 Corinthians 14 the speech was unintelligible and an interpreter was necessary. Thirdly, they were different in *purpose*. In Acts *glossolalia* seems to be evidential, an initial 'sign' given to all, bearing witness to their reception of the Spirit, while in 1 Corinthians it is edificatory, a continuing 'gift' bestowed on some for the building up of the church.

Others, however, point out that the Greek words and expressions are the same throughout the New Testament. *Glōssa* ('tongue') has only two meanings (the organ in the mouth and a language) and *hermēneuō* ('interpret') usually means to translate a language. They therefore conclude that the Acts and 1 Corinthians passages refer to the same thing, namely languages. Even some who think the *purpose* is different, go on to affirm that the *character* is the same. For example, the Assemblies of God commentator Stanley M. Horton writes that 'the tongues here (*sc.* in Acts 2) and the tongues in 1 Corinthians chapters 12–14 are the same'.[19] As the official *Statement* of the Assemblies of God puts it (para. 8), they are 'the same in essence', but 'different in purpose and use'. To sum up, rejecting the liberal approach, which is to declare Corinthian *glossolalia* to be unintelligible utterance and to assimilate the Acts phenomenon to it, it is better to make the opposite proposal, namely that the Acts phenomenon was intelligible languages and that the 1 Corinthians experience must be assimilated to it. The

[18] 1 Cor. 14:2; *cf.* vv 14–17, 28. [19] Horton, p. 33, footnote 11.

main argument for this is that, although *glossolalia* is mentioned without explanation in several New Testament passages, Acts 2 is the only passage in which it is described and explained; it seems more reasonable to interpret the unexplained in the light of the explained than vice versa.[20]

Discussion about the nature of *glossolalia* must not distract our attention from Luke's understanding of its significance on the Day of Pentecost. It symbolized a new unity in the Spirit transcending racial, national and linguistic barriers. So Luke is at pains to emphasize the cosmopolitan character of the crowd, not least by the expression 'from every nation under heaven' (5). Although all the nations of the world were not present *literally*, they were *representatively*. For Luke includes in his list descendants of Shem, Ham and Japheth, and gives us in Acts 2 a 'Table of the Nations' comparable to the one in Genesis 10. Bishop Stephen Neill has made this point: 'Most of the peoples mentioned by Luke fall under the heading of the Semites, Elam being the first of the Semitic nations mentioned in Genesis 10; but Luke is careful also to add Egypt and Libya which come under the heading of the Hamites, and Cretans (Kittim) and dwellers in Rome who belong to the section under Japheth. . . . Luke does not draw attention to what he is doing; but in his own subtle way he is saying to us that on that Day of Pentecost the whole world was there in the representatives of the various nations.'[21]

Nothing could have demonstrated more clearly than this the multi-racial, multi-national, multi-lingual nature of the kingdom of Christ. Ever since the early church fathers, commentators have seen the blessing of Pentecost as a deliberate and dramatic reversal of the curse of Babel. At Babel human languages were confused and the nations were scattered; in Jerusalem the language barrier was supernaturally overcome as a sign that the nations would now be gathered together in Christ, prefiguring the great day when the redeemed company will be drawn 'from every nation, tribe, people and language'.[22] Besides, at Babel earth proudly tried to ascend to heaven, whereas in Jerusalem heaven humbly descended to earth.

[20] The debate continues as to whether the contemporary experience of *glossolalia* is, or sometimes includes, speaking in recognizable languages. Claims to this are put forward by *e.g.* Morton T. Kelsey in *Speaking with Tongues* (1964; Epworth, 1965) and John L. Sherrill in *They Speak with Other Tongues* (1964; Hodder, 1965). On the other hand, two fair, objective, socio-linguistic investigations have reached the conclusion that there have been no scientifically confirmed records of *glossolalia* being an unlearned foreign language. These are William J. Samarin's *Tongues of Men and Angels* (MacMillan, 1972) and John P. Kildahl's *The Psychology of Speaking in Tongues* (Hodder and Stoughton, and Harper and Row, 1972).

[21] *Call to Mission* by Stephen C. Neill (Fortress, 1970, p. 12).

[22] Gn. 11:1–9; Rev. 7:9.

2. Peter's sermon: the explanation of Pentecost (2:14–41)

Before we are ready to study Peter's sermon in particular, it is necessary to consider the Acts' speeches in general.

a. The speeches in Acts

Every reader of Acts is struck by the prominent position occupied in Luke's text by speeches. We observe again how incomplete the book's title is, whether the 'Acts' are thought of as those of Christ, the Spirit or the apostles. For it contains as many 'addresses' as 'acts'. Luke is true to his intention of recording what Jesus continued (after his ascension) both 'to do and to teach' (1:1). No fewer than nineteen significant Christian speeches occur in his second volume (omitting the non-Christian speeches by Gamaliel, the Ephesian town clerk and Tertullus). There are eight by Peter (in chapters 1, 2, 3, 4, 5, 10, 11 and 15), one each by Stephen and James (in chapters 7 and 15), and nine by Paul (five sermons in chapters 13, 14, 17, 20 and 28, and four defence speeches in chapters 22 to 26). Approximately 20% of Luke's text is devoted to addresses by Peter and Paul; if Stephen's speech is added, the percentage rises to about 25%.

But are these speeches genuine utterances by the people to whom they are attributed? Are they accurate? There are three possible responses.

First, probably nobody has ever imagined that the Acts' speeches are *verbatim* accounts of what was said on each occasion. There are several reasons for rejecting this idea. They are much too short to be complete (Peter's Pentecost sermon, as recorded by Luke, would have taken three minutes to deliver, and Paul's in Athens one and a half); Luke specifically says at the end of his account of Peter's sermon that he went on exhorting the crowd 'with many other words' (40); there was of course no recording equipment in those days, even if shorthand was being developed; and Luke was in any case not present to hear every speech himself, so that he must have depended on summaries given him later either by the speaker or by one of his listeners. He cannot be claiming, therefore, to be giving more than a reliable digest of each address.

Secondly, the modern critical approach, developed and popularized between the wars by H. J. Cadbury in the English-speaking world and by Martin Dibelius in Germany, is much more sceptical. Their assertion of the substantial unreliability of the speeches is based on two main arguments. First, if one compares the speeches with each other and with Luke's narrative passages, the whole of his text reflects the same style and vocabulary, while many of the speeches contain the same shape, theological emphasis and Scripture quotations; the natural explanation of this sameness is that it all comes from Luke's mind and pen, rather than from the different speakers. The second argument is that 'a prevailing convention among ancient historians was the custom of inserting speeches of the leading characters in the narrative',[23] and of freely composing these speeches themselves. Thus, the speeches in Greek history had the same interpretative function as the chorus in Greek drama. Moreover, the authors assumed that their readers understood and accepted this literary artifice, which was employed by both Greek and Jewish historians.

The Greek example most frequently quoted is Thucydides, the historian of the Peloponnesian War in the fifth century BC. The key passage from his chronicle includes the following statement:

> As to the speeches . . . , it was hard for me, and for others who reported them to me, to recollect the exact words. I have therefore put into the mouth of each speaker the sentiments proper to the occasion, expressed as I thought he would be likely to express them, while at the same time I endeavoured, as nearly as I could, to give the general purport of what was actually said.[24]

Because of Thucydides' references to his fallible memory of what was said and to his personal opinion of what would have been said, his statement has usually been taken to mean that he simply invented the speeches he records. The Jewish example quoted is generally Josephus, who seems to have been far less conscientious than Thucydides, even totally unprincipled. H. J. Cadbury describes how he sometimes merely transforms the Old Testament narrative 'into his own prosy platitudes', sometimes 'inserts in inappropriate scenes long diatribes of his own composing', and in the case of more contemporary history has 'evidently invented speeches'.[25] Summing up this tradition of Greek and Jewish history, Cadbury wrote: 'From Thucydides downwards, speeches reported by the historians are confessedly pure imagination.'[26] This having been the supposedly universal convention in the writing of Greek and Jewish history, the biblical critics assume that Luke as a Christian historian was no different. 'The presumption . . . is strong', wrote Cadbury, 'that his speeches are generally without basis of definite information – even when the accompanying narrative seems thoroughly reliable'.[27]

The third approach to the Acts' speeches, rejecting both extreme literalism and extreme scepticism, is to regard them as reliable

[23] Cadbury, p. 184.
[24] *Thucydides*, translated into English by Benjamin Jowett (Oxford: Clarendon Press, 1881), vol. I, I.22.
[25] *BC*, V, p. 405. [26] *BC*, II, p. 13. [27] *BC*, V, p. 406.

summaries of what was said on each occasion. A threefold critique of the Cadbury-Dibelius reconstruction may be made. First, it is not fair to all ancient historiography. Josephus and some Greek historians do seem to have regarded the speeches they include as belonging more to rhetoric than to history. This is not so of Thucydides, however. Conservative commentators argue that Thucydides has been misinterpreted. On the one hand, insufficient attention has been paid to the final sentence of the statement already quoted, namely that he kept as nearly as he could to the general gist of 'what was actually said' (a clause which, F. F. Bruce has written, expresses 'Thucydides' historical conscience'[28]). On the other hand, the quotation has not been continued as it should have been. For Thucydides went on:

> Of the events of the war I have not ventured to speak from any chance information, nor according to any notion of my own; I have described nothing but what I either saw myself, or learned from others of whom I made the most careful and particular enquiry. The task was a laborious one. . . .[29]

A. W. Gomme summarized this chapter of Thucydides in these words: 'I have tried to relate these events as accurately as possible, both the speeches and the deeds done, difficult as this was.'[30]

Dr Ward Gasque also points out that Polybius, the second-century BC Greek historian, 'time and again explicitly condemns the custom of the free invention of speeches by historians'. Dr Gasque concludes that 'the free invention of speeches was not a universally accepted practice among historians in the Graeco-Roman world'.[31]

Secondly, critical scepticism regarding the Acts' speeches is not fair to Luke either. For Luke claimed in his preface, as we have seen, that he was writing carefully researched history, and at the beginning of his second volume that his concept of history included words as well as deeds. It is therefore as antecedently unlikely that

[28] Bruce, *Speeches* (2), p. 54. [29] Thucydides, *ibid.*, I.22.

[30] Gomme, I, p. 157. See also Colin Hemer's chapter 3 on 'Ancient Historiography' (pp. 63–100), and his appendix on the Acts' speeches (pp. 415–427). Conrad Gempf stresses in his Conclusion to Hemer's book that 'contrary to modern opinion on the subject, ancient historians were capable of very rigorous and critical methods and principles' (p. 411).

[31] Gasque, *History*, pp. 226–228. See also Gasque, 'Book', pp. 58–63; Longenecker, *Acts*, pp. 212–214 and 229–231; and A. W. Gomme, 'The Speeches in Thucydides', in his *Essays in Greek History and Literature* (Oxford, 1937), p. 166 and his *A Historical Commentary on Thucydides*, I, pp. 140–141, 157. Colin Hemer refers to Polybius' 'devastating exposure' of the faults of Timaeus as a historian in his words 'Timaeus *actually invents speeches*'. Hemer concludes: 'Polybius explodes with indignation against such an indefensible proceeding' (p. 75).

he would make up speeches as that he would make up events. It is also gratuitous to assume that, because some – even many – ancient historians took liberties with their sources, Luke must have done the same. On the contrary, we know from his gospel the conscientious respect with which he treated his main source, Mark. Even Cadbury conceded that in his gospel 'he transfers speech material from his source to his own manuscript with a minimum of verbal alteration'.[32] So, even though the Acts' speeches differ from the sayings and parables of Jesus, there is every reason to believe that Luke would handle the former with the same reverence that he gave to the latter. In addition, he actually heard a number of Paul's speeches himself, and met people who heard other speeches which he records, so that he was considerably closer to the originals than other historians are.

Thirdly, the sceptical critics are not fair in their evaluation of the variety and appropriateness of the Acts' speeches. As we read Peter's first sermons in Acts 2 – 5, we are conscious of hearing the earliest apostolic formulation of the gospel. H. N. Ridderbos has drawn attention to their decidedly 'old-fashioned' character, because 'neither the Christological terminology nor the remarkable method of citing Scripture in these speeches . . . bear the marks of later development'.[33] And when we read Paul's sermons, we marvel at his adaptability, as he addresses Jews in the synagogue of Pisidian Antioch (chapter 13), pagans in the open air at Lystra (chapter 14), philosophers on the Areopagus in Athens (chapter 17), and the elders of the church of Ephesus in Miletus (chapter 20). Each is different and each is appropriate. Are we really to suppose that Luke had such rich theological insight, historical sense and literary skill that he made them all up? Is it not much more reasonable to suppose that he is summarizing genuinely Pauline utterances, although in the process his own style and vocabulary naturally show through? As F. F. Bruce has written: 'Taken all in all, each speech suits the speaker, the audience, and the circumstances of delivery; and this . . . gives good ground . . . for believing these speeches to be, not inventions of the historian, but condensed accounts of speeches actually made, and therefore valuable and independent sources for the history and theology of the primitive Church.'[34]

b. Peter's quotation of Joel (2:14–21)

Then Peter stood up with the Eleven, raised his voice and addressed the crowd: 'Fellow Jews and all of you who live in Jerusalem, let me explain this to you; listen carefully to what I say. [15]*These men*

[32] *BC*, V, p. 416. [33] Ridderbos, p. 10. [34] Bruce, *Speeches* (1), p. 27

are not drunk, as you suppose. It's only nine in the morning! [16]*No, this is what was spoken by the prophet Joel:*

> [17]'"*In the last days, God says,*
> *I will pour out my Spirit on all people.*
> *Your sons and daughters will prophesy,*
> *your young men will see visions,*
> *your old men will dream dreams.*
> [18]*Even on my servants, both men and women,*
> *I will pour out my Spirit in those days,*
> *and they will prophesy."'*

What Luke has described in verses 1–13 Peter now explains. The extraordinary phenomenon of Spirit-filled believers declaring God's wonders in foreign languages is the fulfilment of Joel's prediction that God would pour out his Spirit on all flesh. Peter's exposition is similar to what in the Dead Sea Scrolls is called a 'pesher' or 'interpretation' of an Old Testament passage in the light of its fulfilment. So (i) Peter introduces his sermon with the words 'this is that' (16, AV), *i.e.* 'this' which his hearers have witnessed is 'that' which Joel foretold; (ii) he deliberately changes Joel's 'afterwards' (as the time when the Spirit will be poured out) to 'in the last days' in order to emphasize that with the Spirit's coming the last days have come; and (iii) he applies the passage to Jesus, so that 'the Lord' who brings salvation is no longer Yahweh who shelters survivors on Mount Zion,[35] but Jesus who saves from sin and judgment everyone who calls on his name (21).[36]

It is the unanimous conviction of the New Testament authors that Jesus inaugurated the last days or Messianic age, and that the final proof of this was the outpouring of the Spirit, since this was the Old Testament promise of promises for the end-time. This being so, we must be careful not to re-quote Joel's prophecy as if we are still awaiting its fulfilment, or even as if its fulfilment has been only partial, and we await some future and complete fulfilment. For this is not how Peter understood and applied the text. The whole Messianic era, which stretches between the two comings of Christ, is the age of the Spirit in which his ministry is one of abundance. Is not this the significance of the verb 'pour out'? The picture is probably of a heavy tropical rainstorm, and seems to

[35] Joel 2:32.

[36] R. N. Longenecker shows (in *Exegesis*) that 'pesher' interpretation was characteristic of Jesus' own teaching. 'The "this is that" fulfilment motif, which is distinctive to pesher exegesis, repeatedly comes to the fore in the words of Jesus' (p. 70). Moreover, the apostles learned this method from him, as they were led by the Spirit. Consequently, 'most characteristic in their treatment of Scripture is pesher interpretation' (p. 98). See also pp. 38–45, 70–75 and 129–132.

illustrate the generosity of God's gift of the Spirit (neither a drizzle nor even a shower but a downpour), its finality (for what has been 'poured out' cannot be gathered again) and its universality (widely distributed among the different groupings of humankind). Peter goes on to stress this universality. *All people* (*pasa sarx*, 'all flesh', 17a) means not everybody irrespective of their inward readiness to receive the gift, but everybody irrespective of their outward status. There are still spiritual conditions for receiving the Spirit, but there are no social distinctions whether of sex (*Your sons and daughters*, 17b), or of age (*your young men . . . your old men . . .*, 17c) or of rank (*even on my servants, both men and women*, 18 – who are not just 'servants', as in the Hebrew, but whom God dignifies as belonging to him).

And they will prophesy (18). This seems to be an umbrella-use of the verb 'to prophesy'. As Luther put it, 'prophesying, visions and dreams are *all one thing*'.[37] That is, the universal gift (the Spirit) will lead to a universal ministry (prophecy). Yet the promise is surprising because elsewhere in Acts – and in the New Testament generally – only some are called to be prophets. How then shall we understand a universal prophetic ministry? If in its essence prophecy is God speaking, God making himself known by his Word, then certainly the Old Testament expectation was that in New Covenant days the knowledge of God would be universal, and the New Testament authors declare that this has been fulfilled through Christ.[38] In this sense all God's people are now prophets, just as all are also priests and kings. So Luther understood prophecy here as 'the knowledge of God through Christ which the Holy Spirit kindles and makes to burn through the word of the gospel',[39] while Calvin wrote that it 'signifies simply the rare and excellent gift of understanding'.[40] In fact, it is this universal knowledge of God through Christ by the Spirit which is the foundation of the universal commission to witness (1:8). Because we know him, we must make him known.

Peter continues the quotation from Joel: ' "*I will show wonders in the heaven above and signs on the earth below, blood and fire and billows of smoke* (19). *The sun will be turned to darkness and the moon to blood before the coming of the great and glorious day of the Lord*" ' (20). It is possible to understand these predictions either literally as uphcavals of nature (which already began on Good Friday,[41] and more of which Jesus foretold before the end[42]), or metaphorically as convulsions of history (since this is traditional

[37] Quoted by Lenski, p. 74

[38] Je. 31:34, 'they will all know me'; 1 Thes. 4:9, 'you yourselves have been taught by God'; 1 Jn. 2:27, 'his anointing teaches you about all things'.

[39] Lenski, p. 75 [40] Calvin, I, p. 59. [41] Lk. 23:44–45. [42] Lk. 21:11

apocalyptic imagery for times of social and political revolution[43]). Meanwhile, between the Day of Pentecost (when the Spirit came, inaugurating the last days) and the day of the Lord (when Jesus will come, concluding them) there stretches a long day of opportunity, during which the gospel of salvation will be preached throughout the world: ' "*And everyone who calls on the name of the Lord will be saved*" ' (21).

c. *Peter's testimony to Jesus (2:22–41)*

The best way to understand Pentecost, however, is not through the Old Testament prediction, but through the New Testament fulfilment, not through Joel but through Jesus. As Peter summons the *men of Israel* to *listen* to him, his first words are *Jesus of Nazareth*, and he goes on to tell the story of Jesus in six stages:

(i) His life and ministry (2:22)

He was truly *a man*, yet he was *accredited by God* to them through supernatural works, which are given three names – *miracles* or literally 'powers' (*dynameis*, their nature being a demonstration of the power of God), *wonders* (*terata*, their effect being to arouse astonishment) *and signs* (*sēmeia*, their purpose being to embody or signify spiritual truth). *God did* these *through him*, and publicly (*among you*), *as you yourselves know*.

(ii) His death (2:23)

Peter describes *this man* as having been killed, partly because he had been *handed over* to them not by Judas (though the same verb is used of his betrayal) but *by God's set purpose and foreknowledge*, and partly because they *with the help of wicked men* (presumably the Romans) had then *put him to death by nailing him to the cross*. Thus the same event, the death of Jesus, is attributed simultaneously both to the purpose of God and to the wickedness of men. No developed doctrine of the Atonement is yet expressed, but there is already an understanding that through Jesus' death God's saving purpose was being worked out.

(iii) His resurrection (2:24–32)

'But God raised him from the dead, freeing him from the agony of death, because it was impossible for death to keep its hold on him. [25]*David said about him:*

> *' "I saw the Lord always before me.*
> *Because he is at my right hand,*
> *I will not be shaken.*

[43] *E.g.* Is. 13:9ff.; 34:1ff.; Ezk. 32:7ff.; Am. 8:9; Mt. 24:29; Lk. 21:25–26; Rev 6:12ff.

[26]Therefore my heart is glad and my tongue rejoices;
my body also will live in hope,
[27]because you will not abandon me to the grave,
nor will you let your Holy One see decay.
[28]You have made known to me the paths of life;
you will fill me with joy in your presence."

[29]'Brothers, I can tell you confidently that the patriarch David
died and was buried, and his tomb is here to this day. [30]But he was
a prophet and knew that God had promised him on oath that he
would place one of his descendants on his throne. [31]Seeing what was
ahead, he spoke of the resurrection of the Christ, that he was not
abandoned to the grave, nor did his body see decay. [32]God has
raised this Jesus to life, and we are all witnesses of the fact.'

It was impossible for death to keep its hold on him (24; Peter sees this moral impossibility without explaining it). So although men had killed him, *God raised him from the dead*, and thereby freed him *from the agony of death*. 'Agony' means literally 'birth pains', so that his resurrection is pictured as a regeneration, a new birth out of death into life.

Peter next confirms the truth of Jesus' resurrection by appealing to Psalm 16:8–11 in which, he claims, it was foretold. David cannot have been referring to himself, when he wrote that God would not abandon him to the grave or let his Holy One see decay (27), because David had *died and was buried*, and his tomb was still in Jerusalem (29). Instead, being a prophet and remembering God's promise to place a distinguished descendant on his throne,[44] *he spoke of the resurrection of the Christ* (30–31). Peter's use of Scripture probably sounds strange to us, but we need to bear three points in mind. First, all Scripture bears witness to Christ, especially to his death, resurrection and world-wide mission. That is its character and purpose. Jesus himself said so both before and after his resurrection.[45] In consequence, secondly, not least because of Jesus' post-resurrection teaching, his disciples came naturally to see Old Testament references to God's anointed or king, to David and his royal seed, as finding their fulfilment in Jesus.[46] This is what Dom Jacques Dupont has called 'the radically christological character of early Christian exegesis'.[47] And, thirdly, once this foundation is granted, a Christian use of the Old Testament like Peter's of Psalm 16 is 'scrupulously logical and internally coherent'.[48]

[44] *Cf.* 2 Sa. 7:16; Ps. 89:3ff.; 132:11–12.
[45] *E.g.* Lk. 4:21; Jn 5:39–40; Lk. 24:27, 44ff.
[46] *E.g.* Psalm 2:8; 16:10; 110:1. [47] Dupont, p. 120.
[48] *Ibid.*, p. 109; and pp. 103–128, 136, 154–157. See also Dr Longenecker's comments in *Acts*, pp. 279–280, and in *Exegesis*, especially pp. 85–103 and 205–209

Having quoted these verses of Psalm 16 and applied them to the resurrection of Jesus, Peter adds: *God has raised this Jesus to life, and we are all witnesses of the fact* (32). Thus the spoken testimony of the apostles and the written prediction of the prophets converged. Or, as we would say, the Old and New Testament Scriptures coincided in their witness to the resurrection of Christ.

(iv) His exaltation (2:33–36)

Peter now jumps straight from Jesus' resurrection from the dead to his exaltation to God's right hand. From this position of supreme honour and absolute power, having received the promised Spirit from the Father, Jesus has poured out the Spirit.

'Exalted to the right hand of God, he has received from the Father the promised Holy Spirit and has poured out what you now see and hear. [34]For David did not ascend to heaven, and yet he said,

' "The Lord said to my Lord:
'Sit at my right hand
[35]until I make your enemies
a footstool for your feet." '

[36]'Therefore let all Israel be assured of this: God has made this Jesus, whom you crucified, both Lord and Christ.'

Peter again clinches his argument with an apt Old Testament quotation. As he has applied Psalm 16 to the Messiah's resurrection, so he now applies Psalm 110 to the Messiah's ascension. For David *did not ascend to heaven* (34), any more than he had been preserved from decay by resurrection. Yet he designated as 'my lord' him whom Yahweh had instructed to sit at his right hand. Jesus had already applied this verse to himself,[49] as did Paul and the writer to the Hebrews later.[50] Peter's conclusion is that all Israel should now be assured that *this Jesus*, whom they had repudiated and crucified, God had made *both Lord and Christ*. Not of course that Jesus became Lord and Christ only at the time of his ascension, for he was (and claimed to be) both throughout his public ministry. It is rather that now God exalted him to be in reality and power what he already was by right.

(v) His salvation (2:37–39)

Luke now describes the crowd's response to Peter's sermon, together with Peter's reply.

When the people heard this, they were cut to the heart and said to Peter and the other apostles, 'Brothers, what shall we do?'

[49] Mk. 12:35–37; Lk 20:41–44. [50] 1 Cor. 15:25; Heb. 1:13.

[38]*Peter replied, 'Repent and be baptised, every one of you, in the name of Jesus Christ for the forgiveness of your sins. And you will receive the gift of the Holy Spirit.* [39]*The promise is for you and your children and for all who are far off – for all whom the Lord our God will call.'*

Cut to the heart, that is, convicted of sin and conscience-stricken, Peter's hearers asked anxiously what they should do (37). Peter replied that they must *repent*, completely changing their mind about Jesus and their attitude to him, and *be baptised* in his name, submitting to the humiliation of baptism, which Jews regarded as necessary for Gentile converts only, and submitting to it in the name of the very person they had previously rejected. This would be a clear, public token of their repentance – and of their faith in him. Though Peter does not specifically call on the crowd to believe, they evidently did so, since they are termed 'believers' in verse 44, and in any case repentance and faith involve each other, the turn from sin being impossible without the turn to God, and vice versa (*cf.* 3:19). And both are signified by baptism in Christ's name, which means 'by his authority, acknowledging his claims, subscribing to his doctrines, engaging in his service, and relying on his merits'.[51]

Then they would receive two free gifts of God – the forgiveness of their sins (even of the sin of rejecting God's Christ) and the gift of the Holy Spirit (to regenerate, indwell, unite and transform them). For they must not imagine that the Pentecostal gift was for the apostles alone, or for the 120 disciples who had waited ten days for the Spirit to come, or for any élitist group, or even for that nation or that generation alone. God had placed no such limitations on his offer and gift. On the contrary (39), *the promise* – or 'gift' or 'baptism' – of the Spirit (1:4; 2:33) was for them also (who were listening to Peter), and for their children (of the next and subsequent generations), and for all who were far off (certainly the Jews of the dispersion and perhaps also prophetically the distant Gentile world[52]), indeed *for all* (without exception) *whom the Lord our God will call*. Everyone God calls to himself through Christ receives both gifts. The gifts of God are coextensive with the call of God.

(vi) His new community (2:40–41)

Luke adds that this was not the end of Peter's sermon, for *with many other words* he both *warned them* and *pleaded with them*. And the essence of his warnings and pleadings was the appeal: '*Save yourselves from this corrupt generation*' (40). That is, Peter was not asking for private and individual conversions only, but for

[51] Alexander, I, p. 85. [52] As in Is. 49:1, 12; 57:19; *cf.* Eph. 2:13, 17.

a public identification with other believers. Commitment to the Messiah implied commitment to the Messianic community, that is, the church. Indeed, they would have to change communities, transferring their membership from one that was old and *corrupt* to one that was new and *being saved* (47).

The amazing response to Peter's appeal is now recorded. Large numbers of people *accepted his message* (*i.e.* repented and believed), and in consequence *were baptised.* In fact, *about three thousand were added to their number* that day (41). The body of Christ in Jerusalem multiplied twenty-six times, from 120 to 3,120. They must also, according to Peter's promise, have received forgiveness and the Spirit, although this time apparently with no supernatural signs. At least Luke makes no mention of phenomena like wind or fire, or of languages.

d. The gospel for today

We have seen that Peter focused on Christ and told his story in six stages. (i) He was a man, though divinely attested by miracles; (ii) he was put to death by wicked hands, though according to God's purpose; (iii) he was raised from the dead, as the prophets had foretold and the apostles had witnessed; (iv) he was exalted to God's right hand, and from there poured out the Spirit; (v) he now gives forgiveness and the Spirit to all who repent, believe and are baptized; and (vi) he thus adds them to his new community.

Numerous reconstructions of this material have been attempted. Special mention must be made of C. H. Dodd's famous lectures at King's College, London, on the *kerygma* of Peter and Paul, and their coincidence, which were published under the title *The Apostolic Preaching and its Developments.*[53] He summarized the sermons of Peter as follows: (i) the age of fulfilment, the Messianic age, has dawned; (ii) this has happened through the ministry, death and resurrection of Jesus, as testified by the Scriptures; (iii) Jesus has been exalted to God's right hand as Lord, and as head of the New Israel; (iv) the Holy Spirit's activity in the church is the sign of Christ's present power and glory; (v) the Messianic age will shortly reach its consummation in the return of Christ; and (vi) forgiveness and the Spirit are offered to those who repent.[54]

Our struggle today is how to be faithful to this apostolic gospel, while at the same time presenting it in a way which resonates with modern men and women. What is immediately clear is that, like the apostles, we must focus on Jesus Christ. Peter's beginning

[53] *The Apostolic Preaching and its Developments* by C. H. Dodd (Hodder and Stoughton, 1936).

[54] *Ibid.*, pp. 38–45.

'listen to this: Jesus . . .' (22) must be our beginning too. It is impossible to preach the gospel without proclaiming Christ. But how? I have myself found it an aid to faithfulness to express the apostles' message in the following framework:

First, *the gospel events*, namely the death and resurrection of Jesus. It is true that Peter referred to Jesus' life and ministry (22) and went on to his exaltation (33), and elsewhere to his return as judge. The apostles felt free to rehearse his whole saving career. Yet they concentrated on the cross and the resurrection (23–24), both as historical happenings and as significant saving events. Although a full doctrine of the atonement is not yet developed, it is already implied by the references to God's purpose (23), to the suffering servant passages (3:13, 18), and to the 'tree', the place of the divine curse (5:30; 10:39; 13:29).[55] The resurrection had saving significance too, since by it God reversed the human verdict on Jesus, snatched him from the place of a curse and exalted him to the place of honour.

Secondly, *the gospel witnesses*. The apostles did not proclaim the death and resurrection of Jesus in a vacuum, but in the context of Scripture and history. They appealed to a twofold evidence to authenticate Jesus, so that in the mouth of two witnesses the truth might be established. The first was the Old Testament Scriptures, which he fulfilled. In Acts 2 Peter appeals to Psalm 16, Psalm 110 and Joel 2 in order to illuminate his teaching about Jesus' resurrection, exaltation and gift of the Spirit. The second was the testimony of the apostles. 'We are witnesses', Peter kept repeating (*e.g.* 2:32; 3:15; 5:32; 10:39ff.), and this eyewitness experience was indispensable to the apostolate. Thus the one Christ has a double attestation. We have no liberty to preach a Christ of our own fantasy, or even to focus on our own experience, since we were not eyewitnesses of the historical Jesus. Our responsibility is to preach the authentic Christ of the Old and New Testament Scriptures. The primary witnesses to him are the prophets and apostles; ours is always secondary to theirs.

Thirdly, *the gospel promises*. The gospel is good news not only of what Jesus *did* (he died for our sins and was raised, according to the Scriptures) but also of what he *offers* as a result. He promises to those who respond to him both the forgiveness of sins (to wipe out the past) and the gift of the Spirit (to make us new people). Together these constitute the freedom for which many are searching, freedom from guilt, defilement, judgment and self-centredness, and freedom to be the persons God made and meant us to be. Forgiveness and the Spirit comprise 'salvation', and both are pub-

[55] *Cf.* Gal. 3:13.

licly signified in baptism, namely the washing away of sin and the outpouring of the Spirit.

Fourthly, *the gospel conditions*. Jesus Christ does not impose his gifts upon us unconditionally. What the gospel demands is a radical turn from sin to Christ, which takes the form inwardly of repentance and faith, and outwardly of baptism. For submission to baptism in the name of the Christ we have formerly repudiated gives public evidence of penitent faith in him. Additionally, by this same repentance, faith and baptism we change allegiance, as we are transferred into the new community of Jesus.

Here, then, is a fourfold message – two events (Christ's death and resurrection), as attested by two witnesses (prophets and apostles), on the basis of which God makes two promises (forgiveness and the Spirit), on two conditions (repentance and faith, with baptism). We have no liberty to amputate this apostolic gospel, by proclaiming the cross without the resurrection, or referring to the New Testament but not the Old, or offering forgiveness without the Spirit, or demanding faith without repentance. There is a wholeness about the biblical gospel.

It is not enough to 'proclaim Jesus'. For there are many different Jesuses being presented today. According to the New Testament gospel, however, he is *historical* (he really lived, died, rose and ascended in the arena of history), *theological* (his life, death, resurrection and ascension all have saving significance) and *contemporary* (he lives and reigns to bestow salvation on those who respond to him). Thus the apostles told the same story of Jesus at three levels – as historical event (witnessed by their own eyes), as having theological significance (interpreted by the Scriptures), and as contemporary message (confronting men and women with the necessity of decision). We have the same responsibility today to tell the story of Jesus as fact, doctrine and gospel.

3. The church's life: the effect of Pentecost (2:42–47)

Having first described in his own narrative what happened on the day of Pentecost, and then supplied an explanation of it through Peter's Christ-centred sermon, Luke goes on to show us the effects of Pentecost by giving us a beautiful little cameo of the Spirit-filled church. Of course the church did not begin that day, and it is incorrect to call the Day of Pentecost 'the birthday of the church'. For the church as the people of God goes back at least 4,000 years to Abraham. What happened at Pentecost was that the remnant of God's people became the Spirit-filled body of Christ. What evidence did it give of the presence and power of the Holy Spirit? Luke tells us.

They devoted themselves to the apostles' teaching and to the fellowship, to the breaking of bread and to prayer. [43]*Everyone was filled with awe, and many wonders and miraculous signs were done by the apostles.* [44]*All the believers were together and had everything in common.* [45]*Selling their possessions and goods, they gave to anyone as he had need.* [46]*Every day they continued to meet together in the temple courts. They broke bread in their homes and ate together with glad and sincere hearts,* [47]*praising God and enjoying the favour of all the people. And the Lord added to their number daily those who were being saved.*

a. *It was a learning church*

The very first evidence Luke mentions of the Spirit's presence in the church is that *they devoted themselves to the apostles' teaching*. One might perhaps say that the Holy Spirit opened a school in Jerusalem that day; its teachers were the apostles whom Jesus had appointed; and there were 3,000 pupils in the kindergarten! We note that those new converts were not enjoying a mystical experience which led them to despise their mind or disdain theology. Anti-intellectualism and the fullness of the Spirit are mutually incompatible, because the Holy Spirit is the Spirit of truth. Nor did those early disciples imagine that, because they had received the Spirit, he was the only teacher they needed and they could dispense with human teachers. On the contrary, they sat at the apostles' feet, hungry to receive instruction, and they persevered in it. Moreover, the teaching authority of the apostles, to which they submitted, was authenticated by miracles: *many wonders and miraculous signs were done by the apostles* (43). The two references to the apostles, in verse 42 (their teaching) and in verse 43 (their miracles), can hardly be an accident.[56] Since the teaching of the apostles has come down to us in its definitive form in the New Testament, contemporary devotion to the apostles' teaching will mean submission to the authority of the New Testament. A Spirit-filled church is a New Testament church, in the sense that it studies and submits to New Testament instruction. The Spirit of God leads the people of God to submit to the Word of God.

b. *It was a loving church*

They devoted themselves . . . to the fellowship (*koinōnia*). *Koinōnia* (from *koinos*, 'common') bears witness to the common life of the church in two senses. First, it expresses what we share in together. This is God himself, for 'our fellowship is with the Father and with his Son, Jesus Christ',[57] and there is 'the fellowship of the

[56] *Cf.* 2 Cor. 12:12; Heb. 2:1–4. [57] 1 Jn. 1:3.

Holy Spirit'.[58] Thus *koinōnia* is a Trinitarian experience; it is our common share in God, Father, Son and Holy Spirit. But secondly, *koinōnia* also expresses what we share out together, what we give as well as what we receive. *Koinōnia* is the word Paul used for the collection he was organizing among the Greek churches,[59] and *koinōnikos* is the Greek word for 'generous'. It is to this that Luke is particularly referring here, because he goes on at once to describe the way in which these first Christians shared their possessions with one another: *all the believers were together and had everything in common* (*koina*). *Selling their possessions and goods* (probably meaning their real estate and their valuables respectively), *they gave to anyone as he had need* (44–45). These are disturbing verses. Do they mean that every Spirit-filled believer and community will follow their example literally?

A few miles east of Jerusalem the Essene leaders of the Qumran community were committed to the common ownership of property. According to its Damascus Rule all members of 'the Covenant', wherever they lived, were obliged to 'succour the poor, the needy, and the stranger',[60] but the candidate for initiation into membership of the monastic community accepted a stricter discipline: 'his property and earnings shall be handed over to the Bursar of the Congregation . . .; his property shall be merged . . .'.[61] This arrangement, comments Geza Vermes, 'bears a close resemblance to the custom adopted by the primitive Church of Jerusalem'.[62]

So did the early Christians imitate them, and should we do so today? At different times in church history some have thought so and done so. And I do not doubt that Jesus still calls some of his disciples, as he did the rich young ruler, to a life of total, voluntary poverty. Yet neither Jesus nor his apostles forbade private property to all Christians. Even the sixteenth-century Anabaptists in the so-called 'radical reformation', who wanted fellowship and brotherly love to be added to the Reformers' definition of the church (in terms of word, sacraments and discipline), and who talked much about Acts 2 and 4 and 'the community of goods', recognized that this was not compulsory. The Hutterite Brethren in Moravia seem to have been the only exception, for they did make complete common ownership a condition of membership. But Menno Simons, the most influential leader of the movement, pointed out that the Jerusalem experiment was neither universal nor permanent, and wrote 'we . . . have never taught nor practised community of goods'.[63]

[58] 2 Cor. 13:14. [59] 2 Cor. 8:4; 9:13. [60] Vermes, p. 103.
[61] Community Rule VI, *ibid.*, p. 82. [62] *Ibid.*, p. 30.
[63] See *Every Need Supplied: Mutual Aid and Christian Community in the Free Churches 1525–1675*, ed. Donald F. Durnbaugh (Philadelphia: Temple University Press, 1974).

It is important to note that even in Jerusalem the sharing of property and possessions was voluntary. According to verse 46, *they broke bread in their homes*. So evidently many still had homes; not all had sold them. It is also noteworthy that the tense of both verbs in verse 45 is imperfect, which indicates that the selling and the giving were occasional, in response to particular needs, not once and for all. Further, the sin of Ananias and Sapphira, to which we shall come in Acts 5, was not greed or materialism but deceit; it was not that they had retained part of the proceeds of their sale, but that they had done so while pretending to give it all. Peter made this plain when he said to them: 'Didn't it belong to you before it was sold? And after it was sold, wasn't the money at your disposal?' (5:4).

At the same time, although the selling and the sharing were and are voluntary, and every Christian has to make conscientious decisions before God in this matter, we are all called to generosity, especially towards the poor and needy. Already in the Old Testament there was a strong tradition of care for the poor, and the Israelites were to give a tenth of their produce to 'the Levite, the alien, the fatherless and the widow'.[64] How can Spirit-filled believers possibly give less? The principle is stated twice in the Acts: *they gave to anyone as he had need* (45), and 'there were no needy persons among them . . . the money . . . was distributed to anyone as he had need' (4:34–35). As John was to write later, if we have material possessions and see a brother or sister in need, but do not share what we have with him or her, how can we claim that God's love dwells in us?[65] Christian fellowship is Christian caring, and Christian caring is Christian sharing. Chrysostom gave a beautiful description of it: 'This was an angelic commonwealth, not to call anything of theirs their own. Forthwith the root of evils was cut out. . . . None reproached, none envied, none grudged; no pride, no contempt was there. . . . The poor man knew no shame, the rich no haughtiness.'[66] So we must not evade the challenge of these verses. That we have hundreds of thousands of destitute brothers and sisters is a standing rebuke to us who are more affluent. It is part of the responsibility of Spirit-filled believers to alleviate need and abolish destitution in the new community of Jesus.

c. *It was a worshipping church*

They devoted themselves . . . to the breaking of bread and to prayer (42). That is, their fellowship was expressed not only in caring for each other, but in corporate worship too. Moreover, the definite article in both expressions (literally, 'the breaking of the bread and

[64] Dt. 26:12. [65] 1 Jn. 3:17. [66] Chrysostom, Homily VII, p. 47.

the prayers') suggests a reference to the Lord's Supper on the one hand (although almost certainly at that early stage as part of a larger meal) and prayer services or meetings (rather than private prayer) on the other. There are two aspects of the early church's worship which exemplify its balance.

First, it was both formal and informal, for it took place both *in the temple courts and in their homes* (46), which is an interesting combination. It is perhaps surprising that they continued for a while in the temple, but they did. They did not immediately abandon what might be called the institutional church. I do not believe they still participated in the sacrifices of the temple, for already they had begun to grasp that these had been fulfilled in the sacrifice of Christ, but they do seem to have attended the prayer services of the temple (*cf.* 3:1), unless, as has been suggested, they went up to the temple to preach, rather than to pray. At the same time, they supplemented the temple services with more informal and spontaneous meetings (including the breaking of bread) in their homes. Perhaps we, who get understandably impatient with the inherited structures of the church, can learn a lesson from them. For myself, I believe that the Holy Spirit's way with the institutional church, which we long to see reformed according to the gospel, is more the way of patient reform than of impatient rejection. And certainly it is always healthy when the more formal and dignified services of the local church are complemented with the informality and exuberance of home meetings. There is no need to polarize between the structured and the unstructured, the traditional and the spontaneous. The church needs both.

The second example of the balance of the early church's worship is that it was both joyful and reverent. There can be no doubt of their joy, for they are described as having *glad and sincere hearts* (46), which literally means 'in exultation [*agalliasis*] and sincerity of heart'. The NEB unites the two words by translating 'with unaffected joy'. Since God had sent his Son into the world, and had now sent them his Spirit, they had plenty of reason to be joyful. Besides, 'the fruit of the Spirit is . . . joy',[67] and sometimes a more uninhibited joy than is customary (or even acceptable) within the staid traditions of the historic churches. Yet every worship service should be a joyful celebration of the mighty acts of God through Jesus Christ. It is right in public worship to be dignified; it is unforgivable to be dull. At the same time, their joy was never irreverent. If joy in God is an authentic work of the Spirit, so is the fear of God. *Everyone was filled with awe* (43), which seems to include the Christians as well as the non-Christians. God had

[67] Gal. 5:22.

visited their city. He was in their midst, and they knew it. They bowed down before him in humility and wonder. It is a mistake, therefore, to imagine that in public worship reverence and rejoicing are mutually exclusive. The combination of joy and awe, as of formality and informality, is a healthy balance in worship.

d. *It was an evangelistic church*

So far we have considered the study, the fellowship and the worship of the Jerusalem church, for it is to these three things that Luke says the first believers *devoted themselves*. Yet these are aspects of the interior life of the church; they tell us nothing about its compassionate outreach to the world. Tens of thousands of sermons have been preached on Acts 2:42, which well illustrates the danger of isolating a text from its context. On its own, verse 42 presents a very lopsided picture of the church's life. Verse 47b needs to be added: *And the Lord added to their number daily those who were being saved*. Those first Jerusalem Christians were not so preoccupied with learning, sharing and worshipping, that they forgot about witnessing. For the Holy Spirit is a missionary Spirit who created a missionary church. As Harry Boer expressed it in his challenging book *Pentecost and Missions*,[68] the Acts 'is governed by one dominant, overriding and all-controlling motif. This motif is the expansion of the faith through missionary witness in the power of the Spirit. . . . Restlessly the Spirit drives the church to witness, and continually churches rise out of the witness. The church is a missionary church'.[69]

From these earliest believers in Jerusalem, we can learn three vital lessons about local church evangelism. First, the Lord himself (that is, Jesus) did it: *the Lord added to their number*. Doubtless he did it through the preaching of the apostles, the witness of church members, the impressive love of their common life, and their example as they were *praising God and enjoying the favour of all the people* (47a). Yet he did it. For he is the head of the church. He alone has the prerogative to admit people into its membership and to bestow salvation from his throne. This is a much needed emphasis, for many people talk about evangelism today with reprehensible self-confidence and even triumphalism, as if they think the evangelization of the world will be the ultimate triumph of human technology. We should harness to the evangelistic task all the technology God has given us, but only in humble dependence on him as the principal evangelist.

Secondly, what Jesus did was two things together: he *added to*

[68] *Pentecost and Missions* by Harry Boer (Lutterworth, 1961).
[69] *Ibid.*, pp. 161–162.

their number . . . those who were being saved (the present participle *sōzomenous* either being timeless or emphasizing that salvation is a progressive experience culminating in final glorification). He did not add them to the church without saving them (no nominal Christianity at the beginning), nor did he save them without adding them to the church (no solitary Christianity either). Salvation and church membership belonged together; they still do. Thirdly, the Lord added people *daily*. The verb is an imperfect ('kept adding'), and the adverb ('daily') puts the matter beyond question. The early church's evangelism was not an occasional or sporadic activity. They did not organize quinquennial or decennial missions (missions are fine so long as they are only episodes in an ongoing programme). No, just as their worship was daily (46a), so was their witness. Praise and proclamation were both the natural overflow of hearts full of the Holy Spirit. And as their outreach was continuous, so continuously converts were being added. We need to recover this expectation of steady and uninterrupted church growth.

Looking back over these marks of the first Spirit-filled community, it is evident that they all concerned the church's relationships. First, they were related to the apostles (in submission). They were eager to receive the apostles' instruction. A Spirit-filled church is an apostolic church, a New Testament church, anxious to believe and obey what Jesus and his apostles taught. Secondly, they were related to each other (in love). They persevered in the fellowship, supporting each other and relieving the needs of the poor. A Spirit-filled church is a loving, caring, sharing church. Thirdly, they were related to God (in worship). They worshipped him in the temple and in the home, in the Lord's Supper and in the prayers, with joy and with reverence. A Spirit-filled church is a worshipping church. Fourthly, they were related to the world (in outreach). They were engaged in continuous evangelism. No self-centred, self-contained church (absorbed in its own parochial affairs) can claim to be filled with the Spirit. The Holy Spirit is a missionary Spirit. So a Spirit-filled church is a missionary church.

There is no need for us to wait, as the one hundred and twenty had to wait, for the Spirit to come. For the Holy Spirit did come on the Day of Pentecost, and has never left his church. Our responsibility is to humble ourselves before his sovereign authority, to determine not to quench him, but to allow him his freedom. For then our churches will again manifest those marks of the Spirit's presence, which many young people are specially looking for, namely biblical teaching, loving fellowship, living worship, and an ongoing, outgoing evangelism.

3. The outbreak of persecution *3:1–4:31*

Luke has painted an idyllic picture of the early Christian community in Jerusalem. Its members, having received forgiveness and the Holy Spirit, were conscientious in their learning from the apostles, their worship of God, their care of one another and their witness to those as yet outside their fellowship. Everything was sweetness and light. Love, joy and peace reigned. Commissioned by Christ and empowered by his Spirit, they stood on the threshold of the great missionary adventure which Luke is going to describe. The good ship *Christ-church* was ready to catch the wind of the Spirit and to set sail on her voyage of spiritual conquest. But almost immediately a perilous storm blew up, a storm of such ferocity that the church's very existence was threatened.

Alternatively, we might say that, if the chief actor in the story of Acts 1 and 2 is the Holy Spirit, the chief actor in Acts 3 – 6 almost seems to be Satan. True, he is identified only once by name, but his activity may be discerned throughout. His one specific mention is when Peter confronts Ananias: 'Ananias, how is it that Satan has so filled your heart that you have lied to the Holy Spirit . . . ?' (5:3). Here the Holy Spirit and that evil spirit often called the devil stand in opposition to one another. According to outward appearance, two men faced each other, and one of them lied to the other, but Peter had the spiritual discernment to see behind the appearance to the unseen reality: Satan had lied to God (5:3–4). Indeed, Satan had 'filled' Ananias' heart to induce him to do so – a kind of diabolical equivalent to Peter's being filled with the Spirit.

For a full understanding of the early church we need to read *The Acts of the Apostles* and *The Book of Revelation* side by side. Both tell much the same tale of the church and its experience of conflict, but from a different perspective. Luke in the Acts chronicles what unfolded on the stage of history before the eyes of observers; John in the Revelation enables us to see the hidden forces at work. In the Acts human beings oppose and undermine the church; in the Revelation the curtain is lifted and we see the hostility of the devil himself, depicted as an enormous red dragon, aided and abetted by two grotesque monsters and a lewd prostitute. Indeed the Revelation is a vision of the age-long battle between the Lamb and the dragon, Christ and Satan, Jerusalem the holy city and Babylon the great city, the church and the world. Moreover, it can hardly be a coincidence that the symbolism of the dragon's three allies in Revelation corresponds to the devil's three weapons wielded against the church in the early chapters of the Acts, that is, persecution, moral compromise, and the danger of exposure to false teaching when the apostles became distracted from their chief responsibility, namely 'the ministry of the Word and prayer'.

The devil's crudest weapon was physical violence, and Luke describes two outbreaks of persecution by the Sanhedrin. In the first Peter and John are arrested, jailed, tried, forbidden to preach, warned and released (4:1–22); in the second they and others ('the apostles' in general) are arrested, jailed and tried, and this time flogged before being again forbidden to preach and released. Luke sees this as a fulfilment of Jesus' own predictions, which he has recorded in his Gospel, that his disciples would be hated, insulted and rejected (Lk. 6:22, 26), brought to trial before 'rulers and authorities' (Lk. 12:11), and persecuted and imprisoned on account of his name (Lk. 21:12ff.).

It is noteworthy that the structure Luke adopts in chapters 3 and 4 is the same as in chapter 2. First, he describes from a spectator's viewpoint a miraculous event – in chapter 2 the coming of the Spirit (2:1–13), in chapter 3 the healing of a cripple (3:1–10). The story is told in an objective, matter-of-fact way, although in both cases the crowd are said to have been utterly amazed and 'unable to explain' what had happened.[1] Secondly, Luke records a speech by Peter which takes the miraculous event as its text and interprets it in such a way as to glorify Christ, whom his hearers had killed, but God had raised, as the apostles had witnessed. In addition, the now-exalted Christ had both poured out the Spirit and healed the cripple, thus demonstrating the power of his name to those who believe (2:23–39; 3:13–16; 4:12). In each case Peter concluded his speech with an appeal to the crowd to repent, so that they might receive the promised blessings (2:38ff. and 3:17ff.). Thirdly, Luke describes the consequences of the miraculous event and Peter's explanation of it, namely a Spirit-filled church which in the first case learns, worships, shares and witnesses (2:42–47) and in the second is persecuted, but also prays and shares (4:1–37).

[1] JB, 2:7, 12; 3:10.

As Luke develops this second vignette of the post-Pentecost church, he focuses successively on the cripple who was healed (3:1–10), on the apostle Peter who addressed the crowd (3:11–26), on the council which arrested and arraigned the apostles (4:1–22), and on the church which turned to God in prayer (4:23–31).

1. A congenital cripple is healed (3:1–10)

What triggered the opposition of the Jewish authorities was the healing of the cripple, together with Peter's sermon which followed it. Luke began his second volume by telling his readers that he was going to record what Jesus continued, after his ascension, 'to do and to teach' through his apostles (1:1–2). He has also told us that 'many wonders and miraculous signs were done by the apostles' (2:43). Now he supplies a particularly dramatic example. *Peter and John were going up to the temple*. The date is not given (it happened *one day*), but the time is, namely, *at three in the afternoon*, which is *the time of prayer* (1). This took place shortly after the evening sacrifice and was observed by all pious Jews like Daniel and 'God-fearers' like Cornelius.[2] The apostles' arrival at the temple coincided with the arrival of *a man crippled from birth*, who *was being carried* there, presumably by friends and/or relatives, so that he could beg from those who came to worship and who thought (incidentally) that they would gain some merit by their almsgiving.

The beggar's pitch, Luke says, was *the temple gate called Beautiful*. Commentators mostly identify this as the Nicanor Gate, which was the main eastern entrance to the temple precincts from the Court of the Gentiles. Because Luke names it 'the Beautiful Gate', it is probably the one made of Corinthian brass which Josephus said 'greatly excelled those that were only covered over with silver and gold'.[3] It was about seventy-five feet high and had huge double doors. But at the foot of this magnificent gate the cripple sat begging. Luke's medical interest seems to be betrayed in the brief clinical history he gives. It was a congenital case, he tells us; the man was now *over forty years old* (4:22); and he was so severely handicapped that he had to be carried and *put every day to beg from those going into the temple courts* (2). As *Peter and John* were *about to enter* the temple, *he asked them for money* (3). The apostles stopped and *looked straight at him*, and Peter gave him two commands. First, '*Look at us!*' (4). *So the man gave them his attention, expecting to get something from them* (5). But by his second command Peter told him he had something better to give him than money: '*Silver or gold I do not have, but what I have I give you.*

[2] Dn. 9:20–21; Acts 10:2, 22. [3] Josephus, *Wars*, V.5.3.

In the name of Jesus Christ of Nazareth, walk' (6). The apostle did not then stand back and watch the man struggle to his feet; he leaned forward and, *taking him by the right hand, he helped him up* (7a). As Thomas Walker comments, 'the power was Christ's, but the hand was Peter's'.[4] It was not a gesture of unbelief, but of love. Besides, it was something Peter had seen Jesus do when he took Jairus' daughter by the hand.[5] Then *instantly*, Dr Luke continues, *the man's feet and ankles became strong* (7b) – so strong and agile that *he jumped to his feet and began to walk*, which he had never done before. Not only so, but he now accompanied the apostles *into the temple courts*, all the time *walking and jumping, and praising God* (8). It was an outstanding fulfilment of the Messianic prophecy: 'Then will the lame leap like a deer.'[6]

A crowd quickly gathered. For they *saw him walking and praising God* (9). This is the fourth time that Luke describes the man as *walking*, as if to emphasize the incredible fact that his poor crippled legs and feet were now for the first time fully operational. *They recognised him as the same man who* had been a familiar sight for decades, since he *used to sit* every day *begging at the temple gate called Beautiful, and they were filled with wonder and amazement at what had happened to him* (10).

2. The apostle Peter preaches to the crowd (3:11–26)

While the beggar held on to Peter and John, cured but still clinging to them and not yet confident, *all the people were astonished and came running to them*, and assembled *in the place called Solomon's Colonnade* (11). This was a cloister or 'portico' (NEB), formed by a double row of marbled columns and roofed with cedar, which ran all the way along the eastern wall of the outer court. Jesus himself sometimes walked and taught in it.[7]

Peter seized the opportunity to preach. Just as the Pentecost event had been the text for his first sermon, so the cripple's healing became the text for his second. Both were mighty acts of the exalted Christ. Both were signs which proclaimed him Lord and Saviour. Both aroused the crowd's amazement.

Peter began by ascribing all the credit to Jesus. '*Men of Israel, why does this surprise you?*' he asked (12), presumably pointing to the healed cripple. And '*Why do you stare at us*, presumably making a gesture which pointed to themselves, *as if* it had been *by our own power or godliness* that *we had made this man walk?*' (12). Instead, he redirected their gaze to Jesus, by whose powerful name the miracle had taken place. For '*The God of Abraham, Isaac and*

[4] Walker, p. 67. [5] Lk. 8:54. [6] Is. 35:6. [7] Jn. 10:23.

Jacob, the God of our fathers, has glorified his servant Jesus' (13a). Peter's designation of God expressed his conviction that what was new in Jesus nevertheless enjoyed a direct continuity with the Old Testament. Then, in contrast to the honour that God had given to Jesus, Peter is outspoken in describing the fourfold dishonour which the inhabitants of Jerusalem have shown him: (i) *You handed him over to be killed, and* (ii) *you disowned him before Pilate* (as indeed Peter had himself 'disowned' or 'denied' him before a servant girl and others[8]), *though he had decided to let him go* (13b). (iii) *You disowned the Holy and Righteous One and asked that a murderer be released to you* (14), thus demanding both 'the condemnation of the innocent' and 'the acquittal of the guilty'.[9] (iv) *You killed the author of life*, a striking oxymoron, in which the pioneer or giver of life (*archēgos* could mean either) is himself deprived of life, *but God*, wonderfully reversing this fourfold rejection of Jesus, *raised him from the dead*, and of this mighty resurrection *we* (apostles) *are witnesses* (15). So then, it is *by faith in the name of Jesus*, of the once rejected but now resurrected and reigning Jesus, that *this* crippled *man whom you see and know was made strong*. Peter goes on to repeat it for emphasis, this time separating the name and the faith which apprehends it. For it was *Jesus' name* (all he is and has done), together with *the faith that comes through him*, being aroused by him in those who grasp the implications of his name, which *has given this complete healing to him, as you can all see*' (16).

The most remarkable feature of Peter's second sermon, as of his first, is its Christ-centredness. He directed the crowd's attention away from both the healed cripple and the apostles to the Christ whom men disowned by killing him but God vindicated by raising him, and whose name, having been appropriated by faith, was strong enough to heal the man completely. Moreover, in his testimony to Jesus Peter attributed to him a cluster of significant titles. He began by calling him 'Jesus Christ of Nazareth' (6), but went on to style him God's 'servant' (13), who first suffered and then was glorified in fulfilment of Isaiah 52:13ff. (*cf.* 18 and 26; 4:27, 30). Next he was 'the Holy and Righteous One' (14) and 'the author [or pioneer] of life' (15), while in the concluding part of the sermon Peter called him the 'prophet' foretold by Moses (22) and before the Sanhedrin the rejected stone which has become the capstone (4:11). Servant and Christ, Holy One and source of life, Prophet and Stone – these titles speak of the uniqueness of Jesus in his sufferings and glory, his character and mission, his revelation

[8] *Cf.* Lk. 22:54–62. [9] Alexander, I, p. 109.

and redemption. All this is encapsulated in his 'Name' and helps to explain its saving power.

Having exalted the name of Jesus, Peter ended his sermon by challenging his hearers (*brothers*, he calls them) with the necessity and the blessings of repentance. '*I know*', he says, '*that you acted in ignorance, as did your leaders*' (17). His purpose in saying this was neither to excuse their sin, nor to imply that forgiveness was unnecessary, but to show why it was possible. Peter was echoing the Old Testament distinction between sins of 'ignorance' and sins of 'presumption'.[10] Next, although they did not know what they were doing, God knew what he was doing. For what happened to Jesus was the fulfilment of prophecy, for '*this is how God fulfilled what he had foretold through all the prophets*, especially *that his Christ would suffer* (18). Neither their ignorance nor God's predictions exonerated them, however. They must *repent . . . and turn to God*' (19a). Then three successive blessings would take place.

The first is *that your sins may be wiped out* (19b), even their sin of doing to death the author of life. *Exaleiphō* means to wash off, erase, obliterate. It is used in the book of Revelation both of God who wipes away our tears[11] and of Christ who refuses to erase our name from the book of life.[12] William Barclay explains the allusion: 'Ancient writing was upon papyrus, and the ink used had no acid in it. It therefore did not bite into the papyrus as modern ink does; it simply lay upon the top of it. To erase the writing a man might take a wet sponge and simply wipe it away.'[13] Just so, when God forgives our sins, he wipes the slate clean.[14]

The second promised blessing is *that times of refreshing may come from the Lord* (19c). The Greek word *anapsyxis* can mean rest, relief, respite or refreshment. It seems here to be the positive counterpart to forgiveness, for God does not wipe away our sins without adding his refreshment for our spirits.

The third promised blessing is *that he may send the Christ who has been appointed for you – even Jesus* (20). Although during the present interim period he continuously gives us his forgiveness and his refreshment, yet he himself *must remain in heaven until the time comes for God to restore everything, as he promised long ago through his holy prophets* (21). Some commentators believe that the word 'everything' in this sentence refers not to the universe which God will 'restore' but to the promises which he will 'establish'. Thus the RSV translates the verse: 'until the time for establishing all that God spoke by the mouth of his holy prophets . . .' But *apokatastasis* is more naturally understood of the eschatological

[10] *E.g.* Nu. 15:27ff., and *cf.* Lk. 23:34; 1 Cor. 2:8; 1 Tim. 1:13.
[11] Rev. 7:17; 21:4. [12] Rev. 3:5. [13] Barclay, p. 32. [14] *Cf.* Is. 43:25

'restoration', which Jesus called a 'regeneration',[15] when nature will be liberated from its bondage to pain and decay[16] and God will make a new heaven and earth.[17] This final perfection awaits the return of Christ.

These Christ-centred promises of total forgiveness (sins wiped out), spiritual refreshment and universal restoration were all adumbrated in the Old Testament. So Peter concludes with more significant quotations and allusions. He refers to three major prophetic strands which are associated with Moses, Samuel (and his successors) and Abraham. First, '*Moses said, "The Lord your God will raise up for you a prophet like me from among your own people; you must listen to everything he tells you* (22), for *anyone who does not listen to him will be completely cut off from among his people*" ' (23).[18] Secondly, '*all the prophets from Samuel on, as many as have spoken, have foretold these days*', the days of the Messiah (24). Although this is a very general statement, perhaps the chief reference is to God's promise, which began with Samuel, to establish the kingdom of David.[19] At all events, Peter assured his hearers, '*you are heirs of the prophets and of the covenant God made with your fathers*' (25a). It is impressive that Peter regards the many and varied strands of Old Testament prophecy as a united testimony, applying to 'these days' because fulfilled in Christ and his people. Thirdly, God '*said to Abraham, "Through your offspring all peoples on earth will be blessed*" ' (25b).[20] This was a foundation promise of the Old Testament. Consider both the beneficiaries and the nature of the promised blessing. As for the beneficiaries, '*When God raised up his servant* Jesus, *he sent him first to you to bless you*' (26a), the physical descendants of Abraham, as is several times emphasized by Paul.[21] But later Paul argues, especially in his letters to the Romans and the Galatians, that the promised blessing is for all believers, including Gentiles who by faith have become Abraham's spiritual children. And what is the blessing? It is not forgiveness only, but righteousness. For God sent Jesus Christ his servant '*to bless you by turning each of you from your wicked ways*' (26).

Looking back over Peter's Colonnade sermon, it is striking that he presents Christ to the crowd 'according to the Scriptures' as successively the suffering servant (13, 18), the Moses-like prophet (22–23), the Davidic king (24) and the seed of Abraham (25–26). And if we add his Pentecost sermon, and glance on to his speech before the Sanhedrin (4:8ff.), it is possible to weave a biblical tapestry which forms a thorough portrait of Christ. Arranged chronologically according to the events of his saving career, the

[15] Mt. 19:28. [16] Rom. 8:19ff. [17] 2 Pet. 3:13; Rev. 21:5.
[18] Dt. 18:15ff., *cf.* Lk. 9:35. [19] *Eg.* 2 Sa. 7:12ff. [20] Gn. 12:3; 22:18; 26:4.
[21] 'First for the Jew', *e.g.* Rom. 1:16; 2:9–10; 3:1–2.

Old Testament texts declare that he was descended from David (Ps. 132:11 = 2:30); that he suffered and died for us as God's servant (Is. 53 = 2:23; 3:18); that the stone the builders rejected has nevertheless become the capstone (Ps. 118:22 = 4:11), for God raised him up from the dead (Is. 52:13 = 2:25ff.), since death could not hold him and God would not abandon him to decay (Ps. 16:8ff. = 2:24, 27, 31); that God then exalted him to his right hand, to wait for his final triumph (Ps. 110:1 = 2:34–35); that meanwhile through him the Spirit has been poured out (Joel 2:28ff. = 2:16ff., 33); that now the gospel is to be preached world-wide, even to those afar off (Is. 57:19 = 2:39), although opposition to him has been foretold (Ps. 2:1ff. = 4:25–26); that people must listen to him or pay the penalty of their disobedience (Dt. 18:18–19 = 3:22–23); and that those who do listen and respond will inherit the blessing promised to Abraham (Gn. 12:3; 22:18 = 3:25–26).

This comprehensive testimony to Jesus as rejected by men but vindicated by God, as the fulfilment of all Old Testament prophecy, as demanding repentance and promising blessing, and as the author and giver of life, physically to the healed cripple and spiritually to those who believe, aroused the indignation and antagonism of the authorities. The devil cannot endure the exaltation of Jesus Christ. So he stirred up the Sanhedrin to persecute the apostles.

3. The council brings the apostles to trial (4:1–22)

The priests and the captain of the temple guard and the Sadducees came up to Peter and John while they were speaking to the people. [2]They were greatly disturbed because the apostles were teaching the people and proclaiming in Jesus the resurrection of the dead. [3]They seized Peter and John, and because it was evening, they put them in jail until the next day. [4]But many who heard the message believed, and the number of men grew to about five thousand.

Luke makes it plain that both waves of persecution were initiated by the Sadducees (4:1 and 5:17). They were the ruling class of wealthy aristocrats. Politically, they ingratiated themselves with the Romans, and followed a policy of collaboration, so that they feared the subversive implications of the apostles' teaching. Theologically, they believed that the Messianic age had begun in the Maccabean period; so they were not looking for a Messiah. They also denied the doctrine of *the resurrection of the dead*, which the apostles proclaimed *in Jesus* (2b). They thus saw the apostles as both agitators and heretics, both disturbers of the peace and enemies of the truth. In consequence, they were *greatly disturbed*, 'annoyed' (RSV), even 'exasperated' (NEB), by what the apostles were teaching the people (2a), for this was 'unauthorized preaching by unprofessional preachers'.[22]

Led by *the captain of the temple guard* (1), that is, the chief of the temple police, who was responsible for the maintenance of law and order, and who held a priestly rank second only to the high priest, *they seized Peter and John* and, *because it was evening* and too late to convene the council, *they put them in jail* overnight (3). Luke assures his readers immediately that the opposition of men did not hinder the Word of God. The Sadducees could arrest the apostles, but not the gospel. On the contrary, *many who heard the message believed, and the number of men grew to about five thousand* (4) – not counting the women and children, he seems to mean.

The next day the rulers (that is, the Sanhedrin, which consisted of seventy-one members, presided over by the high priest), including both the *elders* (probably clan leaders) and the *teachers of the law* (the scribes who copied, conserved and interpreted it), *met in Jerusalem* (5). *Annas . . . was there*, Luke tells us. He also calls him *the high priest* because, although the Romans had deposed him in AD 15, he retained among the Jews his prestige, influence and title.[23] *Caiaphas* was there too, Annas' son-in-law. Both men had figured prominently in the trial and condemnation of Jesus.[24] Luke also mentions *John* and *Alexander* (of whom nothing is known for certain) and *the other men of the high priest's family* (6). As they sat in their customary semi-circle, and *Peter and John* were *brought before them* (7a), memories of the trial of Jesus must have flooded the apostles' minds. Was history to repeat itself? They could hardly expect justice from *that* court, which had listened to false witnesses and unjustly condemned their Lord. Were they to suffer the same fate? Would they too be handed over to the Romans and crucified? They must have asked themselves such questions.

a. Peter's defence (4:8–12)

The court began their interrogation with a straight question to Peter and John: '*By what power or what name did you do this* [*i.e.* heal the cripple]*?*' One is reminded of the Jewish leaders, who had asked Jesus by what authority he had cleansed the temple.[25] In reply, the apostles bore witness to Jesus Christ. Whether they were preaching to the crowd in the temple or answering accusations in court, their preoccupation was not their own defence but the honour and glory of their Lord. In that moment of need, and in fulfilment of Jesus' promise that 'words and wisdom' would be given them whenever they were brought to trial,[26] Peter was freshly

[22] Neil, p. 88. [23] *Cf.* Lk. 3:2. [24] *Cf.* Jn. 18:12ff.
[25] Lk. 20:1–2. [26] Lk. 21:12ff.

filled with the Holy Spirit and *said: 'Rulers and elders of the people!* (8) *If we are being called to account today for an act of kindness shown to a cripple* (for what could be objectionable about that?) *and are asked how he was healed* (9), *then know this, you and all the people of Israel: It is by the name of Jesus Christ of Nazareth, whom you crucified but whom God raised from the dead, that this man stands before you healed* (10). *He is "the stone you builders rejected, which has become the capstone" '* (11). This is the third time that Peter has used the graphic formula 'you killed him, but God raised him' (2:23–24; 3:15), for Jesus is the stone of Psalm 118 which the builders rejected but God has promoted to be the capstone (11), a text which Jesus himself had quoted.[27] Moreover, '*salvation is found in no-one else, for there is no other name under heaven given to men by which we must be saved*' (12). We notice the ease with which Peter moves from healing to salvation, and from the particular to the general. He sees one man's physical cure as a picture of the salvation which is offered to all in Christ. His two negatives (*no-one else* and *no other name*) proclaim the positive uniqueness of the name of Jesus. His death and resurrection, his exaltation and authority constitute him the one and only Saviour, since nobody else possesses his qualifications.

b. The court's decision (4:13–22)

When they saw the courage of Peter and John and realised that they were unschooled, ordinary men, they were astonished and they took note that these men had been with Jesus. [14]But since they could see the man who had been healed standing there with them, there was nothing they could say. [15]So they ordered them to withdraw from the Sanhedrin and then conferred together. [16]'What are we going to do with these men?' they asked. 'Everybody living in Jerusalem knows they have done an outstanding miracle, and we cannot deny it. [17]But to stop this thing from spreading any further among the people, we must warn these men to speak no longer to anyone in this name.'

[18]Then they called them in again and commanded them not to speak or teach at all in the name of Jesus. [19]But Peter and John replied, 'Judge for yourselves whether it is right in God's sight to obey you rather than God. [20]For we cannot help speaking about what we have seen and heard.'

[21]After further threats they let them go. They could not decide how to punish them, because all the people were praising God for what had happened. [22]For the man who was miraculously healed was over forty years old.

[27] Lk. 20:17.

The court was *astonished* by *the courage of Peter and John*, particularly because they were *unschooled* (*agrammatoi*, meaning not that they were illiterate, but that they had received no proper training in Rabbinic theology) and *ordinary men* (*idiōtai*, meaning 'laymen' or 'non-professionals'). But then *they took note that these men had been with Jesus*, who also lacked both a formal theological education[28] and professional status as a Rabbi (13). Nevertheless, they could also see before their eyes the incontrovertible evidence of the healed cripple. Although it was well known in the city that he had never walked in his life, there he was *standing* with the apostles. So *there was nothing they could say* (14). They could not deny it and they would not acknowledge it. Embarrassed, they ordered them out of court, so that they could confer in private (15).

Liberal critics have enjoyed themselves in asking how Luke could have known what went on in the Sanhedrin's confidential discussion. 'The author reports the closed deliberations', comments Haenchen sarcastically, 'as if he had been present'.[29] But Paul may have been there. More likely, Gamaliel was, and he could have told Paul later what happened. At all events, the Council was in a real quandary. On the one hand, *an outstanding miracle* had been performed, as *everybody living in Jerusalem* knew well; so they could *not deny it* (16). On the other hand, they must *stop this thing from spreading any further among the people* (17a). (We note in passing that they made no attempt to discredit the apostles' witness to the resurrection, although they knew that it was the centre of their message, verse 2.) So what could they do? All they could think of was to warn them, as a legal admonition before witnesses, *to speak no longer to anyone in this name* (17b) – the powerful name by which the cripple had been healed, which Peter had preached, and which they were reluctant even to pronounce.

So *they called* the apostles *in again* and solemnly forbade them *to speak or teach at all in the name of Jesus* (18). To this prohibition Peter and John made the spirited reply that the court must judge whether the accused would be right in God's sight to obey them or God (19), for, they added: '*we cannot help speaking about what we have seen and heard*' (20). The court threatened them further, and then *let them go*. It did not seem possible *to punish them, because all the people were praising God for what had happened* (21), especially because the cripple who had been miraculously cured *was over forty years old* (22).

[28] Jn. 7:15. [29] Haenchen, p. 218.

4. The church prays (4:23–31)

On their release, Peter and John went back to their own people and reported all that the chief priests and elders had said to them. [24]*When they heard this, they raised their voices together in prayer to God. 'Sovereign Lord,' they said, 'you made the heaven and the earth and the sea, and everything in them.* [25]*You spoke by the Holy Spirit through the mouth of your servant, our father David:*

' "Why do the nations rage
and the peoples plot in vain?
[26]*The kings of the earth take their stand*
and the rulers gather together
against the Lord
and against his Anointed One."

[27]*Indeed Herod and Pontius Pilate met together with the Gentiles and the people of Israel in this city to conspire against your holy servant Jesus, whom you anointed.* [28]*They did what your power and will had decided beforehand should happen.* [29]*Now, Lord, consider their threats and enable your servants to speak your word with great boldness.* [30]*Stretch out your hand to heal and perform miraculous signs and wonders through the name of your holy servant Jesus.'*

[31]*After they prayed, the place where they were meeting was shaken. And they were all filled with the Holy Spirit and spoke the word of God boldly.*

What was the apostles' reaction to the Council's ban and threats? *On their release*, Luke tells us, they went straight *to their own people*, their relatives and friends in Christ, *reported* everything the Council had said to them (23), and then immediately turned together *in prayer to God* (24a). Here is the Christian *koinōnia* in action. We have seen the apostles in the Council; now we see them in the church. Having been bold in witness, they were equally bold in prayer. Their first word was *Despotēs, Sovereign Lord*, a term used of a slave owner and of a ruler of unchallengeable power. The Sanhedrin might utter warnings, threats and prohibitions, and try to silence the church, but their authority was subject to a higher authority still, and the edicts of men cannot overturn the decrees of God.

Next we observe that, before the people came to any petition, they filled their minds with thoughts of the divine sovereignty. First, he is the God of creation, who *made the heaven and the earth and the sea, and everything in them* (24). Secondly, he is the God of revelation, who *spoke by the Holy Spirit through the mouth of . . . David*, and in Psalm 2 (already in the first century BC recognized as Messianic) had foretold the world's opposition to his Christ, with nations raging, peoples plotting, kings standing and rulers assembling against the Lord's Anointed (25–26). Thirdly, he is the God of history, who had caused even his enemies (Herod and Pilate, Gentiles and Jews, united in a conspiracy against Jesus, verse 27) to do what his *power and will had decided beforehand should happen* (28). This, then, was the early church's understanding of God, the God of creation, revelation and history, whose characteristic actions are summarized by the three verbs 'you made' (24), 'you spoke' (25) and 'you decided' (28).

Only now, with their vision of God clarified, and themselves humbled before him, were they ready at last to pray. Luke tells us their three main requests. The first was that God would *consider their threats* (29a). It was not a prayer that their threats would fall under divine judgment, nor even that they would remain unfulfilled, so that the church would be preserved in peace and safety, but only that God would *consider* them, would bear them in his mind. The second petition was that God would enable them his *servants* (literally, 'slaves') to speak his Word *with great boldness* (29b), undeterred by the Council's prohibition and unafraid of their threats. The third prayer was that God would *stretch out* his *hand to heal*, and to *perform miraculous signs and wonders* in and *through the name of . . . Jesus* (30). As Alexander pointed out, 'their demand is not now for miracles of vengeance or destruction, such as fire from heaven,[30] but for miracles of mercy'.[31] Moreover, the word and the signs would go together, the signs and wonders confirming the word proclaimed with boldness.

In answer to their united and earnest prayers, (i) *the place . . . was shaken*, and as Chrysostom commented, 'that made them the more unshaken';[32] (ii) *they were all* again *filled with the Holy Spirit*; and (iii), in response to their specific request (29), they *spoke the word of God boldly* (31). Nothing is said in this context of an answer to their other specific prayer, namely for miracles of healing (30), but it would probably be legitimate to see 5:12 as the answer: 'The apostles performed many miraculous signs and wonders among the people.'

Conclusion: signs and wonders

Perhaps the three most notable features of Luke's narrative in Acts 3 and 4 are (i) the spectacular healing miracle and the prayer for more, (ii) the Christ-centred preaching of Peter, and (iii) the out-

[30] Lk. 9:54. [31] Alexander, I, p. 172. [32] Chrysostom, Homily XI, p. 73.

break of persecution. Because Peter's testimony to Christ has already been considered in some detail during the exposition, and because we will revert in the next chapter to the subject of persecution, we will concentrate now on the other topic of miracles.

The current controversy over signs and wonders should not lead us into a naïve polarization between those who are for them and those who are against. Instead, the place to begin is the wide area of agreement which exists among us. All biblical Christians believe that, although the Creator's faithfulness is revealed in the uniformity and regularities of his universe, which are the indispensable bases of the scientific enterprise, he has also sometimes deviated from the norms of nature into abnormal phenomena we call 'miracles'. But to think of them as 'deviations from nature' is not to dismiss them (as did the eighteenth-century deists), as 'violations of nature' which cannot happen, and therefore did not and do not happen. No, our biblical doctrine of the creation, that God has made everything out of an original nothing, precludes this kind of scepticism. As Campbell Morgan put it, 'granted the truth of the first verse in the Bible, and there is no difficulty with the miracles'.[33] Moreover, since we believe that the miracles recorded in the Bible, and not least in the Acts, did happen, there is no *a priori* ground for asserting that they cannot recur today. We have no liberty to dictate to God what he is permitted to do and not to do. And if we have hesitations about some claims to 'signs and wonders' today, we must make sure that we have not confined both God and ourselves in the prison of Western, rationalistic unbelief.[34]

The popular exponent of 'signs and wonders' teaching today is John Wimber of the Vineyard Fellowship in California. He and Kevin Springer have summarized his position in *Power Evangelism* (1985) and *Power Healing* (1986). Although it is impossible to do justice to it in a few sentences, its leading ideas are (i) that Jesus inaugurated the kingdom of God, demonstrated its arrival by signs and wonders, and means us similarly both to proclaim and to dramatize its advance; (ii) that signs and wonders were 'everyday occurrences in New Testament times' and 'a part of daily life',[35] so that they should characterize 'the normal Christian life' for us too; and (iii) that church growth in the Acts was largely due to the prevalence of miracles. 'Signs and wonders occurred fourteen times

[33] Morgan, p. 91.

[34] John Wimber, to whom reference is made in the rest of this chapter, is right to warn us in both *Power Evangelism* (Hodder and Stoughton, 1985; chapter 5, 'Signs and Wonders and Worldviews') and *Power Healing* (Hodder and Stoughton, 1986; pp. 28 and 30) against 'the pervasive influence of a secularized western worldview', lest we become 'caught in the web of western secularism'.

[35] *Power Evangelism*, p. 117.

in the book of Acts in conjunction with preaching, resulting in church growth. Further, on twenty occasions church growth was a direct result of signs and wonders performed by the disciples.'[36]

John Wimber argues his case with sincerity and force. But some unanswered questions remain. Let me ask three, especially in relation to our study of the Acts. First, is it certain that signs and wonders are the main secret of church growth? John Wimber supplies a table of fourteen instances in the Acts in which, he claims, signs and wonders accompanied the preaching and 'produced evangelistic growth in the church'. One or two cases are indisputable, as when the Samaritan crowds 'heard Philip and saw the miraculous signs he did' and so 'paid close attention to what he said' (8:6, 12). In a number of other cases, however, the connection between miracles and church growth is made by John Wimber not by Luke. For example, to take the only two cases he gives from the chapters we have so far considered, there is no evidence in the text that the Pentecostal phenomena of wind, fire and languages (2:1–4) were the direct cause of the three thousand converts of verse 41, nor that the healing of the congenital cripple (3:1ff.) was the direct cause of the increase to five thousand (4:4), as John Wimber's Table claims. Luke seems rather to attribute the growth to the power of Peter's preaching. In this sense all true evangelism is 'power evangelism', for conversion and new birth, and so church growth, can take place only by the power of God through his Word and Spirit.[37]

Secondly, is it certain that signs and wonders are meant by God to be 'everyday occurrences' and 'the normal Christian life'? I think not. Not only are miracles by definition 'abnorms' rather than norms, but the Acts does not provide evidence that they were widespread. Luke's emphasis is that they were performed mostly by the apostles (2:43; 5:12), and especially by the apostles Peter and Paul on whom he focuses our attention. True, Stephen and Philip also did signs and wonders, and perhaps others did. But it can be argued that Stephen and Philip were special people, not so much because the apostles had laid hands on them (6:5–6) as because each was given a unique role in laying the foundations of the church's world-wide mission (see 7:1ff. and 8:5ff.). Certainly the thrust of the Bible is that miracles clustered round the principal organs of revelation at fresh epochs of revelation, particularly Moses the lawgiver, the new prophetic witness spearheaded by Elijah and Elisha, the Messianic ministry of Jesus, and the apostles, so that Paul referred to his miracles as 'the things that mark an apostle'.[38] There may well be situations in which miracles are appro-

[36] *Ibid.*, p. 117. [37] *E.g.* 1 Cor. 2:1–5; 1 Thes. 1:5. [38] 2 Cor. 12:12.

priate today, for example, on the frontiers of mission and in an atmosphere of pervasive unbelief which calls for a power encounter between Christ and Antichrist. But Scripture itself suggests that these will be special cases, rather than 'a part of daily life'.

Thirdly, is it certain that today's claimed signs and wonders are parallel to those recorded in the New Testament? Some are, or seem to be. But in his public ministry by turning water into wine, stilling a storm, multiplying loaves and fishes, and walking on water, Jesus gave a preview of nature's final, total subservience to him – a subservience which belongs not to the 'already' but to the 'not yet' of the kingdom. We should not, therefore, expect to do these things ourselves today. Nor should we expect to be miraculously rescued from prison by the angel of the Lord or to see church members struck dead like Ananias and Sapphira. Even the healing miracles of the Gospels and the Acts had features which are seldom manifested even in the signs and wonders movement today.

Let me come back to the Acts to illustrate this, and take the healing of the cripple as my example. It is the first and longest miraculous cure described in the book. It had five noteworthy characteristics, which together indicate what the New Testament means by a miracle of healing. (i) The healing was of a grave, organic condition, and could not be regarded as a psychosomatic cure. Luke is at pains to tell us that the man had been a cripple from birth (3:2), was now more than forty years old (4:22), and was so handicapped that he had to be carried everywhere (3:2). Humanly speaking, his case was hopeless. Doctors could do nothing for him. (ii) The healing took place by a direct word of command in the name of Christ, without the use of any medical means. Not even prayer, the laying on of hands or anointing with oil were used. True, Peter gave the man a helping hand (3:7), but this was not part of the cure. (iii) The healing was instantaneous, not gradual, for 'instantly the man's feet and ankles became strong', so that he jumped up and began to walk (3:7–8). (iv) The healing was complete and permanent, not partial or temporary. This is stated twice. The man had been given 'this complete healing', Peter said to the crowds (3:16), and later stood before the Council 'completely healed' (4:10, 1978 edition of NIV). (v) The healing was publicly acknowledged to be indisputable. There was no doubt or question about it. The crippled beggar was well known in the city (3:10, 16). Now he was healed. It was not only the disciples of Jesus who were convinced, but also the enemies of the gospel. The as-yet-unbelieving crowd were 'filled with wonder and amazement' (3:10), while the Council called it 'an outstanding miracle' which they could not deny (4:14, 16).

If, then, we take Scripture as our guide, we will avoid opposite extremes. We will neither describe miracles as 'never happening', nor as 'everyday occurrences', neither as 'impossible' nor as 'normal'. Instead, we will be entirely open to the God who works both through nature and through miracle. And when a healing miracle is claimed, we will expect it to resemble those in the Gospels and the Acts and so to be the instantaneous and complete cure of an organic condition, without the use of medical or surgical means, inviting investigation and persuading even unbelievers. For so it was with the congenital cripple. Peter took his miraculous healing as the text of both his sermon to the crowd and his speech to the Council. Word and sign together bore testimony to the uniquely powerful name of Jesus. The healing of the cripple's body was a vivid dramatization of the apostolic message of salvation.

4. Satanic counter-attack 4:32–6:7

We noted at the beginning of chapter 3 that, as soon as the Spirit came upon the church, Satan launched a ferocious counter-attack. Pentecost was followed by persecution. An alternative title for this chapter might be 'The strategy of Satan'. His strategy was carefully developed. He attacked on three fronts. His first and crudest tactic was physical violence; he tried to crush the church by persecution. His second and more cunning assault was moral corruption or compromise. Having failed to destroy the church from outside, he attempted through Ananias and Sapphira to insinuate evil into its interior life, and so ruin the Christian fellowship. His third and subtlest ploy was distraction. He sought to deflect the apostles from their priority responsibilities of prayer and preaching by preoccupying them with social administration, which was not their calling. If he had been successful in this, an untaught church would have been exposed to every wind of false doctrine. These then were his weapons – physical (persecution), moral (subversion) and professional (distraction).

Now I claim no very close or intimate familiarity with the devil. But I am persuaded that he exists, and that he is utterly unscrupulous. Something else I have learned about him is that he is peculiarly lacking in imagination. Over the years he has changed neither his strategy, nor his tactics, nor his weapons; he is still in the same old rut. So a study of his campaign against the early church should alert us to his probable strategy today. If we are taken by surprise, we shall have no excuse.

Luke is concerned, however, not only to expose the devil's malice, but also to show how he was overcome. First, the hypocrisy of Ananias and Sapphira was not allowed to spread, for God's judgment fell on them, and the church grew by leaps and bounds (5:12–16). Secondly, when the Sanhedrin again resorted to violence, they were restrained from killing the apostles by the cautious counsel of Gamaliel (5:17–42). Thirdly, when the widows' dispute threatened to occupy all the time and energies of the apostles, the social work was delegated to others, the apostles resumed their priority tasks, and the church again began to multiply (6:1–7).

1. The believers enjoy a common life (4:32–37)

All the believers were one in heart and mind. No-one claimed that any of his possessions was his own, but they shared everything they had. [33]*With great power the apostles continued to testify to the resurrection of the Lord Jesus, and much grace was upon them all.* [34]*There were no needy persons among them. For from time to time those who owned lands or houses sold them, brought the money from the sales* [35]*and put it at the apostles' feet, and it was distributed to anyone as he had need.*

[36]*Joseph, a Levite from Cyprus, whom the apostles called Barnabas (which means Son of Encouragement),* [37]*sold a field he owned and brought the money and put it at the apostles' feet.*

Luke has just recorded that, in answer to their prayers, the believers were freshly 'filled with the Holy Spirit' (31). The immediate result was that they 'spoke the word of God boldly'. With this we should perhaps link verse 33: *with great power the apostles continued to testify to the resurrection of the Lord Jesus*, which was one of their primary apostolic responsibilities (*cf.* 1:22). Thus they ignored the Sanhedrin's ban, and their witness was characterized by both boldness and power. Indeed, *much grace was with them all*, an expression which may describe their 'wonderful spirit of generosity' (JBP), or refer to the fact that they were 'held in high esteem' (NEB), or be a more general statement that God's grace was sustaining them.

Luke does not leave it there, however. He is concerned to show that the fullness of the Spirit is manifest in deed as well as word, service as well as witness, love for the family as well as testimony to the world. So, just as after the first coming of the Spirit he describes the characteristics of the Spirit-filled community (2:42–47), so after they are again filled with the Spirit he provides a second description (4:32–37). Moreover in both cases his emphasis is the same. *All the believers*, he begins, in 4:32 as in 2:44, formed a closely knit group. They 'were together' (2:44), as they devoted themselves to 'the fellowship' (2:42), and they *were one in heart and mind* (4:32). This was the fundamental solidarity of love which the believers enjoyed, and their economic sharing was but one expression of the union of their hearts and minds.

It is instructive to compare Luke's two pictures of the same united, Spirit-filled church in Jerusalem. Although the accounts are verbally independent of one another, he mentions in each the same three consequences of their mutual commitment. The first I will call their radical attitude, in particular to their possessions. They 'had everything in common' (2:44); *no-one claimed that any of his possessions was his own, but they shared everything they had* (4:32b). Both verses contain the two key words *hapanta koina*, 'all things in common'. In the light of Peter's later statement to Ananias that his property was his own (5:4), we cannot press these words into meaning that the believers had literally renounced private, in favour of common, ownership. Perhaps the important phrase is that *no-one claimed* his possessions as his own. Although in fact and in law they continued to own their goods, yet in heart and mind they cultivated an attitude so radical that they thought of their possessions as being available to help their needy sisters and brothers.

Secondly, their radical attitude led to sacrificial action, namely that *from time to time those who owned lands or houses sold them*, and then put the sale money *at the apostles' feet*, so that they might distribute it (34b–35). The same actions of selling and distributing are referred to in 2:45. In both cases the selling was voluntary and sporadic (*from time to time*), as the need for ready cash arose.

Thirdly, both the radical attitude and the practical action were based on the equitable principle that distribution was proportionate to genuine need. The two accounts use the identical words *kathoti an tis chreian eixen*, meaning 'according as anyone had need' (35b, *cf.* 2:45). Only in the second description, however, does Luke state the consequence of the principled distribution of relief, namely *there were no needy persons among them* (34a).

Calvin wrote in his commentary:

> We must have hearts that are harder than iron if we are not moved by the reading of this narrative. In those days the believers gave abundantly of what was their own; we in our day are content not just jealously to retain what we possess, but callously to rob others. . . . They sold their own possessions in those days; in our day it is the lust to purchase that reigns supreme. At that time love made each man's own possessions common property for those in need; in our day such is the inhumanity of many, that they begrudge to the poor a common dwelling upon earth, the common use of water, air and sky.[1]

In seeking to evaluate the so-called 'Jerusalem experiment', we shall be wise to avoid extreme positions. We have no liberty to dismiss it as a rash and foolish mistake, motivated by the false

[1] Calvin, I, p. 130.

expectation of an imminent Parousia and causing the poverty which Paul had later to remedy by his collection from the Greek churches. Luke gives no hint of these things. Nor can we say, however, that the Jerusalem church, being filled with the Spirit, laid down an obligatory model – a kind of primitive Christian 'communism' – which God wants all Spirit-filled communities to copy. The fact that the selling and giving were voluntary is enough to dispose of this. What we should surely do, instead, is to note and seek to imitate the care of the needy and the sacrificial generosity which the Holy Spirit created. Of course many societies have dreamed of the ending of poverty. The Greeks, for example, looked back to a golden age in which all property was public, and Pythagoras is said to have practised it with his disciples, and to have coined the epigram 'among friends everything is common' (*koina*). Plato later incorporated this ideal in his vision of a utopian republic. Then Josephus wrote that the Essenes, whom we know as the Qumran community, 'live the same kind of life as do those whom the Greeks call Pythagoreans'.[2] Yet the inspiration for the common life and love of the Jerusalem church will have come neither from Pythagoras, nor from Plato, nor from the Essenes, but from the Old Testament, as illumined by Jesus. For the law was quite clear on the matter: 'there should be no poor among you' (Dt. 15:4). In addition, Luke stressed Jesus' teaching that the gospel of the kingdom was good news for the poor.[3] But how could it be so unless it offered them justice as well as salvation, the abolition of their poverty as well as the remission of their sins?

Having portrayed the solidarity of love enjoyed by the Jerusalem church, Luke supplies his readers with two contrasting examples: Barnabas whose generosity and openness fulfilled the ideal (4:36–37) and Ananias and Sapphira whose greed and hypocrisy contradicted it (5:1ff.). 'Barnabas' (*Son of Encouragement*) was actually the nickname which the apostles gave, on account of his helpfulness, to *Joseph, a Levite from Cyprus* (36). He *sold a field he owned*, presumably in Cyprus, and laid the money *at the apostles' feet* (37). It was an act of liberality fully in keeping with his character as it later emerges in the Acts narrative. Luke deliberately introduces him here.

2. Ananias and Sapphira are punished for their hypocrisy (5:1–11)

The story of the deceit and death of this married couple is important for several reasons. It illustrates the honesty of Luke as a historian;

[2] Josephus, *Antiquities*, XV.10.4. [3] *E.g.* Lk. 4:18; 6:20; 7:22

he did not suppress this sordid episode. It throws light on the interior life of the first Spirit-filled community; it was not all romance and righteousness. It is also a further example of the strategy of Satan. Several commentators have suggested a parallel between Ananias and Achan – the Achan who stole money and clothing after the destruction of Jericho. Thus Bengel wrote: 'the sin of Achan and that of Ananias were in many respects similar, at the beginning of the churches of the Old and New Testament respectively'.[4] F. F. Bruce sees a further analogy: 'The story of Ananias is to the book of Acts what the story of Achan is to the book of Joshua. In both narratives an act of deceit interrupts the victorious progress of the people of God.'[5]

What we are told is that *a man named Ananias, together with his wife Sapphira*, first *sold a piece of property* (1) and then, *with his wife's full knowledge* (or 'connivance', JB), *he kept back part of the money for himself, but brought the rest and put it at the apostles' feet* (2). To all appearances, Barnabas and Ananias did the same thing. Both sold a property. Both brought the proceeds of the sale to the apostles, and both committed it to their disposal. The difference was that Barnabas brought all the sale money, while Ananias brought only a proportion. Thus Ananias and Sapphira perpetuated a double sin, a combination of dishonesty and deceit. At first sight, there was nothing wrong in their withholding part of the sale money. As Peter plainly said later, their property was their own both before and after the sale (see verse 4 below). So they were under no obligation to sell their piece of land or, having sold it, to give away any – let alone all – of the proceeds. That is not the whole story, however. There is something else, something half-hidden. For Luke, in declaring that Ananias *kept back* part of the money for himself, chooses the verb *nosphizomai*, which means to 'misappropriate' (BAGD). The same word was used in LXX of Achan's theft,[6] and in its only other New Testament occurrence it means to steal.[7] We have to assume, therefore, that before the sale Ananias and Sapphira had entered into some kind of contract to give the church the total amount raised. Because of this, when they brought only some instead of all, they were guilty of embezzlement.

It was not on this sin that Peter concentrated, however, but on the other, hypocrisy. The apostle's complaint was not that they lacked honesty (bringing only a part of the sale price) but that they lacked integrity (bringing only a part, while pretending to bring the whole). They were not so much misers as thieves and – above all – liars. They wanted the credit and the prestige for sacrificial

[4] Bengel, p. 556. [5] Bruce, *English*, p. 110. [6] Jos. 7:1. [7] Tit. 2:10.

generosity, without the inconvenience of it. So, in order to gain a reputation to which they had no right, they told a brazen lie. Their motive in giving was not to relieve the poor, but to fatten their own ego.

Peter saw behind Ananias' hypocrisy the subtle activity of Satan. He confronted Ananias: '*Ananias, how is it that Satan has so filled your heart that you have lied to the Holy Spirit and have kept for yourself* [*nosphizomai*, again] *some of the money you received for the land?*' (3). Peter accused him both of misappropriation and of falsehood, both of stealing and then of lying about it. But there was no need for either sin. '*Didn't it belong to you before it was sold? And after it was sold, wasn't the money at your disposal? What made you think of doing such a thing? You have not lied to men but to God*' (4). We note in passing that Peter assumes the deity of the Holy Spirit, since to lie to him (3) was to lie to God (4).

5When Ananias heard this, he fell down and died. And great fear seized all who heard what had happened. 6Then the young men came forward, wrapped up his body, and carried him out and buried him.

7About three hours later his wife came in, not knowing what had happened. 8Peter asked her, 'Tell me, is this the price you and Ananias got for the land?'

'Yes,' she said, 'that is the price.'

9Peter said to her, 'How could you agree to test the Spirit of the Lord? Look! The feet of the men who buried your husband are at the door, and they will carry you out also.'

10At that moment she fell down at his feet and died. Then the young men came in and, finding her dead, carried her out and buried her beside her husband. 11Great fear seized the whole church and all who heard about these events.

No reply from Ananias to Peter's indictment and questions is recorded. Luke tells us only that God's judgment fell upon him: 'he dropped dead' (5a, NEB). Understandably *great fear*, the solemnity which is experienced in the presence of the holy God, *seized all who heard what had happened* (5b), even while certain *young men* attended to the burial (6). *About three hours later* the incident repeated itself. Ignorant of her husband's death, Sapphira *came in*. Peter gave her the chance to repent by asking her to state the price they had received for the land, but she merely identified herself with his duplicity (7–8). Peter protested that they had conspired *to test the Spirit of the Lord*, presuming to see whether they could get away with their deception, and warned her that those who had buried her husband would bury her too (9), whereupon *she fell down at his feet and died*, and the young men buried her *beside her husband* (10). For the second time Luke refers to the *great fear* which *seized the whole church*, and indeed *all who heard about these events* (11).

Many readers of this story are offended by what they regard as the severity of God's judgment. Some even say they 'hope that Ananias and Sapphira are legendary'.[8] Or they try to exonerate God by attributing the death of Ananias and Sapphira instead to Peter who, they say, either laid a curse on them or put them under undue psychological pressure, thus anticipating the use of a modern lie detector. But, even if the anguish of a violated conscience contributed to their death on the human level, Luke clearly intends us to understand that it was a work of divine judgment. Once this has been accepted, there are at least three valuable lessons for us to learn.

First, the gravity of their sin. Peter stressed this by repeating that their lie was not directed primarily against him, but against the Holy Spirit, that is, against God. And God hates hypocrisy. Luke has recorded Jesus' denunciation of it,[9] together with his warning that those who blaspheme against the Holy Spirit (in deliberate defiance of known truth) will not be forgiven (Lk. 12:10). Yet the sin of Ananias and Sapphira was also against the church. Is it intentional that Luke here uses for the first time the word *ekklēsia* (11)? He thus affirms the continuity of the Christian community with God's redeemed and gathered people in the Old Testament.[10] Luke seems to be underlining the great evil of sinning against God's people. Falsehood ruins fellowship. If the hypocrisy of Ananias and Sapphira had not been publicly exposed and punished, the Christian ideal of an open fellowship would not have been preserved, and the modern cry 'there are so many hypocrites in the church' would have been heard from the beginning.

The second lesson to be learned concerns the importance, even the sacredness, of the human conscience. Luke will later record Paul's claim before Felix that he always strove to keep his 'conscience clear before God and man' (Acts 24:16). This seems to be what John meant by 'walking in the light'. It is to live a transparent life before God, without guile or subterfuge, whose consequence is that 'we have fellowship with one another'.[11] The 'brethren' of the East African revival, who lay great stress on this teaching, amusingly illustrate it by expressing their desire to 'live in a house without ceiling or walls', that is, to permit nothing to come between

[8] W. L. Knox, quoted by Haenchen, p. 237.
[9] *E.g.* Lk. 6:42; 12:1, 56; 13:15.
[10] *Cf. ekklēsia* in 7:38 and in LXX of, *e.g.*, Jos. 8:35. [11] 1 Jn. 1:7.

them and either God or other people. It was this openness which Ananias and Sapphira failed to maintain.

Thirdly, the incident teaches the necessity of church discipline. Although physical death may have continued in some situations as a penalty for those sins which 'despise the church of God',[12] it came to be associated with excommunication.[13] The church has tended to oscillate in this area between extreme severity (disciplining members for the most trivial offences) and extreme laxity (exercising no discipline at all, even for serious offences). It is a good general rule that secret sins should be dealt with secretly, private sins privately, and only public sins publicly. Churches are also wise if they follow the successive stages taught by Jesus.[14] Usually the offender will be brought to repentance before the final stage of excommunication is reached. But offences which are serious in themselves, have become a public scandal, and have not been repented of, should be judged. Presbyterians are right to 'fence the table', that is, to make access to the Lord's Supper conditional. For, although the Lord's table is open to sinners (who else either needs or wishes to come to it?), it is open only to penitent sinners.

We have now seen that, if the devil's first tactic was to destroy the church by force from without, his second was to destroy it by falsehood from within. He has not given up the attempt, whether by the hypocrisy of those who profess but do not practise, or by the stubbornness of those who sin but do not repent. The church must preserve its vigilance.

3. The apostles heal many people (5:12–16)

Luke is about to record the second wave of persecution by which the devil attempted to annihilate the church. As he does so, he will highlight various developing attitudes, especially 'the deepening jealousy and antagonism of the Sadducees, the moderation of the Pharisees, and the increasing joy and confidence of the Christians'.[15] But before this he refers to the fact that *the apostles performed many miraculous signs and wonders among the people*, especially Peter (12a). Having given an account of their message, he now describes the extraordinary signs which authenticated it. They seem to have taken place in *Solomon's Colonnade*, the eastern cloister in which Peter had preached his second sermon (3:11) and in which now *all the believers used to meet together* (12b). The miracles had two interesting and opposite results. On the one hand, *no-one else dared join them, even though they were highly regarded by the*

[12] *E.g.* 1 Cor. 11:22, 30. [13] *E.g.* 1 Cor. 5:5; 1 Tim. 1:20.
[14] Mt. 18:15ff. [15] Longenecker, *Acts*, p. 316.

people (13). This might just mean that the opposition lacked the courage to 'join in disputation with them',[16] but the context suggests simply that they preferred to keep aloof rather than to associate with them. On the other hand, *more and more* people, both *men and women*, having no such fears, *believed in the Lord and were added to their number* (14). 'On the one hand an awestruck reserve', as Haenchen puts it, and 'on the other great missionary successes'.[17] This paradoxical situation has often recurred since then. The presence of the living God, whether manifest through preaching or miracles or both, is alarming to some and appealing to others. Some are frightened away, while others are drawn to faith.

As the movement grew, Luke continues, *people brought the sick into the streets*, presumably their sick relatives, friends and neighbours, *and laid them on beds and mats* in such a way *that at least Peter's shadow might fall on some of them as he passed by* (15). Their action may have been somewhat superstitious, but I see no reason to condemn it as tantamount to belief in magic, any more than was the woman's faith that a touch of the hem of Jesus' garment would be enough to heal her. No, the people had been deeply impressed by the words and works of Peter, had recognized him as a man of God and an apostle of Christ, and believed that through close proximity to him they could be healed. It may be significant that the verb *episkiazō*, which Luke chooses, meaning to 'overshadow', he has used twice in his Gospel of the overshadowing of God's presence.[18]

Now *crowds gathered also from the towns around Jerusalem, bringing* not only *their sick* people but also *those tormented by evil spirits* (Luke does not confuse the two conditions), and *all of them were healed* (16). It was a remarkable demonstration of the power of God to heal and free human beings, as the Ananias and Sapphira episode had been of his power to judge them.

4. The Sanhedrin intensifies its opposition (5:17–42)

The apostolic healing mission provoked the second attack by the authorities, much as the healing of the congenital cripple had provoked the first. Angered by the failure of their first assault on the apostles, dismayed to see that they had ignored the court's prohibition and threats, and *filled with jealousy* (17) of their power and popularity, *the high priest and all his associates, who were members of the party of the Sadducees*, resolved to take further action.

[16] Neil, p. 95. [17] Haenchen, p. 244. [18] Lk. 1:35; 9:34.

a. The imprisonment (5:18–25)

They arrested the apostles and put them in the public jail. [19]*But during the night an angel of the Lord opened the doors of the jail and brought them out.* [20]*'Go, stand in the temple courts,' he said, 'and tell the people the full message of this new life.'*

[21]*At daybreak they entered the temple courts, as they had been told, and began to teach the people.*

When the high priest and his associates arrived, they called together the Sanhedrin – the full assembly of the elders of Israel – and sent to the jail for the apostles. [22]*But on arriving at the jail, the officers did not find them there. So they went back and reported,* [23]*'We found the jail securely locked, with the guards standing at the doors; but when we opened them, we found no-one inside.'* [24]*On hearing this report, the captain of the temple guard and the chief priests were puzzled, wondering what would come of this.*

[25]*Then someone came and said, 'Look! The men you put in jail are standing in the temple courts teaching the people.'*

This time they arrested not only Peter and John but *the apostles*, most if not all of them (see 29), and *put them in the public jail* (18). But *during the night* they were rescued by *an angel of the Lord*. William Neil speculates that this was 'a sympathetic warder' or 'a secret sympathizer among the guardroom staff', who came later to be seen as 'an angel in disguise'.[19] But we have no liberty to demythologize what Luke evidently intends his readers to believe was a heavenly visitor, who not only *opened the doors of the jail* and brought the apostles out (19), but instructed them to *stand in the temple courts* and publicly proclaim *the full message of this new life* (20). *At daybreak* they entered the temple *as they had been told, and began to teach the people* (21a). We note that they disobeyed the Sanhedrin, who had told them not to speak in the name of Jesus (4:17), in order to obey the angel who told them to speak the words of life.

Meanwhile, the Sanhedrin, which Luke describes as *the full assembly of the elders* (or 'senate', JB) *of Israel*, was convened (21). And they were humiliated to discover, on sending for the apostles, that they were no longer in the prison where they had consigned them, although it was *securely locked, with the guards standing at the doors* (22–24). Instead, they were *in the temple courts teaching the people* (25), which they had been forbidden to do.

[19] Neil, pp. 96, 97.

b. The trial (5:26–39)

At that, the captain went with his officers and brought the apostles. They did not use force, because they feared that the people would stone them.

[27]*Having brought the apostles, they made them appear before the Sanhedrin to be questioned by the high priest.* [28]*'We gave you strict orders not to teach in this name,' he said. 'Yet you have filled Jerusalem with your teaching and are determined to make us guilty of this man's blood.'*

[29]*Peter and the other apostles replied: 'We must obey God rather than men!* [30]*The God of our fathers raised Jesus from the dead – whom you had killed by hanging him on a tree.* [31]*God exalted him to his own right hand as Prince and Saviour that he might give repentance and forgiveness of sins to Israel.* [32]*We are witnesses of these things, and so is the Holy Spirit, whom God has given to those who obey him.'*

[33]*When they heard this, they were furious and wanted to put them to death.* [34]*But a Pharisee named Gamaliel, a teacher of the law, who was honoured by all the people, stood up in the Sanhedrin and ordered that the men be put outside for a little while.* [35]*Then he addressed them: 'Men of Israel, consider carefully what you intend to do to these men.* [36]*Some time ago Theudas appeared, claiming to be somebody, and about four hundred men rallied to him. He was killed, all his followers were dispersed, and it all came to nothing.* [37]*After him, Judas the Galilean appeared in the days of the census and led a band of people in revolt. He too was killed, and all his followers were scattered.* [38]*Therefore, in the present case I advise you: Leave these men alone! Let them go! For if their purpose or activity is of human origin, it will fail.* [39]*But if it is from God, you will not be able to stop these men; you will only find yourselves fighting against God.'*

The captain of the temple guard and his officers re-arrested the apostles, although *they did not use force* because they were afraid *that the people would stone them* (26). They then *made them appear before the Sanhedrin* a second time for questioning (27). The way the high priest addressed them was in reality an admission of the court's powerlessness before the purpose of God. For the Sanhedrin had condemned and liquidated Jesus, given the apostles *strict orders not to teach in this name* (which they still preferred not to pronounce), and locked them up in prison. All the power and authority seemed clearly to be on their side. Yet, in contempt of court and in defiance of its authority, the apostles had successfully *filled Jerusalem* with their teaching, and (in the court's opinion) were determined to fasten on them the guilt of *this man's blood* (28), which at the time (they seem to have forgotten) they had urged the people to call down on themselves and their children.[20]

The apostles' response took the form of a mini-sermon, for their concern was still not to defend themselves but to uplift Christ. *We must obey God rather than men!* they said (29), and in so doing laid down the principle of civil and ecclesiastical disobedience. To be sure, Christians are called to be conscientious citizens and generally speaking, to submit to human authorities.[21] But if the authority concerned misuses its God-given power to command what he forbids or forbid what he commands, then the Christian's duty is to disobey the human authority in order to obey God's.

Having stated that their primary responsibility was to obey God, the apostles emphasized three truths about him. First, *God*, who is *the God of our fathers, raised Jesus from the dead*, whom the Jewish leaders *had killed by hanging him on a tree* (30). It is the familiar contrast: you killed him, but God raised him; you rejected him, but God vindicated him. Secondly, *God exalted him to his own right hand as Prince* (*archēgos* again, as in 3:15) *and Saviour*, so that from this supreme position of honour and power he is able to *give repentance and forgiveness of sins* (which are both gifts of God) *to Israel* (31). Moreover, of the death and resurrection of Jesus the apostles were *witnesses*, not just eye-witnesses but mouth-witnesses, for they were called to bear witness to what they had seen. Yet the chief witness to Jesus Christ is *the Holy Spirit,*[22] *whom God has given* (literally 'gave') *to those who obey him* (32). That is the apostles' third affirmation about God. He raised Jesus from the dead, exalted him as Saviour and gave the Holy Spirit to his obedient people. Thus the sermon began and ended with a reference to obeying God. God's people are under obligation to obey him, and if they do so, even though they may suffer when they have to disobey human authorities, they will be richly rewarded by the ministry of the Holy Spirit.

Hearing these words of defiance and triumph, the Council was *furious* ('touched . . . on the raw', NEB), and but for the diplomatic intervention of Gamaliel, they would probably have fulfilled their wish *to put them to death* (33). Gamaliel was a Pharisee, and as such exhibited a more tolerant spirit than the rival party of the Sadducees. Grandson and follower of the famous liberal Rabbi Hillel, he was given the honorific and affectionate title 'Rabban', 'our teacher', and Saul of Tarsus had been one of his pupils (22:3). He had a reputation for scholarship, wisdom and moderation, and *was honoured by all the people*. His behaviour on this occasion

[20] Mt. 27:25. [21] *E.g.* Rom. 13:1ff.; Tit. 3:1; 1 Pet. 2:13ff.
[22] *Cf.* Jn. 15:26.

was fully in keeping with his public image. He stood up and gave instructions for the apostles to be *put outside for a little while*, so that the Council might confer in private session (34). He then proceeded to restrain their anger and to counsel caution (35) on account of certain historical precedents. He gave two examples, namely men called Theudas and Judas the Galilean.

The account which Gamaliel is recorded as giving of their careers is brief. When Theudas arose, *claiming to be somebody, about four hundred men rallied* to his cause. But he himself *was killed, all his followers were dispersed*, and his movement *came to nothing* (36). Following him, *Judas the Galilean* arose *in the days of the census* (always an inflammatory event, a symbol of Roman rule by taxation), and 'induced some people to revolt under his leadership' (NEB). But he also perished, 'and his whole following melted away' (JBP, 37). Gamaliel thus sketched their histories in parallel. Both men *appeared*, advanced claims and won a following. But then each *was killed, all his followers* were scattered, and his movement faded away.

Commentators have understandably consulted Josephus for confirmation and/or amplification of these revolts, and have found references to two rebels with the same names. There was, he says, 'a certain magician' named Theudas, when Fadus was procurator of Judea, who persuaded many to 'follow him to the River Jordan, for he told them he was a prophet, and that he would by his own command divide the river'. But he was captured and beheaded.[23] Then Josephus also describes 'a certain Galilean' named Judas, who prevailed on his countrymen to revolt, because he told them they would be 'cowards if they would endure to pay a tax to the Romans' and thus 'submit to mortal men as their lords', when tribute should be paid to God alone.[24] He was the forerunner of the zealots.

So far, then, there are slight similarities between Gamaliel and Josephus. The problem arises when we look at the dates. The taxation census against which Judas revolted was introduced by Cyrenius (Quirinius) when he came from Rome to Judea in about AD 6. Josephus' Theudas, however, rebelled not *before* Judas (as Luke records Gamaliel as saying, verses 36–37) but during the procuratorship of Fadus (AD 44–46), which was about forty years *after* him, and indeed a decade or more after Gamaliel was speaking!

How we react to the discrepancy will depend on our basic presuppositions. Liberal commentators jump to the conclusion that Luke was guilty of an anachronism amounting to a major error,

[23] Josephus, *Antiquities*, XX.5.1.
[24] Josephus, *Wars*, II.8.1; *cf. Antiquities*, XVIII.1.1.

which must fatally undermine our confidence in him as a reliable historian. Conservatives, on the other hand, reach the opposite conclusion: 'we cannot suppose that St Luke could have made the gross blunder attributed to him in the face of his usual accuracy.'[25] If there is a mistake, it is more likely to have been made by Josephus (who was 'far from being an infallible historian'[26] than by Luke. A better alternative explanation is that Josephus and Luke were each referring to a different Theudas. The stories they tell are divergent (Josephus does not mention that his followers numbered four hundred, nor Luke that he led them to the River Jordan). The only similarities are that both men were named Theudas, and led a revolt which was crushed. But Josephus tells us that after the death of Herod the Great 'there were ten thousand other disorders in Judea, which were like tumults',[27] and Theudas was not an uncommon name. So perhaps neither Luke nor Josephus made a mistake, but Gamaliel was referring to a Theudas whom Josephus does not describe, who revolted about 4 BC, and who was indeed followed, among others, by Judas the Galilean in AD 6.

At all events, Gamaliel took the failure of both revolts as an object lesson which justified a policy of *laissez-faire*. His advice to the Council is given in verse 38: *Leave these men alone! Let them go! For if their purpose or activity is of human origin, it will fail. If*, on the other hand, *it is from God, you will not be able to stop these men; you will only find yourselves fighting against God* (39). We should not be too ready to credit Gamaliel with having uttered an invariable principle. To be sure, in the long run what is from God will triumph, and what is merely human (let alone diabolical) will not. Nevertheless, in the shorter run evil plans sometimes succeed, while good ones conceived in accordance with the will of God sometimes fail. So the Gamaliel principle is not a reliable index to what is from God and what is not.

c. The conclusion (5:40–42)

The Council accepted Gamaliel's reasoning, however. *His speech persuaded them*. Having *called the apostles in*, they first *had them flogged* (presumably administering the terrible 'forty lashes minus one'). *Then they ordered them* (for the second time) *not to speak in the name of Jesus, and let them go* (40).

The apostles' reaction arouses our admiration. They *left the Sanhedrin*, their backs cruelly lacerated and bleeding, yet *rejoicing because they had been counted worthy of suffering disgrace for the Name* (41). Luke's expression is 'a beautiful antithesis (the honour

[25] Knowling, p. 158. [26] Neil, p. 99.

[27] *Antiquities*, XVII.10.4; *cf. Wars*, II.4.1.

to be dishonoured, the grace to be disgraced)'.[28] They were in fact doing what in the Sermon on the Mount Jesus had told them to do, namely rejoicing in persecution.[29] Moreover, they again boldly defied the court's prohibition, for *day after day*, in public and in private, *in the temple courts and from house to house, they never stopped teaching and proclaiming the good news that Jesus is the Christ* (42).

Luke has now concluded his account of the two waves of persecution which broke over the infant church. In the first the Council issued a prohibition and a warning, which led the apostles to pray to the sovereign Lord for boldness to go on preaching; in the second they received a prohibition and a beating, which led them to praise God for the honour of suffering for Christ.

The devil has never given up the attempt to destroy the church by force. Under Nero (AD 54–68) Christians were imprisoned and executed, including probably Paul and Peter. Domitian (AD 81–96) oppressed Christians who refused to pay him the divine honours he demanded; under him John was exiled to Patmos. Marcus Aurelius (AD 161–180), believing that Christianity was dangerous and immoral, turned a blind eye to severe local outbreaks of mob violence. Then in the third century what had so far been sporadic became systematic. Under Decius (AD 249–251) thousands died, including Fabian, Bishop of Rome, for refusing to sacrifice to the imperial name. The last persecuting emperor before the conversion of Constantine was Diocletian (AD 284–305). He issued four edicts which were intended to stamp out Christianity altogether. He ordered churches to be burned, Scriptures to be confiscated, clergy to be tortured, and Christian civil servants to be deprived of their citizenship and, if stubbornly unrepentant, executed. Still today, especially in some Marxist, Hindu and Moslem countries, the church is often harassed. But we need not fear for its survival. Tertullian, addressing the rulers of the Roman Empire, cried out: 'Kill us, torture us, condemn us, grind us to dust. . . . The more you mow us down, the more we grow; *the seed is the blood of Christians.*'[30] Or, as Bishop Festo Kivengere said in February 1979, on the second anniversary of the martyrdom of Archbishop Janani Luwum of Uganda: 'Without bleeding the church fails to bless.' Persecution will refine the church, but not destroy it. If it leads to prayer and praise, to an acknowledgment of the sovereignty of God and of solidarity with Christ in his sufferings, then – however painful – it may even be welcome.

[28] Alexander, I, p. 239. [29] Mt. 5:10–12; Lk. 6:22–23.
[30] Tertullian, *Apology*, chapter 50.

5. The Seven are chosen and commissioned (6:1–7)

The devil's next attack was the cleverest of the three. Having failed to overcome the church by either persecution or corruption, he now tried distraction. If he could preoccupy the apostles with social administration, which though essential was not their calling, they would neglect their God-given responsibilities to pray and to preach, and so leave the church without any defence against false doctrine.

a. The problem (6:1)

The situation is clear. On the one hand, *in those days . . . the number of the disciples was increasing*. On the other, the excitement of church growth was tempered by a regrettable *goggysmos*, a 'complaint . . . expressed in murmuring' (BAGD). The cognate verb is used in LXX to denote the 'murmuring' of the Israelites against Moses,[31] and evidently the Jerusalem church members were murmuring against the apostles, who received the relief money (4:35, 37) and were therefore expected to distribute it equitably. But such grumbling is inappropriate in Christians.[32]

The complaint concerned the welfare of the widows, whose cause God had promised in the Old Testament to defend.[33] Assuming that they were unable to earn their own living and had no relatives to support them,[34] the church had accepted the responsibility, and a daily distribution of food was made to them. But there were two groups in the Jerusalem church, one called *Hellēnistai* and the other *Hebraioi*, and the former *complained against* the latter *because their widows were being overlooked in the daily distribution of food* (1). It is not suggested that the oversight was deliberate ('the Hebrew widows were being given preferential treatment', JBP); more probably the cause was poor administration or supervision.

What exactly was the identity of these two groups? It has usually been supposed that they were distinguished from each other by a mixture of geography and language. That is, the *Hellēnistai* came from the diaspora, had settled in Palestine and spoke Greek, while the *Hebraioi* were natives of Palestine and spoke Aramaic. This is an inadequate explanation, however. Since Paul called himself *Hebraios*,[35] in spite of the fact that he came from Tarsus and spoke Greek, the distinction must go beyond origin and language to culture. In this case the *Hellēnistai* not only spoke Greek but thought and behaved like Greeks, while the *Hebraioi* not only spoke Aramaic but were deeply immersed in Hebrew culture. This

[31] *E.g.* Ex. 16:7; Nu. 14:27; 1 Cor. 10:10. [32] *E.g.* Phil. 2:14; 1 Pet. 4:9.
[33] *E.g.* Ex. 22:22ff.; Dt. 10:18. [34] *Cf.* 1 Tim. 5:3–16.
[35] 2 Cor. 11:22; Phil. 3:5.

being so, *Grecian Jews* is a good rendering, while *the Aramaic-speaking community* is not, since it refers to language only and not culture. 'What is needed here', writes Richard Longenecker, 'is some such translation as "Grecian Jews" and "Hebraic Jews".'[36] There had always, of course, been rivalry between these groups in Jewish culture; the tragedy is that it was perpetuated within the new community of Jesus who by his death had abolished such distinctions.[37]

The issue was more, however, than one of cultural tension. The apostles discerned a deeper problem, namely that social administration (both organizing the distribution and settling the complaint) was threatening to occupy all their time and so inhibit them from the work which Christ had specifically entrusted to them, namely preaching and teaching.

b. The solution (6:2–6)

The Twelve did not impose a solution on the church, however, but *gathered all the disciples together* in order to share the problem with them. They said, '*It would not be right for us to neglect the ministry of the word of God in order to wait on tables*' (2). There is no hint whatever that the apostles regarded social work as inferior to pastoral work, or beneath their dignity. It was entirely a question of calling. They had no liberty to be distracted from their own priority task. So they made a proposal to the church: '*Brothers, choose seven men from among you who are known to be full of the Spirit and wisdom* [JBP, "both practical and spiritually-minded"]. *We will turn this responsibility over to them* (3) *and will give our attention to prayer and the ministry of the word*' (4). It is noteworthy that now the Twelve have added prayer to preaching (probably meaning public as well as private intercession) in specifying the essence of the apostles' ministry. They form a natural couple, since the ministry of the word, without prayer that the Spirit will water the seed, is unlikely to bear fruit. This delegation of social welfare to the Seven is commonly thought to have been the origin of the diaconate. It may be so, for the language of *diakonia* is used in verses 1 and 2, as we shall see later. Nevertheless, the Seven are not actually called *diakonoi*.[38]

The church saw the point of the apostles' plan: *This proposal pleased the whole group*. So they put it into effect. *They chose Stephen, a man full of faith and of the Holy Spirit; also Philip, Procorus, Nicanor, Timon, Parmenas, and Nicholas from Antioch,*

[36] *Acts*, p. 332. Dr Longenecker gives a thorough discussion of the options on pp. 326–329.

[37] *E.g.* Gal. 3:28; Eph. 2:14ff.; Col. 3:11.

[38] *Cf.* Rom. 16:1; Phil. 1:1; 1 Tim. 3:8, 12; 4:6.

a convert (NEB, 'a former convert') *to Judaism* (5), *i.e.* a proselyte. It has been pointed out that all seven had Greek names. They may all, therefore, have been *Hellēnistai*, deliberately chosen to satisfy this group who were complaining. But this is speculative. It seems more likely *a priori* that 'some of both classes of Jews were elected, the only fair and proper course'.[39] Whether they were deacons or not, and whether they were *Hellēnistai* or not, the church *presented these men to the apostles, who prayed and laid their hands on them* (6), thus commissioning and authorizing them to exercise this ministry.

c. *The principle*

A vital principle is illustrated in this incident, which is of urgent importance to the church today. It is that God calls all his people to ministry, that he calls different people to different ministries, and that those called to 'prayer and the ministry of the word' must on no account allow themselves to be distracted from their priorities.

It is surely deliberate that the work of the Twelve and the work of the Seven are alike called *diakonia* (1, 4), 'ministry' or 'service'. The former is 'the ministry of the word' (4) or pastoral work, the latter 'the ministry of tables' (2) or social work. Neither ministry is superior to the other. On the contrary, both are Christian ministries, that is, ways of serving God and his people. Both require spiritual people, 'full of the Spirit', to exercise them. And both can be full-time Christian ministries. The only difference between them lies in the form the ministry takes, requiring different gifts and different callings.

We do a great disservice to the church whenever we refer to the pastorate as 'the ministry', for example when we speak of ordination in terms of 'entering the ministry'. This use of the definite article implies that the ordained pastorate is the only ministry there is. But *diakonia* is a generic word for service; it lacks specificity until a descriptive adjective is added, whether 'pastoral' , 'social', 'political', 'medical' or another. All Christians without exception, being followers of him who came 'not to be served but to serve', are themselves called to ministry, indeed to give their lives in ministry. But the expression 'full-time Christian ministry' is not to be restricted to church work and missionary service; it can also be exercised in government, the media, the professions, business, industry and the home. We need to recover this vision of the wide diversity of ministries to which God calls his people.

In particular, it is vital for the health and growth of the church

[39] Lenski, p. 246.

that pastors and people in the local congregation learn this lesson. True, pastors are not apostles, for the apostles were given authority to formulate and teach the gospel, while pastors are responsible to expound the message which the apostles have bequeathed to us in the New Testament. Nevertheless, it is a real 'ministry of the word' to which pastors are called to dedicate their life. The apostles were not too busy for ministry, but preoccupied with the wrong ministry. So are many pastors. Instead of concentrating on the ministry of the word (which will include preaching to the congregation, counselling individuals and training groups), they become overwhelmed with administration. Sometimes it is the pastor's fault (he wants to keep all the reins in his own hands), and sometimes the people's (they want him to be a general factotum). In either case the consequences are disastrous. The standards of preaching and teaching decline, since the pastor has little time to study or pray. And the lay people do not exercise their God-given roles, since the pastor does everything himself. For both reasons the congregation is inhibited from growing into maturity in Christ. What is needed is the basic, biblical recognition that God calls different men and women to different ministries. Then the people will ensure that their pastor is set free from unnecessary administration, in order to give himself to the ministry of the word, and the pastor will ensure that the people discover their gifts and develop ministries appropriate to them.

d. The result (6:7)

As a direct result of the action of the apostles in delegating the social work, in order to concentrate on their pastoral priority, *the word of God spread* (7a). But of course! The word cannot spread when the ministry of the word is neglected. Conversely, when pastors devote themselves to the word, it spreads. Then, as a further result, *the number of disciples in Jerusalem increased rapidly, and* (a remarkable development) *a large number of priests became obedient to the faith* (7b). The two verbs 'spread' and 'increased' are in the imperfect tense, indicating that both the spread of the word and the growth of the church were continuous. This verse is the first of six summaries of growth, with which Luke intersperses his narrative. They come at crucial points in his unfolding story: after the apostles' decision to give their attention to prayer and preaching (6:7);[40] after the dramatic conversion of Saul of Tarsus (9:31); after the equally wonderful conversion of the first Gentile, Cornelius, followed by the overthrow of Herod Agrippa I (12:24); after Paul's first missionary journey and the Jerusalem Council (16:5); after the

[40] *Cf.* Acts 2:47; 4:4; 5:14; 6:1.

second and third missionary journeys (19:20); and at the end of the book after Paul's arrival in Rome, where he preached 'boldly and without hindrance' (28:30–31). In each of these verses we read either that the word was spreading or that the church was growing or both. God was at work; neither humans nor demons could stand in his way.

We have now seen the three tactics which the devil employed in his overall strategy to destroy the church. First, he tried through the Jewish authorities to suppress it by force; secondly through the married couple Ananias and Sapphira to corrupt it by hypocrisy; and thirdly through some squabbling widows to distract its leadership from prayer and preaching, and so expose it to error and evil. If he had succeeded in any of these attempts, the new community of Jesus would have been annihilated in its infancy. But the apostles were sufficiently alert to detect 'the devil's schemes'.[41] We need their spiritual discernment today to recognize the activity of both the Holy Spirit and the evil spirit (*cf.* 5:3). We also need their faith in the strong name of Jesus, by whose authority alone the powers of darkness can be overthrown.[42]

[41] Eph. 6:11. [42] *Cf.* Acts 3:6, 16; 4:7, 10, 12, 18.

to be converted and welcomed into the church. The gift of the Spirit to him plainly authenticated his inclusion in the Messianic community on the same terms as Jews, and so overcame the narrow Jewish prejudice of the apostle Peter.

Only after these four men had played their part in Luke's developing story was the scene set for the first missionary journey recorded in Acts 13 and 14.

Luke has already introduced Stephen. As one of the Seven, he was 'full of the Spirit and wisdom' (6:3). He himself is then described as 'full of faith and of the Holy Spirit' (6:5), and now he is re-introduced as *a man full of God's grace and power* (6:8a). Filled with the Spirit, and so filled also with wisdom, faith, grace and power, he evidently gave people an impression of plenitude. 'Grace and power' form a striking combination, which Campbell Morgan explains as 'sweetness and strength . . . merged in one personality'.[1] Certainly 'grace' seems to indicate a gracious, Christ-like character, while his 'power' was seen in the *great wonders and miraculous signs* which he did *among the people* (8b). So far signs and wonders have been credited by Luke only to Jesus (2:22) and the apostles (2:43; 5:12); now for the first time others are said to perform them. Some conclude that Stephen (6:8) and Philip (8:6) were special cases, both because the apostles had laid their hands on them (6:6), thus including them within their own apostolic ministry, and because they occupied a special place in salvation history, in the transition from Jewish movement to world mission. But this cannot be proved. Stephen and Philip are certainly witnesses to the fact that, even if according to Luke signs and wonders were mainly limited to the apostles, this restriction was not absolute.

Yet in spite of all Stephen's outstanding qualities, his ministry provoked fierce antagonism. We are not yet told why, but it is explained that the *opposition arose . . . from members of the Synagogue of the Freedmen (as it was called)*. Also mentioned are *Jews of Cyrene and Alexandria as well as the provinces of Cilicia and Asia* (9a). The 'freedmen' (*libertinoi*, a Greek transliteration of a Latin word) were freed slaves and their descendants. But who were the Jews from Cyrene, Alexandria, Cilicia and Asia? Some think that they composed four distinct synagogues, with the freedmen making a fifth. Others think two, three or four synagogues are in mind. But perhaps it is best to understand with the NIV that Luke is referring to only one synagogue (for the word is in the singular). The NEB also takes it in this way, describing the synagogue as 'comprising' people from the four places mentioned. Because they

[1] Morgan, pp. 142–143.

B. FOUNDATIONS FOR WORLD MISSION
Acts 6:8–12:24

5. Stephen the martyr
6:8–7:60

After the coming of the Spirit and the counter-attack of Satan (whose overthrow Luke has celebrated in 6:7), the church is almost ready to initiate its world-wide mission. So far it has been composed only of Jews and restricted to Jerusalem. Now, however, the Holy Spirit is about to thrust his people out into the wider world, and the apostle Paul (Luke's hero) is to be God's chosen instrument to pioneer this development. But first, in the next six chapters of the Acts, Luke explains how the foundations of the Gentile mission were laid by two remarkable men (Stephen the martyr and Philip the evangelist), followed by two remarkable conversions (Saul the Pharisee and Cornelius the centurion). These four men, each in his own way, together with Peter, through whose ministry Cornelius was converted, made an indispensable contribution to the global expansion of the church.

Stephen the martyr came first (6:8 – 8:2). His preaching aroused strenuous Jewish opposition, but in his carefully reasoned defence before the Sanhedrin he emphasized the freedom of the living God to go where he pleases and to call his people to go forth too. Although he failed to convince the Council and was stoned to death, his martyrdom seems to have had a profound influence on Saul of Tarsus. It also led to the scattering of the disciples throughout Judea and Samaria.

Philip the evangelist (8:4–40) had the distinction of being both the first to share the good news with the despised Samaritans and the means by which the Jewish-Samaritan barrier was broken. He then led the first African to Christ, the Ethiopian eunuch, and baptized him.

The simultaneous conversion and commissioning of Saul the Pharisee (9:1–31) were an indispensable prelude to the Gentle mission, since he was called to be pre-eminently the apostle to the Gentiles.

Cornelius the centurion (10:1 – 11:18) was the very first Gentile

had been freed from slavery, they must have been foreign Jews who had now come to live in Jerusalem. Perhaps those from Cilicia even included Saul of Tarsus. At all events, Stephen's appointment as one of the Seven, entrusted with the care of the widows, did not necessitate his resignation as a preacher, for it was to his message that these synagogue members objected.

First, *these men began to argue with Stephen* (9b). *But* they had not reckoned with the calibre of the man they were opposing, for *they could not stand up against his wisdom or the Spirit by which he spoke* (10), meaning perhaps 'the inspired wisdom with which he spoke' (NEB). This was a fulfilment of the promise of Jesus, which Luke has recorded, that he would give his followers 'words and wisdom' which their adversaries would be unable to resist or contradict.[2]

Secondly, thwarted in open debate, Stephen's opponents started a smear campaign against him, for when arguments fail, mud has often seemed an excellent substitute. So *they secretly persuaded some men* – presumably by bribery – to allege '*We have heard Stephen speak words of blasphemy against Moses and against God*' (11). In this way *they stirred up the people and the elders and the teachers of the law* (12a).

Thirdly, *they seized Stephen and brought him before the Sanhedrin* (12b), and then *produced false witnesses* (13a).

Thus the opposition degenerated from theology through slander to violence. The same order of events has often been repeated. At first there is serious theological debate. When this fails, people start a personal campaign of lies. Finally, they resort to legal or quasi-legal action in an attempt to rid themselves of their adversary by force. Let others use these weapons against us; may we be delivered from resorting to them ourselves!

After this introduction to Stephen, Luke first clarifies the accusation which was levelled against him (6:13–15), then summarizes the defence he made before the Council (7:1–53), and finally describes the summary sentence which was carried out, in other words his death by stoning (7:54–60).

1. Stephen is accused (6:13–15)

The rumour which had been circulated was that Stephen had blasphemed against Moses and against God (11). Now before the Sanhedrin the false witnesses elaborated the charge: '*This fellow never stops speaking against the holy place and against the law*' (13). We pause to note that this was an extremely serious double

[2] Lk. 21:15; *cf.* 12:12.

accusation. For nothing was more sacred to the Jews, and nothing more precious, than their temple and their law. The temple was the 'holy place', the sanctuary of God's presence, and the law was 'holy scripture', the revelation of God's mind and will. Therefore, since the temple was God's house and the law was God's word, to speak against either was to speak against God or, in other words, to blaspheme.

But in what sense did Stephen speak against the temple and the law? The false witnesses explained: '*For we have heard him say that this Jesus of Nazareth will destroy this place and change the customs Moses handed down to us*' (14). Stephen's words against the temple and the law are thus seen to be his teaching about what Jesus of Nazareth would do to both. But was Stephen right? Was Jesus an iconoclast, who had threatened to destroy the temple and change the law, thus robbing Israel of her two most treasured possessions and even opposing God who gave them? Certainly Jesus had been accused of this, and it is safe to assume that Stephen was faithfully echoing his teaching.

So what did Jesus say about the temple and the law? First, he said that he would replace the temple. 'We heard him say,' false witnesses had testified, ' "I will destroy this man-made temple and in three days will build another, not made by man." '[3] His hearers thought he meant this literally, and asked: 'It has taken forty-six years to build this temple, and you are going to raise it in three days?'[4] 'But', John comments, 'the temple he had spoken of was his body',[5] both his resurrection body which was raised on the third day, and also his spiritual body, the church, which would take the place of the material temple. Thus Jesus dared to speak of himself as God's new temple replacing the old. 'I tell you', he declared, 'that one greater than the temple is here.'[6] In consequence, although in the past the people came together to the temple to meet God, in future the meeting place with God would be himself.

Secondly, Jesus said that he would fulfil the law. He was of course accused of disrespect for the law, for example in relation to the sabbath. But the scribes and Pharisees did not understand him. What he did was to contradict the scribal misinterpretations of Moses, and so sweep away all the traditions of the elders. But he was never disrespectful to the law itself. On the contrary, he said: 'Do not think that I have come to abolish the Law or the Prophets; I have not come to abolish them but to fulfil them.'[7] In particular, his resolve to lay down his life for us would fulfil all priesthood and sacrifice.

[3] Mk. 14:58; *cf.* 15:29; Mt. 26:61. [4] Jn. 2:20.
[5] Jn 2:21. [6] Mt. 12:6. [7] Mt. 5:17.

What Jesus taught, then, was that the temple and the law would be superseded, meaning not that they had never been divine gifts in the first place, but that they would find their God-intended fulfilment in him, the Messiah. Jesus was and is himself the replacement of the temple and the fulfilment of the law. Moreover, to affirm that both temple and law pointed forward to him and are now fulfilled in him is to magnify their importance, not to denigrate it.

So far as we can tell, Stephen was teaching much the same as Jesus taught. The false witnesses accused him of saying that Jesus of Nazareth would destroy the temple and change the law. That is, they portrayed the work of Christ in negative, destructive terms. But what Stephen was really doing was preaching Christ, positively and constructively, as the One in whom all that the Old Testament foretold and foreshadowed is fulfilled, including the temple and the law.

At this point *all who were sitting in the Sanhedrin looked intently at Stephen, and they saw that his face was like the face of an angel* (15). It is surely significant that the Council, gazing at the prisoner in the dock, should see his face shining like an angel's, for this is exactly what happened to Moses' face when he came down from Mount Sinai with the law.[8] Was it not God's deliberate purpose to give the same radiant face to Stephen when he was accused of opposing the law as he had given to Moses when he received the law? In this way God was showing that both Moses' ministry of the law and Stephen's interpretation of it had his approval. Indeed God's blessing on Stephen is evident throughout. The grace and power of his ministry (8), his irresistible wisdom (10) and his shining face (13) were all tokens that the favour of God rested upon him.

2. Stephen makes his defence (7:1–53)

Many students of Stephen's speech have criticized it as rambling, dull and even incoherent. A good example is George Bernard Shaw in his preface to *Androcles and the Lion*. Calling Stephen 'a quite intolerable young speaker' and 'a tactless and conceited bore', he describes him as having 'delivered an oration to the council, in which he . . . inflicted on them a tedious sketch of the history of Israel, with which they were presumably as well acquainted as he'.[9] Others have found his speech lacking not only in interest but in point. Dibelius, for instance, wrote of 'the irrelevance of most of

[8] Ex. 34:29ff.

[9] Preface to *Androcles and the Lion* by George Bernard Shaw (1912; Constable 1916), p. lxxxv.

this speech'.[10] Such negative assessments of Stephen's oratory are by no means universal, however. William Neil even calls his speech 'a subtle and skilful proclamation of the gospel'.[11]

It is important to bear in mind the nature and purpose of Stephen's speech. After the two serious accusations had been levelled at him, the high priest challenged him with the direct question: *Are these charges true?* (7:1). So Stephen needed to defend himself against them in such a way as to develop an *apologia* for his radical gospel. What he did was not just to rehearse the salient features of the Old Testament story, with which the Sanhedrin were as familiar as he, but to do so in such a way as to draw lessons from it which they had never learned or even noticed. His concern was to demonstrate that his position, far from being 'blasphemous' because disrespectful to God's word, actually honoured it. For Old Testament Scripture itself confirmed his teaching about the temple and the law, especially by predicting the Messiah, whereas by rejecting him it was they who disregarded the law, not he. Stephen's mind had evidently soaked up the Old Testament, for his speech is like a patchwork of allusions to it.

a. The temple

It was not because of its architectural magnificence that the Jews prized the temple, but because God had promised to 'put his Name' there and meet his people there. Several psalms bear witness to Israel's consequent love for the temple. For example, 'One thing I ask of the Lord, this is what I seek: that I may dwell in the house of the Lord all the days of my life, to gaze upon the beauty of the Lord and to seek him in his temple.'[12] This was right. But many drew a false conclusion. They conceived of Yahweh as so completely identified with the temple that its existence guaranteed his protection of them, while its destruction would mean that he had abandoned them. It was against these notions that the prophets inveighed.[13] Long before them, however, as Stephen pointed out, the great figures of the Old Testament never imagined that God was imprisoned in a building.

What Stephen did was to pick out four major epochs of Israel's history, dominated by four major characters. First he highlighted Abraham and the patriarchal age (7:2–8); then Joseph and the Egyptian exile (9–19); thirdly Moses, the Exodus and the wilderness wanderings (20–44); and lastly David and Solomon, and the establishment of the monarchy (45–50). The connecting feature of these four epochs is that in none of them was God's presence limited to

[10] Dibelius, pp. 167 and 169. [11] Neil, p. 107.

[12] Ps. 27:4; *cf.* Pss. 15, 42 – 43, 84, 122, 134, 147, 150. [13] *E.g.* Je. 7:4.

any particular place. On the contrary, the God of the Old Testament was the living God, a God on the move and on the march, who was always calling his people out to fresh adventures, and always accompanying and directing them as they went.

(i) Abraham (7:2–8)

Here is Stephen's summary of the first or patriarchal epoch, in which Abraham was the key figure:

'The God of glory appeared to our father Abraham while he was still in Mesopotamia, before he lived in Haran. [3]"Leave your country and your people," God said, "and go to the land I will show you."

[4]'So he left the land of the Chaldeans and settled in Haran. After the death of his father, God sent him to this land where you are now living. [5]He gave him no inheritance here, not even a foot of ground. But God promised him that he and his descendants after him would possess the land, even though at that time Abraham had no child. [6]God spoke to him in this way: "Your descendants will be strangers in a country not their own, and they will be enslaved and ill-treated for four hundred years. [7]But I will punish the nation they serve as slaves," God said, "and afterwards they will come out of that country and worship me in this place." [8]Then he gave Abraham the covenant of circumcision. And Abraham became the father of Isaac and circumcised him eight days after his birth. Later Isaac became the father of Jacob, and Jacob became the father of the twelve patriarchs.'

It is no accident that Stephen describes Yahweh as *the God of glory*, for his 'glory' is his self-manifestation, and Stephen is about to give details of how he made himself known to Abraham. He *appeared* to him first *while he was still in Mesopotamia*, specifically in Ur of the Chaldeans,[14] while he and his family 'worshipped other gods'.[15] Yet even in that idolatrous context God appeared and spoke to Abraham, telling him to uproot himself from his home and people and migrate to another country which he would later show him. Some commentators regard Stephen as having made a mistake in this, because they deduce from Genesis 11:31 – 12:1 that God's command to Abraham was given him at Haran, not Ur. But Genesis 12:1 can be translated, 'The Lord had said to Abram' (NIV), suggesting that what he told him in Haran was actually a confirmation of what he had already said to him in Ur. Certainly God later announced himself to Abram as 'the Lord, who brought you out of Ur of the Chaldeans . . .', and both Joshua and Nehemiah bear

[14] Gn. 11:28. [15] Jos. 24:2.

witness to this.[16] So Abram left Ur *and settled in Haran*. But from there *God sent him* on the next stage of his journey to the land of Canaan. *He gave him no inheritance* in it, however, *not even a foot of ground*, but instead *promised* that *his descendants* (though at the time he had no child) *would possess the land*. At the same time, even they would not inherit it immediately, for first they were to be *strangers in a country not their own*, where they would be both *enslaved and ill-treated for four hundred years* (Stephen is content with a round figure, although the precise length of their slavery was 430 years).[17] Even during their cruel servitude God had neither forgotten nor forsaken them; he intervened to *punish the nation* which had enslaved them and so to rescue them from their bondage (7).

We cannot miss Stephen's emphasis on the divine initiative. It was God who appeared, spoke, sent, promised, punished and rescued. From Ur to Haran, from Haran to Canaan, from Canaan to Egypt, from Egypt back to Canaan again, God was directing each stage of his people's pilgrimage. Although the whole fertile crescent from the River Euphrates to the River Nile was the scene of their migrations, God was with them. Why was this? It was because *he gave Abraham the covenant of circumcision* (8), that is, made a solemn promise to Abraham to bless him and his posterity, and gave him circumcision to signify and seal this covenant. So, long before there was a holy place, there was a holy people, to whom God had pledged himself. He then renewed the promise he had made to Abraham, first to his son Isaac, then to his grandson Jacob, and then to his great-grandsons *the twelve patriarchs* (8b). Thus Stephen makes the transition from Abraham to Joseph, the second great figure of the Old Testament he singles out (9–16).

(ii) Joseph (7:9–16)

'Because the patriarchs were jealous of Joseph, they sold him as a slave into Egypt. But God was with him [10]*and rescued him from all his troubles. He gave Joseph wisdom and enabled him to gain the goodwill of Pharaoh king of Egypt; so he made him ruler over Egypt and all his palace.*

[11]*'Then a famine struck all Egypt and Canaan, bringing great suffering, and our fathers could not find food.* [12]*When Jacob heard that there was grain in Egypt, he sent our fathers on their first visit.* [13]*On their second visit, Joseph told his brothers who he was, and Pharaoh learned about Joseph's family.* [14]*After this, Joseph sent for his father Jacob and his whole family, seventy-five in all.* [15]*Jacob went down to Egypt, where he and our fathers died.* [16]*Their bodies*

[16] Gn. 15:7; Jos. 24:3; Ne. 9:7. [17] *Cf.* Gn. 15:13; Ex. 12:40–41.

were brought back to Shechem and placed in the tomb that Abraham had bought from the sons of Hamor at Shechem for a certain sum of money.'

We note at once that, if Mesopotamia was the surprising context in which God appeared to Abraham (7:2), Egypt was the equally surprising scene of God's dealings with Joseph. Six times in seven verses Stephen repeats the word 'Egypt', as if to make sure that his hearers have grasped its significance. This was the 'country not their own' in which Abraham's descendants would be strangers and slaves for 400 years (6), and it was owing to the patriarchs' jealousy of their younger brother Joseph that the migration took place (9). Though Joseph was now a foreigner and a slave in Egypt, however, *God was with him* (9). In consequence, *God rescued him from all his troubles* (the 'troubles' being a euphemism for his unjust imprisonment by Potiphar), and *gave* him *wisdom* (especially to interpret dreams), so that he gained *the goodwill of Pharaoh* and was promoted to be *ruler over Egypt* (10).

God was not only with Joseph but also with all his family, for he saved them from starvation during the famine (11). The venue for this divine deliverance was Egypt too. Stephen outlines the three visits to Egypt paid by Joseph's brothers, the first to get grain (12), the second when Joseph made himself known to them (13), and the third when they brought their father Jacob with them, together with their wives and children, making *seventy-five in all* (14). This is the number given in the LXX translation of Genesis 46:27 and Exodus 1:5, although the Hebrew text in both verses has seventy, the discrepancy being probably due to whether Joseph's sons are included in the total or not. It is difficult for us to imagine, and indeed Stephen does not mention, how traumatic this descent into Egypt must have seemed to Jacob. He surely knew that in an earlier famine the Lord had specifically forbidden his father Isaac to 'go down to Egypt', telling him instead to remain in the promised land.[18] Did this ban include Jacob too? It was doubtless to allay Jacob's qualms that at Beersheba, near the border between Canaan and Egypt, God told him in a night vision not to be afraid to 'go down to Egypt', for he would go down with him, bless him there and ultimately bring him back.[19] So *Jacob went down to Egypt* (15). And there he and all his sons died, far from the promised land, to which they never returned. Only *their bodies were brought back* to be buried (16).

There were two patriarchal burial grounds in Canaan. The first was the field and cave of Machpelah near Hebron, which Abraham bought from Ephron the Hittite;[20] the second was a plot of ground

[18] Gn. 26:1ff. [19] Gn. 46:1ff.; *cf.* 28:10ff. [20] Gn. 23.

near Shechem, which Jacob bought from the sons of Hamor.[21] Some commentators have made fun of Stephen (or Luke) for confusing these, since he speaks of Abraham buying the Shechem tomb, instead of Jacob. But it is antecedently unlikely that Stephen, with his intimate knowledge of the Old Testament, would have made this mistake. It is better to conclude either that Jacob bought the Shechem burial ground in Abraham's name, since he was still alive at the time, or that, in giving an omnibus account of the burial of all the patriarchs, Stephen deliberately conflated the two sites, since Jacob was buried at his own request in the field of Machpelah,[22] whereas Joseph's bones were buried many years later at Shechem.[23]

(iii) Moses (7:17–43)

Stephen's third epoch (17–43) was dominated by Moses, through whose ministry God kept his promises to Abraham which had seemed to be in abeyance. Perhaps Stephen's handling of Moses' career (which he divides into three forty-year periods) is longer and fuller than his account of the others because he had been accused of speaking against Moses (6:11). He leaves his judges in no doubt of his immense respect for Moses' leadership and law-giving.

'As the time drew near for God to fulfil his promise to Abraham,
the number of our people in Egypt greatly increased. 18Then another
king, who knew nothing about Joseph, became ruler of Egypt. 19He
dealt treacherously with our people and oppressed our forefathers
by forcing them to throw out their newborn babies so that they
would die.

20'At that time Moses was born, and he was no ordinary child.
For three months he was cared for in his father's house. 21When he
was placed outside, Pharaoh's daughter took him and brought him
up as her own son. 22Moses was educated in all the wisdom of the
Egyptians and was powerful in speech and action.

23'When Moses was forty years old, he decided to visit his fellow
Israelites. 24He saw one of them being ill-treated by an Egyptian,
so he went to his defence and avenged him by killing the Egyptian.
25Moses thought that his own people would realise that God was
using him to rescue them, but they did not. 26The next day Moses
came upon two Israelites who were fighting. He tried to reconcile
them by saying, "Men, you are brothers; why do you want to hurt
each other?"

27'But the man who was ill-treating the other pushed Moses aside

[21] Gn. 33:18–20. [22] Gn. 47:29–30; 49:29–33; 50:12–14.
[23] Gn. 50:26; Jos. 24:32.

and said, "Who made you ruler and judge over us? 28Do you want
to kill me as you killed the Egyptian yesterday?" 29When Moses
heard this, he fled to Midian, where he settled as a foreigner and
had two sons.

30'After forty years had passed, an angel appeared to Moses in the
flames of a burning bush in the desert near Mount Sinai. 31When
he saw this, he was amazed at the sight. As he went over to look
more closely, he heard the Lord's voice: 32"I am the God of your
fathers, the God of Abraham, Isaac and Jacob." Moses trembled
with fear and did not dare to look.

33'Then the Lord said to him, "Take off your sandals; the place
where you are standing is holy ground. 34I have indeed seen the
oppression of my people in Egypt. I have heard their groaning and
have come down to set them free. Now come, I will send you back
to Egypt."

35'This is the same Moses whom they had rejected with the words,
"Who made you ruler and judge?" He was sent to be their ruler
and deliverer by God himself, through the angel who appeared to
him in the bush. 36He led them out of Egypt and did wonders and
miraculous signs in Egypt, at the Red Sea and for forty years in the
desert. 37This is that Moses who told the Israelites, "God will send
you a prophet like me from your own people." 38He was in the
assembly in the desert, with the angel who spoke to him on Mount
Sinai, and with our fathers; and he received living words to pass
on to us.

39'But our fathers refused to obey him. Instead, they rejected him
and in their hearts turned back to Egypt. 40They told Aaron, "Make
us gods who will go before us. As for this fellow Moses who led us
out of Egypt – we don't know what has happened to him!" 41That
was the time they made an idol in the form of a calf. They brought
sacrifices to it and held a celebration in honour of what their hands
had made. 42But God turned away and gave them over to the
worship of the heavenly bodies. This agrees with what is written in
the book of the prophets:

' "Did you bring me sacrifices and offerings
for forty years in the desert, O house of Israel?
43You have lifted up the shrine of Molech
and the star of your god Rephan,
the idols you made to worship.
Therefore I will send you into exile" beyond Babylon.'

The Israelites' exile and slavery in Egypt lasted for four bitter centuries. Had God forgotten his people, and his promise to bless them? No. He had warned Abraham of their 400 years of enslavement and mistreatment (6). But now at last *the time drew near* (the set time, for God is the lord of history) *for God to fulfil his promise to Abraham* (17a). God had actually made Abraham two promises, namely to give him both a seed (numerous descendants) and a land (Canaan).[24] The first promise was being fulfilled even during their Egyptian captivity, for *the number of our people in Egypt greatly increased* (17b). But how would the promise of the land be fulfilled? Only after much suffering. For another Pharaoh *became ruler of Egypt* who, knowing nothing about Joseph, 'exploited' (JB) the Israelites and *oppressed* them, even *forcing them to throw out their newborn babies* (18–19).

It was *at that time*, when the people's sufferings were greatest and their prospects bleakest, that *Moses was born*, their God-appointed deliverer. 'No ordinary child' is NIV's rendering of an expression which combines the ideas of his being beautiful and pleasing to God (20). For the first *three months* of his life he was nurtured by his own mother, but was then brought up in the Egyptian palace as the adopted son of Pharaoh's daughter (21). He was thus *educated in all the wisdom of the Egyptians* and became *powerful in speech and action* (22).

At the age of forty, *he decided to visit his fellow Israelites*, in the sense of investigating their plight and seeking to remedy it (23). Witnessing two cases of injustice, he took things into his own hands. First, he tried to defend an Israelite, and killed the Egyptian who was ill-treating him (24). The following day he tried to reconcile two Israelites who were fighting, and appealed to them to remember that they were brothers who on that account should not hurt one another (26). In both cases he thought *his own people would realise* and acknowledge his God-given vocation *to rescue them* (25). *But they did not.* Instead, the Israelite who was ill-treating the other challenged Moses' authority to be their *ruler and judge*, and enquired if he intended to kill him as he had killed the Egyptian (27–28). Alarmed that his act of murder was known, Moses *fled to Midian*, where he settled down *as a foreigner*, married, and had *two sons* (29). This was the beginning of his second forty-year period.

At the end of it came the turning-point in his career, when God met and commissioned him. True, it is said to have been *an angel* who *appeared to Moses in the flames of a burning bush in the desert near Mount Sinai* (30). Yet it was *the Lord's voice* which called him, and which announced that he was *the God of Abraham, Isaac and Jacob*, so that *Moses trembled with fear and did not dare to look* (31–32). The divine voice then told him to remove his sandals because the place where he was standing, in the very presence of

[24] See Gn. 12:1–3; 15:18–21; 22:15–18.

the living God, was *holy ground* (33). This statement was central to Stephen's thesis. There was holy ground outside the holy land. Wherever God is, is holy. Moreover, the same God who met Moses in the desert of Midian was also present in Egypt, for he had *seen* his people's *oppression* there, had *heard their groaning*, had actually *come down* in person *to set them free*, and was now sending Moses *back to Egypt* to effect their liberation (34). *The same Moses*, whom the Israelites had rejected as their *ruler and judge*, was now appointed *their ruler and deliverer by God himself, through the angel who appeared to him in the bush* (35).

Moses' third forty-year period was spent in the desert after he had *led them out of Egypt*. Moreover, alike *in Egypt, at the Red Sea* and . . . *in the desert* his unique ministry as their deliverer and lawgiver had been authenticated (like the equally unique ministry of the apostles) *by wonders and miraculous signs* (36). *This is that Moses*, continued Stephen, wishing to magnify his ministry, who foretold the coming of the Messiah as a prophet like him,[25] who was *in the assembly* (*ekklēsia*) *in the desert*, along with the people and with *the angel who spoke to him on Mount Sinai*, and who *received living words*, oracles from God, to pass on to his people (37–38). True (and here Stephen anticipates how his defence will end), this greatly privileged nation *refused to obey* God. They not only *in their hearts turned back to Egypt*, but, rejecting Moses' leadership, commissioned Aaron to make them substitute gods to go before them into the promised land (39–40). They then *brought sacrifices* to the golden calf and *held a celebration in honour of what their hands had made* (41), which provoked God to turn away from them and to give them up instead to *the worship of the heavenly bodies* (42a). Although Stephen backs up his accusation with a quotation from Amos 5 which dates from several centuries later, it nevertheless refers to the corrupt worship of Israel during their forty years in the desert. Their *sacrifices and offerings* were not in reality brought to Yahweh, whatever their claim may have been, but rather to pagan idols (42b–43).

Stephen has traced the life and ministry of Moses through its Egyptian, Midianite and wilderness periods, and has shown that in each period and place God was with him. Chrysostom understood the import of this. Both when Moses was being educated in the Egyptian palace and when God appeared to him in the desert of Midian, there is 'not a word of temple, not a word of sacrifice' (Chrysostom repeats this phrase). In fact the 'holy ground' at the burning bush was 'far more wonderful . . . than . . . the Holy of Holies', for God is nowhere said to have appeared in the inner

[25] Dt. 18:15.

sanctuary in Jerusalem as he did in the burning bush. So the lesson to learn from the experience of Moses is that 'God is everywhere present' and that 'the holy place is there wherever God may be'.[26]

(iv) David and Solomon (7:44–50)

It is in Stephen's fourth epoch (44–50), which includes the settlement of the promised land and the establishment of the monarchy, that a religious structure is mentioned for the first time, namely *the tabernacle of the Testimony which* the people had *with them in the desert* (44).

'Our forefathers had the tabernacle of the Testimony with them in the desert. It had been made as God directed Moses, according to the pattern he had seen. [45]*Having received the tabernacle, our fathers under Joshua brought it with them when they took the land from the nations God drove out before them. It remained in the land until the time of David,* [46]*who enjoyed God's favour and asked that he might provide a dwelling-place for the God of Jacob.* [47]*But it was Solomon who built the house for him.*

[48]*'However, the Most High does not live in houses made by men. As the prophet says:*

> [49]*' "Heaven is my throne,*
> *and the earth is my footstool.*
> *What kind of house will you build for me? says the Lord.*
> *Or where will my resting place be?*
> [50]*Has not my hand made all these things?" '*

In referring to the tabernacle and the temple, Stephen is derogatory to neither. On the contrary, they were associated with some of the greatest names of Israelite history – Moses, Joshua, David and Solomon. Further, the tabernacle was constructed *as God directed Moses* and *according to the pattern he had seen* (44). Then the *fathers under Joshua brought it with them* into the land they took from the nations they dispossessed (45a). For a long period it *remained in the land* as a focus of national life, even *until the time of David* (45b), who *enjoyed God's favour* and asked permission to build God a more substantial and permanent *dwelling place* (47). His request was refused, however, and *it was Solomon who built the house for him* (47). In this story of the transition from tabernacle to temple, Stephen is seen by some as showing a bias towards the former because it was mobile. But he expresses neither a preference for the tabernacle nor a distaste for the temple. For both were constructed in accordance with God's will. Does this not contradict Stephen's thesis, however? No, Stephen's point is not that it was

[26] Chrysostom, Homilies XVI and XVII, pp. 100–112.

wrong to construct either the tabernacle or the temple, but that they should never have been regarded as in any literal sense God's home. For *the Most High does not live in houses made by men* (48). Paul was to make the same point to the Athenian philosophers (17:24). And, although this sentiment is not expressed in the Old Testament in so many words, Solomon himself understood it. After the temple had been built he prayed: 'But will God really dwell on earth? The heavens, even the highest heaven, cannot contain you. How much less this temple I have built!'[27] Instead of quoting this, however, Stephen cites Isaiah 66:1–2 where God says: *Heaven is my throne and the earth is my footstool.* So *what kind of house* or *resting place* could be built for him? God is himself the Creator; how can the Maker of everything be confined within man-made structures? (49–50).

It is not difficult, then, to grasp Stephen's thesis. A single thread runs right through the first part of his defence. It is that the God of Israel is a pilgrim God, who is not restricted to any one place. Key assertions in his speech are that the God of glory appeared to Abraham while he was still in heathen Mesopotamia (2); that God was with Joseph even when he was a slave in Egypt (9); that God came to Moses in the desert of Midian, and thereby constituted the place 'holy ground' (30, 33); that, although in the wilderness God had been 'moving from place to place with a tent as [his] dwelling',[28] yet 'the Most High God does not live in houses made by men' (48). It is evident then from Scripture itself that God's presence cannot be localized, and that no building can confine him or inhibit his activity. If he has any home on earth, it is with his people that he lives. He has pledged himself by a solemn covenant to be their God. Therefore, according to his covenant promise, wherever they are, there he is also.

b. The law

The false witnesses had accused Stephen of two blasphemies, namely of 'speaking against this holy place and against the law' (6:13). In response to both accusations he developed a similar defence, namely that in each area he was more biblical than they. That is, the Old Testament Scriptures laid less emphasis on the temple, and more emphasis on the law, than they did. We have followed his argument in relation to the temple; now in relation to the law he turns the tables on his judges. It is not he, he maintains, who has shown a disregard for the law, but they, like their fathers before them. The accused assumes the role of the accuser.

This theme has already been sketched in the earlier part of

[27] 1 Ki. 8:27; *cf.* 2 Ch. 6:18. [28] 2 Sa. 7:6; *cf.* 1 Ch. 17:5.

Stephen's speech. His respect for Moses and the law was unambiguous. His acknowledgement of Moses' divine vocation has been plain beyond question. Moses' birth and early education were superintended by God (20–22). His call came direct from God, who spoke to him out of the burning bush (31–32). His appointment as Israel's ruler and deliverer was made 'by God himself' (35), and from the same God 'he received living words' to pass on to the people (38). The shocking disrespect which Moses received, then, came not from Stephen but from the Israelites themselves. It was they who failed to recognize him as their heaven-sent deliverer (25), who 'pushed Moses aside' (27), who rejected his leadership (35), and who in the desert 'refused to obey him'; instead, in their hearts they turned back to Egypt and became idolaters (39ff.). It was similar with the prophets. Stephen quoted two of them with approval (Amos in verses 42–43, and Isaiah in verses 48–50), but in both citations the prophets were rebuking Israel.

So now, having exposed Israel's past unfaithfulness to the law and the prophets, Stephen went on to accuse his judges of the same sin.

[51]*'You stiff-necked people, with uncircumcised hearts and ears! You are just like your fathers: You always resist the Holy Spirit!* [52]*Was there ever a prophet your fathers did not persecute? They even killed those who predicted the coming of the Righteous One. And now you have betrayed and murdered him –* [53]*you who have received the law that was put into effect through angels but have not obeyed it.'*

We notice how Stephen boldly called the Sanhedrin *stiff-necked*, meaning stubborn, an epithet which both Moses and the prophets had applied to Israel.[29] And though they insisted on bodily circumcision, he described them as having *uncircumcised hearts and ears*, another expression which was common to Moses and the prophets[30] and which implied that they were 'heathen still at heart and deaf to the truth' (NEB). Indeed, in their wilful rejection of God's word, he said to them: *you are just like your fathers* (51).

Pressing home his indictment in greater detail, Stephen declared them guilty of sinning against the Holy Spirit, the Messiah and the law. First, *you always resist the Holy Spirit* (51) by rejecting his appeals. Secondly, whereas their fathers had persecuted every prophet,[31] and even *killed those who predicted the coming of the Righteous One*, they had been still worse, for they had *betrayed and murdered him* whom the prophets had predicted (52). Thirdly,

[29] *E.g.* Ex. 32:9; 33:3, 5; 34:9; Dt. 9:6, 13; 10:16; 31:27; 2 Ch. 30:8; Je. 17:23.
[30] *E.g.* Lv. 26:41; Dt. 10:16; 30:6; Je. 6:10; 9:26; Ezk. 44:7
[31] *Cf.* Lk. 6:23; 11:49ff.; 13:34

although they had been specially privileged to receive the law through the mediation of angels, they had *not obeyed it* (53).

Stephen's speech was not so much a self-defence as a testimony to Christ. His main theme was positive, that Jesus the Messiah had come to replace the temple and fulfil the law, which both bore witness to him. As Calvin put it, 'No harm can be done to the temple and the law, when Christ is openly established as the end and truth of both.'[32]

3. Stephen is stoned (7:54–60)

When they heard this, they were furious and gnashed their teeth at him. [55]*But Stephen, full of the Holy Spirit, looked up to heaven and saw the glory of God, and Jesus standing at the right hand of God.* [56]*'Look,' he said, 'I see heaven open and the Son of Man standing at the right hand of God.'*

[57]*At this they covered their ears and, yelling at the top of their voices, they all rushed at him,* [58]*dragged him out of the city and began to stone him. Meanwhile, the witnesses laid their clothes at the feet of a young man named Saul.*

[59]*While they were stoning him, Stephen prayed, 'Lord Jesus, receive my spirit.'* [60]*Then he fell on his knees and cried out, 'Lord, do not hold this sin against them.' When he had said this, he fell asleep.*

Stephen was ready to be the first true *martys*, who sealed his testimony with his blood. His death was full of Christ. Luke records three further sentences which he spoke, the first of which referred to Christ, while the remaining two were addressed to Christ.

First, when the Sanhedrin, infuriated by his accusations, ground their teeth at him (54), snarling like wild animals, Stephen, filled with the Spirit, had a vision of the glory of God (55), and cried out: '*Look, . . . I see heaven open and the Son of Man standing at the right hand of God*' (56). Several guesses have been made why Jesus was *standing* (repeated in verses 55 and 56), instead of sitting,[33] at God's right hand. It may have been that the son of man, who in Daniel's vision[34] was led into the presence of God, stood before him to receive authority and power. But it seems likely that Christ's standing related more directly to Stephen, and that he had stood up either as his heavenly advocate or to welcome his first martyr. As F. F. Bruce has put it, 'Stephen has been confessing Christ before men, and now he sees Christ confessing his servant before God.'[35]

[32] Calvin, I, p. 212. [33] Ps. 110:1; *cf.* Lk. 22:69; Acts 2:34–35.
[34] Dn. 7:13–14. [35] Bruce, *English*, p. 168.

Unwilling to listen to Stephen's testimony to the exaltation of Jesus, the Council both *covered their ears* and sought to drown his voice by their yelling. Worse, they were determined to silence him. So they *rushed at him* (57), *dragged him out of the city and began to stone him* (58a). Since the Romans had taken away the Jews' right of capital punishment,[36] it seems that Stephen's stoning was more a mob lynching than an official execution. Yet it had a small semblance of justice, since according to the law,[37] the first to begin stoning the condemned person must be 'the witnesses', which means his accusers, whether in Stephen's case these were the false witnesses of 6:13 or Sanhedrin members. At all events, they *laid their clothes at the feet of a young man named Saul* (58b), an experience he never forgot (22:20). Thus discreetly does Luke introduce into his narrative the man who is soon to dominate it.

It was during his actual stoning that Stephen uttered his second sentence: '*Lord Jesus, receive my spirit*' (59). His prayer was similar to that which Luke has recorded Jesus as praying just before he died, 'Father, into your hands I commit my spirit.'[38] Yet this was not to be Stephen's last word. He spoke a third sentence when *he fell on his knees*. He *cried out, 'Lord, do not hold this sin against them'* (60a). It was reminiscent of the first word from the cross which Luke has recorded, 'Father, forgive them, for they do not know what they are doing.'[39] Whether it was Stephen who deliberately imitated his Master, or whether it was Luke who observed and highlighted the fact, there are several parallels between the death of Jesus and the death of Stephen. In both cases false witnesses were produced and the charge was one of blasphemy. In both cases too the execution was accompanied by two prayers, as each prayed for the forgiveness of his executioners and for the reception of his spirit as he died. Thus did the disciple – whether consciously or unconsciously – reflect his Master. The only difference was that Jesus addressed his prayers to the Father, while Stephen addressed them to Jesus, calling him 'Lord' and putting him on a level with God.

Luke concludes his story with a dramatic contrast between Stephen and Saul. Stephen *fell asleep* (60b), which Bengel called 'a mournful but sweet word'[40] and F. F. Bruce 'an unexpectedly beautiful and peaceful description of so brutal a death'.[41] By contrast, *Saul was there, giving approval to his death* (8:1a). We shall return later to Stephen's influence on Saul. At this stage it is enough to note how brightly Stephen's tranquil faith shines against the dark background of Saul's murderous anger (8:1, 3).

[36] Jn. 18:31. [37] Dt. 17:7. [38] Lk. 23:46. [39] Lk. 23:34
[40] Bengel, p. 584. [41] Bruce, *English*, p. 172.

Conclusion

What interests many people most about Stephen is that he was the first Christian martyr. Luke's main concern lies elsewhere, however. He emphasizes the vital role Stephen played in the development of the world-wide Christian mission through both his teaching and his death.

Stephen's teaching, misunderstood as 'blasphemy' against the temple and the law, was that Jesus (as he himself had claimed) was the fulfilment of both. Already in the Old Testament God was tied to his people, wherever they were, not to buildings. So now Jesus is ready to accompany his people wherever they go. When soon Paul and Barnabas set out into the unknown on the first missionary journey, they will find (as Abraham, Joseph and Moses had found before them) that God is with them. That is exactly what they reported on their return (14:27; 15:12). Indeed, this assurance is indispensable to mission. Change is painful to us all, especially when it affects our cherished buildings and customs, and we should not seek change merely for the sake of change. Yet true Christian radicalism is open to change. It knows that God has bound himself to his church (promising that he will never leave it) and to his word (promising that it will never pass away). But God's church means people not buildings, and God's word means Scripture not traditions. So long as these essentials are preserved, the buildings and the traditions can if necessary go. We must not allow them to imprison the living God or to impede his mission in the world.

Stephen's martyrdom supplemented the influence of his teaching. Not only did it deeply impress Saul of Tarsus, and contribute to his conversion which led to his becoming the apostle to the Gentiles, but it also occasioned 'a great persecution' which led to the scattering of the disciples 'throughout Judea and Samaria' (8:1b).

The church was shocked, even stunned, by the martyrdom of Stephen and by the violent opposition which followed. But, with the benefit of hindsight, we can see how God's providence used Stephen's testimony, in word and deed, through life and death, to promote the church's mission.

6. Philip the evangelist
8:1-40

Luke seems to have regarded Stephen and Philip as a pair. Both men belonged to the Seven, and so had social responsibilities in the Jerusalem church (6:5). Yet both were also preaching evangelists (6:10; 8:5), and both performed public signs and wonders (6:8; 8:6). In addition, Luke saw the ministry of both men as helping to pave the way for the Gentile mission. Stephen's contribution lay in his teaching about the temple, the law and the Christ, and in the effects of his martyrdom, while Philip's lay in his bold evangelization of the Samaritans and of an Ethiopian leader. For the Jews regarded the Samaritans as heretical outsiders and Ethiopia as 'the extreme boundary of the habitable world in the hot south'.[1]

A notable feature of this chapter is the currency it gives to two distinctively Christian words for evangelism. Luke has already described the apostles as bearing witness to Christ, announcing (*katangellein*, 4:2) their message, devoting themselves to the ministry of the word of God, and teaching the people. But now he introduces the verb *kērysso* ('to herald') in relation to Philip's proclamation of Christ (5), and popularizes the verb *euangelizō* ('to bring good news'). The latter he has used once before (5:42), but in this chapter it occurs five times. Twice the object of the verb is the towns or villages evangelized (25, 40), while the other three times the object is the message itself, namely the good news of 'the word' (4), of 'the kingdom of God and the name of Jesus Christ' (12), and simply of 'Jesus' (35). This is a salutary reminder that there can be no evangelism without an evangel, and that Christian evangelism presupposes the good news of Jesus Christ. Effective evangelism becomes possible only when the church recovers both the biblical gospel and a joyful confidence in its truth, relevance and power.

[1] Hengel, p. 80.

In the first four verses Luke sets the scene for the evangelistic exploits of Philip which he is about to narrate, beginning with this statement: *And Saul was there* (at Stephen's martyrdom), *giving approval to his death* (1a). Luke appears to be drawing attention to a threefold chain of cause and effect.

First, Stephen's martyrdom brought *a great persecution ... against the church at Jerusalem.* It began *on that day,* the day of Stephen's death, and it *broke out* with the ferocity of a sudden storm (1b). True, not every inhabitant of the city was in opposition, for there were *godly men* (probably pious Jews rather than believers) who *buried Stephen and mourned deeply for him* (2), deploring the injustice of his death. They will have taken a considerable personal risk by thus identifying with Stephen. In contrast, Saul, who had approved of Stephen's stoning (1a, *cf.* 22:20), now *began to destroy the church* (3a). The verb *lumainō* expresses 'a brutal and sadistic cruelty'.[2] Making a *house-to-house* search for believers, *he dragged off men and women and put them in prison* (3b). Not only did he not spare the women, but he did not stop short of seeking – and securing – his victims' death (9:1; 22:4; 26:10). Saul of Tarsus had blood on his hands, for several others followed Stephen into martyrdom.

Secondly, the great persecution led to a great dispersion: *all except the apostles were scattered throughout Judea and Samaria* (1c). Luke remembers how the risen Lord commanded his followers to be his witnesses 'in all Judea and Samaria' (1:8), as well as in Jerusalem; now he shows how the commission was fulfilled as a result of persecution. We are very familiar with the Jewish diaspora, which had led to the propagation of Judaism; 'this was the beginning of the Dispersion of the New Israel',[3] which led to the dissemination of the gospel. Stephen's speech had been truly prophetic. Jerusalem and the temple now begin to fade from view, as Christ calls his people out and accompanies them. No blame is attached to the apostles for staying behind. Jerusalem would still for a while be the headquarters of the new Christian community, and they evidently saw it as their duty to remain there. Besides, it would have been dangerous for them to leave, even if the persecution was directed more against 'Hellenists' like Stephen than against 'Hebraists' like them.

Thirdly, if Stephen's martyrdom led to persecution, and the persecution to the dispersion, the dispersion now resulted in widespread evangelism. The scattering of the Christians was followed by the scattering of the good seed of the gospel. For *those who*

[2] Barclay, p. 64.

[3] Neil, p. 119; *diaspeiro* is the word translated 'scattered' in both verses 1 and 4.

had been scattered, as they fled, far from going into hiding, or even maintaining a prudential silence, *preached the word wherever they went* (4). Up to this point it was the apostles who had given the lead in evangelism, in defiance of the Sanhedrin's ban, violence and threats; now, however, as the apostles stayed in Jerusalem, it was the generality of believers who took up the evangelistic task. Not that they all became 'preachers' or 'missionaries' as a full-time vocation. The statement that they 'preached the word' is misleading; the Greek expression does not necessarily mean more than 'shared the good news'. Philip was soon to preach to the Samaritan crowds (6); it is better to think of the other refugees as lay witnesses ('nameless amateur missionaries'[4]).

What is plain is that the devil (who lurks behind all persecution of the church) over-reached himself. His attack had the opposite effect to what he intended. Instead of smothering the gospel, persecution succeeded only in spreading it. As Bengel comments, 'the wind increases the flame'.[5] An instructive modern parallel is what happened in 1949 in China when the National Government was defeated by the Communists. Six hundred and thirty-seven China Inland Mission missionaries were obliged to leave. It seemed a total disaster. Yet within four years 286 of them had been redeployed in South-East Asia and Japan, while the national Christians in China, even under severe persecution, began to multiply and now total thirty or forty times the number they were when the missionaries left (the exact figures are not known).

Having set the scene in the first four verses of the chapter, Luke goes on to give us two examples of early Christian evangelism, in both of which Philip was the chief actor. He may have obtained the facts from the lips of Philip himself, for about twenty years later he stayed in his home in Caesarea (21:8).

1. Philip the evangelist and a Samaritan city (8:5–25)

Philip went down to a city in Samaria and proclaimed the Christ there. [6]*When the crowds heard Philip and saw the miraculous signs he did, they all paid close attention to what he said.* [7]*With shrieks, evil spirits came out of many, and many paralytics and cripples were healed.* [8]*So there was great joy in that city.*

[9]*Now for some time a man named Simon had practised sorcery in the city and amazed all the people of Samaria. He boasted that he was someone great,* [10]*and all the people, both high and low, gave him their attention and exclaimed, 'This man is the divine power known as the Great Power.'* [11]*They followed him because he had*

[4] Green, *Evangelism*, p. 180; *cf.* p. 208. [5] Bengel, p. 585.

amazed them for a long time with his magic. [12]But when they
believed Philip as he preached the good news of the kingdom of
God and the name of Jesus Christ, they were baptised, both men
and women. [13]Simon himself believed and was baptised. And he
followed Philip everywhere, astonished by the great signs and miracles he saw.

[14]When the apostles in Jerusalem heard that Samaria had accepted
the word of God, they sent Peter and John to them. [15]When they
arrived, they prayed for them that they might receive the Holy
Spirit, [16]because the Holy Spirit had not yet come upon any of them;
they had simply been baptised into the name of the Lord Jesus.
[17]Then Peter and John placed their hands on them, and they received
the Holy Spirit.

[18]When Simon saw that the Spirit was given at the laying on of
the apostles' hands, he offered them money and said, [19]'Give me
also this ability so that everyone on whom I lay my hands may
receive the Holy Spirit.'

[20]Peter answered: 'May your money perish with you, because you
thought you could buy the gift of God with money! [21]You have no
part or share in this ministry, because your heart is not right before
God. [22]Repent of this wickedness and pray to the Lord. Perhaps he
will forgive you for having such a thought in your heart. [23]For I
see that you are full of bitterness and captive to sin.'

[24]Then Simon answered, 'Pray to the Lord for me so that nothing
you have said may happen to me.'

[25]When they had testified and proclaimed the word of the Lord,
Peter and John returned to Jerusalem, preaching the gospel in many
Samaritan villages.

It is hard for us to conceive the boldness of the step Philip took in preaching the gospel to Samaritans. For the hostility between Jews and Samaritans had lasted a thousand years. It began with the break-up of the monarchy in the tenth century BC when ten tribes defected, making Samaria their capital, and only two tribes remained loyal to Jerusalem. It became steadily worse when Samaria was captured by Assyria in 722 BC, thousands of its inhabitants were deported, and the country was re-populated by foreigners. In the sixth century BC, when the Jews returned to their land, they refused the help of the Samaritans in the rebuilding of the temple. Not till the fourth century BC, however, did the Samaritan schism harden, with the building of their rival temple on Mount Gerizim and their repudiation of all Old Testament Scripture except the Pentateuch. The Samaritans were despised by the Jews as hybrids in both race and religion, as both heretics and schismatics. John summed up the situation in his simple statement that 'Jews do not associate with Samaritans'.[6] Jesus' sympathy for them, however, is already apparent in Luke's Gospel.[7] Now in Acts 8 Luke is obviously excited by the evangelization of the Samaritans and their incorporation in the Messianic community.

It is uncertain which city Philip evangelized, since some manuscripts read *a city in Samaria* (as NIV) and others 'the city of Samaria'. The better attested reading has the definite article, in which case 'the city' (presumably meaning 'the capital city' or 'the principal city') is likely to have been either the Old Testament town called 'Samaria', which Herod the Great had renamed 'Sebastos' in honour of the emperor Augustus, or the ancient Shechem, which by then was called 'Neapolis' and is now 'Nablus'. On the other hand, *a city in* (the province of) *Samaria* may be correct, since neither in this verse nor in verse 25 does Luke seem concerned to identify the city or villages in question.

Luke's concern is rather to tell us what happened in the city. He unfolds the story in five stages.

a. Philip evangelizes the city (8:5–8)

The evangelist both *proclaimed the Christ* to the Samaritans (5), since they too were expecting a Messiah,[8] and performed *miraculous signs* (6), exorcizing *evil spirits*, which uttered wild *shrieks* as they left their victims, and healing *many paralytics and cripples* (7). Some think of these miracles as special to Philip; others think of them as demonstrating a norm for evangelism. What is certain is that, since neither Stephen nor Philip was an apostle, Scripture does not warrant a rigid restriction of miracles to the apostles. At any rate, hearing Philip's message and seeing his signs, *the crowds . . . all paid close attention to what he said* (6), and the combination of salvation and healing brought *great joy* to the city (8).

b. Simon Magus professes faith (8:9–13)

For some time before Philip arrived in the city, it had been under a very different influence. *A man named Simon had practised sorcery in the city.* He had *amazed all the people of Samaria*, even in the region beyond the city, not only by his magic arts (11) but also by his extravagant claims (9). For *he boasted that he was someone great*, even 'momentous' (JB). And *all the people*, 'eminent citizens and ordinary people alike' (JB), who seem to have been a gullible group, actually stated that *this man is the divine power known as*

[6] Jn. 4:9.

[7] *E.g.* Lk. 9:52–56; 10:30–37; 17:11–19; *cf.* Jn. 4. Jesus' prohibition of evangelism in any Samaritan town (Mt. 10:5) was restricted to the period of his public ministry; it had now been rescinded.

[8] *Cf.* Jn. 4:25.

the Great Power (10). Commentators are not agreed about the meaning of this phrase. Haenchen considers it clear 'that "the great power" was a Samaritan designation for the supreme deity', and that 'Simon declared that this deity had come to earth in his person for the redemption of men'.[9] Others think it more probable that Simon regarded himself, and came to be regarded, as some kind of emanation or representative of the divine being. Certainly in the middle of the second century Justin Martyr, who himself came from Samaria, described 'a Samaritan, Simon', who 'did mighty acts of magic', so that 'he was considered a god' and was worshipped not only by 'almost all the Samaritans' but even by some in Rome who erected a statue in his honour.[10] Towards the end of the second century Irenaeus represented him both as 'glorified by man as if he were "a god" ' and as the author of 'all sorts of heresies',[11] while by the third century he had come to be seen as the originator of Gnosticism and the arch-enemy of the apostle Peter. But this is more romance than history.

Now, however, in Samaria, Simon found himself challenged by Philip. It is not just that Philip's miracles rivalled Simon's magic. It is rather that, whereas Simon boasted of himself, Philip *preached the good news of the kingdom of God and the name of Jesus Christ* (12). The people first 'paid close attention to what he said' (6a), and then *believed Philip*. Luke seems to mean that they believed Philip's gospel, in other words were converted, for they then *were baptised, both men and women* (12b). It is less clear what Luke intends us to understand by his next statement that *Simon himself believed and was baptised and followed Philip everywhere, astonished by the great signs and miracles he saw* (13). He who had amazed others was himself now amazed. There is no need to suppose that he was only pretending to believe. Nor, on the other hand, did he exercise saving faith, for Peter was later to declare that his heart was 'not right before God' (21). Calvin suggests that we should seek 'some middle position between faith and mere pretence'.[12] Probably 'the sorcerer believed to all appearances as the rest did; he professed belief, became a convert in the view of others, and in the customary way, by submitting to the rite of baptism'.[13] New Testament language does not always distinguish between believing and professing to believe.[14]

c. The apostles send Peter and John (8:14–17)

The apostles in Jerusalem heard that Samaria had accepted the word

[9] Haenchen, p. 303. [10] Justin Martyr, *Apology*, I.26.
[11] Irenaeus, *Against Heresies*, 1.23.1–5. For a thorough summary of later traditions and legends about Simon Magus, see the note by R. P. Casey in *BC*, V, pp. 151–163.
[12] Calvin, I, p. 233. [13] Alexander, I, p. 329. [14] *Cf.* Jas. 2:19.

of God (14). This is more than a matter-of-fact statement; it seems to be almost a technical expression by which Luke signals an important new stage in the advance of the gospel. He has used it in reference to the Day of Pentecost when three thousand Jews 'accepted his [Peter's] message' (2:41). He uses it here of the first Samaritans who 'accepted the word of God'. And he will use it again after the conversion of Cornelius, when the apostles heard that 'the Gentiles also had received the word of God' (11:1). Further, in all three developments Peter played a decisive role, using the keys of the kingdom (though Luke does not refer to this) to open it successively to Jews, Samaritans and Gentiles.

When the apostles heard about the conversion of Samaritans, *they sent* two of their number, *Peter and John*, to investigate (14). It was particularly appropriate that one of them was John, since Luke describes him in his gospel as wanting on one occasion to call fire down from heaven to consume a Samaritan city.[15] Now his desire is to see the Samaritans saved, not destroyed. *When they arrived*, they discovered (we are not told how) that, although the Samaritans had received both the gospel and Christian baptism, they had not yet received the Spirit. So *they prayed for them that they might receive the Holy Spirit* (15), *because* (Luke explains) he *had not yet come upon any of them; they had simply been baptised into the name* (that is, into the allegiance, even into the ownership) *of the Lord Jesus* (16). In addition to praying for them, *Peter and John placed their hands on them*, thus identifying the people for whom they prayed, and in answer to their prayers, *they received the Holy Spirit* (17). Luke is as unforthcoming about how the apostles knew that the people had received the Spirit as he was about how they knew that they had previously not received him. Some attribute their knowledge to the gift of discernment; others suggest that there was visible public evidence, whether speaking in tongues as on the Day of Pentecost, or their exalted joy or bold testimony.

I think Professor Howard Marshall is right to call verse 16 ('the Holy Spirit had not yet come upon any of them; they had simply been baptised into the name of the Lord Jesus') 'perhaps the most extraordinary statement in Acts'.[16] For Peter had promised the gift of the Spirit to those who repented (the corollary of faith) and were baptized (2:38). How, then, could the Samaritans have believed and been baptized and *not* received the Spirit? The question has caused Christian readers much puzzlement and division, and we will return to it shortly.

[15] Lk. 9:51–56. [16] Marshall, *Acts*, p. 157.

d. Simon tries to buy power (8:18–24)

When he *saw that the Spirit was given at the laying on of the apostles' hands*, Simon the sorcerer, whom we might also call Simon the superstitious, to whom the apostles appeared 'extraordinarily gifted practitioners of religious magic',[17] *offered them money* (18) in exchange for the power to bestow the Spirit on people through the laying-on of his hands (19).

Peter immediately rebuked him, outspokenly and publicly, for imagining that God's gift could be bought (20). He added that Simon could have *no part or share in this ministry* because his *heart* was *not right before God* (21). He therefore called on him to *repent of this wickedness and pray to the Lord*, for *perhaps* then the Lord would forgive him for entertaining such an evil thought in his mind (22), even though he was *full of bitterness and captive to sin* (23). Ever since that day, the attempt to turn the spiritual into the commercial, to traffic in the things of God, and especially to purchase ecclesiastical office, has been termed 'simony'.

Simon's response to Peter's rebuke was not encouraging. He showed no sign of repentance, or even of contrition. Instead of praying for forgiveness, as Peter had urged him to do (22), he felt so incapable of praying, or so distrustful of his own prayers, that he asked Peter to pray for him instead. What really concerned him was not that he might receive God's pardon, but only that he might escape God's judgment, with which Peter had threatened him (24). It is true that the Bezan text adds that he 'did not stop weeping copiously'. But these words are not original; and if they were, Simon's tears will have been tears of remorse or rage, not of repentance.[18]

e. Peter and John evangelize many Samaritan villages (8:25)

Once the apostolic mission was fulfilled, and the Samaritans had received the Spirit, *Peter and John* stayed on for an unspecified period to proclaim *the word of the Lord*, presumably teaching the new converts. Then they *returned to Jerusalem*. Not directly, however. They visited *many Samaritan villages* on the way, in order to preach the gospel in them also, and so to gather in more Samaritan converts (25).

2. Philip, the Samaritans, the apostles and the Holy Spirit

We return now to the questions about the gift of the Spirit which the Samaritan story raises. How is it that through the ministry of Philip the Samaritan believers received only baptism, 'that and

[17] Bruce, *English*, p. 183. [18] See Metzger, pp. 358–359.

nothing more' (16, NEB), and that they received the Holy Spirit later through the ministry of the apostles Peter and John? What did the apostles have which Philip did not? How are we to understand the interlocking relationships between Philip, the Samaritans, the apostles and the Holy Spirit?

Behind these questions, moreover, lies another and more crucial one. Does Luke intend his readers to understand the Samaritans' divided experience (first faith-baptism, later the gift of the Spirit) as typical or atypical, normal or abnormal? Is it set before us as the usual pattern for Christian experience today, or as an exception which we should not expect to be repeated?

Opposite answers are given to this central question. According to the first, Christian initiation or becoming a Christian is a two-stage process, consisting first of conversion and water-baptism and secondly of the gift or baptism of the Spirit, so that the Samaritan experience must be judged normal. According to the second, initiation into Christ is a one-stage event, comprising repentance/faith, water-baptism and Spirit-baptism, so that what happened in Samaria must be judged abnormal.

a. Two-stage initiation

Acts 8 is a major proof text for two large groups at opposite ends of the ecclesiastical spectrum, on the one hand 'catholic' people (Roman Catholics and some Anglican Catholics) and on the other 'pentecostal' people (classical Pentecostalists, together with some neo-pentecostal or charismatic Christians in the older denominations). Both claim warrant from this passage for their belief that Christian initiation is in two stages, the second (receiving the Spirit) being accompanied by the laying-on of hands with prayer. True, there are differences between them, in that the catholic scheme is largely outward and ceremonial, while the pentecostal scheme is largely inward and spiritual. Yet a striking parallel remains.

Catholics believe that the first stage of initiation is baptism, and the second is confirmation by a bishop regarded as a successor of the apostles, through whose imposition of hands the Spirit is given. This position can be traced back to Hippolytus and Cyprian in the third century. Cyprian commented on the Samaritan incident thus: 'Exactly the same thing happens with us today; those who have been baptized in the church are presented to the bishops of the church so that by our prayer and the imposition of our hands they may receive the Holy Spirit.'[19] Modern Roman Catholic writers tend to give similar teaching. For example, George D. Smith writes

[19] Cyprian, *Letters*, 73.9; from *Early Latin Theology*, translated and edited by S. L. Greenslade, vol. V of The Library of Christian Classics (SCM, 1956).

that the Samaritan episode 'bears all the marks of a normal procedure'.[20] Relying on the same passage, Ludwig Ott systematizes the Catholic position in this way: '(a) The Apostles performed a sacramental rite, consisting of the imposition of hands and prayer; (b) The effect of this outward rite was the communication of the Holy Ghost . . .'; (c) The Apostles acted in the mandate of Christ. . . . The (*sc.* their) matter-of-course manner . . . presupposes its ordinance by Christ.'[21] Similarly R. B. Rackham, the devout Anglo-Catholic commentator, reasoned that because in Acts 8 the Spirit was given through apostolic hands, 'the church has accepted this as the normal method', and has perpetuated it in the rite of episcopal confirmation.[22] The Anglican Prayer Book of 1928 gives the same impression. True, the text of its Order of Confirmation speaks only of the Holy Spirit 'strengthening' those he has already 'regenerated'. Nevertheless, the preface to the service declares that 'in ministering confirmation the church doth follow the example of the apostles of Christ', quotes the Acts 8 passage as warrant, and explains it as teaching that 'a special gift of the Holy Spirit is bestowed through laying on of hands with prayer', without clarifying what this 'special gift' is.

The Pentecostal churches, together with some (but by no means all) Charismatics, also teach a two-stage Christian initiation, but formulate it differently. To them the first stage consists of conversion (the human turn of repentance and faith) and regeneration (the divine work of new birth), while the second is 'baptism in or of the Spirit', often (not always) associated with the laying-on of hands by a pentecostal leader. For example, paragraph 7 of the Assemblies of God 'Statement of Fundamental Truths' reads 'All believers are entitled to, and should ardently expect, and earnestly seek, the Baptism in the Holy Ghost and fire, according to the command of our Lord Jesus Christ. This was the normal experience of all in the early Christian church . . .'. Similarly, Myer Pearlman, an Assemblies of God Bible teacher writes: 'While freely admitting that Christians have been born of the Spirit, and workers anointed with the Spirit, we maintain that not all Christians have experienced the charismatic operation (*i.e.* baptism) of the Spirit, followed by a sudden supernatural utterance.'[23]

In seeking to evaluate these viewpoints, we are concerned at this

[20] *The Teaching of the Catholic Church* by George D. Smith (Burns and Oates, 2nd ed., 1952), p. 816.

[21] *Fundamentals of Catholic Dogma* by Ludwig Ott (Mercier Press, 6th ed., 1963), p. 362.

[22] Rackham, p. 117.

[23] *Knowing the Doctrines of the Bible* by Myer Pearlman (Gospel Publishing House, Springfield, Missouri, revised ed. 1981), p. 313.

point to ask only one question: is the two-stage Samaritan experience to be regarded as the norm for Christian initiation? We do not deny that the Samaritan experience did, in fact, take place in two stages. Nor have we any right to deny that, having happened once, it could happen again, especially if the circumstances are similar. We must not infringe the sovereignty of the Holy Spirit. But we press the question: is it God's normal purpose that the reception of the Spirit is a second experience subsequent to conversion and baptism?

To this question we need to give a negative answer (we come to the positive alternative later), because what happened in Samaria diverged from the plain and general teaching of the apostles. Initiation into Christ, according to the New Testament, is a single-stage experience, in which we repent, believe, are baptized, and receive both the forgiveness of sins and the gift of the Holy Spirit, after which by the indwelling power of the Spirit we grow into Christian maturity. During this period of growth there may indeed be many deeper, fuller, richer experiences of God; it is the insistence on a two-stage stereotype which we should reject. Moreover, no imposition of human hands is necessary for the accomplishment of the initial saving work of God. To be sure, the laying-on of hands is a significant gesture accompanying prayer for somebody, whether for blessing, comfort, healing or commissioning. And the Anglican Church has retained it in episcopal confirmation, although its purpose in this context is to assure candidates of God's acceptance of them and to introduce them into full church membership, and emphatically not to bestow the Holy Spirit on them.

Therefore the Samaritan situation, in which there was a two-stage experience, together with an apostolic imposition of hands, was exceptional and is not to be taken as a norm for us today, either in Catholic or in Pentecostal terms.

b. One-stage initiation

One possible way to handle the first half of Acts 8 is to say that even the Samaritans' experience, although in two stages, was not the two-stage initiation which at first sight it appears to be, because either the first or the second stage was not initiatory.

Some argue that the Samaritans' first stage was not a genuine conversion at all, but a spurious one. Campbell Morgan interprets their having 'accepted the word of God' (14) as a merely intellectual assent: 'they had not received the Spirit which brings regeneration, the beginning of the new life'.[24] In our day Professor Dunn has provided a thorough development of this thesis. He suggests that

[24] Morgan, p. 157.

the Samaritans got carried along 'by the herd-instinct of a popular mass-movement'. They are said only to have 'believed Philip' (12), which he thinks does not mean that they believed in Jesus Christ; and their baptism (like Simon's) was form without reality. Besides, since 'in New Testament times the possession of the Spirit was *the* hallmark of the Christian', we simply cannot regard the Samaritans at that stage as having been Christians at all. Therefore their second stage was really their first. It was through Peter and John, not through Philip, that they became Christians.[25]

It is an ingenious reconstruction, but it has not won general agreement. The main objection to it is that Luke gives no hint that he considers the Samaritans' original response inadequate, although he is clear that Simon Magus' profession was bogus. No, Luke writes that outstanding blessing attended Philip's ministry (4–8); that the Samaritans 'believed Philip as he preached the good news of . . . Jesus Christ' (12), so that it is inadmissible to divorce believing Philip from believing the Christ Philip preached; that they 'had accepted the word of God' (14) in the believing sense in which he uses this phrase elsewhere (*e.g.* 2:41 and 11:1); and that the apostles gave no indication that they thought Philip's ministry or the Samaritans' faith to be defective.

Others argue that the Samaritans did truly believe in Jesus, and that they must therefore have received the Spirit at that point in accordance with New Testament teaching. In consequence, what they received through the laying-on of the apostles' hands was not the initial gift of the Spirit (which they had received at their conversion), but rather some charismatic manifestations of the Spirit. Calvin taught this: 'To sum up, since the Samaritans had the Spirit of adoption conferred on them already, the extraordinary graces of the Spirit are added as a culmination.'[26] And reformed commentators have tended to follow him. They may be correct. Certainly the statement that the Spirit 'had not yet fallen on any of them' (16, RSV) could refer to special gifts and graces. On the other hand, Luke never says that the Samaritans received the Spirit when they believed and were baptized, whereas he does use the language of 'giving' and 'receiving' the Spirit (15, 17–19) as synonymous with the Spirit 'falling on' them, which suggests that what they received through the ministry of the apostles was the initial gift of the Spirit.

Although these two reconstructions are mutually exclusive, they have one thing in common. They both affirm that the Samaritans'

[25] Dunn, *Baptism*, pp. 63–68.

[26] Calvin, I, p. 236. Similarly, B. B. Warfield wrote that what the Samaritans received through the ministry of Peter and John was 'the extraordinary gifts of the Spirit' (*Miracles Yesterday and Today* [1918; Eerdmans, 1965], p. 22).

initiation into Christ was a one-stage event, because they deny that the other stage was initiatory. According to the first view, stage one was a spurious conversion and irregular baptism, so that stage two was the full initiation, including faith and the gift of the Spirit. According to the second view, stage one was the Samaritans' full initiation, including their conversion and reception of the Spirit, so that stage two was not initiatory but a subsequent charismatic endowment. In both cases, by eliminating one of the two stages (either declaring the first bogus or the second supplementary), the same result is achieved, namely a one-stage initiation into Christ.

Neither reconstruction is satisfactory, however, since Luke does seem to understand stage one as a genuine conversion, and stage two as the initial reception of the Spirit. In that case, because Luke describes a two-stage initiation in Samaria, the alternative explanation is to regard it as having been altogether unusual. There are two main indications of this, namely that it deviated both from the normal teaching and from the normal practice of the apostles.

Take the apostles' teaching. It is always dangerous to isolate any passage of Scripture, and always wise to interpret Scripture by Scripture. What, then, is the general teaching of Scripture about receiving the Spirit? According to Peter's first sermon, forgiveness and the gift of the Spirit are twin initial blessings which God bestows on everyone whom he calls, and who repents, believes and is baptized (2:38–39). Further, Paul agrees with Peter. God gives his Spirit to all his children, so that 'if anyone does not have the Spirit of Christ, he does not belong to Christ'.[27]

Now Luke must have been very familiar with this apostolic teaching, for he was Paul's constant travelling companion, and it is he who records Peter's instruction in Acts 2:38–39. No wonder, therefore, that we detect a note of surprise in his narrative when he describes the Samaritans as not having received the Spirit, but as having 'simply' (NIV) or 'only' (RSV) been baptized into Christ. '*Only* implies that the two things were expected or accustomed to go together.'[28] But, contrary to expectation, water-baptism had been received without Spirit-baptism, the sign without the thing signified. There was, Luke implies, something distinctly odd about their separation. It was because of this irregularity, Professor Dunn writes, that 'the two senior apostles came down hot-foot from Jerusalem to remedy a situation which had gone seriously wrong somewhere'.[29]

The second deviation was from the apostles' practice. Luke tells us that on this occasion the college of the apostles, if we may so

[27] Rom. 8:9; *cf.* Rom. 8:14–16; 1 Cor. 6:19; Gal. 3:2, 14; 4:6.
[28] Alexander, I, p. 332. [29] Dunn, *Baptism*, p. 58.

call them, sent a delegation of its two leading members to evaluate what was going on in Samaria. This was unique. The apostles did not normally cast themselves in the role of 'inspectors of evangelism'. On other occasions when people received the gospel, the apostles did not come and investigate, or feel it necessary to add their imprimatur to what had been done. They did not do it with regard to either the evangelism of other Christians mentioned at the beginning of this chapter (1, 4) or the conversion of the Ethiopian related at its end (26–40). 'The picture of apostles scurrying hither and thither up and down the eastern end of the Mediterranean in an attempt to keep up with the rapid expansion of the Christian gospel, with little time for anything but "confirmation services", is amusing but incredible.'[30] So why was it necessary for an official apostolic delegation to scrutinize and confirm the work of Philip? And why in any case was the Spirit not given through Philip himself who had done the preaching and the baptizing? For what special reason could God have withheld the Spirit? There is no indication that Philip's teaching was defective. Otherwise the apostles would have supplemented it, whereas what they did was pray for and lay hands on the Samaritans, not instruct them.

The most natural explanation of the delayed gift of the Spirit is that this was the first occasion on which the gospel had been proclaimed not only outside Jerusalem but inside Samaria. This is clearly the importance of the occasion in Luke's unfolding story, since the Samaritans were a kind of half-way house between Jews and Gentiles. Indeed, 'the conversion of Samaria was like the first-fruits of the calling of the Gentiles'.[31] The nearest equivalents to the investigation by Peter and John were when the Gentiles first believed. When Cornelius was converted, the apostles asked Peter to explain his actions (11:1–18), and when Greeks turned to the Lord in Antioch, Barnabas was sent there to reconnoitre the situation (11:20–24).

As we saw earlier, the Samaritan schism had lasted for centuries. But now the Samaritans were being evangelized, and were responding to the gospel. It was a moment of significant advance, which was also fraught with great peril. What would happen now? Would the long-standing rift be perpetuated? The gospel had been welcomed by the Samaritans, but would the Samaritans be welcomed by the Jews? Or would there be separate factions of Jewish Christians and Samaritan Christians in the church of Jesus Christ? The idea may seem unthinkable in theory; in practice it might well have happened. There was a real 'danger . . . of their tearing Christ apart, or at least of forming a new and separate church for themselves'.[32]

[30] Ibid., p. 59. [31] Calvin, I, p. 225. [32] *Ibid.*, p. 235.

Is it not reasonable to suggest (in view of this historical background) that, in order to avoid just such a disaster, God deliberately withheld the Spirit from these Samaritan converts? The delay was only temporary, however, until the apostles had come down to investigate, had endorsed Philip's bold policy of Samaritan evangelism, had prayed for the converts, had laid hands on them as 'a token of fellowship and solidarity',[33] and had thus given a public sign to the whole church, as well as to the Samaritan converts themselves, that they were *bona fide* Christians, to be incorporated into the redeemed community on precisely the same terms as Jewish converts. To quote Geoffrey Lampe again, 'at this turning-point in the mission something else was required in addition to the ordinary baptism of the converts. It had to be demonstrated to the Samaritans beyond any shadow of doubt that they had really become members of the church, in fellowship with the original "pillars".... An unprecedented situation demanded quite exceptional methods'.[34]

This seems to be the only explanation which takes account of all the data of Acts 8, reads the story in its historical context of the developing Christian mission, and is consistent with the rest of the New Testament. It is also becoming increasingly accepted on both sides of the charismatic divide. Although J. I. Packer calls it no more than a 'guess', he adds that it 'seems rational and reverent'.[35] Similarly, Michael Green sees the delay as 'a divine veto on schism in the infant church, a schism which could have slipped almost unnoticed into the Christian fellowship, as converts from the two sides of the "Samaritan curtain" found Christ without finding each other. That would have been the denial of the one baptism and all it stood for'.[36]

At all events, the action of the apostles appears to have been effective. Henceforward, Jews and Samaritans were to be admitted into the Christian community without distinction. There was one body because there was one Spirit.

To sum up, the Samaritan happening provides no biblical warrant either for the doctrine of a two-stage Christian initiation as the norm, or for the practice of an imposition of hands to inaugurate the supposed second stage. The official visit and action of Peter and John were historically exceptional. These things have no precise parallels in our day, because there are no longer any Samaritans or any apostles of Christ. Today, because we are not Samaritans, we receive forgiveness and the Spirit together the moment we believe.

[33] *The Seal of the Spirit* by G. W. H. Lampe (SPCK, second ed., 1967), p. 70.
[34] *Ibid.*, pp. 69–70.
[35] *Keep in Step with the Spirit* by J. I. Packer (IVP, 1984), p. 204.
[36] Green, *I believe in the Holy Spirit*, p. 168.

As for the laying-on of hands, although it can be an appropriate and helpful gesture in various contexts, its use as the means by which the Spirit is given and received lacks authority, whether in episcopal confirmation or in charismatic ministry, because neither bishops nor pentecostal leaders are apostles comparable to Peter and John, any more than Philip was, although directly appointed by them.

3. Philip the evangelist and an Ethiopian leader (8:26–40)

Now an angel of the Lord said to Philip, 'Go south to the road –
the desert road – that goes down from Jerusalem to Gaza.' 27So he
started out, and on his way he met an Ethiopian eunuch, an import-
ant official in charge of all the treasury of Candace, queen of the
Ethiopians. This man had gone to Jerusalem to worship, 28and on
his way home was sitting in his chariot reading the book of Isaiah
the prophet. 29The Spirit told Philip, 'Go to that chariot and stay
near it.'

30Then Philip ran up to the chariot and heard the man reading
Isaiah the prophet. 'Do you understand what you are reading?'
Philip asked.

31'How can I,' he said, 'unless someone explains it to me?' So he
invited Philip to come up and sit with him.

32The eunuch was reading this passage of Scripture:

> *'He was led like a sheep to the slaughter,*
> *and as a lamb before the shearer is silent,*
> *so he did not open his mouth.*
> *33In his humiliation he was deprived of justice.*
> *Who can speak of his descendants?*
> *For his life was taken from the earth.'*

34The eunuch asked Philip, 'Tell me, please, who is the prophet
talking about, himself or someone else?' 35Then Philip began with
that very passage of Scripture and told him the good news about
Jesus.

Soon after the departure of Peter and John from the Samaritan city, Philip was given another evangelistic commission. He was told to 'Go south.' The person who gave him this instruction is called *an angel of the Lord*, although in later stages of the story, it is 'the Spirit' who directed him to the Ethiopian (29) and 'the Spirit of the Lord' who then took him away again (39). Philip was sent to (and along) *the desert road that goes down* about sixty miles *from Jerusalem to Gaza*, which was the most southerly of the five Philistine cities, and near the Mediterranean coast. Whether the Gaza in question was 'old Gaza' which had been destroyed in 93 BC, or 'new Gaza' which had been built further south some thirty-five years later, we are not told. In either case, the road was well used, for it continued past Gaza to Egypt and so to the African continent.

a. Philip meets the Ethiopian (8:27–29)

The 'Ethiopia' of those days corresponded to what we call 'the Upper Nile', reaching approximately from Aswan to Khartoum. The man from that region to whom Luke introduces us was not only a *eunuch* (as were most courtiers at that period) but *an important official in charge of all the treasure of Candace, queen of the Ethiopians* (27). 'Candace' is known to have been not a personal name but a dynastic title for the Queen Mother who performed certain functions on behalf of the king. The Ethiopian official to whom Philip was sent was her treasurer or chancellor of the exchequer, presumably a black African. But he *had gone to Jerusalem to worship*, a pilgrim at one of the annual festivals, and now *on his way home* was *sitting in his chariot reading* the scroll of *Isaiah the prophet* (28). This may mean that he was actually Jewish, either by birth or by conversion, for the Jewish dispersion had penetrated at least into Egypt and probably beyond, and perhaps by now the promise to eunuchs of Isaiah 56:3–4 had superseded the ban of Deuteronomy 23:1. It seems unlikely that he was a Gentile, since Luke does not present him as the first Gentile convert; that distinction he reserves for Cornelius. He regards the Ethiopian's conversion rather as another example of the loosening of bonds with Jerusalem (foreseen by Stephen in his speech) and of the liberation of the word of God to be the gospel for the world. It is especially significant that this African, who *had gone to Jerusalem* to worship, was now leaving it and would not return there. The story ends with Luke's statement that 'he went on his way rejoicing' (39), distanced from Jerusalem although accompanied by Christ.

b. Philip shares the good news with the Ethiopian (8:30–35)

Told to '*go to that chariot and stay near it*' (29), *Philip ran* alongside it, close enough to hear *the man reading Isaiah the prophet* (because everybody read aloud in those days), and close enough to shout to him the question, '*Do you understand what you are reading?*' (30). Replying that he could not understand *unless someone explains it* to him, *he invited Philip to come up and sit with him* in his carriage (31).

Calvin contrasts the Ethiopian's modesty, in that he 'acknowledges his ignorance freely and frankly', with a person who is 'swollen-headed with confidence in his own abilities'. He goes on: 'That is also why the reading of Scripture bears fruit with such a few people today, because scarcely one in a hundred is to be found who gladly submits himself to teaching.'[37] The fact is that God has given us two gifts, first the Scriptures and secondly teachers to open up, explain, expound and apply the Scriptures. It is wonderful to note God's providence in the Ethiopian's life, first enabling him to obtain a copy of the Isaiah scroll and then sending Philip to teach him out of it. As Professor Howard Marshall writes, 'The way in which the story is told bears some structural resemblances to another story in which a Stranger joined two travellers and opened up the Scriptures to them, took part in a sacramental act, and then disappeared from view (Lk. 24:13–35).'[38]

So we are to picture the Ethiopian with the scroll of Isaiah 53 spread out on his lap, and with Philip now sitting beside him, as the carriage jolted its way further south. The verses Luke quotes[39] speak of a human sufferer who is *led like a sheep to the slaughter* and like *a lamb before the shearer* is silent. He experiences deep *humiliation*, is *deprived of justice*, and is killed (32–33). The Ethiopian asks who *the prophet* is *talking about, himself or someone else*? (34). In reply, beginning *with that very passage of Scripture*, Philip *told him the good news about Jesus* (35). Now there is no evidence that anyone in first-century Judaism was expecting a suffering rather than a triumphant Messiah. No, it was Jesus who applied Isaiah 53 to himself, and understood his death in the light of it.[40] It was, therefore, from him that the early Christians learned to read Isaiah 53 in this way. So well prepared by the Holy Spirit was the Ethiopian's heart that it seems he believed immediately, and went on to ask for baptism.

Chrysostom contrasts the conversion of the Ethiopian with that of Saul of Tarsus, recorded in Acts 9. 'Verily', he says, 'one has reason to admire this eunuch.' For, unlike Saul, he had no supernatural vision of Christ. Yet he believed, 'so great a thing is the careful reading of the Scriptures!'[41]

c. *Philip baptizes the Ethiopian (8:36–39a)*

As they travelled along the road, they came to some water, presumably in a wayside wadi, and the Ethopian said: '*Look, here is water. Why shouldn't I be baptised*?' (36). The following verse (37), found in the text of AV and NIV margin, is a Western addition, not found in the earlier manuscripts: 'Philip said, "If you believe with all your heart, you may." The eunuch answered, "I believe that Jesus Christ is the Son of God." ' The two sentences seem to have belonged to an early baptismal liturgy. They were probably inserted

[37] Calvin, I, p. 247. [38] Marshall, *Acts*, p. 161. [39] Is. 53:7–8.
[40] *E.g.* Mk. 10:45; 14:24ff.; Lk. 22:37. [41] Chrysostom, Homily XIX, p. 126.

into the text by a scribe who felt certain that Philip, before baptizing the Ethiopian, would have made sure that he had believed in his heart, in contrast to Simon Magus, whose heart was 'not right before God' (21). At all events, the Ethiopian *gave orders to stop the chariot. Then both Philip and the eunuch went down into the water*, and *Philip baptised him* (38). The water was a visible sign of the washing away of his sins and of his baptism with the Spirit. Incidentally, the words 'went down into the water', as J. A. Alexander comments, 'can prove nothing as to its extent or depth'.[42] Total immersion *may* be implied, but in that case the baptizer and the baptized will have been submerged together, since the same statement is made of them both. So the expression may rather mean, as the earliest paintings and baptistries suggest, that they went down into the water up to their waist, and that Philip then poured water over the Ethiopian.[43] Several MSS add that 'the Holy Spirit fell on the eunuch', and some scholars accept these words as original. But it seems more likely that they were added specially 'to make explicit that the baptism of the Ethiopian was followed by the gift of the Holy Spirit'.[44]

d. Philip is parted from the Ethiopian (8:39b–40)

Luke implies that immediately after *they came up out of the water, the Spirit of the Lord suddenly took Philip away* (39) . . . and he *appeared at Azotus*, that is, Ashdod (40a). Some understand this trip as 'a supersonic ride',[45] undertaken 'with miraculous velocity',[46] and, to be sure, the Greek verb for 'took away' (*harpazō*) normally means to 'snatch' (NEB) or 'seize', as at the rapture.[47] But I think Campbell Morgan was right: 'It is not at all necessary that this should be accounted a miracle. I am never anxious to read miracles in, where they are not; any more than I am anxious to rule out miracles, where they are in.'[48] At any rate, *the eunuch did not see him* (Philip) *again, but went on his way rejoicing* (39b), without the evangelist but with the evangel, without human aid but with the divine Spirit who not only gave him joy but also, according to Irenaeus, gave him courage and power in his own country 'to preach what he had himself believed'.[49] Philip also went on evangelizing, working his way north along the coast, *preaching the gospel in all the towns until he reached Caesarea* (40b), where, later if not already, he made his home (21:8).

[42] Alexander, I, p. 350. [43] See Hanson, pp. 107, 111.
[44] Metzger, pp. 360–361. [45] Horton, p. 112. [46] Bengel, p. 592.
[47] 1 Thes. 4:17. [48] Morgan, p. 171. [49] Irenaeus, *Against Heresies*, 3.12.8.

4. Some lessons about evangelism

Luke has brought together for us two examples of Philip's evangelistic labours, and it is instructive to compare and contrast them. The similarities are plain. In both instances the same pioneer spirit was shown by Philip, who won the first Samaritans and the first African to Christ. To both audiences the same message was proclaimed, namely the good news of Jesus Christ (12, 35), for there is only one gospel. In both situations the same response was given, for the hearers believed and were baptized (12, 36–38). And in both cases, the same result is recorded, namely joy (8, 39).

The differences are striking too. I am not now thinking of how the Spirit was received, or of the apostolic delegation to Samaria which had no parallel in the conversion of the Ethiopian. I am thinking rather of the people evangelized and of the methods employed.

Take the people evangelized. The people with whom Philip shared the good news were different in race, rank and religion. The Samaritans were of mixed race, half-Jewish and half-Gentile, and Asiatic, while the Ethiopian was a black African, though probably a Jew by birth or a proselyte. As for rank, the Samaritans were presumably ordinary citizens, whereas the Ethiopian was a distinguished public servant in the employment of the Crown. That brings us to religion. The Samaritans revered Moses but rejected the prophets. Recently they had come under the spell of Simon the sorcerer and his occult powers. They had 'paid attention' to him (10) before they 'paid attention' to Philip (6). The Ethiopian, on the other hand, had a strong attachment to Judaism, perhaps as a convert, and this led him both to go on a pilgrimage to Jerusalem and to read one of the very prophets the Samaritans rejected. So the Samaritans were unstable and credulous, while the Ethiopian was a thoughtful seeker after the truth. Yet despite their differences in racial origin, social class and predisposing religious condition, Philip presented them both with the same good news of Jesus.

Consider next the methods Philip employed. His mission to the Samaritans was an early example of 'mass evangelism', for 'the crowds' heard his message, saw his signs, paid attention to him, believed and were baptized (6, 12). Philip's conversation with the Ethiopian, however, was a conspicuous example of 'personal evangelism', for here was one man sitting alongside another man, and talking to him out of the Scriptures, privately and patiently, about Jesus. It is also noteworthy that the same evangelist was adaptable enough to use both methods, namely public proclamation and private testimony. But, although he could alter his method, he did not alter his basic message.

It is this combination of change (in relation to contexts and methods) and changelessness (in relation to the gospel itself), together with the ability to discern between them, which is one of Philip's abiding legacies to the church.

7. The conversion of Saul
9:1-31

Now that Stephen and Philip have contributed their pioneer preparations for the world mission of the church, Luke is ready to tell the story of the two notable conversions which launched it. The first was of Saul of Tarsus, who became the apostle to the Gentiles,[1] and the second of Cornelius the centurion, who was the first Gentile to be converted. Saul's conversion belongs to this chapter, and Cornelius' to the next.

Saul's experience on the road to Damascus is the most famous conversion in church history. Luke is so impressed with its importance, that he includes the story three times, once in his own narrative and twice in Paul's speeches. He is evidently anxious, as the Book of Common Prayer puts it, that we should 'have his wonderful conversion in remembrance'.

As we read it, however, a crucial question forms in our minds. Does Luke intend us to regard Saul's conversion as typical of Christian conversion today, or as exceptional? Many people dismiss it as having been altogether unusual, and as constituting no possible norm for conversion today. 'I've had no Damascus Road experience,' they say. Certainly some features of it were atypical. On the one hand, there were the dramatic, supernatural events, like the flash of lightning and the voice which addressed him by name. On the other hand, there were the historically unique aspects, like the resurrection appearance of Jesus, which Paul later claimed it was, although the last (9:17, 27 and 1 Cor. 15:8), and his commissioning to be an apostle, like the call of Isaiah, Jeremiah and Ezekiel to be prophets, and more particularly to be the apostle to the Gentiles.[2] In order to be converted, it is not necessary for us to be

[1] Rom. 11:13.

[2] *Cf.* Acts 9:5; 22:14–15; 26:17–18, 20; Rom. 1:1, 5, 13; 11:13; 15:15–18; Gal. 1:15–16; 2:2, 7–8; Eph. 3:1–8; Col. 1:24–29. For the analogy between Saul's conversion and the call of the Old Testament prophets see *Paul and the Salvation of Mankind* by Johannes Munck (English translation, John Knox, Richmond, VA,

struck by divine lightning, or fall to the ground, or hear our name called out in Aramaic, any more than it is necessary to travel to precisely the same place outside Damascus. Nor is it possible for us to be granted a resurrection appearance or a call to an apostleship like Paul's.

Nevertheless, it is clear from the rest of the New Testament that other features of Saul's conversion and commissioning are applicable to us today. For we too can (and must) experience a personal encounter with Jesus Christ, surrender to him in penitence and faith, and receive his summons to service. Provided that we distinguish between the historically particular and the universal, between the dramatic outward accompaniments and the essential inward experience, what happened to Saul remains an instructive case study in Christian conversion. Moreover, Christ's display of 'unlimited patience' towards him was meant to be an encouraging 'example' to others.[3]

Another kind of assault on the story of Saul's conversion has to be considered, however, namely the attempt to eliminate its supernatural element altogether. In the last century, some commentators speculated that Saul was overcome by sunstroke or by an epileptic seizure. In our generation a partly psychological and partly physiological explanation of his conversion has been proposed, especially by Dr William Sargant in his book *Battle for the Mind*.[4] Subtitled 'a physiology of conversion and brainwashing', the book's object is 'to show how beliefs . . . can be forcibly implanted in the human brain, and how people can be switched to arbitrary beliefs altogether opposed to those previously held', while the book's conclusion is 'that simple physiological mechanisms of conversion do exist'.[5] Basing his thesis on Pavlov's experiments with dogs and on his own wartime treatment of patients who had broken down under 'combat exhaustion', Dr Sargant conjectured that something similar happened to Saul. After 'his acute stage of nervous excitement' came 'total collapse, hallucinations and an increased state of suggestibility',[6] made more intense by three days of fasting. In this condition new beliefs, exactly contradictory to those he held before, were implanted in him first by Ananias and then by 'the necessary period of indoctrination' by the Christians in Damascus.[7]

1959), pp. 24–30. Similarly, Krister Stendahl in his right emphasis on Saul's call goes too far in denying that it was also his conversion (*Paul among Jews and Gentiles* [Fortress, 1976; SCM, 1977]), pp. 7–23.

[3] 1 Tim. 1:16.

[4] *Battle for the Mind* by William Sargant (Heinemann, 1957; revised edition by Pan Books, 1959).

[5] *Ibid.*, p. 20. [6] *Ibid.*, p. 106. [7] *Ibid.*, p. 106.

We have no quarrel with Dr Sargant's general analysis of the terrible technique of brainwashing, in which the mind is incessantly bombarded with alien ideas until it breaks down and becomes totally docile and suggestible. Nor do we deny that something of this kind happens both through the rhythmic drumming and dancing of primitive religious cults and even through some forms of manipulative, emotional evangelism. Our disagreement is with Dr Sargant's artificial attempt to fit Saul's conversion into this pattern. For the facts do not support his reconstruction. There is no evidence of any 'technique' having been used by anybody to 'bombard' Saul until he collapsed, unless it be Jesus himself. But that would posit a supernatural explanation, which would undermine Dr Sargant's thesis. Also, the conversion experiences in the Acts are so varied that they cannot all be explained away in physiological or psychological terms.[8]

In complete contrast to the attempts by unbelievers to discredit Saul's conversion, I would like to mention an eighteenth-century letter from Baron George Lyttelton to Gilbert West, which was published under the title *Observations on the Conversion and Apostleship of Saint Paul*.[9] He was so convinced of the authenticity of Saul's conversion that he believed it was in itself, aside from other arguments, 'a demonstration sufficient to prove Christianity to be a divine revelation'.[10] Drawing attention to Paul's references to his conversion in both his speeches and his letters, he worked out his case in considerable detail. Since Saul was neither 'an impostor, who said what he knew to be false, with an intent to deceive', nor 'an enthusiast, who by the force of an over-heated imagination imposed on himself', nor 'deceived by the fraud of others', therefore 'what he declared to have been the cause of his conversion, and to have happened in consequence of it, did all happen, and therefore the Christian religion is a divine revelation'.[11]

So then, accepting the fact that Saul's conversion did take place on account of an intervention by Jesus Christ, and accepting the need to distinguish between its essential and its exceptional features, we are now in a position to examine its cause and its effects. We shall look successively at Saul himself in his pre-conversion state, at Saul and Jesus in their encounter on the road, at Saul and Ananias who welcomed him into the church in Damascus, and at Saul and Barnabas, who introduced him to the apostles in Jerusalem.

[8] See *Conversions, Psychological and Spiritual* by D. M. Lloyd-Jones (IVP, 1960); 'Dr William Sargant's Writings on Conversion' by Gaius Davies, in *In the Service of Medicine* (CMF, vol. 22, no. 84, Jan. 1976); and *Psychology and Christianity: the view both ways* by Malcolm A. Jeeves (IVP, 1976), especially pp. 133–139.

[9] Published in Edinburgh, revised edition, 1769.

[10] *Ibid.*, p. 3. [11] *Ibid.*, pp. 9–10.

1. Saul himself: his pre-conversion state in Jerusalem (9:1–2)

Meanwhile, Saul was still breathing out murderous threats against the Lord's disciples. He went to the high priest [2]*and asked him for letters to the synagogues in Damascus, so that if he found any there who belonged to the Way, whether men or women, he might take them as prisoners to Jerusalem.*

If we ask what caused Saul's conversion, only one answer is possible. What stands out from the narrative is the sovereign grace of God through Jesus Christ. Saul did not 'decide for Christ', as we might say. On the contrary, he was persecuting Christ. It was rather Christ who decided for him and intervened in his life. The evidence for this is indisputable.

Consider first Saul's state of mind at the time. Luke has already mentioned him three times, and each time as a bitter opponent of Christ and his church. He tells us that at Stephen's martyrdom 'the witnesses laid their clothes at the feet of a young man named Saul' (7:58), that 'Saul was there, giving approval to his death' (8:1), and that then 'Saul began to destroy the church' (8:3), making a house-to-house search for Christians, dragging men and women off to prison. Now Luke resumes Saul's story by saying that he *was still breathing out murderous threats against the Lord's disciples* (9:1). He had not changed since Stephen's death; he was *still* in the same mental condition of hatred and hostility.

Worse than that. Saul had evidently hoped to contain the followers of Jesus in Jerusalem, in order to destroy them there (8:3). But some had escaped his net and fled to Damascus, where several synagogues served a large Jewish colony. Determined to pursue these fugitive disciples to foreign cities, Saul hatched a plot for their liquidation and persuaded the high priest to sanction it (9:1b–2). This self-appointed inquisitor then left Jerusalem, armed with written authority to the Damascus synagogues that, *if he found any there who belonged to the Way* (a very interesting early description of Jesus' followers, which we will consider later), *whether men or women, he might take them as prisoners to Jerusalem* (2). In modern idiom, the high priest issued him with an extradition order.

Some of the language Luke uses to describe Saul in his pre-conversion state seems deliberately to portray him as 'a wild and ferocious beast'.[12] The verb *lymainomai*, whose only New Testament occurrence is in 8:3 of Saul's 'destroying' the church, is used in Psalm 80:13 (LXX) of wild boars devastating a vineyard; and it especially refers to 'the ravaging of a body by a wild

[12] Calvin, I, p. 256.

beast'.[13] A little later the Damascus Christians depicted him as having 'caused havoc in Jerusalem' (21), where the verb is *portheō* (as in Gal. 1:13, 23), which C. S. C. Williams translates 'mauled'.[14] Continuing the same picture, J. A. Alexander suggested that Saul's 'breathing out murderous threats' (1) was 'an allusion to the panting or snorting of wild beasts',[15] while later God's grace is seen, according to Calvin, 'not only in such a cruel wolf being turned into a sheep, but also in his assuming the character of a shepherd'.[16]

This, then, was the man (more wild animal than human being) who in a few days' time would be a converted and baptized Christian. But he was in no mood to consider the claims of Christ. His heart was filled with hatred and his mind was poisoned by prejudice. In his own language later, a 'raging fury' obsessed him (26:11, RSV). If we had met him as he left Jerusalem and (with the benefit of hindsight) had told him that before he reached Damascus he would have become a believer, he would have ridiculed the idea. Yet this was the case. He had left out of his calculations the sovereign grace of God.

2. Saul and Jesus: his conversion on the Damascus Road (9:3–9)

As he neared Damascus on his journey, suddenly a light from heaven
flashed around him. 4He fell to the ground and heard a voice say
to him, 'Saul, Saul, why do you persecute me?'
5'Who are you, Lord?' Saul asked.
'I am Jesus, whom you are persecuting,' he replied. 6'Now get up
and go into the city, and you will be told what you must do.'
7The men travelling with Saul stood there speechless; they heard
the sound but did not see anyone. 8Saul got up from the ground,
but when he opened his eyes he could see nothing. So they led him
by the hand into Damascus. 9For three days he was blind, and did
not eat or drink anything.

The second piece of evidence that Saul's conversion was due to God's grace alone is Luke's narrative of what happened. We will draw from all three accounts in the Acts, although in a later chapter we will compare and contrast them. Saul and his escort (we are not told who they were) had nearly completed their journey of about 150 miles. It would have taken them approximately a week. When they approached Damascus, a beautiful oasis surrounded by desert,

[13] Bruce, *English*, p. 175, n. 8. He is referring to *BC*, IV, p. 88, where Lake and Cadbury say it is used 'particularly of the mangling by wild beasts, *e.g.* lions'.

[14] Williams, pp. 124–125. [15] Alexander, I, p. 355.

[16] Calvin, I, pp. 256, 260.

at about noon (22:6), suddenly it happened: *a light from heaven flashed around him* (3), brighter than the midday sun (26:13). It was such an overwhelming experience that it both blinded him (8–9) and knocked him over. *He fell to the ground* (4), 'prostrate at the feet of his conqueror'.[17] Then *a voice* addressed him personally and directly (in Aramaic, 26:14): '*Saul, Saul* [Luke preserves the original Aramaic *Saoul*], *why do you persecute me?*' And, in answer to Saul's enquiry about the speaker's identity, the voice continued: '*I am Jesus, whom you are persecuting*' (5). At once Saul must have grasped, from the extraordinary way in which Jesus identified with his followers, so that to persecute them was to persecute him, that Jesus was alive and his claims were true. So he promptly obeyed the order *get up and go into the city* (6), where further instructions would be given him. Meanwhile, *the men travelling with Saul stood there speechless*, for *they heard the sound*, but they *did not see anyone* (7), nor did they understand the invisible speaker's words (22:9). Nevertheless, *they led him by the hand into Damascus* (8). He who had expected to enter Damascus in the fullness of his pride and prowess, as a self-confident opponent of Christ, was actually led into it, humbled and blinded, a captive of the very Christ he had opposed. There could be no misunderstanding what had happened. The risen Lord had appeared to Saul. It was not a subjective vision or dream; it was an objective appearance of the resurrected and now-glorified Jesus Christ.[18] The light he saw was the glory of Christ, and the voice he heard was the voice of Christ. Christ had interrupted his headlong career of persecution and had turned him round to face in the opposite direction.

The third piece of evidence which attributes Saul's conversion to God's grace is the apostle's own later references to the event. He never mentioned his conversion without making this clear. 'It pleased God', he wrote, 'to reveal his Son in me.'[19] God took the initiative according to his own will and pleasure. And this truth Paul went on to illustrate by at least three dramatic images. First, Christ 'took hold of' him,[20] or 'seized' him, the verb *katalambanō* perhaps even suggesting that Christ 'arrested' him before he had the chance to arrest any Christians in Damascus. Secondly, he likened his inward illumination to the creative command, 'Let there be light'[21] or 'Let light shine out of darkness'.[22] And thirdly, he wrote of God's mercy 'overflowing' towards him, like a river in spate, flooding his heart with faith and love.[23] Thus God's grace arrested him, shone into his heart and swept over him like a flood.

[17] Walker, p. 207 [18] Acts 9:17, 27; *cf.* 22:14–15; 26:16; 1 Cor. 9:1; 15:8.
[19] Gal. 1:15–16. [20] Phil. 3:12. [21] Gn. 1:3 [22] 2 Cor 4:6.
[23] 1 Tim. 1:14

This variety of images reminds me of another series of metaphors, which C. S. Lewis uses in the last chapters of his autobiography. Sensing God's relentless pursuit of him, he likens him to 'the great Angler' playing his fish, to a cat chasing a mouse, to a pack of hounds closing in on a fox, and finally to the divine chess player manoeuvering him into the most disadvantageous positions until in the end he concedes 'checkmate'.[24]

To ascribe Saul's conversion to God's initiative can easily be misunderstood, however, and needs to be qualified in two ways, namely that the sovereign grace which captured Saul was neither sudden (in the sense that there had been no previous preparation) nor compulsive (in the sense that he needed to make no response).

First, Saul's conversion was not at all the 'sudden conversion' it is often said to have been. To be sure, the final intervention of Christ was sudden: 'Suddenly a light from heaven flashed around him' (3), and a voice addressed him. But this was by no means the first time Jesus Christ had spoken to him. According to Paul's own later narrative, Jesus said to him: 'It is hard for you to kick against the goads' (26:14). By this proverb (which seems to have been fairly common in both Greek and Latin literature) Jesus likened Saul to a lively and recalcitrant young bullock, and himself to a farmer using goads to break him in. The implication is that Jesus was pursuing Saul, prodding and pricking him, which it was 'hard' (painful, even futile) for him to resist. What were these goads, with which Jesus had been pricking him, and against which Saul had been kicking? We are not specifically told what they were, but the New Testament gives us a number of hints.

One goad was surely his doubts. With his conscious mind he repudiated Jesus as an impostor, who had been rejected by his own people and had died on a cross under the curse of God. But subconsciously he could not get Jesus out of his mind. Had he ever seen him, met him? 'There are those who categorically . . . deny the possibility', writes Donald Coggan, but 'I cannot be among their number.' Why not? Because it is 'more than likely that they were contemporaries pretty close in age to one another'. It is therefore probable that they both visited Jerusalem and the temple at the same time, in which case 'is it not possible, indeed highly likely, that the young teacher from Galilee and the younger Pharisee from Tarsus would have looked into one another's eyes, and that Saul would have heard Jesus teach?'[25] Even if they did not meet, Saul will have heard reports of Jesus' teaching and miracles, character and claims, together with the persistent rumour from

[24] *Surprised by Joy* by C. S. Lewis (Geoffrey Bles, 1955; Collins reprint, 1986), pp. 169–183.

[25] Coggan, pp. 33–34.

many witnesses that he had been raised from death and seen.

Another goad will have been Stephen. This was no hearsay, for Saul had been present at his trial and his execution. He had seen with his own eyes both Stephen's face shining like an angel's (6:15), and his courageous non-resistance while being stoned to death (7:58–60). He had also heard with his own ears Stephen's eloquent speech before the Sanhedrin, as well perhaps as his wisdom in the synagogue (6:9–10), his prayer for the forgiveness of his executioners, and his extraordinary claim to see Jesus as the Son of Man standing at God's right hand (7:56). It is in these ways that 'Stephen and not Gamaliel was the real master of St Paul'.[26] For Saul could not suppress the witness of Stephen. There was something inexplicable about those Christians – something supernatural, something which spoke of the divine power of Jesus. The very fanaticism of Saul's persecution betrayed his growing inner uneasiness, 'because fanaticism is only found', wrote Jung, 'in individuals who are compensating secret doubts'.[27]

But the goads of Jesus were moral as well as intellectual. Saul's bad conscience probably caused him more inner turmoil even than his nagging doubts. For although he could claim to have been 'faultless' in external righteousness,[28] he knew that his thoughts, motives and desires were not clean in God's sight. In particular, the tenth commandment against covetousness convicted him. The other commandments he could obey in word and deed, but covetousness was neither a word nor a deed, but a disposition of the heart which he could not control.[29] So he had neither power nor peace. Yet he would not admit it. He was kicking violently against the goads of Jesus, and it was hurting him to do so. His conversion on the road to Damascus was, therefore, the sudden climax of a long-drawn-out process in which 'the Hound of Heaven' had been pursuing him. The stiff neck of the self-righteous Pharisee bowed. The ox had been broken in.

If God's grace was not sudden, it was not compulsive either. That is, the Christ who appeared to him and spoke to him did not crush him. He humbled him, so that he fell to the ground, but he did not violate his personality. He did not demean Saul into a robot or compel him to perform certain actions in a kind of hypnotic trance. On the contrary, Jesus put to him a probing question, 'Why do you persecute me?' He thus appealed to his reason and conscience, in order to bring into his consciousness the folly and evil of what he was doing. Jesus then told him to get up and go

[26] Rackham, p. 88.

[27] *Contributions to Analytical Psychology* by C. G. Jung (Routledge and Kegan Paul, 1928), p. 257.

[28] Phil. 3:6. [29] Rom. 7:7ff.

into the city, where he would be told what to do next. And Saul was not so overwhelmed by the vision and the voice as to be deprived of speech and unable to reply. No, he answered Christ's question with two counter-questions: first, 'Who are you, Lord?' (5) and secondly, 'What shall I do, Lord?' (22:10). His response was rational, conscientious and free. *Kyrios* ('Lord') could have meant no more than 'sir'. Yet, since he realized that he was talking to Jesus, and that he had risen from the dead, it must already have begun to acquire the theological overtones which it was later to have in Paul's letters.

To sum up, the cause of Saul's conversion was grace, the sovereign grace of God. But sovereign grace is gradual grace and gentle grace. Gradually, and without violence, Jesus pricked Saul's mind and conscience with his goads. Then he revealed himself to him by the light and the voice, not in order to overwhelm him, but in such a way as to enable him to make a free response. Divine grace does not trample on human personality. Rather the reverse, for it enables human beings to be truly human. It is sin which imprisons; it is grace which liberates. The grace of God so frees us from the bondage of our pride, prejudice and self-centredness, as to enable us to repent and believe. One can but magnify the grace of God that he should have had mercy on such a rabid bigot as Saul of Tarsus, and indeed on such proud, rebellious and wayward creatures as ourselves.

C. S. Lewis, whose sense of God's pursuit of him has already been mentioned, also expressed his sense of freedom in responding to God:

> I became aware that I was holding something at bay, or shutting something out. Or, if you like, that I was wearing some stiff clothing, like corsets, or even a suit of armour, as if I were a lobster. I felt myself being, there and then, given a free choice. I could open the door or keep it shut; I could unbuckle the armour or keep it on. Neither choice was presented as a duty; no threat or promise was attached to either, though I knew that to open the door or to take off the corset meant the incalculable. The choice appeared to be momentous but it was also strangely unemotional. I was moved by no desires or fears. In a sense I was not moved by anything. I chose to open, to unbuckle, to loosen the rein. I say 'I chose,' yet it did not really seem possible to do the opposite. On the other hand, I was aware of no motives. You could argue that I was not a free agent, but I am more inclined to think this came nearer to being a perfectly free act than most I have ever done. Necessity may not be the opposite of freedom, and perhaps a man is most free when, instead of

producing motives, he could only say, 'I am what I do.'[30]

3. Saul and Ananias: his welcome into the church in Damascus (9:10–25)

In Damascus there was a disciple named Ananias. The Lord called to him in a vision, 'Ananias!'

'Yes, Lord,' he answered.

[11]*The Lord told him, 'Go to the house of Judas on Straight Street and ask for a man from Tarsus named Saul, for he is praying.* [12]*In a vision he has seen a man named Ananias come and place his hands on him to restore his sight.'*

[13]*'Lord,' Ananias answered, 'I have heard many reports about this man and all the harm he has done to your saints in Jerusalem.* [14]*And he has come here with authority from the chief priests to arrest all who call on your name.'*

[15]*But the Lord said to Ananias, 'Go! This man is my chosen instrument to carry my name before the Gentiles and their kings and before the people of Israel.* [16]*I will show him how much he must suffer for my name.'*

[17]*Then Ananias went to the house and entered it. Placing his hands on Saul, he said, 'Brother Saul, the Lord – Jesus, who appeared to you on the road as you were coming here – has sent me so that you may see again and be filled with the Holy Spirit.'* [18]*Immediately, something like scales fell from Saul's eyes, and he could see again. He got up and was baptised,* [19]*and after taking some food, he regained his strength.*

Following the story as Luke tells it, we turn from the causes to the consequences of Saul's conversion. It is wonderful to see the transformation of his attitudes and character which immediately began to be apparent, and especially of his relationships to God, to the Christian church and to the unbelieving world.

First, Saul had a new reverence for God. Ananias, instructed to go and minister to the new convert, was told 'behold, he is praying' (11, RSV). Three days had elapsed since his encounter on the road with the risen Lord, during which he *did not eat or drink anything* (9). Presumably, then, he spent those days in fasting and praying, that is, abstaining from nourishment in order to give himself without distraction to prayer. Not that he had never fasted and prayed before. Like the Pharisee in Jesus' parable, he will have gone up to the temple to pray, and like him too could probably have claimed, 'I fast twice a week.'[31] But now through Jesus and his cross Saul had been reconciled to God, and consequently enjoyed a new and

[30] *Surprised by Joy*, p. 179 [31] Lk 18:10, 12

immediate access to the Father, as the Spirit witnessed with his spirit that he was the Father's child.[32] What was the content of his prayers? We can guess that he prayed for the forgiveness of all his sins, especially his self-righteousness and his cruel persecution of Jesus through his followers; for wisdom to know what God wanted him to do now; and for power to exercise whatever ministry he was to be given. No doubt also his prayers included worship, as he poured out his soul in praise that God should have had mercy on him. The very same mouth, which had been 'breathing out murderous threats against the Lord's disciples' (1), was now breathing out praises and prayers to God. 'The raging lion has been changed into a bleating lamb.'[33]

Still today the first fruit of conversion is always a new awareness of the fatherhood of God, as the Spirit enables us to cry 'Abba, Father',[34] together with a gratitude for his mercy and a longing to know, please and serve him better. This is 'godliness', and no claim to conversion is genuine if it does not issue in a godly life.

Secondly, Saul had a new relationship to the church, into which Ananias now introduced him. No wonder William Barclay calls Ananias 'one of the forgotten heroes of the Christian church'.[35] At first, however, when told to minister to Saul, Ananias demurred. He was very reluctant to do any 'follow-up work' (to use the modern jargon), and his hesitation was understandable. To go to Saul would be tantamount to giving himself up to the police. It would be suicidal. For he had *heard many reports about this man and all the harm* he had done to Jesus' people in Jerusalem (13). Ananias also knew that Saul had come to Damascus *with authority from the chief priests to arrest* all believers (14). But Jesus repeated his command *'Go!'* and added that Saul was his *chosen instrument* to carry his name *before the Gentiles and their kings and before the people of Israel* (15) – a ministry which would involve him in much suffering for the sake of the same name (16).

So Ananias went to *Straight Street* (11), which is still Damascus' main east-west thoroughfare, and to the house of Judas, indeed to the very room where Saul was. There he placed his hands on him (17), perhaps to identify with him as he prayed for the healing of his blindness and for the fullness of the Spirit to empower him for his ministry. Even more, I suspect that this laying-on of hands was a gesture of love to a blind man, who could not see the smile on Ananias' face, but could feel the pressure of his hands. At the same time, Ananias addressed him as 'Brother Saul' or 'Saul, my brother' (NEB). I never fail to be moved by these words. They may well have been the first words which Saul heard from Christian lips

[32] Rom. 8:16. [33] Lenski, p. 360. [34] Rom. 8:15. [35] Barclay, p. 74.

after his conversion, and they were words of fraternal welcome. They must have been music to his ears. What? Was the arch-enemy of the church to be welcomed as a brother? Was the dreaded fanatic to be received as a member of the family? Yes, it was so. Ananias explained how the same Jesus, who had appeared to him on the road, had sent him to him so that he might both recover his sight *and be filled with the Holy Spirit* (17). Immediately *something like scales fell from Saul's eyes*, and *he could see again* (Dr Luke uses some medical terminology here). After this he *was baptised* (18), presumably by Ananias, who thus received him visibly and publicly into the community of Jesus. Only then did he take *some food*, so that after his three-day fast *he regained his strength* (19a). Did Ananias prepare and serve the meal, as well as baptize him? If so, he recognized that the young convert had physical as well as spiritual needs.

The next thing we are told is that *Saul spent several days with the disciples in Damascus* (19b). He knew that he now belonged to the very company which he had previously been trying to destroy, and he showed this plainly by beginning to *preach in the synagogues that Jesus is the Son of God* (20). It is amazing that he was accepted. Indeed, the people who heard him preach were *astonished* ('staggered', JBP), asking if he was not *the man who caused havoc in Jerusalem* among believers and who had come to Damascus *to take them as prisoners to the chief priests* (21). Luke does not tell us how their anxious questions were answered, but perhaps Ananias helped to reassure them. Meanwhile, Saul himself *grew more and more powerful* as a witness and apologist, to such an extent that he *baffled the Jews . . . in Damascus by proving that Jesus* was *the Christ* (22).

Saul did not settle down with the Damascus Christians for any length of time, however. Luke goes on to describe how he left the city *after many days had gone by* (23a). It is an intentionally vague time reference, but we know from Galatians 1:17–18 that these 'many days' actually lasted three years, and that during this period Saul was in Arabia. He need not have travelled far, because at that time the north-west tip of Arabia reached nearly to Damascus. But why did he go to Arabia? Some think he went on a preaching mission, but others suggest more cogently that he needed time to be quiet, and that Jesus now revealed to him those distinctive truths of Jewish-Gentile solidarity in the body of Christ which he would later call 'the mystery made known to me by revelation', 'my gospel' and 'the gospel . . . I received by revelation from Jesus Christ'.[36] Some have even conjectured that those three years in

[36] *E.g.* Eph. 3:3; Rom. 16:25; Gal. 1:11–12.

Arabia were a deliberate compensation for the three years with Jesus which the other apostles had had but Saul had not. At all events, after his time in Arabia Saul returned to Damascus.[37] Not for long, though. For *the Jews conspired to kill him* (23b) and *day and night . . . kept close watch on the city gates in order to kill him* (24). Somehow or other Saul *learned of their plan*, and in the end *his followers* (an interesting indication that his leadership was already recognized and had attracted a following) *lowered him in a basket through an opening in the wall* (25), so that he escaped to Jerusalem.

4. Saul and Barnabas: his introduction to the apostles in Jerusalem (9:26–31)

When he came to Jerusalem, he tried to join the disciples, but they
were all afraid of him, not believing that he really was a disciple.
27 But Barnabas took him and brought him to the apostles. He told
them how Saul on his journey had seen the Lord and that the Lord
had spoken to him, and how in Damascus he had preached fearlessly
in the name of Jesus. 28 So Saul stayed with them and moved about
freely in Jerusalem, speaking boldly in the name of the Lord. 29 He
talked and debated with the Grecian Jews, but they tried to kill
him. 30 When the brothers learned of this, they took him down to
Caesarea and sent him off to Tarsus.
31 Then the church throughout Judea, Galilee and Samaria enjoyed
a time of peace. It was strengthened; and encouraged by the Holy
Spirit, it grew in numbers, living in the fear of the Lord.

Saul's experience in Jerusalem was similar to his experience in Damascus. On his arrival in the capital city, *he tried to join the disciples*, since he knew he was one of them, but they were filled with scepticism and fear: *they were all afraid of him, not believing that he really was a disciple* (26). Presumably they had not heard of him for three years. But this time Barnabas came to the rescue. True to his disposition and his name, he *took him and brought him to the apostles* (in particular to Peter and James according to Gal. 1:18–20), and told them how he *had seen the Lord, the Lord had spoken to him*, and *in Damascus he had preached fearlessly in the name of Jesus* (27). As a result of this testimonial, Saul was accepted as a Christian brother. He *stayed with them and moved about freely in Jerusalem* during the two weeks we know that he spent there.[38]

Thus Saul was clear about his membership of the new society of Jesus. First in Damascus, then in Jerusalem, he sought out 'the disciples' (19, 26). True, both groups hesitated, but their initial

[37] Gal. 1:17. [38] Gal. 1:18.

scepticism was overcome. Thank God for Ananias who introduced Saul to the fellowship in Damascus, and for Barnabas who did the same thing for him later in Jerusalem. But for them, and the welcome they secured for him, the whole course of church history might have been different.

True conversion always issues in church membership. It is not only that converts must join the Christian community, but that the Christian community must welcome converts, especially those from a different religious, ethnic or social background. There is an urgent need for modern Ananiases and Barnabases who overcome their scruples and hesitations, and take the initiative to befriend newcomers.

In addition to his new reverence for God, and new relationship to the church, Saul recognized that he had a new responsibility to the world, especially as a witness. According to his own account of his conversion, it was already on the Damascus road that Jesus appointed him 'as a servant and as a witness' and indeed as the apostle to the Gentiles (26:16ff.). Jesus then confirmed to Ananias that Saul was his 'chosen instrument' (15), and Ananias passed on to Saul Jesus' commission to 'be his witness to all men' of what he had seen and heard (22:15). Several characteristics of his witness are noteworthy. First, it was Christ-centred. In Damascus Saul both 'preached' that Jesus was the Son of God (20) and 'proved' that he was the Christ (22). The arguments from Old Testament Scripture and from his own experience coincided. They both focused on Christ, and this is the task of the Christian witness. Testimony is not a synonym for autobiography. To witness is to speak of Christ. Our own experience may illustrate, but must not dominate, our testimony.

Secondly, Saul's witness to Christ was given in the power of the Holy Spirit (17), so that he 'grew more and more powerful' (22). No wonder, for the supreme function of the Spirit is to bear witness to Christ.[39]

Thirdly, his witness was courageous. Twice Luke alludes to the 'boldness' of his preaching, first in Damascus (27), in the very synagogues to which the high priest had addressed letters authorizing Saul to arrest Christians (2, 20), and then in Jerusalem itself (28), the seat of the Sanhedrin from whom the authority had come. He also debated with the Grecian Jews or Hellenists (29), like Stephen and perhaps in the same synagogue (6:8ff.).

Fourthly, Saul's witness was costly. He suffered for his testimony, as Jesus had warned that he would: 'I will show him how much he must suffer for my name' (16). Already in Damascus he

[39] *E.g.* Jn. 15:26–27.

went in danger of his life (23–24) so that, when all the city's exits were sealed, he had to make that ignominious escape in a basket (25).[40] In Jerusalem too some Hellenists tried to kill him (29), so that Jesus warned him to leave the city immediately (22:17–18). So his Christian brothers personally *took him down to Caesarea* on the coast and from there *sent him off* by ship *to Tarsus*, his home town, where he stayed incognito for the next seven or eight years.

Thus the story of Saul's conversion in Acts 9 begins with him leaving Jerusalem with an official mandate from the high priest to arrest fugitive Christians, and ends with him leaving Jerusalem as a fugitive Christian himself. Saul the persecutor has become Saul the persecuted. And in the rest of the Acts story Luke tells us more of his hero's sufferings, how he was stoned in Lystra and left for dead, beaten and imprisoned in Philippi, the centre of a public riot in Ephesus, arrested and imprisoned in Jerusalem, shipwrecked in the Mediterranean, and finally held in custody in Rome. Witness to Christ involves suffering for Christ. It is not an accident that the Greek word for witness (*martys*) came to be associated with martyrdom. 'Suffering, then, is the badge of true discipleship', wrote Bonhoeffer.[41]

Yet the world's opposition did not impede the spread of the gospel or the growth of the church. On the contrary, Luke ends his narrative of Saul's conversion, which culminated in his providential escape from danger, with another of his summary verses (31). He describes the church, which has now spread throughout *Judea, Galilee* and *Samaria*, as having five characteristics – peace (free from external interference), strength (consolidating its position), encouragement (enjoying *paraklēsis*, the special ministry of the Holy Spirit, the Paraclete), growth (multiplying numerically) and godliness (*living in the fear of the Lord*).

Conclusion

We have been considering the cause and effects of Saul's conversion. Our overall impression has been of the grace of God which could be the cause of such great effects, laying hold of such an obstinate rebel and completely transforming him 'from a wolf to a sheep'.[42] Luke's story should persuade us to expect more from God in relation to both the unconverted and the newly converted.

As for the unconverted, there are many Sauls of Tarsus in the world today. Like him they are richly endowed with natural gifts of intellect and character; men and women of personality, energy,

[40] *Cf.* 2 Cor. 11:32–33.
[41] *The Cost of Discipleship* by Dietrich Bonhoeffer (Macmillan, 1963), p. 100.
[42] Calvin, II, p. 273.

initiative and drive; having the courage of their non-Christian convictions; utterly sincere, but sincerely mistaken; travelling, as it were, from Jerusalem to Damascus instead of from Damascus to Jerusalem; hard, stubborn, even fanatical, in their rejection of Jesus Christ. But they are not beyond his sovereign grace. We need more faith, more holy expectation, which will lead us to pray for them (as we may be sure the early Christians prayed for Saul) that Christ will first prick them with his goads and then decisively lay hold of them.

But we should never be satisfied with a person's conversion. That is only the beginning. The same grace which brings a person to new birth is able to transform him or her into Christ's image.[43] Every new convert becomes a changed person, and has new titles to prove it, namely a 'disciple' (26) or 'saint' (13), newly related to God, a 'brother' (17) or sister, newly related to the church, and a 'witness' (22:15; 26:16), newly related to the world. If these three relationships – to God, the church and the world – are not seen in professed converts, we have good reason to question the reality of their conversion. But whenever they are visibly present, we have good reason to magnify the grace of God.

[43] *E.g.* 2 Cor. 3:18.

8. The conversion of Cornelius *9:32–11:18*

From the conversion of Saul to be the apostle to the Gentiles, Luke proceeds to the conversion of Cornelius, the first Gentile to become a believer. Both conversions were essential foundations on which the Gentile mission would be built. And prominent in both was a leading apostle, the first conversion having Paul as its subject, the second having Peter for its agent. Both apostles (despite their different callings)[1] had a key role to play in liberating the gospel from its Jewish clothing and opening the kingdom of God to the Gentiles. Luke therefore makes an abrupt transition in 9:32 from Paul to Peter. He leaves Paul in Tarsus for a while (9:30), temporarily out of sight, until he is ready to bring him to the centre of the stage with the first missionary journey (13:1ff.). Meanwhile for more than three chapters (9:32 – 12:25), although he mentions Paul twice (11:25–30; 12:25), he concentrates on Peter. So, if his book narrates 'Acts of Apostles', this section records some specific 'Acts of Peter', after which Peter drops from the scene altogether.

The three Peter-stories Luke selects are (i) a double miracle story (how Aeneas was healed and Tabitha raised from death), (ii) a conversion story (how Cornelius was brought to faith), and (iii) an escape story (how Peter was rescued from prison and so from Herod's evil intentions). Each may be seen as a confrontation – with disease and death, with Gentile alienation and with political tyranny. Moreover, in each case conflict gave place to victory – the cure of Aeneas, the resuscitation of Tabitha, the conversion of Cornelius, and the removal of Herod. The apostle Peter is portrayed as an effective agent through whom the risen Lord by his Spirit continued to act and to teach. Leaving Peter's imprisonment and deliverance until the next chapter, we will focus in this one on his ministry to Aeneas, Tabitha and Cornelius.

[1] Gal. 2:1ff.

1. Peter heals Aeneas and raises Tabitha (9:32–43)

As Peter travelled about the country, he went to visit the saints in Lydda. [33]There he found a man named Aeneas, a paralytic who had been bedridden for eight years. [34]'Aeneas,' Peter said to him, 'Jesus Christ heals you. Get up and tidy up your mat.' Immediately Aeneas got up. [35]All those who lived in Lydda and Sharon saw him and turned to the Lord.

[36]In Joppa there was a disciple named Tabitha (which, when translated, is Dorcas), who was always doing good and helping the poor. [37]About that time she became sick and died, and her body was washed and placed in an upstairs room. [38]Lydda was near Joppa; so when the disciples heard that Peter was in Lydda, they sent two men to him and urged him, 'Please come at once!'

[39]Peter went with them, and when he arrived he was taken upstairs to the room. All the widows stood around him, crying and showing him the robes and other clothing that Dorcas had made while she was still with them.

[40]Peter sent them all out of the room; then he got down on his knees and prayed. Turning towards the dead woman, he said, 'Tabitha, get up.' She opened her eyes, and seeing Peter she sat up. [41]He took her by the hand and helped her to her feet. Then he called the believers and the widows and presented her to them alive. [42]This became known all over Joppa, and many people believed in the Lord. [43]Peter stayed in Joppa for some time with a tanner named Simon.

Peter is introduced as engaged in an itinerant ministry: he *travelled about the country* (32a). Previously, when persecution had broken out, the apostles had deemed it prudent to remain in Jerusalem (8:1b). Now that the church was enjoying a time of peace (31), however, they felt free to leave the city. Peter's purpose was not only to preach the gospel, but also *to visit the saints* (32b), in order to teach and encourage them. On one of his tours he was itinerating towards and then along the western seaboard, when two incidents took place which Luke evidently regarded as a complementary pair. In Lydda, about twelve miles south-east of Joppa, there lived a man named Aeneas, who had been paralysed and *bedridden for eight years* (33). In Joppa, the modern Jaffa and the nearest sea port to Jerusalem, there lived a woman named Tabitha or Dorcas (the Aramaic and Greek words respectively for a 'gazelle'), whom Luke describes as *a disciple . . . who was always doing good and helping the poor* (36). In particular, she seems to have made both undergarments and outer clothing, 'shirts and coats' (29, NEB) for the needy. But she *became sick and died* (37). Such was the basic situation in these two cases. It seems that, by the way in which he recorded the miracles which then took place, Luke deliberately portrayed Peter as an authentic apostle of Jesus Christ, who performed 'the signs of a true apostle'.[2] Similar miracles had endorsed the prophetic ministry of Elijah and Elisha.[3] Four factors support this suggestion.

First, both miracles followed *the example of Jesus*. Aeneas is reminiscent of that other paralytic, who lived in Capernaum. As Jesus had said to him, 'Get up, take your mat and go home,'[4] so Peter said to Aeneas, 'Get up and tidy up your mat' (34). And the raising of Tabitha recalls the raising of Jairus' daughter. Because the people were weeping noisily, Peter 'sent them all out of the room', just as Jesus had done. Further, the words spoken to the dead person were almost identical. Indeed, as several commentators have pointed out, if Peter spoke Aramaic on this occasion, only a single letter would have been different, for Jesus had said *Talitha koum!*,[5] whereas Peter would have said *Tabitha koum!* (40).

Secondly, both miracles were performed by *the power of Jesus*. Peter knew that he could not overcome disease and death by his own authority or power. So he did not attempt to do so. Instead, to the paralysed, bedridden Aeneas he said, 'Jesus Christ heals you' (34), while before addressing the dead Tabitha 'he got down on his knees and prayed' (40), a detail which must have come from Peter, since nobody else was present.

Thirdly, both miracles were signs of *the salvation of Jesus*. Because of his confidence in the power of Christ, Peter dared to address the diseased man and the dead woman with the same word of command: *anastēthi*, 'Get up!' (34, 40). Yet *anistēmi* is the verb used of God raising Jesus, which can hardly have been an accident. This is not to forget that Tabitha was 'resuscitated' to her old life (only to die again), whereas Jesus was 'resurrected' to a new life (never to die again). It is rather to point out that recovery from paralysis and resuscitation from death were both visible signs of that new life into which by the power of the resurrection we sinners are raised.

Fourthly, both miracles redounded to *the glory of Jesus*. When Aeneas was healed, *all those who lived in Lydda and Sharon* (the coastal plain) *saw him and turned to the Lord* (35). Not that we need interpret the 'all' as meaning literally every single inhabitant, for, as Calvin wisely comments, 'when Scripture mentions *all*, it is not embracing, to a man, the whole of whatever it is describing, but uses "all" for many, for the majority, or for a crowd of people'.[6] Similarly, when Tabitha was restored to life, *this became known*

[2] 2 Cor. 12:12, RSV. [3] 1 Ki. 17:17–24; 2 Ki. 4:32–37.
[4] Mk. 2:11. [5] Mk. 5:41, 'Little girl, get up!' [6] Calvin, I, p. 277.

all over Joppa, and many people believed in the Lord (42). In accordance with the purpose of the signs, which was to authenticate and illustrate the salvation message of the apostle, people heard the word, saw the signs, and believed.

2. Peter is sent for by Cornelius (10:1–8)

At Caesarea there was a man named Cornelius, a centurion in what was known as the Italian Regiment. 2He and all his family were devout and God-fearing; he gave generously to those in need and prayed to God regularly. 3One day at about three in the afternoon he had a vision. He distinctly saw an angel of God, who came to him and said, 'Cornelius!'

4Cornelius stared at him in fear. 'What is it, Lord?' he asked.

The angel answered, 'Your prayers and gifts to the poor have come up as a memorial offering before God. 5Now send men to Joppa to bring back a man named Simon who is called Peter. 6He is staying with Simon the tanner, whose house is by the sea.'

7When the angel who spoke to him had gone, Cornelius called two of his servants and a devout soldier who was one of his attendants. 8He told them everything that had happened and sent them to Joppa.

Peter has responded boldly to the challenges of sickness and death; how will he respond to the challenge of racial and religious discrimination? Luke may be hinting at his comparative openness by ending the story of Aeneas and Tabitha with the information that 'Peter stayed in Joppa for some time with a tanner named Simon' (9:43). For, since tanners worked with dead animals, in order to convert their skins into leather, they were regarded as ceremonially unclean. But Peter disregarded this, which 'seems to show that [he] was already in a state of mind which would fit him for the further revelation of the next chapter, and for the instructions to go and baptize the Gentile Cornelius'.[7]

At all events, we who now read Acts 10 remember that Jesus had given Peter 'the keys of the kingdom', although it is Matthew who tells us this not Luke.[8] And we have already watched him use these keys effectively, opening the kingdom to Jews on the Day of Pentecost and then to Samaritans soon afterwards. Now he is to use them again to open the kingdom to Gentiles; by evangelizing and baptizing Cornelius, the first Gentile convert (*cf.* Acts 15:7).

Cornelius was stationed at Caesarea, a garrison city named after

[7] Knowling, p. 249. See Nu. 19:11–13; Strack and Billerbeck, *Kommentar zum Neuen Testament aus Talmud und Midrasch*, vol. 2 (1924), p. 695; and Edersheim's *Jewish Social Life*, p. 158. [8] Mt. 16:19.

Augustus Caesar, the administrative capital of the province of Judea, boasting a splendid harbour built by Herod the Great. Luke introduces him as *a centurion in what was known as the Italian Regiment* (1). 'Regiment' translates *speira*, usually 'cohort', which consisted of six 'centuries' (100 men), each under the command of a 'centurion'. Ten cohorts made up a legion. So a centurion corresponded approximately to a 'captain' or 'company commander' in our day.

In addition, he seems to have been an exemplary *pater familias*, for *he and all his family* were *devout*, their godliness being expressed both in generosity to the needy (JB, 'to Jewish causes') and in regular prayer to God (2). Whether 'God-fearing' is to be understood in a general sense that Cornelius was religious (as in verse 35) or in the more technical sense that he had become 'a God-fearer' (*e.g.* 13:16, 26), 'a proselyte of the gate', is disputed.[9] If the latter is correct, it means that he had accepted the monotheism and ethical standards of the Jews, and attended synagogue services, but had not become a full proselyte and been circumcised. So, although later (22) he is described as 'respected by all the Jewish people', he was still a Gentile, an outsider, excluded from God's covenant with Israel.

It is difficult for us to grasp the impassable gulf which yawned in those days between the Jews on the one hand and the Gentiles (including even the 'God-fearers') on the other. Not that the Old Testament itself countenanced such a divide. On the contrary, alongside its oracles against the hostile nations, it affirmed that God had a purpose for them. By choosing and blessing one family, he intended to bless all the families of the earth.[10] So psalmists and prophets foretold the day when God's Messiah would inherit the nations, the Lord's servant would be their light, all nations would 'flow' to the Lord's house, and God would pour out his Spirit on all humankind.[11] The tragedy was that Israel twisted the doctrine of election into one of favouritism, became filled with racial pride and hatred, despised Gentiles as 'dogs', and developed traditions which kept them apart. No orthodox Jew would ever enter the home of a Gentile, even a God-fearer, or invite such into his home (see verse 28). On the contrary, 'all familiar intercourse with Gentiles was forbidden' and 'no pious Jew would of course have sat down at the table of a Gentile'.[12]

This, then was the entrenched prejudice which had to be overcome before Gentiles could be admitted into the Christian com-

[9] See Conrad Gempf's essay on 'The God-fearers', being Appendix 2 in Hemer, pp. 444–447. [10] Gn. 12:1–4.

[11] Ps. 2:7–8; 22:27–28; Is. 2:1ff.; 42:6; 49:6; Joel 2:28ff.

[12] Edersheim, *Jewish Social Life*, pp. 25–29.

munity on equal terms with Jews, and before the church could become a truly multi-racial, multi-cultural society. We saw in Acts 8 the special steps God took to prevent the perpetuation of the Jewish-Samaritan schism in the church; how would he prevent a Jewish-Gentile schism? Luke regards this episode as being so important that he narrates it twice, first in his own words (Acts 10), and then in Peter's when the latter explained to the Jerusalem church what had happened (11:1–18).

It is first made clear that Peter is to be God's instrument in this development, for Cornelius was instructed to send for him. *One day at about three in the afternoon*, which Luke has already identified as a time of prayer among Jews (3:1), *he had a vision* in which *he distinctly saw* an angel who called him by name (3). In response to his terrified question, the angel told him that his *prayers and gifts to the poor* had *come up as a memorial offering before God* (4), so that he had taken note of them, and that he must *send men to Joppa*, about thirty-two miles along the coast to the south, to fetch Simon Peter who was staying *by the sea* with his namesake, Simon the tanner (5–6). It was at Joppa, centuries previously, that the disobedient prophet Jonah had boarded a ship in his foolish attempt to run away from God.[13] But Cornelius the centurion, who was himself used to giving commands, immediately obeyed this one, sending two servants and one soldier to Joppa (7–8). The angel did not preach the gospel to the centurion; that privilege was to be entrusted to the apostle Peter.

This initial incident set the stage for what followed. For the primary question was how God would deal with Peter. How would he succeed in breaking down Peter's deep-seated racial intolerance? The principal subject of this chapter is not so much the conversion of Cornelius as the conversion of Peter.

3. Peter receives a vision (10:9–23)

On the *following day* after Cornelius' vision, at *about noon* (*i.e.* twenty-one hours later), even as Cornelius' men *were approaching the city* of Joppa, Peter *went up on the* flat *roof* of the tanner's house *to pray* (9). *He became hungry and wanted something to eat, and while the meal was being prepared, he fell into a trance* (10) and had an extraordinary vision. *He saw heaven opened and something like a large sheet being let down to earth by its four corners* (11). Some commentators have speculated that in his hunger-induced trance on the seaside rooftop what Peter really saw was not a sheet but the sail of a boat passing by. And certainly *othonē*

[13] Jon. 1:3.

could be translated 'sail-cloth' (11, NEB). The main point of his vision, however, was what the sheet *contained*, namely *all kinds of four-footed animals, as well as reptiles of the earth and birds of the air* (12, NEB, 'whatever walks or crawls or flies'), evidently a mixture of clean and unclean creatures calculated to disgust any orthodox Jew. Yet, having seen the vision, he now heard *a voice* which issued the shocking order: *'Get up, Peter. Kill and eat'* (13). *'Surely not, Lord!' Peter replied*, as he had done twice during Jesus' public ministry,[14] adding *'I have never eaten anything impure or unclean'* (14). So *the voice spoke to him a second time, 'Do not call anything impure that God has made clean'* (15). After this it seems that the whole vision of the sheet was repeated *three times, immediately* after which *the sheet was taken back to heaven* (16).

The vision itself left Peter confused. But *while* he *was wondering* (RSV, 'inwardly perplexed') *about the meaning of the vision*, the delegation *sent by Cornelius found out where Simon's house was and stopped at the gate* (17). *They called out, asking if Simon who was known as Peter was staying there* (18). Then, *while Peter was still thinking about the vision, the Spirit said to him* (in some direct, unmistakable way), *'Simon, three men are looking for you* (19). *So get up and go downstairs. Do not hesitate to go with them, for I* [the Spirit] *have sent them'* (20). The key expression *mēden diakrinomenos* in 10:20 and *mēden diakrinanta* in 11:12 is usually translated 'without hesitation' (RSV) or 'without misgiving' (JBP, NEB), but it could mean 'making no distinction' (11:12, RSV), that is, 'making no gratuitous, invidious distinction between Jew and Gentile'.[15] Thus, although the vision challenged the basic distinction between clean and unclean foods, which Peter had been brought up to make, the Spirit related this to the distinction between clean and unclean people, and told him to stop making it. That Peter grasped this is clear from his later statement: 'God has shown me that I should not call any man impure or unclean' (28).

So *Peter went down and said to the men* who had come from Cornelius: *'I'm the one you're looking for. Why have you come?'* (21). *The men replied, 'We have come from Cornelius, the centurion. He is a righteous and God-fearing man, who is respected by all the Jewish people. A holy angel told him to have you come to his house so that he could hear what you have to say* (22). At this *Peter invited the* three *men into the house to be his guests* (23a). This seems to mean that he 'gave them a night's lodging' (NEB), even though they were uncircumcised Gentiles.

We note how perfectly God dovetailed his working in Cornelius and in Peter. For while Peter was praying and seeing his vision,

[14] Mt. 16:22; Jn. 13:8. [15] Alexander, I, p. 398.

the men from Cornelius were approaching the city (9–16); while Peter was perplexed about the meaning of what he had seen, they arrived at his house (17–18); while Peter was still thinking about the vision, the Spirit told him that the men were looking for him and he must not hesitate to go with them (19–20); and when Peter went down and introduced himself to them, they explained to him the purpose of their visit (21–23).

4. Peter preaches to Cornelius' household (10:23b–48)

The next day Peter started out with them, and some of the brothers from Joppa went along. [24]*The following day he arrived in Caesarea. Cornelius was expecting them and had called together his relatives and close friends.* [25]*As Peter entered the house, Cornelius met him and fell at his feet in reverence.* [26]*But Peter made him get up. 'Stand up,' he said, 'I am only a man myself.'*

[27]*Talking with him, Peter went inside and found a large gathering of people.* [28]*He said to them: 'You are well aware that it is against our law for a Jew to associate with a Gentile or visit him. But God has shown me that I should not call any man impure or unclean.* [29]*So when I was sent for, I came without raising any objection. May I ask why you sent for me?'*

[30]*Cornelius answered: 'Four days ago I was in my house praying at this hour, at three in the afternoon. Suddenly a man in shining clothes stood before me* [31]*and said, "Cornelius, God has heard your prayer and remembered your gifts to the poor.* [32]*Send to Joppa for Simon who is called Peter. He is a guest in the home of Simon the tanner, who lives by the sea."* [33]*So I sent for you immediately, and it was good of you to come. Now we are all here in the presence of God to listen to everything the Lord has commanded you to tell us.'*

The next day, Peter and his entourage set out north along the coastal road to Caesarea. They were a party of ten, the three Gentiles from Cornelius, Peter himself and *some of the brothers from Joppa* (23b), who numbered six (11:12). If they went on foot, it must have taken them a good nine or ten hours, apart from stops. So it was the following day that they reached their destination. They found a considerable company awaiting them, for *Cornelius was expecting them* and had assembled not only his personal household but also *his relatives and close friends* (24). His spiritual humility and receptivity may be judged from the fact that, *as Peter entered the house*, he 'threw himself at his feet – as if he were a heavenly visitant'.[16] It was an inappropriate gesture, how-

[16] Haenchen, p. 350.

ever. Peter *made him get up*, affirming that he was himself only a man.[17]

If Cornelius' act of falling down before Peter was unbecoming, so too according to Jewish tradition was Peter's act of entering a Gentile home. *It is against our law*, Peter said (28). This is not the best translation of *athemitos*, however, which 'denotes what is contrary to ancient custom or prescription (*themis*), rather than to positive enactment (*nomos*)'.[18] In fact, the word describes what is 'taboo'.[19] But now Peter felt at liberty to break this traditional taboo and to enter Cornelius' house, because God had shown him that no human being was unclean in his sight.

Whether consciously or unconsciously, Peter had just now repudiated both extreme and opposite attitudes which human beings have sometimes adopted towards one another. He had come to see that it was entirely inappropriate either to worship somebody as if divine (which Cornelius had tried to do to him) or to reject somebody as if unclean (which he would previously have done to Cornelius). Peter refused both to be treated by Cornelius as if he were a god, and to treat Cornelius as if he were a dog.

Peter went on to say that, having been sent for, he had come, *without raising any objection* (29), or 'without demur' (NEB). Why, then, had Cornelius sent for him?

In reply, Cornelius told the story of his vision of the angel (30–33) which had taken place four days previously. His account is identical with Luke's (3–6), except that he now calls the angel *a man in shining clothes* and omits any reference to the terror he had experienced at the time (4). He then thanked Peter for coming and added: *Now we are all here in the presence of God to listen to everything the Lord has commanded you to tell us* (33). It was a remarkable acknowledgement that they were in God's presence, that the apostle Peter was to be the bearer of God's word to them, and that they were all ready and open to listen to it. No preacher today could ask for a more attentive audience.

Peter began his sermon with a solemn personal statement of what he had learned through his experiences of the previous few days. He stated it both negatively and positively. First, '*I now realise how true it is that God does not show favouritism*' (34). *Prosōpolēmpsia* means 'partiality'. It was forbidden to judges in LXX, who were not to pervert justice by discriminating in favour of either the rich or the poor.[20] For with the divine judge 'there is no injustice or partiality or bribery'.[21] Peter's statement, however, has a wider connotation. He means that God's attitude to people is not

[17] *Cf.* Acts 14:11ff.; Rev. 19:10; 22:8–9. [18] Alexander, I, p. 403.
[19] Bruce, *English*, p. 222. [20] *E.g.* Lv. 19:15. [21] 2 Ch. 19:7.

determined by any external criteria, such as their appearance, race, nationality or class. Instead, and positively, God *accepts men from every nation who fear him and do what is right* (35). Better, and more literally, 'in every nation whoever fears God and works righteousness is acceptable (*dektos*) to him'. I will leave for the time being a full examination of this statement. It is enough now to draw attention both to its context in Acts 10 and to its contrast with 'no favouritism'. The emphasis is that Cornelius' Gentile nationality was acceptable so that he had no need to become a Jew, not that his own righteousness was adequate so that he had no need to become a Christian. For God is 'not indifferent of religions but indifferent of nations'.[22] As Lenski asks: 'If his honest pagan convictions had been sufficient, why did he seek the synagogue? If the synagogue had been enough, why was Peter here?'[23] Peter will soon teach him the necessity of faith for salvation (43).

After this introduction, affirming that 'there is no racial barrier to Christian salvation',[24] Luke summarizes Peter's sermon (36–43). Although it was addressed to a Gentile audience, its content was substantially the same as what he had been preaching to Jews. Indeed Peter said so, calling it both *the message God sent to the people of Israel* and *the good news of peace* (reconciliation with God and neighbour) *through Jesus Christ, who is Lord of all*, not just of Israel (36). It related to certain recent events, which Peter's audience knew about, because they had been public, and whose place and time Peter was able to pin-point: '*You know what has happened throughout Judea, beginning in Galilee after the baptism that John preached*' (37; *cf.* 1:22). These events centred on the historical Jesus, on the successive stages of his saving career, and on the salvation he offers in consequence.

First, Peter alluded to Jesus' life and ministry, *how God anointed Jesus of Nazareth* for his work as the Messiah, not with oil like the kings of Israel and Judah but *with the Holy Spirit and power*, that is, with the power of the Spirit.[25] Thus anointed, *he went around doing good and healing all who were under the power of the devil*, or 'tyrannized' by him,[26] so that his power was seen to be greater than the devil's, *because God was with him* (38; *cf.* 2:22). Moreover, Peter continued, '*we are witnesses* [eyewitnesses in fact] *of everything he did in the country of the Jews and in Jerusalem*' (39a), and are therefore able to give firsthand evidence or testimony. It is clear from this that 'some kind of an account of the life and character of Jesus formed an integral part of the early church's

[22] Bengel, p. 605. [23] Lenski, p. 419. [24] Haenchen, p. 351.
[25] Lk. 4:18. [26] Lenski, p. 422.

preaching, especially its initial evangelism'.[27]

Next came Jesus' death. The authorities *killed him* by crucifixion. But Peter hints, as he had done in his earlier sermons (2:23; 5:30), that behind the historical event lay a theological significance, behind the human execution a divine plan. For they had killed him *by hanging him on a tree* (39b). Peter was under no necessity to call the cross 'a tree'; he did it by design, in order to indicate that Jesus was bearing in our place the 'curse' or judgment of God on our sins.[28]

The third event was the resurrection (40–41). Peter emphasized that it was both a divine act (*they killed him . . . but God raised him from the dead*, the same dramatic contrast as in 2:23–24 and 5:30–31), and datable (*on the third day*). It was also physically verified, because God deliberately *caused him to be seen, not* indeed *by all the people, but by* special *witnesses whom God had already chosen*, especially by *us* apostles. Moreover, the resurrection body the apostles saw, although wonderfully transfigured and glorified, could nevertheless materialize, so that they *ate and drank with him*, and he with them, *after he rose from the dead*.[29]

The life, death and resurrection of Jesus were more than significant events; they also constituted the gospel, which *he commanded us* (the apostles again) *to preach*, in the first instance *to the people*, *i.e.* the Jews. But the scope of the gospel was universal. So the apostles were also to proclaim him as 'Lord of all' (36), as judge of all and as Saviour of all who believe. They were *to testify that* he would return on the judgment day, since *he is the one whom God appointed as judge of the living and the dead* (42; *cf.* 17:31). All will be included; none can escape. Yet we need not fear the judgment of Christ, since he is also the one who bestows salvation. Long before the apostles began to testify to him as Saviour, *all the prophets* did so in the Old Testament, and still do through their written words: they *testify about him*, the unique, historical, incarnate, crucified and resurrected Jesus, *that everyone who believes in him receives forgiveness of sins through his name* (43), that is, through the efficacy of who he is and what he has done. This 'everyone' includes Gentiles as well as Jews: the phrase 'crashes through the barrier' of race and nationality.[30]

[27] Stanton, p. 13. Against the insistence of Bultmann and others that the early church was concerned only about the risen Lord and not the historical Jesus, Professor Stanton takes what he calls the 'unfashionable' view that 'the early church was interested in the past of Jesus' (p. 186), that his life and character were part and parcel of its initial evangelistic preaching (p. 30), and that 'the resurrection faith of the church did not obscure' these things (p. 191).

[28] Dt. 21:22–23; *cf.* Gal. 3:10–13; 1 Pet. 2:24.

[29] *Cf.* Lk. 24:30, 41ff; Jn. 21:13; Acts 1:4.

[30] Haenchen, p. 353.

It was a marvellously comprehensive message, a précis of the good news according to Peter which Mark would later record more fully in his gospel, and which Luke incorporated in his. Focusing on Jesus, Peter presented him as a historical person, in and through whom God was savingly at work, who now offered to believers salvation and escape from judgment. Thus history, theology and gospel were again combined, as in other apostolic sermons. As Cornelius, his family, relatives, friends and servants listened, their hearts were opened to grasp and believe Peter's message, and so to repent and believe in Jesus.

Then, *while Peter was still speaking these words*, and before he had finished (11:15), *the Holy Spirit came on all* those Gentiles *who heard the message* and believed (44), which was the condition Peter had just mentioned (43). The small group of Jewish Christians (*circumcised believers*) *who had come with Peter* was *astonished* ('absolutely amazed', JBP) *that the gift of the Holy Spirit had been poured out even on the Gentiles* (45), whom they had regarded as uncircumcised outsiders. But they could not deny the evidence of their eyes and ears, *for they heard them speaking in tongues and praising God* (46), as had happened on the Day of Pentecost. It was 'a type of the reconciliation between Jew and Gentile, whose alienation had for ages been secured and symbolized by differences of language'.[31]

Peter was quick to draw the inevitable deduction. Since God had accepted these Gentile believers, which indeed he had (15:8), the church must accept them too. Since God had baptized them with his Spirit (11:16), '*Can anyone keep* [them] *from being baptised with water? They have received the Holy Spirit just as we have*' (47). How could the sign be denied to those who had already received the reality signified? Chrysostom expatiated on this logic. By giving the Spirit to Cornelius and his household before their baptism, God gave Peter an *apologia megalē* (a mighty reason or justification) for giving them water-baptism.[32] Yet in a sense their baptism 'was completed already',[33] for God had done it. Peter was clear that 'in no one point was he the author, but in every point God'. It was as if Peter said: 'God baptized them, not I.'[34]

So Peter *ordered that they be baptised in the name of Jesus Christ. Then*, having been welcomed into God's household, *they asked Peter to stay with them* in their household *for a few days* (48), no doubt in order to nurture them in their new faith and life. The gift of the Spirit was insufficient; they needed human teachers too. And Peter's acceptance of their hospitality demonstrated

[31] Alexander, I, p. 417. [32] Chrysostom, Homily XXIV, p. 155.
[33] *Ibid.*, p. 157. [34] *Ibid.*, p. 158.

the new Jewish-Gentile solidarity which Christ had established.

5. Peter justifies his actions (11:1–18)

The apostles and the brothers throughout Judea heard that the Gentiles also had received the word of God. [2]So when Peter went up to Jerusalem, the circumcised believers criticised him [3]and said, 'You went into the house of uncircumcised men and ate with them.'

[4]Peter began and explained everything to them precisely as it had happened: [5]'I was in the city of Joppa praying, and in a trance I saw a vision. I saw something like a large sheet being let down from heaven by its four corners, and it came down to where I was. [6]I looked into it and saw four-footed animals of the earth, wild beasts, reptiles, and birds of the air. [7]Then I heard a voice telling me, "Get up, Peter. Kill and eat."

[8]'I replied, "Surely not, Lord! Nothing impure or unclean has ever entered my mouth."

[9]'The voice spoke from heaven a second time, "Do not call anything impure that God has made clean." [10]This happened three times, and then it was pulled up to heaven again.

[11]'Right then three men who had been sent to me from Caesarea stopped at the house where I was staying. [12]The Spirit told me to have no hesitation about going with them. These six brothers also went with me, and we entered the man's house. [13]He told us how he had seen an angel appear in his house and say, "Send to Joppa for Simon who is called Peter. [14]He will bring you a message through which you and all your household will be saved."

[15]'As I began to speak, the Holy Spirit came on them as he had come on us at the beginning. [16]Then I remembered what the Lord had said, "John baptised with water, but you will be baptised with the Holy Spirit." [17]So if God gave them the same gift as he gave us, who believed in the Lord Jesus Christ, who was I to think that I could oppose God?'

[18]When they heard this, they had no further objections and praised God, saying, 'So then, God has even granted the Gentiles repentance unto life.'

The news that *the Gentiles also had received the word of God* spread far and wide. *The apostles and the brothers throughout Judea* heard about it. It is understandable that, just as the apostles needed to endorse the evangelization of the Samaritans who 'had accepted the word of God' (8:14), so now they were concerned about the conversion and baptism of the first Gentiles, who had similarly received it (1). Not that they summoned Peter to give an account of himself. Luke writes only that *Peter went up to Jerusalem* of his own accord (2). And the editor of the Bezan text, anxious to put this beyond question, added that Peter had 'for a considerable time wished to journey to Jerusalem', that he eventually did so on his own initiative, and that he 'reported to them the grace of God'.[35]

At all events, on arrival in Jerusalem, *the circumcised believers criticised him* for having entered *the house of uncircumcised men* and having eaten with them (3). Some have suggested that Peter's critics were 'the circumcision party' (JBP), that is, 'the right-wing Jewish Christians', 'the extremists' or 'the rigorists'.[36] But the Greek phrase need only mean 'those who were of Jewish birth' (NEB), namely the whole Christian community in Jerusalem, all of whom up to that time were Jews. Recent events in Caesarea had naturally disturbed them.

In verses 4–17 Peter *explained everything to them precisely as it had happened* (4). In fact Luke now rehearses the whole story a second time, but more briefly, with a different order of events, and through the lips of Peter. Luke's own narrative had followed the chronology of the four days, beginning with Cornelius' vision of the angel. Peter, however, because he is recounting things as he himself experienced them, begins with his own vision of the sheet, and does not mention Cornelius' vision until the fourth day, when he heard it from Cornelius' lips (although the three men from Cornelius had already mentioned it, 10:22). Peter's order of events is important because it helps us to live through his experience with him, and so to learn just how God had shown him that he should not call anybody impure or unclean (10:28). It took four successive hammer-blows of divine revelation before his racial and religious prejudice was overcome, as he explains to the Jerusalem church.

First came *the divine vision* (4–10) of the sheet containing animals, reptiles and birds. In verse 6 the *wild beasts* are an addition, and so is Peter's statement that he 'looked into' the sheet 'intently' (NEB). The vision was followed by the voice which gave Peter the startling order to *Get up . . . Kill and eat* and, after his protest, rebuked him that he was not to *call anything impure that God has made clean*. The whole vision, including the order and the rebuke, was repeated three times, so that the heavenly voice addressed him six times altogether with the same basic message. In consequence, Peter grasped that the clean and unclean animals (a distinction which Jesus had abolished)[37] were a symbol of clean and unclean, circumcised and uncircumcised persons. As Rackham put it, 'the sheet is the church', which will 'contain all races and classes without any distinction at all',[38] even though the full import of this dawned on Peter only later.

[35] Metzger, pp. 382–384. [36] Neil, pp. 141–142. [37] Mk. 7:19.
[38] Rackham, p. 153.

The second hammer-blow was *the divine command* (11–12) to accompany the three men who had come from Caesarea to fetch him. For 'at that very moment' (RSV), immediately after the vision had ended, Cornelius' men arrived at Peter's house, and the Spirit told him to go with them without hesitation or distinction (12), even though they were uncircumcised Gentiles. Indeed *these six brothers*, who were now with Peter in Jerusalem, had previously escorted him from Joppa to Caesarea (10:23), and so were witnesses of what had taken place. With Peter they made a group of seven, which William Barclay thought was significant, for 'in Egyptian law, which the Jews would know well, seven witnesses were necessary completely to prove a case', while 'in Roman law, which they would also know well, seven seals were necessary to authenticate a really important document like a will'.[39]

The third hammer-blow was *the divine preparation* (13–14). That is, as Peter and his party entered Cornelius' house, Cornelius told them how God had prepared him for their visit. An angel had appeared to him and told him to send to Joppa for Simon Peter, who would bring him a message of salvation. In Luke's own account the content of Cornelius' message to Peter had not been mentioned (10:5–6, 22, 32–33), but Peter knew what the angel had led Cornelius to expect.

As Peter retold to the Jerusalem church the story of the two visions, he must have been freshly impressed by the chronology. For God had been working at both ends, in Cornelius and in Peter, deliberately arranging for them to meet, and preparing for it by granting to each on successive days a special, independent and appropriate vision. He told Cornelius in Caesarea to send for Peter in Joppa, and Peter in Joppa to go to Cornelius in Caesarea, and he perfectly synchronized the two events. Haenchen thinks that Luke overdoes God's supernatural interventions, that he thereby 'virtually excludes all human decision' and turns the obedience of faith into 'very nearly the twitching of puppets'.[40] But this is unfair. To be sure, the divine intervention is plain, in the lives of both Cornelius and Peter, but neither of them was manipulated in such a way as to bypass his mind or will. On the contrary, they reflected on what they saw and heard, interpreted its significance, and deliberately chose to obey.

The fourth and final revelation to Peter was *the divine action* (15–17). For as Peter *began to speak*, or at least (since commentators warn us not to take this semitic construction too literally) while he was still speaking (10:44), *the Holy Spirit came on them* just as, he added, *he had come on us at the beginning*. It was the

[39] Barclay, pp. 91–92. [40] Haenchen, p. 362.

extraordinary similarity of the two events which struck him. He remembered what the risen Jesus had said after his resurrection (1:5), namely *John baptised with water, but you will be baptised with the Holy Spirit*. In other words, this was the Gentile Pentecost in Caesarea, corresponding to the Jewish Pentecost in Jerusalem.

Here, then, were the four divine hammer-blows which were all aimed deftly at Jewish racial prejudice, and especially at Peter's – the vision, the command, the preparation and the action. Together they demonstrated conclusively that God had now welcomed believing Gentiles into his family on equal terms with believing Jews. Peter was convinced. He at once drew the correct deduction from the fact that God had given the same gift of the Spirit to Gentiles as to Jews. He asked two rhetorical questions. The first was at the time: 'Can anyone keep these people from being baptised with water? They have received the Holy Spirit just as we have' (10:47). The second he addressed to his critics in Jerusalem: 'If God gave them the same gift as he gave us . . . , who was I to think that I could oppose God?' (11:17). Both questions were unanswerable. And they were the more striking because both contain an almost identical Greek expression, namely *dynatai kōlysai* (10:47) and *dynatos kōlysai* (11:17), literally 'able to forbid, refuse or prevent'. Water-baptism could not be forbidden to these Gentile converts, because God could not be forbidden to do what he had done, namely give them Spirit-baptism. The argument was irrefutable. Peter had been 'confronted with a divine *fait accompli*'.[41] To be sure, to give Christian baptism to an uncircumcised Gentile was a bold, innovative step, but to withhold it would be to 'stand in God's way' (NEB).

If Peter had been convinced by the evidence, so now was the Jerusalem church: *they had no further objections* (literally, 'they remained silent') *and praised God*. As F. F. Bruce neatly puts it, 'their criticism ceased; their worship began'.[42] And they had good reason to glorify God for, they concluded, *God has granted even the Gentiles repentance unto life* (11:18).

6. Lessons to learn

Luke tells the story of the conversion of Cornelius with great dramatic skill. But has it any abiding significance? There are no Roman centurions in the world today, and Gentiles have been full members of the church for centuries. So has this incident any more than a historical – even antiquarian – interest? Yes, it speaks directly to some modern questions about the church, the Holy Spirit, non-

[41] Bruce, *English*, p. 230. [42] *Ibid.*, p. 236.

Christian religions and the gospel.

a. The unity of the church

The fundamental emphasis of the Cornelius story is that, since God does not make distinctions in his new society, we have no liberty to make them either. Yet, tragic as it is, the church has never learned irrevocably the truth of its own unity or of the equality of its members in Christ. Even Peter himself, despite the fourfold divine witness he had received, later had a bad lapse in Antioch, withdrew from fellowship with believing Gentiles, and had to be publicly opposed by Paul.[43] Even then, the circumcision party continued their propaganda, and the Council of Jerusalem had to be called to settle the issue (Acts 15). Even after that, the same ugly sin of discrimination has kept reappearing in the church, in the form of racism (colour prejudice), nationalism ('my country, right or wrong'), tribalism in Africa and casteism in India, social and cultural snobbery,[44] or sexism (discriminating against women). All such discrimination is inexcusable even in non-Christian society; in the Christian community it is both an obscenity (because offensive to human dignity) and a blasphemy (because offensive to God who accepts without discrimination all who repent and believe). Like Peter, we have to learn that 'God does not show favouritism' (10:34).

b. The gift of the Spirit

Luke, whose keen interest in the ministry of the Holy Spirit we have already noted, gives much prominence to him in the Cornelius story. This rebukes those Christians who overlook or underplay his work today. Even if the speech in foreign languages, which characterized both the Jewish and the Gentile Pentecost (2:4; 10:46), is not a universal Christian blessing, the gift of the Spirit himself is. Yet this story also poses awkward questions to those who insist on a two-stage Christian initiation, since it is certain that Luke is describing Cornelius' conversion, and not a second, post-conversion baptism of the Spirit. For Peter preached the gospel to him, and Cornelius is said to have repented (11:18) and believed (15:7, 9). What he experienced is also called interchangeably either 'receiving' the gift of the Spirit (10:45, 47; 11:17) or being 'baptized' with the Spirit (11:16). In fact, Cornelius' water-baptism signified and sealed the total salvation (11:14) which God had given him, including both the forgiveness of sins and the gift of the Spirit (10:43, 45), as on the Day of Pentecost (2:38).

[43] Gal. 2:11ff. [44] Jas. 2:1ff.

c. *The status of non-Christian religions*

The story of Cornelius has developed a fresh importance in relation to the new pluralism of many societies and the contemporary assessment of non-Christian religions. Some argue that it is 'perhaps the most powerful pointer to the inclusiveness of God's saving activity' and contains statements which are 'important clues for a Christian understanding of the status before God of those who are not Christians in our day'.[45] We need, therefore, to examine carefully this 'pointer' and these 'clues'.

It is true that Luke describes Cornelius as a 'devout' (*eusebēs*, 'godly') and 'God-fearing' man, who 'gave generously to those in need and prayed to God regularly' (10:2). Later his own servants portray him as 'a righteous [*dikaios*] and God-fearing man, who is respected by all the Jewish people' (10:22), while Peter includes him among those who 'fear God and do what is right' (10:35). More than this, God is represented as being pleased with him. His prayers and gifts had 'come up as a memorial offering before God' (10:4, 31). This phrase 'memorial offering' translates *mnēmosynos*, a sacrificial word used in the LXX of the so-called 'memorial portion' of an offering which was burned.[46] Does this mean that Cornelius' prayers and alms had been 'accepted as a sacrifice in the sight of God' (31, JB)?[47] And what did Peter mean when he stated that God 'accepts' (*dektos*) in every nation those 'who fear him and do what is right' (10:35)? What kind of 'acceptability' to God is implied by this word *dektos* and by the use of sacrificial imagery in 10:4 and 31?

One possibility is that *dektos* refers to the acceptance called 'justification', but that fearing God and doing right (35) are 'not meritorious conditions or prerequisites to the experience of divine grace, but its fruits and evidences', and that Peter is describing believers rather than unbelievers (as, for example, Paul does in Rom. 2:10). The emphasis then is that God accepts whoever fears him and does right, not irrespective of their faith in Jesus (because they have believed and now show their faith by their works), but irrespective of their race and rank. 'The essential meaning is that whatever is acceptable to God in one race is acceptable in any other.'[48] An alternative explanation, however, seems to me to fit the context better. This is that *dektos* means not 'accepted' in the

[45] *Towards a Theology for Inter-Faith Dialogue* (Anglican Consultative Council, 1984; second edition, 1986), pp. 24–25. [46] *E.g.* Lv. 2:2, 9, 16.

[47] Some point to Is. 56:6ff. and Mal. 1:10–11 as teaching that God will accept the sacrifices of Gentiles. But in the former text the 'foreigners' in view are those who bind themselves to Yahweh, love his name and hold fast to his covenant, while in the latter Yahweh rejects the offerings of Israel and instead accepts the offerings of those nations among whom his 'name is great'. [48] Alexander, I, p. 409.

absolute sense of justified, but 'acceptable' in a comparative sense, because in everybody God prefers righteousness to unrighteousnes and sincerity to insincerity, and in the case of Cornelius God provided for him to hear the saving gospel.

What Peter emphatically did not mean is that anybody of any nation or religion who is devout ('fears God') and upright ('does right') is thereby justified. Calvin rightly dismisses this notion as 'an exceedingly childish error'.[49] Not only does it contradict Paul's gospel, which Luke faithfully echoes in the Acts, but it is refuted by the rest of the Cornelius story. For this devout, God-fearing, upright, sincere and generous man still needed to hear the gospel, to repent (11:18) and to believe in Jesus (15:7). Only then did God in his grace (15:11) save him (11:14, 15:11), give him forgiveness of sins (10:43), the gift of the Spirit (10:45; 15:8) and life (11:18), and purify his heart by faith (15:9). Moreover, only then was he baptized and thus visibly and publicly received into the Christian community.

It is, then, a misuse of Acts 10 and 11 to suggest that already before he heard Peter, Cornelius was in right relationship with God, or 'justified'. The essence of the story is that (negatively) God shows no favouritism (10:34) and makes no distinction between races (10:20, 29; 11:12; 15:9), and that (positively) he gave and gives the same Spirit to all alike, not irrespective of faith, but irrespective of circumcision.

d. *The power of the gospel*

Luke has now recounted the conversions of Saul and Cornelius. The differences between these two men were considerable. In race Saul was a Jew, Cornelius a Gentile; in culture Saul was a scholar, Cornelius a soldier; in religion Saul was a bigot, Cornelius a seeker. Yet both were converted by the gracious initiative of God; both received forgiveness of sins and the gift of the Spirit; and both were baptized and welcomed into the Christian family on equal terms. This fact is a signal testimony to the power and impartiality of the gospel of Christ, which is still 'the power of God for the salvation of everyone who believes; first for the Jew, then for the Gentile'.[50]

[49] Calvin, I, p. 288. [50] Rom. 1:16.

9. Expansion and opposition *11:19–12:24*

Luke ended his previous section with the words 'then to the Gentiles also God has granted repentance unto life' (18, RSV). It was an epoch-making declaration by the conservative Jewish leaders of the Jerusalem church. As Peter had become convinced by circumstantial evidence that God intended Gentiles to be welcomed into the redeemed community, so Peter's critics had been convinced by his rehearsal of the evidence. God himself had put the matter beyond dispute by bestowing his Spirit on a Gentile household.

The inclusion of the Gentiles is to be Luke's main theme in the rest of Acts, and with chapter 13 he begins to chronicle Paul's missionary exploits. Before this, however, he gives his readers two vignettes, which form a transition between the conversion of the first Gentile (through Peter) and the systematic evangelization of Gentiles (by Paul). The first (11:19–30) depicts the expansion of the church northwards, as a result of evangelistic activity by anonymous missionaries. The scene is Antioch, and Paul figures in the story, although Barnabas is more prominent. The second (12:1–25) depicts opposition to the church by King Herod Agrippa I, who concentrates his attack on members of the apostolic circle. The scene is Jerusalem, and Peter occupies the centre of the stage. In fact, this is Luke's final Peter-story before his leadership role is taken over by Paul, and Jerusalem is eclipsed by the goal of Rome.

1. Expansion: the church in Antioch (11:19–30)

The key expression at the end of the last paragraph was 'to the Gentiles also' (18, RSV); the key expression of this paragraph is 'to the Greeks also' (20, RSV). The addition in both verses of 'also' (*kai*) is important. It is not that the evangelization of the Jews must stop, but that the evangelization of the Gentiles must begin. As Paul was later to write (it was almost a refrain in the early chapters of Romans), the gospel was intended 'first for the Jew, then for the Gentile'.[1]

a. The Greek mission is initiated by unnamed evangelists (11:19–21)

Luke has written in 8:1 that, as a result of the persecution which broke out after Stephen's martyrdom, 'all except the apostles were scattered [*diesparēsan*] throughout Judea and Samaria'. He now resumes his narrative: *Now those who had been scattered* (*diasparentes*) *by the persecution in connection with Stephen travelled as far as Phoenicia, Cyprus and Antioch* (19a). In both cases he represents this fanning out of believers as a Christian 'diaspora' or dispersion. In both cases the result was the same, namely that 'those who had been scattered preached the word wherever they went' (8:4), *telling the message* (19b). And in both cases he leaves the evangelists unnamed, except for stating that they were not apostles (8:1) and mentioning Philip (8:5ff.).

Luke now shows how the outward movement of the gospel expanded in two ways, geographical and cultural. Geographically, the mission spread north beyond 'Judea and Samaria' (8:1b) *as far as Phoenicia*, corresponding to Lebanon today, the island of *Cyprus* and the city of Syrian *Antioch* (19). Culturally, the mission spread beyond Jews to Gentiles. Most of the missionaries were *telling the message only to Jews*, 'to Jews only and to no others' (19c, NEB). *Some of them, however, men* who came *from Cyprus* (which incidentally was Barnabas' home, 4:36) *and Cyrene* on the North African coast (did they perhaps include 'Lucius of Cyrene' mentioned in 13:1?) *went to Antioch and began to speak to Greeks also, telling them the good news about the Lord Jesus* (20), proclaiming Jesus, that is, not now as 'the Christ', but as 'the Lord'. Moreover their bold innovation was richly blessed by God, for *the Lord's hand was with them* (his power confirming his word), so that *a great number of people believed and turned to the Lord* (21) in that combination of repentance and faith which is commonly called 'conversion'. Some speculate that Luke himself was one of these converts, because the Western text introduces verse 28 with the words 'when *we* were gathered together', indicating that Luke was present, and because a tradition can be traced back to the end of the second century that Luke was a native of Antioch.

Is it certain, however, that these 'daring spirits'[2] did evangelize Greeks in Antioch, and not just Hellenists, that is, Greek-speaking Jews? This question has long occupied scholars. The slightly better

[1] Rom. 1:16; 2:9–10; *cf.* 3:29; 9:24; 10:12; 1 Cor. 1:24; 12:13; Col. 3:11.
[2] Bruce, *English*, p. 238.

attested reading in verse 20 is not *Hellēnas*, 'Greeks', but *Hellēnistas*, 'Hellenists'.

So who were they? The word itself (*Hellēnistēs*) does not tell us, for it 'is found nowhere in previous Greek literature or in Hellenistic-Jewish literature', writes Dr Bruce Metzger, and 'in the New Testament it occurs only here and in 6:1 and 9:29'. All that can be affirmed with confidence is that it 'appears to be a new formation from *hellēnizein*, "to speak Greek" or "to practise Greek ways" ';[3] it thus indicates the culture of the people in question, but not their nationality.

If, then, the meaning of the word is in itself uncertain, the context must decide. Yet even this is to a degree ambiguous. Some argue that the contrast between 'only to Jews' (19) and 'to Greeks also' (20) settles the matter. There would have been nothing remarkable about preaching to Greek-speaking Jews, for it had been going on from the beginning. It would not have called for a specal investigation from Jerusalem. So, they conclude, the context requires us (like most of the church fathers) to take *Hellēnistas* as a synonym for *Hellēnas* and to translate it 'Greeks', 'Gentiles', or (NEB, 1961 edition) 'pagans'.

Others point out, however, that, even if the narrower context is clear (the contrast in verses 19–20 between 'only Jews' and 'also Greeks'), the wider context is not. There would, in fact, be an anachronism in representing the full-scale Gentile mission as having been pioneered by anonymous evangelists in Antioch, since Luke reserves this innovation for Paul on his first missionary journey (Acts 13). He could hardly have intended to anticipate it here (Acts 11).

Since there is ambiguity in both word and context, it seems wise to look for a compromise solution between Greek-speaking Jews on the one hand and complete pagans on the other. Linguistically, we can be sure only that *Hellēnistas* denotes people whose language and culture are Greek; the word does not indicate their ethnic origin, whether 'the person be a Jew or a Roman or any other non-Greek'.[4] It certainly does not require that the person is a Jew. Contextually, Richard Longenecker suggests that the *Hellēnistas* were indeed Gentiles, but Gentiles 'who had some kind of relationship with Judaism', perhaps 'God-fearers'. His conclusion is 'that Luke did not look on the Greeks in verse 20 as simply Gentiles unaffected by the influence of Judaism and that he did not view the Hellenistic Christians' approach to them as pre-empting the uniqueness of Paul's later Gentile policy'.[5] Instead, *Hellēnistas* 'is to be understood in the broad sense of "Greek-speaking persons",

[3] Metzger, p. 386. [4] Ibid., p. 388. [5] Longenecker, *Acts*, pp. 400–401.

meaning thereby the mixed population of Antioch in contrast to the *Joudaioi* of verse 19'.[6] It is clear from both Acts 15:1 and Galatians 2:11ff. that in the church of Antioch Jews and Gentiles, the circumcised and the uncircumcised, were at that time enjoying table fellowship with one another.

This new outreach took place in *Antioch*, Luke tells us (20), and no more appropriate place could be imagined, either as the venue for the first international church or as the springboard for the world-wide Christian mission. The city was founded in 300 BC by Seleucus Nicator, one of Alexander the Great's generals. He named it 'Antioch' after his father Antiochus, and its port, fifteen miles west along the navigable river Orontes, 'Seleucia' after himself. Over the years it became known as 'Antioch the Beautiful' because of its fine buildings, and by Luke's day was famous for its long, paved boulevard, which ran from north to south and was flanked by a double colonnade with trees and fountains. Although it was a Greek city by foundation, its population, estimated as at least 500,000, was extremely cosmopolitan. It had a large colony of Jews, attracted by Seleucus' offer of equal citizenship, and orientals too from Persia, India and even China, earning it another of its names, 'the Queen of the East'. Since it was absorbed into the Roman Empire by Pompey in 64 BC, and became the capital of the imperial province of Syria (to which Cilicia was later added), its inhabitants included Latins as well. Thus Greeks, Jews, Orientals and Romans formed the mixed multitude of what Josephus called 'the third city of the empire', after Rome and Alexandria.[7]

b. The Greek mission is endorsed by Barnabas (11:22–24)

News of this fresh development *reached the ears of the church at Jerusalem*, much as they had previously heard 'that Samaria had accepted the word of God' (8:14) and 'that the Gentiles [*sc.* Cornelius and his household] also had received the word of God' (11:1). Luke seems to be hinting that they felt the need to assure themselves that all was well, in addition to helping nurture this young, multi-cultural church. This time they did not send an apostle, however. Instead, *they sent Barnabas to Antioch* (22), whom Barclay called 'the man with the biggest heart in the church',[8] and who was known to be true to his name 'Son of Encouragement' (4:36). *When he arrived* in Antioch, he immediately *saw* for himself *the evidence of the grace of God* in the converts' changed lives and new international community, and in consequence he both *was glad*, presumably expressing his joy in praise, *and encouraged them all* ('encouraged' being perhaps a deliberate play on his name) *to*

[6] Metzger, pp. 388–389. [7] Josephus, *Wars*, III.2.4. [8] Barclay, p. 95.

remain true to the Lord with all their hearts (23). It was an exhortation both to perseverance and to whole-heartedness. Luke was obviously impressed with Barnabas' Christian character, and attributed his ministry to it: for (it is a pity that NIV does not translate this connecting particle *hoti*) *he was a good man, full of the Holy Spirit and faith*. It is no wonder that *a great number of people were brought* (literally 'added', as RSV) *to the Lord* (24).

The verb for 'added' in verse 24 (*prostithēmi*) has become for Luke an almost technical word for church growth. He used it twice in relation to the Day of Pentecost, first of the three thousand who were added that day (2:41) and then of the daily additions which followed (2:47). Later he wrote of 'more and more men and women' believing in the Lord and being added to the church (5:14), while in Syrian Antioch 'a great number of people' were added (11:24). This use of the verb *prostithēmi* led the famous Dutch theologian Abraham Kuyper to propose the word 'prosthetics' to define missiology (although today it applies to the surgical replacement of limbs and organs), since it should be concerned with the expansion of the church by additions to its membership. Hermann Bavinck responded that it would not be an appropriate term, however, because in the New Testament it is the Lord who does the adding (2:47), not human missionaries.[9] We might also comment that the additions are not just to the church but to the Lord (11:24). When we see 'the Lord adding to the Lord', so that he is both subject and object, source and goal, of evangelism, we have to repent of all self-centred, self-confident concepts of the Christian mission.

c. *The Greek mission is consolidated by Saul (11:25–26)*

Barnabas' next action was to go *to Tarsus to look for Saul* (25), for Tarsus was Saul's home town to which the Jerusalem believers had sent him, when his life was threatened (9:28–30). That was seven or eight years previously. What he had been doing meanwhile we do not know, although in his letter to the Galatians he seems to indicate that he was preaching in Syria and Cilicia.[10] Some commentators have suggested that it was during this period that he suffered some of the physical persecutions to which he later referred,[11] and was disinherited by his family.[12]

We cannot help admiring Barnabas' humility in wanting to share the ministry with Saul, and his sense of strategy also. He must have known of Saul's calling to be the apostle to the Gentiles (9:15, 27), and it may well have been the Gentile conversions in Antioch

[9] See *An Introduction to the Science of Missions* by J. H. Bavinck, 1954 (Presbyterian and Reformed Publishing Co., 1960), p. xvii.

[10] Gal. 1:21ff. [11] 2 Cor. 11:23ff. [12] Phil. 3:8

which made him think of Saul. At all events, *when* Barnabas *found him, he brought him to Antioch*, and then *for a whole year Barnabas and Saul met with the church*, most of whose members were young and uninstructed believers, *and taught great numbers of people* (26a).

They must have taught about Christ, making sure that the converts knew both the facts and the significance of his life, death, resurrection, exaltation, Spirit-gift, present reign and future coming. Is it because the word 'Christ' was constantly on their lips that *the disciples were called Christians first at Antioch* (26b)? Luke has so far referred to them as 'disciples' (6:1), 'saints' (9:13), 'brethren' (1:16; 9:30), 'believers' (10:45), those 'being saved' (2:47) and the people 'of the Way' (9:2). Now it seems to have been the unbelieving public of Antioch, famed for their wit and nicknaming skill, who, supposing that 'Christ' was a proper name rather than a title (the Christ or Messiah), coined the epithet *Christianoi.* It was probably more familiar and jocular than derisory. Although it does not seem to have caught on initially, since elsewhere it appears only twice in the New Testament (Acts 26:28 and 1 Pet. 4:16), it at least emphasized the Christ-centred nature of discipleship. For the word's formation was parallel to *Hērōdianoi* (Herodians) and *Kaisarianoi* (Caesar's people); it marked out the disciples as being above all the people, the followers, the servants of Christ.

d. The Greek mission is authenticated by good works (11:27–30)

It was *during this time*, Luke continues, that *some prophets came down from Jerusalem to Antioch* (27). *One of them, named Agabus, stood up and through the Spirit predicted that a severe famine would spread over the entire Roman world* (the *oikoumenē* or 'inhabited earth' being regarded as more or less coterminous with the empire). Luke adds in parenthesis that this predicted famine *happened during the reign of Claudius* (28). Claudius ruled from AD 41 to 54, but historians do not record 'a severe and world-wide famine' (NEB) during this period. F. F. Bruce therefore proposes the more general expression 'great dearth' (AV), adding that this period 'was indeed marked by a succession of bad harvests and serious famines in various parts of the empire'.[13] For example, Josephus wrote of a great famine which during the reign of Claudius oppressed the people of Judea, so that 'many people died for want of what was necessary to procure food withal', although Queen Helena bought and distributed large quantities of corn and figs.[14]

Luke's concern, however, is not so much with the fulfilment of

[13] Bruce, *Greek*, p. 239; *English*, p. 243.
[14] Josephus, *Antiquities*, XX.2.5; *cf.* XX.5.2 and III.15.3.

Agabus' prophecy as with the generous response of Antioch's church. For *the disciples, each according to his ability, decided to provide help for the brothers living in Judea* (29). Moreover, their decision led to action. They were soon *sending their gift to the elders by Barnabas and Saul* (30), who, having ministered as evangelists and teachers, were glad now to minister as social workers also. This second visit of Saul's to Jerusalem, which Luke here records, seems (although not all scholars agree with this) to be the same as the second visit which Paul himself mentions in Galatians 2:1–10. The parallels are striking. He writes there that he travelled 'with Barnabas', that he went 'in response to a revelation' (*i.e.* Agabus' prophecy), and that the leaders urged him to 'continue to remember the poor', which was 'the very thing' he was 'eager to do', namely in bringing the famine relief.

One naturally wonders why, apart from the famine, the Jerusalem church was now so poor as to need this relief, and whether perhaps their extreme generosity which Luke has described in Acts 2 and 4 was a contributory factor. At all events, it was now the turn of the Antiochene believers to be generous. They gave *each according to his ability*,[15] just as the Jerusalem believers had previously distributed 'to anyone as he had need' (2:45; 4:35). I have often wondered if Marx knew these two passages and bracketed them in his mind. For in his famous 'Critique of the Gotha Programme' (1875), that is, of the united policy of the two wings of German socialism, he called for something much more radical than they proposed, when society can 'inscribe on its banners: from each according to his ability, to each according to his needs!'[16]

Whatever our political and economic convictions may be, these are plainly biblical principles, that is, ability on the one hand, need on the other, and how to relate them to each other. These principles should characterize the family of God. It is not an accident that the Jerusalem recipients of Antiochene relief are called 'brothers' (29). More important still, this brotherhood or family included both Jewish and Gentile believers, and the fellowship between them was illustrated in the relations between their two churches. The church of Jerusalem had sent Barnabas to Antioch; now the church of Antioch sent Barnabas, with Saul, back to Jerusalem. This famine relief anticipated the collection which Paul was later to organize, in which the affluent Greek churches of Macedonia and Achaia contributed to the needs of the impoverished churches of Judea.[17] Its importance to Paul was that it was a symbol of Gentile-Jewish solidarity in Christ, 'for if the Gentiles have shared in the Jews'

[15] *Cf.* 2 Cor. 8:3.
[16] *Karl Marx: Selected Writings*, ed. David McLellan (OUP, 1977), pp. 564–569
[17] 2 Cor. 8 – 9

spiritual blessings', he wrote, 'they owe it to the Jews to share with them their material blessings'.[18]

2. Opposition: the church in Jerusalem (12:1–25)

Luke has been recording one marvellous conversion after another – the three thousand on the Day of Pentecost, the Samaritans, the Ethiopian eunuch, Saul of Tarsus, the Gentile centurion Cornelius and the mixed crowd in Antioch. In concentric circles the word of God was spreading. Luke is about to describe that great leap forward we call the first missionary journey. But first he has to chronicle a serious setback in the death of James and the imprisonment of Peter, both of whom were apostles and leaders of the Jerusalem church. Herod Agrippa I was the tyrant responsible for this double assault upon the work of God. At the time it must have seemed a grave crisis, although Luke is able to go on to chronicle the rescue of Peter by the intervention of God. Thus the destructive power of Herod and the saving power of God are contrasted. Indeed, throughout church history the pendulum has swung between expansion and opposition, growth and shrinkage, advance and retreat, although with the assurance that even the powers of death and hell will never prevail against Christ's church, since it is built securely on the rock.

Herod Agrippa I was the grandson of Herod the Great. He shared some of his grandfather's characteristics, and after the emperors Caligula and Claudius had given him successive portions of Palestinian territory, his kingdom was as extensive as his grandfather's.

a. Herod's plot (12:1–4)

It was about this time (Luke is deliberately vague, and scholars dispute the exact order of the events he chronicles in Acts 10 to 12) *that King Herod* (Luke accurately uses the title which the emperor Caligula had given him) *arrested some who belonged to the church, intending to persecute them* (1). He must have been well informed about Jesus and his followers, for his uncle Antipas had known and tried Jesus.[19] He is also known to have been anxious to preserve the Roman peace in Palestine and therefore to have disliked minorities which threatened to disrupt it. It is fully in keeping with this policy that he sought to ingratiate himself with the Jews (who naturally despised him for his Roman upbringing and Edomite ancestry) by conscientiously observing the law and now by persecuting the church. So *he had James, the brother of*

[18] Rom. 15:27. [19] Lk. 23:7ff.; Acts 4:27.

John, put to death with the sword (2) or 'beheaded' (NEB). Jesus had warned both James and John, who had asked for the best seats in his kingdom, that they would drink his cup and share his baptism,[20] that is, participate in his sufferings. But it belongs to the mystery of God's providence why this was to mean execution for James and exile for John,[21] whereas for the time being Peter escaped James' fate which Herod intended for him also. For *when he saw that this pleased the Jews, he proceeded to seize Peter also. This happened during the Feast of Unleavened Bread* (3), which immediately followed Passover, and during which Jewish law permitted neither trials nor sentencing. *After arresting him*, therefore, Herod *put him in prison*, perhaps in the Tower of Antonia at the north-west corner of the temple area, *handing him over to be guarded*, in a maximum security arrangement, *by four squads of four soldiers each*, working by shifts so that each squad would be on duty for six hours at a time, or perhaps for only three hours during the night watches. *Herod intended to bring him out for public trial*, what today we might call a 'show trial', *after the Passover*, including the days which the festival of unleavened bread lasted (4). Peter's trial would then, of course, be followed by his execution.

The situation looked extremely bleak, even hopeless. There appeared to be no possibility of Peter's escape. What could the little community of Jesus, in its powerlessness, do against the armed might of Rome?

b. Herod's defeat (12:5–19a)

The Jerusalem church will not have forgotten Peter's two previous imprisonments, although they had been at the hand of the Sanhedrin (4:3; 5:18). Nor will they have forgotten how Peter and John, after their first release, had joined the rest of the church in prayer, affirming that God was sovereign and that Herod Antipas and Pontius Pilate, the Gentiles and the Jews, had conspired against Jesus to do only what his 'power and will had decided beforehand should happen' (4:23–28). As for the apostles' second imprisonment, an angel of the Lord had opened the doors of the jail and set them free (5:19); could he not do it again? *So*, even while *Peter was kept in prison, the church was earnestly praying to God for him* (5). Luke uses the adverb *ektenōs* (JB, 'unremittingly'; NEB, 'fervently'), which he has previously applied to Jesus' intense agony in Gethsemane.[22] They believed that somehow, whether or not by another miracle, God could grant release to the jailed apostle in answer to their prayers.[23] Here then were two communities, the world and the church, arrayed against one another, each wielding

[20] Mk. 10:38–39. [21] Rev. 1:9. [22] Lk. 22:44. [23] *Cf.* Phil. 1:19; Phm. 22.

an appropriate weapon. On the one side was the authority of Herod, the power of the sword and the security of the prison. On the other side, the church turned to prayer, which is the only power which the powerless possess.

The night before Herod was to bring him to trial, Peter was sleeping between two soldiers, bound with two chains, and sentries stood guard at the entrance (6). Luke deliberately stresses the thoroughness with which the apostle was being guarded against escape or rescue. Normally it was considered enough for a prisoner to be handcuffed to one soldier, but as a special precaution Peter had a soldier each side of him and both his wrists were manacled, while outside the cell the other two soldiers of the squad were on duty. In spite of the seeming impossibility of liberation, and the extreme likelihood that on the following day he would suffer the same fate as James (in fulfilment of Jesus' prophecy that he would die as a martyr),[24] Peter showed no sign of anxiety, let alone alarm. On the contrary, he fell fast asleep. Later Paul, in a similar situation in Philippi, was to pray and sing to God (16:25). This leads Chrysostom to comment: 'It is beautiful that Paul sings hymns, whilst here Peter sleeps.'[25] Both Luke's heroes, Peter and Paul, showed themselves to be equally defiant of death.

Then *suddenly an angel of the Lord appeared*. Our understanding of who this 'angel' was will depend largely on our presuppositions, and in particular whether we believe in the existence of angels and the possibility of the miraculous. It is true that the word *angelos* can be translated simply 'messenger' and that Luke used it of human beings several times in his Gospel, for example of the messengers John the Baptist sent to Jesus (Lk. 7:24), of John the Baptist himself (7:27) and of those Jesus sent on ahead to get things ready for him (9:52). Consequently, I suppose one could just argue that a human messenger is meant here. Moreover, according to William Neil, some would regard Peter's release 'as no less of a "miracle" if it was engineered by sympathizers among the guard'.[26] And R. P. C. Hanson finds it 'reasonable' to understand that Peter 'managed to escape because of bribery, negligence or simply a change of mind on the part of the authorities'.[27] But the key hermeneutical question is what Luke himself intended us to understand, and of that there is little doubt. He has already referred to supernatural angelic beings on about fifteen occasions in his Gospel and the early chapters of Acts, and his emphasis in this story is on a divine intervention through a heavenly agent. So, as if to make this fact unequivocal, *a light shone in the cell*, and the release was

[24] Jn. 21:18–19. [25] Chrysostom, Homily XXVI, p. 172. [26] Neil, p. 149.
[27] Hanson, pp. 133–134.

accomplished in a succession of swift actions, while Peter was still half asleep and uncertain if he was dreaming. Luke's narrative needs no further comment:

[7]*Suddenly an angel of the Lord appeared and a light shone in the cell. He struck Peter on the side and woke him up. 'Quick, get up!' he said, and the chains fell off Peter's wrists.*

[8]*Then the angel said to him, 'Put on your clothes and sandals.' And Peter did so. 'Wrap your cloak around you and follow me,' the angel told him.* [9]*Peter followed him out of the prison, but he had no idea that what the angel was doing was really happening; he thought he was seeing a vision.* [10]*They passed the first and second guards and came to the iron gate leading to the city. It opened for them by itself, and they went through it. When they had walked the length of one street, suddenly the angel left him.*

[11]*Then Peter came to himself and said, 'Now I know without a doubt that the Lord sent his angel and rescued me from Herod's clutches and from everything the Jewish people were anticipating.'*

When this had dawned on him, for Peter was fully awake now, *he went to the house of Mary the mother of John, also called Mark* (12). That it was natural for him to go straight there suggests that it was a well-known (even the principal) meeting place of the Jerusalem believers. The Mary to whom it belonged is known only as the mother of John Mark, a cousin of Barnabas,[28] who is here mentioned by Luke for the first time and who is soon to feature in his story again as the renegade member of the first missionary journey (12:25; 13:5, 13). Some commentators have speculated that this house of Mary contained the 'large upper room, furnished and ready', which Mark himself mentions[29] as the place where Jesus ate the passover with the Twelve before his arrest, trial and crucifixion. Perhaps it was also the house where the Twelve lived, and they and others met to pray, during the ten days between the Ascension and Pentecost (1:12–14). It was certainly spacious, for it had an outer entrance or vestibule where Peter knocked, and presumably a courtyard between this and the main house. It was here, at all events, although it was in the middle of the night, that *many people had gathered and were praying* (12).

When *Peter knocked at the outer entrance*, the praying group must immediately have imagined that they had received a visit from the secret police. As they waited in suspense, *a servant girl named Rhoda* (who figured so prominently in this episode that her name was remembered and recorded) *came to answer the door* (13). *When she recognised Peter's voice*, because it was customary in those days

[28] Col. 4:10. [29] Mk. 14:15.

for visitors to call out as well as to knock, *she was so overjoyed* that *she ran back*, leaving Peter standing outside the door, *without opening it, and exclaimed, 'Peter is at the door!'* (14). *'You're out of your mind,'* they told her. It is ironical that the group who were praying fervently and persistently for Peter's deliverance should regard as mad the person who informed them that their prayers had been answered! Rhoda's simple joy shines brightly against the dark background of the church's incredulity. *When she kept insisting that it was so*, because she was sure she had rightly identified Peter's voice, they changed their tune and said, *'It must be his angel'* (15), referring to what are rather loosely called 'guardian angels'.[30] As F. F. Bruce puts it, 'The angel is here conceived of as a man's spiritual counterpart, capable of assuming his appearance and being mistaken for him.'[31] *But Peter kept on knocking, and when*, at last, *they opened the door and saw him, they were astonished* (16). They must also have broken into a chorus of noisy greetings, for *Peter motioned with his hand for them to be quiet*, perhaps fearful of the danger if the clamour woke the neighbours, *and described how the Lord had brought him out of prison.* He then gave them a single instruction: *'Tell James* [that is, the Lord's brother, who seems already to be recognized as the leader of the Jerusalem church, *cf.* 15:13, 21:18; Gal. 1:19; 2:9, 12] *and the brothers* [the rest of the Christian assembly in Jerusalem] *about this.' Then he left for another place* (17). This was definitely not Rome, as the apocryphal *Acts of Peter* suggested, and as some Roman Catholic commentators used to argue, adding that he stayed there for twenty-five years as the first pope. Luke means simply that he went into temporary hiding, whether or not anybody knew where. What we do know is that a year or two later he was in Antioch,[32] and then back in Jerusalem for the meeting of the Council (15:7ff.).

Perhaps the most important statement of the whole narrative of Peter's deliverance is in verse 17: 'the Lord had brought him out of prison.' The dramatic details Luke includes all seem to emphasize the intervention of God and the passivity of Peter. Peter was asleep, and the angel had to nudge him awake. His chains fell off. The order to dress was given as though by numbers: 'Get up; put on your clothes and sandals; wrap your cloak round you; and follow me.' They passed the guards on duty in the corridor, who were presumably in a deep sleep, and the external prison gate opened automatically. Peter himself did not know if it was all fact or fantasy, reality or dream.

In the morning, on the very day on which Peter was to be tried

[30] *Cf.* Mt. 18:10. [31] Bruce, *Greek*, p. 247. [32] Gal. 2:11.

and executed, *there was no small commotion among the soldiers as to what had become of Peter*, for their prisoner was nowhere to be found (18). When the news reached *Herod*, he first *had a thorough search made for him*, and then, when he *did not find him, he cross-examined the guards and*, because in Roman law a gaoler who allowed his charge to escape was liable to the penalty to which the prisoner had been condemned (*cf.* 16:27; 27:42), *ordered that they be executed* (19a).

c. *Herod's death (12:19b–24)*

Although Herod's victim had escaped his clutches, Herod himself was still at large. So Luke ends this part of his chronicle by describing the tyrant's death. He *went from Judea to Caesarea*, the provincial capital, *and stayed there a while* (19b). Luke then sketches the history behind the incident he is about to relate. Herod *had been quarrelling with the people of Tyre and Sidon* on the Phoenician coast, or was 'furiously angry' (NEB) with them. So *they now joined together and sought an audience with him*. For this they needed an intermediary. So *having secured the support* (perhaps by a bribe) *of Blastus*, who is identified as *a trusted personal servant of the king* or 'the royal chamberlain' (NEB), *they asked for peace*. It was urgent for them to be restored to Herod's favour, *because they depended on the king's country for their food supply*, especially Galilean corn.

That was the background. Now *on the appointed day*, on which Blastus was to present their case to him, *Herod, wearing his royal robes, sat on his throne and delivered a public address to the people* or 'harangued them' (NEB, 21). The crowd shouted, '*This is the voice of a god, not of a man*' (22). And *immediately, because Herod did not give praise to God*, and had in fact 'usurped the honour due to God' (NEB), *an angel of the Lord struck him down, and he was eaten by worms and died* (23).

Josephus also described in graphic detail the circumstances surrounding Herod's death.[33] His account and Luke's differ from one another in a few details, which shows that they are independent. But their general outline is the same. Both agree that Herod was in Caesarea at the time, although Josephus said he had gone there to participate in a festival in honour of Caesar, which was attended by a large crowd of leading citizens. Both mention the royal robes he was wearing, while Josephus adds the detail that his garment was 'made wholly of silver and of a contexture truly wonderful', which shone so brightly in the morning sun that the people hailed him as a god. 'Upon this', Josephus continued, 'the king did neither

[33] Josephus, *Antiquities*, XIX.8.2.

rebuke them, nor reject their impious flattery.' Luke and Josephus agree, therefore, that God's judgment fell upon him because he glorified himself instead of God. Although Luke says 'he was eaten by worms', Josephus is content with the more general statement that 'a severe pain . . . arose in his belly', which became so violent that he was carried into his palace, where five days later he died. Their description is reminiscent of the last days of that arch-persecutor Antiochus Epiphanes who in his arrogance 'had thought to grasp the stars of heaven', but 'was seized with an incurable pain in his bowels and with excruciating internal torture', until he died.[34]

Dr A. Rendle Short, who was professor of surgery at Bristol University and wrote a book entitled *The Bible and Modern Medicine*, stated that a great many people in Asia 'harbour intestinal worms', which can form a tight ball and cause 'acute intestinal obstruction'. This may have been the cause of Herod's death.[35]

It is in striking contrast to the death of the tyrant, that Luke adds one of his summary verses: *But the word of God continued to increase and spread* (24, *cf.* 6:7; 9:31). Indeed, one cannot fail to admire the artistry with which Luke depicts the complete reversal of the church's situation. At the beginning of the chapter Herod is on the rampage – arresting and persecuting church leaders; at the end he is himself struck down and dies. The chapter opens with James dead, Peter in prison and Herod triumphing; it closes with Herod dead, Peter free, and the word of God triumphing. Such is the power of God to overthrow hostile human plans and to establish his own in their place. Tyrants may be permitted for a time to boast and bluster, oppressing the church and hindering the spread of the gospel, but they will not last. In the end, their empire will be broken and their pride abased.

[34] 2 Macc. 9:5ff. (JB).
[35] *The Bible and Modern Medicine* by Rendle Short (Paternoster, 1955), pp. 66–68.

C. THE APOSTLE TO THE GENTILES
Acts 12:25–21:17

10. The first missionary journey
12:25–14:28

Luke has reached a decisive turning point in his narrative. In keeping with the risen Lord's prophecy (1:8), witness has been borne to him 'in Jerusalem' and 'in all Judea and Samaria': now the horizon broadens to 'the ends of the earth'. The two deacon-evangelists have prepared the way – Stephen by his teaching and his martyrdom, Philip by his bold evangelization of the Samaritans and the Ethiopian. So have the two major conversions which Luke has documented, that of Saul, who was also commissioned as the apostle to the Gentiles, and that of Cornelius through the instrumentality of the apostle Peter. Unnamed evangelists have also preached the gospel to 'Hellenists' in Antioch. But all the time the action has been limited to the Palestinian and Syrian mainland. Nobody has yet caught the vision of taking the good news to the nations overseas, although indeed Cyprus has been mentioned in 11:19. Now at last, however, that momentous step is to be taken.

1. Barnabas and Saul are sent out from Antioch (12:25 – 13:4a)

These two men have been south in Jerusalem, in order to hand over the famine relief money contributed by the church of Antioch (11:30). Now that they *had finished this mission, they returned from Jerusalem* (12:25). It is true that the better reading is '*to* Jerusalem', in which case the verse would have to read that 'they returned after they had fulfilled at Jerusalem their mission'. But this is clumsy, and the textual evidence needs to be overridden by the demands of the context, namely that Barnabas and Saul, who had travelled *to* Jerusalem from Antioch with their gift (11:30), now returned *from* Jerusalem to Antioch after they had delivered it (12:25).[1] Moreover, they took *with them John, also called Mark*,

[1] See Metzger, pp. 398–400.

who will accompany them when they set out on the first missionary expedition.

The cosmopolitan population of Antioch was reflected in the membership of its church, and indeed in its leadership, which consisted of five resident *prophets and teachers*. Luke explains neither how he understood the distinction between these ministries, nor whether all five men exercised both or (as some have suggested) the first three were prophets and the last two teachers. What he does tell us is their names. The first was *Barnabas*, whom he has earlier described as 'a Levite from Cyprus' (4:36). Secondly, there was *Simeon* (a Hebrew name) *called Niger* ('black') who was presumably a black African, and just conceivably none other than Simon of Cyrene who carried the cross for Jesus[2] and who must have become a believer, since his sons Alexander and Rufus were known to the Christian community.[3] The third leader, *Lucius of Cyrene*, definitely came from North Africa, but the conjecture of some early church fathers that Luke was referring to himself is extremely improbable, since he carefully preserves his anonymity throughout the book. Fourthly, there was *Manaen*, who is called in the Greek the *syntrophos* of *Herod the tetrarch*, that is, of Herod Antipas, son of Herod the Great. The word may mean that Manaen was 'brought up with' him in a general way, or more particularly that he was his 'foster-brother' or 'intimate friend'. In either case, since Luke knew a lot about Herod's court and family, Manaen may well have been his informant. The fifth church leader was *Saul*, who of course came from Tarsus in Cilicia. These five men, therefore, symbolized the ethnic and cultural diversity of Antioch.

It was *while they were worshipping the Lord and fasting* that *the Holy Spirit said* to them, '*Set apart for me Barnabas and Saul for the work to which I have called them*' (2). So important was this occasion, that it may be helpful to ask some questions about it.

First, to whom did the Holy Spirit reveal his will? Who is the 'they' who were worshipping and fasting, and to whom he spoke? It seems unlikely that we are meant to restrict them to the small group of five leaders, for that would entail three of them being instructed about the other two. It is more probable that the church members as a whole are in mind, since both they and the leaders are mentioned together in verse 1, and on the not dissimilar occasion when the seven were to be chosen, it was the local church as a whole who acted (6:2–6). Moreover, when Paul and Barnabas returned, 'they gathered the church together'. They reported to the church because they had been commissioned by the church (14:26–27). Further, if the Holy Spirit disclosed his purpose to the

[2] Lk. 23:26. [3] Mk. 15:21 and perhaps Rom. 16:13.

church, there is no need to except Barnabas and Saul themselves. Rather the reverse. Does not the Holy Spirit's instruction to set them apart 'for the work to which I have called them' imply that he had already called them before he made it known to the church?

Secondly, what was it that the Holy Spirit revealed to the church? It was very vague. The nature of the work to which he had called Barnabas and Saul was not specified. It was not unlike the call of Abram. To him God had said, 'Go to the land I will show you.'[4] To the Antiochene church God said, 'Set apart for me Barnabas and Saul for the work to which I have called them.' In both cases the call to go was clear, while the land and the work were not. So in both cases the response to God's call required an adventurous step of faith.

Thirdly, how was God's call disclosed? We are not told. The most likely guess is that God spoke to the church through one of the prophets. But his call could have been inward rather than outward, that is, through the Spirit's witness in their hearts and minds. However it came to them, their first reaction was to fast and pray, partly (it seems) to test God's call and partly to intercede for the two who were to be sent out. We notice that in neither reference to fasting does it occur alone. It is linked with worship in verse 2 and with prayer in verse 3. For seldom if ever is fasting an end in itself. It is a negative action (abstention from food and other distractions) for the sake of a positive one (worshipping or praying). Then, *after they had fasted and prayed*, and so assured themselves of God's call and prepared themselves to obey it, *they placed their hands on them and sent them off* (3). This was not an ordination to an office, still less an appointment to apostleship (since Paul insists that this was 'not from men nor by man'[5]), but rather a valedictory commissioning to missionary service.

Who, then, commissioned the missionaries? That is our fourth question. According to verse 4, Barnabas and Saul were *sent on their way by the Holy Spirit* , who had previously instructed the church to set them apart for him (2). But according to verse 3 it was the church which, after the laying-on of hands, *sent them off*. It is true that the latter verb could be translated 'let them go' (NEB), discharging them from their teaching responsibilities in the church at Antioch, in order to make them available for a wider ministry. For Luke sometimes uses the verb *apolūo* in the sense of 'release'.[6] But he also uses it for 'dismiss'.[7] So, in our anxiety to do justice to the Holy Spirit's initiative, we should not depict the church's role as having been entirely passive. Would it not be true to say

[4] Gn. 12:1. [5] Gal. 1:1. [6] *E.g.* Acts 3:13; 5:40; 16:35–36.
[7] *E.g.* Acts 15:30, 33; 19:40.

both that the Spirit sent them out, by instructing the church to do so, and that the church sent them out, having been directed by the Spirit to do so? This balance will be a healthy corrective to opposite extremes. The first is the tendency to individualism, by which a Christian claims direct personal guidance by the Spirit without any reference to the church. The second is the tendency to institutionalism, by which all decision-making is done by the church without any reference to the Spirit. Although we have no liberty to deny the validity of personal choice, it is safe and healthy only in relation to the Spirit and the church. There is no evidence that Barnabas and Saul 'volunteered' for missionary service; they were 'sent' by the Spirit through the church. Still today it is the responsibility of every local church (especially of its leaders) to be sensitive to the Holy Spirit, in order to discover whom he may be gifting and calling.

2. Barnabas and Saul in Cyprus (13:4b–12)

The two of them, missionaries from the church of Antioch, *sent on their way by the Holy Spirit, went down to Seleucia*, the port near the mouth of the River Orontes, about fifteen miles away, *and sailed from there to Cyprus* (4). We are not told why Cyprus was chosen as their first destination, although we know that Barnabas was a Cypriot (4:36). In what follows Luke is inevitably selective. To begin with, he concentrates on Paul's exploits to the west and north, with his eyes on Rome, and says nothing about the church's expansion east and south, or about the missionary adventures of other apostles, for example of Thomas who, according to the Syrian Orthodox and Mar Thoma churches of Kerala, travelled from Syria to India. Even in Paul's travels Luke is selective, according both to his available sources and to his editorial purposes. Thus in the first missionary journey, although he sketches the whole itinerary, he focuses on three main incidents. He portrays Paul evangelizing the proconsul and confronting the sorcerer in Paphos, the provincial capital of Cyprus, preaching the gospel in the synagogue in Pisidian Antioch in south Galatia, and addressing a pagan crowd in the open air in Lystra. They illustrate the extraordinary versatility of the apostle in adapting himself to different situations; he appeared to be equally at ease with individuals and crowds, Jews and Gentiles, the religious and the irreligious, the educated and the uneducated, the friendly and the hostile.

When they arrived at Salamis, a commercial city on the east coast of Cyprus, *they proclaimed the word of God in the Jewish synagogues* there. But Luke tells us no more than this, except that *John* (*i.e.* Mark, 12:25) *was with them as their helper* (5). We would like to know what kind of help he gave them, and whether we are correct in supposing that, whereas Barnabas and Saul had been specially chosen and sent by the Holy Spirit, John Mark had been chosen by them, without a similar direct divine call. All we can say is that the word *hypēretēs* was used of a servant or assistant of doctors, army officers, priests and politicians, and does not tell us whether Mark's service was pastoral (*e.g.* instructing enquirers and nurturing converts) or practical (*e.g.* cooking and cleaning).

On leaving Salamis, *they travelled through the whole island until they came to Paphos* (6a). This took them from the east coast to the west coast, a journey of about ninety miles, which Ramsay argued from Luke's use of the verb *dierchomai* was 'a preaching tour through the whole island'.[8] *There*, in Paphos, *they met* a man whom Luke immediately characterizes as *a Jewish sorcerer and false prophet named Bar-Jesus*, 'son of salvation' (6). By profession he *was an attendant of* (literally just 'with') *the proconsul, Sergius Paulus*, that is, a kind of court wizard. *The proconsul*, whom Luke describes as *an intelligent man*, in spite of his evident fascination for superstitious and occult practices, *sent for Barnabas and Saul because* in his intellectual and spiritual hunger *he wanted to hear the word of God* (7). Without doubt the missionaries responded to his summons, and we are free to imagine Paul the Christian apostle sharing with Paul the Roman proconsul the good news of Jesus Christ.

But Elymas the sorcerer (for that is what his name means) opposed them. Luke now refers to him by a different name, and the words in parenthesis have perplexed the commentators. JB may be right to translate them simply 'Elymas Magos – as he was called in Greek'. Alternatively, if Luke is explaining the meaning of the word 'Elymas', it may have been originally an Arabic word for somebody 'skilful' or 'expert', in other words a *magos* or wise man. At all events, Elymas saw in the Christian missionaries a threat to his prestige and livelihood. So he *tried to turn the proconsul from the faith* (8). This attempt the apostle saw as an extremely serious attack by the evil one, so that he now confronted Elymas Magus as Peter had confronted Simon Magus in Samaria (8:20ff.). Luke chooses this moment to inform us that *Saul . . . was also called Paul*. It was common for Jews to take a Greek or Roman second name, like Joseph Barsabbas (1:23) and John Mark (12:12, 25), and it was appropriate for Luke to mention Saul's now as he moves into increasingly non-Jewish contexts. He does not call Paul 'Saul' again. Next, he tells us that Paul was freshly *filled with the Holy Spirit*, to show that his boldness, outspokenness and power in

[8] Ramsay, *St Paul*, p. 73.

condemning Elymas were all from God. Thus endowed, he *looked straight at Elymas*, fixing him with his eye, *and said* (9): '*You are a child of the devil and an enemy of everything that is right! You are full of all kinds of deceit and trickery. Will you never stop perverting the right ways of the Lord? Now the hand of the Lord is against you. You are going to be blind, and for a time you will be unable to see the light of the sun*' (10–11a).

Paul's condemnation of Elymas was that he belied his name, 'Bar-Jesus', being rather a child of the devil than of salvation, and that he was the enemy of both goodness and truth, being an 'utter impostor and charlatan' (NEB, 1961 edition). In keeping with his character, he made crooked the straight paths of the Lord, and was guilty of causing 'perversion' (*diastrephō*, 8, 10), instead of 'conversion' (*epistrephō, e.g.* 9:35; 11:21; 14:15).

God's judgment of him was fitting. For those 'who put darkness for light and light for darkness'[9] forfeit the light they originally had. *Immediately*, therefore, *mist and darkness* (Dr Luke uses two contemporary medical terms) *came over him, and he groped about, seeking someone to lead him by the hand* (11b). Paul must have remembered the day not many years previously when he himself had been blinded, albeit by the glory of the Lord, and been led by the hand into Damascus.

When the proconsul saw what had happened, he believed, for he was amazed ('deeply impressed', NEB; 'shaken to the core', JBP) *at the teaching about the Lord* (12). What astonished him was the combination of word and sign, of the apostle's teaching and the sorcerer's defeat. There is no need to argue, as some have done, that because no baptism is mentioned the proconsul was not truly converted, or that the missionaries 'may have mistaken courtesy for conversion'.[10] The statement that *he believed* is plain enough and is in keeping with Luke's general usage elsewhere (*e.g.* 14:1; 17:34; 19:18). He gives no indication, as he did in relation to Simon Magus (8:13, 18ff.), that the proconsul's faith was profession without reality. No, he brings before his readers a dramatic power encounter, in which the Holy Spirit overthrew the evil one, the apostle confounded the sorcerer, and the gospel triumphed over the occult. More than that, Luke surely intends us to view Sergius Paulus as the first totally Gentile convert, who had no religious background in Judaism. Paul's direct approach to Gentiles was 'the great innovative development of this first missionary journey'.[11]

[9] Is. 5:20. [10] *BC*, IV, p. 147. [11] Longenecker, *Acts*, p. 420.

3. Paul and Barnabas in Pisidian Antioch (13:13–52)

From Paphos, Paul and his companions sailed north *to Perga in Pamphylia* (13a). In so doing, they crossed from 'Barnabas's native island' to the south coast of 'Paul's native land, Asia Minor'.[12] They probably landed at Attalia and then walked approximately twelve miles inland to Perga.

Here in Perga they suffered a setback: *John left them to return to Jerusalem* (13b). Luke announces the fact in a matter-of-fact manner and appears to apportion no blame. But it becomes clear in 15:38 that he sees Mark as having 'deserted them'. Later, however, he recovered and again became 'helpful' to Paul in his ministry.[13] Why then did he desert? A variety of conjectures has been made. Was he homesick, missing his mother, her spacious Jerusalem home, and the servants? Did he resent the fact that the partnership of 'Barnabas and Saul' (2, 7) had become 'Paul and Barnabas' (13, 46, *etc.*), since Paul was now taking the lead and eclipsing his cousin? Did he, as a loyal member of Jerusalem's conservative Jewish church, disagree with Paul's bold policy of Gentile evangelism? Was it even he who, on his return to Jerusalem, provoked the Judaizers into opposing Paul (15:1ff.)? Or did Mark simply not relish the stiff climb over the Taurus mountains which were known to be infested with brigands (*cf.* Paul's 'in danger from bandits'[14])? We do not know.

Or was it that Paul was sick and that Mark thought it foolhardy that he was determined to go north over the mountains? We do know that, when Paul reached the cities of the south Galatian plateau, he was suffering from a debilitating illness ('it was because of an illness that I first preached the gospel to you'[15]). It seems to have disfigured him in some way, so that the Galatians might have treated him with contempt,[16] and to have affected his eyesight, so that if possible they would have given him their own eyes.[17] Sir William Ramsay suggested that Paul suffered from 'a species of chronic malaria fever' (which the ancient Greeks and Romans both knew and feared); that it involved 'very distressing and prostrating paroxysms', together with stabbing headaches 'like a red-hot bar thrust through the forehead' (perhaps his 'thorn in the flesh'[18]); and that it was his fever which necessitated leaving the enervating climate of the low-lying coastal plain, in spite of the rigorous climb involved, in order to seek the bracing cool of the Taurus plateau some 3,500 feet above sea level.[19] Perhaps it was this hurry which explains why the missionaries did not stay to evangelize Perga,

[12] Bruce, *English*, p. 266. [13] Col. 4:10; 2 Tim. 4:11. [14] 2 Cor. 11:26.
[15] Gal. 4:13. [16] Gal. 4:14. [17] Gal. 4:15. [18] 2 Cor. 12:7.
[19] Ramsay, *St Paul*, pp. 92–97; *cf. Church*, pp. 62–64.

which they did on their return journey.

At all events, for whatever reason, Mark left them, and Paul and Barnabas continued without him. *From Perga they went on to Pisidian Antioch*, more than 100 miles north beyond the mountains. It was a Roman colony, a few arches of whose first-century aqueduct are still standing. It was also 'the governing and military centre of the southern half of the vast province of Galatia'.[20] Although politically it belonged to Galatia, in language and geography it belonged to Phrygia. *On the Sabbath they entered the synagogue and sat down* (14). The synagogue service will have begun with a recitation of the *Shema* ('The Lord your God is one Lord, and you shall love the Lord your God . . .') and some prayers, continued with two lessons, one from the Pentateuch and the other from the prophets, followed by an expository sermon, and concluded with a blessing. *After the reading from the Law and the Prophets* (which, it has been suggested because of Paul's quotations, may that day have been Deuteronomy 1 and Isaiah 1), *the synagogue rulers sent word to them*, perhaps recognizing from his dress that Paul was a Rabbi, *saying, 'Brothers, if you have a message of encouragement for the people, please speak'* (15).

Luke now provides his first full summary of one of Paul's sermons. Although some Gentile God-fearers are present, it is essentially an address to a Jewish audience. Luke will later give two samples of Paul's sermons to Gentiles, that is, to the pagans of Lystra and the philosophers of Athens. But now the whole atmosphere is Jewish. The day is the sabbath, the venue is the synagogue, the lessons are from the Law and the Prophets, the listeners are 'men of Israel' (16), and the theme is how 'the God of the people of Israel' (17) 'has brought to Israel the Saviour Jesus, as he promised' (23). Luke is evidently anxious to demonstrate that Paul's message to the Jews was substantially the same as Peter's; that Paul did not turn to the Gentiles until after he had offered the gospel to the Jews and been rebuffed; and that, far from being an innovator, Paul was declaring only what God had promised in Scripture and had now fulfilled in Jesus.

a. The sermon's introduction: the Old Testament preparation (13:16–25)

Standing up, Paul motioned with his hand and said: 'Men of Israel and you Gentiles who worship God, listen to me! [17]The God of the people of Israel chose our fathers; he made the people prosper during their stay in Egypt, with mighty power he led them out of that country, [18]he endured their conduct for about forty years in the

[20] Ramsay, *Church*, p. 25.

desert, [19]he overthrew seven nations in Canaan and gave their land to his people as their inheritance. [20]All this took about 450 years.

'After this, God gave them judges until the time of Samuel the prophet. [21]Then the people asked for a king, and he gave them Saul son of Kish, of the tribe of Benjamin, who ruled for forty years. [22]After removing Saul, he made David their king. He testified concerning him: "I have found David son of Jesse a man after my own heart: he will do everything I want him to do."

[23]'From this man's descendants God has brought to Israel the Saviour Jesus, as he promised. [24]Before the coming of Jesus, John preached repentance and baptism to all the people of Israel. [25]As John was completing his work, he said: "Who do you think I am? I am not that one. No, but he is coming after me, whose sandals I am not worthy to untie."'

In this brief recapitulation of the history of Israel from the patriarchs to the monarchy, Paul's emphasis is on God's initiative of grace. For he is the subject of nearly all the verbs. God *chose our fathers, he made the people prosper . . . in Egypt*, and then *with mighty power he led them out* (17). In the desert he *endured their conduct* (18, that is, 'bore with them', RSV, an echo of Dt. 1:31),[21] and in Canaan *he overthrew seven nations* and *gave their land to his people* (19). *All this took about 450 years*, Paul adds, pausing for breath. It is a round number, of course, and is probably intended to include 400 years in exile, forty in the desert, and ten in conquering the land. After the settlement *God gave them judges* (20), God *gave them Saul* as their first king (21), and then God *made David their king*, calling him '*a man after my own heart*' (22). Now, having reached David, Paul jumps straight to the promised *Saviour Jesus*, who was descended from David (23),[22] and mentions John the Baptist as his immediate forerunner, who pointed away from himself to Jesus (24–25). Paul is now able to follow the Baptist's example and direct his hearers' attention to the same Jesus.

b. The sermon's focus: the death and resurrection of Jesus (13:26–37)

'Brothers, children of Abraham, and you God-fearing Gentiles, it is to us that this message of salvation has been sent. [27]The people of Jerusalem and their rulers did not recognise Jesus, yet in condemning him they fulfilled the words of the prophets that are read every Sabbath. [28]Though they found no proper ground for a death sentence, they asked Pilate to have him executed. [29]When they had carried out all that was written about him, they took him down

[21] See Metzger, pp. 405–406.
[22] *Cf.* Lk. 1:32, 69; 2:4; *cf.* Rom. 1:3; 2 Tim. 2:8.

from the tree and laid him in a tomb. 30*But God raised him from*
*the dead,*31*and for many days he was seen by those who had trav-*
elled with him from Galilee to Jerusalem. They are now his wit-
nesses to our people.

32*'We tell you the good news: What God promised our fathers*
33*he has fulfilled for us, their children, by raising up Jesus. As it is*
written in the second Psalm:

> *' "You are my Son;*
> *today I have become your Father."*

34*The fact that God raised him from the dead, never to decay, is stated in these words:*

> *' "I will give you the holy and sure blessings promised to David."*

35*So it is stated elsewhere:*

> *' "You will not let your Holy One see decay."*

36*'For when David had served God's purpose in his own genera-*
tion, he fell asleep; he was buried with his fathers and his body
decayed. 37*But the one whom God raised from the dead did not see*
decay.'

Paul tells the story of Jesus, as he has told the story of Israel. In doing so, he concentrates on the two great saving events, his death and his resurrection, and demonstrates that both were fulfilments of what God had foretold in Scripture. He concedes that the people and rulers of Jerusalem *did not recognise Jesus*. Nevertheless, he adds, *in condemning him they fulfilled the words of the prophets* which they knew well, since they are read every sabbath in the synagogue (27). Although they could find no adequate ground for condemning him, *they asked Pilate to have him executed* (28). And again in so doing, though without realizing it, they were carrying out *all that was written about him*, including the transfer of his body from *the tree* (the place of a divine curse) to the *tomb* (29). But *God raised him from the dead* (30), and made it possible for him to be *seen* by those who had accompanied him from Galilee to Jerusalem (1:21–22), namely the apostles. *They are now his witnesses* (31). Paul says 'they' not 'we', because he was not one of the Twelve who could bear witness to him from what they had seen and heard during his public ministry. Yet now he moves from 'they' to 'we', including himself: *We tell you the good news*, that in the resurrection (as in the cross) God has fulfilled for us what he promised to our fathers (32–33). In order to substantiate this claim, Paul goes on to quote three Old Testament scriptures –

Psalm 2:7 about God's Son, probably linked in his mind with God's promise to David that his descendant whose throne would be established would be his son;[23] Isaiah 55:3 about *the holy and sure blessings promised to David* (34), which could be 'sure', *i.e.* permanent, only because of the resurrection of David's son; and Psalm 16:10 about God's holy one not being allowed to decay (35). David died, was buried, and decayed (36), but the son of David whom God resurrected *did not see decay* (37). All three texts may have been regarded as Messianic in pre-Christian Judaism (the evidence is not clear in each case); all three related to David from whom 'God has brought to Israel the Saviour Jesus' (23).

c. *The sermon's conclusion: the choice between life and death (13:38–41)*

Having brought Scripture and history together, and shown how what God foretold in Scripture he has fulfilled in Jesus' death and resurrection, Paul comes to his appeal:

'Therefore, my brothers, I want you to know that through Jesus the forgiveness of sins is proclaimed to you. [39]*Through him everyone who believes is justified from everything you could not be justified from by the law of Moses.* [40]*Take care that what the prophets have said does not happen to you:*

> [41]' *"Look, you scoffers,*
> *wonder and perish,*
> *for I am going to do something in your days*
> *that you would never believe,*
> *even if someone told you." '*

The choice is stark. On the one hand, there is the promise *through Jesus* crucified and raised of *the forgiveness of sins* (38). For *through him* (repeated, because he is the only mediator) *everyone who believes is justified*, that is, declared righteous before God. Through *the law of Moses* there is no justification for anybody, since we all break the law and the law condemns law-breakers; through Jesus, however, there is justification for everybody who believes, that is, trusts in him (39). We need to remember that Paul is addressing Galatians. Only a few months or so later he will be writing his Letter to the Galatians. It is very striking, therefore, that he brings together here at the conclusion of his sermon five of the great words which will be foundation stones of his gospel as he expounds it in his Letter. Having referred to Jesus' death on the tree (29),[24] he goes on to speak of sin (38), faith, justification, law (39) and grace (43). W. C. van Unnik felt able to assert that 'Luke has no

[23] 2 Sa. 7:13–14. [24] *Cf.* Gal. 3:10–13.

understanding of the doctrine of justification by faith as the centre of Pauline thought'.[25] But I think Luther was nearer the truth when he wrote in his *Preface to the Acts of the Apostles* (1533):

> It should be noted that by this book St Luke teaches the whole of Christendom . . . that the true and chief article of Christian doctrine is this: We must all be justified alone by faith in Jesus Christ, without any contribution from the law or help from our works. This doctrine is the chief intention of the book and the author's principal reason for writing it.[26]

On the other hand, over against the offer of forgiveness, Paul issues a solemn warning to those who reject it. He reminds his hearers of the prophets' denunciations. In particular, he quotes Habakkuk (Hab. 1:5), who predicted the rise of the Babylonians as instruments of divine judgment upon Israel (40–41).

As we look back over the three parts of Paul's sermon, we cannot fail to note its similarity to the outline of the apostolic *kerygma* which appears in 1 Corinthians 15:3–4. Here, as there, we find the same four events: he died, was buried, was raised and was seen – together with the same insistence that both the major ones, his death and resurrection, were 'according to the Scriptures'. The structure is also practically identical with that of Peter's sermon on the Day of Pentecost, in which we detected the gospel events (the cross and the resurrection), the gospel witnesses (Old Testament prophets and New Testament apostles), the gospel promises (the new life of salvation in Christ, through the Spirit) and the gospel conditions (repentance and faith).

d. The sermon's consequences: a mixed reaction (13:42–52)

The immediate reaction was extraordinarily favourable:

As Paul and Barnabas were leaving the synagogue, the people invited them to speak further about these things on the next Sabbath. [43]*When the congregation was dismissed, many of the Jews and devout converts to Judaism followed Paul and Barnabas, who talked with them and urged them to continue in the grace of God.*

The concern of the people had been aroused. They 'begged' (RSV) to hear more. Both Jews and proselytes surrounded the missionaries, anxious even before the next Sabbath to obtain further instruction. At least some of them had actually believed and received God's grace, for Paul and Barnabas *urged them to continue in the grace of God* (43b).

[25] Keck and Martyn, p. 26.

[26] From *Luther's Works*, vol. 35, ed. E. Theodore Bachman (American edition: Muhlenberg Press, 1960), p. 363.

When *the next Sabbath* came, *almost the whole city gathered to hear the word of the Lord* (44). Luke's enthusiasm has perhaps led him into a little harmless exaggeration. He does not exaggerate the opposition, however. When *the Jews saw the crowds, they were filled with jealousy*, or 'with jealous resentment' (NEB), that the visitors could draw a huge congregation which they could never muster, and they *talked abusively against*, in fact 'contradicted' (RSV), *what Paul was saying* (45).

[46]*Then Paul and Barnabas answered them boldly: 'We had to speak the word of God to you first. Since you reject it and do not consider yourselves worthy of eternal life, we now turn to the Gentiles.* [47]*For this is what the Lord has commanded us:*

' "I have made you a light for the Gentiles,
that you may bring salvation to the ends of the earth." '

[48]*When the Gentiles heard this, they were glad and honoured the word of the Lord; and all who were appointed for eternal life believed.*

Only a few comments on this text seem to be needed. Paul and Barnabas were clear that 'it was necessary' (RSV, NEB) that the word of God should be declared *to you* (*i.e.* you Jews) *first*. For that was God's will (3:26, 'first to you'). And this order was to remain, as Paul later wrote: 'first for the Jew, then for the Gentile.'[27] The same priority continued in Paul's missionary expeditions described in the Acts, even after he had begun to evangelize Gentiles also.[28] Yet it was Jewish opposition to the gospel which led him to turn to the Gentiles and to find scriptural warrant for this epoch-making decision in Isaiah 49:6 ('a light for the Gentiles'), which he quoted freely from the LXX. Luke has already recorded how this verse was applied to Jesus by Simeon[29] and will soon record Jesus applying it to Paul (Acts 26:17–18). This is not a contradiction, however, for the Lord's suffering servant is the Messiah, who gathers round him a Messianic Community to share in his ministry to the nations.

Those who responded to the word and believed are described as having been *appointed for eternal life* (48). Some commentators, offended by what they regard as an extreme predestinarianism in this phrase, have tried in various ways to soften it. But the Greek verb *tassō* means to 'ordain' (AV, RSV), sometimes in the sense of to 'assign someone to a (certain) classification' (BAGD). F. F. Bruce refers to the papyrus evidence that it can mean 'inscribe' or 'enrol',[30]

[27] Rom. 1:16; 2:9–10.
[28] *E.g.* Acts 14:1, 'as usual'; 16:13; 17:2, 'as his custom was'; 17:10, 17; 18:4, 19; 19:8; 28:17, 23. [29] Lk. 2:32.
[30] Bruce, *English*, p. 283; *cf. Greek*, p. 275.

in which case it is a reference to the 'Book of Life'.[31] Certainly those who have believed in Jesus and received eternal life from him all ascribe the credit to God's grace, not to their own merit. The converse is not so, however. It is significant that in this very passage those who rejected the gospel are regarded as having done so deliberately, because they did not 'consider [themselves] worthy of eternal life' (46).

Later developments in Pisidian Antioch followed the same pattern of acceptance and rejection:

> [49]*The word of the Lord spread through the whole region.* [50]*But the Jews incited the God-fearing women of high standing and the leading men of the city. They stirred up persecution against Paul and Barnabas, and expelled them from their region.* [51]*So they shook the dust from their feet in protest against them and went to Iconium.* [52]*And the disciples were filled with joy and with the Holy Spirit.*

Nothing could stop the spread of the Lord's word; *the whole region* heard it (49). Yet at the same time persecution increased. Paul himself suffered from it. This is hinted at in verse 50, for the expulsion of the missionaries was probably violent. It is confirmed by Paul's own later statement that Timothy knew all about his persecutions and sufferings 'in Antioch, Iconium and Lystra'.[32] The missionaries for their part *shook the dust from their feet*, a public protest against those who rejected the gospel, in acordance with the teaching of Jesus.[33] Notwithstanding the opposition, *the disciples were filled with joy and with the Holy Spirit*, for, as Paul was soon to write to the Galatians, 'the fruit of the Spirit is . . . joy'.[34]

4. Paul and Barnabas in Iconium (14:1–7)

Nearly one hundred miles south-east of Pisidian Antioch, commanding the broad plateau which lies between the Taurus and the Sultan mountain ranges and which is well watered by their rivers, is situated the very old city of Iconium, which today is Turkey's fourth largest town of Konya. It was still a Greek city when Paul and Barnabas visited it, and was a centre of agriculture and commerce.

Although *as usual* the missionaries *Paul and Barnabas . . . went* first *into the Jewish synagogue*, their mission in Iconium was plainly not directed to Jews alone. On the contrary, *they spoke so effectively that a great number of Jews and Gentiles believed* (1). *But* if some Jews and Gentiles were united in faith, others were united

[31] See Lk 10:20; Phil. 4:3; Rev. 13:8; 20:12–13; 21:27. [32] 2 Tim. 3:10–11.
[33] Lk. 9:5; 10:11. [34] Gal. 5:22.

in opposition. For *the Jews who refused to believe* (literally 'disobeyed', since faith and obedience go together, as do unbelief and disobedience), *stirred up the Gentiles and poisoned their minds against the brothers* (2) by an unscrupulous slander campaign.

So, undeterred by this propaganda, and even (it is implied) because of it, *Paul and Barnabas* stayed on and *spent considerable time there*, correcting the false witness and bearing a true one, *speaking boldly for the Lord*, or, more accurately, 'in reliance on the Lord' (*epi*, NEB), *who confirmed the message of his grace*, 'a noble definition of the gospel',[35] *by enabling them to do miraculous signs and wonders* (3). Once again we notice the close association between words and signs, the latter confirming the former. As Calvin commented, 'God hardly ever allows them (*sc.* miracles) to be detached from his Word.' Their 'true use' is 'the establishing of the Gospel in its full and genuine authority'.[36]

The people of the city were deeply divided, for the gospel both unites and divides; *some sided with the Jews*, believing their evil slander, while *others* sided *with the apostles* (4), persuaded by the truth of their words and wonders. The attribution of the title 'apostles' to Barnabas as well as Paul, both here and in verse 14, is perplexing, until we remember that the word is used in the New Testament in two senses. On the one hand, there were the 'apostles of Christ', personally appointed by him to be witnesses of the resurrection, who included the Twelve, Paul and probably James (1:21; 10:41).[37] There is no evidence that Barnabas belonged to this group. On the other hand, there were the 'apostles of the churches',[38] sent out by a church or churches on particular missions, as Epaphroditus was an apostle or messenger of the Philippian church.[39] So too Paul and Barnabas were both apostles of the church of Syrian Antioch, sent out by them, whereas only Paul was also an apostle of Christ.

Slander against the missionaries deteriorated into planned violence. *There was a plot afoot among the Gentiles and Jews, together with their leaders*, that is, 'with the connivance of the city authorities' (NEB, JB), not only to *ill-treat them* (*hybrizō* implies insult and humiliation) but actually to *stone them* (5). *But they found out about it*, with the result that they *fled to the Lycaonian cities of Lystra and Derbe and to the surrounding country* (6). Luke is correct is locating these two small towns in Lycaonia, which was one of the regions (Phrygia and Pisidia were others) into which the Roman province of Galatia was divided. But why did the missionaries select them for evangelization? Neither town had a large

[35] Bengel, p. 639. [36] Calvin, II, p. 3. [37] 1 Cor. 9:1; 15:7–9.
[38] 2 Cor. 8:23; RSV margin. [39] Phil. 2:25.

population or lay on an important trade route, and the local Lycaonians were largely uneducated, even illiterate. Ramsay could even describe Lystra as a 'quiet backwater'.[40] Perhaps they were temporary refuges to which they 'fled' (6 and 19–20). At all events, here *they continued to preach the good news* (7), for nothing could silence them.

5. Paul and Barnabas in Lystra and Derbe (14:8–20)

Luke concentrates on what happened in Lystra, and gives us no details of the mission in Derbe.

a. The healing of the cripple (14:8–10)

In Lystra there sat a man crippled in his feet, who was lame from birth and had never walked. 9He listened to Paul as he was speaking. Paul looked directly at him, saw that he had faith to be healed 10and called out, 'Stand up on your feet!' At that, the man jumped up and began to walk.

Luke evidently sees the dramatic healing of this man as a counterpart to the healing of the congenital cripple in Jerusalem (3:1ff.), since several expressions in the two stories are identical (*e.g. lame from birth* and *looked directly at him*). But in Jerusalem Peter was the agent of the divine healing; here it is Paul. The reaction of the crowd is different too.

b. The attempt to worship Paul and Barnabas (14:11–15a)

When the crowd saw what Paul had done, they shouted in the Lycaonian language, 'The gods have come down to us in human form!' 12Barnabas they called Zeus, and Paul they called Hermes because he was the chief speaker. 13The priest of Zeus, whose temple was just outside the city, brought bulls and wreaths to the city gates because he and the crowd wanted to offer sacrifices to them.

14But when the apostles Barnabas and Paul heard this, they tore their clothes and rushed out into the crowd, shouting: 15'Men, why are you doing this? We too are only men, human like you.'

The crowd's superstitious and even fanatical behaviour is hard to comprehend, but some local background throws light on it. About fifty years previously the Latin poet Ovid had narrated in his *Metamorphoses* an ancient local legend. The supreme god Jupiter (Zeus to the Greeks) and his son Mercury (Hermes) once visited the hill country of Phrygia, disguised as mortal men. In their incognito they sought hospitality but were rebuffed a thousand

[40] Ramsay, *Cities*, p. 408.

times. At last, however, they were offered lodging in a tiny cottage, thatched with straw and reeds from the marsh. Here lived an elderly peasant couple called Philemon and Baucis, who entertained them out of their poverty. Later the gods rewarded them, but destroyed by flood the homes which would not take them in. It is reasonable to suppose both that the Lystran people knew this story about their neighbourhood and that, if the gods were to revisit their district, they were anxious not to suffer the same fate as the inhospitable Phrygians. Apart from the literary evidence in Ovid, two inscriptions and a stone altar have been discovered near Lystra, which indicate that Zeus and Hermes were worshipped together as local patron deities.[41]

Since it was *in the Lycaonian language* that the people shouted out their belief that the gods had visited them again, and named Barnabas Zeus and Paul Hermes, it is understandable that the missionaries did not at first understand what was happening (11–12). It dawned on them only when *the priest of Zeus . . . brought bulls and wreaths*, intending *to offer sacrifices to them* (13). At this the missionaries *tore their clothes*, to express their horror at the people's blasphemy,[42] and *rushed out into the crowd*, protesting against their intention, and insisting that they were human like them (14–15).

c. *The sermon Paul preached (14:15b–18)*[43]

'We are bringing you good news, telling you to turn from these worthless things to the living God, who made heaven and earth and sea and everything in them. [16]*In the past, he let all nations go their own way.* [17]*Yet he has not left himself without testimony: He has shown kindness by giving you rain from heaven and crops in their seasons; he provides you with plenty of food and fills your hearts with joy.'* [18]*Even with these words, they had difficulty keeping the crowd from sacrificing to them.*

Although what Luke includes is only a very brief abstract of Paul's sermon, it is of great importance as his only recorded address to illiterate pagans. It invites comparison with his sermon to religious and educated Jews in the synagogue at Pisidian Antioch, which is the only other one that Luke chronicles during the first missionary journey. One can but admire the flexibility of Paul's evangelistic

[41] The details and references are given both by Bruce (*Greek*, p. 281; *English*, pp. 291–292) and by Longenecker (*Acts*, p. 435).

[42] *Cf.* Mk. 14:63.

[43] It is true that in the narrative Paul and Barnabas both 'rushed out into the crowd, shouting . . .' (14). So Luke may be attributing the sermon to both of them. They certainly shared in the gospel preaching (1, 3, 7, 21, 24, 27). On the other hand, Luke's purpose throughout these chapters is to delineate Paul's ministry, and in Lystra he specifies Paul as speaking (9a), healing (9b–11a) and being stoned (19).

approach. I do not doubt that wherever he went his message included the good news of Jesus Christ, which does not change. This must be what Luke means when he says that the missionaries preached 'the word of God',[44] the 'message of salvation' (13:26), 'the message of his grace' (14:3) or 'the good news' (or 'the gospel').[45] Nevertheless, although the substance of his message was invariable, he varied his approach and emphasis. The context within which he preached to the Jews in Antioch was Old Testament Scripture, its history, prophecies and law. But with the pagans in Lystra he focused not on a Scripture they did not know, but on the natural world around them, which they did know and could see. He begged them to turn from the vanity of idolatrous worship to the living and true God. He spoke of the living God as the Creator of heaven, earth and sea, and of everything in them (15). Did he gesture to the sky, to the Taurus mountains to the south, and to the Great Sea beyond them? Moreover, he who made all things has not been inactive since. Although in the past *he let all nations go their own way* (16), yet he has never at any time or in any place *left himself without testimony*. On the contrary, he has borne a consistent witness to himself by his *kindness* to all humankind, including Paul's listeners. He has given them *rain from heaven* and *crops* on earth *in their seasons*, thus providing them with *plenty of food* for their bodies and filling their *hearts with joy* (17). Overawed by the majesty of this perspective, the crowd were restrained only with difficulty *from sacrificing to them* (18).

We need to learn from Paul's flexibility. We have no liberty to edit the heart of the good news of Jesus Christ. Nor is there ever any need to do so. But we have to begin where people are, to find a point of contact with them. With secularized people today this might be what constitutes authentic humanness, the universal quest for transcendence, the hunger for love and community, the search for freedom, or the longing for personal significance. Wherever we begin, however, we shall end with Jesus Christ, who is himself the good news, and who alone can fulfil all human aspirations.

d. The stoning of Paul (14:19–20)

Then some Jews came from Antioch and Iconium and won the crowd over. They stoned Paul and dragged him outside the city, thinking he was dead. [20]*But after the disciples had gathered round him, he got up and went back into the city. The next day he and Barnabas left for Derbe.*

The stoning which had been plotted in Iconium (5) took place now in Lystra. It was not a judicial execution, but a lynching. As the

[44] Acts 13:5, 7, 44, 46, 48–49. [45] Acts 13:32; 14:7, 15, 21.

stones were hurled at him, did Paul remember Stephen, and even pray Stephen's prayer? This must have been the occasion to which he was later to refer, 'Once I was stoned.'[46] The enemies of the gospel had not killed him, however; they only thought that *he was dead* (19). Luke is not claiming that what happened next was a resuscitation. The disciples, having followed those who dragged his body outside the city, now *gathered round him*, hoping to be able to minister to him, certainly praying for him, when suddenly *he got up*. It was a vivid illustration of another verse Paul was later to write in 2 Corinthians: 'Struck down but not destroyed'[47] or 'we may be knocked down but we are never knocked out' (JBP). He was not only resilient; he was courageous. He *went back into the city* which had rejected him, to stay the night there (20a).

Next morning, Luke writes in his matter-of-fact way, Paul and Barnabas *left for Derbe* (20b). It was at least a sixty-mile trudge. How could Paul's battered body manage it? 'I bear on my body the marks of Jesus,' he was soon to write to the Galatians;[48] was he thinking of the wounds he had received in Lystra? 'I once saw the track of a bleeding hare across the snow,' said Dr J. H. Jowett; 'that was Paul's track across Europe.'[49] Of course the companionship of Barnabas will have encouraged him. But as I once traced his route from Lystra to Derbe, I could not help wondering if his spirit had also been cheered by the spectacular, snow-capped mountain peaks around him, by the White Storks nesting on the village rooftops and by the pretty song of the Calandra Larks.

One is amazed at the fickleness of the crowd. One day they tried to sacrifice to Paul and Barnabas as if they were gods, while soon after they joined in stoning Paul as if he were a felon. Yet Luke has recorded something similar of the Jerusalem crowd who with loud voices first acclaimed Jesus and then demanded his execution.[50] Like Jesus, Paul remained unmoved. His steadfastness of character was upset neither by flattery nor by opposition.

6. Paul and Barnabas return to Syrian Antioch (14:21–28)

They preached the good news in that city and won a large number of disciples. Then they returned to Lystra, Iconium and Antioch, [22]*strengthening the disciples and encouraging them to remain true to the faith. 'We must go through many hardships to enter the kingdom of God,' they said.* [23]*Paul and Barnabas appointed elders for them in each church and, with prayer and fasting, committed them to the Lord in whom they had put their trust.* [24]*After going*

[46] 2 Cor. 11:25. [47] 2 Cor. 4:9. [48] Gal. 6:17.
[49] Heard and quoted by W. E. Sangster in *The Craft of the Sermon* (Epworth, 1954), p. 214. [50] Lk. 19:37–40; 23:23.

through Pisidia, they came into Pamphylia, [25]*and when they had preached the word in Perga, they went down to Attalia.*

[26]*From Attalia they sailed back to Antioch, where they had been committed to the grace of God for the work they had now completed.* [27]*On arriving there, they gathered the church together and reported all that God had done through them and how he had opened the door of faith to the Gentiles.* [28]*And they stayed there a long time with the disciples.*

All Luke tells us about the mission in Derbe is that the missionaries *preached the good news* there and *won a large number of disciples.* Perhaps the converts included 'Gaius from Derbe' (20:4). Then they retraced their steps, revisiting (in spite of the danger) the same three Galatian cities which they had evangelized on their outward journey – Lystra, Iconium and Pisidian Antioch (21). It was a ministry of *strengthening* (*epistērizontes*) and *encouraging* (*parakalountes*). Both verbs were almost technical terms for establishing and fortifying new converts and churches.[51] But encouragement did not exclude warning, for we have to pass through *many hardships*, the missionaries said, if we are to *enter the kingdom of God* (22). It was Paul's own sufferings 'in Antioch, Iconium and Lystra' which led him later to assert that 'everyone who wants to live a godly life in Christ Jesus will be persecuted'.[52]

In addition to encouraging the converts *to remain true to the faith* (22), *Paul and Barnabas appointed elders for them* (23a), who would continue to teach them the faith. Then, just as the missionaries had been sent forth from Antioch with prayer and fasting, so *with prayer and fasting* the elders of the Galatian churches were *committed . . . to the Lord* (23b).

After their return visit to the Galatian cities in which they had planted churches, the missionaries now headed home. They crossed the pass over the Taurus mountains and climbed down to the coastal swamps of Pamphylia (24). This time they did not bypass Perga, but *preached the word* there, and then went on to Attalia (25), the port from which *they sailed back to Antioch*, having completed the work for which they had been committed to God's grace (26).

On arrival they gathered the church and reported what *God had done through them*, literally 'with them', 'in conjunction with them, as his instruments, his agents, his co-workers'.[53] In particular, they reported the great innovation, how God *had opened the door of faith to the Gentiles* (27). If by any chance the Western text of 11:28 is correct, reading 'when we were gathered together' and

[51] *E.g.* Acts 9:31; 15:32, 41; 18:23. [52] 2 Tim. 3:11–12.
[53] Alexander, II, p. 68.

indicating Luke's presence on that occasion, then Luke will probably have been present on this occasion too and heard the missionaries' exciting report. They will have been away for the best part of two years. So *they stayed there* in Syrian Antioch *a long time with the disciples* (28).

7. Paul's missionary policy

'The first and most striking difference between his (*sc.* Paul's) action and ours is that he founded "Churches" whilst we found "Missions".' 'Nothing can alter or disguise the fact that St Paul did leave behind him at his first visit complete Churches.' Indeed, 'in little more than ten years St Paul established the Church in four provinces of the Empire, Galatia, Macedonia, Achaia and Asia. Before AD 47 there were no Churches in these provinces; in AD 57 St Paul could speak as if his work there was done.'[54] These three quotations are from the eloquent pen of Roland Allen, the High Church Anglican missionary in North China from 1895 to 1903, whose two main books *Missionary Methods: St Paul's or Ours?* (1912) and *The Spontaneous Expansion of the Church and the Causes which Hinder it* (1927) continue to be read and debated today, and whose principles have been remarkably vindicated in recent years in the very China he loved and served.

Roland Allen's main assertion is indisputable, namely that on his missionary journeys Paul left churches behind him. This was so from the beginning. After he and Barnabas had retraced their steps through Derbe, Lystra, Iconium and Pisidian Antioch, 'strengthening' and 'encouraging' the converts, they did not set up a mission organization; they left them and went home. On what foundations, then, did Paul's indigenization policy rest? There were three.

a. Apostolic instruction

Paul exhorted the church members *to remain true to the faith* (22), which they had received from him. A number of similar expressions are used in different parts of the New Testament to indicate that there was a recognizable body of doctrine, a cluster of central beliefs, which the apostles taught. Here it is called 'the faith', elsewhere 'the tradition', 'the deposit', 'the teaching', or 'the truth'. Doubtless the two missionaries on their return journey will have reminded the Galatians of it. To some extent we can reconstruct it from the apostles' letters. It will have included the doctrines of the living God, the Creator of all things, of Jesus Christ his Son, who

[54] *Missionary Methods: St Paul's or Ours?* by Roland Allen (1912; 6th ed., Eerdmans, 1962), pp. 83, 87, 3.

died for our sins and was raised according to the Scriptures, now reigns and will return, of the Holy Spirit who indwells the believer and animates the church, of the salvation of God, of the new community of Jesus and the high standards of holiness and love he expects from his people, of the sufferings which are the path to glory, and of the strong hope laid up for us in heaven. These truths, perhaps already in some simple structure which later became the Apostles' Creed, Paul left behind him, and then elaborated in his letters. Each church would begin to collect apostolic letters,[55] alongside the Old Testament Scriptures they already had, and in their public worship on the Lord's Day extracts from both would be read aloud.

b. Pastoral oversight

Paul and Barnabas also *appointed elders for them in each church* (23). This arrangement was made from the first missionary journey onwards, and became universal. Although no fixed ministerial order is laid down in the New Testament, some form of pastoral oversight (*episkopē*), doubtless adapted to local needs, is regarded as indispensable to the welfare of the church. We notice that it was both local and plural – local in that the elders were chosen from within the congregation, not imposed from without, and plural in that the familiar modern pattern of 'one pastor one church' was simply unknown. Instead, there was a pastoral team, which is likely to have included (depending on the size of the church) full-time and part-time ministers, paid and voluntary workers, presbyters, deacons and deaconesses. Their qualifications Paul laid down in writing later.[56] These were mostly matters of moral integrity, but loyalty to the apostles' teaching and a gift for teaching it were also essential.[57] Thus the shepherds would tend Christ's sheep by feeding them, in other words care for them by teaching them.

Such was Paul's double – and only – human provision for these young churches: on the one hand a standard of doctrinal and ethical instruction, safeguarded by the Old Testament and the apostles' letters, and on the other pastors to teach the people out of these written resources and to care for them in the name of the Lord. Just the Scriptures and the pastorate; that was all. Yet there was a third – and divine – provision.

c. Divine faithfulness

Indigenous principles rest ultimately on the conviction that the church belongs to God and that he can be trusted to look after his

[55] *Cf.* Col. 4:16; 1 Thes. 5:27. [56] 1 Tim. 3 and Tit 1
[57] Tit. 1:9; 1 Tim. 3:2

own people. So before leaving the Galatian churches, Paul and Barnabas *committed them* (members as well as elders) *to the Lord, in whom they had put their trust* (23b), just as previously they had urged the Antiochene converts 'to continue in the grace of God' (13:43).

These are the reasons why Paul believed that the churches could confidently be left to manage their own affairs. They had the apostles to teach them (through 'the faith' and their letters), pastors to shepherd them, and the Holy Spirit to guide, protect and bless them. With this threefold provision (apostolic instruction, pastoral oversight and divine faithfulness) they would be safe.

Although Roland Allen did not specifically expound this passage in Acts, or appeal to it, it is surely significant that he developed the same three arguments. First, 'St Paul seems to have left his newly-founded churches with a simple system of Gospel teaching, two sacraments, a tradition of the main facts of the death and resurrection, and the Old Testament'.[58] Secondly, he ordained elders by a combination of election and appointment.[59] And thirdly, he trusted the Holy Spirit and so 'did not shrink from risks'.[60] 'He believed in the Holy Ghost . . . as a Person indwelling his converts. He believed therefore in his converts. He could trust them. He did not trust them because he believed in their natural virtue or intellectual sufficiency. But he believed in the Holy Ghost in them. He believed that Christ was able and willing to keep that which he had committed to him.'[61] He must therefore 'retire from his converts to give place for Christ'.[62]

Roland Allen lived and worked in the heyday of colonialism, when missionaries tended to be paternalistic. 'Everywhere', Allen wrote in 1912, 'Christianity is still an exotic (*sc.* plant) . . . Everywhere our missions are dependent . . . Everywhere we see the same types . . . We desire to see Christianity established in foreign climes putting on a foreign dress and developing new forms of glory and of beauty.'[63] Bishop Lesslie Newbigin agrees with him. Missionaries have to distinguish, he writes, between the *traditum* (what we have in fact received) and the *tradendum* (the essentials which *must* be passed on). Roland Allen 'waged war against everything that had been confused with these essentials, everything that makes missions look like a piece of western imperialism – the whole apparatus of a professional ministry, institutions, church buildings, church organisations, diocesan offices – everything from harmoniums to archdeacons'.[64]

Of course Roland Allen was not the first to raise these questions.

[58] *Missionary Methods*, p. 90. [59] *Ibid.*, pp. 99–107. [60] *Ibid.*, p. 91.
[61] *Ibid.*, p. 149. [62] *Ibid.*, p. 148. [63] *Ibid.*, pp. 141–142.
[64] *The Finality of Christ* by Lesslie Newbigin (SCM, 1969), p. 107.

In the middle of the last century those transatlantic friends, Henry Venn of London and Rufus Anderson of Boston, both cherished the vision of indigenous churches. In an 1851 memorandum Venn wrote of 'the settlement of a Native Church under Native Pastors upon a self-supporting, self-governing and self-extending system'. He specified four stages in this development until at last 'the Mission will have attained its euthanasia'.[65] Anderson used the same three 'self' adjectives but in the opposite order, and saw the establishment of churches as the beginning not the goal.

The Venn-Anderson-Allen theme is not immune to criticism, however. First, it is not radical enough in relation to the church's identity. Their three principles were 'self-supporting, self-governing, self-extending', but the authentic selfhood of a church goes beyond finance, administration and evangelism to the totality of its cultural self-expression, including its theology, worship and lifestyle. Indigenization (local autonomy) should lead to contextualization (cultural identity). Secondly, it is not imaginative enough in relation to missionaries. Henry Venn thought that, once the national church was established, missionaries should leave. But no. The call for a moratorium, issued in 1974 by John Gatu, the Presbyterian leader in Kenya, was not intended to mean that missionaries are redundant, but rather that *some* missionaries hinder the national church's growth into self-reliance. Once the church has established its own selfhood, however, then foreign missionaries will be welcome as guests, to work under national leadership, to offer specialist skills and to demonstrate the international nature of the church. Thirdly, Roland Allen's vision is not flexible enough in relation to its expectations. The selfhood of churches is attainable at different rates in different circumstances. Probably Allen did not sufficiently recognize the unique position of Paul's Jewish and God-fearing converts, who already had a strong Old Testament background in doctrine and ethics. Joachim Jeremias wrote of Judaism as 'the first great missionary religion to make its appearance in the Mediterranean world' and of the 'unparalleled period of missionary activity' which followed. In consequence, the Christian missionaries found proselytes and God-fearers everywhere. 'The overwhelming success of the mission of the apostle Paul, who in the space of ten years had established centres of the Christian faith throughout almost the whole of the contemporary world, depended partly on the fact that everywhere he was able to build on ground prepared by the Jewish mission.'[66] It is doubtful if after only a

[65] *To Apply the Gospel: Selections from the Writings of Henry Venn*, ed. Max Warren (Eerdmans, 1971), p. 28.

[66] *Jesus' Promise to the Nations* by Joachim Jeremias (1956; English translation, SCM, 1958), pp. 11 and 16.

few months Paul could have appointed elders in a congregation composed entirely of ex-pagans and ex-idolators. In such cases there would almost certainly have been a period of transition from mission to church, while elders were being taught and trained.

In conclusion, and reverting to the first missionary journey, its most notable feature was the missionaries' sense of divine direction. It was the Holy Spirit of God himself who told the church of Antioch to set Barnabas and Saul apart, who sent them out, who led them from place to place, and who gave power to their preaching, so that converts were made and churches planted. The sending church had committed them to the grace of God for their work (14:26), and on their return they reported 'all that God had done through them and how he had opened the door of faith to the Gentiles' (14:27). True, he had done the work 'with them' (literally), in co-operation or partnership with them, but he had done it, and they gave him the credit. The grace had come from him; the glory must go to him.

11. The Council of Jerusalem *15:1–16:5*

For several years now Gentiles had been brought to faith in Christ and welcomed into the church by baptism. It began with that God-fearing centurion in Caesarea, Cornelius. Not only – in quite extraordinary circumstances – did he come to hear the good news, believe, receive the Spirit and be baptized, but the Jerusalem leaders, once the full facts were presented to them, instead of raising objections, 'praised God' (11:18). Next came the remarkable movement in Syrian Antioch when unnamed missionaries 'began to speak to Greeks also' (11:20), a great number of whom believed. The Jerusalem church heard about this too and sent Barnabas to investigate, who 'saw the evidence of the grace of God' and rejoiced (11:23). The third development which Luke chronicles was the first missionary journey, during which the first complete outsider believed (Sergius Paulus, proconsul of Cyprus) and later Paul and Barnabas responded to Jewish unbelief with the bold declaration 'we now turn to the Gentiles' (13:46). Thereafter, wherever they went, both Jews and Gentiles believed (*e.g.* 14:1), and on their return to Syrian Antioch, the missionaries were able to report that 'God . . . had opened the door of faith to the Gentiles' (14:27).

All that was fairly straightforward. After the conversion of both Cornelius and the Antiochene Greeks the Jerusalem leaders had been able to reassure themselves that God was in it. How would they now react to the even more audacious policy of Paul? The Gentile mission was gathering momentum. The trickle of Gentile conversions was fast becoming a torrent. The Jewish leaders had no difficulty with the general concept of believing Gentiles, for many Old Testament passages predicted their inclusion. But now a particular question was forming in their minds: what means of incorporation into the believing community did God intend for Gentiles? So far it had been assumed that they would be absorbed into Israel by circumcision, and that by observing the law they would be acknowledged as *bona fide* members of the covenant people of God. Something quite different was now happening, however, something which disturbed and even alarmed many. Gentile converts were being welcomed into fellowship by baptism without circumcision. They were becoming Christians without also becoming Jews. They were retaining their own identity and integrity as members of other nations. It was one thing for the Jerusalem leaders to give their approval to the conversion of Gentiles: but could they approve of conversion-without-circumcision, of faith in Jesus without the works of the law, and of commitment to the Messiah without inclusion in Judaism? Was their vision big enough to see the gospel of Christ not as a reform movement within Judaism but as good news for the whole world, and the church of Christ not as a Jewish sect but as the international family of God? These were the revolutionary questions which some were daring to ask.

No wonder Haenchen can write: 'Chapter 15 is the turning point, "centrepiece" and "watershed" of the book, the episode which rounds off and justifies the past developments, and makes those to come intrinsically possible.'[1] This is not an exaggeration. Luke draws attention to it by silent shifts of emphasis. In this chapter Jerusalem is still the focus of interest, and Peter makes his final appearance in the story. But from now on Peter disappears, to be replaced by Paul, and Jerusalem recedes into the background as Paul pushes on beyond Asia into Europe, and Rome appears on the horizon. Indeed we ourselves, from our later perspective of church history, can see the crucial importance of this first ecumenical Council held in Jerusalem. Its unanimous decision liberated the gospel from its Jewish swaddling clothes into being God's message for all humankind, and gave the Jewish-Gentile church a self-conscious identity as the reconciled people of God, the one body of Christ. And although the whole Council affirmed it, Paul claimed that it was a new understanding granted specially to him, the 'mystery' previously hidden but now revealed, namely that through faith in Christ alone Gentiles stand on equal terms with Jews as 'heirs together, members together, sharers together' in his one new community.[2]

1. The point at issue (15:1–4)

The tranquillity of the Christian fellowship in Syrian Antioch was shattered by the arrival of a group Paul later dubs 'trouble makers'.[3] *Some men came down from Judea to Antioch* (1). Before going on

[1] Haenchen, p. 461. [2] Eph. 3:2–6; *cf.* Col. 1:26–27; Rom. 16:25–27.
[3] Gal. 1:7 and 5:10, RSV.

to consider who they were and what they were teaching, I need to share with my readers that I hold the so-called 'South Galatian' view, namely that Paul's Letter to the Galatians was written to the South Galatian churches of Pisidian Antioch, Iconium, Lystra and Derbe, which he and Barnabas had just visited on their first missionary journey; that he dictated it during the height of this theological crisis before the Council settled it (for he does not refer in his letter to the 'apostolic decree'); that he was writing it probably on his way up to Jerusalem for the Council, which would be his third visit to the city, although he does not mention it in *Galatians* because it has not yet taken place; and that therefore the situation Luke describes at the beginning of Acts 15 is the same as that to which Paul refers in Galatians 2:11–16.[4]

If that is correct, then the statement that *some men came down from Judea to Antioch* (1) corresponds to 'certain men came from James' to Antioch.[5] Not that James had actually sent them, for he later disclaims this (24), but that was their boast. They were trying to set two apostles against each other, claiming James as their champion and framing Paul as their opponent. They were 'Pharisees' (5), and 'zealous for the law' (21:20). And this is what they *were teaching the brothers: 'Unless you are circumcised, according to the custom taught by Moses, you cannot be saved'* (1). Nor was the circumcision of Gentile converts their only demand; they went further. Gentile converts, they insisted, were also *required to obey the law of Moses* (5). Because they could not accept conversion without circumcision as adequate, they had organized themselves into a pressure group, whom we often term 'Judaizers' or 'the circumcision party'. They were not opposed to the Gentile mission, but were determined that it must come under the umbrella of the Jewish church, and that Gentile believers must submit not only to baptism in the name of Jesus, but, like Jewish proselytes, to both circumcision and law-observance as well. It is hardly surprising that *this* teaching of theirs *brought Paul and Barnabas into sharp dispute and debate with them* (2a).

We need to be clear what they were saying, and what the point at issue was. They were insisting, in Luke's tell-tale summary, that without circumcision converts could *not be saved*. Of course circumcision was the God-given sign of the covenant, and doubtless the Judaizers were stressing this; but they were going further and making it a condition of salvation. They were telling Gentile con-

[4] See Colin Hemer's chapter 7, 'Galatia and the Galatians' (pp. 277–307). His view 'embodies a synthesis of three elements: (1) a South Galatian destination of the epistle; (2) an early, pre-Jerusalem Council dating of the epistle; (3) a straightforward identification of the visits to Jerusalem, Acts 9 with Gal. 1, Acts 11 with Gal. 2, Acts 15 being later than the epistle' (p. 278).

[5] Gal. 2:11–12.

verts that faith in Jesus was not enough, not sufficient for salvation: they must add to faith circumcision, and to circumcision observance of the law. In other words, they must let Moses complete what Jesus had begun, and let the law supplement the gospel. The issue was immense. The way of salvation was at stake. The gospel was in dispute. The very foundations of the Christian faith were being undermined.

The apostle Paul saw this with great clarity, and was outraged. His indignation increased when the Judaizers won over a notable convert in the apostle Peter, who was also in Antioch at the time. Before they arrived, as Paul explains in Galatians 2:11–14, Peter 'used to eat with the Gentiles'. True, they had not been circumcised, but they had been converted. They had believed, received the Spirit and been baptized. So Peter, remembering Cornelius, was entirely happy to associate with them freely, and even to eat with them, doubtless including the Lord's Supper, recognizing them as brothers and sisters in the Lord. But when the circumcision party arrived in Antioch, they persuaded Peter to withdraw 'and separate himself from the Gentiles'.

Unfortunately, that was only the beginning. What happened next Paul rehearses in Galatians 2. The rest of the Jewish believers followed Peter's bad example and 'joined him in his hypocrisy' (for Paul knew Peter was acting from fear, not conviction), and even Barnabas, in spite of everything he had seen during the first missionary journey, was carried away by the flood and 'led astray'. Paul was hot with anger – not from personal pique, because his position was losing ground, but out of concern for the truth. He saw that Peter and his followers were 'not acting in line with the truth of the gospel'. So he 'opposed him [Peter] to his face, because he was in the wrong', and rebuked him publicly for his inconsistency. His behaviour was a disgraceful contradiction of the gospel. So he said to him: 'We . . . know [you and I, Peter and Paul, are agreed about this] that a man is not justified by observing the law, but by faith in Jesus Christ. So we, too, have put our faith in Christ Jesus that we may be justified by faith in Christ and not by observing the law, because by observing the law no-one will be justified.'[6] How then, if we know this and have ourselves experienced it, can we preach a different gospel to Gentiles? Further, if God has accepted them by faith, as he has accepted us, how can we break fellowship with one another? How dare we reject those whom God has accepted? Paul's logic was incontrovertible. His courageous confrontation of Peter evidently had the desired result. For by the time Peter reached Jerusalem for the Council, he had regained his

[6] Gal. 2:15–16.

theological equilibrium and went on to bear faithful witness during the assembly to the gospel of grace and its consequences for Gentile-Jewish fellowship. Barnabas had recovered too.

The issue can be clarified by a series of questions. Is the sinner saved by the sheer grace of God in and through Christ crucified, when he or she simply believes, that is, flees to Jesus for refuge? Has Jesus Christ by his death and resurrection done everything necessary for salvation? Or are we saved partly through the grace of Christ and partly through our own good works and religious performance? Is justification *sola fide*, 'by faith alone', or through a mixture of faith and works, grace and law, Jesus and Moses? Are Gentile believers a sect of Judaism, or authentic members of a multi-national family? It was not some Jewish cultural practices which were at stake, but the truth of the gospel and the future of the church.

We are not surprised, therefore, by the 'fierce dissension and controversy' (2, NEB) which arose. We may be thankful that the church of Antioch grasped the nettle, and took practical steps to ensure a resolution of the issue. The calling of a Council can be extremely valuable, if its purpose is to clarify doctrine, end controversy and promote peace. *So Paul and Barnabas were appointed, along with some other believers, to go up to Jerusalem to see the apostles and elders about this question* (2). *The church sent them on their way, and as they travelled through Phoenicia and Samaria, they told how the Gentiles had been converted. This news made all the brothers very glad* (3). *When they came to Jerusalem, they were welcomed by the church and the apostles and elders, to whom they reported everything God had done through them* (4).

2. The debate in Jerusalem (15:5–21)

No sooner had the delegation from Antioch been given a warm welcome by the Jerusalem church, especially by the apostles and elders, than the controversy broke out afresh. *Then some of the believers who belonged to the party of the Pharisees stood up and said, 'The Gentiles must be circumcised and required to obey the law of Moses'* (5). They were entirely biblical to value circumcision and the law as gifts of God to Israel. But they went further and made them obligatory for everyone, including Gentiles. We note their word 'must', as we did the word 'cannot' in verse 1. Circumcision and law-observance, they insisted, were essential for salvation. So *the apostles and elders met to consider this question* (6), although others were present too. Luke gives no details of the *much discussion* (7a) which took place, but he summarizes the decisive speeches which were made successively by the three apostles involved – the apostle Peter (7–11), the apostle Paul supported by Barnabas (12) and the apostle James (13–21).

a. Peter (15:7–11)

Peter's contribution was to remind the assembly of the Cornelius incident, in which he had been the chief human factor, and which had taken place *some time ago*, probably about ten years previously. He humbly attributed the whole initiative to God. First, he said, *God made a choice among you that the Gentiles might hear from my lips the message of the gospel and believe* (7). The choice had been God's, the privilege his. Secondly, *God, who knows the heart* (the word *kardiōgnostēs*, 'heart-knower', had been used of Jesus in 1:24), *showed that he accepted them* (literally, he 'bore witness to them', meaning 'showed his approval of them', NEB, JB) *by giving the Holy Spirit to them, just as he did to us* (8). This proves that Peter's earlier statement that 'God . . . accepts men from every nation who fear him . . .' (10:35) meant that there is no racial barrier to conversion; but God 'accepted them' in the sense of welcoming them into his family only when he gave them his Spirit. Thirdly, God *made no distinction between us and them, for he purified their hearts by faith* (9), demonstrating that it is the inward purity of the heart which makes fellowship possible, not the external purity of diet and ritual. It is also a purification by faith, not works.

This threefold work of God (choosing Peter, giving the Spirit, purifying the heart) led to an unavoidable conclusion. In expressing it, Peter addressed the opposition direct: *Now then, why do you try to test God* (that is, why do you provoke him by resisting what he has clearly revealed?) *by putting on the necks of the disciples a yoke that neither we nor our fathers have been able to bear?* (10). We Jews have not obtained salvation by obedience to the law; so how can we expect Gentiles to do so? '*No!*' Peter concludes, '*We believe it is through the grace of our Lord Jesus that we are saved, just as they are*' (11).

As he makes this final affirmation, we notice that he is echoing, perhaps quite unconsciously, the gospel statement which Paul had made to him in Antioch, while publicly challenging him. Together they make it plain that salvation is 'through the grace of Jesus Christ' and 'by faith in Jesus Christ'. Grace and faith cannot be separated.

Paul: 'We know that a man is . . . justified . . . by faith in Jesus Christ. So we, too, have put our faith in Christ Jesus' (Gal. 2:16).

Peter: 'We believe it is through the grace of our Lord Jesus that we are saved, just as they are' (Acts 15:11).

The central theme of Peter's testimony was not just that Gentiles had heard the gospel, believed in Jesus, received the Spirit and been purified by faith, but that at each stage God *made no distinction between us and them* (9, *cf*. 10:15, 20, 29; 11:9, 12, 17). Four times in Luke's condensed report of Peter's speech the theme of 'us-them' or 'we-they' is repeated. God gave the Spirit to them as to us (8) and made no distinction between us and them (9). So why lay on them a yoke we could not bear? (10). We conclude that we are saved by grace as they are (11). If only the Judaizers could grasp that God makes no distinctions between Jews and Gentiles, but saves both by grace through faith, they would not make distinctions either. Grace and faith level us; they make fraternal fellowship possible.

b. Paul and Barnabas (15:12)

The whole assembly became silent, evidently out of deep respect, *as they listened to Barnabas and Paul* (perhaps the priority of Barnabas is because he was better known in Jerusalem than Paul) *telling about the miraculous signs and wonders God had done among the Gentiles through them*. Previously God was said to work 'with' them (*meta* in 14:27 and 15:4, RSV); now 'through' them (*dia*) as his agents. This extremely brief résumé may be due to the fact that Luke's readers were already fully acquainted with the details of the first missionary journey from having read Acts 13 and 14. And probably the emphasis on the signs and wonders is intended not to denigrate the preaching of the word, but because they confirmed and validated it.

c. James (15:13–21)

The James who spoke next was 'James the Just', as he came later to be known because of his reputation for godly righteousness, one of the brothers of Jesus, who had probably come to believe in him through being granted a resurrection appearance.[7] In his New Testament letter he would later emphasize that saving faith always issues in good works of love and that heavenly wisdom is 'peace-loving, considerate, submissive, full of mercy and good fruit, impartial and sincere'.[8] He manifested some of that wisdom now. Almost certainly an apostle,[9] and already recognized as a (even 'the') leader of the Jerusalem church (12:17),[10] he was evidently the moderator of the assembly. He waited until the leading missionary apostles

[7] Mk. 6:3; Acts 1:14; 1 Cor. 15:7. [8] Jas. 3:17. [9] Gal. 1:19.
[10] Gal. 2:9; *cf*. Acts 21:18.

Peter and Paul had completed their evidence. Then, *when they finished,* he *spoke up* (NEB, 'summed up'), addressing his audience as *Brothers* and requesting them: *listen to me* (13). Then, referring to Peter by his Hebrew name (an authentic touch), he summarized his testimony in these words: '*Simon* [literally, *Symeon*] *has described to us how God at first showed his concern by taking from the Gentiles a people for himself*' (14).

His statement is considerably more significant than it looks at first sight, for the expressions 'people' (*laos*) and 'for himself' (literally, 'for his name') are regularly applied in the Old Testament to Israel. James was expressing his belief that Gentile believers now belonged to the true Israel, called and chosen by God to belong to his one and only people and to glorify his name. He did not refer also to the testimony of Paul and Barnabas, perhaps because it was their mission policy which was on trial. Instead he went straight from the apostolic evidence to the prophetic word: *The words of the prophets are in agreement with this* (15). Councils have no authority in the church unless it can be shown that their conclusions are in accord with Scripture. To substantiate his claim, James quoted Amos 9:11–12:

> 16' "*After this I will return*
> *and rebuild David's fallen tent.*
> *Its ruins I will rebuild,*
> *and I will restore it,*
> 17*that the remnant of men may seek the Lord,*
> *and all the Gentiles who bear my name,*
> *says the Lord, who does these things*"
> 18 *that have been known for ages.*'

As it stands, this quotation from Amos is a powerful statement of two related truths. God promises first to restore David's fallen tent and rebuild its ruins (which Christian eyes see as a prophecy of the resurrection and exaltation of Christ, the seed of David, and the establishment of his people) so that, secondly, a Gentile remnant will seek the Lord. In other words, through the Davidic Christ Gentiles will be included in his new community.[11]

[11] The difficulty with James's citation of Amos is that the text quoted is almost exactly that of the LXX, whereas in the Masoretic (Hebrew) text the first promise refers to a restored Israel and the second to Israel's possession of Edom and all the nations. To be sure, the Masoretic text would still have been an appropriate quotation for James to use, understanding Edom as an example of the nations to be 'possessed' or embraced by the true Israel. But which text was James using? Critics argue that, being the Hebrew leader of the Hebrew church, he would never have used the Greek LXX. Perhaps not. On the other hand, 'like all Galileans he would be bilingual' (Neil, p. 173), and the proceedings of the Council are likely to have been in Greek. If, however, he was speaking Aramaic, then probably he was using

Thus James, whom the circumcision party had claimed as their champion, declared himself in full agreement with Peter, Paul and Barnabas. The inclusion of the Gentiles was not a divine afterthought, but foretold by the prophets. Scripture itself confirmed the facts of the missionaries' experience. There was an 'agreement' between what God had done through his apostles and what he had said through his prophets. This correspondence between Scripture and experience, between the witness of prophets and apostles, was for James conclusive. He was ready to give his *judgment.* The Greek verb *krinō* could mean merely to 'express an opinion'. But the context demands something stronger than that. 'I rule, then' (JB), on the other hand, is too strong, as is Kirsopp Lake's explanation that 'it is the definite sentence of a judge, and the *ego* implies that he is acting by an authority which is personal'.[12] So we need a word stronger than 'opinion' and weaker than 'decree', perhaps 'conviction', since James was making a firm proposal, which in fact the other leaders endorsed, so that the decision was unanimous and the letter went out in the name of 'the apostles and elders, with the whole church' (22).

What, then, was the decision? In general, it was *that we should not make it difficult for* ('impose no irksome restrictions on', NEB) *the Gentiles who are turning to God* (19). *Instead we should write to them, telling them to abstain from food polluted by idols, from sexual immorality, from the meat of strangled animals and from blood* (20). Putting these two sentences together, James was saying that they must recognize and embrace Gentile believers as brothers and sisters in Christ, and not burden them by asking them to add to their faith in Jesus either circumcision or the whole code of Jewish practices. At the same time, having established the principle that salvation is by grace alone through faith alone, without works, it was necessary to appeal to these Gentile believers to respect the consciences of their Jewish fellow-believers by abstaining from a few practices which might offend them. *For,* James went on to explain, *Moses has been preached in every city from the earliest times and is* still being *read in the synagogues on every Sabbath* (21). In such contexts, where Moses' teachings were well known and highly respected, Jewish scruples were sensitive and out of charity should not be violated.

A degree of uncertainty, however, surrounds what is sometimes referred to, at least in Anglican circles, as 'the Jerusalem Quadrilateral', that is, the four requested abstentions. At first sight, they

---

a Hebrew text different from the Masoretic, which presumably lay behind the LXX translation, and which, in a form almost identical to the LXX wording, the Qumran community seem to have known. [12] *BC*, IV, p. 177.

appear to be an odd mixture of moral and ceremonial matters, since sexual immorality belongs to the former category, and idol-meats, 'things strangled' (AV) and blood to the latter. How could James combine them, as if they were of equal importance? Besides, sexual chastity is an elementary ingredient in Christian holiness; so why state the obvious by including it in the list? In addition, verse 20 raises complex textual questions, as variant Greek readings reflect variant interpretations. Two main solutions have been proposed, both aimed at separating the ethical from the ritual.

The first is to regard the requested abstentions as being all moral. Since the third ('the meat of strangled animals') cannot by any feat of imagination or ingenuity be turned into an ethical matter, it is proposed to follow the Western text and omit it. We are then left with three. 'Food polluted by idols' (20) or 'food sacrificed to idols' (29) is understood as idolatry; 'blood' is interpreted as blood-shedding, that is, murder; and 'sexual immorality' retains its moral meaning. These three (idolatry, murder and immorality) were in Jewish eyes the main moral offences which human beings can commit. It seems a neat solution, but it raises more problems than it solves. (i) The textual warrant for dropping 'the meat of strangled animals' is very weak; (ii) the interpretation of the unqualified word 'blood' as meaning murder is far-fetched; (iii) the three sins are so grave, that a special apostolic decree was not necessary to outlaw them; (iv) the choice of only three moral prohibitions raises the question whether Gentile converts were permitted to break the rest of the Ten Commandments, *e.g.* to steal, bear false witness and covet. It may be this lacuna which led a scribe to add the Golden Rule in negative form, preserved in the Western text: 'and not to do to others what one would not have done to oneself.'

The alternative solution is the opposite, namely to regard the four abstentions as being all ceremonial, all matters of external purity. In this case, the first is not actual idolatry but the eating of idol-meats, to which Paul was later to refer in Romans 14 and 1 Corinthians 8. 'Blood' refers not to shedding it, but to eating it, which was forbidden in Leviticus, while 'the meat of strangled animals' related to 'animals killed without having the blood drained from them, whose flesh the Jews were forbidden to eat (Lv. 17:13–14)'.[13] In place of these two, the Gentile believers would be expected to eat 'kosher' food, prepared according to Jewish dietary rules. This leaves the fourth item, sexual immorality. It now seems to be the moral exception to a list of ceremonial requirements, just as 'things strangled' was the ceremonial exception to a list of moral requirements. One way of dealing with the problem is to omit the

[13] BAGD.

word, and there seems to have been at least one manuscript in existence which did this, and which was known to Origen in the third century. But the evidence for this is extremely flimsy. The better way is to interpret *porneia* (which covers, in any case, 'every kind of unlawful sexual intercourse', BAGD) as referring here 'to all the irregular marriages listed in Leviticus 18' (JB margin), in particular to 'marriage within degrees of blood-relationship or affinity forbidden by the legislation of Leviticus 18'.[14] A number of other commentators agree with this interpretation.

If this reconstruction is correct, then all four requested abstentions related to ceremonial laws laid down in Leviticus 17 and 18, and three of them concerned dietary matters which could inhibit Jewish-Gentile common meals. To abstain would be a courteous and temporary (although in some circumstances 'necessary', 28, RSV) concession to Jewish consciences, once circumcision had been declared unnecessary, and so the truth of the gospel had been secured and the principle of equality established. 'The abstinence here recommended must be understood . . . not as an essential Christian duty, but as a concession to the consciences of others, *i.e.* of the Jewish converts, who still regarded such food as unlawful and abominable in the sight of God'.[15]

3. The Council's letter (15:22–29)

The Council agreed with James's summary. The combination of prophetic Scripture and apostolic experience seemed conclusive to them, as it had done to him. And James's proposal of Gentile Christian abstinence in four cultural areas seemed a wise policy to promote mutual tolerance and fellowship. So *then the apostles and elders, with the whole church, decided to choose some of their own men* (*i.e.* members of the Jerusalem church) *and send them to Antioch with Paul and Barnabas. They chose Judas (called Barsabbas)*, evidently a Hebrew-speaking believer, of whom nothing else is known, unless by chance he was a brother of Joseph Barsabbas (1:23), *and Silas,* whose Latin name was Silvanus, a Hellenist who was also a Roman citizen (16:37) and who later became closely associated with both Paul[16] and Peter.[17] These *two men* Luke describes as *leaders among the brothers* (22). The church did not decide only to choose emissaries to send to the church of Antioch, however, from whom the request had come to adjudicate in this controversy, but also to write a letter to the churches with a Gentile membership, in order to convey the decisions. A letter can seem

[14] Bruce, *English*, p. 315; he mentions 1 Cor. 5:1 as an example, where *porneia* means 'incest'. [15] Alexander, II, p. 84.

[16] Acts 15:40; 2 Cor. 1:19; 1 Thes. 1:1; 2 Thes. 1:1. [17] 1 Pet. 5:12.

impersonal; it was wise to send people with it who could explain its origin, interpret its meaning and secure its acceptance.

The letter has justly been described as 'a masterpiece of tact and delicacy'.[18] It began in a markedly brotherly manner: *With them* (*sc.* Judas Barsabbas and Silas) *they sent the following letter:*

The apostles and elders, your brothers,

To the Gentile believers in Antioch, Syria and Cilicia:

Greetings. (23)

The NIV text conceals, however, that the Greek text reads 'The apostles and elders, your brothers, to the Gentile brothers in Antioch, Syria and Cilicia.' Whenever brothers communicate with brothers, one has good reason to expect to find a conciliatory spirit. This was the case here. The text of the letter was as follows:

> [24]*We have heard that some went out from us without our authorisation and disturbed you, troubling your minds by what they said.* [25]*So we all agreed to choose some men and send them to you with our dear friends Barnabas and Paul –* [26]*men who have risked their lives for the name of our Lord Jesus Christ.* [27]*Therefore we are sending Judas and Silas to confirm by word of mouth what we are writing.* [28]*It seemed good to the Holy Spirit and to us not to burden you with anything beyond the following requirements.* [29]*You are to abstain from food sacrificed to idols, from blood, from the meat of strangled animals and from sexual immorality. You will do well to avoid these things.*
>
> *Farewell.*

The Jerusalem church and its leaders made three important points in their letter. First, they disassociated themselves from the circumcision party and therefore, by clear implication, from the requirement of circumcision. These men *went out from us* but *without our authorisation* (RSV, 'although we gave them no instructions'). The unauthorized message, moreover, had *disturbed* their hearers (24, the verb is *tarassō*, to trouble, upset or throw into confusion, interestingly the very word which Paul uses of them in Galatians 1:7 and 5:10). Secondly, they made it abundantly clear that the men they had now *agreed to choose . . . and send . . .* (25), namely *Judas and Silas*, did have their full approval and support. They would not only deliver the letter, but also *confirm by word of mouth* what it contained (27). Thirdly, they enunciated their unanimous decision (made by *the Holy Spirit and . . . us*) *not to burden* Gentile converts *with anything* (certainly not with circumcision) *beyond*

[18] Rackham, p. 255.

the following requirements (28), namely the four specified abstentions, which we have already considered. The letter's conclusion, which expresses more a recommendation than a command, was: *You will do well to avoid these things* (29).

4. The sequel to the Council (15:30 – 16:5)

Having shared with his readers the text of the letter, Luke now documents its reception by the largely Gentile churches, first in Syrian Antioch (15:30–35), secondly in Syria and Cilicia (15:36–40), and thirdly in Galatia (16:1–5).

a. Antioch receives the letter (15:30–35)

Antioch was named at the head of the letter as its first recipient, because it was there that the original controversy had broken out and from there that the appeal for help had come.

The men were sent off and went down to Antioch, where they gathered the church together and delivered the letter. [31]*The people read it and were glad for its encouraging message.* [32]*Judas and Silas, who themselves were prophets, said much to encourage and strengthen the brothers.* [33]*After spending some time there, they were sent off by the brothers with the blessing of peace to return to those who had sent them.* [35]*But Paul and Barnabas remained in Antioch, where they and many others taught and preached the word of the Lord.*

This gathering together of the church in Antioch must have reminded them of a similar meeting some time previously (14:27). Paul and Barnabas were present on both occasions. Then it had been to receive a report of the first missionary journey with its wonderful news of the conversion of Gentiles; now it was to receive the Jerusalem letter with its equally wonderful news that Gentiles who had believed in Jesus were to be accepted as Christians, without the need to become Jews as well. Small wonder that, on hearing the contents of the letter, *the people . . . were glad for its encouraging message* (31). *Judas and Silas,* now identified as *prophets,* stayed on for some time *and said much to encourage and strengthen the brothers* (32), but they then returned to Jerusalem, sent on their way *with the blessing of peace* (33). The statement of verse 34 that 'Silas decided to remain there' (NIV margin, *cf.* AV) is obviously a gloss. The best manuscripts omit it. It was probably added to explain how in verse 40 Silas was in Antioch, but it contradicts the plain statement of verse 33 that he and Judas both left. *Paul and Barnabas* stayed, however, and with *many others taught and preached* (literally, 'evangelized') *the word of the Lord* (35).

b. Syria and Cilicia receive the letter (15:36–41)

The single province of Syria (to which Antioch belonged) and Cilicia (in which Tarsus was situated) had been the scene of some of Paul's earliest evangelistic endeavours (9:30).[19] It evidently had some Gentile churches, for they are specifically named at the head of the Jerusalem letter (23). But before Luke can narrate how the letter reached them, he is obliged in his honesty to tell the sad story of how Paul and Barnabas came to separate.

Some time later Paul said to Barnabas, 'Let us go back and visit the brothers in all the towns where we preached the word of the Lord and see how they are doing.' 37*Barnabas wanted to take John, also called Mark, with them,* 38*but Paul did not think it wise to take him, because he had deserted them in Pamphylia and had not continued with them in the work.* 39*They had such a sharp disagreement that they parted company. Barnabas took Mark and sailed for Cyprus,* 40*but Paul chose Silas and left, commended by the brothers to the grace of the Lord.* 41*He went through Syria and Cilicia, strengthening the churches.*

We observe that it was *some time later* (perhaps when winter gave place to spring and travel became feasible again) that Paul made his proposal to Barnabas that they should revisit the Galatian converts and see how they were getting on (36). Barnabas agreed, but wanted to take his cousin John Mark with them, perhaps to give him a second chance (37). But Paul considered this unwise, for he took a serious view of Mark's desertion and lack of perseverance (38). The disagreement between them was so sharp that they parted company, Barnabas taking Mark and sailing for his home country Cyprus (39), while Paul chose Silas, whose recent ministry in Antioch had evidently impressed him, and they were *commended* by the church *to the grace of the Lord* (40), just as Paul and Barnabas had been for their missionary journey (14:26). God certainly overruled 'this melancholy disagreement',[20] since as a result of it 'out of one pair two were made', as Bengel commented.[21] But this example of God's providence may not be used as an excuse for Christian quarrelling. It was now that *he* (Paul, though with Silas, as we have just learned) *went through Syria and Cilicia,* which would involve their walking through the majestic, narrow pass in the Taurus mountains known as the 'Cilician Gates', *strengthening* (JB, 'consolidating') *the churches* (41), without doubt by delivering the letter as well as by their teaching and encouragement.

[19] Gal. 1:21, 23. [20] Calvin, II, p. 60. [21] Bengel, p. 654.

c. Galatia receives the letter (16:1–5)

He came to Derbe and then to Lystra, where a disciple named Timothy lived, whose mother was a Jewess and a believer, but whose father was a Greek. [2]The brothers at Lystra and Iconium spoke well of him. [3]Paul wanted to take him along on the journey, so he circumcised him because of the Jews who lived in that area, for they all knew that his father was a Greek. [4]As they travelled from town to town, they delivered the decisions reached by the apostles and elders in Jerusalem for the people to obey. [5]So the churches were strengthened in the faith and grew daily in numbers.

Lystra and Derbe were the last Galatian towns to have been visited on the first missionary journey. So now, as Paul approached them from the east, Derbe and Lystra were of course the first to be revisited. The most notable event took place in Lystra. Here lived Timothy (*a disciple*) and his mother Eunice,[22] who was a *Jewess*, but had become a *believer*. Presumably both mother and son had been converted during Paul's previous visit about five years previously.[23] Timothy's father, however, was a Greek (1), and because in verse 3 the verb 'was' (*hypērchen*) is in the imperfect tense, some commentators surmise that he was now dead. Since Timothy had an excellent reputation with the Christians in both Iconium and Lystra (2), Paul wanted to recruit him into his mission team, not just as a companion, but as a worker, perhaps to take Mark's place, as Silas had taken Barnabas'. His Jewish-Greek parentage would give him an entrée into both communities. But, although he will have been brought up by his mother in the Jewish faith, he had never been circumcised. So Paul circumcised him *because of* (NEB, 'out of consideration for') *the Jews who lived in that area*, and to make his ministry acceptable to them, since they knew about his Greek father (3) and would have guessed that he was uncircumcised. It is really marvellous that, so soon after Paul's hot indignation over the Judaizers in Antioch (15:1), and his vehement statements against circumcision in his Letter to the Galatians,[24] he should now be prepared to circumcise Timothy. Little minds would have condemned him for inconsistency. But there was a deep consistency in his thought and action. Once the principle had been established that circumcision was not necessary for salvation, he was ready to make concessions in policy. What was unnecessary for acceptance with God was advisable for acceptance by some human beings.

Probably Timothy was also 'ordained' before leaving Lystra. At

[22] 2 Tim. 1:5, *cf.* 2 Tim. 3:15. [23] 1 Cor. 4:17.
[24] *E.g.* Gal. 1:6–9; 3:1–5; 5:2–6. [25] 1 Tim. 4:14; 2 Tim. 1:6.

least Paul and the church elders laid their hands on him,[25] presumably to commission him for his ministry. Now, as Paul, Silas and Timothy *travelled from town to town, they delivered the decisions* contained in the letter, and in consequence the churches *were strengthened in the faith and grew daily in numbers* (as in 2:47).

It is noteworthy that in each of these three paragraphs which describe the reception of the Jerusalem letter, Luke makes a similar statement about the church. In Antioch Judas and Silas spoke the word in order to *strengthen the brothers* (15:32). Then Paul and Silas went through Syria and Cilicia, *strengthening the churches* (15:41), and as they journeyed on through and beyond Galatia, *the churches were strengthened* (16:5). The first two verbs are both *epistērizō*, as in 14:22, where we noted that it is almost a technical term for the establishing or consolidating of Christian individuals and churches; the third is a similar verb *stereoō*, to make strong or firm. So wise and healthy was the Jerusalem Council's decision, incorporated in their letter, that wherever its good news went, the churches grew in stability and steadfastness.

5. Permanent lessons

Students who read Acts 15 today are tempted to dismiss it impatiently as being of purely antiquarian interest. There is no circumcision party nowadays trying to impose Mosaic rituals on anybody, and it would be ludicrous to expect any contemporary Christian group to accept the four apostolic abstentions, although some of them (like eating kosher food) could still apply to Christians living among conservative Jews. Otherwise, the whole incident appears remote, even irrelevant. Yet it contains at least two lessons of permanent value, the first relating to salvation, and the second to fellowship.

a. Salvation: an issue of Christian truth

The Judaizers were arguing that circumcision was necessary for salvation (1). There was, therefore, a danger of the church breaking up into competing theological factions, with different apostles teaching different gospels, and the church's unity destroyed. The danger was real enough. The Judaizers claimed the authority of James and contradicted Paul. Peter was led astray and was opposed by Paul. The three apostles appeared to be at loggerheads, with James and Paul on opposite sides and Peter oscillating between them. The situation was critical. So Luke was at great pains to describe how in the Council Peter spoke first, then Paul, then James; how Scripture and experience coincided; and how the apostles (Peter, Paul and James), the elders and the whole church reached a unanimous decision (22, 28). Thus the unity of the gospel preserved the unity of the church. In spite of its rich diversity of formulation and emphasis in the New Testament, there is only one apostolic gospel. We must resist modern theologians who set the New Testament writers at variance with each other, and who talk about Pauline, Petrine and Johannine positions as if they were incompatible gospels. Even Paul and James, who were reconciled at the Council, can be reconciled in their New Testament letters too. They taught the same way of salvation.

Moreover, the gospel of Christ's apostles is the gospel of God's free grace, of his undeserved love for sinners in the death of his Son in our place. Further, it is the gospel of God's sufficient grace. It cannot be regarded either as a supplement to something else (*e.g.* Judaism) or as needing to be supplemented by something else (*e.g.* circumcision), without being undermined. Yet this was exactly the Judaizers' mistake. To them faith in Jesus was not enough; circumcision and law works had to be added. Today people try to add works of a different kind, philanthropy perhaps or religious observances, or a particular ceremony or experience. In each case it is a 'Jesus plus' gospel, which is derogatory to the adequacy of his work. We need to echo Peter: 'We believe it is through the grace of our Lord Jesus that we are saved, just as they' (11). We and they, Jews and Gentiles, are saved in the same way, through the one and only apostolic gospel of God's grace.

b. Fellowship: an issue of Christian love

It was one thing to secure the gospel from corruption; it was another to preserve the church from fragmentation. Paul was resolutely unwilling to compromise 'the truth of the gospel'.[26] He resisted the Judaizers, rebuked Peter publicly, and wrote a passionate appeal to the Galatians.[27] At the same time, he was extremely anxious to maintain Jewish-Gentile solidarity in the one body of Christ. So how could he unite the church without compromising the gospel, or defend the integrity of the gospel without sacrificing the unity of the church? His answer reveals the greatness of his mind and heart. Once the theological principle was firmly established, that salvation is by grace alone, and that circumcision was not required but neutral, he was prepared to adjust his practical policies. He made two notable concessions, both for the same conciliatory reason. First, he accepted the four cultural abstentions proposed by Jewish leaders to Gentile converts, because Moses was widely read and preached, and this Gentile restraint would ease Jewish consciences and facilitate Jewish-Gentile social intercourse.

[26] Gal. 2:14. [27] *E.g.* Gal. 1:6–9; 3:1–5; 5:2–6.

Secondly, he circumcised Timothy (he who had just been fulminating against circumcision!), out of consideration for the Jews who would be offended if he remained uncircumcised.

Some commentators have been so astonished by the apparent discrepancy between Paul the inflexible, who opposed circumcision, and Paul the flexible who circumcised Timothy, that they have pronounced them irreconcilable. This was the main reason why F. C. Baur wrote: 'the Paul of the Acts is manifestly quite a different person from the Paul of the Epistles'.[28] But the fact is that the discrepancy is found within the Acts narrative itself. Besides, Paul's concessions in Acts 15 and 16 are entirely in keeping with the conciliatory teaching of his letters. He urged Christians with a 'strong' (or educated) conscience not to violate the consciences of the 'weak' (or over-scrupulous). A strong conscience gives us liberty of behaviour, but we should limit our liberty out of love for the weak.[29] Again, though free, Paul was willing to make himself a slave to others. To those under the law he was prepared to become like one under the law, in order to win those under the law.[30] Was that not exactly what he was doing when he circumcised Timothy, as also when some years later he accepted James' proposal in Jerusalem that he join in certain Jewish purification rites (21:17–26)?

We may say, then, that the Jerusalem Council secured a double victory – a victory of truth in confirming the gospel of grace, and a victory of love in preserving the fellowship by sensitive concessions to conscientious Jewish scruples. As Luther put it, Paul was strong in faith, and soft in love. So, 'as concerning faith we ought to be invincible, and more hard, if it might be, than the adamant stone; but as touching charity, we ought to be soft, and more flexible than the reed or leaf that is shaken with the wind, and ready to yield to everything'.[31] Or as John Newton once said during a meeting of the Eclectic Society in 1799, 'Paul was a reed in non-essentials, – an iron pillar in essentials.'[32]

[28] Baur, *Paul*, I, p. 11. See also (to the contrary) W. W. Gasque, 'Book', pp. 64–70.

[29] *E.g.* Rom. 14 and 1 Cor. 8. [30] 1 Cor. 9:19–20.

[31] *Commentary on the Epistle to the Galatians* by Martin Luther, based on lectures delivered in 1531 (James Clarke, 1953), p. 112.

[32] *The Thought of the Evangelical Leaders*, Notes of the Discussions of the Eclectic Society, London, during the years 1798–1814, ed. John H. Pratt (1856; reprinted by Banner of Truth Trust, 1978), p. 151.

12. Mission in Macedonia *16:6–17:15*

The most notable feature of Paul's second missionary expedition, which Luke narrates in these chapters, is that during it the good seed of the gospel was now for the first time planted in European soil. Of course there was in those days no line of demarcation between 'Asia' and 'Europe', and the missionaries sailing across the northern part of the Aegean Sea were conscious of travelling only from one province to another, not from one continent to another, since both shores of the Aegean belonged to the Roman Empire. Nevertheless, I agree with Campbell Morgan who wrote: 'That invasion of Europe was not in the mind of Paul, but it was evidently in the mind of the Spirit.'[1] With the benefit of hindsight, knowing that Europe became the first Christian continent and was until fairly recently the main base for missionary outreach to the rest of the world, we can see what an epoch-making development this was. It was from Europe that in due course the gospel fanned out to the great continents of Africa, Asia, North America, Latin America and Oceania, and so reached the ends of the earth.

What Paul and his companions were conscious of doing was to establish new churches in three Roman provinces during the second missionary journey, which they had not penetrated during the first. In the first they had concentrated exclusively on Cyprus and Galatia; in the second they reached Macedonia and Achaia, the provinces of northern and southern Greece respectively, and they just touched the province of Asia by visiting Ephesus, promising to return during their next journey. Moreover, in each case the missionaries included the capital city in their itinerary – Thessalonica being Macedonia's capital, Corinth being Achaia's, and Ephesus being Asia's. In addition, to each of the churches in these capital cities Paul was later to write, namely his letters to the Thessalonians, the Corinthians and the Ephesians. In this chapter we focus on

[1] Morgan, p. 287.

his mission in Macedonia, which involved visits to three principal Macedonian cities, Philippi, Thessalonica and Berea.

How, then, did the missionaries come to reach Europe? Paul had set out from Syrian Antioch, again commended by the church to God's grace, not primarily in order to plant new churches, but to nurture and strengthen those planted several years previously during his first expedition. The verb translated 'visit' in 15:36 (*episkeptomai*) is linked with *episkopē*, pastoral oversight, and is used of visiting the sick[2] and of looking after widows and orphans.[3] Paul was more than a pioneer missionary; he was concerned to see churches and believers grow into maturity. So he and his companions spent time first in Derbe and Lystra, and then in Iconium and Pisidian Antioch, which is probably what Luke meant by *the region of Phrygia and Galatia*, namely 'the Phrygian region of the province of Galatia'.[4] It is very instructive to see how God guided them in their next moves.

Paul and his companions travelled throughout the region of Phrygia
and Galatia, having been kept by the Holy Spirit from preaching
the word in the province of Asia. 7When they came to the border
of Mysia, they tried to enter Bithynia, but the Spirit of Jesus would
not allow them to. 8So they passed by Mysia and went down to
Troas. 9During the night Paul had a vision of a man of Macedonia
standing and begging him, 'Come over to Macedonia and help us.'
10After Paul had seen the vision, we got ready at once to leave for
Macedonia, concluding that God had called us to preach the gospel
to them.

Pisidian Antioch, the centre of the Phrygian region, was also very close to the border of the province of Asia. It was natural, therefore, that the missionaries' eyes should look south-west along the *Via Sebaste* which led to Colosse (about 150 miles) and then to the coast at Ephesus (almost as many miles beyond). In fact, they seem to have travelled some way along this road, but in some undefined way were prevented by the Holy Spirit *from preaching the word in the province of Asia* (6). With the south-westerly route blocked, they turned north, until they reached *the border of Mysia*, which was not a Roman administrative region but an old name for much of Asia Minor's north-westerly bulge. Here they tried to continue north and enter Bithynia, the province situated on the southern shore of the Black Sea, including towns like Nicea and Nicomedia. But again, in some way which Luke does not explain, *the Spirit of Jesus would not allow them to* (7). It has been conjectured from

[2] Mt. 25:36, 43. [3] Jas. 1:27.
[4] Ramsay, *St Paul*, pp. 194, 196. *Cf. Church*, p. 93.

the fact that Peter later wrote to the Christian dispersion in these parts, including Asia and Bithynia,[5] that Paul was kept from evangelizing there in order to make way for Peter. But how the Holy Spirit did his preventive work on these two occasions we can only guess. It may have been through giving the missionaries a strong, united inward impression, or through some outward circumstance like illness, Jewish opposition or a legal ban, or through the utterance of a Christian prophet, perhaps Silas himself (15:32). At all events, having come from the east, and having found the south-westerly and northerly roads obstructed, the only direction left open to them was north-west. So they went 'through' Mysia (JB) or *passed by* it, which could mean either that they 'neglected' it, in the sense that they did not stop to evangelize there,[6] or that they 'skirted' it (NEB), because there was no main road straight through its territory to the coast.[7] Whichever precise route they took, they arrived in the Aegean port of *Troas* (8), close to the Hellespont, which we call the Dardanelles. They had come a long way, in fact all the way from the south-east to the north-west extremities of Asia Minor, and by a strangely circuitous route. They must have been in a state of considerable perplexity, wondering what God's plan and purpose were, for so far their guidance had been almost entirely negative. Only now did they receive a positive lead.

One night in Troas Paul had a dream or vision in which he saw *a man of Macedonia standing and begging him* in some posture of appeal, perhaps beckoning, and heard him saying, '*Come over to Macedonia* [across the Aegean Sea] *and help us*' (9). William Barclay made the improbable suggestion that the man in the dream was Alexander the Great, partly because 'the district was permeated with memories of Alexander' and partly because Alexander's aim had been 'to marry the east to the west' and so make one world, while Paul's vision was to make 'one world for Christ'.[8] Sir William Ramsay argued that the Macedonian was Luke, whom Paul had just met in Troas, possibly consulting him as a doctor. It is likely that Luke had some personal connection with Philippi, and certain that he was in Troas at the time, since in the next verse (10) he begins the first of the 'we-sections' by which, quietly but deliberately, he draws attention to his presence at the time. The identification of the Macedonian with Luke is entirely conjectural, however, and Ramsay admitted that some would regard it as 'moonstruck fancy'.[9]

What we do know is that the following morning Paul told his

[5] 1 Pet. 1:1. [6] Ramsay, *St Paul*, pp. 195, 197.

[7] See Paul Bowers' note on Acts 16:8 entitled 'Paul's Route through Mysia' in *The Journal of Theological Studies*, Vol. XXX, Part 2, 1979, pp. 507–511.

[8] Barclay, p. 132. [9] Ramsay, *St Paul*, p. 204.

companions his vision, that together they discussed its meaning and implications, and that they concluded that God had called them to preach the gospel to the Macedonians. So they *got ready at once to leave for Macedonia* (10). A. T. Pierson in his *The Acts of the Holy Spirit* drew attention to what he called 'the double guidance of the apostle and his companions', namely, 'on the one hand *prohibition and restraint*, on the other *permission and constraint*. They are forbidden in one direction, invited in another; one way the Spirit says "go not"; the other he calls "Come".' Pierson went on to give some later examples from the history of missions of this same 'double guidance': Livingstone tried to go to China, but God sent him to Africa instead. Before him, Carey planned to go to Polynesia in the South Seas, but God guided him to India. Judson went to India first, but was driven on to Burma. We too in our day, Pierson concludes, 'need to trust him for guidance and rejoice equally in his restraints and constraints'.[10]

Some important principles of divine guidance are, in fact, exemplified in the experience of Paul and his companions. God led them by a combination of factors, over a period of time, ending when they pondered their meaning together. First came the double prohibition, somehow barring their way into both Asia and Bithynia, and leading them to Troas, whose harbour faced west to Macedonia. This was followed by the night vision calling to Paul for help. These circumstances were the basis for their discussion, as they asked themselves and each other what these things indicated. They then put two and two together, the negative (the block to Asia and Bithynia) and the positive (the appeal to Macedonia), and concluded that through these various experiences God was calling them to go over to Macedonia to 'help', that is, to preach the gospel there. From this we may learn that usually God's guidance is not negative only but also positive (some doors close, others open); not circumstantial only, but also rational (thinking about our situation); not personal only, but also corporate (a sharing of the data with others, so that we can mull over them together and reach a common mind). Indeed the verb *symbibazō* in verse 10, translated 'assuredly gathering' (AV), 'concluding' (RSV, NIV, NEB) and 'convinced' (JBP, JB), means literally to 'bring together', to 'put together in one's mind' (GT), and so to infer something from a variety of data.

1. The mission in Philippi (16:11–40)

From Troas we put out to sea and sailed straight for Samothrace, and the next day on to Neapolis. [12]*From there we travelled to*

[10] Pierson, pp. 120–122.

Philippi, a Roman colony and the leading city of that district of Macedonia. And we stayed there several days.

Luke 'has the true Greek feeling for the sea', wrote Sir William Ramsay,[11] for, as he (Luke) has now joined the missionary team and travels with them, he gives some details of their voyage across the Aegean. He mentions *Samothrace*, a rocky island whose peak rises to 5,000 feet, where they probably made an overnight stop, and *Neapolis*, the modern port of Kavalla, where *the next day* they landed (11). They must have enjoyed a favourable wind to complete their 150-mile journey in only two days, since it took them five days on their return (20:6). From Neapolis they had a ten-mile walk inland to Philippi along the *Via Egnatia*, which ran right across the Greek peninsula from the Aegean to the Adriatic. Its massive paving stones can still be seen, worn down by the traffic of the centuries.

Philippi was given its name by Philip of Macedon in the 4th century BC. After about two centuries as a Greek colony, it became part of the Roman Empire, and towards the end of the first century BC it was made *a Roman colony* and settled with numerous veterans. Luke also knows that the province of Macedonia had been divided into four districts, and calls Philippi *the leading city of that district of Macedonia*. Other scholars translate 'a leading city of the district of Macedonia', while yet others suggest a conjectural emendation of the text, which then reads 'a city of the first district of Macedonia'.[12] Whichever is correct, Luke is expressing pride in what was probably his own city. In this city the missionary team stayed for *several days* (12), indeed almost certainly several weeks. During this period of mission there must have been many converts. But Luke selects only three for mention, not (it seems) because they were particularly notable in themselves, but because they demonstrate how God breaks down dividing barriers and can unite in Christ people of very different kinds.

a. A business woman named Lydia (16:13–15)

On the Sabbath we went outside the city gate to the river, where we expected to find a place of prayer. We sat down and began to speak to the women who had gathered there. [14]*One of those listening was a woman named Lydia, a dealer in purple cloth from the city of Thyatira, who was a worshipper of God. The Lord opened her heart to respond to Paul's message.* [15]*When she and the members of her household were baptised, she invited us to her home. 'If you consider me a believer in the Lord,' she said, 'come and stay at my*

[11] Ramsay, *St Paul*, p. 205.
[12] See the full discussion in Metzger, pp. 444–446.

house.' And she persuaded us.

There seems to have been no synagogue in Philippi, but there was *a place of prayer* (as the missionaries had expected there would be), which was just over a mile *outside the city gate*. It may have been an enclosure of some kind, or just an open air site. It was close to the small river Gangites, whose proximity would have been useful for ceremonial ablutions. Since Luke adds that the congregation consisted of women, it is usually assumed that this explains the non-existence of a synagogue: a quorum of ten men was necessary before a synagogue could be constituted. Anyway, Paul and his friends joined the women for worship *on the Sabbath*, and *sat down* waiting to be invited to speak (13).

One of the women, *named Lydia*, came from Thyatira which was situated in the Lycus Valley on the other side of the Aegean, within provincial Asia. Because that area was previously the ancient kingdom of Lydia, it is possible that 'Lydia' was not so much her personal name as her trade name; she may have been known as 'the Lydian lady'. Thyatira had been famed for centuries for its dyes, and an early inscription refers to a guild of dyers in the town. Lydia herself specialized in cloth treated with an expensive purple dye, and was presumably the Macedonian agent of a Thyatiran manufacturer. She was also *a worshipper of God*, believing and behaving like a Jew without having become one. As she listened to Paul's message, *the Lord opened her heart to respond* (14). That is, he opened her inner eyes to see and to believe in the Jesus Paul proclaimed. We note that, although the message was Paul's, the saving initiative was God's. Paul's preaching was not effective in itself; the Lord worked through it. And the Lord's work was not itself direct; he chose to work through Paul's preaching. It is always the same.

Soon after her conversion Lydia *and the members of her household (oikos) were baptised*. This is the second household baptism Luke records.[13] The household is likely to have included her servants. Whether it also included her children (assuming that she was a widow) is a moot point, although it is worth mentioning that *oikos* is certainly used sometimes for a family with children.[14] Lydia then invited Paul and his companions into her house (which probably became the Christians' meeting place), for once the heart is opened, the home is opened too. If they considered her *a believer in the Lord*, she said, it would surely be appropriate for her to entertain them. She was very persuasive, in fact 'she insisted' (15, NEB, JBP). This has led to several rumours, for example that the

[13] *Cf.* Acts 10:33; 16:33; 18:8; 1 Cor. 1:16. [14] *E.g.* 1 Tim. 3:4–5, 12; 5:4.

Lydian lady was either Euodia or Syntyche[15] or Paul's 'true yoke-fellow',[16] and even that, as such, she and Paul had married. But these are nothing but wild speculations.

b. An anonymous slave girl (16:16–18)

Once when we were going to the place of prayer, we were met by a slave girl who had a spirit by which she predicted the future. She earned a great deal of money for her owners by fortune-telling.
[17]This girl followed Paul and the rest of us, shouting, 'These men are servants of the Most High God, who are telling you the way to be saved.' [18]She kept this up for many days. Finally Paul became so troubled that he turned round and said to the spirit, 'In the name of Jesus Christ I command you to come out of her!' At that moment the spirit left her.

On another sabbath, when Paul and his friends were going *to the place of prayer*, they were *met by a slave girl*, who evidently stood in their way. Luke tells us two things about her. First, she *had a spirit by which she predicted the future*, or, literally, she had 'a spirit of a python' or 'a python spirit'. The reference is to the snake of classical mythology which guarded the temple of Apollo and the Delphic oracle at Mount Parnassus. Apollo was thought to be embodied in the snake and to inspire 'pythonesses', his female devotees, with clairvoyance, although other people thought of them as ventriloquists. Luke does not commit himself to these superstitions, but he does regard the slave girl as possessed by an evil spirit. The second thing he tells us is that as a slave she was exploited by her owners, for whom she made a lot of money *by fortune-telling* (16). As Paul and his friends continued their walk, the girl followed them screaming: '*These men are servants of the Most High God*' (a term for the Supreme Being which was applied by Jews to Yahweh and by Greeks to Zeus), '*who are telling you the way to be saved*' (17). Since salvation was a popular topic of conversation in those days, even if it meant different things to different people, it is not in the least strange that the girl should have hailed the missionaries as teachers of 'the way of salvation'. Nor is it strange that the evil spirit should have cried out in recognition of God's messengers, for Luke has documented the same thing during the public ministry of Jesus.[17] But why should a demon engage in evangelism? Perhaps the ulterior motive was to discredit the gospel by associating it in people's minds with the occult.

The girl's shrieks continued *for many days* until *finally* Paul was provoked to take action. He was *troubled*, Luke says, which cer-

[15] Phil 4:2 [16] Phil 4:3 [17] Lk. 4:33–34, 41; 8:27–28

tainly means that he was deeply 'disturbed' (BAGD). The verb *diaponeomai* could be translated 'annoyed' (RSV), but it is gratuitous to say that Paul had 'a burst of irritation' (JBP) or 'lost his temper' (JB). It is better to understand that he was 'grieved' (AV), indeed indignant, because of the poor girl's condition, and also dismayed by this inappropriate and unwelcome kind of publicity. His distress led him to turn round and command the evil spirit in the name of Jesus Christ to come out of her, which it immediately did (18). Although Luke does not explicitly refer to either her conversion or her baptism, the fact that her deliverance took place between the conversions of Lydia and the gaoler leads readers to infer that she too became a member of the Philippian church.

c. *The Roman gaoler (16:19–40)*

The deliverance of the slave girl was too much for her owners, however, who realized that, if the evil spirit had gone out of her (*exēlthen*), *their hope of making money was gone*, or had 'gone out' too (*exēlthen*). The repetition of the verb is surely deliberate. As F. F. Bruce comments: 'When Paul exorcized the spirit that possessed her, he exorcized their source of income as well.'[18] Their fury had some very unpleasant consequences for the missionaries, especially for Paul and Silas.

When the owners of the slave girl realised that their hope of making money was gone, they seized Paul and Silas and dragged them into the market-place to face the authorities. [20]*They brought them before the magistrates and said, 'These men are Jews, and are throwing our city into an uproar* [21]*by advocating customs unlawful for us Romans to accept or practise.'*

[22]*The crowd joined in the attack against Paul and Silas, and the magistrates ordered them to be stripped and beaten.* [23]*After they had been severely flogged, they were thrown into prison, and the jailer was commanded to guard them carefully.* [24]*Upon receiving such orders, he put them in the inner cell and fastened their feet in the stocks.*

[25]*About midnight Paul and Silas were praying and singing hymns to God, and the other prisoners were listening to them.* [26]*Suddenly there was such a violent earthquake that the foundations of the prison were shaken. At once all the prison doors flew open, and everybody's chains came loose.* [27]*The jailer woke up, and when he saw the prison doors open, he drew his sword and was about to kill himself because he thought the prisoners had escaped.* [28]*But Paul shouted, 'Don't harm yourself! We are all here!'*

[29]*The jailer called for lights, rushed in and fell trembling before*

[18] Bruce, *English*, p. 335.

Paul and Silas. [30]*He then brought them out and asked, 'Sirs, what must I do to be saved?'*

[31]*They replied, 'Believe in the Lord Jesus, and you will be saved – you and your household.'* [32]*Then they spoke the word of the Lord to him and to all the others in his house.* [33]*At that hour of the night the jailer took them and washed their wounds; then immediately he and all his family were baptised.* [34]*The jailer brought them into his house and set a meal before them; he was filled with joy because he had come to believe in God – he and his whole family.*

[35]*When it was daylight, the magistrates sent their officers to the jailer with the order: 'Release those men.'* [36]*The jailer told Paul, 'The magistrates have ordered that you and Silas be released. Now you can leave. Go in peace.'*

[37]*But Paul said to the officers: 'They beat us publicly without a trial, even though we are Roman citizens, and threw us into prison. And now do they want to get rid of us quietly? No! Let them come themselves and escort us out.'*

[38]*The officers reported this to the magistrates, and when they heard that Paul and Silas were Roman citizens, they were alarmed.* [39]*They came to appease them and escorted them from the prison, requesting them to leave the city.* [40]*After Paul and Silas came out of the prison, they went to Lydia's house, where they met with the brothers and encouraged them. Then they left.*

Luke's account of what happened in Philippi accurately reflects the situation in a Roman colony. The slave owners dragged Paul and Silas into the *agora*, which was not only *the market-place* but the centre of a city's public life (19). They then brought them before the *stratēgoi*, that is, the two *praetors* who acted as magistrates in a Roman colony. The charge was that *these men are Jews* who '. . . disturb our city and introduce . . . customs which it is not allowed to us Romans to adopt and practise'. The accusations of causing a riot and introducing an alien religion were serious. 'Officially the Roman citizen may not practise any alien cult that has not received the public sanction of the state, but customarily he might do so as long as his cult did not otherwise offend against the laws and usages of Roman life, *i.e.* so long as it did not involve political or social crimes' (20–21).[19] The slave owners were very clever. They not only concealed the real reason for their anger, which was economic, but also presented their legal charge against the missionaries 'in terms that appealed to the latent anti-Semitism of the people ("these men are Jews") and their racial pride ("us Romans")' and so 'ignited the flames of bigotry'.[20]

The crowd then *joined in the attack against Paul and Silas*, and

[19] Sherwin-White, p. 79. [20] Longenecker, *Acts*, p. 463

the praetors ordered their lictors to strip and beat them publicly (22). It was a severe flogging, perhaps the first of the three Paul later mentioned,[21] and it was followed by their being *thrown into prison*, with an instruction to the gaoler to keep them under close guard (23). He therefore confined them *in the inner cell* and *in the stocks* (24). It is wonderful that in such pain, with lacerated backs and aching limbs, Paul and Silas at *about midnight* were *praying and singing hymns to God*. Not groans but songs came from their mouths. Instead of cursing men, they blessed God. No wonder *the other prisoners were listening to them* (25).

Then suddenly the prison's foundations were shaken by *such a violent earthquake* that *all the prison doors flew open*, the prisoners' chains *came loose* (26), and the gaoler *woke up*. Seeing the prison doors open, and imagining that the inmates had escaped, he was about to commit suicide (27), because he would have been held responsible, when Paul shouted to him not to harm himself because the prisoners were all there (28). Haenchen refers to this whole episode as 'a nest of improbabilities',[22] and so indeed it must appear to those who approach it with sceptical presuppositions. But the eye of faith, which believes in a gracious, sovereign God, sees probabilities instead, as he works all things together for good, in this case the conversion of the gaoler and the release of the missionaries. Convicted of sin, the gaoler *fell trembling before Paul and Silas* and asked what he had to do to be saved (29–30). Perhaps he had heard of the slave girl shouting about 'the way to be saved', or perhaps he was simply expressing the longing of his heart. In either case the missionaries first gave him a straight answer, that he must trust personally in the Lord Jesus and he would be saved, with his household (31), and then *spoke the word of the Lord* to him and his household, opening up the way of salvation more fully (32). He not only believed, but repented also. And as a token of his penitence, there and then he *washed their wounds*, and immediately afterwards *he and all his family were baptised*, perhaps in a well or fountain in the prison courtyard, or perhaps using the same bowl from which he had cleaned their wounds (33). Thus, as Chrysostom pointed out, the washing was reciprocal: 'he washed them and was washed; those (*sc.* the imprisoned missionaries) he washed from their stripes, himself was washed from his sins.'[23] The baptized family now welcomed Paul and Silas into their home, just as Lydia had done into hers, *and set a meal before them*. And this celebratory feast was but an external expression of the inward *joy* which *the whole family* experienced, *because*

[21] 2 Cor. 11:23, 25. [22] Haenchen, p. 501.
[23] Chrysostom, Homily XXXVI, p. 225.

they *had come to believe in God* (34).

Early the following morning, the praetors sent their lictors to the gaoler with the order to release Paul and Silas (35), and the gaoler passed the message on to the prisoners. No doubt the authorities thought that a public flogging and a night in gaol were a sufficient punishment, and hoped that the prisoners had learned their lesson and would leave quietly. But Paul reacted differently. He claimed for himself and Silas their rights as Roman citizens. Perhaps they had done so before in the agora, and had been either not heard or not believed. But now a grave injustice had been done to them. For 'according to the text of the *lex Julia* . . . , the Roman citizen might not be beaten or bound by a magistrate *adversus provocationem* or by any other person in any circumstances',[24] let alone untried and uncondemned. The citizen had only to say *civis Romanus sum* and he would be immune to punishment; heavy penalties were prescribed for those who violated these citizenship privileges. So Paul replied to the officers: '*They beat us publicly without a trial, even though we are Roman citizens, and threw us into prison. And now do they want to get rid of us quietly?*', 'push us out on the quiet' (JB) or 'smuggle us out privately' (NEB). '*No! Let them come themselves* in person *and escort us* out' (37). 'Paul seems to have been responsible', writes A. N. Triton, 'for the first recorded "sit-in". He refused to move until the authorities came and apologized. . . . He wanted to compel the authorities to recognize and to fulfil their God-appointed task. This may have been very important for the freedom of the church he left behind.'[25]

When the lictors reported back, the praetors *were alarmed* (38), came to the prison to apologize, and *escorted them from the prison*, as they had demanded, though at the same time, no doubt for the sake of public order, *requesting them to leave the city* (39). This Paul and Silas did, having first returned to *Lydia's house*, in order to meet the church members, encourage them and say goodbye. *Then they left* (40), though without Luke (20:5), satisfied that they had been vindicated and that their mission had been cleared of illegality.

d. The unifying power of the gospel

It would be hard to imagine a more disparate group than the business woman, the slave girl and the gaoler. Racially, socially and psychologically they were worlds apart. Yet all three were changed by the same gospel and were welcomed into the same church.

Take their different *national* origins first. Philippi was a very cosmopolitan city, having been Greek before it was Roman, and

[24] Sherwin-White, p. 71 [25] *Whose World?* by A. N. Triton (IVP, 1970), p. 48.

sitting astride the great east-west *Via Egnatia*. Lydia was an Asiatic, not perhaps in our sense of the word, but in the sense that she came from Asia Minor. She was an immigrant in Philippi, not a native. The slave girl was presumably Greek and a resident. She could have been a foreigner, since slaves were imported from everywhere, but there is nothing in the story to indicate this. The gaoler was probably like most gaolers at that time a retired soldier or army veteran, and, like all officials in the legal administration of a Roman colony, he was doubtless a Roman himself. Each of the three had been brought up in a different national culture. True, they were already united politically by the Roman Empire, but now in Jesus Christ they found a deeper unity still.

Or take their different *social* backgrounds. Lydia is likely to have been a wealthy woman, who had made her money in what we jocularly call 'the rag trade'. She certainly had a large enough house to accommodate the four missionaries in addition to her own household (15). The slave girl came from the opposite end of the social spectrum. You could not sink much lower in public estimation than to be a female slave. She owned nothing, not even herself. She had no possessions, rights, liberty or life of her own. Even the money she earned by fortune-telling went straight into her masters' pockets. Then the gaoler was socially half-way between the two women. Although he had a responsible post in the local prison, he was still only a subordinate official in government service. One might say that he belonged to the respectable middle class. Yet these three were foundation members of the Philippian church, admitted into it on the same terms with no distinction. The head of a Jewish household would use the same prayer every morning, giving thanks that God had not made him a Gentile, a woman or a slave. But here were representatives of these three despised categories redeemed and united in Christ. For truly, as Paul had recently written to the Galatians: 'There is neither Jew nor Greek, slave nor free, male nor female, for you are all one in Christ Jesus.'[26]

Thirdly, consider their different *personal* needs. Lydia could be said to have had an intellectual need. At least the point Luke makes about her is that, as she 'kept listening' (14, literally), the Lord opened her heart, meaning really her mind, to attend to what Paul was saying, just as he had opened the minds of his disciples to understand the Scriptures.[27] Perhaps she was first a disenchanted oriental, and was then attracted to Judaism. But still she was not satisfied. The slave girl had a psychological need. True, she had an evil spirit which needed to be exorcized, but being possessed, then as now, can have terrible psychological consequences. She had lost

[26] Gal. 3:28. [27] Lk. 24:45.

her identity, her individuality, as a human being. If socially she belonged as a slave to her masters, psychologically she belonged to the spirit which controlled her. She was in double bondage. But in finding Christ (for I think Luke means us to understand that she was converted as well as delivered), she found herself. She became an integrated person again. As for the gaoler, we could say that his need was moral. At least, we know that his conscience had been to some degree aroused, since he cried out to know how to be saved. The needs of human beings do not change much with the changing years, but Jesus Christ can meet them and fulfil our aspirations.

It is wonderful to observe in Philippi both the universal appeal of the gospel (that it could reach such a wide diversity of people) and its unifying effect (that it could bind them together in God's family). Of course the gospel also divides a community, because some reject it, but it unifies those who accept it. It is touching to see that Luke ends his Philippian narrative with a reference to 'the brothers' (40). The wealthy business woman, the exploited slave girl and the rough Roman gaoler had been brought into a brotherly or sisterly relationship with each other and with the rest of the church's members. True, they experienced some tensions, and in his later Letter to the Philippians Paul had to exhort them to 'stand firm in one spirit', and to be 'like-minded, having the same love, being one in spirit and purpose'.[28] Nevertheless, they all belonged to the one fellowship of Christ. We too, who live in an era of social disintegration, need to exhibit the unifying power of the gospel.

2. The mission in Thessalonica (17:1–9)

In spite of having 'suffered and been insulted in Philippi', Paul and Silas received strength from God to preach the gospel in Thessalonica. That is what they wrote in their first Thessalonian letter.[29] Calvin referred to Paul's 'unconquerable mental courage and indefatigable endurance of the cross'.[30] It was a one-hundred-mile journey from Philippi to Thessalonica, following the *Via Egnatia* all the way in a south-westerly direction. They *passed through Amphipolis and Apollonia* (1a), not stopping in either town except perhaps to rest for the night, for their destination was *Thessalonica*, the capital of the province of Macedonia. It was a harbour town, situated at the head of the Thermaic Gulf. Commanding trade by sea across the Aegean and by land along the east-west *Via Egnatia*, it was a flourishing commercial centre, and was proud of having been made a free city in 42 BC. Here too *there was a Jewish*

[28] Phil. 1:27; 2:2 [29] 1 Thes. 2:2. [30] Calvin, II, p. 91

synagogue (1b). So Paul followed *his custom* (even after deciding to 'turn to the Gentiles', 13:46), *and went into the synagogue* first, where *on three Sabbath days* running he preached the gospel (2a).

Although Paul and his friends must have stayed in Thessalonica for several months, as is clear from his two Thessalonian letters, and although most of the converts must have been Gentiles, even pagan idolators,[31] Luke concentrates on his Jewish mission, which lasted only three weeks, and tells us how his argument developed.

First, Paul *reasoned with them from the Scriptures, explaining and proving that the Christ* (*i.e.* the expected Messiah) *had to suffer and rise from the dead* (2b–3a). This was the standard Christian apologetic towards Jewish people. The precedent for it was set by Jesus, as Luke himself has recorded. During his public ministry he kept predicting that the Son of Man must suffer, die and be raised.[32] Then after his resurrection he first rebuked his Emmaus disciples for their slowness to believe the prophetic witness, which he traced through 'all the Scriptures', that the Christ had to suffer before entering his glory,[33] and secondly he re-emphasized the teaching of the Old Testament and of his earlier ministry that the Christ must suffer and rise.[34] Naturally, therefore, this became the heart of the apostolic *kērygma*, which Peter had unfolded already on the Day of Pentecost (2:22ff.) and which Paul summarized later (13:26ff.).[35] There can be little doubt that in the Thessalonian synagogue the Scriptures to which Paul turned were those already quoted in the apostles' earlier sermons, especially Psalms 2:1–7; 16:8–11; 110:1; 118:22; Isaiah 52 – 53, and probably also Deuteronomy 21:22–23.

Secondly, Paul was engaged in *proclaiming . . . Jesus* (3b). That is to say, he told the story of Jesus of Nazareth: his birth, life and ministry, his death and resurrection, his exaltation and gift of the Spirit, his present reign and future return, his offer of salvation and warning of judgment. There is no reason to doubt that Paul gave a thorough account of the saving career of Jesus from beginning to end.

Thirdly, he identified the Jesus of history with the Christ of Scripture, boldly declaring: '*This Jesus I am proclaiming to you is the Christ*' (3b). It was a typical 'pesher' or 'this is that' use of the Old Testament, like Peter's on the Day of Pentecost (2:16). It is worth noting that the Greek verb for *proving* near the beginning of verse 3 is *paratithēmi*. Since it means literally to 'place beside', it may refer to Paul's argument in 'setting the fulfilment alongside the predictions'.[36] At all events, the identification of history with

[31] 1 Thes. 1:9–10. [32] *E.g.* Lk. 9:22. [33] Lk. 24:25–27.
[34] Lk. 24:44–46. [35] *Cf.* 1 Cor. 15:3–4. [36] Bruce, *English*, p. 343.

Scripture, Jesus with Christ, was essential to Paul's apologetic. It remains an indispensable part of Christian testimony in our day in which some theologians are attempting to drive a wedge between the historical Jesus of the gospels and a mystical Christ of Christian theology and experience.

Luke goes on to describe the divided response which Paul's ministry received. On the one hand, because his gospel was preached 'not simply with words, but also with power',[37] many believed. For example, *some of the Jews were persuaded*, convinced by Paul's careful arguments, *and joined Paul and Silas*, perhaps withdrawing from the synagogue to become members of a Christian house church, *as did a large number of God-fearing Greeks and not a few prominent women* (4) . Because 'God-fearing Greeks' seems tautologous (all 'God-fearers' being Gentiles), Luke may be referring to two groups (God-fearers and Greeks) rather than one, as the Western text indicates and William Ramsay argued.[38] In this case the converts were drawn from four sections of the community – Jews, Greeks, God-fearers and well-known women. Among them were Aristarchus and Secundus, who later became Paul's fellow-travellers, and even, in the case of Aristarchus, his fellow-prisoner (20:4; 27:2).[39]

On the other hand, the unbelieving *Jews were jealous; so they rounded up some bad characters from the market-place* (louts or layabouts), *formed a mob and started a riot in the city. They rushed to Jason's house in search of Paul and Silas*, Jason being their host or landlord (see verse 7), *in order to bring them out to the crowd* (5). 'Crowd' here translates *dēmos*, which may refer to 'the People's Assembly' (JB) or citizens' council, of which Thessalonica as a free city was justly proud. *But when they did not find them*, that is, the missionaries they were looking for, *they dragged Jason and some other brothers before the city officials* (*politarchas*) instead (6a). Luke's accuracy in calling the city magistrates 'politarchs' has been confirmed from a number of contemporary Macedonian inscriptions. 'From five inscriptions referring to Thessalonica, it appears that a body of five politarchs ruled the city during the first century AD.'[40] The charge against Paul and Silas was very serious: '*These men who have caused trouble all over the world* [*oikoumenē*, the known inhabited earth, in practice the Roman Empire] *have now come here* (6b), *and Jason has welcomed them into his house. They are all defying Caesar's decrees, saying that there is another king, one called Jesus*' (7). *When they heard this, the crowd and the city officials were thrown into turmoil* (8). The general accusation

[37] 1 Thes. 1:5. [38] Ramsay, *St Paul*, p. 227. [39] Col. 4:10.
[40] Longenecker, *Acts*, p. 469.

levelled against the missionaries was that they had *caused trouble* (6). This means not (in the familiar and appealing AV expression) that they had 'turned the world upside down', but that they were causing a radical social upheaval. The verb *anastatoō* has revolutionary overtones and is used in 21:38 of an Egyptian terrorist who 'started a revolt'. In particular, Paul and Silas were charged with high treason. It is hard to exaggerate the danger to which this exposed them, for 'the very suggestion of treason against the Emperors often proved fatal to the accused'.[41] Just as Jesus had been accused before Pilate of sedition, of 'subverting' the nation by claiming himself to be 'Christ, a king',[42] so Paul's teaching about the kingdom of God (14:22) and about Christ's *parousia* (the official term for an imperial visit), which we know from the letters to the Thessalonians he had emphasized when he was with them, were misinterpreted. Since the emperor was sometimes called *basileus* ('king'),[43] as well as *kaisar* ('emperor'), how could the attribution of *basileus* to Jesus (7) not be a treasonable offence? The ambiguity of Christian teaching in this area remains. On the one hand, as Christian people, we are called to be conscientious and law-abiding citizens, not revolutionaries. On the other hand, the kingship of Jesus has unavoidable political implications since, as his loyal subjects, we must refuse to give to any ruler or ideology the supreme homage and total obedience which are due to him alone.

The politarchs' alarm led them to *put Jason and the others on bail* and then *let them go* (9). The magistrates' action was probably more than to release the accused on bail. Luke's expression refers to 'the offering and giving of security, in civil and criminal procedures'.[44] 'They bound over Jason and the others' (NEB), in the sense of extracting an undertaking from them that Paul and Silas would leave town and not return, with severe penalties if the agreement were broken. It was probably this legal ban which Paul saw as Satan preventing him from returning to Thessalonica;[45] 'this ingenious device put an impassable chasm between Paul and the Thessalonians'.[46]

3. The mission in Berea (17:10–15)

As soon as it was night, the brothers sent Paul and Silas away to Berea, smuggling them out of Thessalonica under cover of darkness, in order to ensure no further public disturbance. *On arriving there*, following a fifty-mile journey in a south-westerly direction, though no longer on the Egnatian Way, the missionaries again *went* first

[41] Ramsay, *St Paul*, p. 229. [42] Lk. 23:2.
[43] *E.g.* Jn. 19:12; 1 Pet. 2:13, 17. [44] Sherwin-White, p. 95.
[45] 1 Thes. 2:18. [46] Ramsay, *St Paul*, p. 231.

to the Jewish synagogue (10), in order to share with its members the good news of Jesus. *Now* these Jews, whom Luke calls *the Bereans, were of more noble character* (more 'open-minded', JB, BAGD) *than the Thessalonians*, that is, their co-religionists in Thessalonica, *for they received the message with great eagerness and examined the Scriptures every day*, meeting Paul for a daily dialogue and not just a weekly one on the Sabbath, *to see if what Paul said was true* (11). Luke obviously admires their enthusiasm for Paul's preaching, together with their industry and unprejudiced openness in studying the Scriptures. They combined receptivity with critical questioning. The verb for 'examine' (*anakrinō*) is used of judicial investigations, as of Herod examining Jesus,[47] the Sanhedrin Peter and John (4:9), and Felix Paul (24:8). It implies integrity and absence of bias. Ever since then, the adjective 'Berean' has been applied to people who study the Scriptures with impartiality and care.

The Bereans' listening and studying did not result, however, in a unanimous acceptance of the gospel. As in Thessalonica, there was a division. *Many of the Jews believed, as did also a number of prominent Greek women and many Greek men* (12), who probably included Sopater son of Pyrrhus (although he is not named until 20:4). At the same time, *when the Jews in Thessalonica learned that Paul was preaching the word of God at Berea, they went there too, agitating the crowds and stirring them up* (13). This time *the brothers* did not wait and risk another public furore, but *immediately sent Paul to the coast*, while *Silas and Timothy stayed at Berea* (14) for the time being. *The men who escorted Paul brought him to Athens*, presumably by sea, a voyage of more than 300 miles, *and then left with instructions for Silas and Timothy to join him as soon as possible* (15).

4. Some concluding reflections

Luke chronicles the Thessalonian and Berean missions with surprising brevity. Yet one important aspect of them, to which he seems to be drawing his readers' attention, is the attitude to the Scriptures adopted by both speaker and hearers, as evidenced by the verbs he uses. In Thessalonica Paul 'reasoned', 'explained', 'proved', 'proclaimed' and 'persuaded', while in Berea the Jews eagerly 'received' the message and diligently 'examined' the Scriptures. It was inevitable in Jewish evangelism that the Old Testament Scriptures should be both the textbook and the court of appeal. What is impressive is that neither speaker nor hearers used Scripture in a superficial,

[47] Lk. 23:14–15.

unintelligent or proof-texting way. On the contrary, Paul 'argued' out of the Scriptures and the Bereans 'examined' them to see if his arguments were cogent. And we may be sure that Paul welcomed and encouraged this thoughtful response. He believed in doctrine (his message had theological content), but not in indoctrination (tyrannical instruction demanding uncritical acceptance). As Bengel wrote about verse 11, 'a characteristic of the true religion is that it suffers itself to be examined into, and its claims to be so decided upon'.[48] Thus Paul's arguments and his hearers' studies went hand in hand. I do not doubt that he also bathed both in prayer, asking the Holy Spirit of truth to open his mouth to explain, and his hearers' minds to grasp, the good news of salvation in Christ.

[48] Bengel, p. 662.

13. Paul in Athens *17:16-34*

There is something enthralling about Paul in Athens, the great Christian apostle amid the glories of ancient Greece. Of course he had known about Athens since his boyhood. Everybody knew about Athens. Athens had been the foremost Greek city-state since the fifth century BC. Even after its incorporation into the Roman Empire, it retained a proud intellectual independence and also became a free city. It boasted of its rich philosophical tradition inherited from Socrates, Plato and Aristotle, of its literature and art, and of its notable achievements in the cause of human liberty. Even if in Paul's day it 'lived on its great past',[1] and was a comparatively small town by modern criteria, it still had an unrivalled reputation as the empire's intellectual metropolis.

Now for the first time Paul visited the Athens of which he had heard so much, arriving by sea from the north. His friends, who had given him a safe escort from Berea, had gone. He had asked them to send Silas and Timothy to join him as soon as possible (17:15). He was hoping to be able to return to Macedonia, for it was to Macedonia that he had been called (16:10). Meanwhile, as he waited for their arrival, he found himself alone in the cultural capital of the world. What was his reaction? What should be the reaction of a Christian who visits or lives in a city which is dominated by a non-Christian ideology or religion, a city which may be aesthetically magnificent and culturally sophisticated, but morally decadent and spiritually deceived or dead? There were four parts to Paul's reaction. Luke tells us what he saw, felt, did and said.

1. What Paul saw

While Paul was waiting for them in Athens, that is, for Silas and Timothy, *he was greatly distressed to see that the city was full of*

[1] Haenchen, p. 517.

idols (16) or 'given over to idolatry' (JB). Of course he could have walked round Athens as a tourist, as we would probably have done, in order to see the sights of the town. He could have been determined, now that at last he had the opportunity, to 'do' Athens thoroughly and tick its spectacles one by one. For the buildings and monuments of Athens were unrivalled. The acropolis, the town's ancient citadel, which was elevated enough to be seen from miles around, has been described as 'one vast composition of architecture and sculpture dedicated to the national glory and to the worship of the gods'.[2] Even today, although now a partial ruin, the Parthenon has a unique grandeur. Or Paul could have lingered in the *agora*, with its many porticoes painted by famous artists, in order to listen to the debates of its contemporary statesmen and philosophers, for Athens was well known for its democracy. And Paul was no uncultured philistine. In our terms he was a graduate of the universities of Tarsus and Jerusalem, and God had endowed him with a massive intellect. So he might have been spellbound by the sheer splendour of the city's architecture, history and wisdom.

Yet it was none of these things which struck him. First and foremost what he saw was neither the beauty nor the brilliance of the city, but its idolatry. The adjective Luke uses (*kateidōlos*) occurs nowhere else in the New Testament, and has not been found in any other Greek literature. Although most English versions render it 'full of idols', the idea conveyed seems to be that the city was 'under' them. We might say that it was 'smothered with idols' or 'swamped' by them. Alternatively, since *kata* words often express luxurious growth, what Paul saw was 'a veritable forest of idols'.[3] As he was later to say, the Athenians were 'very religious' (22). Xenophon referred to Athens as 'one great altar, one great sacrifice'.[4] In consequence, 'there were more gods in Athens than in all the rest of the country, and the Roman satirist hardly exaggerates when he says that it was easier to find a god there than a man'.[5] There were innumerable temples, shrines, statues and altars. In the Parthenon stood a huge gold and ivory statue of Athena, 'whose gleaming spear-point was visible forty miles away'.[6] Elsewhere there were images of Apollo, the city's patron, of Jupiter, Venus, Mercury, Bacchus, Neptune, Diana and Aesculapius. The whole Greek pantheon was there, all the gods of Olympus. And they were beautiful. They were made not only of stone and brass, but of gold, silver, ivory and marble, and they had been elegantly fashioned by the finest Greek sculptors. There is no need to suppose

[2] Quoted by Conybeare and Howson, p. 275.
[3] R. E. Wycherley; quoted by Marshall, *Acts*, p. 283.
[4] Quoted by Alexander, II, p. 145. [5] Conybeare and Howson, p. 280.
[6] Blaiklock, *Acts*, p. 137.

that Paul was blind to their beauty. But beauty did not impress him if it did not honour God the Father and the Lord Jesus Christ. Instead, he was oppressed by the idolatrous use to which the God-given artistic creativity of the Athenians was being put. This is what Paul saw: a city submerged in its idols.

2. What Paul felt

He was greatly distressed (16). The Greek verb *paroxynō*, from which 'paroxysm' comes, originally had medical associations and was used of a seizure or epileptic fit. It also meant to 'stimulate', especially to 'irritate, provoke, rouse to anger' (GT). Its only other occurrence in the New Testament is in Paul's first letter to the Corinthian church, where he describes love as 'not easily angered'.[7] Did Paul then not practise in Athens what he preached to Corinth? Was he roused to sinful anger by the city's idolatry? Is it right to say that he was 'irritated' (Moffatt), and even 'exasperated' (NEB, JBP)? No, I think not. To begin with, the verb is in the imperfect tense, which expresses not a sudden loss of temper but rather a continuous, settled reaction to what Paul saw. Besides, he was alone. Nobody witnessed his paroxysm. So this must have been the word which he himself used when later describing his feelings to Luke; evidently he was not ashamed of them.

The clue to interpreting the nature of Paul's emotion is that *paroxynō* is the verb which is regularly used in the LXX of the Holy One of Israel, and in particular (such is the consistency of Scripture) of his reaction to idolatry. Thus, when the Israelites made the golden calf at Mount Sinai, when later they were guilty of gross idolatry and immorality in relation to the Baal of Peor, and when the Northern Kingdom made another calf to worship in Samaria, they 'provoked' the Lord God to anger. Indeed, he described Israel as 'an obstinate people . . . who continually provoke me to my very face'.[8] So Paul was 'provoked' (RSV) by idolatry, and provoked to anger, grief and indignation, just as God is himself, and for the same reason, namely for the honour and glory of his name. Scripture sometimes calls this emotion 'jealousy'. For example, it is written that Yahweh, 'whose name is Jealous, is a jealous God'.[9] Now jealousy is the resentment of rivals, and whether it is good or evil depends on whether the rival has any business to be there. To be jealous of someone who threatens to outshine us in beauty, brains or sport is sinful, because we cannot claim a monopoly of talent in those areas. If, on the other hand, a third party enters a marriage,

[7] 1 Cor. 13:5. [8] Is. 65:2–3; see Dt. 9:7, 18, 22; Ps. 106:28–29; Ho. 8:5.
[9] Ex. 34:14.

the jealousy of the injured person, who is being displaced, is righteous, because the intruder has no right to be there. It is the same with God, who says, 'I am the Lord, that is my name! I will not give my glory to another or my praise to idols.'[10] Our Creator and Redeemer has a right to our exclusive allegiance, and is 'jealous' if we transfer it to anyone or anything else. Moreover, the people of God, who love God's name, should share in his 'jealousy' for it. For example, Elijah at a time of national apostasy said, 'I have been very jealous for the Lord, the God of hosts',[11] so distressed was he that God's honour was being profaned. Similarly, Paul wrote to the backsliding Corinthians, 'I am jealous for you with a godly jealousy';[12] he longed for them to remain loyal to Jesus, to whom he had betrothed them.

So the pain or 'paroxysm' which Paul felt in Athens was due neither to bad temper, not to pity for the Athenians' ignorance, nor even to fear for their eternal salvation. It was due rather to his abhorrence of idolatry, which aroused within him deep stirrings of jealousy for the Name of God, as he saw human beings so depraved as to be giving to idols the honour and glory which were due to the one, living and true God alone. 'His whole soul was revolted at the sight of a city given over to idolatry' (JB).

Moreover this inward pain and horror, which moved Paul to share the good news with the idolaters of Athens, should similarly move us. Incentives are important in every sphere. Being rational human beings, we need to know not only what we should be doing, but why we should be doing it. And motivation for mission is specially important, not least in our day in which the comparative study of religions has led many to deny finality and uniqueness to Jesus Christ and to reject the very concept of evangelizing and converting people. How then, in the face of growing opposition to it, can Christians justify the continuance of world evangelization? The commonest answer is to point to the Great Commission, and indeed obedience to it provides a strong stimulus. Compassion is higher than obedience, however, namely love for people who do not know Jesus Christ, and who on that account are alienated, disorientated, and indeed lost. But the highest incentive of all is zeal or jealousy for the glory of Jesus Christ. God has promoted him to the supreme place of honour, in order that every knee and tongue should acknowledge his lordship. Whenever he is denied his rightful place in people's lives, therefore, we should feel inwardly wounded, and jealous for his name. As Henry Martyn expressed it in Moslem Persia at the beginning of the last century, 'I could not endure existence if Jesus was not glorified; it would be hell to

[10] Is. 42:8. [11] 1 Ki. 19:10 (RSV). [12] 2 Cor. 11:2ff.

me, if he were to be always . . . dishonoured.'[13]

3. What Paul did

So (*men oun;* 'therefore', AV) *he reasoned in the synagogue with the Jews and the God-fearing Greeks, as well as in the market-place day by day with those who happened to be there* (17). *A group of Epicurean and Stoic philosophers began to dispute with him* (18a). Paul's reaction to the city's idolatry was not negative only (horror and dismay) but also positive and constructive (witness). He did not merely throw up his hands in despair, or weep helplessly, or curse and swear at the Athenians. No, he shared with them the good news of Jesus. He sought by the proclamation of the gospel to prevail on them to turn from their idols to the living God and so to give to him and to his Son the glory due to their name. The stirrings of his spirit with righteous indignation opened his mouth in testimony. We observe the three groups with whom Luke tells us he spoke. First, following his usual practice, he went to the synagogue on the sabbath and 'reasoned' there with both Jews and God-fearers. As in Thessalonica, so in Athens, he will have delineated the Christ of Scripture, proclaimed the Jesus of history, and identified the two as the heaven-sent Saviour of sinners. Secondly, he went into the *agora*, which has now been completely excavated and restored, and which did duty as both market-place and centre of public life, and argued there with 'casual passers-by' (NEB), not now on the sabbath but *day by day*. He seems deliberately to have adopted the famous Socratic method of dialogue, involving questions and answers; he was, in fact, a kind of Christian Socrates, although with a better gospel than Socrates ever knew.

Thirdly, Epicurean and Stoic philosophers began to dispute with him, and he with them. These were contemporary but rival systems. The Epicureans, or 'philosophers of the garden', founded by Epicurus (died 270 BC), considered the gods to be so remote as to take no interest in, and have no influence on, human affairs. The world was due to chance, a random concourse of atoms, and there would be no survival of death, and no judgment. So human beings should pursue pleasure, especially the serene enjoyment of a life detached from pain, passion and fear. The Stoics, however, or 'philosophers of the porch' (the *stoa* or painted colonnade next to the *agora* where they taught), founded by Zeno (died 265 BC), acknowledged the supreme god but in a pantheistic way, confusing him with the 'world soul'. The world was determined by fate, and human beings

[13] *Henry Martyn: Confessor of the Faith* by Constance E. Padwick (IVF, 1953), p. 146.

must pursue their duty, resigning themselves to live in harmony with nature and reason, however painful this might be, and develop their own self-sufficiency. To oversimplify, it was characteristic of Epicureans to emphasize chance, escape and the enjoyment of pleasure, and of the Stoics to emphasize fatalism, submission and the endurance of pain. In Paul's later speech to the Areopagus we hear echoes of the encounter between the gospel and these philosophies, as he refers to the caring activity of a personal Creator, the dignity of human beings as his 'offspring', the certainty of judgment and the call to repentance.

One cannot help admiring Paul's ability to speak with equal facility to religious people in the synagogue, to casual passers-by in the city square, and to highly sophisticated philosophers both in the *agora* and when they met in Council. Today the nearest equivalent to the synagogue is the church, the place where religious people gather. There is still an important place for sharing the gospel with church-goers, God-fearing people on the fringe of the church, who may attend services only occasionally. The equivalent of the *agora* will vary in different parts of the world. It may be a park, city square or street corner, a shopping mall or market-place, a 'pub', neighbourhood bar, café, discothèque or student cafeteria, wherever people meet when they are at leisure. There is a need for gifted evangelists who can make friends and gossip the gospel in such informal settings as these. As for the Areopagus, it has no precise equivalent in the contemporary world. Perhaps the nearest is the university, where many of the country's intelligentsia are to be found. Neither church evangelism nor street evangelism would be appropriate for them. Instead, we should develop home evangelism in which there is free discussion, 'Agnostics Anonymous' groups in which no holds are barred, and lecture evangelism, which contains a strong apologetic content. There is an urgent need for more Christian thinkers who will dedicate their minds to Christ, not only as lecturers, but also as authors, journalists, dramatists and broadcasters, as television script-writers, producers and personalities, and as artists and actors who use a variety of art forms in which to communicate the gospel. All these can do battle with contemporary non-Christian philosophies and ideologies in a way which resonates with thoughtful, modern men and women, and so at least gain a hearing for the gospel by the reasonableness of its presentation. Christ calls human beings to humble, but not to stifle, their intellect.

4. What Paul said

Paul's evangelistic dialogue with Jews, God-fearers, passers-by and philosophers may well have continued for many days. It led to one of the greatest opportunities of his whole ministry, the presentation of the gospel to the world-famous, supreme council of Athens, the Areopagus. How did this come about? The Epicurean and Stoic philosophers reacted to Paul's message in two ways. *Some of them* insulted him. They *asked*, *'What is this babbler trying to say?'* (18b). *Babbler* translates *spermologos*, which Ramsay calls 'a word of characteristically Athenian slang'.[14] Its literal meaning is a 'seed-picker', and it was used of various seed-eating or scavenging birds, the rook for instance in Aristophanes' comedy *The Birds*. Hence the suggested rendering 'cock sparrow'.[15] From birds it was applied to human beings, vagrants or beggars who live off scraps of food they pick up in the gutter, 'gutter-snipes'. Then thirdly it was used particularly to describe teachers who, not having an original idea in their own heads, unscrupulously plagiarize from others, picking up scraps of knowledge from here and there, 'zealous seekers of the second-rate at second hand',[16] until their system is nothing but a ragbag of other people's ideas and sayings. Hence this 'ignorant plagiarist',[17] 'this charlatan' (NEB), 'this parrot' (JB), this 'intellectual magpie'.[18]

Others (among the philosophers) *remarked, 'He seems to be advocating foreign gods'*, which was one of the charges brought against Socrates 450 years previously. *They said this*, Luke comments, *because Paul was preaching the good news about Jesus and the resurrection* (18c). The word for *gods* here is *daimonia*, which did not always mean 'demons', but could be used of 'lesser gods', in this case 'foreign divinities' (RSV). It is possible that the philosophers, grasping that the essence of Paul's message was *ton Jēsoun kai tēn anastasin* (*Jesus and the resurrection*) thought that he was introducing into Athens a couple of new divinities, a male god called 'Jesus' and his female consort 'Anastasis'. Chrysostom was the first to make this suggestion,[19] and a number of commentators have followed him. F. F. Bruce goes further and writes: 'In the ears of some frequenters of the Agora these two words sounded as if they denoted the personified and deified powers of "healing" (*iasis*) and "restoration".'[20] It is interesting, as Dr Conrad Gempf has pointed out to me, that both Paul's speeches to pagans in the Acts seem to have been occasioned by a misunderstanding. 'The Athenians imagine two new gods, while the Lystrans think they are seeing two old ones! Could Luke be warning his readers of ways in which pagans misunderstand?'

[14] Ramsay, *St Paul*, p. 242. [15] *BC*, IV, p. 211; JBP.
[16] *BC*, IV, p. 211. [17] Ramsay, *St Paul*, p. 241.
[18] Hanson, p. 176. [19] Chrysostom, Homily XXXVIII, p. 233.
[20] Bruce, *English*, p. 351; *Greek*, p. 333.

Whatever the precise motive of the philosophers may have been, *they took him and brought him to a meeting of the Areopagus, where they said to him, 'May we know what this new teaching is that you are presenting?* (19). *You are bringing some strange ideas to our ears, and we want to know what they mean'* (20). *(All the Athenians and the foreigners who lived there spent their time doing nothing but talking about and listening to the latest ideas)* (21).

The word 'Areopagus' means literally 'the Hill (*pagos*) of Ares (the Greek equivalent of Mars)', so 'Mars' Hill'. Situated a little north-west of the Acropolis, it was formerly the place where the most venerable judicial court of ancient Greece met. For this reason the name came to be transferred from the place to the court. By Paul's day, although cases were sometimes heard there, the court had become more a council, with its legal powers diminished. Its members were rather guardians of the city's religion, morals and education, and it normally met in the 'Royal Porch' of the Agora. Two questions now face us. First, was Paul brought to the hill, or before the court/council, or both? Various answers are given, but surely the expressions that he stood 'in the midst' of the Areopagus (22, literally) and later went out 'from their midst' (33, literally) would more naturally refer to people than to a place. It seems almost certain, then, that he addressed that august senate, and it does not matter much where the meeting took place.

Secondly, was Paul's speech before the court of the Areopagus a defence or a sermon? Some students, especially those who consider his address to have been an inadequate presentation of the gospel (since the cross does not appear to have been central to it), try to protect Paul's reputation by arguing that he was defending himself, not preaching Christ. This is certainly a possibility, since the court did still have some judicial functions. In particular, it had jurisdiction over religion in the city and, since Paul was being accused of introducing new gods (18), it would have to take cognizance and adjudicate. So the statement in verse 19 that *they took him* could be translated 'they took hold of him' (RSV) in the sense of arresting him. But the case against this proposal is strong. The 'context is without a vestige of judicial process'.[21] There seem to have been no legal charge, no prosecutor, no presiding judge, no verdict and no sentence. At the same time, although Paul was not subjected to any formal interrogation, he was asked to give an account of his teaching. One may therefore regard the situation as 'an informal inquiry by the education commission', who regarded him with 'slightly contemptuous indulgence',[22] so that 'he might either receive the freedom of the city to preach or be censored and

[21] Alexander, II, p. 149. [22] Gärtner, p. 65.

silenced'.[23] Consequently, he told the court what he believed and taught, but in so doing made a quite personal statement of the gospel. As we have already seen when Peter and John stood before the Sanhedrin, and as we shall see again in trial scenes in Jerusalem and Caesarea, the apostles seemed incapable of defending themselves without at the same time preaching Christ. As for Paul in Athens, it required an uncommon degree of courage to speak as he spoke, for it would be hard to imagine a less receptive or more scornful audience.

Paul then stood up in the meeting of the Areopagus and said: 'Men of Athens! I see that in every way you are very religious (22). *For as I walked around and looked carefully at your objects of worship, I even found an altar with this inscription:* TO AN UNKNOWN GOD. *Now what you worship as something unknown I am going to proclaim to you'* (23). The apostle took as his text, or rather as his point of contact with them, the anonymous altar he had come across. Reference to such altars, inscribed to an unknown god, have been found in ancient literature. Pausanias, for example, who travelled extensively in about AD 175 and wrote in his *Tour of Greece* his admiring account of the glory, history and mythology of that country, began his itinerary in Athens. Landing on the rocky peninsula called Piraeus, five miles south-west of the city, he found near the harbour a number of temples, together with 'altars of the gods named Unknown'.[24] Having seen such an altar himself, Paul was able to make his opening courteous remark about their religiosity. He was not ready yet to challenge the folly of Athenian idolatry. But he did take up their own acknowledgement of their ignorance. How then shall we interpret his statement that 'what' they were worshipping 'as something unknown' he was about to proclaim to them? Was he thereby acknowledging the authenticity of their pagan worship, and should we regard with equal charity the cultus of non-Christian religions? For example, is Raymond Panikkar justified, in *The Unknown Christ of Hinduism*, in writing: 'In the footsteps of St Paul, we believe that we may speak not only of the unknown God of the Greeks but also of the hidden Christ of Hinduism'?[25] Is he further justified in concluding that 'the good and bona fide Hindu is saved by Christ and not by Hinduism, but it is through the sacraments of Hinduism, through the message of morality and the good life, through the mysterion that comes down to him through Hinduism, that

[23] Longenecker, *Acts*, p. 474.

[24] *Pausanias' Description of Greece* in 6 volumes, of the Loeb Classical Library, ed. W. H. S. Jones, vol. I, 1918, Book I.1.4.

[25] *The Unknown Christ of Hinduism* by Raymond Panikkar (Darton, Longman and Todd, 1964), p. 137.

Christ saves the Hindu normally'?[26]

No, this popular reconstruction cannot be maintained. We certainly agree that there is only one God. It is also true that converts, who turn to Christ from a non-Christian religious system, usually think of themselves not as having transferred their worship from one God to Another, but as having begun now to worship in truth the God they were previously trying to worship in ignorance, error or distortion. But N. B. Stonehouse is right that what Paul picked out for comment was the Athenians' open acknowledgement of their ignorance, and that 'the ignorance rather than the worship is thus underscored'.[27] Moreover, Paul made the bold claim to enlighten their ignorance (a Jew presuming to teach ignorant Athenians!), using the *egō* of apostolic authority, and insisting thereby that special revelation must control and correct whatever general revelation seems to disclose. He then went on to proclaim the living and true God in five ways, and so to expose the errors, even horrors, of idolatry.

First, God is the Creator of the universe: *The God who made the world and everything in it is the Lord of heaven and earth and does not live in temples built by hands* (24). This view of the world is very different from either the Epicurean emphasis on a chance combination of atoms or the virtual pantheism of the Stoics. Instead, God is both the personal Creator of everything that exists and the personal Lord of everything he has made. It is absurd, therefore, to suppose that he who made and supervises everything lives in shrines which human beings have built. Any attempt to limit or localize the Creator God, to imprison him within the confines of manmade buildings, structures or concepts, is ludicrous.

Secondly, God is the Sustainer of life: *And he is not served by human hands, as if he needed anything, because he himself gives all men life and breath and everything else* (25). God continues to sustain the life which he has created and given to his human creatures. It is absurd, therefore, to suppose that he who sustains life should himself need to be sustained, that he who supplies our need should himself need our supply. Any attempt to tame or domesticate God, to reduce him to the level of a household pet dependent on us for food and shelter, is again a ridiculous reversal of roles. We depend on God; he does not depend on us.

Thirdly, God is the Ruler of all the nations: *From one man* (the Western text 'of one blood' is surely mistaken; Adam is in view as the single progenitor of the human race) *he made every nation of men, that they should inhabit the whole earth; and he determined the times set for them and the exact places where they should live*

[26] *Ibid.*, p. 54. [27] Stonehouse, p. 19.

(26). *God did this so that men would seek him and perhaps reach out for him and find him, though he is not far from each one of us* (27). *'For in him we live and move and have our being'* (28a). Some commentators think that Paul's reference here to 'times' and 'places' (26) is to God's preparation of the planet earth to be our human habitation, and to his provision of the regular seasons, which Paul had mentioned in Lystra (14:17). The nations' 'times' and 'places', however, seem to be more particular than this, and to refer rather to 'the epochs of their history and the limits of their territory' (NEB). Thus, although God cannot be held responsible for the tyranny or aggression of individual nations, yet both the history and the geography of each nation are ultimately under his control. Further, God's purpose in this has been so that the human beings he has made in his own image might *seek him, and perhaps reach out for him*, or 'feel after him' (RSV), a verb which 'denotes the groping and fumbling of a blind man',[28] *and find him*. Yet this hope is unfulfilled because of human sin, as the rest of Scripture makes clear. Sin alienates people from God even as, sensing the unnaturalness of their alienation, they grope for him. It would be absurd, however, to blame God for this alienation, or to regard him as distant, unknowable, uninterested. For *he is not far from each one of us*. It is we who are far from him. If it were not for sin which separates us from him, he would be readily accessible to us. For '*in him we live and move and have our being*' – a quotation from the 6th century BC poet Epimenides of Cnossos in Crete.

Fourthly, God is the Father of human beings: *As some of your own poets have said, 'We are his offspring'* (28b). *Therefore since we are God's offspring, we should not think that the divine being is like gold or silver or stone – an image made by man's design and skill* (29). This second quotation comes from the 3rd century Stoic author Aratus, who came from Paul's native Cilicia, although he may have been echoing an earlier poem by the Stoic philosopher Cleanthes. It is remarkable that Paul should thus have quoted from two pagan poets.[29] His precedent gives us warrant to do the same, and indicates that glimmerings of truth, insights from general revelation, may be found in non-Christian authors. At the same time we need to exercise caution, for in stating that 'we are his offspring', Aratus was referring to Zeus, and Zeus is emphatically not identical with the living and true God. But is it right that all human beings are God's offspring (*genos*)? Yes, it is. Although in redemption terms God is the Father only of those who are in Christ, and we are his children only by adoption and grace, yet in creation terms

[28] Williams, p. 204.

[29] Paul also quoted from Menander (1 Cor. 15:33) and again from Epimenides (Tit. 1:12).

God is the Father of all humankind, and all are his offspring, his creatures, receiving their life from him. Moreover, because we are his offspring, whose being derives from him and depends on him, it is absurd to think of him as *like gold or silver or stone*, which are lifeless in themselves and which owe their being to human imagination and art. Paul quotes their own poets to expose their own inconsistency.

These are powerful arguments. All idolatry, whether ancient or modern, primitive or sophisticated, is inexcusable, whether the images are metal or mental, material objects of worship or unworthy concepts in the mind. For idolatry is the attempt either to localize God, confining him within limits which we impose, whereas he is the Creator of the universe; or to domesticate God, making him dependent on us, taming and taping him, whereas he is the Sustainer of human life; or to alienate God, blaming him for his distance and his silence, whereas he is the Ruler of nations, and not far from any of us; or to dethrone God, demoting him to some image of our own contrivance or craft, whereas he is our Father from whom we derive our being. In brief, all idolatry tries to minimize the gulf between the Creator and his creatures, in order to bring him under our control. More than that, it actually reverses the respective positions of God and us, so that, instead of our humbly acknowledging that God has created and rules us, we presume to imagine that we can create and rule God. There is no logic in idolatry; it is a perverse, topsy-turvy expression of our human rebellion against God. It leads to Paul's last point.

Fifthly, God is the Judge of the world: *In the past God overlooked such ignorance, but now he commands all people everywhere to repent* (30). *For he has set a day when he will judge the world with justice by the man he has appointed. He has given proof of this to all men by raising him from the dead* (31). Paul reverts at the end of his address to the topic with which he began: human ignorance. The Athenians have acknowledged in their altar inscription that they are ignorant of God, and Paul has been giving evidence of their ignorance. Now he declares such ignorance to be culpable. For God has never 'left himself without testimony' (14:17). On the contrary, he has revealed himself through the natural order, but human beings 'suppress the truth by their wickedness'.[30] *In the past God overlooked such ignorance*. It is not that he did not notice it, nor that he acquiesced in it as excusable, but that in his forbearing mercy he did not visit upon it the judgment it deserved.[31] *But now he commands all people everywhere to repent*. Why? Because of the certainty of the coming judgment. Paul tells

[30] Rom. 1:18. [31] *Cf.* Rom. 3:25.

his listeners three immutable facts about it. First, it will be universal: God *will judge the world*. The living and the dead, the high and the low, will be included; nobody will be able to escape. Secondly, it will be righteous: *he will judge . . . with justice*. All secrets will be revealed. There will be no possibility of any miscarriage of justice. Thirdly, it will be definite, for already the day has been set and the judge has been appointed. And although the day has not yet been disclosed, the identity of the judge has been (10:42). God has committed the judgment to his Son,[32] and *he has given proof of this* publicly to everybody *by raising him from the dead*. By the resurrection Jesus was vindicated, and declared to be both Lord and Judge. Moreover this divine judge is also *the man*. All nations have been created from the first Adam; through the last Adam all nations will be judged.

This mention of the resurrection, which had prompted the philosophers to ask to hear more (18), was now enough to bring the meeting to an abrupt end. *When they heard about the resurrection of the dead, some of them sneered*, even 'burst out laughing' (JB), perhaps the Epicureans, *but others said*, whether sincerely or not, perhaps the Stoics, '*We want to hear you again on this subject*' (32). *At that, Paul left the Council* (33), for the meeting was adjourned. However, *a few men became followers of Paul and believed. Among them was Dionysius, a member of the Areopagus*, whom Eusebius later identified (though on insufficient evidence) as Athens' first Christian bishop and martyr, *also a woman named Damaris, and a number of others* (34). These must all have responded to the summons to repent, and 'turned to God from idols to serve the living and true God'.[33]

As we reflect on Paul's address to the Areopagus, we have to face two criticisms of it, first that it was not authentic, and secondly that it was not adequate. Earlier in this century Martin Dibelius concluded that the speech was intended by Luke to be a sample of the kind of preaching to pagans which he considered appropriate, that it was composed by Luke not Paul, and that it is a 'Hellenistic' speech about the knowledge of God, which is not Christian until its conclusion.[34] Some years later, Hans Conzelmann wrote: 'In my own opinion the speech is the free creation of the author (*sc.* Luke), for it does not show the specific thoughts and ideas of Paul.'[35] In 1955, however, the Swedish scholar Bertil Gärtner decisively answered Dibelius in an essay entitled *The Areopagus Speech and Natural Revelation*. His thesis was (i) that the background to the speech is to be found rather in Hebrew than in Greek thought,

[32] *Cf.* Jn. 5:27. [33] 1 Thes. 1:9.

[34] Dibelius, 'Paul on the Areopagus', in *Studies*, pp. 26–77.

[35] From Conzelmann's contribution to Keck-Martyn, p. 218.

and especially in the Old Testament; (ii) that it has parallels in the apologetic preaching of Hellenistic Judaism; and (iii) that it is genuinely Pauline in the sense that its main features reflect Paul's thought in his letters,[36] although of course Luke has abbreviated it and put it into its present literary form. So it is not difficult to affirm with a good conscience that the voice we hear in the Areopagus address is the voice of the authentic Paul. Nor is it difficult to find Old Testament passages which anticipate the main themes of the sermon – God as Creator of heaven and earth, in whose hand is the breath of all living things, who does not live in man-made temples, who overrules the history of nations, who is not to be likened to graven or carved images, which are dead and dumb, and who warns of judgment and summons to repentance.

The second criticism concerns the adequacy of the sermon as a gospel presentation. Ramsay popularized the notion in his day that Paul 'was disappointed and perhaps disillusioned by his experience in Athens', since the results were negligible. So 'when he went on from Athens to Corinth, he no longer spoke in the philosophic style', but ' "determined not to know anything save Jesus Christ, and him crucified" (1 Cor. 2:2)'.[37] This is a gratuitous theory, however, which I think Stonehouse was fair to pronounce 'quite untenable'.[38] First, there is no trace in Luke's narrative that he is displeased with Paul's performance in Athens, whether we are to regard his address to the Areopagus as a defence or a sermon or a bit of both. On the contrary, Luke records three of Paul's speeches in the Acts as samples respectively of his proclamation to Jews and God-fearers (Pisidian Antioch, chapter 13), to illiterate pagans (Lystra, chapter 14) and now to cultured philosophers (Athens, chapter 17). Secondly, it is inaccurate to dub Paul's visit to Athens a failure. In addition to the two named converts, Luke says that there were 'a number of others' (34). Besides, 'it is most precarious to engage in rationalizing from the number of converts to the correctness of the message'.[39] Thirdly, I believe Paul did preach the cross in Athens. Luke provides only a short extract from his speech, which takes less than two minutes to read. Paul must have filled out this outline considerably, and his conclusion (30–31) must have included Christ crucified. For how could he proclaim the resurrection without mentioning the death which preceded it? And how could he call for repentance without mentioning the faith in Christ which always accompanies it? Fourthly, what Paul renounced in Corinth was not the biblical doctrine of God as Creator, Lord and Judge, but the wisdom of the world and the

[36] *E.g.* Rom. 1:18ff. [37] Ramsay, *St Paul*, p. 252.
[38] Stonehouse, p. 33. [39] *Ibid.*, p. 34.

rhetoric of the Greeks. His firm 'decision' to preach nothing but Jesus Christ and him crucified was taken because of the anticipated challenges of proud Corinth, not because of his supposed failure in Athens. Besides, as Luke shows in his narrative, Paul did not change his tactic in Corinth, but continued to teach, argue and persuade (18:4–5).

5. How Paul challenges us

The Areopagus address reveals the comprehensiveness of Paul's message. He proclaimed God in his fullness as Creator, Sustainer, Ruler, Father and Judge. He took in the whole of nature and of history. He passed the whole of time in review, from the creation to the consummation. He emphasized the greatness of God, not only as the beginning and the end of all things, but as the One to whom we owe our being and to whom we must give account. He argued that human beings already know these things by natural or general revelation, and that their ignorance and idolatry are therefore inexcusable. So he called on them with great solemnity, before it was too late, to repent.

Now all this is part of the gospel. Or at least it is the indispensable background to the gospel, without which the gospel cannot effectively be preached. Many people are rejecting our gospel today not because they perceive it to be false, but because they perceive it to be trivial. People are looking for an integrated world-view which makes sense of all their experience. We learn from Paul that we cannot preach the gospel of Jesus without the doctrine of God, or the cross without the creation, or salvation without judgment. Today's world needs a bigger gospel, the full gospel of Scripture, what Paul later in Ephesus was to call 'the whole purpose of God' (20:27, NEB).

It is not only the comprehensiveness of Paul's message in Athens which is impressive, however, but also the depth and power of his motivation. Why is it that, in spite of the great needs and opportunities of our day, the church slumbers peacefully on, and that so many Christians are deaf and dumb, deaf to Christ's commission and tongue-tied in testimony? I think the major reason is this: we do not speak as Paul spoke because we do not feel as Paul felt. We have never had the paroxysm of indignation which he had. Divine jealousy has not stirred within us. We constantly pray 'Hallowed be your Name', but we do not seem to mean it, or to care that his Name is so widely profaned.

Why is this? It takes us a stage further back. If we do not speak like Paul because we do not feel like Paul, this is because we do not see like Paul. That was the order: he saw, he felt, he spoke. It all began with his eyes. When Paul walked round Athens, he did not just 'notice' the idols. The Greek verb used three times (16, 22, 23) is either *theōreō* or *anatheōreō* and means to 'observe' or 'consider'. So he looked and looked, and thought and thought, until the fires of holy indignation were kindled within him. For he saw men and women, created by God in the image of God, giving to idols the homage which was due to him alone.

Idols are not limited to primitive societies; there are many sophisticated idols too. An idol is a god-substitute. Any person or thing that occupies the place which God should occupy is an idol. Covetousness is idolatry.[40] Ideologies can be idolatries.[41] So can fame, wealth and power, sex, food, alcohol and other drugs, parents, spouse, children and friends, work, recreation, television and possessions, even church, religion and Christian service. Idols always seem particularly dominant in cities. Jesus wept over the impenitent city of Jerusalem. Paul was deeply pained by the idolatrous city of Athens. Have we ever been provoked by the idolatrous cities of the contemporary world?

[40] Eph. 5:5.

[41] See, for example, *Idols of our Time* by Bob Goudzwaard (1981: IVP, 1984).

14. Corinth and Ephesus *18:1–19:41*

'The rise of urban civilization', wrote Professor Harvey Cox in *The Secular City*, is one of the 'hallmarks of our era'.[1] 'Urbanization', he continued, 'constitutes a massive change in the way men live together', as they have moved from tribe to town to technopolis. The urban experience includes a cluster of things like communications and mobility, the disintegration of traditional religion, impersonality and anonymity, human planning, control and bureaucracy. And in the decayed inner cities of our time we would have to add economic neglect, racial disadvantage, unemployment, poor housing and education, crime, violence, family breakdown, and tensions between the police and the community.

In 1850 there were only four 'world class cities' of more than a million inhabitants; in 1980 there were 225, and by the year 2000 there may be 500. Or consider the so-called 'megalopolis' or 'megacity' of more than ten million people. In 1950 only London and New York qualified. But by AD 2000 it is calculated that there will be twenty-three cities of this size, with Mexico City taking the lead at nearly thirty million inhabitants, and Sao Paulo and Tokyo following at nearly twenty-five million. Most of these megacities will be in the Third World; only four will be in Europe and the United States. Already two-fifths of the world's population are city-dwellers; by the end of the century the ratio will be more like one half.[2]

This process of urbanization, as a significant new fact of this century, constitutes a great challenge to the Christian church. On the one hand, there is an urgent need for Christian planners and architects, local government politicians, urban specialists, developers and community social workers, who will work for justice, peace, freedom and beauty in the city. On the other, Christians

[1] *The Secular City* by Harvey Cox (Macmillan, 1965), p. 1.

[2] See *World Population Trends and Policies: 1987 Monitoring Report*, United Nations Publication, 1988.

need to move into the cities, and experience the pains and pressures of living there, in order to win city-dwellers for Christ. Commuter Christianity (living in salubrious suburbia and commuting to an urban church) is no substitute for incarnational involvement.

It seems to have been Paul's deliberate policy to move purposefully from one strategic city-centre to the next. What drew him to the cities was probably that they contained the Jewish synagogues, the larger populations and the influential leaders. So on his first missionary expedition he visited Salamis and Paphos in Cyprus, and Antioch, Iconium, Lystra and Derbe in Galatia; on his second he evangelized Philippi, Thessalonica and Berea in Macedonia, and Athens and Corinth in Achaia; while during the greater part of his third journey he concentrated on Ephesus. Indeed Luke deliberately describes how the gospel spread 'by the gradual establishment of radiating centres or sources of influence at certain salient points throughout a large part of the Empire'.[3]

It is true that some of the towns Paul visited were small and insignificant. This could not be said of Athens, Corinth and Ephesus, however. It has been reckoned that Athens may have had less than 10,000 inhabitants, but that Ephesus had half a million, and that Corinth at its zenith had nearly three-quarters of a million. All three were leading cities of the Roman Empire, situated round the shores of the Aegean Sea, while Corinth and Ephesus were also provincial capitals. They could perhaps be characterized as follows.

Athens was the *intellectual* centre of the ancient world, as we saw in the last chapter, the city where Socrates, Plato, Aristotle, Epicurus and Zeno had all expounded their respective philosophies. It was also the birthplace of democracy, and of the three famous universities of antiquity (Alexandria, Tarsus and Athens), Athens was the most distinguished. Although it had now declined from the peak of its brilliance, the brightest students still flocked to it from all parts of the Empire. For the world's younger intelligentsia it retained an almost irresistible magnetism.

Corinth was above all a great *commercial* centre, a world-famous emporium. Situated close to the isthmus which joined mainland Greece to the Peloponnesian peninsula, it commanded the trade routes in all directions, not only north-south by land but also east-west by sea. For before the Corinthian canal was cut for three and a half miles across the isthmus, there was a *diolkos* or slipway along which cargoes and even small vessels could be hauled, thus saving 200 miles of perilous navigation round the southern tip of the peninsula. In consequence, Corinth boasted two ports, Lechaeum on the Corinthian Gulf to the west and Cenchrea on the Saronic

[3] Alexander, II, p. xiii.

Gulf to the east. Thus 'through its two harbours Corinth bestrode the isthmus, with one foot planted in each sea', which led Horace to call it *bimaris* or 'two-sea'd'.[4] So Corinth was a city of seafarers, of maritime merchants, and it is hardly surprising that Poseidon, the Greek god of the sea, whom the Romans called Neptune, was worshipped there. F. W. Farrar imagined its markets stocked with cosmopolitan goods – 'Arabian balsam, Egyptian papyrus, Phoenician dates, Libyan ivory, Babylonian carpets, Cilician goats'-hair, Lycaonian wool, Phrygian slaves'.[5] Paul must have seen its strategic importance. If trade could radiate from Corinth in all directions, so could the gospel.

Ephesus was also famed for its commerce. Barclay calls it 'the market of Asia Minor'.[6] It had political importance as well, as the capital of the Roman province of Asia. But in particular Ephesus was one of the principal *religious* centres of the Graeco-Roman world. The imperial cult flourished there, and at one time the city boasted as many as three temples dedicated to the worship of the Emperor. Above all, Ephesus was famed as 'the guardian of the temple of Artemis' (19:35). In classical mythology Artemis (whom the Romans called Diana) was a virgin huntress, but in Ephesus she had somehow become identified with an Asian fertility goddess. Ephesus guarded with immense pride both her grotesque many-breasted image (probably in origin a meteorite) and the magnificent temple which housed it. This structure had more than one hundred Ionic pillars, each sixty feet high, and supporting a white marble roof. Being four times the size of the Parthenon in Athens, and adorned by many beautiful paintings and sculptures, it was regarded as one of the seven wonders of the world. In addition, under Diana's patronage, superstitions and occult practices of all kinds flourished. And the magic words and formulae, which were sold to the credulous, were known as 'Ephesian Letters'.

Here, then, were three major cities of the Graeco-Roman world, all of them in differing degrees being centres of learning, trade and religion. Luke plainly understands their significance for the spread of the gospel. Having portrayed the apostle Paul among the philosophers in Athens (17:16ff.), he now describes his visits to Corinth (18:1ff.) and to Ephesus (18:18bff. and 19:1ff.). These visits followed a similar pattern, namely the evangelization of Jews, their opposition to the gospel, the apostle's deliberate turn to the Gentiles, and the multiple vindication of his dramatic decision. This is Luke's underlying theme in chapters 18 and 19.

First, in both cities Paul began with a serious and sustained attempt to 'persuade' his Jewish hearers in the synagogue that Jesus

[4] Ramsay in *HDB*. [5] Farrar, p. 315. [6] Barclay, p. 152.

was the Christ (18:4–5; 19:8).

Secondly, in both cities Paul responded to Jewish rejection of the gospel by leaving the synagogue and turning to Gentile evangelism, using as his base the house of Titius Justus in Corinth and the lecture hall of Tyrannus in Ephesus (18:6–7; 19:9).

Thirdly, in both cities Paul's bold step was vindicated by many people hearing and believing the gospel (18:8; 19:10).

Fourthly, in both cities Jesus confirmed his word and encouraged his apostle – in Corinth by a night vision and in Ephesus by extraordinary miracles (18:9–10; 19:11–12).

Fifthly, in both cities the Roman authorities dismissed the opposition and declared the legitimacy of the gospel – in Corinth through the proconsul Gallio and in Ephesus through the town clerk (18:12ff.; 19:35ff.).

1. Paul in Corinth (18:1–18a)

After this (that is, following his Areopagus speech and its aftermath) *Paul left Athens and went to Corinth* (1). It was about this journey (as was noted at the end of the last chapter), in anticipation of his mission in Corinth, that Paul later wrote: 'I resolved to know nothing while I was with you except Jesus Christ and him crucified. I came to you in weakness and fear, and with much trembling.'[7] We need to penetrate deeper into the causes of Paul's fear and the reasons for his resolve. What was it about Corinth which occasioned his alarm and necessitated his decision to preach only Christ and his cross?

It was surely the pride and immorality of the Corinthian people which intimidated Paul, since the cross comes into direct collision with both. To begin with, the Corinthians were a proud people. Their intellectual arrogance emerges clearly in Paul's correspondence with them. They were also proud of their city, which Julius Caesar had beautifully rebuilt in 46 BC. They boasted of its wealth and culture, of the world-famous Isthmian games which it hosted every other year, and of its political prestige as the capital of provincial Achaia, taking precedence even over Athens. But the cross undermines all human pride. It insists that we sinners have absolutely nothing with which to buy, or indeed contribute to, our salvation. No wonder that not many wise, influential or upper-class Corinthians responded to the gospel![8]

Secondly, Corinth was associated in everybody's mind with immorality. Behind the city, nearly 2,000 feet above sea level, rose the rocky eminence called the Acrocorinth. On its flat summit

[7] 1 Cor. 2:2–3. [8] 1 Cor. 1:26ff.

stood the temple of Aphrodite or Venus, the goddess of love. A thousand female slaves served her and roamed the city's streets by night as prostitutes. The sexual promiscuity of Corinth was proverbial, so that *korinthiazomai* meant to practise immorality, and *korinthiastēs* was a synonym for a harlot. Corinth was 'the Vanity Fair of the Roman Empire'.[9] But the gospel of Christ crucified summoned the Corinthians to repentance and holiness, and warned them that the sexually immoral would not inherit the kingdom of God.[10]

It is in these ways that Christ's cross, in its call for self-humbling and self-denial, is a stumbling-block to the proud and the sinful. Hence Paul's 'weakness, fear and much trembling' and his necessary decision in Corinth 'to know nothing . . . except Jesus Christ and him crucified'.[11]

a. Paul stays with Aquila and Priscilla (18:2–6)

There, in Corinth, *he met a Jew named Aquila, a native of Pontus, who had recently come from Italy with his wife Priscilla, because Claudius had ordered all the Jews to leave Rome* (2a). This married couple, whom Paul later called his 'fellow-workers in Christ Jesus', who had 'risked their lives' for him,[12] exemplified an extraordinary degree of mobility. Born in Pontus on the southern shore of the Black Sea, Aquila had migrated to Italy. We are not told why, nor whether this move was before or after his marriage to Priscilla. It was together, however, that they left Rome for Corinth, and on account of an imperial edict. Suetonius referred to this in his *Life of Claudius* (25:4): 'as the Jews were making constant disturbances at the instigation of Chrestus (*impulsore Chresto*), he banished them from Rome'. The people expelled he called 'Jews', but 'Chrestus' seems to mean Christ (the pronunciation of 'Christus' and 'Chrestus' will have been very similar), in which case the Jews were Christians and the disturbances in the Jewish community had been caused by the gospel. Presumably, then, Aquila and Priscilla were already believers before they reached Corinth. They later undertook a further move, this time from Corinth to Ephesus in the company of Paul, and the church, or a portion of it, met in their house (18:18, 19, 26).[13]

Paul now *went to see them* (2b), *and because he was a tentmaker as they were, he stayed and worked with them* (3). They shared the same trade as well as the same faith. What was it? Virtually all English versions translate *skēnopoios* 'tentmaker', since *skēnē* or *skēnos* is a tent. Some commentators prefer 'leather worker' or

[9] Farrar, p. 315. [10] 1 Cor. 6:9ff. [11] 1 Cor. 2:2–3. [12] Rom. 16:3–4.

[13] 1 Cor. 16:9. For other references to Aquila and Priscilla, see Rom. 16:3 and 2 Tim. 4:19.

'saddler', however, 'since the tents of antiquity were usually made of leather'.[14] Another possibility is 'cloth worker', and it is at least plausible (though not proven) that Paul wove a coarse fabric from the thick goats' hair of his native Cilicia. Called in Latin *cilicium*, it was used for curtains, rugs and clothing as well as tents. What is certain is that he worked with his hands. Indeed, Rabbis were required to learn a trade, and urged all young men to do the same. True, Paul also insisted several times on the right of Christian teachers to be supported by their pupils.[15] But he himself voluntarily renounced this right, partly so as not to be a 'burden' to the churches[16] and partly to undercut the accusation of ulterior motives by preaching the gospel free of charge.[17] 'Tentmaking ministries' have rightly become popular in our day. The expression describes cross-cultural messengers of the gospel, who support themselves by their own professional or business expertise, while at the same time being involved in mission. Dr J. Christy Wilson has written about it in his book *Today's Tentmakers*.[18] The principle of self-support is the same, and the desire not to burden the churches, but the main motivation is different, namely that this may be the only way for Christians to enter those countries which do not grant visas to self-styled 'missionaries'.

While Paul worked at his trade on every weekday, *every Sabbath he reasoned in the synagogue, trying to persuade* (an imperfect tense expressing his persistence) *Jews and Greeks*, the latter being 'God-fearers' who attended synagogue worship (4). *When Silas and Timothy came from Macedonia*, however, after staying in Berea (17:14) and visiting Thessalonica,[19] they brought with them not only the good news of the Thessalonians' faith and love,[20] but also a gift.[21] As a result, Paul was able to give up his tentmaking. Instead, he now *devoted himself exclusively to preaching, testifying to the Jews that Jesus was the Christ* (5), or (RSV, *cf.* NEB) 'that the Christ was Jesus'. Either way, it was the identity of the historical Jesus and the expected Christ which mattered. But this Jewish mission met with stubborn resistance, which led Paul to repeat the drastic step he had taken in Pisidian Antioch (13:46, 51) and to turn to the Gentiles. This time he expressed his decision in a dramatic gesture and statement: *But, when the Jews opposed Paul and became abusive, he shook out his clothes in protest* (so that 'not a speck of dust from the synagogue might adhere to' them)[22] *and said to them,*

[14] *TDNT*, vol. VII, p. 393. [15] *E.g.* Gal. 6:6; 1 Cor. 9:4ff.
[16] 1 Thes. 2:9; 2 Thes. 3:8; 2 Cor. 12:13. [17] 1 Cor. 9:15ff.; 2 Cor. 11:7ff.
[18] *Today's Tentmakers* by J. Christy Wilson (Tyndale, USA, 1979).
[19] 1 Thes. 3:2. [20] 1 Thes. 3:6. [21] *Cf.* Phil. 4:14ff. and 2 Cor. 11:8–9.
[22] Bruce, *English*, p. 371.

echoing Ezekiel,[23] *'Your blood be on your own heads! I am clear of my responsibility. From now on I will go to the Gentiles'* (6).

b. Paul turns to the Gentiles (18:7–11)

Luke's next statement, that *then Paul left the synagogue and went next door to the house of Titius Justus, a worshipper of God* (7), is more than a geographical note. It means rather that the scene of his evangelistic labours changed from public synagogue to private house, and that so the people being evangelized changed from Jews to Gentiles. We know that the house belonged to one Titius Justus, and that he was a God-fearer, but it is pure speculation that his other name was Gaius, and indeed the Gaius mentioned in Romans 16:23 and 1 Corinthians 1:14. It is surprising that the first convert of the Gentile mission was *Crispus, the synagogue ruler*, who was in charge of the services, and that *his entire household believed in the Lord* (8a), but following him *many of the Corinthians*, presumably Gentiles, *who heard him* (Paul) *believed and were baptised* (8b).

Paul's audacious decision to move from synagogue to home, from Jewish to Gentile evangelism, was quickly vindicated by God not only through the conversion and baptism of many (8), but also through a vision of Jesus (9–10) and through the attitude of the Roman authorities (12ff.). *One night the Lord spoke to Paul in a vision* (9a). 'The Lord', according to Luke's consistent usage, means 'the Lord Jesus' (see verse 8 'believed in the Lord'). Yet 'the message is couched in the language used by God himself in the Old Testament when addressing his servants'.[24] Both the prohibition 'Do not be afraid' and the promise 'I am with you' were regularly addressed by Yahweh to his people. Now Jesus said the same things to Paul: '*Do not be afraid; keep on speaking, do not be silent* (9b). *For I am with you, and no-one is going to attack and harm you, because I have many people in this city*' (10). He was to continue witnessing, fortified by the presence and the protection of Christ, and by the assurance that Christ had in Corinth 'many people' (*laos*, the Old Testament word for Israel, now extended to include Gentiles). The expression is reminiscent of the Good Shepherd's statement that he had 'other sheep . . . not of this sheep pen' (Israel), *i.e.* Gentiles.[25] They had not yet believed in him, but they would do so, because already according to his purpose they belonged to him. This conviction is the greatest of all encouragements to an evangelist. Strengthened by it, *Paul stayed for a year and a half* in Corinth, *teaching them the word of God* (11). For the word of God is the divinely appointed means by which people come to put their trust in Christ

[23] See Ezk. 33:1ff. [24] Marshall, *Acts*, p. 296. [25] Jn. 10:16

and so identify themselves as his.

c. Paul is vindicated by Roman law (18:12–18a)

At some point during these eighteen months Jewish opposition to the gospel, which had earlier led Paul to turn to the Gentiles (6), erupted again: *The Jews made a united attack on Paul and brought him into court* (12b), or 'before the tribunal' (RSV, JB), the *bēma*, which was 'a large, raised platform that stood in the *agora* . . . in front of the residence of the proconsul and served as a forum where he tried cases'.[26] It was in keeping with Christ's promise that no-one would harm Paul (10) that the Jews took him to court *while Gallio was proconsul of Achaia* (12a, almost certainly AD 51–52), for Gallio proved to be a friend of justice and truth. He was the younger brother of Seneca, the Stoic philosopher and tutor of the youthful Nero, and Seneca spoke appreciatively of his brother's tolerant kindness. Incidentally, Luke was correct to call Gallio 'proconsul', since 'Achaia was at this time a "senatorial" province of the Empire, and therefore governed by a proconsul – as opposed to an "imperial" province, which was governed by a legate'.[27] The province's status had changed only in AD 44.

Of what offence did the Jews accuse Paul? *'This man', they charged, 'is persuading the people to worship God in ways contrary to the law'* (13). But which law was he supposed to be contravening? Gallio understood them to be referring to what he called 'your own law' (15), but they knew as well as he that debates about the Jewish law were beyond his jurisdiction. So they must have been trying to make out that Paul's teaching was against Roman law, because it was not an authentic expression of Judaism. Judaism was a *religio licita*, an authorized religion. But Paul's teaching was 'something new and un-Jewish . . . ; it was, they urged, a *religio illicita*, which accordingly ought to be banned by Roman law'.[28]

The proconsul gave the accused no opportunity to reply to this charge, for he refused to hear it himself. *Just as Paul was about to speak, Gallio said to the Jews, 'If you Jews were making a complaint about some misdemeanour or serious crime* [that is, an obvious offence against Roman law], *it would be reasonable for me to listen to you* (14). *But since it involves questions* [NEB, "bickering"] *about words and names and your own law – settle the matter yourselves. I will not be a judge of such things'* (15). Having made his decision not to hear the Jews' case, Gallio *had them ejected from the court* (16). An unpleasant example of mob rule followed. Although it is not certain who is meant by *they all* in verse 17, it seems to be the crowd of Gentile onlookers who, 'in an outbreak of the anti-

[26] Longenecker, *Acts*, p. 486. [27] Neil, p. 197. [28] Bruce, *English*, p. 374.

Semitism always near the surface in the Graeco-Roman world',[29] now *turned on Sosthenes*, who had evidently succeeded Crispus as *the synagogue ruler*,[30] *and beat him in front of the court* (17a). Luke's addition that *Gallio showed no concern whatever* (17b) does not mean that he was indifferent to justice, but that he considered it judicious to turn a blind eye to this act of violence.

Gallio's refusal to take seriously the Jewish case against Paul or to adjudicate was immensely important for the future of the gospel. In effect, he passed a favourable verdict on the Christian faith and thus established a significant precedent. The gospel could not now be charged with illegality, for its freedom as a *religio licita* had been secured as the imperial policy. Luke's concluding comment is logical: *Paul stayed on in Corinth for some time* (18a), not now because of his vision of Jesus, but because of the judicial decision of Gallio. Jesus would keep his promise to protect him; the chief means of his protection would be Roman law.

2. Paul in transit (18:18b–28)

Luke now follows Paul from Corinth to Ephesus, Caesarea, Jerusalem, Antioch and back through Galatia to Ephesus again. His narrative is very condensed, either because his information was limited (he was himself still in Philippi) or because his purpose was to get Paul from Achaia to Asia (where he had previously been forbidden by the Spirit to preach, 16:6), from his two years in Corinth to his three years in Ephesus, without dwelling on his intervening months of travel.

a. Paul visits Ephesus, Jerusalem and Antioch (18:18–23)

Some time after Gallio's refusal to take cognizance of the Jewish charge against the apostle, Paul *left the brothers and sailed for Syria* (18a), presumably intending to report back to the church of Syrian Antioch which had sent him out (13:1ff.; 14:26ff.; 15:35ff.), and was *accompanied by Priscilla and Aquila*, who may well have financed his trip. Luke now adds the interesting detail that *before he sailed, he had his hair cut off at Cenchrea*, Corinth's eastern port, *because of a vow he had taken* (18b). Commentators have been perplexed regarding who made this vow, what it was, when it was taken and why. As for the person concerned, although the grammar permits it to be Aquila, the context requires that it was Paul. The reference to his hair makes it almost certain that it was a Nazirite vow,[31] which involved abstinence from drinking wine

[29] Longenecker, *Acts*, p. 486. [30] See also 1 Cor. 1:1.
[31] Nu. 6:1ff.

and from cutting one's hair for a period, at the end of which the hair was first cut and then burned, along with other sacrifices, as a symbol of self-offering to God. If the vow was completed away from Jerusalem, the hair could still be brought there to be burned. Such vows were made 'either in thankfulness for past blessings (such as Paul's safekeeping in Corinth) or as part of a petition for future blessings (such as safekeeping on Paul's impending journey)'.[32] Once Paul had been liberated from the attempt to be justified by the law, his conscience was free to take part in practices which, being ceremonial or cultural, belonged to the 'matters indifferent', perhaps on this occasion in order to conciliate the Jewish Christian leaders he was going to see in Jerusalem (*cf.* 21:23ff., relating to his subsequent visit).

They arrived at Ephesus, where Paul left Priscilla and Aquila. He himself went into the synagogue and reasoned with the Jews (19). His mission was so much more acceptable to the Jews in Ephesus than in Corinth (did this have anything to do with his shaven head?) that they wanted him to stay. But *when they asked him to spend more time with them he declined* (20), adding (according to the Western text), 'I must at all costs keep the coming festival in Jerusalem', which Ramsay declared 'may be confidently understood as the Passover'.[33] Whatever the reason for Paul's haste, *as he left, he promised* to return, saying: *'I will come back if it is God's will.' Then he set sail from Ephesus* (21).

When he landed at Caesarea, Palestine's chief port, *he went up and greeted the church and then went down to Antioch* (22). The church which he greeted on disembarkation was almost certainly not that of Caesarea, but of Jerusalem, about sixty-five miles inland, for 'the terms "going up" and "going down" are used so frequently of the journey to and from Jerusalem as to establish this usage'.[34]

After spending some time in Antioch, probably from the early summer of AD 52 to the early spring of 53, and having doubtless given its church a full account of his second missionary expedition, *Paul set out from there* on what proved to be his third and last. He will have gone first in a northerly direction, then west through the Cilician Gates, over the Taurus range, *and travelled from place to place throughout the region of Galatia and Phrygia, strengthening all the disciples* (23). This must mean that he revisited the churches of Pisidian Antioch, Iconium, Lystra and Derbe, which he had established during his first missionary journey (chapters 13 to 14) and consolidated during his second (16:6).

[32] Marshall, *Acts*, p. 300. [33] Ramsay, *St Paul*, p. 263. [34] *Ibid.*, p. 264.

b. Apollos visits Ephesus (18:24–28)

Meanwhile, during the year or so which must have elapsed since Paul left Corinth, *a Jew named Apollos, a native of Alexandria, came to Ephesus* (24a). Luke goes on to tell us three interesting facts about him. First, *he was a learned man* (though *logios* could mean 'eloquent', as in RSV, NEB), *with a thorough knowledge of the Scriptures* (24b). Alexandria had a huge Jewish population at that time. It was here that the LXX had been produced some 200 years before Christ, and here that the great scholar Philo, Jesus' contemporary, lived and worked, struggling by allegorical interpretation of the Old Testament to reconcile Hebrew religion with Greek philosophy. Did Apollos himself interpret the Old Testament allegorically? Perhaps Luther was right in being the first person to propose Apollos as the author of the Letter to the Hebrews. Secondly, *he had been instructed in the way of the Lord* (*i.e.* the Lord Jesus). He also spoke with great fervour ('fervent in spirit', as in Rom. 12:11, probably meaning 'spiritually fervent'), thus matching erudition with enthusiasm. In addition, he *taught about Jesus accurately*. He was therefore, although Jewish, a Christian teacher (25a). Thirdly, however, *he knew only the baptism of John* (25b), whom Luke knew to have been the Messiah's forerunner[35] and to have belonged to the law and the prophets, not the kingdom.[36] Since Apollos can hardly have known John's baptism without also knowing his teaching, he must have been familiar with John's witness to Jesus as the Messiah. But how much more did he know? At all events, when *he began to speak boldly in the synagogue*, and *Priscilla and Aquila heard him*, they recognized that his understanding was defective, invited him to their home, and *explained to him the way of God more adequately* (26), literally, 'more accurately' (RSV), the comparative of the adverb *akribōs* used in the previous verse.

It is not possible to be sure which Christian truths Apollos knew when he taught 'accurately' and which were explained to him 'more accurately'. On the one hand, Luke could hardly have described him as 'instructed in the way of the Lord' if at that stage he was still completely ignorant of the death and resurrection of Jesus. On the other hand, if his knowledge was largely limited to John's baptism and teaching, his grasp of these events may have been minimal, and he will also have needed to hear about Jesus' commission, exaltation and gift of the Spirit. Such truths as these Priscilla and Aquila taught him. Their ministry was timely and discreet. As Professor Bruce remarks, 'how much better it is to give such private help to a preacher whose ministry is defective than to correct or denounce him publicly!'[37]

[35] Lk. 3:1ff. [36] Lk 16:16. [37] Bruce, *English*, p. 382

Next, *when Apollos wanted to go to Achaia, the brothers encouraged him*, for he was better equipped now for a wider ministry, *and wrote to the disciples there to welcome him. On arriving, he was a great help to those who by grace had believed* (27). *For he vigorously refuted the Jews in public debate, proving from the Scriptures that Jesus was the Christ* (28). Indeed, in 1 Corinthians 1 – 4 Paul himself wrote appreciatively of Apollos' ministry in Corinth and generously acknowledged him as a fellow-worker in God's field. 'I planted the seed,' he wrote; 'Apollos watered it, but God made it grow.'[38]

3. Paul in Ephesus (19:1–41)

While Apollos was at Corinth, Paul took the road through the interior (or 'made his way overland', JB) *and arrived at Ephesus* (1), keeping his promise to return if God willed it (18:21). It was, therefore, during Paul's year of absence from Ephesus that Apollos came, ministered and left again.

a. Paul and John the Baptist's followers (19:1b–7)

On arrival in Ephesus Paul *found some disciples*. At least, that is what they claimed to be. In reality, however, they were disciples of John the Baptist, and were decidedly less well informed than Apollos had been. Luke records the dialogue which developed between them (2–4) and its sequel (5–7).

Paul's first question:	*'Did you receive the Holy Spirit when you believed?'*
Their answer:	*'No, we have not even heard that there is a Holy Spirit.'*
Paul's second question:	*'Then what baptism did you receive?'*
Their answer:	*'John's baptism.'*
Paul's comment:	*'John's baptism was a baptism of repentance. He told the people to believe in the one coming after him, that is, in Jesus.'*

5*On hearing this, they were baptised into the name of the Lord Jesus.* 6*When Paul placed his hands on them, the Holy Spirit came on them, and they spoke in tongues and prophesied.* 7*There were about twelve men in all.*

This incident has become a proof text in some pentecostal and charismatic circles, especially when the inaccurate and unwarranted AV translation of verse 2 is followed, namely 'Have ye received the

[38] 1 Cor. 3:6.

Holy Ghost since ye believed?' From this it is sometimes argued that Christian initiation is in two stages, beginning with faith and conversion, and followed later by receiving the Holy Spirit. But those twelve 'disciples' cannot possibly be regarded as providing a norm for a two-stage initiation. On the contrary, as Michael Green has written, it is 'crystal clear that these disciples were in no sense Christians',[39] having not yet believed in Jesus, whereas through the ministry of Paul they came to believe and were then baptized with water and the Spirit more or less simultaneously.

When Paul first met them, he assumed that they were believers, but noticed that they gave no evidence in their bearing or behaviour of the indwelling of the Holy Spirit. So he asked them his two leading questions, whether they had received the Spirit when they believed, and into what they had been baptized. His first question linked the Spirit with faith, and his second with baptism. That is, his questions expressed his assumptions that those who have believed have received the Spirit,[40] and that those who have been baptized have received the Spirit, for he cannot separate the sign (water) from the thing signified (the Spirit). He took it for granted that baptized believers receive the Spirit, as Peter also taught (2:38–39). Both his questions imply that to have believed and been baptized and not to have received the Spirit constitutes an extraordinary anomaly.

Consider now the answers which Paul received to his questions. In answer to his first, they said that they had 'not even heard that there is a Holy Spirit'. This cannot mean that they had never heard of the Spirit at all, for he is referred to many times in the Old Testament, and John the Baptist spoke of the Messiah as baptizing people with the Spirit. It must rather mean that, although they had heard John's prophecy, they had not heard whether it had been fulfilled. They were ignorant of Pentecost. In answer to Paul's second question, they explained that they had received John's baptism, not Christian baptism. In a word, they were still living in the Old Testament which culminated with John the Baptist. They understood neither that the new age had been ushered in by Jesus, nor that those who believe in him and are baptized into him receive the distinctive blessing of the new age, the indwelling Spirit.

Once they came to understand this through Paul's instruction, they put their trust in Jesus of whose coming their teacher John the Baptist had spoken. They were then baptized into Christ, Paul laid his hands on them (giving his apostolic imprimatur to what was happening, as Peter and John had done in Samaria), the Holy Spirit came on them, and they spoke in tongues and prophesied. In

[39] Green, *I believe in the Holy Spirit*, p. 135. [40] *Cf.* Gal. 3:2.

other words, they experienced a mini-Pentecost. Better, Pentecost caught up on them. Better still, they were caught up into it, as its promised blessings became theirs.

The norm of Christian experience, then, is a cluster of four things: repentance, faith in Jesus, water baptism and the gift of the Spirit. Though the perceived order may vary a little, the four belong together and are universal in Christian initiation. The laying-on of apostolic hands, however, together with tongue-speaking and prophesying, were special to Ephesus, as to Samaria, in order to demonstrate visibly and publicly that particular groups were incorporated into Christ by the Spirit; the New Testament does not universalize them. There are no Samaritans or disciples of John the Baptist left in the world today.

b. Synagogue and lecture hall (19:8–10)

The pattern of Paul's evangelistic ministry in Ephesus was similar to that in Corinth. First, *Paul entered the synagogue*, where he was already known (18:19), *and spoke boldly there for three months, arguing persuasively* (RSV, 'arguing and pleading') *about the kingdom of God* (8). To argue from the Old Testament Scriptures about the kingdom is the same as to argue that Jesus is the Christ, since it is Jesus the Christ who inaugurated the kingdom (*cf.* 28:31). *But*, as in Corinth so in Ephesus, the Jewish people rejected the good news: *some of them became obstinate; they refused to believe and publicly maligned the Way*, as Christian discipleship is again called,[41] since 'Christianity was for the disciples the way of all ways . . . in which to walk'.[42] As a direct result of this stubborn opposition in the synagogue, *Paul left them.* He also *took the disciples with him and had discussions* (*dialegomenos*; RSV, 'argued') *daily in the lecture hall of Tyrannus* (9). In fact this new outreach to the Gentiles in the form of dialogue evangelism *went on for two years, so that all the Jews and Greeks who lived in the province of Asia heard the word of the Lord* (10). It is a bit tantalizing that Luke tells us nothing about Tyrannus. One assumes that he was a philosopher or educator of some kind, who lectured during the cool hours of the morning, but was prepared to rent his school room or lecture hall (*scholē*) to the Christian evangelist during the

[41] *Cf.* Acts 9:2; 19:23; 22:4; 24:14, 22.

[42] Williams, p. 122. It is interesting that Hinduism, Buddhism, Taoism, Judaism and Islam all in differing degrees use the imagery of the 'way' or the 'path'. In the Bible too we are confronted by two ways between which to choose, usually between life and death (*e.g.* Dt. 30:19ff.; Ps. 1; Pr. 2; Mt. 7:13–14). The Qumran community was also familiar with this alternative. But the six occurrences of 'the way' in Acts are all unqualified. The origin of this absolute use is not known. It may go back to Jesus' claim to be the only way to the Father (Jn. 14:6; *cf.* Acts 4:12; 16:17) or it may be declaring that to follow Christ is a uniquely adventurous journey.

heat of the day. Since *tyrannos* means a despot or tyrant, 'one wonders idly if this was the name his parents gave him or the name his pupils gave him!'[43] What is clear is that Paul's daily Christian lecturing for two years led to the evangelization of the whole province.

c. *Some power encounters (19:11–20)*

In Corinth Christ encouraged his apostle and endorsed his teaching through a night vision; in Ephesus through signs and wonders by which Christ's power over disease, demon-possession and magic was demonstrated. *God did extraordinary miracles through Paul* (11). *Handkerchiefs and aprons that had touched him* ('the sweat-rags being used for tying round his head and the aprons for tying round his waist' while he was engaged in his tentmaking)[44] *were taken to the sick, and their illnesses were cured and the evil spirits left them* (12). Liberal commentators are embarrassed by these verses and tend to dismiss them as legendary. At least four points may be made on the other side. First, Luke himself is not content to describe these events as mere 'miracles', *dynameis*, demonstrations of divine power; he adds the adjective *tychousas*, which is variously translated 'special' (AV), 'singular' (NEB), 'remarkable' (JB) and 'extraordinary' (RSV, NIV). He does not regard them as typical, even for 'miracles'. Secondly, he does not regard them as magic either, for he sets them apart from the magical practices which Ephesian believers were soon to confess and renounce as evil (18–19). Thirdly, the wisest attitude to the sweat-rag miracles is neither that of the sceptics who declare them spurious, nor that of the mimics, who try to copy them, like those American televangelists who offer to send to the sick handkerchiefs which they have blessed, but rather that of Bible students who remember both that Paul regarded his miracles as his apostolic credentials[45] and that Jesus himself condescended to the timorous faith of a woman by healing her when she touched the edge of his cloak.[46] Fourthly, as in the Gospels so in the Acts, demon-possession is distinguished from illness, and therefore exorcism from healing.

The mention of exorcism leads Luke to tell of some Jewish exorcists, who attempted to tap the power they believed to inhere in the name of Jesus, with disastrous consequences: *Some Jews who went around driving out evil spirits tried to invoke the name of the Lord Jesus over those who were demon-possessed. They would say, 'In the name of Jesus, whom Paul preaches, I command you to come out'* (13). *Seven sons of Sceva, a Jewish chief priest*, meaning

[43] Bruce, *English*, p. 388, f.n. 18. [44] *Ibid.*, p. 389.
[45] *E.g.* 2 Cor. 12:12; Rom. 15:19. [46] Lk. 8:43–44.

probably that he belonged to a high-priestly family, *were doing this* (14). *The evil spirit answered them, 'Jesus I know and I know about Paul, but who are you?'* (15). *Then the man who had the evil spirit jumped on them and overpowered them all. He gave them such a beating that they ran out of the house naked and bleeding* (16). To be sure, there is power – saving and healing power – in the name of Jesus, as Luke has been at pains to illustrate (*e.g.* 3:6, 16; 4:10–12). But its efficacy is not mechanical, nor can people use it second-hand. Nevertheless, in spite of this misuse of the Name, the incident had a wholesome effect. *When this became known to the Jews and Greeks living in Ephesus, they were all seized with fear* (NEB, 'awestruck'), *and the name of the Lord Jesus was held in high honour* (17).

The power encounter of Jesus with the kingdom of Satan was not yet complete. After healing and exorcism came deliverance from occult practices. *Many of those who believed now came and openly confessed their evil deeds* (18). *A number who had practised sorcery brought their scrolls together and burned them publicly. When they calculated the value of the scrolls, the total came to fifty thousand drachmas* (19), the drachma being a silver coin representing about a day's wage. We have already noted that Ephesus was famous for its 'Ephesian letters' (*grammata*), which were 'written charms, amulets and talismans'.[47] That these young believers, instead of realizing the monetary value of their magic spells by selling them, were willing to throw them on a bonfire, was signal evidence of the genuineness of their conversion. Their example also led to more conversions, for *in this way the word of the Lord spread widely and grew in power* (20).

d. Paul's future plans (19:21–22)

After all this had happened, after the synagogue and lecture-hall evangelism and the power encounters, but before the riot in the theatre, *Paul decided to go to Jerusalem*, first *passing through Macedonia and Achaia* (21a). Luke does not add at this stage the reason for this circuitous route, but we know that he was going to pick up the offering which he had been urging the Christians of Northern and Southern Greece to collect for their poverty-stricken sisters and brothers in Judea.[48] His eyes were not on Jerusalem, however. *'After I have been there,' he said, 'I must visit Rome also'* (21b), and beyond that he was even dreaming of Spain,[49] 'the most westerly outpost of Roman civilization in Europe'.[50] His vision had no limits. As Bengel rightly commented, 'no Alexander, no Caesar,

[47] Alexander, II, p. 200.
[48] See Acts 24:17; Rom. 15:25ff.; 1 Cor. 16:1–8; 2 Cor. 8 – 9.
[49] Rom. 15:24, 28. [50] Bruce, *English*, p. 394.

no other hero, approaches to the large-mindedness of this *little* (a play on his name *Paulos*, "little") Benjamite'.[51] Meanwhile, *he sent two of his helpers, Timothy and Erastus*, ahead of him *to Macedonia*, presumably in order to make last-minute preparations for the offering, *while he stayed in the province of Asia*, indeed in Ephesus itself, *a little longer* (22), because 'a great door for effective work' had opened before him, and many were opposing him.[52] Both the opportunity and the opposition necessitated his continued presence in Ephesus.

e. *The riot in the city (19:23–41)*

Luke gives his readers a graphic account of the riot which Demetrius the silversmith instigated and the town clerk skilfully quelled. Perhaps he obtained his information from Aristarchus and/or Gaius, who found themselves caught up in the uproar (29) and later became Paul's and Luke's travelling companions (20:4–6). Haenchen's presuppositions lead him to find in the story 'a regular tangle of difficulties'.[53] He elaborates six of them. But Howard Marshall is right to say that Haenchen's case 'disappears under scrutiny'. He gives an adequate explanation of each supposed problem.[54] Luke's narrative divides itself naturally into three sections relating to the origin, course and termination of the riot.

First, its origin. It was inevitable that sooner or later the kingly authority of Jesus would challenge Diana's evil sway.

> 23*About that time there arose a great disturbance about the Way.*
> 24*A silversmith named Demetrius, who made silver shrines of Artemis, brought in no little business for the craftsmen.* 25*He called them together, along with the workmen in related trades, and said: 'Men, you know we receive a good income from this business.* 26*And you see and hear how this fellow Paul has convinced and led astray large numbers of people here in Ephesus and in practically the whole province of Asia. He says that man-made gods are no gods at all.*
> 27*There is danger not only that our trade will lose its good name, but also that the temple of the great goddess Artemis will be discredited, and the goddess herself, who is worshipped throughout the province of Asia and the world, will be robbed of her divine majesty.'*

Luke declares that the disturbance arose 'about the Way' (NEB, 'the Christian movement'). At root its cause was neither doctrinal, nor ethical, but economic. Demetrius, whom Ramsay called 'probably Master of the guild (*sc.* of silversmiths) for the year',[55] drew the

[51] Bengel, p. 681. [52] 1 Cor. 16:8–9. [53] Haenchen, p. 576.
[54] Marshall, *Acts*, pp. 315–317. [55] *HDB*, p. 723.

attention of his and other craftsmen to Paul's success in convincing people 'that man-made gods are no gods at all'. In consequence, the sales of 'silver shrines of Artemis' (either miniature models of the temple or statuettes of the goddess) were dwindling and their affluent life-style was threatened. Not that Demetrius played directly on their covetousness, however. He was subtle enough to develop three more respectable motives for concern, namely the dangers that their trade would lose its good name, their temple its prestige, and their goddess her divine majesty (27). Thus 'vested interests were disguised as local patriotism – in this case also under the cloak of religious zeal'.[56]

Demetrius proved to be a skilled rabble-rouser, for the artisans' response was immediate.

[28]*When they heard this, they were furious and began shouting: 'Great is Artemis of the Ephesians!'* [29]*Soon the whole city was in an uproar. The people seized Gaius and Aristarchus, Paul's travelling companions from Macedonia, and rushed as one man into the theatre.* [30]*Paul wanted to appear before the crowd, but the disciples would not let him.* [31]*Even some of the officials of the province, friends of Paul, sent him a message begging him not to venture into the theatre.*

[32]*The assembly was in confusion: Some were shouting one thing, some another. Most of the people did not even know why they were there.* [33]*The Jews pushed Alexander to the front, and some of the crowd shouted instructions to him. He motioned for silence in order to make a defence before the people.* [34]*But when they realised he was a Jew, they all shouted in unison for about two hours: 'Great is Artemis of the Ephesians!'*

'The most impressive ruins in Asia Minor . . . , Ephesus stands dignified and alone in its death', wrote H. V. Morton.[57] The excavated site is magnificent; it is easy to visualize the riot. According to the Bezan text of verse 28, the infuriated craftsmen went 'running into the street' before they started to shout for Diana. This was probably the Arcadian Way, the main thoroughfare of Ephesus, eleven metres wide, marble-paved and colonnaded, leading from the harbour to the theatre. The theatre itself, still in a fine state of preservation, nestling at the foot of Mount Pion and nearly 500 feet in diameter, could accommodate at least 25,000 people. Here the crowd dragged Gaius and Aristarchus. And here Paul (overconfident perhaps in the immunity he believed his Roman citizenship would give him) was prevented from coming by the pleas of both the disciples and by some 'officials of the province' who were

[56] Neil, p. 207. [57] Morton, p. 327.

his friends (31). Luke rightly calls them 'Asiarchs'. These were leading citizens, who were prominent members of the provincial council of Asia, especially its 'annual presidents and perhaps ex-presidents', and/or the city's deputies who served on it, and/or 'the administrators of the various temples of the imperial cult, who were under the charge of high priests appointed by the provincial council'.[58] Paul was fortunate to have the friendship and the advice of some of them. By now confusion reigned in the theatre. Some people were shouting this or that, but most of them had no idea why they were there. A diversion was caused when some Jews tried to put forward their spokesman, no doubt in order to disassociate Jews from Christians, but the crowd, who would not have comprehended the distinction, shouted him down and for two hours resumed their chanting of Diana's name. Indeed, this section begins and ends with the hysterical screams 'Great is Artemis of the Ephesians!' (28, 34). Haenchen is right to comment that 'in final analysis the only thing heathenism can do against Paul is to shout itself hoarse'.[59]

Luke now describes how the crowd's frenzy was calmed by 'the city clerk' (*grammateus*, 35), who was 'the elected head of the city executive'[60] or 'the chief administrative assistant, annually elected, of the magistrates; he had a staff of permanent clerks, responsible for the paper work of the city'.[61]

35*The city clerk quietened the crowd and said: 'Men of Ephesus, doesn't all the world know that the city of Ephesus is the guardian of the temple of the great Artemis and of her image, which fell from heaven?* 36*Therefore, since these facts are undeniable, you ought to be quiet and not do anything rash.* 37*You have brought these men here, though they have neither robbed temples nor blasphemed our goddess.* 38*If, then, Demetrius and his fellow craftsmen have a grievance against anybody, the courts are open and there are proconsuls. They can press charges.* 39*If there is anything further you want to bring up, it must be settled in a legal assembly.* 40*As it is, we are in danger of being charged with rioting because of today's events. In that case we would not be able to account for this commotion, since there is no reason for it.'* 41*After he had said this, he dismissed the assembly.*

This city clerk was evidently a man of high intelligence and of great skill in crowd control. He made four points. First, the whole world knows that Ephesus is the guardian of Artemis' temple and image. Since this is undeniable, no-one is going to deny it, and the

[58] Sherwin-White, p. 90. [59] Haenchen, p. 578.
[60] Sherwin-White, p. 83. [61] *Ibid.*, p. 86.

cult of Artemis is in no danger (35–36). Secondly, 'these men' (Gaius and Aristarchus) are guilty of neither sacrilege (robbing the temple) nor blasphemy (reviling the goddess). They are innocent (37). Thirdly, Demetrius and his colleagues are familiar with statutory legal procedures. If they have a private grievance, they should bring their case to the proconsular assizes. If, on the other hand, their case is more serious and more public, they should refer it to 'a legal assembly', the correct technical term for the regular (three times a month) official meetings of the *dēmos* or city council (38–39). As Dr Sherwin-White comments, Luke 'is very well informed about the finer points of municipal institutions at Ephesus in the first and second centuries AD'.[62] Fourthly, the citizens of Ephesus are themselves in danger of being charged with civil disorder. If this were to happen, they would not be able to justify themselves. Each of these arguments was cogent; the four together were decisive. When the town clerk 'dismissed the assembly', they went home in a very chastened mood.

Luke's purpose in recounting this incident was clearly apologetic or political. He wanted to show that Rome had no case against Christianity in general or Paul in particular. In Corinth the proconsul Gallio had refused even to hear the Jews' charge. In Ephesus the town clerk implied that the opposition was purely emotional and that the Christians, being innocent, had nothing to fear from duly constituted legal processes. Thus the impartiality of Gallio, the friendship of Asiarchs and the cool reasonableness of the city clerk combined to give the gospel freedom to continue on its victorious course.

4. Paul's strategy for urban evangelism

In spite of the obvious cultural differences between first-century cities in the Roman Empire and the great urban complexes of today, there are also similarities. We may learn from Paul in Corinth and Ephesus important lessons about the where, the how and the when of urban evangelism.

a. The secular places he chose

It is true that in both Corinth and Ephesus he began in the Jewish synagogue; that was his custom. But when the Jews rejected the gospel, he withdrew from the synagogue and moved to a neutral building instead. In Corinth he chose a private house, the home of Titius Justus, while in Ephesus he rented the lecture hall of Tyrannus. And easily the greater part of his evangelistic ministry in both

[62] *Ibid.*, p. 87.

cities was spent in these secular situations.

In our day we still have to evangelize the religious. The equivalent to the synagogue in our culture is the church. It is here that the Scriptures are read, prayer is offered, and 'God-fearers' congregate, people on the fringe who are attracted but not committed. The gospel must be proclaimed to them. But we must not limit our evangelism to the religious and neglect the irreligious. If religious people can be reached in religious buildings, secular people have to be reached in secular buildings. Perhaps the equivalent to Paul's use of the house of Titius Justus is home evangelism, and the equivalent to his use of the hall of Tyrannus is lecture evangelism. People will come to a home, to listen to an informal talk and engage in free discussion, who would never darken the door of a church, and there is an important place for apologetic and/or explanatory Christian lectures in the local college or university or in some other neutral, public place.

b. The reasoned presentation he made

Luke uses several verbs to describe Paul's evangelistic preaching. But two of them stand out in these chapters. Each occurs four times, almost equally divided between his ministry in Corinth and in Ephesus. They are the verbs to 'reason' or 'argue' (*dialegomai*) and to 'persuade' (*peithō*). In Corinth 'every Sabbath he *reasoned* in the synagogue, trying to *persuade* Jews and Greeks' (18:4). In consequence, the Jews complained to Gallio that 'this man is *persuading the people* . . .' (18:13). In Ephesus Paul spoke boldly in the synagogue for three months, '*arguing persuasively* [literally, "arguing and persuading"] about the kingdom of God' (19:8), and then after withdrawing from the synagogue he 'had discussions daily' [RSV, '*argued* daily'] in the hall of Tyrannus (19:9). Thus both in the religious context of the synagogue and in the secular context of the lecture hall, Paul combined argument and persuasion. As a result, Demetrius was able to complain that 'this fellow Paul has *convinced* [RSV, "persuaded"] . . . large numbers of people . . .' (19:26). Martin Hengel conjectures plausibly that Paul's letters (especially Romans and parts of 1 and 2 Corinthians) 'contain brief summaries of lectures and . . . the much reduced quintessence of what Paul taught' during those years in Tyrannus' lecture theatre.[63]

This vocabulary shows that Paul's presentation of the gospel was serious, well reasoned and persuasive. Because he believed the gospel to be true, he was not afraid to engage the minds of his hearers. He did not simply proclaim his message in a 'take it or leave it' fashion; instead, he marshalled arguments to support and

[63] Hengel, p. 11.

demonstrate his case. He was seeking to convince in order to convert, and in fact, as Luke makes plain, many were 'persuaded'. Luke indicates, moreover, that this was Paul's method even in Corinth. What he renounced in Corinth[64] was the wisdom of the world, not the wisdom of God, and the rhetoric of the Greeks, not the use of arguments. Arguments of course are no substitute for the work of the Holy Spirit. But then trust in the Holy Spirit is no substitute for arguments either. We must never set them over against each other as alternatives. No, the Holy Spirit is the Spirit of truth, and he brings people to faith in Jesus not in spite of the evidence, but because of the evidence, when he opens their minds to attend to it.

c. *The extended periods he stayed*

Luke is careful to give us the details. In Corinth Paul began by preaching in the synagogue every sabbath, presumably for several weeks or months, and then moved to the house of Titius Justus and 'stayed for a year and a half, teaching . . . the word of God' (18:11). Next, he 'stayed on in Corinth for some time' (18:18), so that probably he was in the city for about two years altogether. In Ephesus he began with three months in the synagogue and then lectured for two years in Tyrannus' lecture hall (19:8, 10). Since later he also 'stayed in the province of Asia a little longer' (19:22), it is understandable that he could later refer to his ministry in Ephesus as having lasted 'for three years' (20:31). Thus he spent two years in Corinth and three years in Ephesus, and in both cases his teaching was comprehensive and thorough.

His use of the lecture hall of Tyrannus was specially remarkable. The accepted text says that he lectured there daily for two years, but the Bezan text adds that he did it 'from the fifth hour to the tenth' (19:9, RSV margin), that is, from 11 o'clock in the morning to 4 o'clock in the afternoon. Dr Bruce Metzger thinks that this addition 'may represent an accurate piece of information, preserved in oral tradition before being incorporated into the text of certain manuscripts'.[65] According to Ramsay, 'public life in the Ionian cities ended regularly at the fifth hour',[66] that is, at 11 a.m., having begun at sunrise and continued during the cool of the early morning. But at 11 the city stopped work, not for 'elevenses', but for an elongated siesta! According to Lake and Cadbury, 'at 1 p.m. there were probably more people sound asleep than at 1 a.m.'[67] But Paul did not sleep in the daytime. Until 11 a.m. he would work at his tentmaking and Tyrannus would give his lectures. At 11, how-

[64] See 1 Cor. 1 and 2. [65] Metzger, p. 470.
[66] Ramsay, *St Paul*, p. 271. [67] *BC*, IV, p. 239.

ever, Tyrannus would go to rest, 'the lecture-room would be disengaged',[68] and Paul would exchange leather-work for lecture-work, continuing for five hours, and stopping only at 4 p.m. when work was resumed in the city. Assuming that the apostle kept one day in seven for worship and rest, he will have given a daily five-hour lecture six days a week for two years, which makes 3,120 hours of gospel argument! It is not surprising that Luke continues: 'all the Jews and Greeks who lived in the province of Asia heard the word of the Lord' (19:10). For all the roads of Asia converged on Ephesus, and all the inhabitants of Asia visited Ephesus from time to time, to buy or sell, visit a relative, frequent the baths, attend the games in the stadium, watch a drama in the theatre, or worship the goddess. And while they were in Ephesus, they heard of this Christian lecturer named Paul, who was both speaking and answering questions for five hours in the middle of every day. Evidently many dropped in, listened and were converted. They then returned to their towns and villages as born-again believers. Thus the gospel must have spread to the Lycus valley and to its chief towns Colosse, Laodicea and Hierapolis, which Epaphras had visited but Paul had not,[69] and perhaps to the remaining five of the seven churches of Revelation 2 and 3, namely Smyrna, Pergamum, Thyatira, Sardis and Philadelphia. This is a fine strategy for the great university and capital cities of the world. If the gospel is reasonably, systematically and thoroughly unfolded in the city centre, visitors will hear it, embrace it and take it back with them to their homes.

When we contrast much contemporary evangelism with Paul's, its shallowness is immediately shown up. Our evangelism tends to be too ecclesiastical (inviting people to church), whereas Paul also took the gospel out into the secular world; too emotional (appeals for decision without an adequate basis of understanding), whereas Paul taught, reasoned and tried to persuade; and too superficial (making brief encounters and expecting quick results), whereas Paul stayed in Corinth and Ephesus for five years, faithfully sowing gospel seed and in due time reaping a harvest.

[68] *Ibid.* [69] Col. 1:7; 2:1; 4:12–13.

15. More about Ephesus
20:1–21:17

Luke now narrates how Paul left Ephesus (20:1), having spent the best part of three years there during his third missionary expedition, and then travelled from place to place until at last he reached Jerusalem (21:17). True, Luke has let us into the secret that Paul was intending after visiting Jerusalem to make for Rome (19:21). Nevertheless, it was Jerusalem which filled his vision at this stage.

In fact, it is hard to resist the conclusion that Luke sees a parallel between Jesus' journey to Jerusalem, which is prominent in his first volume, and Paul's journey to Jerusalem, which he describes in his second. Of course the resemblance is far from being exact, and the mission of Jesus was unique; yet the correspondence between the two journeys seems too close to be a coincidence. (i) Like Jesus, Paul travelled to Jerusalem with a group of his disciples (20:4ff.).[1] (ii) Like Jesus he was opposed by hostile Jews who plotted against his life (20:3, 19).[2] (iii) Like Jesus he made or received three successive predictions of his 'passion' or sufferings (20:22–23; 21:4, 11)[3] including his being handed over to the Gentiles (21:11).[4] (iv) Like Jesus he declared his readiness to lay down his life (20:24; 21:13).[5] (v) Like Jesus he was determined to complete his ministry and not be deflected from it (20:24; 21:13).[6] (vi) Like Jesus he expressed his abandonment to the will of God (21:14).[7] Even if some of these details are not to be pressed, Luke surely intends his readers to envisage Paul as following in his Master's footsteps when he 'steadfastly set his face to go to Jerusalem'.[8]

When the uproar had ended (1), and public order had been restored to the city of Ephesus, *Paul sent for the disciples* to come to him (was he still in hiding?) *and, after encouraging them, he said good-bye*. I imagine that his encouragement took the form of

[1] *Cf.* Lk. 10:38. [2] *Cf.* Lk. 6:7, 11; 11:53–54; 22:1–2.
[3] *Cf.* Lk. 9:22, 44; 18:31–32. [4] *Cf.* Lk. 18:32.
[5] *Cf.* Lk. 12:50; 22:19; 23:46. [6] *Cf.* Lk. 9:51. [7] *Cf.* Lk. 22:42.
[8] Lk. 9:51, AV.

an exhortation similar to the one he would later give to their pastors in Miletus (20:17ff.). He will have urged them to remain loyal to Christ in spite of continuing persecution and 'to live a life worthy of [their] calling' as God's new and holy people.[9] Then he *set out for Macedonia*, intending to catch up with Timothy and Erastus, whom he had sent on ahead of him (19:22). Whether he went by sea or by road, he must have journeyed north, and his first main stop is likely to have been Troas. Here he had expected 'to preach the gospel of Christ', and indeed he 'found that the Lord had opened a door' for him there.[10] Unfortunately, however, he was unable to exploit this opportunity. For he had also expected to find Titus in Troas, whom he had recently sent on an important fact-finding mission to Corinth. But Titus was not there to meet him, and so, because he 'had no peace of mind', instead of staying to evangelize in Troas, he 'went on to Macedonia'.[11] It was later, probably in Philippi, that Paul's longed-for rendez-vous with Titus took place and his anxiety was transformed into joy.[12] The good news Titus brought, along with other information, prompted Paul to write what we call his Second Letter to the Corinthians (which was actually his fourth).

1. Paul in northern and southern Greece (20:2–6)

Paul now *travelled through that area* (2a). He probably spent several months revisiting the Macedonian churches he had founded on his second missionary journey, namely Philippi, Thessalonica and Berea, and Luke characterized his ministry to them as *speaking many words of encouragement to the people*. The word is *paraklēsis* (the noun which is cognate with the verb *parakaleō* in verse 1), and it has a range of meanings from appeal and entreaty through exhortation and encouragement to comfort and consolation. It is a vital ministry in establishing Christian disciples, and the principal means of its exercise is, literally, 'much word'. Nothing encourages and strengthens the people of God like the Word of God. It is likely also to have been during this period that Paul travelled further west along the Egnatian Way than he had previously gone, reaching even Illyricum on the Adriatic coast north of Macedonia.[13]

After these Macedonian journeys Paul *finally arrived in Greece* (2b), *Hellas* being the popular name for Achaia. Here, almost certainly in Corinth, *he stayed three months* (3a). Much had happened in his relations with the Corinthian church since his first visit which Luke has described. He had written them four letters, and even

[9] Eph. 4:1ff. [10] 2 Cor. 2:12. [11] 2 Cor. 2:13. [12] 2 Cor. 7:5–16.
[13] Rom. 15:19.

paid them an interim visit (the so-called 'painful visit' of 2 Cor. 2:1, which Luke does not mention). So he will have had much to talk about with the church's leaders, in the realms of both doctrine and ethics. We also know that he finalized arrangements for the Corinthians' share in the collection for the Judean churches.[14] In addition, it was during this visit to Corinth that Paul wrote his major manifesto of Christian faith and life, his Letter to the Romans. In Romans 15 he explained that he had now 'from Jerusalem all the way around to Illyricum . . . fully proclaimed the gospel of Christ' and that in consequence 'in these regions' there was 'no more place' for him to work. That was why he hoped soon to visit Rome and go on to Spain.[15]

Paul's three months in Corinth are likely to have been during the winter, while he waited for the spring weather to open up navigation on the high seas. His purpose was *to sail for Syria* direct, as he had done after his first visit (18:18). As he was about to embark, however, he heard that *the Jews* had *made a plot against him*. Ramsay imagines the situation: 'Paul's intention must have been to take a pilgrim ship carrying Achaian and Asian Jews to the Passover. . . . With a shipload of hostile Jews, it would be easy to find opportunity to murder Paul'[16] and dump his body overboard. So Paul changed his plan at the last moment and *decided to go back through Macedonia* (3). The Bezan text adds that 'the Spirit told him' to do so. Yet it was his own decision; the two are not incompatible.

At this point Luke interrupts his narrative in order to tell us who Paul's travelling companions were. It is noteworthy that Paul hardly ever travelled alone, and that when he was alone, he expressed his longing for human companionship, for example in Athens[17] and in his final Roman imprisonment.[18] That he favoured team work is specially clear during his missionary journeys. On his first he was accompanied by Barnabas and John Mark (until the latter defected), on his second by Silas and later Timothy, then Luke, and now at the end of his third Luke supplies his readers with a list of Paul's friends. *He was accompanied by Sopater* (perhaps the same as the *Sosipater* who in Romans 16:21 is called one of Paul's 'relatives') *son of Pyrrhus from Berea, Aristarchus* (19:29; 27:2) *and Secundus from Thessalonica, Gaius from Derbe* (probably the same as in 19:29, where one reading makes only Aristarchus a Macedonian, not Gaius), *Timothy also, and Tychicus and Trophimus from the province of Asia.* Trophimus came from Ephesus;[19]

[14] 1 Cor. 16:1–4; *cf.* Acts 24:17.
[15] Rom. 15:17–33; see verses 19, 23, 24 and 28.
[16] Ramsay, *St Paul*, p. 287. [17] Acts 17:15–16; *cf.* 1 Thes. 3:1, 5.
[18] 2 Tim. 4:9, 21. [19] Acts 21:29; *cf.* 2 Tim. 4:20.

perhaps Tychicus did also.[20] In most cases Luke supplies these men's home as well as their name in order both to identify them clearly and also (probably) to indicate how they represented the different regions which were taking part in the collection. Thus, Macedonia was represented by Sopater (Berea), Aristarchus and Secundus (Thessalonica) and perhaps Luke himself (Philippi); Galatia by Gaius (Derbe) and Timothy (Lystra); and Asia by Tychicus and Trophimus (Ephesus). Achaia is missing, but could have been represented by Paul himself, and/or by Titus,[21] who according to Ramsay's conjecture was a relative of Luke's.[22] This would mean that Paul's entourage consisted of at least nine men.

Luke does not actually mention the offering in connection with them, although it must have been in his mind. In our minds, as we reflect on Paul's associates, should be the threefold witness which they bear. The first is to the growth, unity, and even (one might say) 'catholicity' of the church. Already Christian leaders from inland and coastal Asia Minor, from both sides of the Aegean, and from the northern and southern halves of Greece, know that they belong to the same church and in consequence co-operate in the same cause. Secondly, they bear witness to the fruitfulness of Paul's missionary expeditions, since Derbe and Lystra were evangelized during his first, Berea and Thessalonica during his second, and Ephesus during his third. All nine men must have been the fruits of mission. But they then became the agents of mission. For, thirdly, they give evidence of the missionary-mindedness of the young Christian communities, which already gave up some of their best local leadership to the wider work and witness of Christ's church.

Reading between the lines of Luke's compressed narrative, it seems that Paul and his group of associates left Corinth together and reached Philippi together. Perhaps it was here, and not earlier, that Luke joined the party (since the previous 'we-section' left him there, 16:12, and the next 'we-section' begins now in 20:5). Here too the group apparently split into two. *These men*, at least seven or eight of them, *went on ahead and waited for us at Troas* (5). *But we* (just Paul and Luke?) *sailed from Philippi*, that is, from its port Neapolis (16:11), only *after the Feast of Unleavened Bread.* This is unlikely to be a purely chronological note. Nor is Luke clearly saying that, having been foiled in his desire to celebrate the Passover in Jerusalem, Paul celebrated it in Philippi instead. Are we sure that he continued to observe the Jewish feasts, even though for a particular purpose he intended to get to Jerusalem in time for

[20] See Eph. 6:21–22; Col. 4:7–8; 2 Tim. 4:12; Tit. 3:12.
[21] 2 Cor. 8:16–24. [22] Ramsay, *St Paul*, p. 390.

Pentecost (20:16)? I prefer Professor Howard Marshall's explanation: 'It is probable that he was celebrating the Christian Passover, *i.e.* Easter, with the church at Philippi (1 Cor. 5:7f.).'[23] At all events, it was not until after the festival that they left Philippi, and then it was *five days later* that they *joined the others at Troas.* They must have encountered strong head winds, for their voyage in the opposite direction had taken only two days (16:11). Once in Troas, however, they *stayed seven days* (6).

2. A week in Troas (20:7–12)

Luke records only one incident during this week in Troas, namely the dramatic sleep, fall, death and resuscitation of a young man called Eutychus. Because it took place in the context of a worship service, however, the story is also instructive in the area of early Christian worship.

a. The death and resuscitation of Eutychus

On the first day of the week we came together to break bread (7a). How we interpret this 'first day' depends on whether we think Luke followed the Jewish reckoning of a day (from sunset to sunset) or the Roman (from midnight to midnight). It is because the NEB translators opted for the former that they rendered the opening expression 'on the Saturday night'. And certainly the Bezan text of 19:9 'from the fifth hour to the tenth' (11 a.m. to 4 p.m.) is a Jewish calculation, with the day beginning at 6 a.m. But here Luke is following the Roman way of reckoning, since the 'daylight' of verse 11 is already 'the next day' of verse 7. Professor Bruce is surely right, therefore, that Luke's reference to 'the first day of the week', *i.e.* Sunday, 'is the earliest unambiguous evidence we have for the Christian practice of gathering together for worship on that day'.[24] Moreover, the purpose of their assembly was 'to break bread', which Luke understood as the Lord's Supper in the context of a fellowship meal, as in the upper room in Jerusalem.[25] In addition, *Paul spoke to the people and, because he intended to leave the next day, kept on talking* (JBP, 'prolonged his address') *until midnight* (7b).

Luke was himself present on this occasion ('we came together', 7, and 'where we were meeting', 8), so that he was able to supply several eyewitness details which help us to visualize the scene. First, it was an evening service or meeting, for if Paul's address ended at

[23] Marshall, *Acts*, p. 325.

[24] Bruce, *English*, pp. 407–408; see also Mk. 16:2; Jn. 20:19, 26; 1 Cor. 16:2; Rev. 1:10.

[25] Lk. 22:20; 24:30–35; Acts 2:42.

midnight, it can hardly have begun at midday! No, it probably began at about sunset, the congregation assembling for worship at the conclusion of their day's work. Next, the meeting was being held in a private house, upstairs (8), indeed on the third floor (9). Thirdly, *there were many lamps in the upstairs room where we were meeting* (8), so that the atmosphere became stuffy and oily, even for *Eutychus* who was *seated in a window* (9a; NEB, 'was sitting on the window-ledge'), which, being unglazed, gave him some fresh air to breathe. Fourthly, although Eutychus is called 'a young man' (*neanias*) in verse 9, in verse 12 he is only a 'boy' (NEB, JB) or 'lad' (RSV), *pais* normally covering the years from 8 to 14. Fifthly, Luke does not intend us to attach any blame to the boy for falling asleep during the apostle's sermon. For the impression is that he had a protracted struggle with his sleepiness. To begin with, he was gradually *sinking into a deep sleep*, or better 'grew drowsy'; it was only *as Paul talked on and on* that he fell *sound asleep* (NEB, JBP, he was 'completely overcome by sleep') and the accident happened: *he fell to the ground from the third storey and was picked up dead* (9b). The NEB 'picked up for dead', hinting that he might not really have been dead, is definitely wrong. Luke declares that he was dead; as a doctor he could vouch for it.

One can imagine the confusion which then took over, as everybody tried to run downstairs. *Paul* at once suspended his sermon and himself *went down*. Then, surely following the precedent established by Elijah with the son of the widow at Zarephath[26] and by Elisha with the son of the Shunammite woman,[27] he *threw himself on the young man and put his arms around him*, and *said, 'Don't be alarmed. . . . He's alive!'* (10). This was not a statement that he was still alive in spite of his disastrous fall, but that as a result of Paul embracing him he had come alive again. *Then he* (Paul) *went upstairs again and broke bread and ate*, sharing in both the Lord's Supper and the fellowship supper, which had evidently not been served previously. Paul also resumed his sermon and *after talking until daylight, he left* (11). Meanwhile, *the people* (relatives and friends, one may assume) *took the young man home alive and were greatly comforted* (12).

b. Some principles of Christian worship

What can we learn about Christian worship from that Sunday evening service in Troas many centuries ago? We will be wise to exercise due caution in answering this question, for Luke's account is purely descriptive, and is not intended to be prescriptive. We have no liberty, therefore, to be slavish, either in copying what

[26] 1 Ki. 17:19ff. [27] 2 Ki. 4:32–33.

took place (*e.g.* assembling in a house, indeed on the third floor, meeting in the evening, using oil lamps for illumination and listening to an inordinately lengthy sermon) or in omitting what is not mentioned (*e.g.* prayers, psalms, hymns and Scripture readings). Nevertheless, there seem to be principles of public worship here, which are endorsed by biblical teaching elsewhere and are applicable to us today.

First, the disciples met on the Lord's Day for the Lord's Supper. At least verse 7 sounds like a description of the normal, regular practice of the church in Troas. And the evidence is that the Eucharist, as a thankful celebration of the now risen Saviour's death, very early became the main Sunday service, in the context of an *agapē*, that is, a 'love feast' or fellowship meal.

Secondly, in addition to the supper there was a sermon, indeed a very long one, for its first part lasted from sunset to midnight (7), and its second from midnight to sunrise (11). Not that we are to envisage Paul's preaching as purely monologue, since Luke uses the verb *dialegomai* twice (7, 9), which implies discussion, perhaps in the form of questions and answers. The other word he uses is *homileō* (11), which JBP renders 'a long earnest talk' and NEB 'much conversation'. It was clearly more free and open than a formal sermon. But at least the apostle took his teaching responsibility seriously. So should we. 'There is no hint that Paul took the incident as a rebuke for long-windedness.'[28] And since we have no living apostles comparable to Paul to instruct us today, we need to listen to the teaching of Christ's apostles as it has come down to us in the New Testament. From the earliest days local churches began to make their own collection of the memoirs and letters of the apostles, and obeyed the repeated apostolic injunction to read them, alongside the law and the prophets, in the public assembly.[29]

So it is, thirdly, that word and sacrament were combined in the ministry given to the church at Troas, and the universal church has followed suit ever since. For God speaks to his people through his Word both as it is read and expounded from Scripture and as it is dramatized in the two gospel sacraments, baptism and the Lord's Supper. Perhaps 'word and sacrament' is not the best or most accurate coupling, common though it is. For strictly speaking the sacrament itself is a word, a 'visible word' according to Augustine. What builds up the church more than anything else is the ministry of God's word as it comes to us through Scripture and Sacrament (that is the right coupling), audibly and visibly, in declaration and drama.

[28] Longenecker, *Acts*, p. 509.

[29] *E.g.* Col. 4:16; 1 Thes. 5:27; Rev. 1:3; 22:18–19.

3. A coastal voyage to Miletus (20:13–16)

This next brief paragraph in Luke's narrative (only four verses in our English Bibles) is a rather breathless account of Paul's voyage from Troas (where he addressed the local church) to Miletus (where he addressed the pastors of the Ephesian church). He tells us that Paul was 'in a hurry' (16); we get the impression that Luke was in a hurry too. He mentions four coastal or island ports at which Paul and his companions stopped (Assos, Mitylene, Kios and Samos) after leaving Troas and before arriving at Miletus. The we-section which began at verse 5 continues, so that Luke must be drawing on his own daily log of events. The ship evidently sailed each day and anchored each night. 'The reason', Ramsay explained, 'lies in the wind.' During the Aegean summer 'it generally blows from the north, beginning at a very early hour in the morning'. Then 'in the late afternoon it dies away' and 'at sunset there is a dead calm'.[30]

Leaving Troas, Luke writes, *we went on ahead to the ship and sailed for Assos*, a port on the Asian mainland about twenty miles south of Troas, *where we were going to take Paul aboard. He had made this arrangement because he was going there on foot* (13), or perhaps simply 'by land' (RSV) or 'by road' (NEB). Luke shares two facts with us, without explaining them. First, Paul sent his companions on ahead of him. Did he delay his departure from Troas in order first to assure himself that Eutychus was not only alive but well? It is only a guess. Secondly, Paul arranged for his friends to travel to Assos by sea and for himself to go by land. Travel along the coastal road would be quicker than a sea voyage round the cape. But why did he want to be alone? Was it that this was the real beginning of his long journey to Jerusalem? We know that he was anxious both that he would be rescued from unbelievers in Judea and that his offering would be acceptable to the believers in Jerusalem, for he begged the Christians in Rome to join him in praying for these very things.[31] Maybe it was these things which occupied his thoughts and prayers on his lonely walk from Troas to Assos. But again, it is only a guess.

When he met us at Assos, the pre-arranged rendez-vous, *we took him aboard and went on to Mitylene* (14), which was the main city of the island of Lesbos, and was situated on its south-east coast. *The next day we set sail from there and arrived off Kios* (15a), that is, anchored in a mainland port opposite the island of Kios. *The day after that we crossed over to Samos*, an island west of Ephesus, and, 'after stopping at Trogyllium' (JB, following the Bezan text), a promontory at the entrance to the gulf, *on the following day*

[30] Ramsay, *St Paul*, p. 293. [31] Rom. 15:30ff.

arrived at Miletus (15b), the mainland harbour at the mouth of the River Meander. *Paul had decided to sail past Ephesus*, and indeed had now done so in order to reach Miletus, because he wanted *to avoid spending time in the province of Asia*, a quick visit being in his judgment impossible, *for he was in a hurry to reach Jerusalem, if possible, by the day of Pentecost* (16).

4. Paul's address to the Ephesian elders (20:17–38)

From Miletus, Paul sent to Ephesus for the elders of the church (17). As the crow flies, Ephesus was only thirty miles north of Miletus, but the rather circuitous road was longer. It must have taken about three days for a messenger to travel to Ephesus and bring the elders back to Miletus. But in due course *they arrived* (18a).

a. Some introductory points

Before we are ready to study the text of Paul's address to the Ephesian elders, several introductory points need to be made. First, this is the only speech in the Acts which is addressed to a Christian audience. All the others are either evangelistic sermons, whether preached to Jewish people (2:14ff.; 3:12ff.; 13:16ff.) or Gentiles (10:34ff.; 14:14ff.; 17:22ff.), or legal defences, whether made before the Sanhedrin in the early days of the church (4:8ff.; 5:29ff.; 7:1ff.) or the five speeches before the Jewish and Roman authorities, which come near the end of the book (22–26).

Secondly, the leaders addressed are called 'elders' (17), 'pastors' (28a) and 'overseers' (28b), and it is evident that these terms denote the same people. 'Pastors' is the generic term which describes their role. In our day, in which there is much confusion about the nature and purpose of the pastoral ministry, and much questioning whether clergy are primarily social workers, psychotherapists, educators, facilitators or administrators, it is important to rehabilitate the noble word 'pastors', who are shepherds of Christ's sheep, called to tend, feed and protect them. This pastoral responsibility over the local congregation seems to have been shared by both deacons (though in a supportive role)[32] and those who are called either *presbyteroi* (elders), a word borrowed from the Jewish synagogue, or *episkopoi* (overseers), a word borrowed from Greek contexts. These are often – and rightly – referred to as 'presbyter-bishops', in order to indicate that during the apostolic period the two titles referred to the same office. In those days there were only 'presbyter-bishops and deacons'.[33] Those of us who belong to episcopally ordered churches, and believe that a threefold order

[32] 1 Tim. 3:8ff. [33] Phil. 1:1.

(bishops, presbyters and deacons) can be defended and commended from Scripture, do not base our argument on the word *episkopoi*, but on people like Timothy and Titus who, though not called 'bishops', were nevertheless given an oversight and jurisdiction over several churches, with authority to select and ordain their presbyter-bishops and deacons.

Thirdly, the church of Ephesus clearly had a team of presbyter-bishops (*presbyteroi* in verse 17 and *episkopoi* in verse 28 are both in the plural). Similarly Paul appointed 'elders' in every Galatian church (14:23), as we have seen, and later instructed Titus to do the same in Crete.[34] There is no biblical warrant either for the one-man-band (a single pastor playing all the instruments of the orchestra himself) or for a hierarchical or pyramidal structure in the local church (a single pastor perched at the apex of the pyramid). It is not even clear that each of the elders was in charge of an individual house-church. It is better to think of them as a team, some perhaps with the oversight of house-churches, but others with specialist ministries according to their gifts, and all sharing the pastoral care of Christ's flock. We need today to recover this concept of a pastoral team in the church.

Fourthly, Luke himself was present and heard this speech (see the 'we' in 21:1). Perhaps William Neil is correct in suggesting that 'Luke may have made notes at the time'.[35] Certainly the address has an authentically Pauline flavour. What has struck many students is the correspondence, in both vocabulary and content, between the speech and Paul's letters. Themes in his letters which he touches on in his speech are the grace of God (24, 32), the kingdom of God (25), the purpose (*boulē*) of God (27), the redeeming blood of Christ (28), repentance and faith (21), the church of God and its edification (28, 32), the inevitability of suffering (23–24), the danger of false teachers (29–30), the need for vigilance (28, 31), running the race (24) and our final inheritance (32).

b. The message of Paul's speech

It may be helpful to divide Paul's speech into three portions, relating to the past, the future and the present.

(i) His ministry in Ephesus (20:18b–21)

'You know how I lived the whole time I was with you, from the first day I came into the province of Asia. [19]I served the Lord with great humility and with tears, although I was severely tested by the plots of the Jews. [20]You know that I have not hesitated to preach anything that would be helpful to you but have taught you publicly

[34] Tit. 1:5. [35] Neil, p. 213.

and from house to house. [21]*I have declared to both Jews and Greeks that they must turn to God in repentance and have faith in our Lord Jesus.'*

You know how I lived, he says (18b). Again, *You know* (20), although this is a resumptive clause in the English text, which is not in the Greek. Yet again later 'you yourselves know' (34). This repeated emphasis on their knowledge of him is reminiscent of 1 Thessalonians 2, where he wrote 'You know, brothers (1) . . . , as you know (2) . . . , You know (5) . . . , Surely you remember (9) . . . , You are witnesses (10) . . . , For you know (11) . . .'. A vicious smear campaign had been launched against Paul in Thessalonica. Because he had had to be smuggled out of the city by night and had not returned, his critics accused him of insincerity. Something similar seems to have happened in Ephesus during the year or so since he had left the city. So he needed to defend the sincerity of his motives and, as in Thessalonica so in Ephesus, he did it by reminding them of his visit. They knew how he had lived during the whole time he was with them from beginning to end. He appealed to their memory, especially of four aspects of his ministry – his humility (meaning perhaps his humiliations), his tears, his testings on account of 'the machinations of the Jews' (19, NEB), and his faithful preaching-teaching ministry, in public and in private, in which he concentrated on the need for both Jews and Gentiles to repent and to believe in the Lord Jesus.

(ii) His future sufferings (20:22–27)

'And now, compelled by the Spirit, I am going to Jerusalem, not knowing what will happen to me there. [23]*I only know that in every city the Holy Spirit warns me that prison and hardships are facing me.* [24]*However, I consider my life worth nothing to me, if only I may finish the race and complete the task the Lord Jesus has given me – the task of testifying to the gospel of God's grace.*

[25]*'Now I know that none of you among whom I have gone about preaching the kingdom will ever see me again.* [26]*Therefore, I declare to you today that I am innocent of the blood of all men.* [27]*For I have not hesitated to proclaim to you the whole will of God.'*

In this section Luke replaces the 'you know . . . you know . . .' of the previous paragraph with 'I know (23) . . . , I know (25) . . . , I know (29)'. For he turns from the past which they knew to the future which the Holy Spirit was teaching him and which he now shared with them. The same Holy Spirit who warns him in every town (perhaps through prophets) of prison and hardships (23), nevertheless compels him to keep travelling to Jerusalem (22). For his overriding concern is not at all costs to survive, but rather that he may finish the race and complete his Christ-given task of bearing witness to the good news of God's grace (24). And Paul knows something else. His prophetic eyes peer beyond Jerusalem and his sufferings there to the mission visits to Rome and to Spain of which he is still dreaming.[36] It must be for this reason that he knows that none of them will see him again (25). This fact adds a poignant finality to the occasion. He makes a solemn declaration that, as a watchman like Ezekiel,[37] he is innocent of everybody's blood (26). His conscience is clear. He has not shrunk from proclaiming to them God's whole purpose of salvation (27). Consequently, he cannot be held responsible if any of them might perish.

(iii) His exhortation to the elders (20:28–35)

Having looked back to his ministry in Ephesus (which they know) and on to his coming sufferings and separation from them (which he knows), Paul now gives them his final charge. The past and the future will together shape their present ministry. In essence, his appeal is for vigilance: 'Keep watch!' (28) . . . 'Be on your guard!' (31).

'Keep watch over yourselves and all the flock of which the Holy Spirit has made you overseers. Be shepherds of the church of God, which he bought with his own blood. [29]I know that after I leave, savage wolves will come in among you and will not spare the flock. [30]Even from your own number men will arise and distort the truth in order to draw away disciples after them. [31]So be on your guard! Remember that for three years I never stopped warning each of you night and day with tears.

[32]'Now I commit you to God and to the word of his grace, which can build you up and give you an inheritance among all those who are sanctified. [33]I have not coveted anyone's silver or gold or clothing. [34]You yourselves know that these hands of mine have supplied my own needs and the needs of my companions. [35]In everything I did, I showed you that by this kind of hard work we must help the weak, remembering the words the Lord Jesus himself said: "It is more blessed to give than to receive."'

We note that the Ephesian pastors must first keep watch over themselves, and only then over the flock over which the Holy Spirit has made them responsible. For they cannot care adequately for others if they neglect the care and culture of their own souls. They are to 'be shepherds' of God's church, *poimainō* meaning in general to 'tend' a flock and in particular 'to lead a flock to pasture,

[36] Acts 19:21; Rom. 15:23–29. [37] Ezk. 33:1ff.

and so to feed it'. This is the first duty of shepherds. 'Should not the shepherds take care of the flock?'[38] Moreover pastors will be the more diligent in their ministry if they remember that their flock is *the church of God, which he bought with his own blood.* The startling concept of God having and shedding blood, although the church fathers Ignatius and Tertullian spoke of it, seems to have led some scribes to write 'the church of the Lord', meaning the Lord Jesus. But this expression occurs nowhere in the New Testament, whereas 'the church of God' is a regular Pauline expression. It should therefore be retained. Then the rest of the sentence should be translated 'which he bought with the blood of his Own' (RSV margin, NEB margin).[39] This sense of *idios* ('own'), writes F. F. Bruce, 'is well attested by the papyri, where it is "used thus as a term of endearment to near relations" '.[40]

The second need for watchfulness is the wolves, that is, the false teachers who, Paul knows, will after his departure enter and devastate Christ's flock (29). Some of them will arise even from within the church. By distorting the truth, they will induce people to forsake it and follow them instead (30). So the Ephesian pastors must be on their guard, as Paul had constantly warned them while he was with them (31). We have only to read both Letters to Timothy and the Letter to Ephesus in Revelation 2:1ff. to know that what Paul predicted came to pass. Perhaps it would not have done if the pastors had been more vigilant.

After exhorting the Ephesian elders to be watchful both over the sheep and against the wolves, the apostle proceeds to commend them to God and his word of grace (32). Then suddenly, as if to enforce his appeal and commendation, he reminds them again of the example he has set them. Like Samuel in his farewell charge,[41] Paul declares that he has coveted nobody's money or clothing (33). Instead, he has supported himself and his companions. One can imagine his gesture as he refers to 'these hands of mine' (34). And by his hard manual work he has exemplified the truth of an otherwise unknown saying of Jesus, 'It is more blessed to give than to receive' (35).

c. *The farewell (20:36–38)*

When he had said this, he knelt down with all of them and prayed. [37]*They all wept as they embraced him and kissed him.* [38]*What grieved them most was his statement that they would never see his face again. Then they accompanied him to the ship.*

[38] Ezk. 34:2. [39] *Cf.* Rom. 8:32.

[40] Bruce, *English*, p. 416, f.n. 59; Professor Bruce is quoting J. H. Moulton's *Grammar of New Testament Greek* (Edinburgh, 1906), p. 90.

[41] 1 Sa. 12:1ff.

d. Ideals of pastoral ministry

In developing the pastoral metaphor, it is noteworthy that Paul described his own teaching ministry (as their 'shepherd'), warned them of false teachers ('wolves') and affirmed the value of their church members (God's 'sheep').

(i) The example of the apostle (the shepherd)
Several times he reminded the elders of his example. There had been a degree of thoroughness about it, which left his conscience clear. First, he had been thorough in his teaching. He had taught them about God's grace and kingdom (24–25) and the necessity of repentance and faith (21). He had not shrunk from declaring to them either what was profitable to them (20) or God's whole salvation plan (27). Secondly, he had been thorough in his coverage. He was as concerned to reach the whole population of Ephesus as he was to teach the whole purpose of God. He wanted to teach everything to everybody! So he had a ministry to both Jews and Gentiles, both residents and visitors. Thirdly, he was thorough in his methods. He taught both publicly (in synagogue and lecture hall) and privately (in homes), and he continued both day and night (20, 31). He was absolutely indefatigable. In modern terms, Paul's threefold thoroughness was a fine example of 'evangelism in depth'. He shared all possible truth with all possible people in all possible ways. He taught the whole gospel to the whole city with his whole strength. His pastoral example must have been an unfailing inspiration to the Ephesian pastors.

(ii) The rise of false teachers (the wolves)
In the ancient Near East wolves were the chief enemy of sheep. Hunting now singly now in packs, they were a constant threat. Sheep were defenceless against them. Shepherds could not afford to relax their vigilance. Nor can Christian pastors. Jesus himself warned of false prophets; 'wolves in sheep's clothing' he called them.[42]

So the shepherds of Christ's flock have a double duty: to feed the sheep (by teaching the truth) and to protect them from wolves (by warning of error). As Paul put it to Titus, elders must hold firm the sure word according to apostolic teaching, so that they would be able both 'to give instruction in sound doctrine and also to confute those who contradict it' [43] This emphasis is unpopular today We are frequently told always to be positive in our teaching, and never negative But those who say this have either not read the New Testament or, having read it, they disagree with it. For the

[42] Mt 7·15 [43] Tit 1:9, RSV

Lord Jesus and his apostles refuted error themselves and urged us to do the same. One wonders if it is the neglect of this obligation which is a major cause of today's theological confusion. If, when false teaching arises, Christian leaders sit idly by and do nothing, or turn tail and flee, they will earn the terrible epithet 'hirelings' who care nothing for Christ's flock.[44] Then too it will be said of believers, as it was of Israel, that 'they were scattered, because there was no shepherd, and . . . they became food for all the wild animals'.[45]

(iii) The value of the people (the sheep)

Implicit in verse 28 is the truth that the pastoral oversight of the church belongs ultimately to God himself. Indeed, each of the three persons of the Trinity has a share in this oversight. To begin with, the church is 'God's church'. Next, whether we read that he redeemed it 'with his own blood' or 'with the blood of his own', it is plain that the purchase price was the blood of Christ. And over this church, which belongs to God and has been bought by Christ, the Holy Spirit appoints overseers. So the oversight is his too, or he could not delegate it to others. This splendid Trinitarian affirmation, that the pastoral oversight of the church belongs to God (Father, Son and Holy Spirit), should have a profound effect on pastors. It should humble us to remember that the church is not ours, but God's. And it should inspire us to faithfulness. For sheep are not at all the clean and cuddly creatures they may appear. In fact, they are dirty, subject to unpleasant pests, and regularly need to be dipped in strong chemicals to rid them of lice, ticks and worms. They are also unintelligent, wayward and obstinate. I hesitate to apply the metaphor too closely and characterize the people of God as dirty, lousy or stupid! But some people are a great trial to their pastors (and *vice versa*). And their pastors will persevere in caring for them only if they remember how valuable they are in God's sight. They are the flock of God the Father, purchased by the precious blood of God the Son, and supervised by overseers appointed by God the Holy Spirit. If the three persons of the Trinity are thus committed to the welfare of the people, should we not be also?

Richard Baxter's great book *The Reformed Pastor* (1656) is really an exposition of Acts 20:28. He wrote:

> Oh then, let us hear these arguments of Christ, whenever we feel ourselves grow dull and careless: 'Did I die for them, and wilt not thou look after them? Were they worth my blood and are they not worth thy labour? Did I come down from heaven

[44] Jn. 10:12ff. [45] Ezk. 34:5.

to earth, to seek and to save that which was lost; and wilt thou not go to the next door or street or village to seek them? How small is thy labour and condescension as to mine? I debased myself to this, but it is thy honour to be so employed. Have I done and suffered so much for their salvation; and was I willing to make thee a co-worker with me, and wilt thou refuse that little that lieth upon thy hands?'[46]

5. On to Jerusalem (21:1–17)

Saying goodbye to the Ephesian elders had been an emotional scene, especially because they and Paul believed that they would never see one another again. Paul's party had had to 'tear themselves away' from them. And now began the final leg of the journey to Jerusalem, for which again Luke obviously drew on his diary. He mentions three or four stops (Cos, Rhodes, Patara and perhaps Myra), followed by three landings (Tyre, Ptolemais and Caesarea).

a. From Miletus to Tyre (21:1–6)

After we had torn ourselves away from them, we (Luke again unostentatiously draws attention to his presence) *put out to sea and sailed straight to Cos* (1a), a small island due south of Miletus. *The next day we went to Rhodes*, a larger island to the south-east, whose city of the same name was situated at its north-easterly tip, *and from there to Patara* (1b), due east of Rhodes, the Bezan text adding 'and Myra', a bit further east still. Both Patara and Myra are near to the southernmost promontory of the mainland of Asia Minor. Because 'the harbour of Myra seems to have been the great port for the direct cross-sea traffic to the coasts of Syria and Egypt', wrote William Ramsay, 'it may . . . be safely assumed that Myra was visited by Paul's ship'.[47] Here *we found a ship crossing over to Phoenicia*, on the Palestinian coast, so that they transferred themselves to it, *went on board and set sail* (2). Their route now took them south-east into the middle of the Eastern Mediterranean. It was a 400-mile voyage from Myra to Tyre. *After sighting Cyprus and passing to the south of it, we sailed on to Syria.*

We landed at Tyre, where our ship was to unload its cargo (3). At the same time their search for Christians in the town was successful. *Finding the disciples there, we stayed with them seven days*, either because the unloading (and perhaps re-loading) took that long, or because their ship stopped there and they were waiting for another one. During this week the disciples *through the*

[46] *The Reformed Pastor* by Richard Baxter (reprint Epworth Press, 1939), pp. 121–122.

[47] Ramsay, *St Paul*, pp. 298–299

Spirit . . . urged Paul not to go on to Jerusalem (4). *But when our time was up, we left and continued on our way* (5a). I will return later to the apparently contradictory signals which were coming from the Holy Spirit about Paul's journey to Jerusalem. *All the disciples and their wives and children accompanied us out of the city, and there on the beach we knelt to pray* (5). It must have been another emotional parting. *After saying good-bye to each other, we went aboard the ship, and they returned home* (6).

b. From Tyre to Jerusalem (21:7–17)

We continued our voyage from Tyre and landed at Ptolemais, called Acre since the Middle Ages, about twenty-five miles south of Tyre. Here *we greeted the brothers and stayed with them for a day* (7). *Leaving the next day, we reached Caesarea*, a magnificent city built by Herod the Great to serve as the port for Jerusalem, *and stayed at the house of Philip the evangelist* (so-called to distinguish him from Philip the apostle), *one of the Seven* (8). It was here at Caesarea that Philip had settled about twenty years previously (8:40). Since then his family had grown up: *he had four unmarried daughters who prophesied* (9). Luke does not tell us exactly how long Paul and his party stayed in Caesarea, but they will have had much to talk about with Philip and his daughters. Perhaps it was now that Philip revealed the facts about himself and Stephen, which Luke later incorporated into Acts 6 – 8. During their stay, another prophecy of great interest was given.

After we had been there a number of days, a prophet named Agabus (presumably the one who featured in 11:27ff.) *came down from Judea* (10). *Coming over to us*, he copied the miming practice of some of the Old Testament prophets, like Ahijah tearing Jeroboam's cloak into twelve pieces,[48] Isaiah going stripped and barefoot for three years[49] and Ezekiel laying siege to a drawing of Jerusalem.[50] *He took Paul's belt*, and *tied his own hands and feet with it*. This was not a short leather belt: 'to bind himself hand and foot with such a girdle would have been an acrobatic performance'.[51] It must rather have been a long piece of cloth which was worn as a girdle. Then Agabus said: *'The Holy Spirit says, "In this way the Jews of Jerusalem will bind the owner of this belt and will hand him over to the Gentiles" '* (11). This was the second prophecy which seems incompatible with what the Spirit originally said to Paul; I will address this problem at the end of this chapter. *When we heard this* (Agabus' prophecy), Luke continues, *we and the people there* (he specifically includes himself) *pleaded with Paul not*

[48] 1 Ki. 11:29ff. [49] Is. 20:3ff. [50] Ezk. 4:1ff.
[51] Haenchen, p. 601, f.n. 5.

to go up to Jerusalem (12). This time the apostle was outspoken in rejecting their pleas. *Then Paul answered, 'Why are you weeping and breaking my heart* [NEB, "trying to weaken my resolution"]? *I am ready not only to be bound, but also to die in Jerusalem for the name of the Lord Jesus'* (13). His words are almost indentical with Peter's: 'Lord, I am ready to go with you to prison and to death.'[52] The difference was that in the event Peter had faltered and failed (though in the end he suffered and died for Christ), whereas Paul was true to his word. *When he would not be dissuaded, we gave up and said* (not in feeble resignation but as a positive prayer), *'The Lord's will be done'* (14).

After this we got ready, meaning either 'we packed our baggage' (NEB) or 'equipped horses'[53] *and went up to Jerusalem* (15). Since the distance between Caesarea and Jerusalem was sixty-five miles, the journey would take two days, as the Bezan text says, and horses would be necessary. *Some of the disciples from Caesarea accompanied us and brought us to the home of Mnason*, which was in Jerusalem, and *where we were to stay. He was a man from Cyprus and one of the early disciples* (16), *i.e.* probably 'a foundation-member of the Jerusalem church'.[54] *When we arrived at Jerusalem, the brothers received us warmly* (17).

c. *The guidance of the Spirit*

Thus at last, after many weeks of travel and suspense, and in spite of dire warnings, Paul arrived at his destination. But was he right to brush aside his friends who implored him to abandon his plan? What about those messages of the Holy Spirit through prophets? Are we to blame Paul for his obstinacy or admire him for his unshakeable resolve?

At first sight the promptings of the Spirit appear to have been in direct conflict with each other. In Miletus Paul told the Ephesian elders that he was going to Jerusalem 'compelled by the Spirit', in spite of the 'prison and hardships' of which the same Spirit warned him (20:12–13). In Tyre, however, it was 'through the Spirit' that certain disciples urged him (the imperfect *elegon* implies 'again and again', JBP) not to go on to Jerusalem (21:4), while in Caesarea Agabus began his prophecy with the formula 'the Holy Spirit says' (21:11). But Paul ignored both messages. Refusing to be dissuaded (21:14), he continued on his way (21:5).

How can we resolve this problem? Certainly not by concluding that the Spirit contradicted himself, telling Paul to go in chapter 20 and countermanding his instruction in chapter 21. Luke has too high a doctrine of the Holy Spirit to portray him as changing his

[52] Lk 22:33 [53] Ramsay, *St Paul*, pp. 301–302 [54] Bruce, *English*, p. 426

mind. Even if 20:22 should be understood as referring rather to the compulsion of his own spirit than of the Holy Spirit, Paul still appears to go against the voice of the Holy Spirit in chapter 21.

I think we should begin by affirming that Luke believed Paul to be right in going to Jerusalem. Probably he attributes to the Holy Spirit both the decision of 19:21 and the compulsion of 20:22, since both of them were *(en) tō pneumati*, 'in the Spirit'. In addition, we have already suggested that Luke sees Paul's journey to Jerusalem as the disciple following in his Master's footsteps. What then are we to make of 21:4 and 11? Some have argued that the references to the Spirit here simply mean that the speakers were *claiming* inspiration, without necessarily being inspired. But then we would have to interpret other references to the Spirit in the same ambiguous way. The better solution is to draw a distinction between a prediction and a prohibition. Certainly Agabus only predicted that Paul would be bound and handed over to the Gentiles (21:11); the pleadings with Paul which followed are not attributed to the Spirit and may have been the fallible (indeed mistaken) human deduction from the Spirit's prophecy. For if Paul had heeded his friends' pleas, then Agabus' prophecy would not have been fulfilled! It is more difficult to understand 21:4 in this way, since the 'urging' itself is said to be 'through the Spirit'. But perhaps Luke's statement is a condensed way of saying that the warning was divine while the urging was human. After all, the Spirit's word to Paul combined the compulsion to go with a warning of the consequences (20:22–23).

So Luke surely intends us to admire Paul for his courage and perseverance. Like Jesus before him, he set his face steadfastly to go to Jerusalem, and (like Jesus again) the divine predictions of suffering did not deter him.

What fortified Paul in his journey was the Christian fellowship which he and his travel companions experienced in every port. In Tyre they found disciples and stayed with them seven days (21:4). In Ptolemais they greeted their sisters and brothers and stayed with them one day (7). In Caesarea they were accommodated in the home of Philip the evangelist and stayed with him 'a number of days' (8, 10). The disciples from Caesarea then personally escorted Paul and his party to Jerusalem, where they were to stay with the early Cypriot convert Mnason (16), and on arrival in Jerusalem the sisters and brothers 'received [them] warmly' (17). It would be an exaggeration to call this Paul's 'triumphal entry' into Jerusalem But at least his warm reception strengthened him to bear the crowd's shouts a few days later 'Away with him!' (36).

D. ON THE WAY TO ROME
Acts 21:18—28:31

16. Paul's arrest and self-defence
21:18—23:35

So far Luke has portrayed his hero on the offensive, taking bold initiatives under the leading of the Holy Spirit to evangelize most of Asia Minor and Greece. But when Paul arrived in Jerusalem, his whole career abruptly changed. He was assaulted, arrested, bound and brought to trial. He found himself on the defensive. Following his three epic missionary journeys Luke describes the five trials he had to endure. The first was before a Jewish crowd at the north-west corner of the temple area (22:1ff.), the second before the supreme Jewish Council in Jerusalem (23:1ff.), the third and fourth in Caesarea before Felix and Festus, who succeeded one another as the procurator of Judea (24:1ff.; 25:1ff.), and the fifth, also in Caesarea, before King Herod Agrippa II (26:1ff.).

These five trials, including in each case Paul's defence speech, together with the circumstances of his arrest (21:18ff.), take up six chapters in our Bibles or nearly 200 verses. Why did Luke consider it necessary to go into such detail? Of course the material was readily available to him, since he was there throughout. He arrived in Jerusalem with Paul (21:15), and the next 'we-section' (27:1ff.) shows that he sailed with Paul to Rome. During the two years of Paul's custody in Caesarea (24:27), Luke was a free man, and it is natural to assume that he remained in Palestine, gathering information for his two-volume work and personally interviewing some of its chief actors.

But Luke had a better reason for giving such a comparatively full account of Paul's trials than the mere circumstance that he had firsthand material at his disposal. For, we remember, Luke was more than a historian; he was a theologian too. One of the major themes which he has been developing concerns the relations between Jews and Gentiles in the Messianic community. He has shown how Paul, called and commissioned to be the apostle to the Gentiles, has by now on three solemn occasions, in Pisidian Antioch, Corinth and Ephesus, left the synagogue and exchanged Jewish for Gentile evangelism (13:46; 18:6 and 19:8–9). It is not an accident that Luke's story begins in Jerusalem and ends in Rome.

In Acts 21 – 23, therefore, to which we have now come, Luke depicts the reaction to the gospel of two communities – of the Jews who were increasingly hostile to it, and of the Romans who were consistently friendly to it. The two themes of Jewish opposition and Roman justice are interwoven in Luke's narrative, with the Christian apostle caught between them, the victim of the one and the beneficiary of the other.

a. *Jewish opposition*

Jewish opposition had been evident from the beginning. Luke shows no sign of anti-semitism; he is simply recording facts. So he documents how the Sanhedrin imprisoned first Peter and John, then all the apostles, and forbade them with threats to preach or teach in the name of Jesus (4:1 – 5:42), although he also draws attention to the caution, wisdom and justice of Gamaliel (5:34ff.). Then came Stephen's martyrdom (7:54ff.), and the Jewish persecution of the church in Jerusalem (8:1ff.) and of the erstwhile persecutor Saul of Tarsus (9:23ff.), which kept erupting during his subsequent missionary journeys.[1] In Jerusalem, however, what had been spasmodic outbursts became an implacable determination to get rid of him once for all, beginning with an attempt to lynch him (21:27ff.), continuing with a hysterical demand for his death (22:22–23), and concluding with the secret plot under oath of more than forty men to murder him (23:12ff.). Luke's statement that, when the mob dragged Paul out of the temple, 'immediately the gates were shut'(21:30), was surely more than a statement of fact. The slammed gates seemed to symbolize the final Jewish rejection of the gospel. Paul's policy of turning to the Gentiles had been justified.

Luke seems also to be drawing a deliberate parallel between the sufferings ('passion') of Christ and the sufferings of his apostle Paul. We saw in the last chapter the similarity between their respective journeys up to Jerusalem. Now Luke takes it further, although of course Paul's sufferings were not redemptive like Christ's. Nevertheless, both Jesus and Paul (1) were rejected by their own people, arrested without cause, and imprisoned; (2) were unjustly accused and wilfully misrepresented by false witnesses; (3) were slapped in the face in court (23:2); (4) were the hapless victims of secret Jewish plots (23:12ff.); (5) heard the terrifying noise of a frenzied mob screaming 'Away with him' (21:36; *cf.* 22:22); and (6) were subjected to a series of five trials – Jesus by Annas, the

[1] *E.g.* Acts 13:50; 14:2, 19; 17:4ff., 13; 18:6ff., 12ff.; 19:8–9; 20:3, 19.

Sanhedrin, King Herod Antipas and twice by Pilate; Paul by the crowd, the Sanhedrin, King Herod Agrippa II and by the two procurators, Felix and Festus.

b. Roman justice

Luke's second and corresponding theme is Roman justice. He consistently presents the Roman authorities as friends of the gospel, not foes. We have already had occasion to notice this. It is not just that the first Gentile convert was a Roman centurion, Cornelius, or that the first convert of Paul's missionary journeys was the Roman proconsul of Cyprus, Sergius Paulus (13:12). It is rather that, whenever they had the opportunity, the Roman authorities defended the Christian missionaries. For example, in Philippi the magistrates actually apologized to Paul and Silas for having beaten and imprisoned them, Roman citizens, and came personally to the prison to escort them out of it (16:35ff.); in Corinth Gallio, the proconsul of Achaia, refused even to listen to Jewish accusations against Paul and dismissed the case (18:12ff.); and in Ephesus the town clerk declared the Christian leaders innocent, rebuked the crowd for public disorder, and sent them home (19:35ff.). Now, in Jerusalem and Caesarea, Claudius Lysias, the military tribune, took Paul under his protection. He twice rescued him from being lynched by bringing him into custody (21:33ff.; 22:24); he quickly exempted him from a brutal examination by torture, on discovering that he was a Roman citizen (22:25ff.); and he protected him from the murder plot by transferring him to the procurator's jurisdiction in Caesarea (23:23ff.).

This protection by Roman justice is even more clear in Paul's trials. Although he was accused by the Jews, he was tried and exonerated by the Romans. The same had been true of Jesus. Luke finds a third parallel here. What he is at pains to demonstrate is that, although the Jews brought accusations against Jesus and his apostle Paul, the Romans could find no fault in either. In the case of Jesus, Luke records a threefold statement of Pilate that in his opinion Jesus was innocent. To the chief priests and the crowd he said, 'I find no basis for a charge against this man.'[2] To the same people, after Jesus had been tried by Herod, Pilate said: 'I have examined him in your presence and have found no basis for your charges against him. Neither has Herod . . .'.[3] And when the crowd kept shouting, 'Crucify him!', Pilate spoke to them for the third time: 'Why? What crime has this man committed? I have found in him no grounds for the death penalty.'[4]

The parallel in the case of Paul is impressive. Luke is not

[2] Lk. 23:4. [3] Lk. 23:14–15. [4] Lk. 23:22.

pronouncing Roman justice to be perfect (for he mentions the readiness of Felix to be bribed, 24:26), but asserting that Paul had not offended it. It is not only that he declared his own innocence ('I have done nothing wrong against the law of the Jews or against the temple or against Caesar,' 25:8), but that his judges agreed with him. Claudius Lysias, in his letter to Felix, affirmed that 'there was no charge against him that deserved death or imprisonment' (23:29). The procurator Festus told King Agrippa: 'I found he had done nothing deserving of death' (25:25). And Agrippa, when the series of trials was over, summed up in these words: 'This man is not doing anything that deserves death or imprisonment. . . . This man could have been set free, if he had not appealed to Caesar' (26:31–32).

Thus three times in the case of Jesus, and three times in the case of Paul, the accused was declared not guilty in a court of law. Sir William Ramsay made much of this in his *St Paul the Traveller and the Roman Citizen* (1895): 'It is beyond doubt that, on our hypothesis, the amount of space assigned to Paul's imprisonment and successive examinations marks this as the most important part of the book in the author's estimation.'[5] Ramsay went on to argue that, when eventually Paul stood before Caesar, he was acquitted, as the Pastoral Epistles indicate, and that his trial, with its 'formal decision by the supreme court of the Empire', 'was really a charter of religious liberty, and therein lies its immense importance'.[6] He concluded that Luke contemplated a third volume documenting the trial in Rome, the acquittal, the apostle's resumed missionary labours, and his subsequent arrest, imprisonment and death under Nero. For Ramsay believed that Luke was writing during the reign of Domitian, 'when Christians had come to be treated as outlaws or brigands, and the mere confession of the name was recognized as an offence'. In such a situation, the Acts was 'not an apology for Christianity; it was an appeal to the truth of history against the immoral and ruinous policy of the reigning Emperor'.[7]

Whether or not we can accept all the details of Ramsay's reconstruction (including the date of Acts and Luke's intention to write a sequel), we must surely agree over Luke's objective. He deliberately sets out to demonstrate the innocence in the eyes of Roman law of both Jesus (Luke's Gospel) and Paul (the Acts), and to draw attention to the precedent which the outcome of their trials had established for the legality of the Christian faith. Luke's purpose has shown the church of all subsequent times and places how to behave under persecution. It must be able to show that accusations of crimes against the state and against humanity (which were often

[5] Ramsay, *St Paul*, p. 303. [6] *Ibid.*, p. 308. [7] *Ibid.*, p. 309.

alleged in the early centuries) are groundless; that it is innocent of offences against the law; and that its members are conscientious citizens, that is, submissive to the state in so far as their conscience permits them. Then the freedom to profess, practise and propagate the gospel will, inasmuch as it lies with the church, be preserved, and the only offence which Christians give will be the stumbling block of the cross.

1. Paul meets James and accepts his proposal (21:18–26)

We have already noted that, when Paul and his friends arrived in Jerusalem, they received a genuinely warm welcome (17). Now, however, Luke explains the tension underlying this welcome (18ff.). *The next day*, without any delay, *Paul and the rest of us*, who had accompanied him from Corinth, including Luke, *went to see James*. James was still the recognized leader of the church in Jerusalem and indeed of the world-wide Jewish Christian community, especially now that the apostles Peter and John seem to have left the city. Not that James was alone when he received Paul and his friends, for *all the elders were present* (18). Since the Jewish Christians now numbered 'many thousands' (20), a large number of elders must have been needed to pastor them. *Paul greeted them* (19a).

In depicting Paul and James face to face, Luke presents his readers with a dramatic situation, fraught with both risk and possibility. For James and Paul were the representative leaders of two Christianities, Jewish and Gentile. This was not, of course, their first meeting. It was at least their fourth. For Paul had called on James during his first visit to Jerusalem years previously,[8] and again when he went there fourteen years after that.[9] Then they had both been prominent figures at the Jerusalem Council (15:12ff.). During the intervening years, however, the movements they led had grown considerably under God's good hand. Indeed, as they greeted one another now, each was flanked by sample fruits of their respective missions, Paul by his companions from the Gentile churches, and James by the elders of the Jerusalem church. Some people were doubtless asserting that the doctrinal positions of James and Paul were incompatible, as they had done before the Jerusalem Council (15:1–2), Paul teaching salvation by grace, and James salvation by works. Hence later Luther's uneasiness, which led him to dub the Letter of James an 'epistle of straw'. It is not that he wanted to exclude it from the canon, but that he felt he could not include it among the 'chief' books which unambiguously teach justification by faith alone. So when Paul and James faced each other in

[8] Gal. 1:18–19. [9] Gal. 2:1, 9.

Jerusalem, there could have been a painful confrontation.

But both apostles were in a conciliatory frame of mind. Take James first. When Paul *reported in detail what God had done among the Gentiles through his ministry* (19, *i.e.* not what *Paul* had done with God's help), James and his elders not only *heard this*, listening attentively to Paul's account, but *they praised God* together (20a). No murmur of disapproval was heard. As in the case of the conversion of Cornelius (11:18), the evangelization of Greeks in Antioch (11:22–23) and the first missionary journey (14:27; 15:12), the evidence of God's grace towards Gentiles was indisputable, and the only appropriate response was worship. The joyful praise of James and the elders was not even grudging; it was spontaneous and genuine.

But Paul was also anxious to be conciliatory towards the Jewish Christian community, and showed it in two ways. The first, which for some reason Luke mentions only later in 24:17, was the presentation to the Jewish church of the offerings given by the Gentile churches of the west. It seems to me likely that Paul made this at the beginning of his visit to James. Perhaps it partly accounts for the warm reception of verse 17. Certainly the collection was of great importance to Paul. Not only had he been preoccupied with it for several years, but he had even postponed his intended visit to Rome and Spain in order first to deliver it personally in Jerusalem (19:21).[10] The offering was important in itself, and an expression of loving Christian responsibility to the poor.[11] 'The love of money is a root of all kinds of evil';[12] but the use of money can be a tangible token of love. The chief significance of the offering, however, lay in its symbolism. It exemplified the solidarity of Gentile believers with their Jewish sisters and brothers in the body of Christ. That is why representatives of the Gentile churches had travelled all the way from Corinth in order to share in presenting their gifts, and were even now present with Paul. Further, the offering was a humble acknowledgement of reciprocal indebtedness. True, the Gentile churches 'were pleased' to give, out of love, but also (Paul wrote) 'they owe it to them. For if the Gentiles have shared in the Jews' spiritual blessings, they owe it to the Jews to share with them their material blessings'.[13] It was surely because of the symbolic nature of the offering that Paul was so concerned about it. He was anxious that it should not be misunderstood, as an unwelcome paternalism perhaps, or as an attempt to buy favour, and that its acceptance should not be misinterpreted as a kind of capitulation by Jewish Christians to Paul's pro-Gentile stance. This is why he

[10] *Cf.* Rom. 15:23ff. [11] *E.g.* Acts 11:27–30; 20:35; Gal. 2:10; 2 Cor. 8:9ff.
[12] 1 Tim. 6:10. [13] Rom. 15:27.

urged the Roman Christians to pray with him that his 'service in Jerusalem may be acceptable to the saints there'.[14] He wanted to express their fellowship in Christ by giving the gift; would the Jewish Christians reciprocate by receiving it?

Luke concentrates, however, on the second example of Paul's conciliatory spirit, namely the positive way in which he responded to the proposal James put to him. This arose because of the existence of both Jewish believers (20) and Gentile believers (25). The question was how they could be helped to live together in amity, especially in view of Jewish Christian scruples about law observance. James and the elders *said to Paul: 'You see, brother* [a touching, because unself-conscious, acknowledgement of their unity in God's family], *how many thousands of Jews have believed, and all of them are zealous for the law* (20), [that is, "staunch upholders" of it (NEB, JBP, JB)]. *They have been informed* [in fact, misinformed] *that you teach all the Jews who live among the Gentiles* [in the diaspora] *to turn away from Moses, telling them not to circumcise their children or live according to our customs'* (21). What exactly was James's concern, then? First, it was not about the way of salvation (James and Paul were agreed that this was through Christ, not through the law), but about the way of discipleship. Secondly, it was not about what Paul taught Gentile converts (he did teach them that circumcision was unnecessary,[15] and James and the Jerusalem Council had said the same thing), but about what he was teaching 'the Jews who live among the Gentiles' (21). Thirdly, it was not about the moral law (Paul and James were agreed that God's people must live a holy life according to God's commandments),[16] but about Jewish 'customs' (21). In a word, should Jewish believers continue to observe Jewish cultural practices? The rumour was that Paul was teaching them not to.

So '*what shall we do?*' James asked Paul. The law-zealous Jewish Christians '*will certainly hear that you have come* (22), *so do what we tell you. There are four men with us who have made a vow* (23). *Take these men, join in their purification rites and pay their expenses, so that they can have their heads shaved. Then everybody will know there is no truth in these reports about you, but that you yourself are living in obedience to the law*' (24), or 'are a practising Jew' (NEB). The reference to the four Jewish Christians shaving their heads indicates that they had taken a Nazirite vow.[17] James's proposal in relation to them was double. First, Paul should 'join in their purification rites'. Commentators are not agreed about what James had in mind. Perhaps he wanted Paul to identify himself

[14] Rom. 15:31. [15] *E.g.* 1 Cor. 7:19; Gal. 6:15.
[16] *E.g.* Rom. 7:12; 8:4; Jas. 1:25; 2:8. [17] Nu. 6:1ff.; *cf.* Acts 18:18ff.

with the four either at the conclusion of the thirty-day period of their vow or in some special ritual necessary because they had contracted defilement during the same period. Or it may mean that Paul had a seven-day purification ceremony of his own to undergo because during his long absence from Jerusalem the Jews regarded him as having become levitically unclean.[18] Secondly, James proposed that Paul should 'pay their expenses', which could have been quite substantial.

Having referred to the scruples of the Jewish Christians (20–24), James turned to the corresponding responsibility of the Gentile Christians. '*As for the Gentile believers*,' he said, the controversy had been settled some years ago at the Council of Jerusalem, as Paul knew well, for '*we have written to them our decision that they should abstain from food sacrificed to idols, from blood, from the meat of strangled animals and from sexual immorality*' (25; *cf.* 15:20, 29) – four cultural practices, as I argued in chapter 11.

Paul agreed with James's proposal, and began as soon as possible to comply with it. *The next day Paul took the men and purified himself along with them. Then he went to the temple to give notice of the date when the days of purification would end and the offering would be made for each of them* (26).

We can only thank God for the generosity of spirit displayed by both James and Paul. They were already agreed doctrinally (that salvation was by grace in Christ through faith) and ethically (that Christians must obey the moral law). The issue between them concerned culture, ceremony and tradition. The solution to which they came was not a compromise, in the sense of sacrificing a doctrinal or moral principle, but a concession in the area of practice. We have already seen Paul's conciliatory spirit in accepting the Jerusalem decrees and circumcising Timothy. Now, in the same tolerant spirit, he was prepared to undergo some purification rituals in order to pacify Jewish scruples. James seems to have gone too far in expecting Paul to live 'in obedience to the law' (24) in all matters and at all times, if that is what he meant. But Paul was certainly ready to do so on special occasions, for the sake of evangelism for example[19] or – as here – for the sake of Jewish-Gentile solidarity. According to his conviction Jewish cultural practices belonged to the 'matters indifferent', from which he had been liberated, but which he might or might not himself practise according to the circumstances. As F. F. Bruce neatly put it, 'a truly emancipated spirit such as Paul's is not in bondage to its own emancipation'.[20] But James manifested a similarly sweet and gen-

[18] See the full discussion in Bruce, *English*, pp. 430–432; Haenchen, pp. 611–612; Marshall, *Acts*, p. 345; and Longenecker, *Acts*, p. 520.

[19] 1 Cor. 9:20. [20] Bruce, *English*, p. 432, f.n. 39.

erous mind both by praising God for the Gentile mission and by accepting the offering from the Gentile churches. It was not a *quid pro quo*, almost a bargain, as some commentators have represented it ('We will identify with you by accepting the Gentile offering, if you will identify with us by accepting Jewish observances'). It was rather a sensitive, mutual Christian forbearance. The unbending prejudice and fanatical violence of the unbelieving Jews, which Luke describes next, stands out in ugly contrast.

2. Paul is assaulted and arrested (21:27–36)

a. Paul is assaulted by the Jews (21:27–32)

When the seven days were nearly over, some Jews from the province of Asia saw Paul at the temple. They stirred up the whole crowd and seized him, [28]shouting, 'Men of Israel, help us! This is the man who teaches all men everywhere against our people and our law and this place. And besides, he has brought Greeks into the temple area and defiled this holy place.' [29](They had previously seen Trophimus the Ephesian in the city with Paul and assumed that Paul had brought him into the temple area.)

[30]The whole city was aroused, and the people came running from all directions. Seizing Paul, they dragged him from the temple, and immediately the gates were shut. [31]While they were trying to kill him, news reached the commander of the Roman troops that the whole city of Jerusalem was in an uproar. [32]He at once took some officers and soldiers and ran down to the crowd. When the rioters saw the commander and his soldiers, they stopped beating Paul.

It was in connection with the seven-day purification ritual, and near its end, that Paul was in the temple. He was recognized by some Jews from proconsular Asia, probably from Ephesus itself. They seem also to have recognized Trophimus the Ephesian (29). They provoked the worshipping crowd to frenzy by two accusations. The first of these was a misunderstanding, for they represented Paul as teaching everybody everywhere 'against our people and our law and this place' (28a). 'It is ironical', Howard Marshall justly comments, 'that this should have been the charge against Paul at a time when he himself was undergoing purification so that he would not defile the temple!'[21] The charge was similar to that laid against Stephen, who was accused by false witnesses of 'speaking against the holy place and against the law' (6:13). But the Jews misunderstood both Stephen and Paul, just as they had misunderstood Jesus. Jesus spoke of himself as the fulfilment of the temple,

[21] Marshall, *Acts*, p. 347.

the people and the law, and Stephen and Paul followed suit. This was not to denigrate them, however, but to reveal their true glory.

The second accusation, that Paul had brought Greeks into the temple area and so defiled it (28b), was simply untrue. It was not a deliberate lie, Luke charitably adds, but rather an assumption on their part (29). They had seen Trophimus (whom they knew to be a Gentile) with Paul in the city, and had jumped to the conclusion that Paul had also brought him into the temple's inner court, which was forbidden to Gentiles. Gentiles were permitted to enter only the outer court, the Court of the Gentiles. Beyond this, and preventing access into the Court of Israel, there was 'a stone wall for a partition', four and a half feet high, 'with an inscription which forbade any foreigner to go in under pain of death'. This is Josephus' description, and he added that there were many such inscriptions, written in Greek and in Latin, at equal distance from each other.[22] F. F. Bruce adds: 'Two of these notices (both in Greek) have been found – one in 1871 and one in 1935 – the text of which runs: "No foreigner may enter within the barricade which surrounds the temple and enclosure. Anyone who is caught doing so will have himself to blame for his ensuing death." '[23] Titus (the Roman general and later emperor) reminded the Jews that the Romans had even given them 'leave to kill such as go beyond it (*sc.* the barricade), though he were a Roman'.[24] Paul was surely thinking of this barrier when he wrote of 'the dividing wall of hostility' between Jews and Gentiles.[25]

The combination of these two accusations – the one a half-truth and the other an untruth – was enough to bring people 'running from all directions' (30), who proceeded to seize Paul, drag him out of the inner court, and try to kill him. Fortunately, soldiers of the Roman garrison, always on the look-out for public disorder in Jerusalem, saw what was happening and rescued him in the nick of time. Their barracks were in the fortress of Antonia, which Herod the Great had built at the north-west corner of the temple area. The garrison usually consisted of a thousand men. In charge of them was a *chiliarchos*, which can be translated 'military tribune', 'commander of the Roman troops' (NIV) or 'colonel of the regiment' (JBP). At this time we know that he was Claudius Lysias (23:26). Hearing that the city was in an uproar, he rushed down personally with some officers and men, and the rioters at once gave up beating Paul.

[22] Josephus, *Antiquities*, XV.11.5; *Wars*, V.5.2. [23] Bruce, *English*, p. 434.
[24] Josephus, *Wars*, VI.2.4. [25] Eph. 2:14.

b. Paul is arrested by the Romans (21:33–36)

The commander came up and arrested him and ordered him to be bound with two chains. Then he asked who he was and what he had done. [34]*Some in the crowd shouted one thing and some another, and since the commander could not get at the truth because of the uproar, he ordered that Paul be taken into the barracks.* [35]*When Paul reached the steps, the violence of the mob was so great he had to be carried by the soldiers.* [36]*The crowd that followed kept shouting, 'Away with him!'*

It is noteworthy that the same verb *epilambanomai* is used both of the mob 'seizing' Paul (30) and of the commander 'arresting' him (33), although they had opposite objectives. The crowd were bent on lynching him, the military tribune on taking him into protective custody. It is a striking example of Luke's aim to contrast Jewish hostility with Roman justice. When the commander failed to discover who the prisoner was and what he had done, because of the hubbub, he had him taken, indeed (owing to the mob's violence) carried, into the barracks. Meanwhile, the crowd was shouting, 'Away with him', just as nearly thirty years previously another crowd had shouted about another prisoner.[26]

3. Paul defends himself before the crowd (21:37 – 22:22)

As the soldiers were about to take Paul into the barracks, he asked the commander, 'May I say something to you?'

'Do you speak Greek?' he replied. [38]*'Aren't you the Egyptian who started a revolt and led four thousand terrorists out into the desert some time ago?'*

[39]*Paul answered, 'I am a Jew, from Tarsus in Cilicia, a citizen of no ordinary city. Please let me speak to the people.'*

[40]*Having received the commander's permission, Paul stood on the steps and motioned to the crowd. When they were all silent, he said to them in Aramaic:*

[22:1]*'Brothers and fathers, listen now to my defence.'*

[2]*When they heard him speak to them in Aramaic, they became very quiet.*

Then Paul said: [3]*'I am a Jew, born in Tarsus of Cilicia, but brought up in this city. Under Gamaliel I was thoroughly trained in the law of our fathers and was just as zealous for God as any of you are today.* [4]*I persecuted the followers of this Way to their death, arresting both men and women and throwing them into prison,* [5]*as also the high priest and all the Council can testify. I even obtained*

[26] Lk. 23:18; *cf.* Acts 22:22.

letters from them to their brothers in Damascus, and went there to
bring these people as prisoners to Jerusalem to be punished.
6*‘About noon as I came near Damascus, suddenly a bright light*
from heaven flashed around me. 7*I fell to the ground and heard a*
voice say to me, “Saul! Saul! Why do you persecute me?”
8*‘ “Who are you, Lord?” I asked.*
‘ “I am Jesus of Nazareth, whom you are persecuting,” he replied.
9*My companions saw the light, but they did not understand the*
voice of him who was speaking to me.
10*‘ “What shall I do, Lord?” I asked.*
‘ “Get up,” the Lord said, “and go into Damascus. There you
will be told all that you have been assigned to do.” 11*My companions*
led me by the hand into Damascus, because the brilliance of the
light had blinded me.
12*‘A man named Ananias came to see me. He was a devout*
observer of the law and highly respected by all the Jews living there.
13*He stood beside me and said, “Brother Saul, receive your sight!”*
And at that very moment I was able to see him.
14*‘Then he said: “The God of our fathers has chosen you to know*
his will and to see the Righteous One and to hear words from his
mouth. 15*You will be his witness to all men of what you have seen*
and heard. 16*And now what are you waiting for? Get up, be baptised*
and wash your sins away, calling on his name.”
17*‘When I returned to Jerusalem and was praying at the temple,*
I fell into a trance 18*and saw the Lord speaking. “Quick!” he said*
to me. “Leave Jerusalem immediately, because they will not accept
your testimony about me.”
19*‘ “Lord,” I replied, “these men know that I went from one*
synagogue to another to imprison and beat those who believe in
you. 20*And when the blood of your martyr Stephen was shed, I*
stood there giving my approval and guarding the clothes of those
who were killing him.”
21*‘Then the Lord said to me, “Go; I will send you far away to*
the Gentiles.” ’
22*The crowd listened to Paul until he said this. Then they raised*
their voices and shouted, ‘Rid the earth of him! He's not fit to live!’

Claudius Lysias, as an honest, open-minded Roman soldier, compares favourably with the prejudiced Jewish crowd. They had assumed, without taking the trouble to check it, that Paul had brought Trophimus into the inner court of the temple; Claudius Lysias had assumed that Paul was an Egyptian terrorist, but immediately changed his mind when he learned the facts. The revolutionary to whom Lysias was referring was described by Josephus as ‘an Egyptian false prophet’ who, about three years previously, had got together 30,000 men (Josephus was prone to exaggeration!), led them to the Mount of Olives, and promised them that, when the walls of Jerusalem fell flat at his command, they would be able to break into the city and overpower the Romans. But the procurator Felix and his troops intervened, and the *sikarioi* ('dagger men', *i.e.* fanatical nationalist assassins) were killed, captured or scattered.[27] But the Egyptian disappeared, and the commander at first thought that he had now come to light again. But Paul enlightened him about his identity. He spoke proudly of his citizenship of Tarsus, which was 'the first city of Cilicia, not merely in material wealth but in intellectual distinction, as one of the great university cities of the Roman world'.[28] He then asked leave to address the crowd, which was granted.

As Paul boldly made his speech or defence (*apologia*, 22:1) to the hostile crowd from the stone steps which led up from the temple to the fortress of Antonia, he did so with great sensitivity and appropriateness. His sensitivity is seen both in his polite address to his audience as *Brothers and fathers* and in his choice of the Aramaic language, which in itself was enough to quieten them. But was what he said appropriate to the occasion? This is, of course, the second time that Luke has given his readers an account of Paul's conversion. Previously he gave it in his own words, but this time (and the third time before King Agrippa) he gives it in Paul's words. In each case the outline is the same, but the particular emphasis of each testimony is well fitted to its context. To the crowd in Jerusalem, whose angry complaint was that he taught everybody everywhere against the people, the law and the temple (21:28), Paul stressed his personal loyalty to his Jewish origins and faith.

First, he spoke of his Jewish birth and up-bringing, and of his training *in the law of our fathers* under Gamaliel (*cf.* 5:34), the most eminent teacher of that time and the leader of the school of Hillel, whose disciple he had been. So his Jewishness was incontrovertible. He was 'a Hebrew of the Hebrews'.[29] Secondly, he drew attention to his zeal for God, which was as great as theirs, since he had persecuted the followers of the Way, both men and women, even to prison and to death. The Sanhedrin could testify to this, since it was they who had issued him with the extradition order which he took with him to Damascus.

Thirdly, Paul narrated the circumstances of his conversion, which was entirely due to a divine intervention, and not at all to any initiative of his own. A light from heaven had blinded him, and

[27] Josephus, *Antiquities*, XX.8.6; *Wars*, II.13.5.
[28] Sherwin-White, p. 180. [29] Phil. 3:5, AV.

the person who spoke to him had identified himself as Jesus of Nazareth. Fourthly, Paul referred to the ministry of Ananias, whom he deliberately characterized as *a devout observer of the law* and *highly respected by all the Jews living there* in Damascus (12). It was he who restored Paul's sight, who told him that *the God of our fathers* had chosen him to know his will, see the Righteous One, 'hear his very voice' (14, NEB) and be his witness, and who baptized him. Then fifthly, Paul came to his vision, which took place in the very temple he was supposed later to have defiled, and in which *the Lord* (Jesus is not mentioned by name) told him to leave Jerusalem immediately, in spite of his reluctance and objections. '*Go*,' the Lord had said, *'I will send you far away to the Gentiles.'* That is, *exapostelō se*, almost 'I will make you an apostle', indeed the apostle to the Gentiles (21; 26:17).[30]

It was at this point that Paul was interrupted by the crowd, who found their voices again and loudly demanded his death (22). It is important to understand why. In their eyes proselytism (making Gentiles into Jews) was fine; but evangelism (making Gentiles into Christians without first making them Jews) was an abomination. It was tantamount to saying that Jews and Gentiles were equal, for they both needed to come to God through Christ, and that on identical terms.

Looking back over Paul's defence, we may perhaps say that he made two major points. The first was that he himself was a loyal Jew, not only by birth and education but still. True, he was now a witness where before he had been a persecutor. But the God of his fathers was his God still. He had not broken away from his ancestral faith, still less apostatized; he stood in direct continuity with it. Jesus of Nazareth was 'the Righteous One' in whom prophecy had been fulfilled. And Paul's second point was that those features of his faith which had changed, especially his acknowledgment of Jesus and his Gentile mission, were not his own eccentric ideas. They had been directly revealed to him from heaven, the one truth in Damascus and the other in Jerusalem. Indeed, nothing but such a heavenly intervention could have so completely transformed him.

4. Paul is protected by Roman law (22:23–29)

Twice more in this brief section Roman law and justice come to Paul's aid. First Claudius Lysias again rescues him from lynching, and secondly, having discovered his Roman citizenship, from flogging.

[30] *Cf.* Gal. 1:16; 2:7–8.

As they were shouting and throwing off their cloaks and flinging dust into the air, [24]the commander ordered Paul to be taken into the barracks. He directed that he be flogged and questioned in order to find out why the people were shouting at him like this. [25]As they stretched him out to flog him, Paul said to the centurion standing there, 'Is it legal for you to flog a Roman citizen who hasn't even been found guilty?'

[26]When the centurion heard this, he went to the commander and reported it. 'What are you going to do?' he asked. 'This man is a Roman citizen.'

[27]The commander went to Paul and asked, 'Tell me, are you a Roman citizen?'

'Yes, I am,' he answered.

[28]Then the commander said, 'I had to pay a big price for my citizenship.'

'But I was born a citizen,' Paul replied.

[29]Those who were about to question him withdrew immediately. The commander himself was alarmed when he realised that he had put Paul, a Roman citizen, in chains.

a. The rescue from lynching (22:23–24)

The crowd was not content with shouting and screaming (22); they started waving their cloaks about and flinging dust into the air (23). H. J. Cadbury suggested that these gestures may have expressed not so much excitement, anger and hostility as horror in reaction to blasphemy.[31] In any case, the commander forestalled any further attempt by the crowd to get their hands on Paul by giving orders (for the second time) for him to be taken into the barracks. He then 'gave instructions to examine him by flogging' (24, NEB). This ghastly ordeal was the standard way of extracting information from prisoners. 'The scourge (Latin *flagellum*) was a fearful instrument of torture, consisting of leather thongs, weighted with rough pieces of metal or bone, and attached to a stout wooden handle. If a man did not actually die under the scourge (which frequently happened), he would certainly be crippled for life.'[32]

b. The rescue from flogging (22:25–29)

Paul was actually being prepared for the flogging when he divulged his Roman citizenship. Similarly, in Philippi he had not revealed that he was a Roman citizen until after he had been beaten, imprisoned and put in the stocks (16:37). He seems for some reason not to have wanted to take advantage of being a citizen except in some

[31] See Cadbury's Note xxiv, 'Dust and Garments', in *BC*, V, pp. 269–277.
[32] Bruce, *English*, p. 445.

dire extremity. Dr Sherwin-White acknowledges that 'the precise legal situation of Roman citizens in provincial jurisdiction is not well documented at this period'.[33] Nor is it clear precisely what the citizen's privileges were, although it is agreed that he was exempt from examination by flogging, *i.e.* torture without trial. Citizenship tended to be either by right (for those of high status or office) or by reward (for those who had served the Empire well). It was passed on from father to son (which was the case with Paul); it could also be bought, not with a fee but with a bribe to some corrupt official 'in the imperial secretariat or the provincial administration',[34] which was the case with Claudius Lysias. Indeed, such corruption was rife during the reign of the Emperor Claudius, which may explain why the commander had added the *nomen* Claudius, in honour of the Emperor, to his *cognomen* Lysias.

Although the commander *was alarmed when he realised that he had put Paul, a Roman citizen, in chains* (29), he does not seem to have released him from them. At least he was still in chains the following day and subsequently.[35] What is the explanation of this? 'Possibly a distinction is to be made between the heavy chains, a torture in themselves (of which Paul may have been relieved) and the lighter chains to prevent the prisoner from escaping.'[36]

5. Paul stands before the Sanhedrin (22:30 – 23:11)

The next day, since the commander wanted to find out exactly why Paul was being accused by the Jews, he released him and ordered the chief priests and all the Sanhedrin to assemble. Then he brought Paul and had him stand before them.

23:1 *Paul looked straight at the Sanhedrin and said, 'My brothers,*
I have fulfilled my duty to God in all good conscience to this day.'
2 *At this the high priest Ananias ordered those standing near Paul*
to strike him on the mouth. 3 *Then Paul said to him, 'God will strike*
you, you whitewashed wall! You sit there to judge me according to
the law, yet you yourself violate the law by commanding that I be
struck!'

4 *Those who were standing near Paul said, 'You dare to insult God's high priest?'*

5 *Paul replied, 'Brothers, I did not realise that he was the high priest; for it is written: "Do not speak evil about the ruler of your people." '*

6 *Then Paul, knowing that some of them were Sadducees and the others Pharisees, called out in the Sanhedrin, 'My brothers, I am a*

[33] Sherwin-White, p. 57. [34] *Ibid.*, p. 155.
[35] Acts 22:30; 23:18; 24:27; 26:29. [36] JB, verse 29, note j.

Pharisee, the son of a Pharisee. I stand on trial because of my hope in the resurrection of the dead.' [7]*When he said this, a dispute broke out between the Pharisees and the Sadducees, and the assembly was divided.* [8]*(The Sadducees say that there is no resurrection, and that there are neither angels nor spirits, but the Pharisees acknowledge them all.)*

[9]*There was a great uproar, and some of the teachers of the law who were Pharisees stood up and argued vigorously. 'We find nothing wrong with this man,' they said. 'What if a spirit or an angel has spoken to him?'* [10]*The dispute became so violent that the commander was afraid Paul would be torn to pieces by them. He ordered the troops to go down and take him away from them by force and bring him into the barracks.*

[11]*The following night the Lord stood near Paul and said, 'Take courage! As you have testified about me in Jerusalem, so you must also testify in Rome.'*

The commander was determined *to find out exactly why Paul was being accused by the Jews* (22:30). He had tried questioning the crowd, but had got different answers from them (21:33–34). He was about to use torture, but Paul's Roman citizenship blocked that avenue (22:24ff.). So now he opted for a third method – trial by the Sanhedrin (22:30). The high priest Ananias was a thoroughly unsavoury character. He was described by Josephus as 'a great hoarder up of money'; he even 'took away the tithes that belonged to the priests by violence'.[37]

Although Luke's account of this trial is brief, it raises at least three rather perplexing problems, the first two concerning Paul and Ananias, and the third concerning Paul, the Pharisees and the Sadducees.

a. Paul and the high priest Ananias (23:1–5)

First, why was the high priest so enraged by Paul's opening remark that he ordered him to be struck on the mouth? It can hardly have been on a point of order, that Paul spoke before he had been spoken to. Nor does it seem likely that his reason and experience were affronted, inasmuch as anybody who claimed to have lived a consistently conscience-free life was (in his view) a blatant liar. Nor is it easily conceivable that the high priest was exasperated by a plea of 'not guilty'. The most likely explanation is that Ananias understood Paul's words as a claim that, though now a Christian, he was still a good Jew, having served God with a good conscience all his life (since, as well as before, his conversion), even 'to this day'. This was certainly the claim Paul made in 2 Timothy 1:3. It

[37] Josephus, *Antiquities*, XX.9.2.

seemed to Ananias the height of arrogance, even of blasphemy.

Secondly, why was Paul's riposte so rude? Jerome seems to have been the first commentator to draw attention to the contrast between Jesus and Paul before their judges. Jesus answered much more coolly when he was slapped in the face.[38] Besides, Paul had recently written of himself and his associates, 'When we are cursed, we bless; when we are persecuted, we endure it.'[39] It may be that he did lose his temper, for he more or less apologized, indicating that he would have responded differently if he had known he was addressing the high priest. How is it, then, that he did not recognize the high priest? Many answers have been suggested. Indeed, according to Haenchen, Paul's statement is 'so unbelievable that it has driven the theologians to desperate efforts'.[40] Some think that this was an informal meeting of the Sanhedrin and that in consequence Ananias was neither robed, nor presiding, so that he could easily have escaped recognition. Others guess that in the babel of voices in court Paul was not able to identify who it was who had ordered him to be struck. A third interpretation is that Paul was speaking in sarcasm, as if to say, 'I did not realize that a man such as you could be the high priest.'[41] But to me the most likely explanation lies in the poor eyesight which Paul is known to have had.[42] In this case 'you white-washed wall' may have been not so much a reference to hypocrisy[43] as an uncouth allusion to a white-robed figure across the court whom Paul could only dimly perceive.

b. *Paul, the Pharisees and the Sadducees (23:6–10)*

Several questions also confront us when we read this part of the narrative. Was Paul justified in deliberately setting the Pharisees and the Sadducees against one another? And was he correct to call himself a Pharisee? There is certainly no need to attribute to Paul either unworthy motives or an untrue statement. He was genuinely concerned about doctrine, and he did believe (as we should) that the resurrection is fundamental to Christianity.[44] The anti-supernaturalist stance of the Sadducees was incompatible with the gospel. As Jesus himself said, the reason they were wrong was that they knew neither God's word nor God's power.[45] Paul was a Pharisee, however, not only in the sense of his parentage and education (6), but also in the sense that he shared with Pharisees the great truth and hope of the resurrection, on account of which he was on trial.

[38] Jn. 18:22–23; *cf.* 1 Pet. 2:23. [39] 1 Cor. 4:12. [40] Haenchen, p. 640.

[41] Calvin follows Augustine in believing that Paul's explanation was 'ironical'. What he meant was 'I, brethren, recognize nothing priestly about this man'; he was denying Ananias' right to be regarded as a priest of God (Calvin, II, pp. 229–230).

[42] *E.g.* Gal. 4:13–16; 6:11. [43] Ezk. 13:8ff.; Mt. 23:27.

[44] *E.g.* Acts 4:2; 17:18, 31; 24:21; 26:6ff.; 28:20. [45] Lk. 20:27ff.

After the uproar which followed, the Pharisees stood up for Paul, and declared that they could find nothing wrong with him. This seems to have triggered off further argument, which became so violent that for the third time the commander had to rescue him and have him brought into safe custody in the fortress of Antonia.

c. *Paul and the Lord Jesus (23:11)*

After the confrontation between Paul and Ananias, and the heated argument between the Pharisees and the Sadducees, it is a relief to read that during the following night the Lord Jesus came and stood near Paul and spoke to him. The violence of the last two days, and especially the enmity of the Jews, must have made him wonder anxiously about the future. There seemed little prospect of his leaving Jerusalem alive, let alone of his travelling on to Rome. So in this moment of discouragement Jesus comforted him with the straightforward promise that, as he had borne witness to him in Jerusalem, so he must also bear witness to him in Rome. It would be hard to exaggerate the calm courage which this assurance must have brought to Paul during his three further trials, his two years' imprisonment and his hazardous voyage to Rome.

6. Paul is rescued from a Jewish plot (23:12–35)

The next morning the Jews formed a conspiracy and bound themselves with an oath not to eat or drink until they had killed Paul.
13More than forty men were involved in this plot. 14They went to the chief priests and elders and said, 'We have taken a solemn oath not to eat anything until we have killed Paul. 15Now then, you and the Sanhedrin petition the commander to bring him before you on the pretext of wanting more accurate information about his case. We are ready to kill him before he gets here.'

16But when the son of Paul's sister heard of this plot, he went into the barracks and told Paul.

17Then Paul called one of the centurions and said, 'Take this young man to the commander; he has something to tell him.' 18So he took him to the commander.

The centurion said, 'Paul, the prisoner, sent for me and asked me to bring this young man to you because he has something to tell you.'

19The commander took the young man by the hand, drew him aside and asked, 'What is it you want to tell me?'

20He said: 'The Jews have agreed to ask you to bring Paul before the Sanhedrin tomorrow on the pretext of wanting more accurate information about him. 21Don't give in to them, because more than forty of them are waiting in ambush for him. They have taken an oath not to eat or drink until they have killed him. They are ready now, waiting for your consent to their request.'

22The commander dismissed the young man and cautioned him, 'Don't tell anyone that you have reported this to me.'

23Then he called two of his centurions and ordered them, 'Get ready a detachment of two hundred soldiers, seventy horsemen and
two hundred spearmen to go to Caesarea at nine tonight. 24Provide
mounts for Paul so that he may be taken safely to Governor Felix.'

25He wrote a letter as follows:

26Claudius Lysias,

To His Excellency, Governor Felix:

Greetings.

27This man was seized by the Jews and they were about to kill
him, but I came with my troops and rescued him, for I had
learned that he is a Roman citizen. 28I wanted to know why they
were accusing him, so I brought him to their Sanhedrin. 29I found
that the accusation had to do with questions about their law,
but there was no charge against him that deserved death or
imprisonment. 30When I was informed of a plot to be carried out
against the man, I sent him to you at once. I also ordered his
accusers to present to you their case against him.

31So the soldiers, carrying out their orders, took Paul with them
during the night and brought him as far as Antipatris. 32The next
day they let the cavalry go on with him, while they returned to the
barracks. 33When the cavalry arrived in Caesarea, they delivered
the letter to the governor and handed Paul over to him. 34The
governor read the letter and asked what province he was from.
Learning that he was from Cilicia, 35he said, 'I will hear your case
when your accusers get here.' Then he ordered that Paul be kept
under guard in Herod's palace.

a. *The plot is hatched (23:12–22)*

The Asian Jews had been frustrated in their attempts to lynch Paul, and the Sanhedrin had been unable to convict him of any offence. So now a group of more than forty Jewish men hatched a plot to murder him, binding themselves by oath to eat and drink nothing until they had succeeded. They then prevailed on the chief priests to persuade the Sanhedrin to petition the commander to co-operate with them. Their scheme was to have Paul brought back to court along narrow streets where he could easily be intercepted and killed. It seemed that everybody was now involved in the conspiracy and that Paul was in extreme danger.

But even the most careful and cunning of human plans cannot succeed if God opposes them. No weapon forged against him will prevail.[46] On this occasion God's providential intervention involved Paul's nephew. It is tantalizing to read these references to Paul's sister and her son, and to have no further information about them. Were they believers? Did they have some association with Jewish leaders which made it natural for Paul's nephew to learn of the plot without rousing anybody's suspicions? And how is it that he got access into the barracks so easily, especially if (as it seems from verse 19) he was only a youth? Luke does not satisfy our curiosity about any of these matters. What we do know is that the news of the plot spread from Paul's nephew to Paul, from Paul to a centurion, and from the centurion to the commander, who then learned about it from the youth's own lips. Doubtless remembering Paul's Roman citizenship, the commander decided on immediate and resolute action.

b. The plot is foiled (23:23–35)

The detachment of *two hundred soldiers, seventy horsemen and two hundred spearmen* certainly sounds like an extraordinary over-provision, representing about half the garrison. Were four hundred soldiers and seventy horses really necessary for the security of a single prisoner? It is this question which has made scholars wonder whether 'spearmen' is the correct translation of *dexiolaboi*, which occurs nowhere else in biblical or contemporary Greek literature. Kirsopp and Lake guessed that it means 'led horses', which would include both substitute mounts for the long overnight journey of nearly forty miles and pack horses too.[47] Some more recent commentators have adopted his suggestion.

Their destination was Caesarea, which, being the provincial capital of Judea, was where Felix the governor had his residence. Felix ruled as Judea's procurator for seven or eight years from AD 52. He owed his appointment to his brother Pallas, who was a favourite at court, first of the Emperor Claudius, and then of Nero. Felix was utterly ruthless in quelling Jewish uprisings. Though he was a freedman, he seems never to have grown out of a servile mentality, so that Tacitus wrote that 'he exercised the power of a king with the mind of a slave'.[48]

People naturally ask how Luke could have managed to get hold of the tribune's official letter to the procurator, so as to be able to publish its text. It is not impossible that it was read out in court, or that Felix divulged its contents to Paul during one of the

[46] Is. 54:17. [47] *BC*, IV, p. 293.

[48] Tacitus, *Histories*, V.9, quoted *e.g.* by Bruce, *English*, p. 462.

occasions on which he questioned him privately (23:34; 24:24). On the other hand, Luke says that Claudius Lysias wrote to Felix *as follows* (25) or 'to this effect' (RSV, NEB), so that he may be claiming to give no more than the gist of its contents. In any case, as we read the letter, we cannot help smiling. The tribune was substantially accurate in describing how he had rescued Paul, given him special treatment as a Roman citizen, brought him before the Sanhedrin, learned that the charges against him were only religious (about 'Moses and a certain Jesus', according to the Western text of verse 29), not civil or criminal, foiled a Jewish plot against him, sent him to the governor, and ordered his accusers to come and present their case in court. At the same time, Lysias somewhat manipulated the facts in order to portray himself in the most favourable light, putting his discovery that Paul was a Roman citizen before his rescue instead of after it, and drawing a discreet veil of silence over his serious offence in binding, and preparing to torture, a Roman citizen. Nine of the principal verbs in his letter are in the first person singular. The letter was fairly honourable, but decidedly self-centred.

After giving the text of the letter, Luke describes the military transfer of Paul from Jerusalem, via Antipatris, where the troops stopped for the night, to Caesarea, where both letter and prisoner were handed over to Felix. The governor read the letter, enquired about Paul's province in order to be sure that he came within his jurisdiction, determined to hear the case himself when Paul's accusers arrived, and ordered Paul to be kept under guard meanwhile in the rather magnificent palace which Herod the Great had built for himself and which was now the *praetorium*, the governor's official residence. Luke does not explain what *kept under guard* will have meant, but we may be sure that, as a Roman citizen, and with no criminal charges to face, Paul was not ill-treated.

Luke's great skill as a historian-theologian, not to mention the inspiration of the Holy Spirit, is clearly seen in these chapters. The future of the gospel was at stake, as powerful forces ranged themselves for and against it. On the one hand, the Jewish persecutors were prejudiced and violent. On the other, the Romans were open-minded and went out of their way to maintain the standards of law, justice and order of which their best leaders were understandably proud. Four times they rescued Paul from death either by lynching or by murder,[49] taking him into custody until the charges against him could be clarified and, if cogent, presented in court. Then three times in Luke's narrative, as we have seen,

[49] Acts 21:32–33; 22:23–24; 23:10; 23:23ff.

Paul either has been or will be declared innocent.

Between these two powers, religious and civil, hostile and friendly, Jerusalem and Rome, Paul found himself trapped, unarmed and totally vulnerable. One cannot help admiring his courage, especially when he stood on the steps of Fortress Antonia, facing an angry crowd which had just severely manhandled him, with no power but the Word and the Spirit of God. Luke seems to offer him to us as a model of Christian valour so that, as Chrysostom put it at the end of his fifty-fifth and last homily on the Acts, we may 'emulate Paul, and imitate that noble, that adamantine soul'.[50] The source of his courage was his serene confidence in the truth. He was well aware that the Romans had no case against him. He was convinced that the Jews had no case either, because his faith was the faith of his fathers, and the gospel was the fulfilment of the law. And above all he knew that his Lord and Saviour Jesus Christ was with him and would keep his promise that he would bear witness, some day, somehow, in Rome.

[50] Chrysostom, Homily LV, p. 328.

17. Paul on trial
24:1–26:32

Jerusalem and Rome were the centres of two enormously strong power blocs. The faith of Jerusalem went back two millennia to Abraham. The rule of Rome extended some three million square miles round the Mediterranean Sea. Jerusalem's strength lay in history and tradition, Rome's in conquest and organization. The combined might of Jerusalem and Rome was overwhelming. If a solitary dissident like Paul were to set himself against them, the outcome would be inevitable. His chances of survival would resemble those of a butterfly before a steamroller. He would be crushed, utterly obliterated from the face of the earth.

Yet such an outcome, we may confidently affirm, never even entered Paul's mind as a possibility. For he saw his situation from an entirely different perspective. He was no traitor to either church or state, that he should come into collision with them, although this is how his accusers tried to frame him. The enemies of Jesus had followed the same ploy. In their own court they had accused him of threatening to destroy the temple and of blaspheming,[1] while before Pilate they had represented him as guilty of sedition – subverting the nation, opposing taxes to Caesar and claiming to be himself a king.[2] Now Paul's enemies laid similar charges against him, namely that he had offended 'against the law of the Jews', 'against the temple' and 'against Caesar' (25:7–8).

But Paul was as innocent in these areas as Jesus had been. He had no quarrel with the God-given status of either Rome or Jerusalem. On the contrary, as he had written to the Roman Christians, he recognized that the authority given to Rome came from God[3] and that the privileges given to Israel came from God also.[4] The gospel did not undermine the law, whether Jewish or Roman, but rather 'upheld' it.[5] To be sure, the Romans might misuse their God-given authority and the Jews might misrepresent their law as the

[1] Mk. 14:55–64; Lk. 22:66–71. [2] Lk. 23:1–3. [3] Rom. 13:1ff.
[4] Rom. 9:4–5. [5] Rom. 3:31.

means of salvation. In such situations Paul would oppose them. But that was not the issue now. Paul's contention, while on trial, was that in principle the gospel both supports the rule of Caesar (25:8–12) and fulfils the hope of Israel (26:6ff.). His defence before his judges was to present himself as a loyal citizen of Rome and a loyal son of Israel.

Paul's double denial of treason and double insistence on loyalty is the thread which runs through these chapters. So far he has defended himself before a Jewish crowd (21:40ff.) and the Sanhedrin (23:1ff.). Now he will stand trial before the procurator Felix (24:1ff.), the procurator Festus (25:1ff.) and King Agrippa II (25:23ff.). In each of these five trials, in which the charge was now political (sedition), now religious (sacrilege), the judging audience was part Roman and part Jewish. Thus, when Paul spoke to the Jewish crowd and the Jewish Council, Claudius Lysias, the Roman tribune, was present and listening, while when Paul stood before Felix and Festus, the representatives of Rome, it was the Jews who were prosecuting. Then in the fifth trial, which was the grand finale, King Agrippa II combined both authorities within himself, for he had been appointed by Rome but was also an acknowledged authority on Jewish affairs.

1. Paul before Felix (24:1–27)

At the end of the previous chapter Felix, having read the letter from Claudius Lysias, sent to Jerusalem for Paul's accusers and meanwhile kept him in custody in Caesarea. *Five days later*, dating presumably from Paul's arrival, *the high priest Ananias* responded to the procurator's summons and *went down to Caesarea with some of the elders and a lawyer named Tertullus*. As soon as the court convened, *they brought their charges against Paul before the governor* (1). Whether they made their accusations in speech or in writing we are not told, but after the procurator had received them, *Paul was called in* and *Tertullus presented his case before Felix* (2a), or 'opened for the prosecution' (JB).

a. The prosecution by Tertullus (24:2b–9)

As a trained and experienced professional lawyer, Tertullus began with what was called a *captatio benevolentiae*, that is, an endeavour to capture the judge's good will. Traditionally, it was complimentary to the point of hypocrisy and often included a promise of brevity, but on this occasion it descended to 'almost nauseating flattery'.[6] For Tertullus expressed gratitude for the 'peace' Felix

[6] Barclay, p. 184.

had secured and the 'reforms' he had introduced, whereas in reality he had put down several insurrections with such barbarous brutality that he earned for himself the horror, not the thanks, of the Jewish population. Here are Tertullus' words: '*We have enjoyed a long period of peace under you, and your foresight has brought about reforms in this nation. Everywhere and in every way, most excellent Felix, we acknowledge this with profound gratitude. But in order not to weary you further, I would request that you be kind enough to hear us briefly*' (2b–4).

Tertullus went on to enumerate three charges against Paul. First, *we have found this man to be a troublemaker* ('a perfect pest', NEB, JB), *stirring up riots among the Jews all over the world* (5a). This was a serious accusation because of its political overtones. There were many Jewish agitators at that time, Messianic pretenders who threatened the very 'peace' which Tertullus had attributed to Felix.

Secondly, Tertullus continued, Paul *is a ringleader of the Nazarene sect* (5b). The word *hairesis* meant 'sect, party, school' and was applied to both the Sadducees (5:17) and the Pharisees (15:5; 26:5) as traditions within Judaism. It is in this sense that it is now used of Christians. It had not yet come to mean 'heresy', although its use in this chapter (5, 14) and its recurrence in 28:22 'incline towards' the rendering 'heretical sect' (BAGD).

The third charge against Paul was that he *even tried to desecrate the temple* (6), a reference to the belief that he had brought Trophimus the Ephesian within the prohibited precinct (21:29). This was a particularly damaging and dangerous accusation, because the Romans had given the Jews wide powers in dealing with offences against their temple. *So we seized him*, said Tertullus in a dishonest euphemism for the Jews' attempt to lynch him (21:30–31). The Western reading then adds verses 6b–8a, which AV and JB include in their text but NIV relegates to the margin: 'and wanted to judge him according to our law. But the commander, Lysias, came and with the use of much force snatched him from our hands and ordered his accusers to come before you'. The effect of this addition is to complete the reversal of the facts, attributing the violence to Lysias instead of to the Jewish crowd, as the orderly arrest had been ascribed to the crowd instead of to Lysias.

Tertullus concluded his prosecution with a direct appeal to Felix: *By examining him yourself you will be able to learn the truth about all these charges we are bringing against him* (8). When he had finished, *the Jews joined in the accusation, asserting that these things were true* (9).

b. The defence by Paul (24:10–21)

As soon as *the governor motioned for him to speak*, Paul launched into his defence. He also began with a *captatio benevolentiae*, although it was considerably more modest and moderate than Tertullus' had been: *I know that for a number of years you have been a judge over this nation; so I gladly make my defence* (1). He then proceeded to refute the prosecution's allegations one by one.

First, he was emphatically not a troublemaker. *You can easily verify that no more than twelve days ago I went up to Jerusalem to worship* (11). *My accusers did not find me arguing with anyone at the temple, or stirring up a crowd in the synagogues or anywhere else in the city* (12). *And they cannot prove to you the charges they are now making against me* (13). In other words, in the few days at his disposal he had had no time to foment an insurrection; he had had no intention of doing so either, since he went to Jerusalem as a pilgrim to worship, not as an agitator to cause a riot; and his accusers could produce no evidence that in temple, synagogue or city he had caused a disturbance or even engaged in an argument.

Secondly, Paul addressed himself to the charge that he was 'a ringleader of the Nazarene sect'. This led him to affirmation as well as denial. Although he was indeed 'a follower of the Way', this was not a 'sect', as they called it, for he worshipped the God of their fathers and believed the teaching of the Scriptures.

14*'However, I admit that I worship the God of our fathers as a follower of the Way, which they call a sect. I believe everything that agrees with the Law and that is written in the Prophets,* 15*and I have the same hope in God as these men, that there will be a resurrection of both the righteous and the wicked.* 16*So I strive always to keep my conscience clear before God and man.'*

Here was Paul's public confession of faith (*homologō*, 'I confess', 14). It consisted of four affirmations: (i) 'I worship the God of our fathers'; (ii) 'I believe everything that agrees with the Law and . . . the Prophets'; (iii) 'I have the same hope in God as these men'; and (iv) 'I strive always [JB, "as much as they"] to keep my conscience clear . . .'. Paul's purpose in this was not just to make a personal declaration, however, but to insist that he shared it with the whole people of God. He worshipped the same God ('the God of our fathers'), believed the same truths (the Law and the Prophets), shared the same hope (the resurrection of both the righteous and the wicked) and cherished the same ambition (to keep a clear conscience). He was not an innovator, therefore, but loyal to the ancestral faith. Nor was he a sectarian or heretical deviant, for he stood squarely in mainstream Judaism. His worship, faith, hope and goal were no different from theirs. 'The Way' enjoyed a direct continuity with the Old Testament, for the Scriptures bore witness to Jesus Christ as the one in whom

God's promises had been fulfilled.

The third accusation against Paul was that he had profaned the temple (7). This the apostle strenuously denied.

[17]'*After an absence of several years, I came to Jerusalem to bring my people gifts for the poor and to present offerings.* [18]*I was ceremonially clean when they found me in the temple courts doing this. There was no crowd with me, nor was I involved in any disturbance.* [19]*But there are some Jews from the province of Asia, who ought to be here before you and bring charges if they have anything against me.* [20]*Or these who are here should state what crime they found in me when I stood before the Sanhedrin –* [21]*unless it was this one thing I shouted as I stood in their presence: "It is concerning the resurrection of the dead that I am on trial before you today."*'

Far from desecrating the temple, Paul's purpose in visiting Jerusalem had been religious ('to bring my people gifts for the poor and to present offerings', 17) and his condition, when he was found in the temple doing this, had been one of ceremonial purity (18). There was no crowd and no disturbance. It was certain Asian Jews, who had interfered with him and caused a riot (though Paul left his sentence unfinished) just when he was demonstrating his love for his nation and his respect for its laws. Why were these men not in court to press their charges? (19). Their absence was a serious breach of Roman law, which 'was very strong against accusers who abandoned their charges'.[7] Since those Asian Jews were not there as witnesses, then those who were there should state of what crime the Sanhedrin had convicted him (20). The fact is that the Pharisees had declared him innocent of any crime (23:9); only the Sadducees thought him guilty, and that only of a theological belief concerning the resurrection of the dead (21).

c. *The adjournment by Felix (24:22–27)*

Then Felix, who was well acquainted with the Way (perhaps through his Jewish wife, Drusilla), adjourned the proceedings. He found himself on the horns of a dilemma. He could not convict Paul, since Lysias the tribune had found no fault in him (23:29), nor had the Sanhedrin (23:9), nor had Tertullus been able to substantiate his charges. On the other hand, Felix was unwilling to release Paul, partly because he hoped for a bribe (26) and partly because he wanted to curry favour with the Jews (27). The only other option was to postpone his verdict on the pretext that he needed the tribune's advice: *When Lysias the commander comes, I will decide your case* (22). Meanwhile, Felix *ordered the centurion*

[7] Sherwin-White, p. 52.

to keep Paul under guard but to give him some freedom and permit his friends to take care of his needs (23). The Romans had different degrees of imprisonment. Because Paul was a Roman citizen, who had not been convicted of any offence, Felix issued instructions that he should be given *custodia libera*, in which, although he was never left unguarded, his friends enjoyed free access to him. We may guess that Luke visited him, and Philip the evangelist with his four daughters who lived in Caesarea (21:8–9), together with others who were members of the local church.

There was to be no further public hearing for two years (27). During this period, however, Felix conducted a kind of private investigation of his own. The Western text ascribes the initiative to his wife Drusilla, 'who asked to see Paul and hear the word'. 'Wishing therefore to satisfy her', Felix summoned Paul.[8] Drusilla was the youngest daughter of Herod Agrippa I, whose opposition and death Luke has described earlier (12:1–23). She was therefore the sister of King Agrippa II and of Bernice, to whom Luke will introduce us in the next chapters (25:13, 23; 26:30). She had a reputation for ravishing youthful beauty, on account of which Felix, with the aid of a Cypriot magician, had seduced her from her rightful husband and secured her for himself. She was, in fact, his third wife. The lax morals of Felix and Drusilla help to explain the topics on which Paul spoke to them.

[24]*Several days later Felix came with his wife Drusilla, who was a Jewess. He sent for Paul and listened to him as he spoke about faith in Christ Jesus.* [25]*As Paul discoursed on righteousness, self-control and the judgment to come, Felix was afraid and said, 'That's enough for now! You may leave. When I find it convenient, I will send for you.'* [26]*At the same time he was hoping that Paul would offer him a bribe, so he sent for him frequently and talked with him.*

[27]*When two years had passed, Felix was succeeded by Porcius Festus, but because Felix wanted to grant a favour to the Jews, he left Paul in prison.*

In general, Paul focused on *faith in Christ Jesus* (24). Since Drusilla was a Jewess, he must have rehearsed the facts of the life, death and resurrection of Jesus and deployed his customary arguments that this Jesus of Nazareth was the Christ of Scripture. He will also have presented Jesus not only as a figure of history and the fulfilment of prophecy, but also as the Saviour and Lord in whom Felix as well as Drusilla should put their trust. Paul never proclaimed the good news in a vacuum, however, but always in a

[8] Metzger, p. 491.

context, the personal context of his hearers. So he went on to discourse *on righteousness, self-control and the judgment to come* (25). Most commentators relate 'righteousness' or 'justice' to the well-known cruelty and oppression of which Felix was guilty, and 'self-control' to the unbridled lust which had drawn and united him to Drusilla, while 'judgment to come' would be the inevitable penalty for their injustice and immorality. And this may be correct. But it seems to me possible that the *dikaiosynē* ('righteousness') of which Paul spoke was precisely that 'righteousness from God' or divine act of justification which he had elaborated in his Letter to the Romans. In this case the three topics of conversation were what are sometimes called the 'three tenses of salvation', namely how to be justified or pronounced righteous by God, how to overcome temptation and gain self-mastery, and how to escape the awful final judgment of God. It is not surprising that, as these solemn subjects were opened up and pressed home, *Felix was afraid* ('alarmed', RSV, NEB) and declared that he had had enough for the time being.

During the succeeding months, however, Felix (though now, it seems, without Drusilla) *sent for him frequently and talked with him* (26). Luke is explicit that he hoped for a bribe, a practice as common as it was illegal. Ramsay even argued from the heavy expenses Paul must have paid for the purification rites (21:23), the long lawsuit, the appeal to Caesar and his rented accommodation in Rome (28:30), in addition to Felix's hope for a bribe, that the apostle must recently have inherited some family property.[9] At all events, the governor's greed (for which he also had a reputation) was aroused. It would be cynical to suppose, however, that Felix's only motive was to hold Paul to ransom. I think he knew that Paul had something more precious than money, something which money cannot buy. If his conscience had been aroused by Paul's teaching, then he must have been seeking forgiveness and peace. Certainly the release of Felix from sin meant more to Paul than his own release from prison. But unfortunately there is no evidence that Felix ever capitulated to Christ and was redeemed. On the contrary, when Porcius Festus succeeded to the procuratorship, Felix still *left Paul in prison* (27), even beyond the two-year period which was 'the maximum duration of preventive custody',[10] in order to win the Jews' favour, which means that 'he not only coveted money, but also glory'.[11]

[9] Ramsay, *St Paul*, pp. 310–313. [10] JB, note o
[11] Chrysostom, Homily LI, p. 304.

2. Paul before Festus (25:1–22)

According to Josephus, Felix was recalled to Rome in order to explain his savage suppression of a dispute between Jews and Syrians over their respective civil rights in Caesarea, and would have been severely punished but for his brother Pallas' appeal to Nero.[12] Not much is known about Porcius Festus, who replaced him, for he died in office only two years later. But he seems to have been more just and moderate than either his predecessor or his successors.

The new procurator lost no time in acquainting himself with Jewish affairs, including the case against Paul. Luke presents him to his readers as 'a brisk and energetic worker'[13] and summarizes his involvement in the case: (a) he refused the Jewish leaders' request to be allowed to try Paul in Jerusalem, (b) he heard Paul's defence and appeal to Caesar, and (c) he consulted King Agrippa II as to what he should do next.

a. Festus refuses the Jewish leaders' request (25:1–5)

Three days after arriving in the province, Festus went up from Caesarea to Jerusalem, [2]where the chief priests and Jewish leaders appeared before him and presented the charges against Paul. [3]They urgently requested Festus, as a favour to them, to have Paul transferred to Jerusalem, for they were preparing an ambush to kill him along the way. [4]Festus answered, 'Paul is being held at Caesarea, and I myself am going there soon. [5]Let some of your leaders come with me and press charges against the man there, if he has done anything wrong.'

Although Festus was a more conciliatory character than Felix, yet on his first visit to Jerusalem he stood firm. In spite of the urgent pleas of the Jewish leaders to have Paul transferred to Jerusalem to be tried there, Festus refused. Had his suspicions been aroused that they had ulterior motives, even (as Luke divulges) that they were preparing an ambush to kill him (3)? We do not know. What is apparent is that Festus was determined to allow justice to take its course. Roman procedure followed three stages. First, charges had to be formulated and sustained by the prosecutor. Secondly, there would be 'a proper formal act of accusation by the interested party'. Thirdly, the case was heard by 'the holder of the *imperium* in person', in this case the procurator.[14] In this way the accused and his accusers would come face to face (15–16).

[12] Josephus, *Antiquities*, XX.8.7,9; *Wars*, II.13.7.
[13] Haenchen, p. 668. [14] Sherwin-White, pp. 17, 48.

b. Festus hears Paul's defence and appeal to Caesar (25:6–12)

After spending eight or ten days with them, he went down to Caesarea, and the next day he convened the court and ordered that Paul be brought before him. [7]When Paul appeared, the Jews who had come down from Jerusalem stood around him, bringing many serious charges against him, which they could not prove.

[8]Then Paul made his defence: 'I have done nothing wrong against the law of the Jews or against the temple or against Caesar.'

[9]Festus, wishing to do the Jews a favour, said to Paul, 'Are you willing to go up to Jerusalem and stand trial before me there on these charges?'

[10]Paul answered: 'I am now standing before Caesar's court, where I ought to be tried. I have not done any wrong to the Jews, as you yourself know very well. [11]If, however, I am guilty of doing anything deserving death, I do not refuse to die. But if the charges brought against me by these Jews are not true, no-one has the right to hand me over to them. I appeal to Caesar!'

[12]After Festus had conferred with his council, he declared: 'You have appealed to Caesar. To Caesar you will go!'

Luke does not specify what the many serious charges were (7), but Paul's defence indicates that he was accused of offending in three ways, namely against the Jewish law, the temple and the emperor (8). Once again religious and political charges were combined, but on this occasion Caesar is mentioned for the first time. The disturbances which Paul was alleged to have caused were religious in their origin but civil in their character. That is why Caesar's representative was obliged to take note of them. The Jews knew that the Roman governors 'were unwilling to convict on purely religious charges and therefore tried to give a political twist to the religious charge'.[15] And the prolongation of the trial was due to the fact that 'the charge was political . . . and yet the evidence was theological'.[16]

It was this mention of Caesar which determined the course of Paul's trial before Festus. For some reason which is not apparent, except that he wished to do the Jews a favour, Festus gave Paul the option of being tried before him in Jerusalem (9). In making this offer he was within his rights. 'Nothing prevented him from using the Sanhedrin, or members of it, as his own *concilium*. That is what Paul feared.'[17] Paul saw clearly that he could hope for justice and for acquittal only from the Romans, not from the Jews. He had committed no offence against the Jews, as Festus knew perfectly well. If he were guilty of a capital offence, he was willing

[15] *Ibid.*, p. 50. [16] *Ibid.*, p. 51 [17] *Ibid.*, p. 67

to bear the penalty. But if the Jewish accusations were false, no-one – not even the procurator – had the right to hand him over to them. So he had only one option left: *I appeal to Caesar!* (11). Festus seems to have been quite unprepared for this development. What would he do now? He could neither convict and sentence Paul, for fear of offending against Roman justice, nor release him, for fear of offending the Jews. So, after conferring with his *concilium*, his legal advisers, he realized that he had no alternative but to allow the prisoner's appeal to go forward. '*You have appealed to Caesar. To Caesar you will go!*' (12).

This was not the *appellatio* of a later period, which was an appeal to a higher court against a sentence passed by a lower one, but rather the Roman citizen's ancient right of *provocatio*, which protected him 'from summary punishment, execution or torture without trial, from private or public arrest, and from actual trial by magistrates outside Italy'.[18]

If in his trial before Felix Paul had emphasized the continuity of 'the Way' with Judaism, in his trial before Festus he stressed his loyalty to Caesar. Caesar is mentioned eight times in this chapter, five times as *Kaisar*, twice as *Sebastos* (21, 25), the Greek equivalent of Augustus, and once as *ho Kyrios* (26), 'the Lord'. Paul knew that he had not offended against Caesar (8) and that he stood in Caesar's court (10). It was only logical that he should exercise his citizen's right to appeal to Caesar (11, 12, 21).

c. *Festus asks Agrippa's advice (25:13–22)*

A few days later King Agrippa and Bernice arrived at Caesarea to pay their respects to Festus. [14]Since they were spending many days there, Festus discussed Paul's case with the king. He said: 'There is a man here whom Felix left as a prisoner. [15]When I went to Jerusalem, the chief priests and elders of the Jews brought charges against him and asked that he be condemned.

[16]'I told them that it is not the Roman custom to hand over any man before he has faced his accusers and has had an opportunity to defend himself against their charges. [17]When they came here with me, I did not delay the case, but convened the court the next day and ordered the man to be brought in. [18]When his accusers got up to speak, they did not charge him with any of the crimes I had expected. [19]Instead, they had some points of dispute with him about their own religion and about a dead man named Jesus whom Paul claimed was alive. [20]I was at a loss how to investigate such matters; so I asked if he would be willing to go to Jerusalem and stand trial

[18] *Ibid.*, p. 58. See Sherwin-White's full discussion of 'The Citizenship of Paul', pp. 57–70

there on these charges. [21]*When Paul made his appeal to be held over for the Emperor's decision, I ordered him to be held until I could send him to Caesar.'*

[22]*Then Agrippa said to Festus, 'I would like to hear this man myself.'*

He replied, 'Tomorrow you will hear him.'

Herod Agrippa II was the son of Herod Agrippa I of Acts 12 and the great grandson of Herod the Great. Bernice was his sister, and rumours were rife that their relationship was incestuous. Because he had been only seventeen years old when his father died, he was considered too young to assume the kingdom of Judea, which therefore reverted to rule by procurator. Instead, he was given a tiny and insignificant northern kingdom within what is now Lebanon, and this was later augmented by territory in Galilee. He was nevertheless influential in Jewry because the Emperor Claudius had committed to him both the care of the temple and the appointment of the high priest.[19] He and Bernice came to Caesarea to pay their respects to the new procurator, and during their stay Festus raised Paul's case, which he had inherited from Felix. He told the king three things which he had done.

First, on his visit to Jerusalem, he had heard the Jewish leaders accuse Paul and request his condemnation, but had insisted that according to Roman custom the accused must be allowed to face his accusers and defend himself against them (15–16). Secondly, when the Jewish leaders came to Caesarea, Festus had immediately convened the court, only to discover that Paul was not being charged with crimes against the state, but with religious offences, and with the claim that 'a dead man named Jesus . . . was alive' (17–19). Thirdly, because Festus felt out of his depth in religious questions like these, he had asked Paul if he was willing to be tried in Jerusalem, but instead he had appealed to Caesar, and Festus had granted his appeal (20–21).

Intrigued by Festus' summary of the case, Agrippa said that he would like to hear Paul himself, and Festus agreed (22). Paul had aroused his curiosity, much as Jesus had aroused the curiosity of his great-uncle, Herod Antipas.[20]

3. Paul before Agrippa (25:23 – 26:32)

Paul's trial before Agrippa is the longest and most elaborate of the five. Luke sketches the scene with graphic detail, and Paul's defence speech is more polished in structure and language than the others. One wonders if Luke was present in the visitors' gallery. Otherwise

[19] See Josephus, *Antiquities*, XX.9.4,7. [20] Lk. 9:9; 23:8.

Paul (or somebody else) must have rehearsed it all to him later, although Luke may also have had access to the official documentation of the case.

The next day Agrippa and Bernice came with great pomp (23a). 'They would have on their purple robes of royalty and the gold circlet of the crown on their brows. Doubtless Festus, to do honour to the occasion, had donned the scarlet robe which a governor wore on state occasions.'[21] Following them, as they *entered the audience room*, in the pageantry of the procession, were both *the high ranking officers*, the military tribunes who were 'members of the procurator's staff',[22] *and the leading men of the city*. When they had taken their seats, *at the command of Festus, Paul was brought in* (23). According to tradition, he was only a little fellow and unprepossessing in appearance, balding, with beetle brows, hooked nose and bandy legs, yet 'full of grace'.[23] Wearing neither crown nor gown, but only handcuffs and perhaps a plain prisoner's tunic, he nevertheless dominated the court with his quiet, Christ-like dignity and confidence.

a. Festus introduces the case (25:24–27)

Festus said: 'King Agrippa, and all who are present with us, you see this man! The whole Jewish community has petitioned me about him in Jerusalem and here in Caesarea, shouting that he ought not to live any longer. [25]I found he had done nothing deserving of death, but because he made his appeal to the Emperor I decided to send him to Rome. [26]But I have nothing definite to write to His Majesty about him. Therefore I have brought him before all of you, and especially before you, King Agrippa, so that as a result of this investigation I may have something to write. [27]For I think it is unreasonable to send on a prisoner without specifying the charges against him.'

Festus' account of the situation was a mixture of truth and error. It was true that the Jewish community had twice petitioned for Paul's death, and that Festus had not found him guilty of any capital offence (24–25). It was not true, however, that Festus had 'nothing definite to write to His Majesty' about Paul (26) and that he could not 'specify the charges against him' (27). For the Jewish charges, as we have seen, were both definite and specific. What Festus lacked was not charges, but evidence to substantiate them. For lack of this, he should have had the courage to declare Paul innocent and to release him.

[21] Barclay, pp. 191–192. [22] Bruce, *English*, p. 484.
[23] From *The Acts of Paul and Thecla;* see James, p. 273.

b. Paul makes his defence (26:1–23)

Then Agrippa said to Paul, 'You have permission to speak for yourself.'

So Paul motioned with his hand and began his defence: [2]'King Agrippa, I consider myself fortunate to stand before you today as I make my defence against all the accusations of the Jews, [3]and especially so because you are well acquainted with all the Jewish customs and controversies. Therefore, I beg you to listen to me patiently.'

It was a dramatic moment when the holy and humble apostle of Jesus Christ stood before this representative of the worldly, ambitious, morally corrupt family of the Herods, who for generation after generation had set themselves in opposition to truth and righteousness. 'Their founder, Herod the Great', wrote R. B. Rackham, 'had tried to destroy the infant Jesus. His son Antipas, the tetrarch of Galilee, beheaded John the Baptist, and won from the Lord the title of "fox". His grandson Agrippa I slew James the son of Zebedee with the sword. Now we see Paul brought before Agrippa's son.'[24] It was Rackham too who was the first (in 1901) to call Paul's defence before Agrippa his *apologia pro vita sua*.[25] But Paul was not in the least intimidated. For he was accurate in his reference to Agrippa's familiarity with 'Jewish customs and controversies' (3), and the Western reviser's gloss, though not part of Luke's original text, is surely correct in saying that Paul was 'confident, and encouraged by the Holy Spirit' (1).[26]

Paul tells his personal story, drawing attention to its three principal phases. He portrays himself (i) as the strict Pharisee, (ii) as the fanatical persecutor, and (iii) as the commissioned apostle.

First, the apostle describes *his upbringing as a Pharisee.*

[4]'The Jews all know the way I have lived ever since I was a child, from the beginning of my life in my own country, and also in Jerusalem. [5]They have known me for a long time and can testify, if they are willing, that according to the strictest sect of our religion, I lived as a Pharisee. [6]And now it is because of my hope in what God has promised our fathers that I am on trial today. [7]This is the promise our twelve tribes are hoping to see fulfilled as they earnestly serve God day and night. O King, it is because of this hope that the Jews are accusing me. [8]Why should any of you consider it incredible that God raises the dead?'

Saul must have been a familiar figure in Jerusalem when as a young man he sat at the feet of Rabbi Gamaliel (22:3). He is

[24] Rackham, p. 457. [25] *Ibid., e.g.* pp. 458, 462. [26] Metzger, p. 494.

likely to have gained a reputation for scholarship, righteousness and religious zeal. Many Palestinian Jews still alive knew how he had lived as a child, first in Tarsus, then in Jerusalem. More than that, they had known him personally and could testify from their own experience that he had belonged to the strictest party in Judaism, that of the Pharisees (4–5). It was surely anomalous, therefore, that he should now be on trial for his hope in God's promise to the fathers, which he and they shared, namely that God would send his Messiah (foretold and foreshadowed in the Old Testament) to rescue and redeem his people. The twelve tribes were still eagerly expecting the fulfilment of this promise. But he believed it had already been fulfilled in Jesus, whose resurrection was the proof of his Messiahship and the pledge of our resurrection too. Why should anybody think resurrection to be incredible? The Pharisees believed in it. And now God had demonstrated it by raising Jesus from the dead.

Secondly, Paul describes *his fanatical persecution of Christ* (9–11).

[9]*'I too was convinced that I ought to do all that was possible to oppose the name of Jesus of Nazareth.* [10]*And that is just what I did in Jerusalem. On the authority of the chief priests I put many of the saints in prison, and when they were put to death, I cast my vote against them.* [11]*Many a time I went from one synagogue to another to have them punished, and I tried to force them to blaspheme. In my obsession against them, I even went to foreign cities to persecute them.'*

Saul the Pharisee was convinced that it was his solemn duty to oppose the name and the claims of Jesus of Nazareth as those of an impostor. Moreover, he had the courage of his convictions. He began his persecuting programme in Jerusalem. Armed with authority from the chief priests, he not only imprisoned many disciples of Jesus, but even, when they were 'sentenced to death' (JB), cast his vote against them. He searched the synagogues for Christians in order to bring them to punishment. 'The synagogue punishment of whipping will be meant here.'[27] He tried by force to make them blaspheme (the phrase indicates that he by no means always succeeded), and in his 'obsession' (RSV, 'in raging fury') he pursued them even to 'foreign cities'.

Thirdly, Paul describes *his conversion and his commissioning as an apostle* (12–18).

[12]*'On one of these journeys I was going to Damascus with the authority and commission of the chief priests.* [13]*About noon, O King, as I was on the road, I saw a light from heaven, brighter than the*

[27] Haenchen, p. 684.

sun, blazing around me and my companions. [14]*We all fell to the ground, and I heard a voice saying to me in Aramaic, "Saul, Saul, why do you persecute me? It is hard for you to kick against the goads."*

[15]*'Then I asked, "Who are you, Lord?"*

' "I am Jesus, whom you are persecuting," the Lord replied. [16]*"Now get up and stand on your feet. I have appeared to you to appoint you as a servant and as a witness of what you have seen of me and what I will show you.* [17]*I will rescue you from your own people and from the Gentiles. I am sending you to them* [18]*to open their eyes and turn them from darkness to light, and from the power of Satan to God, so that they may receive forgiveness of sins and a place among those who are sanctified by faith in me." '*

Damascus was one of the 'foreign cities' to which Paul travelled, equipped with a high priestly extradition order. But before he reached his destination the divine intervention took place. A heavenly light, more brilliant than the sun at noon, flashed round him and his companions. Together they fell to the ground. Then a voice, addressing Paul in Aramaic, asked why he was persecuting him and, quoting a well-known proverb, declared it painful for him to kick against the goads. Dr Longenecker gives the references in the works of Euripides, Aeschylus, Pindar and Terence, where this saying occurs as a metaphor for useless 'opposition to deity'.[28]

To the anonymous voice's question 'Why are you persecuting me?' Saul responded with the counter-question 'Who are you that I am persecuting?' Although his addition 'Lord' does not necessarily mean more than 'Sir', yet the fact that Paul introduces Jesus' reply with the words 'the Lord replied', so that *kyrie* and *kyrios* stand together in Luke's text, suggests that it did mean more. Surely, when the heavenly voice declared, 'I am Jesus, whom you are persecuting,' at least two truths must have registered instantly in Saul's consciousness. The first is that the crucified Jesus was alive and had thus been vindicated, and the second that the Jesus who identified himself so closely with the Christians that to persecute them was to persecute him, must regard them as being peculiarly his own people.

In Paul's account to Agrippa of what happened on the Damascus road, however, what he stressed was not his conversion, but his commissioning, not his becoming a disciple of Jesus, but his appointment to be an apostle. So Jesus' first word of command to him was '*Now get up and stand on your feet*' (16). This cannot mean that he had been wrong to fall to the ground, for in that fall he both was humbled and humbled himself. Nor is there any hint

[28] Longenecker, *Acts*, p. 552.

that he was now grovelling in a prostrate position inappropriate to a human being and a Christian. No, the command to stand was a necessary preliminary to the command to go; it prefaced his commissioning. One is reminded of Ezekiel. When he saw 'the appearance of the likeness of the glory of the Lord' he 'fell face down'.[29] But God immediately said to him, 'Son of man, stand up on your feet . . . I am sending you to the Israelites . . . You must speak my words to them.'[30] In fact, the commissioning of Saul as Christ's apostle was deliberately shaped to resemble the call of Isaiah, Ezekiel, Jeremiah and others to be God's prophets. In both cases the language of 'sending' was used. As God 'sent' his prophets to announce his word to his people, so Christ 'sent' his apostles to preach and teach in his name, including Paul who was now 'sent' to be the apostle to the Gentiles (17).[31]

Christ's commission of Saul took the form of three verbs, all in the first person singular of direct speech, although respectively in the past, future and present tenses: 'I have appeared to you', 'I will rescue you' and 'I am sending you'. First, *I have appeared to you to appoint you as a servant and as a witness* (16a). The general call to be a 'servant' is narrowed down into the particular call to be a 'witness'. Luke has already combined the ideas of service and witness in reference to the original apostolic eyewitnesses, and used the same word for 'servant' (*hypēretēs*).[32] Also in Paul's ministry as in theirs the emphasis is on being an eyewitness, for he was to bear witness both to what he had seen of Jesus and to what Jesus would later show him (16b). Secondly, *I will rescue you from your own people and from the Gentiles* (17). A similar promise of 'rescue' was made to Jeremiah.[33] This did not guarantee immunity to suffering. On the contrary, it was part of the vocation of prophets and apostles to endure suffering (*cf.* 9:16). But it did mean that their testimony would not be silenced until their God-appointed work was done.

Thirdly, *I am sending you* (*egō apostellō se*). The emphatic *egō* ('I'), the personal *se* ('you') and the verb *apostellō* ('send') could almost be rendered (as in 22:21) 'I myself apostle you', 'I myself make you an apostle'. For this was Paul's commission to be an apostle, especially to be the apostle to the Gentiles, which was comparable to the commission to the Twelve which was renewed by the risen Lord on the first Easter Day in his word 'I am sending you'.[34] And what was Paul being sent to do? In essence, *to open*

[29] Ezk. 1:28b. [30] Ezk. 2:1, 3, 7.

[31] For the Old Testament prophets, see *e.g.* Is. 6:8–9; Jer. 1:4, 7; 7:25; 14:14ff.; 29:9, 19; Ezk. 2:3; 3:4ff.; Amos 7:14–15. For the New Testament apostles, see Mt. 10:1–5, 16; Mk. 3:14; 6:7; Lk. 6:12–13; 9:1–2.

[32] Lk. 1:2. [33] Je. 1:8. [34] Jn. 20:21.

their eyes (18a). For the unbelieving Gentile world was blind to the truth of God in Jesus Christ.[35] Yet this opening of the eyes did not mean intellectual enlightenment only, but conversion: to *turn them from darkness to light, and from the power of Satan to God* (18b). For conversion includes a radical transfer of allegiance and so of environment. It is both a liberation from the darkness of satanic rule and a liberation into the sphere of God's marvellous light and power.[36] In other words, it means entering the kingdom of God. Further, the blessings of the kingdom are the *forgiveness of sins and a place among those who are sanctified by faith* in Christ (18c). The promise of forgiveness was part of the apostolic gospel from the beginning.[37] So was belonging to the Messianic people (2:40–41, 47). For the new life in Christ and the new community of Christ always go together. What was specially significant in Christ's commissioning of Paul was that the Gentiles were to be granted a full and equal share with the Jews in the privileges of those sanctified by faith in Christ, that is, the holy people of God.

Thus, the commissioning formula was 'I am sending you'. And the object of Paul's commission was that he should open blind eyes and convert people from darkness to light and Satan to God. Not of course that he himself had authority or power to do the eye-opening or the converting. These things could be effected by Christ only through his word and Spirit. In addition, the essential equipment for his mission was Christ's appearance to him, so that he could be an eyewitness, and his necessary assurance was that Christ would rescue him from the enemies of the gospel until his course was finished and his ministry fulfilled.

Paul now turns from Christ's commission to his response to it, and in describing this he replaces narrative with a direct address to Agrippa:

> [19]*'So then, King Agrippa, I was not disobedient to the vision from heaven.* [20]*First to those in Damascus, then to those in Jerusalem and in all Judea, and to the Gentiles also, I preached that they should repent and turn to God and prove their repentance by their deeds.* [21]*That is why the Jews seized me in the temple courts and tried to kill me.* [22]*But I have had God's help to this very day, and so I stand here and testify to small and great alike. I am saying nothing beyond what the prophets and Moses said would happen –* [23]*that the Christ would suffer and, as the first to rise from the dead, would proclaim light to his own people and to the Gentiles.'*

Paul begins his statement with a double negative: *I was not*

[35] *Cf.* 2 Cor. 4:4. [36] *Cf.* Col. 1:12–13; 1 Pet. 2:9.
[37] Lk. 24:47; Acts 2:38; 3:19; 13:39.

disobedient. How could he have been? The vision was evidently from heaven, and it was overwhelming. His fanatical opposition was overcome in a moment, and his secret doubts resolved. Christ had appeared to him and commissioned him; his obedience corresponded precisely to the charge he had received. First in Damascus, next in Jerusalem and Judea, then also to the Gentiles, he announced the good news and called on people to *repent and turn to God and prove their repentance by their deeds* (20). The word 'turn' in verse 20 is *epistrephō*, as in verse 18, even though there it is transitive, since it is Paul who is appointed to 'turn' people, while here it is intransitive, since it is the people who are exhorted to do the 'turning' in response to Paul's preaching. These expressions are not contradictory; they explain each other. We notice also that Paul was clear from the beginning that, although salvation was by faith (18), it had to be evidenced by good works.

It was Paul's proclamation and promises to the Gentiles (17, 20–21), indicating that they could receive the new life and join the new community directly, without first needing to become Jews, which had aroused Jewish opposition. Indeed, they had seized him in the temple courts and tried to kill him (21). But he was rescued from their hands, according to Christ's promise (17), and God's help had continued with him to that very day. So '*I stand here*' (22a), he cried (as Martin Luther was to say to the Diet of Worms centuries later), bearing witness (as Jesus had instructed him) *to small and great alike*, the nonentities of 1 Corinthians 1:26ff. as well as the dignitaries who were in court, *saying nothing beyond what the prophets and Moses said would happen* (22b). This renewed claim that Paul was not an innovator, but a faithful exponent of the Scriptures, also had its parallel in Luther and the other sixteenth-century Reformers. They were accused by the Roman Catholic Church of teaching novelties. But they denied it. 'We teach no new thing', Luther claimed, 'but we repeat and establish old things, which the apostles and all godly teachers have taught before us.'[38] Or, as Lancelot Andrewes was to say a century later, 'we are renovators not innovators'.[39]

And what did Moses and the prophets say would happen? They predicted three events: first *that the Christ would suffer*, secondly that he would be *the first to rise from the dead*, and as such, thirdly, that he *would proclaim light to his own people and to the Gentiles* (23).[40] More simply still, Jesus the Christ was Isaiah's 'suffering servant' of the Lord, who would suffer and die for our sins,[41] be

[38] Luther's *Commentary on St Paul's Epistle to the Galatians* (1531; James Clarke, 1953), p. 53.

[39] Lancelot Andrewes, *Works*, vol. III (Oxford, 1843), p. 26.

[40] *Cf.* Lk. 24:45–47. [41] Is. 53:4ff.

raised and highly exalted,[42] and become a light to the Gentiles.[43] Further, as the gospel centres on Christ's atonement, resurrection and proclamation (through his witnesses), the resurrection is seen to be indispensable. Paul kept on referring to it during his trials, not in order to provoke the Pharisees and Sadducees into argument, nor only to show that he was faithful to the Jewish tradition, but because the resurrection of Jesus was the beginning and pledge of the new creation, and so at the very heart of the gospel.

c. *The judges react to the prisoner (26:24–32)*

In the place of an orderly summing up to conclude the trial, Luke records a most unorthodox altercation between the bench and the dock. Its high drama may be captured best if it is set forth as a dialogue:

Festus to Paul (who *at this point interrupted Paul's defence* and *shouted*): '*You are out of your mind, Paul! Your great learning is driving you insane*' (24).

Paul to Festus (replying to him with great composure and dignity): '*I am not insane, most excellent Festus. . . . What I am saying is true and reasonable* (25). *The king is familiar with these things, and I can speak freely to him. I am convinced that none of this has escaped his notice, because it was not done in a corner*' (26), or 'has been no hole-and-corner business' (JBP, NEB).

Paul to Agrippa (boldly confronting the king, of whom he has just been speaking to Festus in the third person): '*King Agrippa, do you believe the prophets? I know you do*' (27).

> The court gasps. Has any prisoner ever before presumed to address His Royal Highness with such impertinence? Agrippa is unhorsed. Too embarrassed to give Paul a direct answer to a direct question, and too proud to allow him to dictate the topic of their dialogue, he takes evasive action with an ambiguous counter-question.

Agrippa to Paul: '*Do you think that in such a short time you can persuade me to be a Christian?*' (28).

> The court gasps again. That was a clever riposte, by which the king regained the initiative. A murmur went round the audience as people discussed exactly what he meant. It was 'variously represented as a trivial jest, a bitter sarcasm, a grave irony, a burst of anger, and an expression of sincere conviction'.[44] How would Paul respond?

[42] Is. 52:13; 53:12. [43] Is. 42:6; 49:6; *cf.* 60:3. [44] Alexander, II, p. 428.

Paul to Agrippa (in no doubt how he will interpret the king's words, and determined to exploit them for the gospel): *'Short time or long – I pray God that not only you but all who are listening to me today may become what I am, except for these chains'* (29).

With those words Paul lifted his hands and rattled the chains which bound him. He was sincere, the prisoner Paul. He really believed what he was talking about. He wanted everybody to be like him, including the king – everybody a Christian, but nobody a prisoner. You could not help admiring his integrity. There was also a finality about his statement, for his judges had nothing more to say. So *the king rose, and with him the governor and Bernice and those sitting with them* (30). *They left the room* (*i.e.* withdrew from the court) and began *talking with one another.*

The judges to each other (perplexed to know what to do): *'This man is not doing anything that deserves death or imprisonment'* (31).

They were all agreed about that. The prisoner may have been mad, but he was certainly not a criminal. Their private verdict of 'not guilty' was unanimous. Agrippa then had the last word, though what he said only increased the governor's dilemma.

Agrippa to Festus: *'This man could have been set free if he had not appealed to Caesar'* (32).

Agrippa was quite right in theory. But to acquit Paul now would be to short-circuit his appeal, and so to invade the Emperor's territory. No provincial judge would dare to do that.[45]

Exeunt

Conclusion

Looking back over these three chapters (24 – 26) and the three trials which they record, it seems that Luke intends to portray Paul in two guises, first and negatively as a defendant, then secondly and positively as a witness.

a. Paul as defendant

Behind all three trials, as we have noted, there lies the double allegation of the Jews that Paul had spoken or acted against Moses on the one hand and against Caesar on the other. But Paul vigorously denied both charges (25:8).

[45] Sherwin-White, p. 65; *cf.* Hemer, p. 132.

Before Felix Paul rejected the charge of sectarianism, and emphasized the continuity of his gospel with the Old Testament Scriptures. He served the God of their fathers with a good conscience.[46] He believed everything written in the law and prophets, and taught no more than they taught.[47] He cherished a firm hope in the fulfilment of God's promises about the Messiah.[48] Not apostasy but continuity summed up his attitude to Moses and the prophets.

Before Festus Paul rejected the charge of sedition. He had not been responsible for any breaches of the peace or of public order. So certain was he that he had done nothing against Caesar that he felt it necessary to appeal to Caesar in order to clear himself (25:8, 11). Not anarchy but loyalty summed up his attitude to Caesar.

Before Agrippa, no fresh charges were produced. Paul seems rather to have been responding to the unspoken question why the Jews were so anxious to get rid of him (25:24; 26:21). It had to do with his ministry to the Gentiles, to which however he was inescapably committed out of obedience to the vision and voice of Jesus.

Paul's three defences were successful. Neither Felix, nor Festus, nor Agrippa found him guilty. Instead, each indicated that he was innocent of the charges made against him.[49] Paul was not content with this, however. He went further. He proclaimed in court his threefold loyalty – to Moses and the prophets, to Caesar, and above all to Jesus Christ who met him on the Damascus road. He was a faithful Jew, a faithful Roman and a faithful Christian.

b. Paul as witness

Luke's purpose in describing the three court scenes was not just apologetic, but evangelistic. He wanted his readers to remember that Paul had been commissioned to be Christ's 'servant and witness' (26:16). During those two years of imprisonment, which had interrupted his missionary career, he must have felt very frustrated. But when opportunities for witness were given him, he seized them with confidence and courage. The main examples Luke gives are the private interview with Felix and the public confrontation with Agrippa. In both cases Paul was fearless.

Felix has been described as 'one of the worst of Roman officials'.[50] Mention has already been made of his cruelty, lust and greed. He seems to have had no moral scruples. But Paul was not afraid of him. Since he spoke to him about righteousness, self-control and future judgment, it is reasonable to assume both that he rebuked the governor for his sins, as courageously as John the

[46] Acts 24:14, 16; *cf.* 22:14; 23:1; *cf.* 2 Tim. 1:3.
[47] Acts 24:14; *cf.* 26:22–23, 27; 28:23; also 1 Cor. 15:3–4.
[48] Acts 24:15; *cf.* 23:6; 26:6–7; 28:20.
[49] *E.g.* Acts 24:22ff.; 25:25; 26:31–32.
[50] Rackham, p. 306.

Baptist had rebuked Herod Antipas,[51] and that he called on him to repent and believe in Jesus.

As for the trial before Agrippa, Paul was not overawed by the show of pomp and power which marked that occasion, or by the assembly of notable personages in court. 'See what an audience is gathered together for Paul!' exclaimed Chrysostom.[52] But Paul made no attempt to ingratiate himself with the authorities. He wanted the king's salvation, not his favour. So he did not stop with the story of his own conversion; he was concerned for Agrippa's conversion too. Three times, therefore, Luke has Paul repeating the elements of the gospel in the king's hearing. First, he summarized Christ's commission to him to bring people into his light, power, forgiveness and new community (18). Secondly, he described his obedience to the heavenly vision in terms of preaching that people should repent, turn to God and do good works (20). Thirdly, he detailed his continuing mission 'to this very day', which was to testify that, as the Scriptures had foretold, Christ died, rose and proclaimed the dawn of the new age (23). Each time Paul thus repeated the gospel in court, he was in fact preaching it to the court. Festus might call him mad, as some had said of Jesus,[53] but Paul knew that he was 'speaking the sober truth' (25, RSV). And when the apostle finally addressed the king directly, he was confident that he not only believed the prophets (27), but was also sufficiently familiar with the facts about Jesus (26) to be persuaded of his truth.

Thank God for Paul's courage! Kings and queens, governors and generals did not daunt him. Jesus had warned his disciples that they would be 'brought before kings and governors' on account of his name, and had promised that on such occasions he would give them 'words and wisdom'.[54] Jesus had also told Ananias (who had presumably passed the information on) that Paul was his 'chosen instrument' to carry his name 'before the Gentiles and their kings and before the people of Israel' (9:15). These predictions had come true, and Paul had not failed.

A note on the three accounts of Saul's conversion

It is surprising that, within the comparatively small compass of his story in Acts, Luke should have included three accounts of Saul's conversion – first as part of his unfolding narrative (9:1–19), secondly in Paul's words to a Jewish crowd in Jerusalem (22:5–16), and

[51] Mk. 6:17ff; Lk. 3:19–20. [52] Chrysostom, Homily LII, p. 308.
[53] Mk. 3:21; Jn. 10:20. [54] Lk. 21:12ff.

thirdly, again in Paul's words, before Agrippa (26:12–18). 'Luke employs such repetitions', wrote Haenchen, 'only when he considers something to be extraordinarily important and wishes to impress it unforgettably on the reader. That is the case here.'[55] If the repetition is explained by the importance of the topic, however, how shall we explain the variations between the three accounts?

They certainly indicate that Luke was no slavish literalist; he saw no need to ensure that each account was a precise, word-perfect replica of the others. On the contrary, since each time the story is told, the audience and therefore the purpose of telling it are different, this is naturally reflected in the detailed presentation. Our study of how a single author (Luke) tells the same story differently will help us to understand how the three synoptic evangelists (Matthew, Mark and Luke) could also tell their same stories differently. In this way Luke's practice throws light on 'redaction criticism', that is, on how the work of a redactor (editor) may be influenced by his theological purpose in writing.

The skeleton of the story of Saul's conversion is identical in all three accounts. All three tell us (i) that Saul had launched a campaign of violent persecution against the followers of Jesus, and that the high priest had sanctioned it; (ii) that on the road from Jerusalem to Damascus a bright light from heaven flashed round him and that he fell to the ground; (iii) that the voice of the risen Jesus addressed him with the question, 'Saul, Saul, why are you persecuting me?', that Saul asked, 'Who are you, Lord?' and that Jesus replied, 'I am Jesus whom you are persecuting'; and (iv) that Saul was told to 'get up', and that he received a subsequent commission, indicating that he had been chosen and appointed to be Jesus' witness to the Gentiles.

But some parts of the story vary widely, each adding details which the others lack. I will refer to the three accounts as successively A (9:1–19), B (22:5–16) and C (26:12–18). As to the place of conversion, A and B say 'near Damascus', C only 'on the road'. As to the time, B and C say 'about noon', while A has no time reference at all. In relation to the light, all three say that it came 'from heaven', but only C describes it as 'brighter than the sun'. In relation to the voice, only C says that it spoke in Aramaic and adds the proverb about kicking against the goads. Only B records Saul's second question, 'What shall I do, Lord?' A and B both say that he was blinded, but only A tells how he was healed, whereas C mentions neither the blinding nor the healing. A and B refer to Saul's baptism, but C does not.

These variations are all fairly trivial; their different details sup-

[55] Haenchen, p. 327.

plement and do not contradict each other. Two others, however, are regarded by some commentators as discrepancies. The first concerns the experience of Saul's companions. A says that they stood speechless, but C that they fell to the ground. B says that they saw the light, but A that they did not see anyone. A says that they heard the voice, but B that they did not hear (or understand) the voice of the one speaking to Paul. It is not difficult to harmonize these apparent discrepancies, however. Presumably the men first fell down with Saul, and then stood up with him also. As for the vision and the voice, they saw the light but not the person of Jesus (as Saul did), and they heard a noise without being able to make out any words.[56] Alternatively, as Chrysostom suggested long ago, 'They . . . heard the voice of Paul, but saw no person to whom he answered.'[57]

The second supposed discrepancy relates to Saul's commission and to the role of Ananias in it. Only A tells the full story of Ananias, how he had a vision of Jesus, was told to go to Saul, raised objections, was reassured that Saul was a chosen instrument to carry Christ's name before Gentiles as well as Jews, and to suffer for the same name, went to Straight Street, laid hands on Saul and welcomed him into the fellowship. B omits the whole conversation between Jesus and Ananias, but says that Ananias came to Saul, restored his sight and relayed to him Christ's commission to be a witness to all men. C, on the other hand, makes no reference to Ananias at all, but gives the impression that Christ commissioned Saul on the road before he entered Damascus, while the terms of the commission are much fuller, and seem to include not only the words of Ananias but also what Jesus said to Paul later in the temple when he fell into a trance (22:17ff.). Luke (or Paul himself) is evidently conflating what Jesus said on the road, to and through Ananias, and later in Jerusalem. If, as seems clear, it is his intention to bring different parts of Christ's commission together, and not to specify where or when each part was given, we must allow him this liberty and not accuse him of inaccuracy.

Finally, it is understandable that in his own narrative Luke should give a detailed account of the role of Ananias, and that Paul, addressing hostile Jews on the steps of Fortress Antonia, should emphasize that Ananias was 'a devout observer of the law and highly respected by all the Jews living there' (22:12). But standing before Agrippa and Festus, Paul omitted Ananias from his story altogether. For one thing, Ananias would not have been known to them. For another, Paul wanted to stress the immediacy of his encounter with Christ. Christ had commissioned him personally

[56] *Cf.* Dt. 4:12; Jn. 12:28–30. [57] Chrysostom, Homily XIX, p. 124.

and directly, and he had not been disobedient to this heavenly vision.

18. Rome at last!
27:1–28:31

Rome, the largest and most splendid of ancient cities, acted like a magnet to its peoples. For Rome was the capital and symbol of the Roman Empire, whose founding has been called 'the grandest political achievement ever accomplished'.[1] Rome presided magisterially over the whole known world. It treated its conquered subjects and their religions with comparatively humane tolerance; it somehow managed to integrate Romans, Greeks, Jews and 'Barbarians' into its social life; it protected the Greek culture and language; it inculcated respect for the rule of law; it gained a reputation for efficient administration and postal communication; and it facilitated travel by its ambitious system of roads and ports, policed by its legions and its navy, so preserving for the benefit of all the long-standing *pax romana*. No wonder people came from far and wide to see the great city from which these blessings emanated! Its buildings were famous – the three circuses and their daring chariot-races, the palaces of the Caesars, the tombs of the illustrious dead, the temples (especially the Pantheon erected by Augustus), the basilicas, theatres, baths and aqueducts, and particularly the bustling forum, the hub of the city's commercial, social, political and religious life.

So Paul longed to visit Rome. True, Seneca had called it 'a cesspool of iniquity' and Juvenal 'a filthy sewer',[2] and Paul had himself described this moral decadence near the beginning of his Letter to the Romans,[3] but all the more urgently did it need the gospel. True, John in the book of Revelation portrayed Rome as a persecuting monster and as 'the mother of prostitutes and of the abominations of the earth',[4] but he was writing at least

[1] S. Angus' article, 'Roman Empire', in *The International Standard Bible Encyclopaedia*, first edition 1915, ed. James Orr.

[2] Quoted by Farrar, p. 187. [3] Rom. 1:21ff. [4] Rev. 13:1ff.; 17:1ff.

twenty years later in Domitian's reign; Nero at the time of Paul's visit had not yet exposed his ugly cruelty. True again, Paul was 'a Hebrew of the Hebrews', who went from Tarsus to Jerusalem to study, but, having inherited Roman citizenship from his father, he must have dreamed since childhood of visiting the city for himself.

We do not know how, or how early, the gospel reached Rome and a church was planted there. Luke has told us that the Jerusalem crowd on the Day of Pentecost included some 'visitors from Rome' (2:10). Perhaps some of them were converted at that time and then took the gospel home with them. At all events, some twenty-five years later Paul was able to address to the church in Rome his great manifesto of the gospel, and when eventually he approached the city, some church members came out to meet him (28:15). If only Rome could be thoroughly evangelized, he must often have thought to himself, and its church enlarged, consolidated and fired with a missionary vision, what a radiating centre for the gospel it could become! 'To a Roman the city of Rome was the centre of the world; from the golden milestone in the Forum at Rome roads went out in all directions to all parts of the Empire.'[5]

So in the Letter to the Romans Paul expressed his anxiety to visit the city and its church. Near the beginning of his letter he told them that he was praying that now at last the way would open for him to visit them,[6] for he longed to see them in order that he might strengthen them and that he and they might be mutually encouraged.[7] Indeed, he had planned many times to visit them in order to reap a harvest among them, but had thus far been prevented.[8] So now he was eager to preach the gospel to them in Rome.[9] Then towards the end of his letter he reverted to the same theme. His ambition was to preach the gospel where Christ was not known, in order not to build on somebody else's foundation. That was why he had been hindered from coming to them.[10] But now that Greece had been evangelized, there was no more room for him in those regions. And since he had been longing for many years to see them, he was hoping and planning to visit them on his way to Spain.[11] First, he had to go to Jerusalem to deliver the collection he had been organizing. But once that task was accomplished, he was confident that he would come to them with Christ's full blessing.[12] So he urged them to join him in his struggle by praying for him both that his service to God's people in Jerusalem might be accepted and that afterwards by God's will he might

[5] From Floyd V. Filson's essay, 'The Journey Motif in Luke-Acts', in Gasque and Martin, p. 76.

[6] Rom. 1:10. [7] Rom. 1:11–12. [8] Rom. 1:13. [9] Rom. 1:15.

[10] Rom. 15:20–22. [11] Rom. 15: 23–24. [12] Rom. 15:25–29.

reach them with joy.[13] What Paul wrote to the Romans was extremely personal: 'I pray . . . I long . . . I am eager . . . I plan . . . I hope . . . I urge . . .'. And it was all self-consistent. His hoping, longing and eagerness became a plan and then a prayer, in which he asked them to join him. The thought of this visit meant so much to him that he must have shared it with Luke and other friends. Rome dominated his horizon.

In fact, Luke appears deliberately to arrange his material in both his Gospel and the Acts in order to highlight what Floyd V. Filson has called 'the journey motif'. Two-fifths of the Gospel describe Jesus' journey from Galilee to Jerusalem,[14] and the final one-third of Acts describes Paul's journey from Jerusalem to Rome (19:21 – 28:31). In this way Luke indicates that Jerusalem and its temple are not indispensable to the church. 'It would capture the essential geographical outlook of Luke to entitle the Gospel of Luke "From Galilee to Jerusalem" and the Book of Acts "From Jerusalem to Rome" ', for Jerusalem was the goal of Jesus' ministry, while Rome was the goal of Paul's.[15] Although the journeys of Jesus and Paul differed from one another in their ultimate direction and destination, they also resembled one another in their pattern, for both included a resolute determination, an arrest, a series of trials in Jewish and Roman courts, and even death and resurrection. For Paul's descent into the darkness and danger of the storm was a kind of grave, while his rescue from shipwreck and later springtime voyage to Rome were a kind of resurrection. Luke's 'highest apology for Paul' was to portray him as 'so conformed to the life of the Lord that even his sufferings and deliverance are parallel'.[16]

1. From Caesarea to Crete (27:1–12)

Many readers of Acts 27 have commented on the precision, accuracy and vividness of the narrative. The explanation is surely not that Luke borrowed from somebody else's firsthand description of a sea voyage and shipwreck (as some liberal scholars have unwarrantably suggested), but rather that he was himself present throughout Paul's journey from Jerusalem to Rome, as indicated by the fourth and final 'we-section' which runs from 27:1 to 28:16, and that he was writing a daily log of the ship's progress, on which he later drew. 'There is no such detailed record of the working of an ancient ship', wrote Thomas Walker, 'in the whole of classical literature.'[17]

The writer who has done most to vindicate Luke's accuracy in

[13] Rom. 15:30–32. [14] Lk. 9:51 – 19:44.
[15] Floyd V. Filson, in Gasque and Martin, p. 75.
[16] Rackham, pp. 477–478. [17] Walker, p. 543.

Acts 27 is James Smith of Jordanhill in Renfrewshire, Scotland, whose book *The Voyage and Shipwreck of St Paul* was published in 1848.[18] He was a soldier by profession, a keen yachtsman of thirty years' experience, an eminent amateur geologist and geographer, and a Fellow of the Royal Society. He lived successively in Gibraltar, Lisbon and Malta, and spent the winter of 1844–45 in Malta while investigating Paul's voyage. He was widely read, he familiarized himself with the weather patterns of the Mediterranean, and he made a study of navigation and seamanship in both the ancient and the modern worlds. His general conclusion was that Acts 27 was the work of an eyewitness who nevertheless was a landlubber, and not a professional seaman: 'no sailor would have written in a style so little like that of a sailor; no man not a sailor could have written a narrative of a sea voyage so consistent in all its parts, unless from actual observation.'[19]

When it was decided that we would sail for Italy, Paul and some other prisoners were handed over to a centurion named Julius, who belonged to the Imperial Regiment.

It is presumed (though not specifically stated) that they set sail from Caesarea, since it was there that Paul had been held in custody for two years and had been tried by Felix, Festus and Agrippa. Who were the *other prisoners* who were also on board? Ramsay suggests that they were 'in all probability already condemned to death, and were going to supply the perpetual demand which Rome made on the provinces for human victims to amuse the populace by their death in the arena.'[20]

No ship seems to have been available to transport the prisoners direct to Italy. In consequence, the voyage from Caesarea to Malta took place in two stages and in two ships, which came respectively from Adramyttium (2) and Alexandria (6).

a. A ship from Adramyttium (27:2–5)

We boarded a ship from Adramyttium about to sail for ports along the coast of the province of Asia, and we put out to sea. Aristarchus, a Macedonian from Thessalonica, was with us.

³The next day we landed at Sidon; and Julius, in kindness to Paul, allowed him to go to his friends so they might provide for his needs. ⁴From there we put out to sea again and passed to the lee of Cyprus because the winds were against us. ⁵When we had sailed across the open sea off the coast of Cilicia and Pamphylia, we landed at Myra in Lycia.

[18] I shall be quoting from the 4th edition of 1880, revised and corrected by Walter E. Smith, and published by Longmans.

[19] *Ibid.*, p. xlvi. [20] Ramsay, *St Paul*, p. 314.

Adramyttium was situated on the north-east shore of the Aegean Sea, not far south of Troas. This ship will have been a coastal vessel on its way back to its home port. But how is it that Luke and Aristarchus (who had travelled with Paul to Jerusalem, 20:4) were permitted to accompany Paul? Ramsay makes the plausible suggestion that 'they must have gone as his slaves'.[21] This may have enhanced Paul's importance in the centurion's eyes and may partly account for the respect in which he was held. On the other hand, Paul was later to refer to Aristarchus as 'my fellow-prisoner'.[22]

Their first port of call was Sidon. It will have been a trading stop for the vessel, but for Paul a valuable opportunity for a few hours' fellowship with Christian friends (3). Since the prevailing winds must have been westerly,[23] to pass 'under the lee of Cyprus' meant to sail to the north of it (4). This also explains how they sailed across open sea and off the coasts of Cilicia (where Paul's home town of Tarsus was situated) and Pamphylia (where they had landed on the first missionary journey), and arrived at Myra (5), which is where they changed ships. According to the Western text, the journey so far had taken a fortnight.

b. A ship from Alexandria (27:6–12)

There the centurion found an Alexandrian ship sailing for Italy and put us on board. 7We made slow headway for many days and had difficulty arriving off Cnidus. When the wind did not allow us to hold our course, we sailed to the lee of Crete, opposite Salmone. 8We moved along the coast with difficulty and came to a place called Fair Havens, near the town of Lasea.

9Much time had been lost, and sailing had already become dangerous because by now it was after the Fast. So Paul warned them, 10'Men, I can see that our voyage is going to be disastrous and bring great loss to ship and cargo, and to our own lives also.' 11But the centurion, instead of listening to what Paul said, followed the advice of the pilot and of the owner of the ship. 12Since the harbour was unsuitable to winter in, the majority decided that we should sail on, hoping to reach Phoenix and winter there. This was a harbour in Crete, facing both south-west and north-west.

It was now that Julius the centurion (who, as Luke's tale unfolds, wins our admiration for his kindness and common sense) found what he had been looking for earlier, namely a ship sailing for Italy. It was carrying a cargo of grain (see verse 38) and came from Alexandria, Egypt being Rome's main granary. Sailing between the mainland and the island of Rhodes, but very slowly because of a contrary wind, they arrived off Cnidus, which is located at the

[21] *Ibid.*, p. 316. [22] Col. 4:10. [23] Smith, p. 68.

south-west tip of Asia Minor. But there, instead of continuing west across the lower end of the Aegean Sea, the wind forced them almost due south towards Crete, and indeed a north-westerly wind 'is precisely the wind which might have been expected in those seas towards the end of summer'.[24] Rounding Cape Salmone, they hugged Crete's south coast until they reached Fair Havens. It was clear to everybody that they could not go on to complete their voyage to Italy; they would have to winter somewhere. The only question was whether they should lay up in Fair Havens or seek a better harbour further west. The adverse weather conditions had occasioned a serious delay. Already the Day of Atonement was past, which according to Ramsay fell on October 5 in AD 59.[25] So they had entered the dangerous season for sailing, which always had to cease by the beginning of November. Paul, who had had a lot of experience of the Mediterranean Sea, warned them that to sail any further would bring loss to cargo, ship and life (10). But the pilot and the ship-owner thought differently, and the centurion agreed with them (11) on the ground that Fair Havens was not a sufficiently protected harbour to winter in. So they decided to sail on a further forty miles to Phoenix, although there is some dispute whether this is to be identified with Lutro (which is open to the east) or Phineka (which faces west). The natural translation of the end of verse 12 is 'facing both south-west and north-west' (NIV) which favours Phineka, although Smith argued for Lutro by translating 'in the same direction as' the south-west and north-west winds, *i.e.* east![26]

2. Storm at sea (27:13–20)

When a gentle south wind began to blow, they thought they had obtained what they wanted; so they weighed anchor and sailed along the shore of Crete. [14]Before very long, a wind of hurricane force, called the 'north-easter', swept down from the island. [15]The ship was caught by the storm and could not head into the wind; so we gave way to it and were driven along. [16]As we passed to the lee of a small island called Cauda, we were hardly able to make the lifeboat secure. [17]When the men had hoisted it aboard, they passed ropes under the ship itself to hold it together. Fearing that they would run aground on the sand-bars of Syrtis, they lowered the sea anchor and let the ship be driven along. [18]We took such a violent battering from the storm that the next day they began to throw the cargo overboard. [19]On the third day, they threw the ship's tackle

[24] *Ibid.*, p. 76. [25] Ramsay, *St Paul*, p. 322.
[26] Smith, p. 88. See also Hemer, p. 139.

overboard with their own hands. [20]*When neither sun nor stars appeared for many days and the storm continued raging, we finally gave up all hope of being saved.*

The gentle southerly breeze which arose deceived them into thinking that they could manage another forty miles (13). But *a wind of hurricane force* (*typhōnikos*, 'typhonic'), called the 'north-easter' (originally '*Eurakylōn*, a hybrid compound of *Euros*, the east wind, and Latin *Aquilo*, the north wind'),[27] swept down from the Cretan mountains (14), forcing the ship to 'scud before it' (15).[28]

Already the vessel was in great danger, for once blown out of the lee of Crete, there were no more harbours, only the open sea. It is fascinating to read the five precautionary measures which the crew now took in their desperate attempt to save their ship. First, briefly exploiting what little shelter Cauda (or Clauda) Island could offer them, they just managed to haul on board their lifeboat or dinghy (16). Actually, Luke writes that 'we' did it, because he lent a hand himself, though only with great difficulty, he adds, 'probably remembering his blisters!'[29] Secondly, they 'frapped' the vessel, either by passing cables under her hull to hold her timbers together, or by lashing her stern and bow together above deck to prevent her from having her back broken (17a).[30] Thirdly, fearing the Syrtis sandbanks, which, although many miles south off the Libyan coast, were dreaded by all Mediterranean sailors, they lowered either 'the mainsail' (NEB) or more probably 'the sea anchor' to act as a brake as they drifted onwards (17b). Fourthly, on the following day, as the relentless battering of the storm continued, they jettisoned some of the cargo (18). Fifthly, on the third day of the tempest, they threw overboard as many parts of the ship's tackle or equipment as could be spared (19). Then finally, after many days (eleven more, to be precise) of raging storm, with neither sun nor stars to guide them, and of course in those days no compass or sextant either, the whole ship's company seems to have given up all hope of being saved. But it was in that crisis of despair that Paul stepped forward with a word of encouragement.

3. Paul's three interventions (27:21–38)

So far in the Acts Luke has depicted Paul as the apostle to the Gentiles, the pioneer of the three missionary expeditions, the prisoner, and the defendant. Now, however, he portrays him in a different light. He is no longer an honoured apostle, but an ordinary man among men, a lonely Christian (apart from Luke himself

[27] Metzger, p. 497. [28] Smith, p. 98. [29] Bruce, *English*, p. 509.
[30] See Cadbury's note xxviii in *BC*, V, pp. 345–354.

and Aristarchus) among nearly three hundred non-Christians, who were either soldiers or prisoners or perhaps merchants or crew. Yet Paul's God-given leadership gifts clearly emerge. 'It is quite certain', writes William Barclay, 'that Paul was the most experienced traveller on board that ship.'[31] Even Haenchen, who scornfully dismisses Luke's portrait of him as 'only . . . a mighty superman',[32] concedes that Luke fails to draw our attention adequately to Paul's expertise as a seasoned seafarer. He catalogues the apostle's eleven voyages on the Mediterranean *before* he set sail for Rome and calculates (although he leaves us to do the addition sum!) that Paul had travelled at least 3,500 miles by sea.[33] Yet it was more than mature experience at sea which made Paul stand out as a leader on board ship; it was his steadfast Christian faith and character.

Paul has already spoken once, when he expressed his view about where the ship should winter, but his warning was overridden (9–12). Now Luke relates his three further interventions, in each of which he issues a clear summons to the ship's company.

a. The call to keep up their courage (27:21–26)

After the men had gone a long time without food, Paul stood up before them and said: 'Men, you should have taken my advice not to sail from Crete; then you would have spared yourselves this damage and loss. [22]*But now I urge you to keep up your courage, because not one of you will be lost; only the ship will be destroyed.* [23]*Last night an angel of the God whose I am and whom I serve stood beside me* [24]*and said, "Do not be afraid, Paul. You must stand trial before Caesar; and God has graciously given you the lives of all who sail with you."* [25]*So keep up your courage, men, for I have faith in God that it will happen just as he told me.* [26]*Nevertheless, we must run aground on some island.'*

I am not sure that we need interpret Paul's 'you should have taken my advice' as a rather cheap way of scoring a point off them (21). After all, his minority stand had been the correct one. Perhaps they would be more respectful of his viewpoint in the future. At all events, he now had absolute confidence in what he had to say. Twice he urged them to keep up their courage (22, 25). On what ground? Because none of them, he said, but only the ship, would be lost (22). How could he be so certain? Because the previous night an angel of the God to whom he belonged, and whom he served, had stood beside him (23), had told him not to be afraid, had promised that he must without fail stand trial before Caesar, and had added that God would give him (in answer to his prayers?) the lives of all his fellow passengers (24). These divine promises

[31] Barclay, p. 201. [32] Haenchen, p. 716. [33] *Ibid.*, pp. 702–703.

were the foundation of Paul's summons to everybody to maintain their courage. For he believed in God, in his character and covenant, and was convinced that he would keep his promises (25), even though first the ship would have to run aground on some island (26).

b. The call to stay together (27:27–32)

On the fourteenth night we were still being driven across the Adriatic Sea, when about midnight the sailors sensed they were approaching land.
28They took soundings and found that the water was one hundred and twenty feet deep. A short time later they took soundings again and found it was ninety feet deep.
29Fearing that we would be dashed against the rocks, they dropped four anchors from the stern and prayed for daylight.
30In an attempt to escape from the ship, the sailors let the lifeboat down into the sea, pretending they were going to lower some anchors from the bow.
31Then Paul said to the centurion and the soldiers, 'Unless these men stay with the ship, you cannot be saved.'
32So the soldiers cut the ropes that held the lifeboat and let it fall away.

It was now a fortnight since the ship had been swept from the shelter of Crete and been drifting helplessly across the Adriatic (a word which in popular ancient usage covered the whole of the east central section of the Mediterranean). But on the fourteenth night at about midnight the sailors sensed the approach of land (27), probably because they could hear waves breaking on the shore. Calculating the direction and speed of the drifting vessel (a necessarily imprecise procedure), Smith concluded that 'a ship starting late in the evening from Clauda would, by midnight on the fourteenth, be less than three miles from the entrance of St Paul's Bay', Malta.[34] So the sailors took soundings, finding first one hundred and twenty fathoms, then ninety (28). Fearing rocks or a reef, they dropped four anchors from the stern, to make sure that they would hold, and prayed for dawn (29). It was now, Luke tells us, that the sailors made an attempt to escape. Pretending that they wanted to drop more anchors, this time from the bow, they launched the lifeboat (30). But Paul somehow knew what was happening, 'either by a natural sagacity, by nautical experience or by special revelation',[35] and said to Julius and his men: '*Unless these men stay with the ship, you cannot be saved*' (31). God's promise to give him the lives of the whole ship's company clearly presupposed that they would stay together. So the soldiers cut the lifeboat free and let it go (32).

[34] Smith, p. 128. [35] Alexander, II, p. 460.

c. The call to take food (27:33–38)

Just before dawn Paul urged them all to eat. 'For the last fourteen days,' he said, 'you have been in constant suspense and have gone without food – you haven't eaten anything. [34]Now I urge you to take some food. You need it to survive. Not one of you will lose a single hair from his head.' [35]After he said this, he took some bread and gave thanks to God in front of them all. Then he broke it and began to eat. [36]They were all encouraged and ate some food themselves. [37]Altogether there were 276 of us on board. [38]When they had eaten as much as they wanted, they lightened the ship by throwing the grain into the sea.

Dawn was about to break when Paul made his third intervention, urging everybody to eat because they had not done so for a fortnight, either because of the *constant suspense* (33), or because of seasickness, or because the food supplies had been saturated, or because cooking had been impossible in the gale. But now he pressed them to eat in order to survive, for, he added, seemingly with an allusion to the teaching of Jesus,[36] none of them would lose even a single hair (34). With that he set them an example, gave thanks publicly for the food, and began to eat. Because of the sequence that he took bread, gave thanks, broke it and ate, some have depicted this as a Eucharist. But neither the occasion nor the gathering of unbelieving soldiers, sailors and prisoners, was appropriate for this. It was surely an ordinary meal, although the food was consecrated by thanksgiving.[37] As a result, the rest of the ship's company were *encouraged* (it is the same word as in verses 22 and 25) and followed his example (36). It is at this point that Luke mentions the number of people on board as 276 (37); had they perhaps been counted for the sake of the distribution of food? Having eaten as much as they wanted, the rest of the grain cargo was jettisoned (38).

Here then are aspects of Paul's character which endear him to us as an integrated Christian, who combined spirituality with sanity, and faith with works. He believed that God would keep his promises and had the courage to say grace in the presence of a crowd of hard-bitten pagans. But his trust and godliness did not stop him seeing either that the ship should not take risks with the onset of winter, or that the sailors must not be allowed to escape, or that the hungry crew and passengers had to eat to survive, or (later) that he needed to gather wood to keep the beach fire burning. What a man! He was a man of God and of action, a man of the Spirit and of common sense.

[36] Lk. 21:18; *cf.* Mt. 10:30. [37] 1 Tim. 4:3–5.

4. Shipwreck on Malta (27:39 – 28:10)

a. The escape from the sea (27:39–44)

When daylight came, they did not recognise the land, but they saw a bay with a sandy beach, where they decided to run the ship aground if they could. [40]Cutting loose the anchors, they left them in the sea and at the same time untied the ropes that held the rudders. Then they hoisted the foresail to the wind and made for the beach. [41]But the ship struck a sand-bar and ran aground. The bow stuck fast and would not move, and the stern was broken to pieces by the pounding of the surf.

[42]The soldiers planned to kill the prisoners to prevent any of them from swimming away and escaping. [43]But the centurion wanted to spare Paul's life and kept them from carrying out their plan. He ordered those who could swim to jump overboard first and get to land. [44]The rest were to get there on planks or on pieces of the ship. In this way everyone reached land in safety.

Although, even when it was light, the crew did not recognize the island, they later found that it was Malta (28:1), and James Smith was convinced that the place of the shipwreck was the traditional site which is known as St Paul's Bay, on the island's north-east coast. Certainly the combination of rocks (29), which he identified as the low rocky point of Koura, the 'bay with a sandy beach' (39), and the 'sand-bar' (41) or 'shoal' (RSV), literally a 'place of two seas', which he believed was the mud-bottomed creek between the islet of Salmonetta and the mainland, led him to say 'how perfectly these features still distinguish the coast'.[38] Of course during the subsequent nineteen centuries bays, beaches, sandbanks and even rocks have probably changed their contours; nevertheless, there seems no reason to question the identification.

The sailors 'slipped the anchors . . . loosened the lashings of the steering-paddles', which in ancient vessels did duty for rudders, 'set the foresail to the wind, and let her drive to the beach' (40, NEB). But the ship struck sand or mud, which was probably submerged, and while the bow was immovable, the surf broke the stern to pieces (41). When the soldiers, acting without orders, intended to kill the prisoners (42), knowing that by Roman law if anyone escaped they would themselves be liable to bear his punishment, the centurion stopped them. He then ordered the swimmers to jump overboard first (43), while the rest were to use planks or pieces of wreckage with which to get ashore. 'So it came true', wrote J. B. Phillips, probably to express the fulfilment of

[38] Smith, p. 141.

God's purpose and promise, 'that everyone reached the shore in safety' (44).

b. The bonfire on the beach (28:1–6)

Once safely on shore, we found out that the island was called Malta. [2]The islanders showed us unusual kindness. They built a fire and welcomed us all because it was raining and cold. [3]Paul gathered a pile of brushwood and, as he put it on the fire, a viper, driven out by the heat, fastened itself on his hand. [4]When the islanders saw the snake hanging from his hand, they said to each other, 'This man must be a murderer; for though he escaped from the sea, justice has not allowed him to live.' [5]But Paul shook the snake off into the fire and suffered no ill effects. [6]The people expected him to swell up or suddenly fall dead, but after waiting a long time and seeing nothing unusual happen to him, they changed their minds and said he was a god.

The noun translated 'islanders' in verses 2 and 4 is *barbaroi*, but the AV rendering 'barbarous people' and 'barbarians' is incorrect. The Greeks used the word for all foreigners who spoke (instead of Greek) their own native language. The *unusual kindness* they showed the shipwrecked seafarers, by building a fire in the cold and rain of the early morning (2), indicates that they were the opposite of uncouth savages. Paul played his part by gathering 'a large bundle of sticks', out of which there slithered a viper, dislodged by the heat. Luke does not explicitly say that Paul was bitten, although perhaps his statements that the snake *fastened itself on his hand* (3) and was *hanging from his hand* (4) are meant to imply this. Certainly the islanders took it for granted that he had been bitten. They then jumped to the conclusion that he was a murderer who, having escaped from drowning, was now being pursued and about to be poisoned by the goddess *Dikē*, the personification of justice and revenge. But as they watched, Paul shook the viper into the fire and neither swelled up nor dropped down dead. Luke is obviously amused that they should immediately change their minds and call him a god. So fickle is the crowd that in Lystra Paul was first worshipped, then stoned (14:11–19), while on Malta he was first called a murderer, then a god. But the truth was at neither extreme. Instead of being drowned or poisoned by *Dikē*, Paul had actually been protected from both fates by Jesus.[39]

c. The healings on the island (28:7–10)

There was an estate near by that belonged to Publius, the chief official of the island. He welcomed us to his home and for three

[39] Lk. 10:19; *cf.* Mk. 16:18.

days entertained us hospitably. [8]*His father was sick in bed, suffering from fever and dysentery. Paul went in to see him and, after prayer, placed his hands on him and healed him.* [9]*When this had happened, the rest of the sick on the island came and were cured.* [10]*They honoured us in many ways and when we were ready to sail, they furnished us with the supplies we needed.*

The land near the beach belonged to a man named Publius whom Luke calls the island's *prōtos*, its 'first' or most prominent person, perhaps its 'chief official' (NIV), 'chief magistrate' (NEB) or even 'governor' (JBP). He opened his home to 'us', Luke says, presumably a selection of the shipwrecked men, not all 276 of them(!), and for three days was lavish in his hospitality (7). While in the house, they became aware that Publius' father was also there, sick in bed. Luke describes his complaint as 'fever and dysentery', which Dr Longenecker tentatively diagnoses as 'Malta fever', which, he adds, 'was long common in Malta, Gibraltar and other Mediterranean locales'. The micro-organism, which causes it, was apparently identified in 1887 and traced to the milk of Maltese goats. Although a vaccine has been developed, the fever lasts on average for four months and sometimes persists even for two or three years.[40] Not in the case of Publius' father, however. For through prayer and the laying-on of hands Paul healed him instantly (8). As the news spread, all the island's sick *came and were cured* (9). Although Luke here employs a different verb (*therapeuō*), which was used for medical treatment, and which he himself will have used for his work as a doctor, there is no hint in his text that he means us to think of Publius' father's healing as miraculous and of the other healings as medical. Supernatural cures were part of the apostle's ministry,[41] and the gratitude of the islanders was expressed in giving gifts and providing supplies (10).

5. Arrival in Rome (28:11–16)

After three months we put out to sea in a ship that had wintered in the island. It was an Alexandrian ship with the figurehead of the twin gods Castor and Pollux. [12]*We put in at Syracuse and stayed there three days.* [13]*From there we set sail and arrived at Rhegium. The next day the south wind came up, and on the following day we reached Puteoli.* [14]*There we found some brothers who invited us to spend a week with them. And so we came to Rome.* [15]*The brothers there had heard that we were coming, and they travelled as far as the Forum of Appius and the Three Taverns to meet us. At the sight of these men Paul thanked God and was encouraged.*

[40] Longenecker, *Acts*, p. 565. [41] *Cf.* 2 Cor. 12:12.

[16]*When we got to Rome, Paul was allowed to live by himself, with a soldier to guard him.*

The shipwrecked men spent the three months of winter on the island, perhaps from mid-November to mid-February. By then navigation would be beginning again, and they were ready to board their third ship, another Alexandrian vessel (*cf.* 27:6), which had itself wintered in one of Malta's safe harbours. Its carved and painted figurehead was a representation of the *Dioskouroi*, that is, 'the Twin Brothers' (RSV) or 'the heavenly twins' (JBP), namely *Castor and Pollux* (11), who in Graeco-Roman mythology were the sons of Jupiter (Zeus), the gods of navigation and patrons of seafarers.

Luke makes use of his log again and plots the remaining part of the journey to Rome, by sea and land, in four stages.

First, they sailed from Malta in a north-easterly direction to Syracuse, the capital of Sicily, where they stayed three days (12).

Secondly, they sailed further north and put in at Rhegium on the 'toe' of Italy (13a). The phrase 'made a circuit' (RSV) or 'sailed round' (NEB) probably means that the winds made a zigzag course or 'tacking' necessary.

Thirdly, the next day they sailed on with the benefit of a southerly wind, and made such excellent progress that by the following day they had travelled the approximately two hundred miles to Puteoli, which is on the Gulf of Naples (13). Here they stayed a week with some Christian brothers and sisters, possibly while Julius was awaiting final instructions regarding his prisoners.

The fourth lap of the journey was by land, not sea. After only a few miles they will have joined the famous Appian Way which led straight north to Rome, and which Richard Longenecker has called 'the oldest, straightest and most perfectly made of all the Roman roads'.[42] Christians in Rome had heard of their coming, however, and a delegation set out to meet Paul and his party. Some of them travelled the thirty and more miles to the Three Taverns, while others persevered a further ten miles to the market town called the Forum of Appius. Being Roman place names, NEB is right to spell them *Tres Tabernae* and *Appii Forum*. It must have been an emotional experience for Paul to meet personally the first residents in the city of his dreams and the first members of the church to which he had addressed his great theological and ethical treatise. It is not surprising that at the sight of them 'he thanked God and took courage' (15b, RSV). They then escorted him back along the Appian Way by which they had come. On arrival, Luke tells us that Paul was accorded *custodia militaris* which permitted him to live in his own lodgings, while remaining under the surveil-

[42] Longenecker, *Acts*, p. 568.

lance of a Roman soldier, to whom he was chained by the right wrist (16). The Western text inserts before this, however, that 'the centurion delivered the prisoners to the *stratopedarch*',[43] which BAGD translates 'military commander, commandant of a camp'. There has been much discussion as to who this was. It used to be thought that the *stratopedarchos* was the Prefect (commander) of the Pretorian (imperial) Guard, who had responsibility for provincial prisoners and was at that time Afranius Burrus. But according to Sherwin-White, 'the most likely identification . . . is . . . with the officer known as *princeps castrorum*, the head administrator of the *officium* of the Pretorian Guard', for 'this official is the person most likely to be in executive control of prisoners awaiting trial at Rome . . .'.[44]

6. The gospel for Jews and Gentiles (28:17–31)

a. *Paul addresses Jews (28:17–23)*

Three days later he called together the leaders of the Jews. When they had assembled, Paul said to them: 'My brothers, although I have done nothing against our people or against the customs of our ancestors, I was arrested in Jerusalem and handed over to the Romans. [18]*They examined me and wanted to release me, because I was not guilty of any crime deserving death.* [19]*But when the Jews objected, I was compelled to appeal to Caesar – not that I had any charge to bring against my own people.* [20]*For this reason I have asked to see you and talk with you. It is because of the hope of Israel that I am bound with this chain.'*

[21]*They replied, 'We have not received any letters from Judea concerning you, and none of the brothers who have come from there has reported or said anything bad about you.* [22]*But we want to hear what your views are, for we know that people everywhere are talking against this sect.'*

[23]*They arranged to meet Paul on a certain day, and came in even larger numbers to the place where he was staying. From morning till evening he explained and declared to them the kingdom of God and tried to convince them about Jesus from the Law of Moses and from the Prophets.*

In accordance with his principle that the gospel is God's power for salvation 'first for the Jew, then for the Gentile',[45] even in the Gentile capital of the world Paul addressed himself to Jews first. Three days after his arrival (he gave himself no longer to recover from his arduous journey) he summoned the Jewish leaders to

[43] Metzger, p. 501 [44] Sherwin-White, p. 110. [45] Rom. 1:16

meet him. He emphasized three points. First, he had himself done nothing against the Jewish people ('our people', he called them) or their ancestral customs ('our customs', he said). Secondly, after being arrested and handed over to the Romans (17), and examined by them, they had wanted to set him free because they could find nothing against him deserving death (18). Thirdly, it was because the Jews had objected to his release that he had felt compelled to appeal to Caesar, although he had nothing against his own people (19). Thus, Paul had done nothing against the Jews, the Romans had nothing against him, and he had nothing (*i.e.* no charge) against the Jews. It was in order to clarify these points that he had asked to see them. He was in every way a loyal Jew; indeed it was because of the hope of Israel, Israel's Messianic expectation fulfilled in Jesus, that he was a prisoner (20).

In reply, the Jewish leaders declared, surprisingly enough, both that no official letters about him had reached them from Judea and that no visiting Jews had said anything bad about him (21). They wanted to learn more about his views, however, because they knew that the Nazarene 'sect' was everywhere spoken against (22).

On the appointed day the Jews assembled in Paul's lodgings in even greater numbers. Then all day long, from morning till evening, Paul concentrated on two things. First, he unfolded by explanation and testimony the character and coming of God's kingdom (did he contrast it with Caesar's?), and secondly he tried to convince them about Jesus out of the Scriptures (23). This is likely to mean, as on previous occasions when he addressed Jewish people, that Paul argued for the necessary identification of the historical Jesus with the biblical Christ.

b. Paul turns to the Gentiles (28:24–28)

Some were convinced by what he said, but others would not believe.
25They disagreed among themselves and began to leave after Paul
had made this final statement: 'The Holy Spirit spoke the truth to your forefathers when he said through Isaiah the prophet:

26' "Go to this people and say,
'You will be ever hearing but never understanding;
you will be ever seeing but never perceiving.'
27For this people's heart has become calloused;
they hardly hear with their ears,
and they have closed their eyes.
Otherwise they might see with their eyes,
hear with their ears,
understand with their hearts
and turn, and I would heal them."

[28]*'Therefore I want you to know that God's salvation has been sent to the Gentiles, and they will listen!'*

Paul's day-long persuasive exposition split his audience in two, as so many times previously. Some were convinced by his reasoning; others 'remained sceptical' (NEB) or, since a deliberate intention seems to be indicated, 'refused to believe' (24). In other words, they were deeply divided among themselves and began to go home – but only after Paul's summing-up, whose note of solemn finality no-one could miss. He boldly applied to them words which the Holy Spirit had spoken to their forefathers in Isaiah's day,[46] and which Jesus had quoted of his unbelieving contemporaries,[47] as also had John.[48] This quotation draws a distinction between hearing and understanding, seeing and perceiving (26), and goes on to attribute people's non-comprehension to their deliberately hard hearts, deaf ears and closed eyes, for otherwise they might see, hear, understand, turn and be saved (27). 'In this fearful process', wrote J. A. Alexander, 'there are three distinguishable agencies expressly or implicitly described, the ministerial agency of the prophet, the judicial agency of God, and the suicidal agency of the people themselves.' In other words, if we ask why people do not understand and turn to God, their unbelief could be attributed (in fact, is attributed in Scripture) now to the evangelist's preaching, now to the judgment of God, and now to the obstinacy of the people. Alexander goes on to point out that in the Isaiah verses the first of these is the most prominent, in John 12:40 the second, and in the Matthew and Mark passages, as here in Acts 28, the third.[49] Although our mind finds it hard to reconcile these perspectives with each other, since it is difficult to ascribe the same situation to three agencies simultaneously, yet all three are true and must be held fast with equal tenacity.

Because of the Jews' deliberate rejection of the gospel, Paul wants them to know that God's salvation has been sent to the Gentiles, and that they will listen with open ears, whereas the Jews have closed theirs. Three times before, stubborn Jewish opposition has led Paul to turn to the Gentiles – in Pisidian Antioch (13:46), in Corinth (18:6), and in Ephesus (19:8–9). Now for the fourth time, in the world's capital city, and in a yet more decisive manner, he does it again (28). Verse 29 belongs to the Western text and says that the Jews then left, 'arguing hotly between themselves'.[50]

c. *Paul welcomes all who visit him (28:30–31)*

For two whole years Paul stayed there in his own rented house and

[46] Is. 6:9–10. [47] Mt. 13:14–15; Mk. 4:11–12. [48] Jn. 12:37ff.
[49] Alexander, II, p. 493. [50] JB, verse 29, note i.

welcomed all who came to see him. [31]*Boldly and without hindrance he preached the kingdom of God and taught about the Lord Jesus Christ.*

In these last two verses of the Acts there is no mention of either Jews or Gentiles, as there has been in the previous paragraphs. The most natural explanation of this is that the 'all' who came to see Paul included both. The terrible verses from Isaiah 6 meant neither that no Jews were converted, nor that those Jews who believed would be rejected. Nevertheless, the emphasis of Luke's conclusion is on the Gentiles who came to Paul, who were symbols and precursors of the vast, hungry Gentile world outside. *They will listen!* Paul had predicted (29). And listen they did. For two whole years they came to him and listened to him, as he stayed on in Rome, in his own rented accommodation, or 'at his own expense' (RSV, NEB). Probably he resumed his tent-making, in order to pay his way. But when visitors came to see him, he laid aside his manual labour for evangelism. And what did he talk to them about? He again spoke about 'the kingdom of God' and 'the Lord Jesus Christ' (as in verse 23), especially in relation to each other. He 'preached' the former and 'taught' the latter, Luke says. This seems to mean that he proclaimed the good news of the breaking into human history of God's gracious rule through Christ and that he linked this with 'the facts about the Lord Jesus Christ' (NEB), which he also taught, the facts of his birth and life, words and works, death and resurrection, exaltation and gift of the Spirit. It was through these saving events that the kingdom of God had dawned. Probably, however, the distinction between 'preaching' and 'teaching' has been over-pressed, for all Paul's preaching had a doctrinal content, while all his teaching had an evangelistic purpose.

The final words of the book (which the NIV misplaces) are the adverbial expression *meta pasēs parrēsias*, 'with all boldness', and the adverb *akōlutōs*, 'without hindrance'. *Parrēsia* has been a characteristic word of Acts ever since the Twelve exhibited boldness and prayed for more (4:13, 31). And Paul had asked the Ephesians to pray that his ministry might bear the same mark.[51] *Parrēsia* denotes speech which is candid (with no concealment of truth), clear (with no obscurity of expression) and confident (with no fear of consequences). 'Without hindrance' means that, although the military surveillance continued, there was no ban by the authorities on Paul's speaking. Though his hand was still bound, his mouth was open for Jesus Christ. Though he was chained, the Word of God was not.[52] Together Luke's two adverbs describe the freedom which the gospel enjoyed, having neither internal nor external

[51] Eph. 6:19–20. [52] *Cf.* 2 Tim. 2:9.

restraint. In consequence, we may be sure that many were converted, including the runaway slave Onesimus.[53]

Conclusion: The providence of God

Many readers of Acts, who have no problem with chapter 28 (Paul's arrival and ministry in Rome), find great difficulty in chapter 27 (the voyage, the storm and the shipwreck). Why on earth did Luke devote so much of his precious space to this graphic, but seemingly unedifying, story? To be sure, his reputation as an accurate chronicler is enhanced by it, and his portraiture of Paul in a crisis situation is helpful. But still the length of the narrative seems out of proportion to its value.

It is this feeling which has prompted some students to look in the story for deeper, spiritual meanings. One such was August van Ryn, who was born in the Netherlands in 1890 but became an American preacher and teacher. In his *Acts of the Apostles: The Unfinished Work of Christ*[54] he developed an elaborate allegory. The ship is the visible church, whose history has been a voyage from 'its pristine perfection' in Jerusalem at Pentecost, through 'much contrary wind and violent storms' (persecution and false doctrine) to 'its moral and spiritual wreck in Rome', that is, in the Roman Catholic Church. Those on board are a mixed multitude. Some resemble the centurion, who believed the captain and owner of the ship (church leaders) 'more than those things which were spoken by Paul', while others, even in the midst of darkness, storm and fear, listen to Paul's teaching and are saved. These also throw the wheat into the sea, casting their bread on the waters, that is, broadcasting gospel seed far and wide. The crew struggle to undergird the ship (well-meaning people who try to hold the church together by union schemes). But they cannot prevent it from being wrecked, from being broken into a thousand fragments. The allegory is far-fetched, van Ryn admitted, but added 'personally I like this far-fetchedness'. I hope my readers do not, however. Unprincipled allegorizations bring Scripture into disrepute, and cause confusion, not enlightenment.

What, then, is the major lesson we are intended to learn from Acts 27 and 28? It concerns the providence of God, who 'works out everything in conformity with the purpose of his will',[55] declares that 'no wisdom, no insight, no plan . . . can succeed against the Lord',[56] and engineers even evil 'for the good of those

[53] Phm. 10.

[54] *Acts of the Apostles: The Unfinished Work of Christ* by August van Ryn (Loixeaux Brothers, New York, 1961).

[55] Eph. 1:11.

[56] Pr. 21:30; *cf.* Is. 8:10; 54:17.

who love him'.[57] This providential activity of God is seen in these chapters in two complementary ways, first in bringing Paul to Rome, his desired goal, and secondly in bringing him there as a prisoner, his undesired condition. It was an unexpected combination of circumstances: what lay behind it?

First, Luke intends us to marvel with him over the safe conduct of Paul to Rome. It is not so much that Paul had said 'I must visit Rome' (19:21), as that Jesus had said to him 'You must testify in Rome' (23:11). Yet circumstance after circumstance seemed calculated to make this impossible. Paul had expressed his intention to proceed straight from Jerusalem to Rome.[58] Instead, he was arrested in Jerusalem, subjected to endless trials, imprisoned in Caesarea, threatened with assassination by the Jews, and then nearly drowned in the Mediterranean, killed by the soldiers and poisoned by a snake! Each incident seemed to be designed to prevent him from reaching his God-planned, God-promised destination. Since Luke concentrates on the storm, we need to remember that the sea, reminiscent of the primeval chaos, was a regular Old Testament symbol of evil powers in opposition to God. It was not the forces of nature (water, wind and snake) or the machinations of men (schemes, plots and threats) which were arrayed against Paul, but demonic forces at work through them. Scripture is full of examples of the devil seeking to thwart God's saving purpose through his people and his Christ. He tried through Pharaoh to drown the baby Moses, through Haman to annihilate the Jews, through Herod the Great to destroy the infant Jesus in Bethlehem, and through the Sanhedrin to stifle the apostolic witness and smother the church at its birth. And now through the storm at sea he attempted to stop Paul bringing his gospel to the capital of the world.

But God obstructed his purpose. Luke increases the excitement of his story by letting us into his secret, namely that Jesus had promised Paul in advance that he would reach Rome (23:11). So we know from the beginning that he will get there. But as the narrative proceeds and the storm becomes ever more violent, until all hope is lost, we wonder how on earth he will be rescued. Will he make it? Yes he will! He does! For he was rescued by the divine overruling, which Luke makes clear by his repeated use of the vocabulary of 'salvation'.[59]

So by God's providence Paul reached Rome safe and sound. But he arrived as a prisoner! Christ's promise that he would testify in Rome had not included that information. How was this compatible with the providence of God? It seems to me legitimate to argue

[57] Rom. 8:28; *cf.* Gn. 50:20. [58] Rom. 15:25–29.
[59] Acts 27:20, 31, 34, 43, 44; 28:1, 4.

that the apostle, who was brought to Rome to witness, found his witness expanded, enriched and authenticated by his two-year custody in the city.

First, his witness was expanded, not only because of the constant flow of people visiting him, but especially because he witnessed to Christ in the presence of Caesar. This has, of course, been questioned. Although 'down to the time of Nero', Sherwin-White writes, 'the emperors themselves heard the cases that fell under their *cognitio*', yet in his early years 'Nero avoided personal jurisdiction, and then only accepted a case for special reasons'. Instead, he normally delegated the trial of capital cases, even though 'the sentences were confirmed by him afterwards'.[60] So was the case of Paul one of the exceptions? I think we should argue that it was. Leaving aside the possibility that Paul's deliverance 'from the lion's mouth' was a reference to his release by Nero,[61] the strongest argument is Jesus' promise to Paul on the ship, 'You must stand trial before Caesar' (27:24). If his first promise to Paul (about reaching Rome) was fulfilled, is it likely that Luke would have included his second promise (about standing before Caesar) unless he knew that it too was fulfilled? I think not. In this case we are permitted to imagine that the prisoner who stood before Felix, Festus and Agrippa, stood before Nero also, and that in the world's most prestigious court, to the world's most prestigious person, he faithfully proclaimed Christ. Yes, Nero himself, that artistic but bloodthirsty genius, heard the gospel from the lips of the apostle to the Gentiles. That would not have been possible if he were not a prisoner on trial.

Secondly, Paul's witness was enriched by those two years. It is difficult for us to conceive how such a congenital activist as Paul managed to endure nearly five years of comparative inactivity (two in the Caesarea prison, two under house arrest in Rome, and about six months in between voyaging from Caesarea to Rome). Were they wasted years? Was he champing at the bit and pawing the ground like a restless and rebellious horse? No, his prison letters breathe an atmosphere of joy, peace, patience and contentment, because he believed in the sovereignty of God. Moreover, however much he longed to get out and serve the contemporary church, yet, as a result of his two years' partial withdrawal in Rome, he has bequeathed to posterity in his four prison letters an even richer spiritual legacy. Probably Paul neither knew nor understood this. But we do.

Of course, Paul did not write all his letters in prison. He wrote to the Galatians in the heat of theological debate on his way up to

[60] Sherwin-White, pp. 110–111. [61] 2 Tim. 4:17.

Jerusalem for the Council; he wrote both letters to the Thessalonians within weeks of his mission in their city; and he wrote to the Corinthians and Romans in the midst of a relentlessly busy ministry. So he did not find it necessary to have a spell in gaol in order to get his writing done! Nevertheless, I maintain that in God's providence there is something distinctive and special about those prison letters. It is not only that he had more time now to reflect and to pray; it is also that the substance of these letters owes something to his prison experience. He was facing trial and possible death, but knew that he had already risen with Christ. He was awaiting the emperor's pleasure, but knew that the supreme authority to whom he bowed was not the Lord Caesar, but the Lord Christ.

So then (the Holy Spirit using his custody to clarify and enforce this truth), the three main prison letters (to the Ephesians, Philippians and Colossians) set forth more powerfully than anywhere else the supreme, sovereign, undisputed and unrivalled lordship of Jesus Christ. The person and work of Christ are given cosmic proportions, for God created all things through Christ and has reconciled all things through Christ. The fullness of the Godhead, which dwelt in Christ, had also worked through him. Christ is the agent of all God's work of creation and redemption. In addition, having humbled himself to the cross, God has highly exalted him. All three prison letters say so. God has given him the name or rank above all others.[62] All things have been put under his feet.[63] It is God's will that in everything he might have the supremacy.[64] Was it not through his very confinement that his eyes were opened to see the victory of Christ and the fullness of life, power and freedom which is given to those who belong to Christ? Paul's perspective was adjusted, his horizon extended, his vision clarified and his witness enriched by his prison experience.

Thirdly, his ministry was authenticated by his sufferings. Nothing proves the sincerity of our beliefs like our willingness to suffer for them. So Paul had to suffer, and be seen to suffer, for the gospel he was preaching. It was not only that in Isaiah the servant who brings light to the nations must suffer, that the vocations to service and to suffering are intertwined, that the witness and the martyr are one (*martys*), and that the seed which multiplies is the seed which dies.[65] It is also that Paul was suffering for 'his' gospel,[66] for the 'mystery' revealed to him that Jews and Gentiles were equal members of the body of Christ. That is why he could write of 'my sufferings for you',[67] and could describe

[62] Phil. 2:9. [63] Eph. 1:22. [64] Col. 1:18. [65] Jn. 12:24.
[66] 2 Tim. 2:8–9. [67] Eph. 3:13; Col. 1:24.

himself as Christ's prisoner 'for the sake of you Gentiles'.[68] Paul's arrest, imprisonment and trials were all due to his uncompromising espousal of the Gentile cause. It was because of his witness to the Gentiles that the Jews rose up in such fury against him. Paul paid dearly for his loyalty to the freeness and universality of the gospel. But his appeals to the churches to live a life worthy of the gospel were all the more authentic because he was himself a prisoner on account of the gospel.[69] He was ready to die for it; they must live to adorn it.

Was Paul released after the 'two whole years' Luke mentions (30)? He clearly expected to be.[70] And the Pastoral Epistles supply evidence that he was, for he resumed his travels for about two more years before being re-arrested, re-tried, condemned and executed in AD 64. By then he could write that he had fought the good fight, finished the race and kept the faith.[71] Now the next generation must step into his shoes and continue to work. Just as Luke's Gospel ended with the prospect of a mission to the nations,[72] so the Acts ends with the prospect of a mission radiating from Rome to the world. Luke's description of Paul preaching 'with boldness' and 'without hindrance' symbolizes a wide open door, through which we in our day have to pass. The Acts of the Apostles have long ago finished. But the acts of the followers of Jesus will continue until the end of the world, and their words will spread to the ends of the earth.

[68] Eph. 3:1; *cf.* Col. 4:3. [69] *E.g.* Eph. 4:1; 6:19–20.
[70] Phil. 1:19–26; Phm. 22. [71] 2 Tim. 4:7. [72] Lk. 24:47; *cf* Acts 1:8.

Study Guide for groups or individuals

Introduction

The aim of this study guide is to help you get to the heart of what the author has written and challenge you to apply what you learn to your own life. The questions have been designed for use both by individuals and also by small groups of Christians meeting, perhaps for an hour or two each week, to study, discuss and pray through the message of Acts.

The guide provides material for the book's preface, introduction and eighteen chapters, nineteen sessions in all. When used by a group with limited time, the leader should decide beforehand which questions are most appropriate for the group to discuss during the meeting and which should perhaps be left for group members to work through by themselves or in smaller groups during the week.

In order to be able to contribute fully and learn from the group meetings, each member of the group should read through the section of Acts to be looked at in each study together with the relevant pages of this book.

It is important not to let these studies become merely academic exercises. Guard against this by making time to think through and discuss how what you discover works out in practice for you. Make sure you begin and end each study with a period of worship and prayer. Ask the Holy Spirit to bring to life what Luke has written and to speak to you through it.

STUDY 1

Preface and Introduction (pages 5-7)

1. Why is Acts such a valuable book (pp. 5f.)?
2. Why is it wrong to "read off" the text as if it was originally addressed to us in our context' (pp. 7f.)?
3. What principles should govern the way we apply the teaching of Acts today?

Read Luke 1:1-4 (pages 21-31).
4. Why is it unnecessary to be sceptical about Luke's historical accuracy (pp. 21ff.)?
5. Luke writes as a historian and also as a diplomat. What evidence does he give to show the Roman authorities that they have nothing to fear from Christians (pp. 26f.)?
6. Some have suggested that Acts was written to paper over the cracks of a fundamental hostility between Peter and Paul. What is unsatisfactory about this view (pp. 27ff.)?
7. How does Luke demonstrate their unity and equality?
8. What is 'redaction-criticism' (p. 29)?
How does it help us in understanding Luke's purpose in writing Acts (pp. 29ff.)?
9. Why is it wrong to insist that Luke pursues his theological concerns (*i.e.* what the events mean) at the expense of historical reliability (*i.e.* what the events actually were) (pp. 29f.)?
10. What is Luke's dominant concern in his writing about Jesus and the early church (p. 30)?
11. What 'three fundamental truths' stand out about this major theme (pp. 30f.)?
12. What significance is there in the fact that Luke is 'the only Gentile contributor to the New Testament' (p. 31)?

Read Acts 1:1-5 (pages 32-37).
13. What is misleading about the terms 'Acts of the Apostles' or 'Acts of the Holy Spirit' (pp. 32ff.)?
14. How do Acts 1:1-2 'set Christianity apart from all other religions' (p. 34)?
15. What implications does this have for you?
16. What is unique about the apostles (pp. 34ff.)?
17. In what sense, if any, might there be 'apostles' today?

PART 1. In Jerusalem. *Acts 1:6—6:7*

STUDY 2

Waiting for Pentecost

Acts 1:6-26 (pages 39-59)

Read Acts 1:6-8 (pages 40-45).

1. This chapter deals with the four events which occupied the apostles during the fifty days between Easter and Pentecost. 'Jesus' two main topics of conversation between his resurrection and his ascension were the kingdom of God and the Spirit of God' (p. 40). How are these two subjects related?
2. What did the apostles understand by 'kingdom of God'?
3. Where had they gone wrong (pp. 41ff.)?
4. In what ways is your thinking about the kingdom distorted by these same wrong ideas?
5. What differences are there between power in God's kingdom and power in human kingdoms (pp. 41f.)?
6. How is this relevant for you?
7. What are the 'radical political and social implications' of the kingdom of God for you (p. 42)?
8. About what must the apostles (and we as well!) 'be willing to be left in ignorance' (p. 44)? Why?
9. What information does Jesus give instead?
10. 'Before the Spirit could come, the Son must go' (p. 45). Why?

Read Acts 1:9-12 (pages 45-51).

11. Compare Acts 1:9-12 with Luke 24:50ff. Are Luke's accounts of the ascension contradictory (pp. 45f.)?
12. What are the main discrepancies and what force do they have?
13. What do the accounts have in common?
14. Do you think the ascension really occurred? Explain.
15. What reasons are given to back up the view that it did not take place?
16. What reasons can we give to support the view that it did take place in the way Luke describes (pp. 47ff.)?
17. What are the two main lessons which the ascension teaches us today (pp. 49ff.)?
18. What two opposite errors did the apostles commit (p. 51)?
19. Which do you tend to fall into?
20. What can you do to guard against this?

Read Acts 1:12-14 (pages 52-54).

21. What does Luke tell us about the way they prayed (pp. 52ff.)?

22. To what extent does your prayer with other Christians reflect these priorities?

Read Acts 1:15-26 (pages 54-59).
23. Some people suggest that Judas' action in betraying Jesus may be excused on the grounds that it was predicted and therefore in some way foreordained. What is wrong with this view (p. 55)?
24. Compare 1:18-19 with Matthew 27:3-5. Is Hanson right to say of these two accounts that 'they cannot both be true' (pp. 55f.)? How do you support your answer?
25. How was it decided that Judas should be replaced (pp. 56f.)?
26. Why were martyred apostles (like James—see 12:2) not replaced?
27. What qualifications for apostleship does Peter mention (pp. 57f.)?
28. Why don't we draw lots when making decisions today (p. 59)?

STUDY 3

The Day of Pentecost
Acts 2:1-47 (pages 60-87)

---

1. 'There are at least four ways in which we may think of the Day of Pentecost.' What are they (pp. 60f.)?
2. What does 'revival' mean (p. 61)?
What priority does it have in your thinking and praying?

Read Acts 2:1-13 (pages 61-68).
3. What significance is there in the fact that the events of this chapter took place on the Jewish Day of Pentecost (pp. 61f.)?
4. What three phenomena accompanied the coming of the Holy Spirit (pp. 62f.)?
5. What did they signify?
6. 'Glossolalia' comes from the Greek for 'speaking in tongues'. What does Luke understand glossolalia *not* to be (pp. 65ff.)?
Why not?
7. What then *does* he mean by glossolalia?
8. What are the arguments (on both sides) for whether glossolalia in Acts 2 is the same as that in 1 Corinthians 12 and 14 (pp. 67f.)?
9. Why is it probably better to interpret other New Testament references to glossolalia with reference to Acts 2 rather than the other way round?
10. What is Luke's understanding of the significance of glossolalia (p. 68)?

Read Acts 2:14-41 (pages 69-81).
11. Acts includes nineteen significant examples of what Jesus 'continued to teach'. On what grounds can it be assumed that the speeches are not

verbatim reports (p. 69)?

12. On what grounds have some questioned their reliability as summaries of what was said (pp. 69ff.)?

How may they be answered?

13. Turning to Peter's speech, he explains what is happening by referring first to Old Testament prediction and then to the story of Jesus. What is the significance of the Spirit being 'poured out on all people' (p. 73)?

14. What is meant here by 'they will prophesy' (pp. 74f.)?

15. What are the six stages of the story of Jesus to which Peter draws attention (pp. 75ff.)?

16. 'Peter's use of Scripture probably sounds strange to us' (p. 76). Why?

How may it be justified?

17. 'It is not enough to "proclaim Jesus" ' (p. 81). Why not?

18. What framework does the author use to help him to remain faithful to the apostles' message (pp. 80f.)?

19. How might this help you too?

Read Acts 2:42-47 (pages 81-87).

20. Why is it 'incorrect to call the Day of Pentecost "the birthday of the church" ' (p. 81)?

21. To what difficulties might this lead?

22. What three strands of evidence point to the Spirit's presence and power in the early church (pp. 82ff.)?

23. How does the church to which you belong measure up?

24. Why are 'anti-intellectualism and the fullness of the Spirit . . . mutually incompatible' (p. 82)?

25. What does this mean for you?

26. How does devotion to the apostles' teaching work out in practice for Christians today (p. 82)?

27. What does *koinōnia* mean (pp. 83f.)?

28. To what extent should we imitate the early church's example of having everything in common (pp. 83f.)? Explain.

29. What aspects of the early church's worship does Luke describe (pp. 85ff.)?

30. How far does your experience of worship reflect this balance? Why is this?

31. Acts 'is governed by one dominant, over-riding and all-controlling motif'. What is this?

32. To what extent would the same be true of an account of your life?

33. What 'three vital lessons about local church evangelism' does Luke draw out here (pp. 86f.)?

34. 'There is no need for us to wait, as the one hundred and twenty had to wait, for the Spirit to come' (p. 87). Why not?

STUDY 4

The Outbreak of Persecution
Acts 3:1—4:31 (pages 88-104)

1. How was the 'church's very existence . . . threatened' (p. 88)?
2. What parallels are there between Acts 1—2 and Acts 3—4 (pp. 88f.)?

Read Acts 3:1-10 (pages 90-91).
3. What is striking about the healing that Luke describes here (pp. 90f.)?

Read Acts 3:11-26 (pages 91-95).
4. What is the 'most remarkable feature of Peter's second sermon, as of his first' (p. 92)?
5. What three blessings result from repentance and turning to God (pp. 93f.)?
6. How does Peter demonstrate the truth of what he is saying (pp. 94f.)?
7. What can we learn from what he does?

Read Acts 4:1-22 (pages 95-98).
8. What do we know about the Sadducees (pp. 95f.)?
9. Why did they react to Peter as they did?
10. What preoccupied the apostles (pp. 96f.)?
11. What preoccupies you?
12. What astonished the court about Peter and John (pp. 97f.)?

Read Acts 4:23-31 (pages 99-100).
13. How did the church respond to threats (p. 99)?
14. What is the significance of their calling God 'Sovereign Lord'?
15. What does the way they pray have to teach us (pp. 99f.)?

Conclusion (pages 100-104).
16. How does the author summarize John Wimber's teaching on signs and wonders (pp. 101f.)?
17. How certain is it that signs and wonders are the 'main secret of church growth' (p. 102)?
18. To what extent should we expect signs and wonders as everyday occurrences (pp. 102f.)?
19. Are the signs and wonders which are claimed today parallel to those recorded in the New Testament (pp. 103f.)? Why?

STUDY 5

Satanic Counter-Attack
Acts 4:32—6:7 (pages 105-124)

Read Acts 4:32-37 (pages 106-108).
1. In this section, Luke exposes Satan's threefold strategy and shows how he may be overcome. 'Luke . . . is concerned to show that the fullness of the Spirit is manifest in deed as well as word.' How does he do this (pp. 106ff.)?
2. What was the so-called 'Jerusalem experiment' (pp. 107f.)?
3. Was it a 'rash and foolish mistake' or is it 'an obligatory model . . . which God wants all Spirit-filled communities to copy'? Explain.
4. Is the way you live out the gospel of the kingdom 'good news for the poor'?

Read Acts 5:1-11 (pages 108-112).
5. Why is this incident so important (pp. 109ff.)?
6. What did Ananias and Sapphira do wrong?
7. What lessons are there for us to learn?

Read Acts 5:12-16 (pages 112-113).
8. What paradoxical results did the miracles described here lead to (pp. 112f.)?
9. What causes such different reactions?

Read Acts 5:17-42 (pages 113-119).
10. Under what circumstances is it the Christian's duty to disobey human authority (pp. 116f.)?
11. Can you think of examples from your own experience?
12. What truths about God do the apostles emphasize in verses 25-32 (p. 116)?
13. How do you react to the discrepancy between the account of Theudas and Judas the Galilean given by Luke and that recorded by Josephus (pp. 117f.)?
14. What is the 'Gamaliel principle'? Do you use it?
15. How accurate is it as an indicator of whether or not something is from God (p. 118)?
16. How did the apostles react to the Council's strictures (pp. 118f.)?
17.'The church is often harassed. But we need not fear for its survival' (p. 119). Why not?

Read Acts 6:1-7 (pages 120-124)
18. What are the problems which this incident reveals (pp. 120f.)?

19. How did the apostles set about finding a solution (pp. 121f.)?
20. How often are decisions in your church made like this? Why?
21. What was the essence of the apostles' ministry (pp. 121f.)?
22. 'A vital principle is illustrated in this incident, which is of urgent importance to the church today' (p. 122). What is the 'vital principle'?
Why is it so important today?
23. What was the result of the reorganization described in these verses (pp. 123f.)?
24. 'We have now seen the three tactics which the devil employed in his overall strategy to destroy the church' (p. 124). Which strategy is he using in the church to which you belong?
How can his plans be thwarted?

PART 2. Foundations for World Mission. *Acts 6:8—12:24.*

STUDY 6

Stephen the Martyr

Acts 6:8—7:60 (pages 125-143)

Read Acts 6:1-12 (pages 125-127).
1. What do we learn about Stephen from these verses (p. 126)?
2. What methods did his opponents use against him (pp. 126f.)?

Read Acts 6:13-15 (pages 127-129).
3. Why was the charge against Stephen so serious (pp. 127ff.)?
4. What significance is there in the observation that Stephen's face 'was like that of an angel' (p. 129)?

Read Acts 7:1-53 (pages 129-141).
5. What is 'the nature and purpose of Stephen's speech' (pp.129f.)?
Why is it important to bear this in mind?
6. Stephen speaks about four major Old Testament characters. Why does he say what he does about each of them (pp. 130ff.)?
7. What does Stephen say in this passage which reveals his respect for the law (pp. 139ff.)?
Of what does he accuse his accusers?

Read Acts 7:54-60 (pages 141-142).
8. What parallels are there between the death of Stephen and the death of Jesus?

Conclusion (p. 143).
9. How and why does Luke emphasize the 'vital role Stephen played in

the development of the world-wide Christian mission' (p. 143)?

STUDY 7

Philip the Evangelist
Acts 8:1-40 (pages 144-164)

Read Acts 8:1-4 (pages 144-146).
1. What is the significance of the words which Luke uses to describe Philip's proclamation of Christ (p. 144)?
2. What 'threefold chain of cause and effect' does Luke describe in these verses (pp. 145f.)?
3. Give some similar contemporary examples of how God frustrates Satan's plans.

Read Acts 8:5-25 (pages 146-158).
4. Why was Philip's preaching the gospel to the Samaritans such a bold step (pp. 147f.)?
5. What would be modern equivalents to that step?
6. How does Luke describe what happened (pp. 148ff.)?
7. 'Some think of these miracles as special to Philip; others think of them as demonstrating a norm for evangelism' (p. 148). What do you think, and why?
8. Why was it 'particularly appropriate' that one of the apostles sent from Jerusalem was John (pp. 149f.)?
9. Peter rebuked Simon for trying to buy power. What is discouraging about Simon's response (p. 151)?
10. Why is verse 16 regarded as 'perhaps the most extraordinary statement in Acts' (p. 150)?
11. What crucial question does the account of what happened to the Samaritan believers give rise to (pp. 151f.)?
12. The author suggests that this two-stage Samaritan experience is not to be regarded as the norm for Christian initiation. Why (pp. 152ff.)?
13. One suggestion is that the first stage, when the Samaritans 'believed Philip', was not initiatory. Why has this 'ingenious reconstruction' not won general agreement (pp. 154f.)?
14. Another suggestion is that the Samaritans received the Spirit when they believed and were baptized by Philip and that the laying-on of the apostles' hands served a different purpose. Why is this view open to criticism (pp. 155f.)?
15. A further suggestion is that the Samaritans represent a special case. What evidence is there for this (pp. 156f.)?
16. Why then 'was it necessary for an official apostolic delegation to scrutinize and confirm the work of Philip'?

Read Acts 8:26-40 (pages 159-164).
17. Why is it that, as Calvin suggested, 'the reading of Scripture bears fruit with such a few people today' (pp. 160f.)?
18. To what extent is this true of you too?
19. Looking back over chapter 8, what are the similarities and differences between Philip's work among the Samaritans and with the Ethiopian (pp. 163f.)?
20. What in our evangelism today must always be flexible and open to change?
And what must always stay the same?

STUDY 8

The Conversion of Saul

Acts 9:1-31 (pages 165-180)

---

1. What in Saul's experience was unique to him and what must be characteristic of every Christian's experience (pp. 165f.)?
2. What is inadequate about the view that Saul's conversion was due to brainwashing (pp. 166ff.)?

Read Acts 9:1-2 (pages 168-169).
3. Given the details in these verses, how likely is it that Saul would have become a Christian (pp. 168f.)?
4. Of all the people you know, who would you say is the least likely ever to become a Christian?
5. What is there about Saul's story to encourage you?

Read Acts 9:3-9; 22:3-11; 26:9-18 (pages 169-174).
6. In these accounts, what evidence is there that Saul's conversion was due to God's grace alone (pp. 168ff.)?
7. But 'to ascribe Saul's conversion to God's initiative can easily be misunderstood . . . and needs to be qualified in two ways' (p. 171). How?
8. Sovereign grace is gradual grace and gentle grace. Illustrate this from your own experience.

Read Acts 9:10-25 (pages 174-177).
9. What changes became evident in Saul's life (pp. 174ff.)?
10. If you had been Ananias, how would you have felt about doing 'follow-up work' with Saul (p. 175)?

Read Acts 9:26-31 (pages 177-179).
11. 'True conversion always issues in church membership' (p. 178). Why was the ministry of Ananias and Barnabas so important?

12. Can you think of people who have recently come along to your church who need to receive similar ministry?
13. Luke focuses on Saul's new sense of responsibility to the world as a third change in his life (pp. 178f.). What characteristics of his witness does he mention?
14. What lessons do these have for us?
15. 'The world's opposition did not impede the spread of the gospel or the growth of the church' (p. 179). What five things characterize the growing church?

Conclusion (pages 179-180).
16. Luke's account of Saul's conversion 'should persuade us to expect more from God in relation both to the unconverted and the newly converted' (p. 179). How does this apply to you and your non-Christian friends and colleagues?

STUDY 9

The Conversion of Cornelius
Acts 9:32—11:18 (pages 181-199)

Read Acts 9:32-43 (pages 182-184).
1. Leaving Paul in the wings for a while, Luke turns now to Peter and his key role in preparing the stage for the gospel to be taken to Gentiles as well as Jews. What is there in this passage which suggests that Luke's intention is to portray Peter 'as an authentic apostle of Jesus Christ' (pp. 182ff.)?

Read Acts 10:1-8 (pages 184-186).
2. What significance is there in the fact that Peter stayed with a tanner (p. 184)?
3. What was the extent of the divide between Jews and Gentiles at this time (pp. 185f.)?
4. Can you think of similar situations in the world today?
5. 'The principal subject of this chapter is not so much the conversion of Cornelius as the conversion of Peter' (p. 186). Are there any similar prejudices which you can find in yourself?

Read Acts 10:9-23a (pages 186-188).
6. 'How perfectly God dovetailed his working in Cornelius and in Peter' (p. 187). What examples of divine 'coincidence' have you experienced recently?

Read Acts 10:23b-48 (pages 188-193).

7. What does Peter include in his address to Cornelius' friends and family (pp. 109ff.)?
8. 'The emphasis is that Cornelius' Gentile nationality was acceptable so that he had no need to become a Jew, not that his own righteousness was adequate so that he had no need to become a Christian' (p. 190). Why is this so important?
9. 'The gift of the Spirit was insufficient; they needed human teachers too' (p. 192). How is this statement relevant to you?

Read Acts 11:1-18 (pages 193-199).
10. 'It took four successive hammer-blows of divine revelation before [Peter's] racial and religious prejudice was overcome' (p. 194). What were they?
11. 'Since God does not make distinctions in his new society, we have no liberty to make them either' (p. 197). Are you making any?
12. What is it that 'rebukes those Christians who overlook or underplay' the work of the Holy Spirit today (p. 197)?
13. Why is it incorrect to say that 'anybody of any nation or religion who is devout and upright is thereby justified' (pp. 198f.)?
14. What does a comparison of Saul and Cornelius tell us about the power of the gospel (p. 199)?

STUDY 10

Expansion and Opposition

Acts 11:19—12:24 (pages 200-213)

Read Acts 11:19-30 (pages 200-207).
1. Luke now takes up again where he left off at 8:1. In what ways was the area conquered by the gospel expanded as a result of the Jerusalem persecution (pp. 201f.)?
2. Were the 'Greeks' in verse 20 pagan Greeks or Greek-speaking Jews (pp. 201f.)?
3. Why is this distinction important?
4. What did Barnabas do in verses 22-24 (pp. 203f.)? Why?
5. What can we learn from what Barnabas did next (pp. 204f.)?
6. What happened to demonstrate that the new Christians in Antioch really were members of the family of God (pp. 205ff.)?

Read Acts 12:1-25 (pages 207-213).
7. After tremendous strides forward, the church now faces a major setback. What lay behind Herod's actions (pp. 207f.)?
8. What can we learn from Peter's attitude to prison (p. 209)?
9. What is unsatisfactory about the view that 'Peter managed to escape

because of bribery, negligence or simply a change of mind' (pp. 209ff.)?
10. 'The dramatic details Luke includes all seem to emphasize the intervention of God and the passivity of Peter' (p. 211). Trace the details to which the author refers.
11. 'The chapter opens with James dead, Peter in prison and Herod triumphing; it closes with Herod dead, Peter free, and the word of God triumphing' (p. 213). What does this have to say to us about those who seek to oppress the church and hinder the spread of the gospel?

PART 3. The Apostle to the Gentiles. *Acts 12:25—21:17.*
STUDY 11

The First Missionary Journey
Acts 12:25—14:28 (pages 215-239)

Read Acts 12:25-13:4a (pages 215-218).
1. 'So important was this occasion . . .' (p. 216). What occasion? Why was it so important?
2. To whom did the Holy Spirit reveal his will (pp. 216f.)? Why?
3. What was it that the Holy Spirit revealed to the church (p. 217)?
4. What is the significance of this for us?
5. What was their response to God's call (p. 217)?
6. How is the way Barnabas and Saul were commissioned relevant to us (pp. 217f.)?

Read Acts 13:4b-12 (pages 218-220).
7. What was it that particularly impressed the consul Sergius Paulus (pp. 218ff.)?

Read Acts 13:13-52 (pages 221-228).
8. What was the nature of the setback that affected Paul and Barnabas in Perga (pp. 221f.)?
9. What is Luke 'evidently anxious to demonstrate' (p. 222)?
10. Paul recounts the history of Israel's history between the patriarchs and the monarchy. What is his major emphasis (pp. 222f.)?
11. What does Paul emphasize in his account of the death and resurrection of Jesus (pp. 223ff.)?
12. What is the main difference which Paul identifies between Christianity and Judaism (pp. 225f.)?
13. How would you answer someone who denied that Luke has any understanding of the doctrine of justification by faith as central in Paul's thought (pp. 225f.)?
14. What is the effect of Jewish opposition to the preaching of the gospel

(pp. 226ff.)?
15. What effect does opposition have on you?

Read Acts 14:1-7 (pages 228-230).
16. What is the effect of the preaching of the gospel (pp. 228f.)?
17. Why is the attribution of the title 'apostle' to Barnabas (14:4, 14) 'perplexing' (p. 229)?
How can it be explained?

Read Acts 14:8-20 (pages 230-233).
18. What is the explanation for the crowd's reaction (pp. 230f.)?
19. Why is what Paul says here of particular importance (pp. 231f.)?
20. What is the main difference between Paul's preaching to the Jews in Antioch and the pagans in Lystra (p. 232)?
21. How can we 'learn from Paul's flexibility'?

Read Acts 14:21-28 (pages 233-239).
22. What did Paul and Barnabas concentrate on during their return trip (pp. 233ff.)? Why?
23. 'On his missionary journeys Paul left churches behind him.' What is the importance of 'apostolic instruction' (pp. 235f.) in beginning a church?
What would you include in a 'cluster of central beliefs'?
24. What pattern of pastoral oversight did Paul establish (p. 236)?
In what ways does this differ from the 'familiar modern pattern'?
25. Why did Paul believe 'that the churches could confidently be left to manage their own affairs' (p. 237)?
26. What does Paul's way of doing things have to say to missionaries today (pp. 237ff.)?

STUDY 12

The Council of Jerusalem

Acts 15:1—16:5 (pages 240-257)

---

1. 'The Jewish leaders had no difficulty with the general concept of believing Gentiles' (p. 240). Why not?
2. What particular difficulty did they have?

Read Acts 15:1-4 (pages 241-244).
3. In what way were the 'very foundations of the Christian faith . . . being undermined' (p. 243)?
4. Why did Paul oppose Peter so strongly (pp. 243f.)?

Read Acts 15:5-21 (pages 244-250).

5. Luke summarizes the three speeches made by Peter, Paul and Barnabas, and James. To what threefold work of God does Peter draw attention (pp. 245f.)?
6. What contribution did Paul and Barnabas make to the debate (p. 246)?
7. What lies behind James's statement that God has taken 'from the Gentiles a people for himself' in verse 13?
8. Why does he quote from the prophet Amos (pp. 246ff.)?
On what does he base his conclusion?
9. James's judgment includes a request that Gentiles abstain from four things (pp. 248ff.). Why these four?
10. Are they moral or ceremonial issues? Explain.

Read Acts 15:22-29 (pages 250-252).
11. What three important points are made in the letter (pp. 251ff.)?

Read Acts 15:30—16:5 (pages 252-257).
12. What led to Paul and Barnabas splitting up (p. 253)?
13. In Galatia, Paul circumcised Timothy. How can he be defended against the charge of being inconsistent in his attitude to Jewish law (pp. 254f.)?
14. What happened to the churches as a result of the Jerusalem Council's decision (p. 255)?
15. What is it that preserves the unity of the church (pp. 255f.)?
16. How did Paul 'unite the church without compromising the gospel' and 'defend the church without sacrificing the unity of the church' (pp. 256f.)?

STUDY 13

Mission in Macedonia
Acts 16:6—17:15 (pages 258-275)

---

1. What 'important principles of divine guidance' are shown in 16:6-10 (pp. 258ff.)?

Read Acts 16:11-40 (pages 261-270).
2. What does Luke tell us about how Lydia, the slave girl and the Roman gaoler came to faith (pp. 262ff.)?
Why is this important?
3. What differences are there between these three individuals (pp. 268ff.)?
4. 'We . . . who live in an era of social disintegration, need to exhibit the unifying power of the gospel' (p. 270). How?

Read Acts 17:1-9 (pages 270-273).
5. What is Paul's strategy in presenting the gospel to the Jews in Thessalonica (pp. 271f.)?

6. What is the response to Paul's message (pp. 272f.)?

Read Acts 17:10-15 (pages 273-275).
7. How did the Jews at Berea display a 'more noble character' (verse 11) (pp. 273f.)?
What was the result?
8. Paul 'believed in doctrine. but not in indoctrination' (p. 275). What are the differences between these two things?

STUDY 14

Paul in Athens

Acts 17:16-34 (pages 276-291)

Read Acts 17:16-34 (pages 276-291).
1. What sort of a place was Athens (p. 276)?
2. 'First and foremost what he saw was neither the beauty nor the brilliance of the city but . . .' (p. 277). What did Paul notice in particular?
3. Why did Paul react as he did to what he saw (pp. 278ff.)?
4. How do you react to modern expressions of the same thing?
5. What is the 'highest incentive of all' for world evangelization (p. 279)?
6. What did Paul's reaction lead him to do (pp. 280f.)?
7. What was distinctive about the beliefs of the Epicureans and the Stoics (p. 280)?
8. What are the modern equivalents of the different groups Paul spoke to in Athens (p. 281)?
9. What led to Paul being invited to speak to the court of the Areopagus (p. 282)?
10. Was Paul's speech a defence or a sermon (pp. 283f.)?
11. By speaking as he does in verse 23, is Paul 'acknowledging the authenticity of their pagan worship' (pp. 284f.)? Explain.
12. What five truths about God does Paul set out (pp. 285ff.)?
13. What three facts about God's judgment does Paul refer to (pp. 287f.)?
14. How may claims that what Luke reports about Paul is inauthentic be answered (pp. 288ff.)?
15. Is what Paul said in Athens an adequate presentation of the gospel (pp. 289f.)? Explain.
16. Why do some people suppose that Paul was 'disappointed and perhaps disillusioned by his experience in Athens'?
What do you think of this view?
17. 'Many people are rejecting our gospel today not because they perceive it to be false, but because they perceive it to be trivial' (p. 290). What can we learn from Paul here?
18. 'We do not speak as Paul spoke because we do not feel as Paul felt' (p. 290). Why is this?

290). Why is this?

STUDY 15

Corinth and Ephesus
Acts 18:1—19:41 (pages 292-314)

1. Why did Paul focus on cities (pp. 292f.)?
2. What was special about Athens, Corinth and Ephesus?
3. What was the 'similar pattern' in Paul's visits to Corinth and Ephesus (pp. 294f.)?

Read Acts 18:1-18a (pages 295-300).
4. Why, as he indicates in 1 Corinthians 2:2-3, was Paul so fearful about his mission to Corinth and so concerned to preach only Christ and the cross (pp. 295f.)?
5. Why did Paul work as a tentmaker (p. 297)?
6. What application is there today in his decision to do this?
7. After meeting resistance from the Jews, Paul turned to the Gentiles. What happened to encourage him that this was the right decision (pp. 297f.)?
8. What was so significant in Gallio's refusal to take seriously the Jewish case against Paul (pp. 299f.)?

Read Acts 18:18b-28 (pages 300-303).
9. What significant things does Luke tell us about Apollos (pp. 302f.)?

Read Acts 19:1-41 (pages 303-314).
10. The disciples Paul met in Ephesus 'cannot possibly be regarded as providing a norm for two-stage initiation' (p. 304). Why not?
11. What four things are 'universal in Christian initiation' (p. 305)?
What things were particular to the situation at Ephesus? Why?
12. Some dismiss the 'extraordinary miracles' (verse 11) as 'legendary' (p. 306). What may be said in response?
13. What else happened to advance the cause of the gospel (p. 307)?
14. What were the reasons for Paul's circuitous route to Jerusalem (pp. 307f.)?
15. What was the root cause of the riot (pp. 308ff.)?
How did Demetrius disguise this?
16. Why does Luke recount this incident in the way he does (p. 311)?
17. What can we learn about urban evangelism from Paul's activity in Corinth and Ephesus (pp. 311ff.)?
18. What is the equivalent to the synagogue in our culture?

19. 'Secular people have to be reached in secular buildings.' How does this apply in your situation?
20. Which two words stand out in these chapters as best describing Paul's evangelistic preaching?
21. 'Paul did not simply proclaim his message in a "take it or leave it" fashion' (p. 312). Why not?
What did he do instead?
22. What was 'specially remarkable' about Paul's use of the lecture hall of Tyrannus in Ephesus (pp. 313f.)?
23. 'When we contrast much contemporary evangelism with Paul's . . .' (p. 314), what do you notice?

STUDY 16

More about Ephesus
Acts 20:1—21:17 (pages 315-333)

---

1. What similarities are there between Paul's journey to Jerusalem and that taken by Jesus?

Read Acts 20:1-6 (pages 316-319).
2. How does Luke characterize Paul's ministry in Macedonia (pp. 316ff.)?
3. Why is it 'noteworthy that Paul hardly ever travelled alone' (p. 317)?

Read Acts 20:7-16 (pages 319-323).
4. What does this incident tell us about early Christian worship (pp. 320f.)?

Read Acts 20:17-38 (pages 323-330).
5. What is unique about this speech (p. 323)?
6. What three terms does Paul use in addressing the church leaders (pp. 323f.)?
7. What does each of these indicate?
8. What is the significance of Luke's use of the plural to describe them?
9. What themes in this speech recur in Paul's letters (p. 324)?
10. What evidence does Paul give of his past sincerity (pp. 324f.)?
Why does he need to do so?
11. What is it that is more important to Paul than his personal survival and comfort (pp. 325f.)? Why is this?
12. What is more important to you than these things?
13. What does Paul urge the Ephesian elders to watch out for (pp. 326f.)? Why?
14. To what extent do you watch out for them too?
15. What is noteworthy about Paul's example as a 'shepherd' (p. 328)?
16. What is the 'double duty' which shepherds of Christ's flock have (pp.

328f.)?
17. What neglected obligation does the author suggest may be a 'major cause of today's theological confusion' (p. 329)?
Why is this so important?
18. What 'should inspire' Christian leaders 'to faithfulness' (pp. 329f.)?

Read Acts 21:1-17 (pages 330-333).
19. What is striking about the prophecy of Agabus (pp. 331f.)?
20. How does Paul react to the pleas of those who wanted to dissuade him from going to Jerusalem (pp. 331f.)?
21. What does this reveal about his priorities?
22. What is the solution to the apparent contradiction between the Spirit's promptings in 20:22-23 and 21:4, 11 (pp. 332f.)?
23. What fortified Paul in his journey (p. 333)?
24. In what ways do you both receive and give this same resource?

PART 4. On the Way to Rome. *Acts 21:18—28:31.*
STUDY 17

Paul's Arrest and Self-Defence
Acts 21:18—23:25 (pages 335-357)

---

1. On Paul's arrival in Jerusalem 'his whole career abruptly changed' (p. 335). How?
2. Why does Luke go into so much detail about the five trials that Paul went through (pp. 335f.)?
3. What evidence of Jewish opposition has Luke recorded so far?
4. What parallels are there between the sufferings of Paul and those of Jesus (pp. 336f.)?
5. What evidence of Roman friendliness to the gospel does Luke present (pp. 337ff.)?
Why does he do so?

Read Acts 21:18-26 (pages 339-343).
6. What was the tension underlying Paul's welcome by the Christians in Jerusalem (pp. 339ff.)?
7. How was James conciliatory to Paul?
How was Paul conciliatory towards James?
8. What exactly was James's concern (p. 341)?

Read Acts 21:27-36 (pages 343-345).
9. What were the two accusations made against Paul (pp. 343f.)?
10. What 'striking example' does Luke give of the contrast between Jewish

hostility and Roman justice (p. 345)?

Read Acts 21:37—22:22 (pages 345-348).
11. What is both sensitive and appropriate in the way Paul speaks to the crowd (pp. 347f.)?
12. Why did the crowd resume their demands for Paul to be put to death (p. 348)?
13. What are the two major points that come out of Paul's defence (p. 348)?

Read Acts 22:23—23:11 (pages 348-353).
14. Why was the high priest so enraged by Paul's opening remark (pp. 351f.)?
15. What explanations have been given for the apparent rudeness of Paul's reply (p. 352)?
16. What distinguished the Sadducees from the Pharisees (pp. 352f.)?
17. What would be 'hard to exaggerate' (p. 353)?

Read Acts 23:12-35 (pages 353-357).
18. 'Even the most careful and cunning of human plans cannot succeed if God opposes them' (p. 355). How is this illustrated in this incident? And in your experience?
19. 'Luke's great skill as a historian-theologian . . . is clearly seen in these chapters' (p. 356). How?
20. What was the secret of Paul's courage (p. 357)?

STUDY 18

Paul on Trial

Acts 24:1—26:32 (pages 358-382)

---

1. What is 'the thread which runs through these chapters' (p. 359)?
2. In what ways do Christians today face similar circumstances?

Read Acts 24:1-27 (pages 359-364).
3. What are the charges which Tertullus brings against Paul (pp. 359f.)?
4. How does Paul refute these allegations and deny the charge that Christianity is a heretical sect (pp. 359f.)?
5. What dilemma did Felix face (pp. 362f.)?
6. What happened over the next two years (pp. 363f.)?
7. What was Felix's response to Paul's message? Why?

Read Acts 25:1-22 (pages 365-368).
8. Of what does Paul's defence suggest he was charged (pp. 366f.)?
9. Why did he appeal to Caesar?

10. What do we know about Agrippa (p. 368)?

Read Acts 25:23—26:32 (pages 368-379).
11. In what way was 'Festus' account of the situation . . . a mixture of truth and error' (p. 369)?
12. What is especially 'dramatic' about Paul's appearance before Agrippa (p. 370)?
13. What are the 'three principal phases' of his life which Paul describes (pp. 370ff.)?
14. What does it mean to 'kick against the goads' (verse 14) (p. 372)?
15. What parallels are there between God's call of his prophets in the Old Testament and Christ's commissioning of Paul (p. 373)?
16. What exactly was Paul sent to do (pp. 373f.)?
What does this mean?
17. Why did the Jews seek to kill him (p. 375)?
18. How did the court react to Paul's defence (pp. 376f.)?
19. What double allegation lies behind all three trials (pp. 377f.)? How did Paul respond?
20. What characterizes Paul's use of opportunities for witness (pp. 378f.)?
21. What characterizes your use of similar opportunities?
22. Is there a difference? If so, why?

Read Acts 9:1-19; 22:6-16; 26:12-18 (pages 379-382).
23. What two discrepancies have been alleged in the three accounts by Paul of his conversion (pp. 379ff.)?
How can they be resolved?

STUDY 19

Rome at Last!

Acts 27:1—28:31 (pages 383-405)

Read Romans 1:3-15; 15:20-32.
1. Why did Paul long to visit Rome (pp. 383ff.)?
2. How does Luke indicate that 'Jerusalem and its temple are not indispensable to the church' (p. 385)?
3. What modern equivalents of Jerusalem and the temple can you think of?
4. In what ways does Paul's journey to Rome parallel that of Jesus to Jerusalem (p. 385)?

Read Acts 27:1-38 (pages 385-392).
5. What emerges from the way Paul deals with the situation (p. 390)?
6. On what did Paul base his call to his fellow-travellers to keep up their

courage (pp. 390f.)?
7. How does Paul's combination of 'spirituality and sanity' emerge in this chapter (p. 392)?

Read Acts 27:39—28:10 (pages 393-395).
8. Why were the soldiers so keen to kill the prisoners (p. 393)?
9. Paul was 'first called a murderer, then a god' (p. 394). Why?
10. What is significant about the way Publius' father was healed (p. 395)?

Read Acts 28:11-31 (pages 395-405).
11. What principle did Paul continue to follow, even in Rome (p. 397)?
12. What did Paul concentrate on during his discussions with the Jews (p. 398)?
13. To what can unbelief in the face of preaching be attributed (p. 399)? How do you respond to this?
14. What did Paul talk about to those who visited him (p. 400)?
15. What is the significance of the final words of the book in the Greek text (misplaced to the beginning of verse 31 in the NIV) (p. 400)?
16. Some have thought of chapter 27 that the 'length of the narrative seems out of proportion to its value'. What is the best way of overcoming this apparent difficulty (pp. 401f.)?
17. How is God's providential activity seen in these chapters (p. 402)?
18. What three main advantages were there in Paul being a prisoner (pp. 403ff.)?
19. Are there any apparently adverse circumstances in your life which look different in the light of Paul's experience?